WOMEN, GAYS, AND THE CONSTITUTION

Women, Gays, AND THE Constitution

The Grounds for Feminism and Gay Rights in Culture and Law

DAVID A. J. RICHARDS

UNIVERSITY OF CHICAGO PRESS

Chicago and London

DAVID A. J. RICHARDS is Edwin D. Webb Professor of Law
and director of the Program for the Study of Law,
Philosophy, and Social Theory at New York University.

The University of Chicago Press, Chicago 60637
The University of Chicago Press, Ltd., London
© 1998 by The University of Chicago
All rights reserved. Published 1998
Printed in the United States of America
07 06 05 04 03 02 01 00 99 98   1 2 3 4 5

ISBN: 0-226-71206-0 (cloth)
ISBN: 0-226-71207-9 (paper)

Library of Congress Cataloging-in-Publication Data

Richards, David A. J.
    Women, gays, and the constitution : the grounds for
feminisim and gay rights in culture and law / David A.J.
Richards.
        p.   cm.
    Includes bibliographical references and index.
    ISBN 0-226-71206-0 (cloth : alk. paper).—ISBN 0-226-
71207-9 (pbk. : alk. paper)
    1. Gays—Legal status, laws, etc.—United States.
2. Sex and law—United States.   3. Feminism—United
States.   I. Title.
KF4754.5.R53   1998
342.73′087—dc21   97-35339
                                                             CIP

For Donald Levy

We made slavery, and slavery makes the prejudice. No christian, who questions his own conscience, can justify himself in indulging the feeling. The removal of this prejudice is not a matter of opinion—it is a matter of *duty*.

—Lydia Maria Child, *An Appeal in Favor of Americans Called Africans*

CONTENTS

ACKNOWLEDGMENTS

This book was largely researched during a mid-sabbatical leave taken from the New York University School of Law during the spring term of 1995 and written and revised during the summers of 1995, 1996, and 1997 and during a sabbatical leave taken during the academic year 1997-98. Both the sabbatical leaves and associated summers were made possible by generous research grants from the New York University School of Law Filomen D'Agostino and Max E. Greenberg Faculty Research Fund. I am very grateful as well to my colleagues and my dean, John Sexton, for forging an academic culture of learning at the School of Law so hospitable to scholarly work.

The manuscript profited from critical discussion on two occasions at the Colloquium on Constitutional Theory at the School of Law, which was brilliantly led by my colleagues, Christopher Eisgruber and Lawrence Sager. My colleague, Peggy Davis, gave me invaluable research advice at crucial stages in this project, and I am grateful for her generosity in sharing her own work and perspectives, embodied in her important recently published book on related matters. Conversations with Anthony Amsterdam, Jerome Bruner, Paulette Caldwell, Ronald Dworkin, Thomas M. Franck, Sylvia Law, William Nelson, and John Reid, my superb colleagues, have been helpful to me over the years. Mary Anne Case, while visiting at the School of Law, made extensive probing comments on the entire manuscript from which I much profited. Conversations with other visitors, Derrick Bell and Deborah Rhode, were also helpful to me. Amy Adler, Yochai Benkler, Norman

Dorsen, Sarah Gordon, Helen Hershkoff, Nan Hunter, Frank Michelman, Liam Murphy, Thomas Nagel, Judith Resnik, and Diane Zimmerman also gave me helpful comments on the manuscript.

Work on this project was aided by excellent research assistants, including Julie Novkov, Wendy Bach, Lisa Rechsteiner, Robert Wilson, Anastasia Fernands, and Jon Pickhardt. I am grateful as well to the stimulation I received from the other students in my classes and seminars at the School of Law over the past years; discussions with them, as well as with my research assistants, shaped many of the arguments of this book. My secretary, Lynn Gilbert, also ably and patiently assisted me both in gathering research materials used in writing this book and in preparing the manuscript for publication.

My work in revising the manuscript was greatly assisted by the comments of Martha Minow and William Rubinstein, readers of this manuscript for the University of Chicago Press. I am grateful to both of them, but especially to Martha Minow, whose extensive sympathetic and critical comments were invaluable to me. Thanks also are due to Douglas Mitchell, senior gay studies editor at the University of Chicago Press, for his ardor and patience in support of this project, and to Robert E. Caceres for his fine work as copyeditor.

I am grateful as well for the love and support of my sister and friend, Diane Rita Richards.

The dedication of this book to Donald Levy marks heartfully twenty-one years of our loving life together: "O miracol d'amore."[1]

New York, N.Y.
May 1, 1997

1. Claudio Monteverdi, "Luci serene e chiare," *Quarto Libro dei Madrigali.*

INTRODUCTION

This book combines interpretive history, political philosophy, and constitutional argument to make sense of the background, development, and growing impact of two of the most important movements for human rights currently on the American constitutional scene: feminism and gay rights.

My interest in this approach has its roots in my past two books, the first of which studied American revolutionary constitutionalism as the background of the Constitution of 1787,[1] and the second, as the background of the Civil War and Reconstruction Amendments.[2] American revolutionary constitutionalism, as I understand it, tests the legitimacy of political power (including constitutional law as a higher-order organization of political power) in terms of respect for inalienable human rights. Both the American Revolution and Civil War are, in my view, reasonably interpreted as expressions of such revolutionary constitutionalism; both are revolts against forms of constitutionalism that failed this test with the aim to replace them with more legitimate forms of constitutionalism (in the one case, ultimately with the Constitution of 1787, as amended by the Bill of Rights; in the other, that Constitution, as further amended by the Reconstruction Amendments).

My study of the second expression of American revolutionary consti-

1. See David A. J. Richards, *Foundations of American Constitutionalism* (New York: Oxford University Press, 1989).

2. See David A. J. Richards, *Conscience and the Constitution: History, Theory, and Law of the Reconstruction Amendments* (Princeton: Princeton University Press, 1993).

tutionalism led me, like all other serious students of this development, to the close study of the abolitionist movement. How, I asked myself, should we interpret these amendments today, in light of the clear impact of some quite radical abolitionist ideas on the Reconstruction Amendments? I offered some initial investigations of this topic in my last book, but the interpretive effort of that book was largely directed to the racial cases and only dealt rather cursorily with issues of gender and sexual preference. The more I studied the abolitionist movement and, in particular, the abolitionist feminists within it, the more it became clear to me that interpreting issues of gender and sexual preference in light of the revolutionary constitutionalism of the Reconstruction Amendments would require an approach different from any I had previously taken. This approach must attend closely to the interpretive claims about American revolutionary constitutionalism of a particularly radical dissenting movement within abolitionism (a movement influential on the claims for gay rights of Walt Whitman): one whose distinctive claims were, if anything, largely ignored and often repudiated not only within abolitionism but, after the Civil War, by leading advocates of suffrage feminism. How, I asked myself, could such a movement (let alone its influence on an iconoclast like Whitman) have interpretive relevance to today's great constitutional debates about gender and sexual preference?

My answer to this question is the subject of this book. It is a book very much about the importance of certain kinds of radical theory and practice of rights-based dissent to the integrity of our revolutionary constitutionalism. I try to explain how and why this has been so in the past and how contemporary constitutional interpretation, at its best, builds upon and elaborates this tradition (chapter 1). It is a book treating feminist argument as interpretive argument about central principles of American revolutionary constitutionalism, beginning with antebellum abolitionist feminists who united common principles condemning slavery and racism and the subjection of women and sexism (chapters 2–3) on what they called the platform of human rights. I examine these antebellum feminists in depth and the degree to which their repudiation by suffrage feminists compromised feminism as a serious rights-based movement until the rebirth of second wave rights-based feminism after World War II (chapter 4). Second wave feminism not only took up again, in the wake of the successes of the antiracist civil rights movement (in which many second wave feminists participated), a theory and practice of rights-based feminism building on abolitionist feminism, but infused their reading of these issues of rights-based principle into constitutional interpretation of the Reconstruction

Amendments. These included both constitutional protection of basic rights (conscience, speech, intimate life, and work) and the increasing suspectness of gender as a ground for state action (chapter 5).

My interest in the subject of gay and lesbian rights has been at the center of my work since I first began teaching law. As a gay man, my conviction has long been that the capacity of American constitutional law to do justice to these issues should be a criterion of its legitimacy: the test, as it must be, of its respect for universal human rights. Much of my work has thus been concerned to explore the normative and interpretive foundations for this claim, and this book offers a perspective on this enterprise inspired by the abolitionist feminists in particular and second wave rights-based feminism in general. The case for gay rights is, I argue, a wholly principled and just interpretation of the demands of American revolutionary constitutionalism both in respect for basic human rights (conscience, speech, intimate life, and work) and in the suspectness of sexual preference on the basis of constitutional principles that condemn (in the areas of religion, race, gender, and sexual preference) the expression through law of forms of rights-denying moral slavery (chapter 6). I use this argument to explain why antigay/lesbian initiatives were properly struck down by the Supreme Court (chapter 7) and why both the exclusion of gays and lesbians from the military and from marriage rights are similarly unconstitutional (chapter 8). I conclude with some reflections on how such a rights-based approach clarifies important issues of contesting identity on grounds of justice central to public controversy today in many domains (chapter 9).

For American constitutional lawyers, the central contribution of the argument of this book is its interpretive proposal for how, in light of the history and political theory of the Reconstruction Amendments, these amendments should be interpreted in contemporary circumstances. The normative conception of *moral slavery* is, I argue, the best interpretation of the prohibition of slavery in the Thirteenth Amendment. Moral slavery, as I understand it (building on the arguments of antebellum abolitionist feminists), condemns a structural injustice marked by its abridgment of the basic human rights of a group on inadequate grounds (involving the dehumanization of the group in question) (chapters 3, 5). The analysis of the prohibition of moral slavery, as the hermeneutic pivot of the Reconstruction Amendments, in turn clarifies the proper interpretation of structurally related principles of the Fourteenth Amendment.

Two such principles are of special interpretive concern to contemporary American public law: the nationalization of the protection of basic human rights against both the state and national governments, and the comparably applicable guarantee of equal protection of the laws. I argue that both these judicially enforceable substantive principles under the Fourteenth Amendment are structurally connected to the prohibition of moral slavery. The great normative prohibition of the Thirteenth Amendment identifies a constitutional evil condemned by the two principles protected by the Fourteenth Amendment: first, that basic human rights must be judicially protected against abridgment both by the state and national governments; and second, certain inadequate grounds cannot be permitted illegitimately to rationalize such abridgments. The prohibition on moral slavery condemns a constitutional evil turning both on the abridgment of such basic human rights and the inadequate grounds on which they have been abridged. Accordingly, a historically informed normative analysis of moral slavery makes possible a corresponding interpretive understanding of the central substantive principles of the Fourteenth Amendment.

With respect to the nationalization of the protection of basic human rights, I argue that a proper understanding of the structural injustice condemned by the Thirteenth Amendment crucially requires the identification and protection of basic human rights of conscience, free speech, intimate life, and work, all of which are abridged by institutions of moral slavery on inadequate grounds. The analysis thus clarifies the important role that these rights have played as judicially enforceable human rights against abridgment both by the state and national governments (see chapters 5–6).

With respect to the equal protection principle of the Fourteenth Amendment, equal protection expresses the general requirement, rooted in abolitionist political theory, that all forms of political power must be reasonably justifiable to all persons in terms of both equal respect for their basic human rights and the pursuit of acceptable public purposes of justice and the common good.[3] It has various dimensions, two of which (fundamental rights and suspect classification analysis) call for heightened scrutiny of laws; outside these categories, its demand for reasonable public justification is much more deferential to democratic politics.[4] Fundamental rights analysis calls for such de-

3. For the classic statement of equal protection as a form of public reasonableness, see Joseph Tussman and Jacobus tenBroek, "The Equal Protection of the Laws," *California Law Review* 37 (1949): 341. For tenBroek's pathbreaking work on the abolitionist antecedents of equal protection, see Jacobus tenBroek, *Equal under Law* (New York: Collier, 1969).

4. On the various modes of strict and rational basis analysis, see "Developments in the Law—Equal Protection," *Harvard Law Review* 82 (1969): 86. For arguments for more aggressive rational basis review, see Gerald Gunther, "Newer Equal Protection," *Harvard Law*

terity, are often not in any genetic, let alone ethnic or racial, relationship to these dissenters. What we find in them is a struggle for personal and ethical meaning in living that sets appropriate standards for our interpretive challenge as Americans today. This normative legacy makes sense only when understood in its own demanding universalistic terms, which apply to us in the same abstract terms they did to them. Only an approach that combines both historical contextualization and abstract normative theory is, in my judgment, adequate to so rich and powerful and engaging a contemporary theme.

My proposal is, in its narrative structure, not only meant to be interpretive of American constitutional law as it currently is, but to offer a normative proposal as well for a critical understanding of other interpretive developments in law that may be mistaken. Any plausible theory of constitutional interpretation must have both explanatory and normative features. My account, though explanatory of a surprisingly wide range of contemporary interpretive developments (including the suspectness of race and gender and, most recently, even sexual preference), sometimes takes up a decidedly normative position (e.g., quite critical of our current constitutional "common sense" about the permissibility of excluding gays and lesbians from the military and from marriage). Normative proposals address the American constitutional conscience, which is the responsibility of each and every American. At this point, my argument stretches beyond law to the interpretive responsibilities of Americans to demand that their law and their public and private culture conform to their best critical understandings of American ideals and traditions. This is why I did not write this account in the hermetic positivistic spirit still characteristic of much work in law.

I speak to the role of radical dissent against majoritarian democracy: the place of dissident African Americans, Jews, women, and homosexuals in forging an alternative vision of American rights-based democracy, and the role of visionary poetry (Whitman) in making space for the silenced and subjugated voice of homosexuals in American public and private culture. My argument is that all these developments have pivotally shaped our sense of proper contemporary constitutional interpretation and inform as well our larger interpretive responsibilities to understand our best traditions and, where necessary, protest political and legal failures properly to give effect to those traditions. For these reasons, my account is deeply historical, narratively structured, broadly interpretive (including progressive anthropologists and gay and other literary figures), and framed by arguments of political philosophy central to the progressive integrity of the rights-based dissidents of my story. Such an interdisciplinary perspective—historical, narrative, broadly interpretive, philosophical—must be as rich, complex, and generous as its large and humane topic, the personally and politically transformative American struggle for justice on the platform of human rights. That struggle touches not only constitutional lawyers, but the hearts and minds of all Americans, indeed (today more than ever) all peoples struggling for justice under and through law. Our individual narratives of identity and change shape and are shaped by the larger constitutional narrative of personal and ethical struggle for and empowerment of authentic moral voice. The study of the moral power of that voice in our public and private culture is my very American theme.

1   The Interpretive Challenge

T he analogy between race and gender plays an increasingly important role in the interpretation of the equal protection clause of
the Fourteenth Amendment.[1] For example, a form of the analogy (including an analogy to religion) may be implicit in the Supreme Court's
recent decision in *Romer v. Evans,*[2] which struck down an amendment
to the Colorado state constitution that not only repealed all state
and local ordinances that protected gays and lesbians against discrimination on grounds of sexual preference, but prohibited all such ordinances.[3]

Yet interpretive arguments about the analogies among race, gender,
sexual preference, and religion make little or no reference to the abolitionist historical background of the Reconstruction Amendments, in-

---

1. For opinions of the Supreme Court which pivotally appeal to interpretations of the
analogy, see *Frontiero v. Richardson,* 411 U.S. 677 (1973); *Regents of University of California
v. Bakke,* 438 U.S. 265 (1978).

2. *Romer v. Evans,* 116 S. Ct. 1620 (1996).

3. On homophobia as a form of sexism, see Suzanne Pharr, *Homophobia: A Weapon
of Sexism* (Inverness, Cal.: Chardon Press, 1988); Elisabeth Young-Bruehl, *The Anatomy of
Prejudices* (Cambridge: Harvard University Press, 1996), 35–36, 148–51. For developments
of constitutional analogies among race, gender, and sexual preference, see Andrew Koppelman, "Why Discrimination against Lesbians and Gay Men Is Sex Discrimination," *New York
University Law Review* 69 (1994): 197; Cass R. Sunstein, "Homosexuality and the Constitution," *Indiana Law Journal* 70 (1994): 39; on the analogy to religion, see David A. J. Richards,
"Sexual Preference as a Suspect (Religious) Classification: An Alternative Perspective on the
Unconstitutionality of Anti-Lesbian/Gay Initiatives," *Ohio Law Journal* 55 (1994): 491.

cluding the abolitionist appeal to rights-based normative principles in its criticism of antebellum constitutionalism.[4] This makes sense if the only legitimate interpretive appeal to history was Raoul Berger's version of originalism (including particular persons and practices), in which the relevant drafters and ratifiers of the pertinent constitutional text would or would not have applied the language in question.[5] On this view, the dominant denotative view in 1866–68 that the equal protection clause did not apply to gender, let alone to sexual preference, would debar any legitimate appeal to interpretive history in the understanding of the analogy between race, gender, sexual preference, and religion in contemporary equal protection jurisprudence. However, the judges, lawyers, and citizens who have used the analogy between race, gender, sexual preference, and religion in the interpretation of the equal protection clause clearly reject Berger's theory of originalism as the measure of the proper use of history in constitutional interpretation.[6] So, we are left with a puzzle about the disuse of relevant history in the interpretation of the analogy between race and gender in equal protection jurisprudence. The only theory that might justify such disuse has been reasonably rejected as a general theory of the use of history in constitutional interpretation, but the theory appears to have uncritical force in the specific interpretive domain of the analogy between race, gender, religion, and sexual preference.

The puzzle cannot be solved by the mere appeal to relevant parallel texts in section two of the Fourteenth Amendment, namely, the three textual references to the word "male" as a defining characteristic of the class of persons subject to the formula for reduced representation specified by that provision. Although leading abolitionist feminists like Elizabeth Cady Stanton and Susan B. Anthony did take the language of section 2 to be a bitter defeat for the role that the text of the Fourteenth Amendment should properly play in advancing feminist objectives (in particular, the enfranchisement of women),[7] neither the judiciary that long refused to accept gender discrimination as a violation

---

4. See David A. J. Richards, *Conscience and the Constitution: History, Theory, and Law of the Reconstruction Amendments* (Princeton: Princeton University Press, 1993).

5. See, for example, Raoul Berger, *Government by Judiciary: The Transformation of the Fourteenth Amendment* (Cambridge: Harvard University Press, 1977).

6. Even Robert Bork, who prominently defended a form of originalism, did not subscribe to Berger's denotative view. He thus defended *Brown v. Board of Education*, 347 U.S. 483 (1954), though, in his view, it failed to square with the Founders' denotations. Robert Bork, *The Tempting of America: The Political Seduction of the Law* (New York: The Free Press, 1990), 75–76, 81–82.

7. See Elizabeth Cady Stanton, Susan B. Anthony, and Matilda Joslyn Gage, eds., *History of Woman Suffrage* (1861–76; New York: Fowler & Wells, 1882), 2:315–32.

of equal protection under section 1[8] nor the judiciary that more recently has accepted such arguments[9] rested their views on section 2.
Section 2 struck a short-term compromise of abolitionist principles (regarding the enfranchisement of the freedmen and women's rights) very
much contextually bound to the circumstances of the nation in the
wake of the Civil War (such as the state of Northern public opinion):
it afforded a formula of reduced representation triggered by the racial
exclusion of citizens from the right to vote in circumstances where
public opinion was unready to mandate enfranchisement of the
freedmen directly (as the Fifteenth Amendment would do for blacks
in 1870 and the Nineteenth Amendment would for women in 1920).
Section 1, in contrast, articulated enduring abolitionist principles of government that were not contextually bound to the terms of a historically
contingent compromise of principle. For this reason, the judiciary has
properly not regarded the constitutionality of gender discrimination as
resting on the kind of historical consensus central to section 2.[10]

The puzzle is a particular intellectual challenge to the state of constitutional law scholarship in light of the increasing importance attached
by many scholars, including myself, to the moral, political, and constitutional arguments forged by the abolitionists in the antebellum period, which is acknowledged to be the crucial hermeneutic background
for the proper interpretation of the Reconstruction Amendments.[11] If
historical arguments of this sort are of general interpretive relevance,
then why aren't such arguments centering on the analogy of race, gender, sexual preference, and religion also relevant?

This lacuna in contemporary constitutional scholarship is all the
more remarkable in light of feminist interest in recovering women's
history[12] and the related struggle of gays and lesbians to articulate their

8. See Justice Bradley's concurring opinion in *Bradwell v. State*, 83 U.S. (16 Wall.) 130
(1873) (appealing to woman's nature as the ground for her reasonable exclusion, under the
equal protection clause, from admission to the legal profession).

9. See *Craig v. Boren*, 429 U.S. 190 (1976) (gender distinctions in state liquor sale law
unreasonably reinforce unjust gender stereotypes).

10. But see *Richardson v. Ramirez*, 418 U.S. 24 (1974) (state disenfranchisement of ex-
felons not subject to equal protection scrutiny under section 1 because historical context of
section 2 clearly contemplates the exclusion of such disenfranchisement from its sanctions
of reduced representation).

11. See David A. J. Richards, *Conscience and the Constitution: History, Theory, and Law
of the Reconstruction Amendments* (Princeton: Princeton University Press, 1993). See also
Akhil Reed Amar, "The Bill of Rights and the Fourteenth Amendment," *Yale Law Journal*
101 (1992): 1193; Peggy Cooper Davis, "Neglected Stories and the Lawfulness of *Roe v.
Wade*," *Harvard Civil Rights–Civil Liberties Law Review* 28 (1993): 299.

12. See, generally, Joan Kelly, *Women, History, and Theory* (Chicago: University of Chicago Press, 1984); Joan Wallach Scott, *Gender and the Politics of History* (New York: Colum-

place in history.[13] Women, who could not vote, nonetheless played an intellectually and politically central role in the abolitionist movement. Abolitionist feminists found it morally necessary to articulate feminist arguments and to apply them equally to the plight of blacks and women.[14] In particular, the great American poet, Walt Whitman, was clearly influenced by feminist arguments of these sorts:[15] in the late antebellum period he published successive editions of his masterwork, *Leaves of Grass*,[16] that celebrated a conception of homoerotic love, or "adhesiveness."[17] "Adhesiveness," he later argued in his essay, *Democratic Vistas*,[18] was a crucial emancipatory aspect of the realization of the rights of moral persons he took to be at the core of the American struggle, including the struggle of the Civil War, for a principled conception of democratic individuality.[19] In Great Britain, figures as di-

bia University Press, 1988); Linda J. Nicholson, *Gender and History: The Limits of Social Theory in the Age of the Family* (New York: Columbia University Press, 1986); *A History of Women in the West*, ed. Georges Duby and Michelle Perrot, trans. Arthur Goldhammer, 5 vols. (Cambridge: Harvard University Press, 1992–94).

13. See, for example, Martin Bauml Duberman, Martha Vicinus, and George Chauncey, Jr., *Hidden from History: Reclaiming the Gay and Lesbian Past* (New York: New American Library, 1989).

14. See, in general, Jean Fagan Yellin, *Women and Sisters: The Antislavery Feminists in American Culture* (New Haven: Yale University Press, 1989).

15. On Whitman's veneration of leading nineteenth-century feminists like Frances Wright, Margaret Fuller, and others, see Justin Kaplan, *Walt Whitman: A Life* (New York: Simon and Schuster, 1980), 57, 63, 100, 164. On Whitman's antebellum abolitionist sympathies, qualified by respect for state's rights on whether and how and when to abolish slavery, see Betsy Erkkila, *Whitman: The Political Poet* (New York: Oxford University Press, 1989), 47–48, 196; on his rather conventional racism, see ibid., 150, 240–42; on his feminism, see ibid., 257–59, 298, 308–17.

16. See Walt Whitman, *Leaves of Grass*, in *Walt Whitman: The Complete Poems*, ed. Frances Murphy (Harmondsworth: Penguin, 1975), 35–568. For an illuminating exploration of the changes in the successive editions of *Leaves of Grass* (first edition, 1855; second edition, 1856; third edition, 1860; fourth edition, 1867), see Michael Moon, *Disseminating Whitman: Revision and Corporeality* in Leaves of Grass (Cambridge: Harvard University Press, 1991).

17. See *Leaves of Grass*, 152.

18. See Walt Whitman, *Democratic Vistas*, in *Walt Whitman: Complete Poetry and Collected Prose*, ed. Justin Kaplan (New York: Library of America, 1982), 929, 981–82.

19. The best evidence for this is surely the poetry and essays. See, in particular, "Calamus," in *Leaves of Grass*, 146–67; *Democratic Vistas*, 929–94, especially 929 (praising John Stuart Mill's *On Liberty*) and 981 (defending "[i]ntense and loving comradeshipe, the personal and passionate attachment of man to men"). Whitman remarked: "Free love? Is there any other kind of love?" Justin Kaplan, *Walt Whitman: A Life* (New York: Simon and Schuster, 1980), 43.

The only contrary evidence is Whitman's puzzling and surely disingenuous 1890 letter to John Addington Symonds in which he disavowed the "morbid inferences" of homosexuality Symonds apparently ascribed to Whitman. For excerpts, see John Addington Symonds, *Male Love: Problem in Greek Ethics and Other Writings* (New York: Pagan Press, 1983), 153 (excerpts quoted in letter of Symonds to Edward Carpenter). For plausible analysis of Whitman's verse as Edward Carpenter, John Addington Symonds, and Havelock Ellis interpreted Whitman as the contemporary prophetic visionary of a conception of the role of freedom in sexuality (including homosexual relations) in a progressive rights-based democracy in the modern world.[20] If an important interpretive challenge to modern constitutional scholarship is its ability to explicate and clarify explicit or implicit analogies among race, gender, sexual preference, and religion as constitutionally acknowledged evils of discrimination, surely it will advance matters to recover arguments of these sorts that enrich understanding of the hermeneutic background of the Reconstruction Amendments as it may bear on these analogies.

This book undertakes the task of making such arguments available (including their later developments) and exploring their current interpretive fertility. Contemporary constitutional interpretation must in its nature make reasonable choices among the complex strands of American constitutional history. A salient feature of the interpretive argument of this book is that our best understanding of the responsibilities of contemporary constitutional interpretation (including the interpretive challenge of construing the analogies among religion, race, gender,

---

possible motives for this letter (including growing American censorship of any candid discussion of sexuality in general, let alone homosexuality in particular), see Edward Carpenter, *Some Friends of Walt Whitman: A Study in Sex-Psychology* (London: J. E. Francis, 1924), 12–13; Kaplan, *Walt Whitman: A Life*, 44–49. On Whitman's remarkably homoerotic, feminist, and democratic art, recent important studies include Betsy Erkkila, "Whitman and the Homosexual Republic," in *Walt Whitman*, ed. Ed Folsom (Iowa City: University of Iowa Press, 1994), 153–71; id., *Whitman the Political Poet* (New York: Oxford University Press, 1989); Michael Moon, *Disseminating Whitman: Revision and Corporeality in Leaves of Grass* (Cambridge: Harvard University Press, 1991); George Kateb, *The Inner Ocean: Individualism and Democratic Culture* (Ithaca: Cornell University Press, 1992), 240–66.

20. See Edward Carpenter, *The Intermediate Sex: A Study of Some Transitional Types of Men and Women* (New York: Mitchell Kennerley, 1912), 37–77, especially 73–75 (criticizing application of criminal sanctions to "an attachment . . . of great value in the national life"). On Carpenter's formative relationship to Whitman, see id., *Days with Walt Whitman: With Some Notes on His Life and Work* (London: George Allen, 1906); id., *Some Friends of Walt Whitman* (London: J. E. Francis, 1924); id., *My Days and Dreams: Being Autobiographical Notes* (London: George Allen, 1921), 30, 64, 86–87, 117; Chushichi Tsuzuki, *Edward Carpenter, 1844–1929: Prophet of Human Fellowship* (Cambridge: Cambridge University Press, 1980), 20–21, 29. For other examples of a similar formative influence of Whitman on major British advocates of sexual reform (especially in the area of homosexuality), see John Addington Symonds, *Walt Whitman: A Study* (1893; New York: Benjamin Blom, 1967); Havelock Ellis, *The New Spirit* (Washington, D.C.: National Home Library Foundation, 1935), 86–127. For the works advocating reform, see John Addington Symonds, *A Problem in Modern Ethics* (London, 1896); id., *A Problem in Greek Ethics,* in id., *Male Love: A Problem in Greek Ethics and Other Writings* (1901; New York: Pagan Press, 1983), 1–73; Havelock Ellis and John Addington Symonds, *Sexual Inversion* (London: Wilson and Macmillan, 1897), 153, 155–56 (homosexual conduct not properly criminal).

and sexual preference) requires us to take an interest in strands of our constitutional tradition that were, in their historical context, at best marginal. Whitman's historical marginality is starkly obvious (*Leaves of Grass* was successfully prosecuted for obscenity in 1882[21]), while the marginality of abolitionist feminism, though less obvious, is still on balance reasonably clear.

Abolitionist feminism was, as I shall later describe it, one strand among many in the abolitionist movement. Its most self-conscious articulation, in a relatively brief period of 1835–39, remained at best a marginal subtheme in the abolitionist movement during the remaining antebellum period culminating in the Civil War and the Reconstruction Amendments, and it affirmed common antiracist and antisexist principles resisted by many later feminists.[22] Indeed, a reasonably cogent historical case can be made that the central claims of abolitionist feminism, including not only the claim to the right to vote but the deeper moral interpretation (both antiracist and antisexist) of what I shall later call "moral slavery," were explicitly rejected by the Reconstruction Congress as reasonable interpretations of the Reconstruction Amendments. Congressional Republicans steadfastly denied, for example, that the condemnation of slavery and involuntary servitude by the Thirteenth Amendment applied to domestic relations.[23] Indeed, contrary to a defining moral claim of abolitionist feminism, the rights of freemen were interpreted to include a property right in his family, including his wife.[24] And, contrary to eloquent abolitionist feminist interpretive arguments that both the Fourteenth and Fifteenth Amendments extended the vote to women (made in 1871 by both Victoria Woodhull[25] and Tennie Claflin,[26] and in 1872 by Susan B. Anthony[27]),

21. For discussion, see Erkkila, *Whitman: The Political Poet,* 308, 310–11.

22. On Abby Kelley's struggle against this development, see Dorothy Sterling, *Ahead of Her Time: Abby Kelley and the Politics of Antislavery* (New York: W. W. Norton, 1991).

23. For historical discussion and analysis of this point, see Amy Dru Stanley, "Conjugal Bonds and Wage Labor: Rights of Contract in the Age of Emancipation," *Journal of American History* 75 (1985): 479–80; Lea S. VanderVelde, "The Labor Vision of the Thirteenth Amendment," *University of Pennsylvania Law Review* 138 (1989): 454–59, 480, 496.

24. See Stanley, "Rights of Contract," 480.

25. See Victoria Woodhull, *A Lecture on Constitutional Equality,* in *The Victoria Woodhull Reader,* ed. Madeleine B. Stern (1871; Weston, Mass.: M & S Press, 1974). Woodhull's argument included the claim that, invoking the text of the Fifteenth Amendment, women's traditional status was a "previous condition of servitude," thus bringing the disenfranchisement of women within the scope of the prohibitions of the amendment. Ibid., 17–18.

26. See Tennie C. Claflin, *Constitutional Equality a Right of Woman* (New York: Woodhull, Claflin & Co., 1871).

27. See Susan B. Anthony, "Constitutional Argument," in *The Elizabeth Cady Stanton– Susan B. Anthony Reader: Correspondence, Writings, Speeches,* ed. Ellen Carol DuBois, rev.

such prominent figures in the Reconstruction Congress as Representative John A. Bingham[28] rejected such an interpretation.[29] What reasonable weight, if any, should abolitionist feminism (let alone Whitman), understood as thus historically marginal, be accorded in the interpretation of these amendments?

Elsewhere I have argued at length[30] that the Reconstruction Amendments must be interpreted against the background of the antebellum moral, political, and constitutional theory of radical constitutional antislavery. If the legitimacy of the American Revolution required a form of constitutionalism (in contrast to the corrupt British Constitution) adequate to its normative demands, the legitimacy of the Civil War likewise required a comparably profound answer to the constitutional decadence found in the dominant interpretation of the Constitution in the antebellum period. Radical antislavery's critical analysis of antebellum constitutional decadence met this need, marking the rebirth of the rights-based constitutional government. Its great appeal for the American constitutional mind was both its radical insistence on the primacy of the revolutionary political theory of human rights of American constitutionalism (as embodied in the Declaration of Independence) and its brilliant reinterpretation of the ingredients of such constitutionalism in light of that political theory and the events surrounding the Civil War. In light of its analysis, radical antislavery supplied the most reasonable interpretation of the Civil War as the second American Revolution and offered, consistent with the genre of American revolutionary constitutionalism, remedies that plausibly could be and were regarded as the most justifiable way to correct central defects in the Constitution of 1787—some of which had been acknowledged by the Founders, like Madison.[31] The Reconstruction Amendments—the most radical change in our constitutionalism in our history—could plausibly thus be understood as a wholly reasonable and conservative way to preserve the legitimacy of the long-standing project of American revolutionary constitutionalism.

---

ed. (Boston: Northeastern University Press, 1992), 152–65. Anthony had been arrested in November, 1872 for "illegal voting" and, in preparation for her trial on these charges, lectured in public on the principles by which she claimed a right to vote.

28. On Bingham's role as architect of section 1 of the Fourteenth Amendment, see Richards, *Conscience and the Constitution,* 121–23.

29. See John A. Bingham, Report of the Committee on the Judiciary, in *Congressional Reports on Woman Suffrage* (New York: Woodhull, Claflin & Co., 1871), in *The Victoria Woodhull Reader,* 96–98.

30. See, in general, Richards, *Conscience and the Constitution.*

31. See David A. J. Richards, *Foundations of American Constitutionalism* (New York: Oxford University Press, 1989), 37–38.

The Reconstruction Amendments contain both negative and positive features: the abolition of slavery and involuntary servitude (Thirteenth Amendment), the prohibition of racial discrimination in voting (Fifteenth Amendment), and the affirmative requirements of citizenship for all Americans and nationally defined and enforceable guarantees applicable against the states of equal protection, privileges and immunities, and due process of law (Fourteenth Amendment). The political theory of these prohibitions and requirements was Lockean political theory as it had been articulated and applied in the antebellum period by radical antislavery: all political power (including now the power of the states) could be legitimate only if it met the requirement of extending to all persons subject to such power nationally enforceable standards of respect for their inalienable human rights and the use of power to pursue the public interest. These guarantees thus textually included the central normative dimensions distinctive of radical antislavery: the demand that all persons subject to the burdens of allegiance to the political power of the United States be accorded both their natural rights as persons and their equal rights as citizens, based on the fundamental egalitarian requirement of politically legitimate government stated by the equal protection clause. If the Constitution of 1787 had made remarkably little textual reference to its background political theory, the Reconstruction Amendments textually affirmed and enforced that political theory with notable focus on the forms of political pathology that had motivated antebellum constitutional decadence—the untrammeled state power over abridgment of human rights that had given rise to the political pathologies of the slave power conspiracy in general and American racism in particular.[32] Both the Thirteenth Amendment's prohibition of slavery and the equal protection clause of the Fourteenth Amendment's prohibition of racist subjugation were thus negative corollaries of the affirmative principle of equal respect for the rights of all persons subject to political power, and thus required the national articulation, elaboration, and enforcement of constitutional principles that defined the supreme law of the land because they secured the politically legitimate terms for the exercise of any political power.

The Reconstruction Amendments responded to the gravest crisis of constitutional legitimacy in our history, and are best interpreted as negative and affirmative constitutional principles responsive to that cri-

32. For a good statement of this general concern at the time of the introduction of the Thirteenth Amendment on the floor of the House of Representatives, see Speech of Representative Henry Wilson, *Congressional Globe*, 38th Cong., 1st sess., March 19, 1864, 1199–1206.

sis and any comparable future ones. Our interpretive attitude must be to make the best sense of them in light of the genre of American revolutionary constitutionalism that they assume and to critically elaborate them in deference to the narrative integrity of the story of the American people and their struggle for politically legitimate government that respects human rights. Abolitionist theory and practice played a crucial role in reviving and retelling this story. For example, in the Lincoln-Douglas Debates of 1858, Abraham Lincoln, who had in 1837 criticized abolitionist advocacy as tending "rather to increase than to abate its [slavery's] evils,"[33] appealed to the central abolitionist moral judgment of the rights-denying evil of slavery. He argued that the long-term ambition of the rights-based Constitution for such an evil was "that it is in the course of ultimate extinction."[34] He also argued that the opinion of Chief Justice Taney in *Dred Scott* (holding unconstitutional a power in Congress to exclude slavery from the territories) was wrong because it flouted this principle,[35] and that Stephen Douglas's theory of popular sovereignty (by which territories could decide whether to have or not have slavery) illegitimately evaded what was, for Lincoln, the central moral question of the rights-denying evil of slavery and its inconsistency with the Declaration of Independence. By undermining the political morality of human rights, Lincoln argued that Douglas

> is blowing out the moral lights around us, when he contends that whoever wants slaves has a right to hold them; that he is penetrating, so far as lies in his power, the human soul, and eradicating the light of reason and the love of liberty, when he is in every possible way preparing the public mind, by his vast influence, for making the institution of slavery perpetual and national.[36]

Thus the antebellum constitutional struggle was a fight over basic issues of political morality and the role of that morality in constitutional interpretation. Lincoln put the point starkly: "If slavery is not wrong, nothing can be wrong."[37] If the nation lost its competence at making and enforcing such rights-based judgments as fundamental constitutional morality, it could stand for nothing and anything. The recovery

33. See Abraham Lincoln, "Protest in the Illinois Legislature on Slavery," in *Abraham Lincoln: Speeches and Writings*, ed. Don E. Fehrenbacher (New York: The Library of America, 1989), 1:18. For commentary, see David Herbert Donald, *Lincoln* (New York: Simon & Schuster, 1995), 63–64.

34. See Robert W. Johannsen, *The Lincoln-Douglas Debates of 1858* (New York: Oxford University Press, 1965), 200.

35. Ibid., 255.

36. Ibid., 233–34.

37. Lincoln to Albert G. Hodges, 4 April 1864, *Speeches and Writings*, 2:585.

of our constitutional moral sanity was how Lincoln, in his Gettysburg Address, gave enduring moral meaning to the sacrifices of the Civil War, namely as "a new birth of freedom."[38]

Lincoln thus morally grounded the Civil War on the abolitionist demands for respect for human rights, on which the legitimacy of the Constitution ultimately rested. The Reconstruction Amendments constitutionally insist on respect for these demands and thus rest on and express abolitionist political morality. Our interpretive attitude today should take account of abolitionist political theory and practice as part of an enriched sense of what our constitutional tradition is and how it should be carried forward on the terms that do justice to it.

The constitutional interpretation of the Reconstruction Amendments must thus give expression to each generation's most reasonable understanding of the demands of human rights in its circumstances. Human rights should be interpreted in Lincoln's terms that "there is no just rule other than that of moral and abstract right!"[39] It cannot do justice to this enriched understanding of our interpretive responsibilities to trivialize our interpretation of the Reconstruction Amendments with some fictive search for the concrete exemplars to which some suitably described majority of the Reconstruction Congress or the ratifying states or, for that matter, advocates of radical antislavery would or would not have applied the relevant clause under interpretation.

In the context of the antebellum crisis of constitutional legitimacy, the political and constitutional theory of the Reconstruction Amendments is rooted in the abstract demands of the antipositivist jurisprudence of radical antislavery.[40] It required an interpretive attitude to the Constitution that would preserve its legitimacy on the grounds of the rights-based theory of human rights central to its claims to be the supreme law of the land. Both Taney's originalism[41] and Stephen

38. Ibid., 536.

39. See Johannsen, *The Lincoln-Douglas Debates*, 221.

40. On this view, since the legitimacy of the Constitution turned on its enforcement of a rights-based political morality, the text of the Constitution must be interpreted, wherever possible, as in service of that morality (irrespective of historical understandings to the contrary). The view was radically antipositivist because it rejected any distinction between the authority of law and rights-based morality. On the variant forms of radical constitutional antislavery, see Richards, *Conscience and the Constitution*, 97–194; on its impact on the Reconstruction Amendments, see ibid., 108–48.

41. Taney argued: "No one, we presume, supposes that any change in public opinion or feeling, in relation to this unfortunate race, in the civilized nations of Europe or in this country, should induce the court to give to the words of the Constitution a more liberal construction in their favor than they were intended to bear when the instrument was framed and adopted." *Dred Scott v. Sanford*, 60 U.S. (19 How.) 393, 426 (1857). In fact, as Justice Curtis

Douglas's majoritarian interpretation of popular sovereignty[42] were, from this perspective, equally illegitimate attempts to evade the interpretive responsibilities of making sense of the supremacy of the Constitution in terms of its protection of the human rights of all persons subject to political power. Taney's use of history and Douglas's majoritarianism substituted positivistic amoral facts or procedures for the deliberative rights-based normative judgments that could alone preserve the Constitution's legitimacy.

Testing the legitimacy of political power in terms of rights-based egalitarian claims must therefore play a central role in the interpretation of the requirements of the Reconstruction Amendments in contemporary circumstances. Such interpretive responsibilities require us to take seriously what our rights are and how they are to be understood and elaborated today on terms of principle.[43] The abolitionists give us a model of the forms of political and constitutional theory and practice that such responsibilities reasonably require us to generate in our circumstances. Such a model of interpretive responsibility is, strikingly, very much more bottom-up rather than top-down; critical rather than celebratory; dissident rather than politically majoritarian; performatively self-defining rather than conventionally conformist. Four features of abolitionist thought and practice are, in this connection, notable.

First, the abolitionists were the most principled and morally independent advocates of the inalienable rights of conscience and free speech in the antebellum period. Set against the hostile tyranny of majoritarian antebellum political complacency so notably anatomized by de Tocqueville,[44] their insistence on giving voice to the morally independent demands of conscience conflicted with convention and public opinion. They brilliantly forged performative spaces in books, newspapers, law courts, speeches, novels, and the like through which they defined themselves (often in vigorous debate with one another) as among the most personally individual Americans of their age. Consistent with this perspective, they demanded, as a matter of prin-

---

points out in dissent, Taney gets even his alleged originalist history of Founders' concrete intentions wrong. Id. at 572–74.

42. Popular sovereignty, irrespective of constitutional or natural rights, allowed states to decide whether they would or would not have slavery; as one commentator observes, "Douglas looked upon popular sovereignty as essentially pragmatic and expedient," Robert W. Johannsen, *Stephen A. Douglas* (New York: Oxford University Press, 1973), 240.

43. See, for example, David A. J. Richards, *Toleration and the Constitution* (New York: Oxford University Press, 1986).

44. See Alexis de Tocqueville, *Democracy in America*, ed. Phillips Bradley (1835; New York: Vintage, 1945), 1:264–80.

ciple, recognition of the just demands of African Americans for a self-authenticating moral voice adequate to their own experiences and struggles.[45] The performative demands of abolitionist self-definition were thus brilliantly embraced by former slaves in such diversely remarkable narratives of liberation from slavery as those of Frederick Douglass[46] and Harriet Jacobs.[47]

Second, their principled commitment to the inalienable right to conscience and free speech enabled the abolitionists, as we shall later see, to elaborate and extend the argument for toleration critically to identify new modes of unjust sectarian oppression of basic rights that could not be reasonably justified on political and constitutional terms. The abolitionist criticism of both slavery and racism depended on the remarkable moral and intellectual independence with which they made and pressed this argument.

Third, the abolitionists generated forms of political and constitutional theory that critically tested conventionally popular moral and constitutional views against the most demanding standards of abstract moral, political, and constitutional argument. Consistent with the argument for toleration, for example, they debunked what they found to be polemical sectarian arguments for deprivation of human rights whose irrationalist political force depended on a vicious circle—failure to allow any fair testing of the empirical and normative claims that allegedly justified the deprivation of basic rights (for example, slavery or racist subjugation).

Fourth, abolitionist argument, while often meeting and surpassing the highest intellectual and moral standards of the age, was generated not by mainstream politicians, judges, or academics, but by remarkably courageous moral, political, and constitutional activists; their concern was not with winning votes or securing judicial or academic tenure, but with confronting the American public mind and conscience with its failures of intellect, of morality, of civic republican fidelity to its

45. For two notable examples of arguments along these lines, see William Ellery Channing, *Slavery*, in *The Works of William E. Channing* (1839; New York: Burt Franklin, 1970), 688–743; Lydia Maria Child, *An Appeal in Favor of Americans Called Africans* (1833; New York: Arno Press and the New York Times, 1968).

46. See Frederick Douglass, *Narrative of the Life of Frederick Douglass: An American Slave Written by Himself* (1845; Harmondsworth: Signet, 1968). For Douglass's two later autobiographies, *My Bondage and My Freedom* (1855) and *Life and Times of Frederick Douglass* (1893), see Henry Louis Gates, Jr., ed., *Frederick Douglass: Autobiographies* (New York: The Library of America, 1994), 103–452, and 453–1045, respectively.

47. See Harriet A. Jacobs, *Incidents in the Life of a Slave Girl Written by Herself*, ed. Jean Fagan Yellin (Cambridge: Harvard University Press, 1987).

revolutionary constitutionalism.[48] The abolitionists show us that the best theory and practice work in tandem, stimulating one another.

These features of abolitionist critical thought and practice illuminate the reasons why the constructive contemporary interpretation of the Reconstruction Amendments cannot be and has not been limited to the views of the Reconstruction Congress on how these amendments are concretely to be interpreted. For one thing, it is wholly unclear that the best interpretation of abolitionist moral and political demands even in the circumstances of 1865–70 would be the dominant consensus of the politicians of the Reconstruction Congress; if anything, the demands of abolitionist theory would suggest skepticism about any simplistic identification of normative demands of principle with actual political consensus. Abolitionist theory (as an elaboration of an argument for human rights grounded, as we shall later see, in toleration) calls for a critical distance between morally independent spheres of critical thought, inquiry, and action and the dominant political orthodoxies whose enforcement through law has unreasonably deprived persons of their basic human rights to such spheres. Because of the compromises of principle often central to securing political consensus (even a consensus on the role abolitionist theory should play in constitutional law), such a consensus may only partially and very imperfectly give interpretive effect to the rights-based skepticism abolitionist theory calls for about certain dominant religio-moral orthodoxies. In effect, a skepticism about one kind of injustice (racism) may not be extended to another (sexism or homophobia) and may indeed thus inflict the very evil it should be remedying. To allow these interpretive demands of abolitionist theory to be diluted to the measure of any contingent political consensus would, for this reason, subvert them. Indeed, the identification of abolitionist demands with political consensus may rationalize intolerance, rather than give effect to the principled force of the underlying argument for toleration, when, as a matter of principle, the enforcement of such consensus through law is most unreasonable and indeed unjust. We shall, in later chapters, have occasion to explore this point repeatedly in various contexts.

Even if the identification of abolitionist theory with political consen-

---

48. For some important recent general studies, see Louis Filler, *The Crusade against Slavery, 1830–1860* (New York: Harper & Row, 1960); James Brewer Stewart, *Holy Warriors: The Abolitionists and American Slavery* (New York: Hill and Wang, 1976); Ronald G. Walters, *The Antislavery Appeal: American Abolitionism after 1830* (New York: W. W. Norton, 1978); Merton L. Dillon, *The Abolitionists: The Growth of a Dissenting Minority* (New York: W. W. Norton, 1974).

sus were more plausible than it in fact is, it does not apply across time. Later generations of Americans make abolitionist rights-based demands, and their interpretive demands of these amendments cannot legitimately track concrete interpretive convictions of an earlier generation that may critically fail to elaborate the rights-based performative demands of abolitionist political morality in contemporary circumstances in a principled way (for example, the failure of the Reconstruction Congress to condemn both racism and sexism). Abolitionist feminism, however historically marginal, may be much more important in our interpretive terms. It made a distinctive normative contribution to each of the four dimensions of the abolitionist project (in particular, articulating common principles of both antiracism and antisexism).

First, its advocates rested their case on the moral independence of their assertion of their rights of conscience, free speech, association, and work against both the racist and sexist orthodoxies of their age. Abolitionist feminists forged a moral identity self-consciously based on grounds of injustice common to both race and gender. That transformative personal and moral experience (deepening a sense of one's own claims of injustice as woman through the struggle to understand and rectify the injustice of racism) was also the experience of many women in the civil rights movement of the 1960s who, like the earlier abolitionist feminists, deepened and revived American feminism in the process.[49]

Second, the principled commitment of abolitionist feminists to such inalienable rights enabled them to elaborate the argument for toleration and to identify critical new modes of sectarian oppression of basic rights that could not be reasonably justified publicly. Their criticism of slavery and the subjection of women was made possible by the astonishing moral and intellectual independence with which they pressed this argument, as we shall later see, against dominant modes of Bible interpretation of their age. Such arguments of Angelina and Sarah Grimke anticipated many of the arguments and practices of later feminists. Their concern with misogynist Bible interpretation was a central preoccupation of Elizabeth Cady Stanton[50] and a growing concern of contemporary feminists.[51] Their emphasis on women's rights of associ-

---

49. See Sara Evans, *Personal Politics: The Roots of Women's Liberation in the Civil Rights Movement and the New Left* (New York: Vintage Books, 1979).

50. See Elizabeth Cady Stanton, *The Woman's Bible* (New York: European Publishing Co., 1895–98).

51. See, for example, Gerda Lerner, *The Creation of Patriarchy* (New York: Oxford University Press, 1986); id., *The Creation of Feminist Consciousness: From the Middle Ages to 1870* (New York: Oxford University Press, 1993); Elaine Pagels, *Adam, Eve, and the Serpent*

ational liberty anticipates the importance of this theme in contemporary feminism, including both the right to abortion services and the right not to associate with men central to arguments against institutions of compulsory heterosexuality.[52] Sarah Grimke's concern for the devaluation of women's work is a theme central to the later work of feminists like Charlotte Perkins Gilman and others.[53]

Third, consistent with the argument for toleration, the abolitionist feminists critically debunked what they found to be polemical sectarian arguments for deprivation of human rights whose irrationalist political force depended on the viciously circular failure to allow any fair testing of the empirical and normative claims that allegedly justified the deprivation of basic rights, for example, racist and sexist subjugation. The same confusion of nature and culture, so unjustly central to American racism, was, in their view, unjustly central to American sexism as well, a theme, as we shall see, developed by later feminist analysis (distinguishing, as it does, biological sex from culturally constructed patterns of gender).[54] The Grimkes' preoccupation with sexism's epistemological injury to moral conscience and consciousness was carried forward as well by feminists from Margaret Fuller[55] to Simone de Beauvoir[56] to Gerda Lerner today.[57] Their concern with political epistemology is central to deepening contemporary feminist absorption in these and related issues.[58] The feminist renaissance and reformation, which they

(New York: Random House, 1998); Rosemary Radford Ruether, *Womanguides: Readings toward a Feminist Theology* (Boston: Beacon Press, 1985); Mary Daly, *Beyond God the Father: Towards a Philosophy of Women's Liberation* (London: Women's Press, 1986); Alicia Suskin Ostriker, *Feminist Revision and the Bible* (Oxford: Blackwell, 1993).

52. See Adrienne Rich, "Compulsory Heterosexuality and Lesbian Existence," in Catharine R. Stimpson and Ethel Spector Person, *Women: Sex and Sexuality* (Chicago: University of Chicago Press, 1980), 62–91.

53. See Charlotte Perkins Gilman, *Women and Economics,* ed. Carl N. Degler (New York: Harper & Row, 1966). For contemporary treatments to similar effect, see Claudia Goldin, *Understanding the Gender Gap: An Economic History of American Women* (New York: Oxford University Press, 1990); Victor R. Fuchs, *Women's Quest for Economic Equality* (Cambridge: Harvard University Press, 1988); Sylvia A. Law, "Women, Work, Welfare, and the Preservation of Patriarchy," *University of Pennsylvania Law* Review 131 (1983): 1249.

54. For a useful historical account of this development, see Rosalind Rosenberg, *Beyond Separate Spheres: Intellectual Roots of Modern Feminism* (New Haven: Yale University Press, 1982).

55. See S. Margaret Fuller, *Woman in the Nineteenth Century,* ed. Madeleine B. Stern (1845; Columbia: University of South Carolina, 1980).

56. See Simone de Beauvoir, *The Second Sex,* ed. H. M. Parshley (New York: Vintage Books, 1974).

57. See Lerner, *The Creation of Patriarchy;* id., *The Creation of Feminist Consciousness.*

58. See, for example, Sandra Harding, *The Science Question in Feminism* (Ithaca: Cornell University Press, 1986); id., *Whose Science? Whose Lives?: Thinking from Women's Lives* (Ithaca: Cornell University Press, 1991); Lorraine Code, *What Can She Know?: Feminist*

argued to be morally necessary for the emancipation of women from their moral slavery, are now very much part of the agenda of our critical public culture.

Fourth, the arguments of abolitionist feminists, while pitched at the highest critical standards of their age, were generated by exiles and outcasts from its dominant political and educational culture, who performatively forged through their own dissenting struggles for moral independence and responsibility, as persons, a prophetic vision of our constitutional principles of respect for the human rights of all persons. This dialectic of theory and practice (a striking continuity between the arguments of the Grimkes and later feminists) is not a matter of merely historical interest. The critical procedures of their abolitionist feminism make possible a principled interpretation of the Reconstruction Amendments in our circumstances, and the most reasonable contemporary rearticulation of these procedures must accordingly frame such contemporary interpretation. The abolitionists' forms of interpretive argument were often employed by activist civil rights advocates who have played a role, in the twentieth century, quite analogous to the abolitionists in the nineteenth century. The abolitionist argument of Frederick Douglass was very much the tradition self-consciously carried forward by a civil rights advocate like Martin Luther King.[59] The abolitionist feminism of Angelina and Sarah Grimke is another aspect of that abolitionist tradition (one prominently embraced by Frederick Douglass himself[60]), a tradition contemporary advocates of basic constitutional justice in matters of gender and sexuality may reasonably

Theory and the Construction of Knowledge (Ithaca: Cornell University Press, 1991); Sandra Harding and Merill B. Hintikka, eds., *Discovering Reality: Feminist Perspectives on Epistemology, Metaphysics, Methodology, and Philosophy of Science* (Dordrecht: D. Reidel, 1983); Anne Fausto-Sterling, *Myths of Gender: Biological Theories about Women and Men* (New York: Basic Books, 1985); Cynthia Fuchs Epstein, *Deceptive Distinctions: Sex, Gender, and the Social Order* (New Haven: Yale University Press, 1988); Sandra Lipsitz Bem, *The Lenses of Gender: Transforming the Debate on Sexual Equality* (New Haven: Yale University Press, 1993).

59. For Frederick Douglass, see Philip S. Foner, ed., *The Life and Writings of Frederick Douglass*, 5 vols. (1950; New York: International Publishers, 1970); for commentary, see William S. McFeely, *Frederick Douglass* (New York: W. W. Norton, 1991); Eric J. Sundquist, *Frederick Douglass: New Library and Historical Essays* (Cambridge: Cambridge University Press, 1990). For Martin Luther King, see James M. Washington, ed., *A Testament of Hope: The Essential Writings of Martin Luther King, Jr.* (San Francisco: Harper & Row, 1986); for commentary, see Taylor Branch, *Parting the Waters: Martin Luther King and the Civil Rights Movement, 1954–63* (London: Papermac, 1990).

60. See, in general, Philip S. Foner, ed., *Frederick Douglass on Women's Rights* (New York: Da Capo Press, 1992).

claim and elaborate as fundamental to the interpretive integrity of our arguments of constitutional principle.

If the recovery of a historically marginal tradition like that of the abolitionist feminists may illuminate contemporary interpretive issues turning on a growing critical self-consciousness of the intersectionalities of injustices of race and gender, the interpretive recovery of Walt Whitman may do no less for sexual preference. Like the abolitionist feminists, Whitman, however radical his historical marginality (indeed his iconoclasm), may offer contemporary constitutional law the most important introductory chapter to the place of gay rights among basic constitutional rights. The interpretive recovery of Whitman does so along each of the four dimensions we have so far discussed.

First, Whitman insistently demands voice, on grounds of American rights-based democracy, for self-defining advocacy of the proper dignity of homoerotic love in an antisexist understanding of the basic rights of moral personality. From this perspective, Whitman's visionary struggle to find and give voice to such claims, against the background of a culture framed by Blackstone's condemnation of the "crime not fit to be named, *'peccatum illud horribile, inter christianos non nominandum,'* "[61] required what he called nothing less than "a language experiment,"[62] to wit, the iconoclastically personal poetry of erotic and political imagination of his masterwork, *Leaves of Grass.* Whitman acknowledged the need performatively to forge a new language and thus a new identity and sense of community because his culture afforded no language that was allowed to give voice to such just claims.[63] To that extent, Whitman's creative iconoclasm was the only reasonably adequate response to the cultural vacuum of unspeakability that he confronted.

Second, Whitman strikingly founded his vision in a wholly original interpretation of "the divinity of sex, the perfect eligibility of the female with the male."[64] Whitman implicitly elaborated the argument of the abolitionist feminists to identify a right of sexual authenticity central to the just equality of men and women that was abridged on inadequate

61. See William Blackstone, *Commentaries on the Laws of England,* ed. Thomas A. Green (1765–69; facsimile ed., Chicago: University of Chicago Press, 1979), 4:216.

62. Betsy Erkkila, *Whitman: The Political Poet* (New York: Oxford University Press, 1989), 82.

63. In his 1876 preface to *Leaves of Grass,* Whitman called the work "the Poem of Identity." Walt Whitman, *Leaves of Grass,* in *Walt Whitman: The Complete Poems,* ed. Frances Murphy (Harmondsworth: Penguin, 1975), 783.

64. Ibid., 770 (1856 letter from Walt Whitman to Ralph Waldo Emerson used as preface to 1856 edition of *Leaves of Grass*).

sectarian grounds. As we shall later see, Whitman thus stated an issue
of rights-based principle on which feminists (men and women) insisted
with growing force to advance the emancipation of women;[65] it is the
argument that sovereignty in love is as fundamental to respect for human rights as such recognized rights as conscience and speech. This
argument has been eloquently made by Stephen Pearl Andrews,[66] Victoria Woodhull,[67] Ezra H. Heywood,[68] Elizabeth Cady Stanton,[69] and
Margaret Sanger.[70] The contemporary principle of constitutional privacy rests, as I shall later argue, on a form of this argument.

Third, Whitman confronted the tradition of unspeakability as a polemically insular failure to allow fair testing of the empirical and normative arguments that allegedly justified deprivation of such basic
rights:

> By silence or obedience the pens of savans [sic], poets, historians, biogra-
> phers, and the rest, have long connived at the filthy law, and books enslaved
> to it, that what makes the manhood of a man, that sex, womanhood, mater-
> nity, desires, lusty animations, organs, acts, are unmentionable and to be
> ashamed of, to be driven to skulk out of literature with whatever belongs to
> them. This filthy law has to be repealed—it stands in the way of great re-
> forms. Of women just as much as men, it is the interest that there should
> not be infidelism about sex, but perfect faith.[71]

Whitman thus laid the cultural foundation for voice that made thinkable the long and continuing struggle for the basic rights of gay and
lesbian persons,[72] including a suggestion of the kinds of historical and

65. For the historical background and development of the argument, see John C. Spurlock, *Free Love: Marriage and Middle-Class Radicalism in America, 1825–1860* (New York:
New York University Press, 1988). For its later development, see Linda Gordon, *Woman's
Body, Woman's Right: A Social History of Birth Control in America* (New York: Penguin,
1976).

66. See Stephen Pearl Andrews, ed., *Love, Marriage, and Divorce* (1853; New York:
Source Book Press, 1972), 33, 66, 68, 86, 89, 95, 97, 106–8.

67. See Victoria C. Woodhull, "A Speech on the Principles of Social Freedom," in *The
Victoria Woodhull Reader,* ed. Madeleine B. Stern (1871; Weston, Mass.: M & S Press, 1974).

68. Ezra H. Heywood, "Uncivil Liberty: An Essay to Show the Injustice and Impolicy
of Ruling Woman against Her Consent," in *The Collected Works of Ezra H. Heywood,* ed.
Martin Blatt (1871; Weston, Mass.: M & S Press, 1985).

69. See Elizabeth Cady Stanton, "Speech on Marriage and Divorce," in *The Search for
Self-Sovereignty: The Oratory of Elizabeth Cady Stanton,* ed. Beth M. Waggenspack (1869;
Greenwood Press: New York, 1989), 121–25; ibid., "The Solitude of Self" (1892), 159–67.

70. See Margaret Sanger, *Woman Rebel,* ed. Alex Baskin (New York: Archives of Social
History, 1976), 25; id., *The Pivot of Civilization* (Elmsford, N.Y.: Maxwell Reprint Co., 1969),
140, 211–19, 259.

71. See Murphy, *Walt Whitman: The Complete Poems,* 770–71 (1856 letter of Walt Whitman to Ralph Waldo Emerson used as preface to 1856 edition of *Leaves of Grass*).

72. For useful studies, see John D'Emilio, *Sexual Politics, Sexual Communities: The Making of a Homosexual Minority in the United States, 1940–1970* (Chicago: University of Chi-

cultural methodologies today developed, like the related forms of contemporary feminist analysis already mentioned, adequately to give
voice to a reasonable contemporary understanding of the injustices
traditionally inflicted on gays and lesbians.[73]

Fourth, Whitman was perhaps the ultimate cultural outcast, and he
performatively created a new visionary language of public identity and
community that enlarges our moral imagination and thus our contemporary understanding of the meaning and scope of human rights. He
did so not because he reflected the dominant political consensus of
his time, but because of the kind of critical distance he achieved from
that consensus—a distance made possible by a morally independent
and indeed compelling appeal to the basic rights of moral personality.
Our interpretive interest today in Whitman is founded on the integrity
of his rights-based arguments of principle and the role they play in a
reasonable contemporary understanding of the basic constitutional
rights of the person.

As I earlier observed, contemporary constitutional interpretation of
the Reconstruction Amendments must reasonably select among complex strands of its historical tradition. These interpretive demands can
no more be satisfied by the concrete interpretive convictions of the
Reconstruction Congress (rejecting, as they did, central claims of abolitionist feminism) here than they can be in general. If we reject the
interpretive convictions of the Reconstruction Congress as the measure of our interpretive responsibilities today,[74] we must reject as well
their repudiation of abolitionist feminism if we find it unreasonable in
our circumstances. If the interpretive convictions of the politicians of
the Reconstruction Congress cannot be the reasonable measure of the
strenuous interpretive demands of abolitionist moral and political theory even in their own circumstances, they cannot, *a fortiori,* be the
measure in our own. Indeed, the Reconstruction Congress's uncritical
rejection of the claims of abolitionist feminism reflected, as we shall
later see, the failure of morally independent criticism of the dominant
sexist orthodoxy that abolitionist moral and political theory, resting on
the argument for toleration, condemns and must condemn. From this

---

cago Press, 1983); Jeffrey Weeks, *Sex, Politics, and Society: The Regulation of Sexuality since
1800,* 2d ed. (London: Longman, 1981).

73. For a useful compendium of such contemporary approaches, see Henry Abelove,
Michele Aina Barale, and David M. Halperin, eds., *The Lesbian and Gay Studies Reader*
(New York: Routledge, 1993).

74. See, for example, *Brown v. Board of Education,* 347 U.S. 483 (1954) (earlier historical
consensus on the constitutionality of state-sponsored racial segregation not dispositive on
constitutional issue in contemporary circumstances).

perspective, appeal to the tradition of abolitionist feminism or of Whitman's version of feminist emancipation may, consistent with abolitionist political and moral theory, better illuminate the strenuous demands of principle imposed on us by the deeper moral vision of the Reconstruction Amendments than can the political compromises of either the Reconstruction Congress or the more mainstream feminist movement of an earlier period (struggling, as it perhaps had to, to make political compromises with racist public opinion to achieve the aims of suffrage feminism).[75] Indeed, such an appeal makes possible reasonable contemporary interpretation of precisely the perils of compromise on issues of principle. It affords a much-needed interpretive perspective on larger patterns of intractable American racism and sexism, our collective failures as a people reasonably to understand our interpretive responsibilities to acknowledge and deal with these interlinked constitutional evils, and the need for us to take an appropriately different perspective on these matters, uniting, as we must (in the spirit of the abolitionist feminists), both antiracist and antisexist arguments of principle on what they called the platform of human rights.

Such a contemporary, necessarily selective appeal to abolitionist feminism or Whitman must interpret such strands of our tradition from the perspective of our contemporary concern to make the best rights-based arguments of principle in our circumstances. Our contemporary concern dictates not only the interpretive interest we take in certain strands of our tradition as opposed to others, but the sense we make of the strands we select (including the appropriately contemporary sense we reasonably make of the claims of abolitionist feminists or Whitman, which will ultimately make sense of these matters in our contextual terms not theirs). Our interest in the abolitionist feminists and Whitman is in their interpretive convictions about the proper understanding of basic American constitutional rights and obligations and the kinds of arguments and methodologies they used to defend and explain their convictions to their fellow Americans. We must identify such dissident interpretive traditions, understand how they achieved such better readings of basic American constitutional principles, and

75. See, for example, William L. O'Neill, *Everyone Was Brave: The Rise and Fall of Feminism in America* (Chicago: Quadrangle Books, 1969), 69–74, 87–88; for more recent treatments, see Sara Hunter Graham, *Woman Suffrage and the New Democracy* (New Haven: Yale University Press, 1996); Suzanne M. Marilley, *Woman Suffrage and the Origins of Liberal Feminism in the United States, 1820–1920* (Cambridge: Harvard University Press, 1996). See also, for general background, Ellen Carol DuBois, *Feminism and Suffrage* (Ithaca: Cornell University Press, 1978); Eleanor Flexner, *Century of Struggle*, rev. ed. (Cambridge: Harvard University Press, Belknap Press, 1975); Nancy F. Cott, *The Grounding of Modern Feminism* (New Haven: Yale University Press, 1987).

carry this tradition forward today in ways that enable us in our circumstances to achieve less flawed and more principled interpretations of basic constitutional values. We must examine and weigh their interpretive convictions as critically as we do any others, acknowledging flaws or incoherences when we discover such failures, understanding such flaws contextually (if we can), and learning from them if it is useful for our contemporary interpretive purposes. Abolitionist feminism was historically associated with many other movements besides abolitionism and feminism, including, in various cases, anarchism, vegetarianism, temperance, purity movements, spiritualism, and the like.[76] Indeed, some of these movements (for example, temperance) were not only much closer to the dominant historical consensus of their times (including to the common sense of most women) than abolitionist feminism,[77] but, as we shall see, subversive of the rights-based claims central to abolitionist feminism. And Whitman was uncritical about his populist racism,[78] believed in phrenology (from which he adapted some of his central ideas about human sexuality),[79] and wrote a private letter late in his life that apparently categorically denied that he (or his work) endorsed homosexual sex acts.[80] Our interpretive interest in abolitionist

76. See, for fuller discussion, Robert H. Abzug, *Cosmos Crumbling: American Reform and the Religious Imagination* (New York: Oxford University Press, 1994); Lawrence J. Friedman, *Gregarious Saints: Self and Community in American Abolitionism, 1830–1870* (Cambridge: Cambridge University Press, 1982).

77. Important studies include Ruth Bordin, *Woman and Temperance: The Quest for Power and Liberty, 1873–1900* (New Brunswick, N.J.: Rutgers University Press, 1990); Jed Dannenbaum, *Drink and Disorder: Temperance Reform in Cincinnati from the Washingtonian Revival to the WCTU* (Urbana: University of Illinois Press, 1984); Ian R. Tyrrell, *Sobering Up: From Temperance to Prohibition in Antebellum America, 1800–1860* (Westport, Conn.: Greenwood Press, 1979); Ian Tyrrell, *Woman's World, Woman's Empire* (Chapel Hill: University of North Carolina Press, 1991); Ross Evans Paulson, *Women's Suffrage and Prohibition: A Comparative Study of Equality and Social Control* (Glenview, Ill.: Scott, Foresman, 1973); Ruth Bordin, *Frances Willard: A Biography* (Chapel Hill: University of North Carolina Press, 1986).

78. See David S. Reynolds, *Walt Whitman's America* (New York: Knopf, 1995), 372–73, 468–74.

79. Ibid., 236, 246–51, 398–99 (shaping Whitman's distinction between amativeness and adhesiveness).

80. Whitman, after being repeatedly pressed on the point by John Addington Symonds, wrote a puzzling and surely disingenuous 1890 letter to Symonds in which he disavowed the "morbid inferences" to homosexuality Symonds ascribed to Whitman. See supra note 19. David Reynolds interprets the letter contextually as resting on Whitman's roots in working class male love and comradeship, which was in the antebellum period (when Whitman wrote *Leaves of Grass*) widely accepted in America, and his distaste for Symonds' way of thinking about these matters (rooted in post-Civil War European pathologizing models that regarded homosexuals as a third sex, a suggestion quite antithetical to Whitman's working class and highly masculine understanding of the love of comrades). See Reynolds, *Walt Whitman's*

feminism and in Whitman is in those interpretive convictions that we can reasonably make use of in our enterprise of reflectively principled constitutional interpretation in our circumstances, not in those we cannot. Historically self-conscious constitutional interpretation is not an enterprise of historicist unreason.

If American constitutional interpretation constitutes our tradition in the terms I have elsewhere called a historically self-conscious community of principle,[81] our contemporary interpretive task must be to regard our reasonable elaboration of arguments of constitutional principle as a continuous elaboration of principles implicit in earlier patterns of constitutional interpretation. We may sometimes thus understand ourselves as giving effect to long-standing arguments of principle, but contextualized differently in the circumstances of quite dissimilar historical periods (e.g., the interpretation of the powers of the states and national government under American federalism).[82] On other occasions, our contemporary interest in the past is in its mistakes—its failures reasonably to apply basic principles even in its own circumstances. In such cases, our interest in regarding ourselves as a community of principle requires us to acknowledge and learn from mistakes, including an examination not only of the mistaken views but of the correct views mistakenly not taken. From our perspective, the best account of our tradition is to regard the correct view (however historically marginal) as articulating the better understanding of our basic principles as a community of democratic equals.

Much of my interest in the abolitionist feminists and in Whitman derives from the latter interpretive imperative, in particular, the light thus shed on pivotal interpretive mistakes in the understanding of our rights-based constitutionalism from which we can and must responsibly learn. We interpretively properly lay claim to the Grimke sisters and to Whitman not only because their views were largely correct (in the way that we might take interest in the truth of a great philosopher whatever her nationality), but because their largely correct interpretive convictions about our rights-based constitutional tradition were responsibly addressed to American public culture (against defective

America, 198, 391, 396–97, 526–27, 577–79. Confirming antebellum tolerance of homosexuality, Reynolds notes that the objections to *Leaves of Grass* centered not on the homosexual poems, but the heterosexual poems. Ibid., 403–5, 540–41, 569. Interestingly, Harold Bloom claims that Whitman's work displays not interest in homosexual sex acts as such, but in autoeroticism. See Harold Bloom, ed., *Walt Whitman* (New York: Chelsea House Publishers, 1985), 5, 133–35.

81. See David A. J. Richards, *Foundations of American Constitutionalism* (New York: Oxford University Press, 1989), 143–71.

82. Ibid., 157–71.

competitive understandings) and are thus part of the American interpretive tradition on which we may reflectively draw to advance our interpretive purposes. Participating in the same historically continuous American community of principle, we may reasonably lay interpretive claim to their alternative interpretive tradition as the theory and practice on which we struggle constructively to build a more principled vindication of basic constitutional rights in our circumstances. The cumulative argument of this book aims to show that that the best contemporary understanding of rights-based arguments of principle builds on strands of our tradition (mistakenly marginalized in their circumstances) that forged and demanded better conceptions of basic human rights against the dominant political orthodoxy of their age. We must understand our own interpretive responsibilities accordingly, in particular, our responsibility to bring to bear on contemporary constitutional interpretation of the Reconstruction Amendments the insights we may gather from laying claim in our circumstances to the theory and practice of such ethically empowering traditions of dissent.

For example, growing interpretive interest in the Thirteenth Amendment as the focus for new forms of arguments against private forms of invidious (including gender-based) discrimination need not and should not disown relevant uses of interpretive history.[83] Such uses of interpretive history have recently become increasingly prominent,[84]

83. For an argument along these lines, see Emily Calhoun, "The Thirteenth and Fourteenth Amendments: Constitutional Authority for Federal Legislation against Private Sex Discrimination," *Minnesota Law Review* 61 (1977): 355–58. For the background of such arguments, see Note, "The 'New' Thirteenth Amendment: A Preliminary Analysis," *Harvard University Law Review* 82 (1969): 1294; Note, "Jones v. Mayer: The Thirteenth Amendment and the Federal Anti-Discrimination Laws," *Columbia Law Review* 69 (1969): 1019. For a classic background historical study arguing for the pivotal role of the Thirteenth Amendment in the structure of the Reconstruction Amendments, see Jacobus tenBroek, "Thirteenth Amendment to the Constitution of the United States: Consummation to Abolition and Key to the Fourteenth Amendment," *California Law Review* 39 (1951): 171.

84. See, for example, Akhil Reed Amar, "Remember the Thirteenth," *Constitutional Commentary* 10 (1993): 403; id., "The Case of the Missing Amendments: R.A.V. v. City of St. Paul," *Harvard University Law Review* 106 (1992): 124; Akhil Reed Amar and Daniel Widawsky, "Child Abuse as Slavery: A Thirteenth Amendment Response to *DeShaney*," *Harvard University Law Review* 105 (1992): 1359; Akhil Reed Amar, "Forty Acres and a Mule: A Republican Theory of Minimal Entitlements," *Harvard Journal of Law and Public Policy* 37 (1990): 37; Douglas L. Colbert, "Challenging the Challenge: Thirteenth Amendment as Prohibition against the Racial Use of Peremptory Challenges," *Cornell Law Review* 76 (1990): 1; Neal Kumar Katyal, "Men Who Own Women: A Thirteenth Amendment Critique of Forced Prostitution," *Yale Law Journal* 103 (1993): 791; Andrew Koppelman, "Forced Labor: A Thirteenth Amendment Defense of Abortion," *Northwestern University Law Review* 84 (1990): 480; Joyce E. McConnell, "Beyond Metaphor: Battered Women, Involuntary Servitude and the Thirteenth Amendment," *Yale Journal of Law and Feminism* 4 (1992): 207; Lea S. VanderVelde, "The Labor Vision of the Thirteenth Amendment," *University of Penn-

but perhaps the most interpretively relevant use of such history (namely, the abolitionist feminists) remains largely unexplored. We need both to make such interpretive history available and to explore its profound interpretive fertility. It is, in my judgment, precisely because abolitionist feminism was, during the period under question, so remarkably critical in the way it was of a pervasive political orthodoxy both of race and gender—and so unsuccessfully at war with the dominant political consensus based on this orthodoxy—that it achieved the kind of enduring critical insights of principle it did. Its very critical distance from and rights-based dissent to the dominant political consensus constitute the keys to its impartiality, and thus to its permanent contribution to our normative understanding of a more principled contemporary interpretation of the Reconstruction Amendments in various domains. We need now to explore what the dimensions of such an interpretive contribution might be.

If we are successful, we will be able to show how principled interpretive convictions today elaborate a tradition of moral dissent central to a reasonable contemporary interpretive understanding of the moral and political theory of the Reconstruction Amendments. The interpretive history most relevant to our concerns is not that of dominant political consensus but that of the outcasts from that consensus; they are, from our perspective, the truer prophets of an interpretive jurisprudence of rights-based integrity that yields contemporary arguments of principle most adequate to respect for human rights when such respect is most called for (i.e., in the case of contemporary minorities most outcast from the dominant political consensus). It is for this reason that this interpretive approach so illuminates, as we will see it does, why such arguments of principle reasonably apply to minorities like gay and lesbian persons who largely remain outcasts from the dominant political consensus.[85]

This book focuses both on the task of making such dissident interpretive traditions available and exploring their interpretive fertility. I focus, in particular, on the arguments of the Grimke sisters, Angelina

---

sylvania Law Review 138 (1989): 437; id., "The Gendered Origins of the Lumley Doctrine: Binding Men's Consciences and Women's Fidelity," Yale Law Journal 101 (1992): 775; Robin West, "Toward an Abolitionist Interpretation of the Fourteenth Amendment," West Virginia Law Review 94 (1991): 111, 138–50; Douglas L. Colbert, "Affirming the Thirteenth Amendment," Annual Survey of American Law (1995): 403. Cf. Michelle J. Anderson, Note, "A License to Abuse: The Impact of Conditional Status on Female Immigrants," Yale Law Journal 102 (1993): 1401, 1428–30.

85. For an argument to precisely this effect, see Bowers v. Hardwick, 478 U.S. 186 (1986) (constitutional right to privacy held inapplicable to homosexuals). But see Romer v. Evans, 116 S. Ct. 1620 (1996).

and Sarah, but begin with the general nature of antiracist abolitionist argument that the Grimkes importantly assume and elaborate (chapter 2). I then argue that the abolitionist feminism of the Grimkes articulated a rights-based normative condemnation of moral slavery that included the enslavement of blacks, racism, the subjection of women, and sexism, and explore similar arguments developed by black women like Sojourner Truth and Harriet Jacobs (chapter 3). The struggle for and success of suffrage feminism with the ratification of the Nineteenth Amendment in 1920 fatally compromised this argument, marginalizing advocacy of basic human rights (by, among others, Victoria Woodhull, Emma Goldman, and Margaret Sanger) central to a reasonable understanding of its demands (chapter 4). The struggle against this reactionary compromise and the rebirth of second wave feminism in the wake of the Civil Rights movement are then interpreted in light of acknowledgment of common principles that condemn racism and sexism; indeed, I argue that such a normative conception is and should be the terms in which we should understand the enduring meaning of the abolition of slavery in the Thirteenth Amendment and related requirements of principle of the other Reconstruction Amendments (chapter 5). I then explore the strand of abolitionist feminist argument developed by Walt Whitman, its later elaboration by, among others, Edward Carpenter, Emma Goldman, and Adrienne Rich, and its place in understanding the place of the rights of gay and lesbian persons among basic constitutional rights of privacy and antidiscrimination (chapter 6). In particular, the argument of moral slavery clarifies the grounds for the unconstitutionality of antigay/lesbian initiatives (chapter 7) and related reasons for regarding sexual preference as a fully suspect class (thus, rendering unconstitutional the exclusion of gays and lesbians from the military and from the right of marriage) (chapter 8). Finally, I explore how the analysis advances discussion of issues of multiple identity in American constitutional and political discourse (chapter 9).

2 Abolitionist Antislavery and Antiracism

A bolitionist feminism is a distinctive development of abolitionist argument in general and antiracist abolitionist argument in particular. We must be clear about both if we are to understand the claims of abolitionist feminism.[1]

The great contribution of the abolitionists to American moral, political, and constitutional thought is found not only in the substantive moral issue on which they aimed to fasten the public attention of the nation, but a mode of argument basic to the integrity of American revolutionary constitutionalism: namely, argument based on the demands of the right of free conscience. The abolitionists opposed the tyranny of unreflective majoritarian opinion of the Age of Jackson, and in turn their voice became its proclaimed public enemy—the object of the anti-abolitionist mobs. These mobs, often led by Jacksonian community leaders, subjected courageous abolitionist leaders like Theodore Weld and William Lloyd Garrison—who asked only to be heard—to unremitting violence, threats of death, insult, ridicule and, in the case of Elijah Lovejoy, murder.[2] Their appeal to conscience was met by the repression of their right to free speech both at the state and national levels. Such repression deprived the South and, for a long

1. I draw directly here upon an earlier argument I've made about the claims of abolitionism in chapter 3 of *Conscience and the Constitution*, which I have somewhat condensed.
2. For an excellent study, see Leonard L. Richards, *"Gentlemen of Property and Standing": Anti-Abolition Mobs in Jacksonian America* (New York: Oxford University Press, 1970).

period, the nation of reasonable public discussion of the moral evils of slavery and of the merits and strategies of abolition.[3] The abolitionist attack on the political and constitutional pathology behind the deprivation of these constitutional liberties eventually awakened the public mind of the nation to the underlying constitutional principles of human rights that condemned equally the repression of conscience and the institution of slavery.[4]

To understand the importance of abolitionist thought to American political and constitutional development, we must interpret their thought in light of the political theory of toleration that motivated their intellectual, moral, and political project. That theory gives pivotal weight to the inalienable right to conscience and to the primacy of ethical reflection, and enables us to understand the power of their ethical criticism of slavery and racism.

ABOLITIONIST ETHICAL CRITICISM OF SLAVERY: THE ANALOGY OF ANTI-SEMITISM

Theodore Weld was one of the most influential of the early abolitionists. In *American Slavery As It Is,* his widely circulated pamphlet,[5] he presented both a factual picture (gathered largely from Southern newspapers) of life in the South under slavery and a normative argument through which those facts should be interpreted.[6]

This argument took it to be fundamental that persons have:

3. See, in general, Russel B. Nye, *Fettered Freedom: Civil Liberties and the Slavery Controversy, 1830–1860* (East Lansing: Michigan State College Park, 1949); Clement Eaton, *The Freedom-of-Thought Struggle in the Old South* (New York: Harper and Row, 1940); William Lee Miller, *Arguing about Slavery: The Great Battle in the United States Congress* (New York: Knopf, 1996).

4. See, in general, Nye, *Fettered Freedom;* Miller, *Arguing about Slavery;* Richard H. Sewell, *Ballots for Freedom: Antislavery Politics in the United States, 1837–1860* (New York: Oxford University Press, 1976).

5. *"American Slavery As It Is* sold more copies than any other antislavery pamphlet ever written: more than 100,000 copies within a year." Dwight Lowell Dumond, *Antislavery: The Crusade for Freedom in America* (Ann Arbor: University of Michigan Press, 1961), 256; cf. Gilbert Hobbs Barnes, *The Antislavery Impulse, 1830–1844* (New York: D. Appleton-Century Co., 1933), 139, 163.

6. On Weld and his importance in the early abolitionist movement, see, in general, Barnes, *The Antislavery Impulse;* for other important works by Weld, see Theodore Dwight Weld, *The Bible against Slavery* (1838; Pittsburgh: United Presbyterian Board of Publication, 1864); id., "The Power of Congress over Slavery in the District of Columbia," in Jacobus tenBroek, *Equal under Law* (1838; New York: Collier, 1965), 243–80; id., "Persons held to Service, Fugitive Slave, &c.", in *The Influence of the Slave Power with other Anti-Slavery Pamphlets,* no. 12 (Westport, Conn.: Negro Universities Press, 1970), 1–8.

inalienable rights, of the ownership of their own bodies, of the use of their own limbs and muscles, of all their time, liberty, and earnings, of the free exercise of choice, of the rights of marriage and parental authority, of legal protection, of the right to be, to do, to go, to stay, to think, to feel, to work, to rest, to eat, to sleep, to learn, to teach, to earn money, and to expend it, to visit, and to be visited, to speak, to be silent, to worship according to conscience, in fine, their rights to be protected by just and equal laws, and to be *amenable to such only.*[7]

The abridgment of such inalienable rights (including "free speech and rights of conscience, their right to acquire knowledge" [7–8]), he argued, had to meet a heavy burden of justification.

Weld identified an important analogy between the inadequacies of the justifications offered by Southerners in support of slavery and the comparably inadequate arguments offered in support of religious persecution, whether Puritan persecutions of the Quakers (112–13) or Roman persecution of Christians or Christian persecutions of pagans and heretics (118–20). He was struck by the fact that persons, just and generous "with those of their own grade, or language, or nation, or hue," practiced "towards others, for whom they have contempt and aversion, the most revolting meanness, perpetrate robbery unceasingly, and inflict the severest privations, and the most barbarous cruelties" (120). In language and thought very similar to Madison's theory of faction and its application by Madison to race prejudice,[8] Weld observed that "[a]rbitrary power is to the mind what alcohol is to the body; it intoxicates. Man loves power. It is perhaps the strongest human passion; and the more absolute the power, the stronger the desire for it" (115). The key to understanding the political evil of both religious persecution and slavery was the intrinsic corruptibility of human nature by political power over certain kinds of questions. The worst corruption was of conscience itself—a fact, he argued, well reflected in the cumulative blinding of Southern public morality to the evils of slavery.[9]

In the most important study of the morality of slavery by an American philosopher in the antebellum period, William Ellery Channing

7. Theodore Dwight Weld, *American Slavery As It Is* (1839; New York: Arno Press and The New York Times, 1968), 123. See also 7–8, 143–44, 151.

8. At the Constitutional Convention, Madison expressly applied his worries about constitutionally untrammeled state factions to the form of property-based faction supporting slavery. In a speech delivered on June 6, 1787, Madison referred to it in the following terms: "the mere distinction of colour made . . . a ground of the most oppressive dominion ever exercised by man over man." See Max Farrand, ed., *The Records of the Federal Convention of 1787* (New Haven: Yale University Press, 1966), 1:135.

9. Weld, *American Slavery As It Is,* 113–17, 120–21, 123–25, 146, 184–86.

had temperately stated the ethical dimensions of the abolitionist case for both the evil of slavery and the need for abolition in a similar way.[10] Like Weld, Channing based his argument on the fact that "[a]ll men have the same rational nature and the same power of conscience" (693). He characterized this capacity for the powers of moral personality, following Kant, as man's nature as "an end in himself" (696); these are moral capacities of responsible moral freedom that reflect that we are "created in God's image . . .; because created to unfold godlike faculties and to govern himself by a divine law written on his heart" (695). Our equal moral capacity to know and effectuate that moral law was "the foundation of human rights in human nature" (698), from which "particular rights may easily be deduced [including] a right to sustain domestic relations, to discharge their duties, and to enjoy the happiness which flows from fidelity to these and other domestic relations" (698–99).

The American constitutional republic, in contrast to the Athenian democracy and Roman republic, rested on the distinctive mission of securing respect for the principles of Lockean political legitimacy (702, 716–18). The fundamental wrong of slavery was that it deprived persons of the very foundation of human rights: freedom of conscience in knowing and acting on one's moral rights and duties. Because the test of the Constitution's political legitimacy was the Lockean test of whether a state respected the inalienable rights that must, in principle, be reserved from political power, the idea that such rights were not reserved from political power was "the logic of despotism" (699, 700, 740). While "the oppressions of ages have nowhere wholly stifled" the idea of human rights (698), the existence of slavery today rested on the subversion of the idea of republican human rights (716–18) whose force "is darkened, weakened among us, so as to be to many little more than a sound."[11] The ultimate degradation was that slaves were so deprived of the "consciousness of rights" that their docility was taken to show they have no rights. In fact, "[t]he quiet of slavery is . . . the stillness of death" (714).

Such subversion required people to ignore the "self-evident truth"

---

10. William Ellery Channing, *Slavery*, in *The Works of William E. Channing* (1836; New York: Burt Franklin 1970), 688–743. See also id., *Remarks on the Slavery Question* (1839), in *Works*, 782–820; id., *Emancipation* (1842), in *Works*, 820–53. For commentary on Channing and his background, see Andrew Delbanco, *William Ellery Channing: An Essay on the Liberal Spirit in America* (Cambridge: Harvard University Press, 1981); Daniel Walker Howe, *The Unitarian Conscience: Harvard Moral Philosophy, 1805–1861* (Middletown, Conn.: Wesleyan University Press, 1988). See also D. H. Meyer, *The Instructed Conscience: The Shaping of the American National Ethic* (Philadelphia: University of Pennsylvania Press, 1972).

11. Channing, *Emancipation*, 843.

(692) that persons cannot be owned, a truth that Channing characterized ("And if this impression [that slavery is wrong] is a delusion, on
what single moral conviction can we rely?" [692–93]) in a way Lincoln
later echoed ("If slavery is not wrong, nothing can be wrong."[12]). In
order to understand such subversion, Channing, like Weld, drew an
analogy to the history of religious persecution, whose injustice was supported by the corruption of conscience.[13] In this connection, Channing
drew an analogy between racism and anti-Semitism, noting that "[f]or
ages the Jews were thought to have forfeited the rights of men, as
much as the African race at the South, and were insulted, spoiled, and
slain, not by mobs, but by sovereigns and prelates, who really supposed
themselves avengers of the crucified Saviour."[14]

Other abolitionists like Frederick Douglass, Charles Sumner, and
James Russell Lowell[15] also drew pointed analogies between the evil
of slavery and the evil of intolerance exemplified by anti-Semitism.
George William Curtis, addressing the abolitionist moral challenge before the nation at the end of the Civil War, spoke of "the bitter prejudice against the colored race, which is as inhuman and unmanly as the
old hatred and contempt of Christendom for the Jews."[16]

We need now to explore this abolitionist argument and the role
played in it by the example of the wrongness of anti-Semitism.

THE ARGUMENT FOR TOLERATION

The argument for toleration assumed by both Weld and Channing was
an American elaboration of the argument for universal toleration that
had been stated, in variant forms, by Pierre Bayle and John Locke.[17]
The context and motivations of the argument were those of radical
Protestant intellectual and moral conscience reflecting on the political

12. Lincoln to Albert G. Hodges, 4 April 1864, *Abraham Lincoln: Speeches and Writings,
1858–1865*, ed. Don E. Fehrenbacher (New York: The Library of America, 1989), 2:585.

13. See Channing, *Slavery*, 704–5; see also ibid., 714, 715, 722; id., *Emancipation*,
839–43.

14. Channing, *Emancipation*, 840.

15. See Frederick Douglass, "Colored Men of America Demand Equal Rights as Americans," Charles Sumner, "Charles Sumner Argues for School Desegregation," and James Russell Lowell, "James Russell Lowell Condemns the Prejudice of Color," in William H. Pease
and Jane H. Pease, *The Antislavery Argument* (Indianapolis: Bobbs-Merrill, 1965), 278, 293,
313.

16. See George William Curtis, "The Good Fight," in *Orations and Addresses of George
William Curtis,* ed. Charles Eliot Norton (New York: Harper & Brothers, 1894), 168.

17. For fuller examination of the argument in Locke and Bayle and its American elaboration notably by Jefferson and Madison, see David A. J. Richards, *Toleration and the Constitution* (New York: Oxford University Press, 1986), 89–128.

principles requisite to protect its enterprise against the oppressions of established churches, both Catholic and Protestant.

That enterprise arose both from a moral ideal of the person and the need to protect that ideal from a political threat that had historically crushed it. The ideal was of respect for persons in virtue of their personal moral powers both rationally to assess and pursue ends and reasonably to adjust and constrain pursuit of ends in light of the equal moral status of persons as bearers of equal rights. The political threat to this ideal of the person was the idea that the moral status of persons was not determined by the responsible expression of their own moral powers, but specified in advance of such reflection (or the possibility of such reflection) by a hierarchical structure of society and nature in which they were embedded. That structure, classically associated with orders of being,[18] defined the roles and status to which people were born and exhaustively specified the responsibilities of living in light of those roles.

The political power of the hierarchical conception was shown not only in the ways in which people behaved, but in the ways it penetrated the human heart and mind, framing a personal, moral, and social identity founded on roles specified by the hierarchical structure. The structure—religious, economic, political—had no need for massive coercion because its crushing force on human personality had been rendered personally and socially invisible by a heart that felt and a mind that imaginatively entertained nothing that could render the structure an object of critical reflection. Nor could anything motivate such reflection, for life was perceived, felt, and lived as richly natural.

In light of the moral pluralism made possible by the Reformation, liberal Protestant thinkers like Bayle and Locke subjected the political power of the hierarchical conception to radical ethical criticism in terms of a moral ideal of the person having moral powers of rationality and reasonableness; the hierarchical conception had subverted the ideal, and, for this reason, distorted the standards of rationality and reasonableness to which the ideal appealed.

Both Bayle and Locke argued as religious Christians, and their argument naturally arose as an intramural debate among interpreters of the Christian tradition about freedom and ethics. An authoritative Pauline strand of that tradition gave great weight to the value of Christian freedom.[19] That tradition, like the Jewish tradition from which it devel-

18. See, in general, Arthur O. Lovejoy, *The Great Chain of Being* (Cambridge: Harvard University Press, 1964).

19. See Richards, *Toleration,* 86–87.

oped, possessed a powerful ethical core of concern for the development of moral personality. Augustine of Hippo thus had interpreted
the trinitarian nature of God, in whose image we are made, on the
model of moral personality, that is, the three parts of the soul—will,
memory, and intelligence (85–88). Indeed, the argument for toleration
arose from an internal criticism by Bayle of Augustine's argument for
the persecution of the heretical Donatists (to wit, Augustine had misinterpreted Christian values of freedom and ethics) (89–95). Religious
persecution had corrupted ethics and, for this reason, corrupted the
essence of Christianity's elevated and simple ethical core of a universal
brotherhood of free people.

The argument for toleration was a response to perceived abuses of
political epistemology. The legitimation of religious persecution by
both Catholics and Protestants (drawing authority from Augustine,
among others) had enforced a politically entrenched view of religious
and moral truth. By the late seventeenth century (when Locke and
Bayle wrote), there was good reason to believe that such views of religious and moral truth (appealing to the authority of the Bible and associated interpretive practices) assumed essentially contestable interpretations of a complex historical interaction between Pagan, Jewish, and
Christian cultures in the early Christian era (25–27, 84–98, 105, 125).

The Renaissance rediscovery of Pagan culture and learning re-
opened the question of how the Christian synthesis of Pagan philosophical and Jewish ethical and religious culture was to be understood.
Among other things, the development of critical historiography and
techniques of textual interpretation had undeniable implications for
reasonable Bible interpretation (125–26). The Protestant Reformation
both assumed and further encouraged these new modes of inquiry and
heightened the appeal of experimentation and experience that were a
matrix for the methodologies associated with the rise of modern science.[20] New approaches to thought and inquiry made possible the recognition of the gap separating them from the politically entrenched
conceptions of religious and moral truth and inquiry, that is, the recognition of a disjunction between the reigning political epistemology and
the new epistemic methodologies.

The crux of the problem was this. Politically entrenched conceptions of truth had, on the basis of the Augustinian legitimation of religious persecution, made themselves the measure both of the standards

20. See, for a recent review of the question, I. Bernard Cohen, ed., *Puritanism and the Rise of Modern Science: The Merton Thesis* (New Brunswick, N.J.: Rutgers University Press, 1990).

of reasonable inquiry and of who could count as a reasonable inquirer after truth. But in light of the new modes of inquiry now available, such political entrenchment of religious truth was reasonably seen often to rest not only on the degradation of reasonable standards of inquiry but on the self-fulfilling degradation of the capacity of persons reasonably to conduct such inquiries. In order to rectify these evils, the argument for toleration forbade, as a matter of principle, the enforcement by the state of any such conception of religious truth. The scope of legitimate political concern must, rather, rest on the pursuit of general ends like life and basic rights and liberties (for example, the right to conscience). The pursuit of such goods was consistent with the full range of ends free people might rationally and reasonably pursue.[21]

A prominent feature of the argument for toleration was its claim that religious persecution corrupted conscience itself. (We have already noted this critique in the American abolitionist thinkers who assume the argument.) Such corruption—a kind of self-induced blindness to the evils one inflicts—is a consequence of the at large political enforcement of a conception of religious truth that immunizes itself from independent criticism in terms of reasonable standards of thought and deliberation. In effect, the conception of religious truth, though perhaps having once been importantly shaped by more ultimate considerations of reason, ceases to be held or to be understood and elaborated *on the basis of reason.*

A tradition that loses the sense of its reasonable foundations will stagnate and depend increasingly for allegiance on question-begging appeals to orthodox conceptions of truth and the violent repression of any dissent from such conceptions (treating them as a kind of disloyal moral treason). The politics of loyalty rapidly degenerates into a politics that takes pride in widely held community values solely because they are community values. Standards of discussion and inquiry become increasingly parochial and insular and serve only a polemical role in the defense of the existing community values; indeed, they become increasingly hostile to any more impartial reasonable assessment in light of independent standards.[22]

Such politics tends to degrade to forms of irrationalism in order to protect its now essentially polemical project: opposing views relevant to reasonable public argument are suppressed, facts distorted or mis-

21. See Richards, *Toleration,* 119–20.
22. See, in general, John Hope Franklin, *The Militant South, 1800–1861* (Cambridge: Harvard University Press, Belknap Press, 1956); Bertram Wyatt-Brown, *Honor and Violence in the Old South* (New York: Oxford University Press, 1986); cf. W. J. Cash, *The Mind of the South* (New York: Vintage Books, 1941).

stated, values disconnected from ethical reasoning, and ultimately, deliberation in politics is denigrated in favor of violence against dissent and the aesthetic glorification of such violence. Paradoxically, the greater the tradition's vulnerability to independent reasonable criticism, the more likely it is to generate forms of political irrationalism (including scapegoating of outcast dissenters) in order to secure allegiance.

I call this phenomenon the *paradox of intolerance*. It may be understood by reference to the epistemic motivations of Augustinian intolerance. A certain conception of religious truth was originally affirmed as true and politically enforced on society at large because it was supposed to be the epistemic measure of reasonable inquiry (i.e., more likely to lead to epistemically reliable beliefs). But the consequence of the legitimation of such intolerance over time was that standards of reasonable inquiry, outside the orthodox measure of such inquiry, were repressed. In effect, the orthodox conception of truth was no longer defended on the basis of reason, but was increasingly hostile to reasonable assessment in terms of impartial standards not hostage to the orthodox conception. Indeed, orthodoxy was defended as an end in itself, increasingly by nonrational and even irrational means of appeal to community identity and the like. The paradox appears in the subversion of the original epistemic motivations of the Augustinian argument: rather than securing reasonable inquiry, the argument now has cut off the tradition from such inquiry. Indeed, the legitimacy of the tradition feeds on irrationalism precisely when it is most vulnerable to reasonable criticism, contradicting and frustrating its original epistemic ambitions (thus, the sense of paradox in such self-defeating epistemic incoherence).

The history of religious persecution amply illustrates these truths; and, as the abolitionists clearly saw, no aspect of that history more clearly so than Christian anti-Semitism. The relationship of Christianity to its Jewish origins has always been a tense and ambivalent one.[23] The fact that many Jews did not accept Christianity was a kind of standing challenge to the reasonableness of Christianity, especially in its early period (prior to its establishment as the church of the late Roman Empire) when Christianity was a proselytizing religion that competed for believers with the wide range of religious and philosophical alternative belief systems available in the late Pagan world.

23. For a useful study of the early Christian period, see John A. Gager, *The Origins of Anti-Semitism: Attitudes toward Judaism in Pagan and Christian Antiquity* (New York: Oxford University Press, 1983). The classic general study is Leon Poliakov, *The History of Anti-Semitism*, 4 vols. (Oxford: Oxford University Press, 1965–85).

In his recent important studies of anti-Semitism,[24] the medievalist Gavin Langmuir characterizes Christianity's long-standing worries about the Jews as "anti-Judaism" because of the way the Jewish rejection of Christianity discredited the reasonableness of the Christian belief system in the Pagan world. Langmuir argues that the Christian conception of the obduracy of the Jews and the divine punishment of them for such obduracy were natural forms of anti-Judaic self-defense, resulting in the forms of expulsion and segregation from Christian society that naturally expressed and legitimated such judgments on the Jews.[25] In contrast to anti-Judaism, "anti-Semitism proper," as I shall call it, identifies what Langmuir describes as the totally baseless and irrational beliefs about ritual crucifixions and cannibalism of Christians by Jews that were "widespread in northern Europe by 1350" (302); such beliefs led to populist murders of Jews usually (though not always) condemned by both church and secular authorities. Their irrationalist nature requires, Langmuir suggests, a distinguishing name: "chimeria," suggesting, from the Greek root, "fantasies, figments of the imagination, monsters that, although dressed syntactically in the cloths of real humans, have never been seen and are projections of mental processes unconnected with the real people of the outgroup" (334).

Langmuir suggests, as does R. I. Moore,[26] that the development of anti-Semitism proper was associated with growing internal doubts posed by dissenters in the period 950–1250 about the reasonableness of certain Catholic religious beliefs and practices (e.g., transubstantiation) and the resolution of such doubts by the forms of irrationalist politics associated with anti-Semitism proper (often centering on fantasies of ritual eating of human flesh that expressed the underlying worries about transubstantiation). The worst ravages of anti-Semitism illustrate the paradox of intolerance, which explains the force of the example for abolitionists. Precisely when the dominant religious tradition gave rise to the most reasonable internal doubts, these doubts were displaced from reasonable discussion and debate into blatant political irrationalism in terms of chimeria against one of the more conspicuous, vulnerable, and innocent groups of dissenters.

Langmuir's distinction between anti-Judaism and anti-Semitism proper is an unstable one. Both attitudes rest on conceptions of reli-

---

24. See Gavin I. Langmuir, *Toward a Definition of Antisemitism* (Berkeley and Los Angeles: University of California Press, 1990); id., *History, Religion, and Antisemitism* (Berkeley and Los Angeles: University of California Press, 1990).

25. Langmuir, *Toward a Definition of Antisemitism,* 57–62.

26. See R. I. Moore, *The Formation of a Persecuting Society: Power and Deviance in Western Europe, 950–1250* (Oxford: Basil Blackwell, 1987).

gious truth that are unreasonably enforced on the community at large; certainly, both the alleged obduracy of the Jews and their just punishment for such obduracy were sectarian interpretations of the facts and not reasonably enforced at large. Believing Jews to be obdurate is certainly not as unreasonable as believing Jews to be cannibals, and racial segregation is not as evil as lynchings or genocide, but both forms of politics are, on grounds of the argument for toleration, unreasonable in principle. More fundamentally, anti-Judaism laid the corrupt political foundation for anti-Semitism. Once it became politically legitimate to enforce at large a sectarian conception of religious truth, reasonable doubts about such truth were displaced from the reasonable discussion and debate they deserved to the irrationalist politics of religious persecution. The Jews have been in the Christian West the most continuously blatant victims of that politics, making anti-Semitism "the oldest prejudice in Western civilization."[27]

The radical criticism of political irrationalism implicit in the argument for toleration, once unleashed, could not be limited to religion. It was naturally extended by John Locke to embrace politics as such.[28] The injustice of religious persecution by established churches was generalized into a larger reflection on how political orthodoxies of hierarchical orders of authority and submission (e.g., patriarchal political theories of absolute monarchy like those of Robert Filmer[29]) had been unreasonably enforced at large. In both religion and political theory, political enforcement at large of one view not only degraded standards of argument to the exclusive measure of the orthodox one; it also retained hold on political power by stunting people's capacity to know, understand, and give effect to their inalienable human rights of reasonable self-government. The generalization of the argument for toleration naturally suggested the political legitimacy of some form of constitutional democracy (in which the principle of toleration would play a foundational central role) as a political decision procedure more likely to secure a reasonable politics that respected human rights and pursued the common interests of all persons alike.[30]

The argument for toleration was motivated by a general political skepticism about enforceable political epistemologies. Such politics enforced sectarian conceptions of religious, moral, and political truth

27. Langmuir, *Toward a Definition of Antisemitism*, 45.
28. See Richards, *Toleration*, 98–102; id., *Foundations of American Constitutionalism* (New York: Oxford University Press, 1989), 82–90.
29. See Robert Filmer, *Patriarcha*, in *Patriarcha and Other Writings*, ed. Johann P. Sommerville (1680; Cambridge: Cambridge University Press, 1991), 1–68.
30. See Richards, *Foundations*, 78–97.

at the expense of denying the moral powers of persons to assess these matters in light of reasonable standards and as reasonable persons. The leading philosophers of toleration thus tried to articulate some criteria or thought experiment in terms of which such sectarian views might be assessed and debunked from a more impartial perspective. Bayle suggested a contractualist test for such impartiality: namely, abstracting from our native prejudices born from the customs in which we were raised, we should ask ourselves "Is such a practice just in itself? If it were a question of introducing it in a country where it would not be in use and where he would be free to take it up or not, would one see, upon examining it impartially that it is reasonable enough to merit being adopted?"[31]

Bayle's use of a contractualist test was generalized by Locke into a comprehensive contractualist political theory.[32] Though Locke is not clear on the point, contractualism has nothing to do with history; nothing in the argument turns on the actual existence of a state of nature, nor on ultimate epistemological skepticism. Neither Locke nor Bayle were moral, political, or religious skeptics; they were concerned, rather, by the unreliable appeals to politically enforceable conceptions of sectarian truths (i.e., politically enforceable epistemologies), and articulated a thought experiment of abstract contractualist reasonableness to assess what might legitimately be enforced through law. Bayle's use of a contractualist test made this point exactly: abstracting from your own aims and the particular customs of your society, what principles of legitimate politics would all persons reasonably accept? The test is, of course, very like John Rawls's abstract contractualist test in the absence of knowledge of specific identity, and serves exactly the same political function.[33]

Such a contractualist test assumes that persons have the twin moral powers of rationality and reasonableness in light of which they may assess human ends, their own and others.[34] The former enables us to reflect on the coherence and complementarity among our ends and on the more effective ways to pursue them subject to principles of epistemic rationality; the latter enables us to regulate the pursuit of our ends in light of the common claims of all persons to the forms of action and forbearance consistent with equal respect for our status

31. Pierre Bayle, *Philosophical Commentary*, trans. Amie Godman Tannenbaum (New York: Peter Lang, 1987), 30.

32. See Richards, *Foundations*, 82–90; id., *Toleration*, 98–102.

33. See John Rawls, *A Theory of Justice* (Cambridge: Harvard University Press, 1971).

34. For a fuller account of these powers, see David A. J. Richards, *A Theory of Reasons for Action* (Oxford: Clarendon Press, 1971).

in the moral community. These self-originating powers of reason enable us not only to think for ourselves from our own viewpoint but also from the moral point of view that gives weight or should give weight to the viewpoints of everyone else.

Reason—epistemic and practical—can have the power that it does in our lives because it enables us to stand back from our ends, to assess critically how they cohere with one another and with the ends of others, and to reexamine and sometimes revise such judgments in light of new insights and experience and to act accordingly. Reason can only reliably perform this role when it is itself subject to revision and correction in light of public standards that are open, accessible, and available to all. Public reason—a resource that enables all persons better to cultivate their moral powers—requires a public culture that sustains high standards of independent, critically tested, revisable argument accessible to all. In order to perform the role that it should play in the exercise of our internal moral powers, public reason cannot be merely or even mainly polemical. It must afford sufficient public space within which we may comfortably express what doubts we may have or should have about our ends, lives, and communities, and deliberatively discuss and resolve such doubts.[35]

Respect for our capacity for reason, thus understood, requires a politics that respects the principle of toleration; forms of traditional wisdom—that have a basis in public reason—will not be politically disallowed. But the principle of toleration does deny that convictions of sectarian truth *can be enforced through law solely on that basis.* (The role of such convictions in private life is, of course, another matter.) The principle of toleration thus limits the force in *political* life of convictions that draw their strength solely from the certainties of group loyalty and identification that tend, consistent with the paradox of intolerance, most to self-insulate themselves from reason when they are most reasonably subject to internal doubts.

Nothing in the account suggests that religious views or even convictions about truth of dominant religions are unreasonable, but only that certain facts of political psychology about human nature in politics lead to a kind of political corruption of the religious enterprise (once it is politicized) as an inquiry into ultimate truth. Exercises of political power enforcing views of religious truth tend not to do so on the basis

35. See, for a useful discussion of all these points, Onora O'Neill, *Constructions of Reason* (Cambridge: Cambridge University Press, 1989). For Kant on public reason, see "An Answer to the Question: 'What is Enlightenment?' " in *Kant's Political Writings,* ed. Hans Reiss (Cambridge: Cambridge University Press, 1970), 55: "The *public* use of man's reason must always be free."

of reason. Indeed, consistent with the paradox of intolerance, when the tradition may need most to entertain, discuss, and resolve reasonable doubts about its truth, it tends to make war on its reasonable doubts by the despicable forms of political irrationalism exemplified by the history of religious persecution.

Contractualism, thus understood as a hypothetical test for public reason in politics, must tend in the nature of its enterprise to identify the more abstract features that characterize our moral powers as reasoning agents. Since the motivation of the entire enterprise is the degree to which the idea and practice of hierarchical orders of authority has been permitted to subvert our moral powers of rationality and reasonableness, the reclamation of such powers requires a demanding test of political legitimacy that constrains and limits political power in the ways that we have good reason, in light of our historical experience, to believe require limitation in order to do justice to the reasonable demands of our moral natures.

Contractualism offers us such a test, asking us to think hypothetically in abstraction from our current particular ends and situations about the more general features of living a rational and reasonable life and what constraints on politics are required in order for all persons to be secure in living such a life. The idea of general goods is a corollary of such a test;[36] it identifies the kind of abstract features of living a life that reasonable persons, in the contractualist choice situation, would regard as properly subject to a distributive principle of a just politics. The principle of toleration is one such principle, making possible both a politics of reason and a conception of political community that dignifies the capacity for reasonableness of all persons to be self-governing moral agents.

SLAVERY AS A POLITICAL EVIL

John Locke began his great refutation of Filmer's patriarchalism with a broad condemnation of the advocacy of natural slavery Filmer espoused as "so vile and miserable an Estate of Man . . . that 'tis hardly

36. See, for example, John Rawls, *A Theory of Justice;* David A. J. Richards, *A Theory of Reasons for Action;* T. M. Scanlon, "Preference and Urgency," *Journal of Philosophy* 72 (1975): 655; Amartya Sen, *The Standard of Living* (Cambridge: Cambridge University Press, 1987); Ronald Dworkin, "What Is Equality? Part I: Equality of Welfare," *Philosophy and Public Affairs* 10 (1981): 185; "What Is Equality? Part II: Equality of Resources," *Philosophy and Public Affairs* 10 (1981): 283; "What Is Equality? Part III: The Place of Liberty," *Iowa Law Review* 73 (1987): 1; "What Is Equality? Part IV: Political Equality," *University of San Francisco Law Review* 22 (1987): 1.

to be conceived, that an *Englishman*, much less a *Gentleman*, should plead for't."[37] Locke's constructive development of a general contractualist political theory calling for the protection of inalienable human rights prominently drew the consequence that "a Man, not having the Power of his own Life, *cannot*, by Compact, or his own Consent, *enslave himself* to any one, nor put himself under the Absolute, Arbitrary Power of another, to take away his Life, when he pleases."[38]

The exception to Locke's general rights-based condemnation of slavery was for cases of forfeiture of rights. Certain kinds of culpable wrongdoing led to forfeiture of rights as just punishment; and if death may be just punishment (e.g., for culpably fighting an unjust war), slavery—a less severe punishment—may be just as well.[39] Locke had drafted the Fundamental Constitutions of Carolina, which provided: "Every freeman of Carolina shall have absolute power and authority over his negro slaves, of what opinion or religion soever."[40] He apparently believed that the African slave trade rested on captives taken in a just war, who had forfeited their lives "by some act that deserves Death."[41]

Locke's judgment about the legitimacy of American black slavery was not supported by the facts even as they were known at the time of his writing. The slave trade was not the product of just wars,[42] and even if it were, the theory could not justify the American practice of continuing the enslavement of offspring; the children of slaves were born as free as any other person by any reading of Locke.[43] Both points were quite clearly made by later highly influential, widely read proponents of Lockean political contractualism like Francis Hutcheson. Hut-

37. See John Locke, *The First Treatise of Government,* in John Locke, *Two Treatises of Government,* ed. Peter Laslett (Cambridge: Cambridge University Press, 1960), 159 (sec. 1).

38. See Locke, *Second Treatise of Government,* in John Locke, *Two Treatises of Government,* ed. Peter Laslett (Cambridge: Cambridge University Press, 1960), 301–2 (secs. 22–23).

39. See Locke, *Second Treatise,* 302–3 (secs. 23–24), 340–41 (sec. 85).

40. See John Locke, "The Fundamental Constitutions of Carolina," in *The Works of John Locke* (London: Tomas Tegg et al., 1823), 10:196.

41. See Locke, *Second Treatise,* 302 (sec. 23). For commentary, see ibid., 302–3 note; David Brion Davis, *The Problem of Slavery in Western Culture* (Ithaca: Cornell University Press, 1967), 118–21.

42. See, on the motives and effects of the Atlantic slave trade, Barbara L. Solow, ed., *Slavery and the Rise of the Atlantic System* (Cambridge: Cambridge University Press, 1991); Joseph E. Inikori and Stanley L. Engerman, eds., *The Atlantic Slave Trade: Effects on Economies, Societies, and Peoples in Africa, the Americas, and Europe* (Durham: Duke University Press, 1992).

43. See Ruth W. Grant, *John Locke's Liberalism* (Chicago: University of Chicago Press, 1987), 68, n. 68.

cheson both demolished the just war argument[44] and underscored the clear wrongness of enslaving the children of slaves.[45]

American contractualists were also influenced by Montesquieu's ethically skeptical way of trying to even state the case for American slavery: "It is impossible for us to suppose these creatures to be men, because, allowing them to be men, a suspicion would follow that we ourselves are not Christians."[46] Montesquieu, consistent with his general interest in climactic determinants of political culture, rejected Aristotle's theory of natural slaves as unsupported (240). He suggested, however, that environmental factors like climate might justify its existence in very warm locales, but again, he urged skepticism in view of the very ease with which the argument came to him: "I know not whether this article be dictated by my understanding or by my heart" (241). Such skepticism appealed to American contractualist thought because it naturally raised the same kinds of questions about the sectarian rationalization of entrenched power and hierarchy as their own revolutionary claims against Great Britain, a point made by James Otis with uncompromising and cogent force.

> The colonists are by the law of nature freeborn, as indeed all men are, white or black. No better reasons can be given for enslaving those of any color than such as Baron Montesquieu has humorously given as the foundation of that cruel slavery exercised over the poor Ethiopians, which threatens one day to reduce both Europe and America to the ignorance and barbarity of the darkest ages. Does it follow that 'tis right to enslave a man because he is black? Will short curled hair like wool instead of Christian hair, as 'tis called by those whose hearts are as hard as the nether millstone, help the argument? Can any logical inference in favor of slavery be drawn from a flat nose, a long or a short face? Nothing better can be said in favor of a trade that is the most shocking violation of the law of nature, has a direct tendency to diminish the idea of the inestimable value of liberty, and makes every dealer in it a tyrant. . . . It is a clear truth that those who every day barter away other men's liberty will soon care little for their own.[47]

Following Otis, the abolitionists—the most principled nineteenth-century advocates of the argument for toleration in the United

44. See Francis Hutcheson, *A System of Moral Philosophy* (1755; Hildesheim: Georg Olms Verlagsbuchhandlung, 1969), 204–5; id., *A Short Introduction to Moral Philosophy* (1747; Hildesheim: Georg Olms Verlagsbuchhandlung, 1969), 273–74.

45. See Hutcheson, *A System of Moral Philosophy*, 210; cf. *A Short Introduction to Moral Philosophy*, 226.

46. See Baron de Montesquieu, *The Spirit of the Laws*, trans. Thomas Nugent (New York: Hafner Publishing Company, 1949), 239.

47. James Otis, *The Rights of the British Colonies Asserted and Proved*, in *Pamphlets of the American Revolution, 1750–1776*, ed. Bernard Bailyn (1764; Cambridge: Harvard University Press, Belknap Press, 1965), 1:439.

States—came to see the abolition of slavery as the central critical test for American contractualism. It was fundamental to their vindication of the right to conscience against majoritarian American complacency. The existence of slavery—resting on the denial of the human rights of some—undermined the kind of value appropriate to respect for any human rights at all.[48] Having the political conviction appropriate to the wrongness of slavery was, for the abolitionists, the test for having any political convictions of moral wrongness at all.

Slavery was a moral wrong of a qualitatively distinctive kind; it deprived persons of their inalienable human rights—rights to freedom of conscience and speech, to intimate family life, to free labor, to security of life and property. Such a wrong could only be justified (if at all) on the basis of public reasons not themselves hostage to the institution under critical assessment. In fact, the failure of American politics to meet this latter requirement or even to take it seriously led abolitionists critically to challenge American identity as a nation that ostensibly took rights seriously. Theodore Parker, abolitionist and transcendentalist, was an exemplary and often profound critic along these lines.

Parker saw the evil of slavery as the test for America's commitment to the principles of the Protestant Reformation. He could see how the Catholic Church could tolerate slavery, but "it seems amazing that American Christians of the puritanic stock, with a philosophy that transcends sensationalism, should prove false to the only principle which at once justifies the conduct of Jesus, of Luther, and the Puritans themselves."[49] Consistent with the arguments of Weld and Channing, analogizing the evil of slavery to a kind of religious persecution, Parker's appeal to Protestant principle used the argument for toleration of Bayle and Locke, which Parker and the abolitionists took to be ethically fundamental.

The task of a life of conscience was to question politically entrenched epistemologies to assess whether they illegitimately degraded

48. For another attack on slavery in light of revolutionary political morality, see Samuel Hopkins, *Timely Articles on Slavery* (1776; Miami: Mnemosyne Publishing Inc., 1969). For a comparable Southern view, see St. George Tucker, *A Dissertation on Slavery with a Proposal for the Gradual Abolition of It, in the State of Virginia* (1796; Westport, Conn.: Negro Universities Press, 1970); reprinted in id., *Blackstone's Commentaries with Notes of Reference to the Constitution and Laws of the Federal Government of the United States and of the Commonwealth of Virginia* (Philadelphia: Birch and Small, 1803), 2:31–89, note H; see also Thomas Jefferson, *Notes on the State of Virginia,* ed. William Peden (New York: W. W. Norton, 1982), 137–43, 162–63.

49. Theodore Parker, "The Rights of Man in America," in Theodore Parker, *The Rights of Man in America,* ed. F. B. Sanborn (1854; Boston: American Unitarian Association, 1911), 359–61.

both standards of argument and persons in order to maintain their power. The demands of ethical impartiality accordingly required the raising of more abstract questions of justification and the application of independent standards of public reason—standards not hostage to the political epistemology under examination. The Bible was, of course, no exception. Parker was thus a leading American Protestant advocate of making available to religious inquiry the broadest range of reasonable methodologies available, including the most advanced German techniques of Bible interpretation and historiography. He brought to the interpretation of the Bible, consistent with Bayle and Locke, an interest primarily in what he took to be its simple and elevated ethical truths of a reasonable respect for the moral powers of all persons as equal bearers of inalienable human rights.[50]

Parker's quest for an ethical impartiality on human rights motivated his neo-Kantian transcendentalism. Our capacity for ethics, he argued, was rooted in the abstract deliberations of our internal moral powers, "a living principle which of itself originates ideas."[51] Ethics demanded abstract respect for these moral powers, however stunted and starved by the unjust coercions of politically entrenched epistemologies. Parker's transcendentalism was thus an appeal for an abstract respect for free moral personality; such ethical deliberation could not be reduced, in the style of proslavery thought, to impersonal facts found in sociology, Biblical literalism, or history (ancient or medieval). Nor could it be reduced to utilitarian aggregation, which was in this case a sensationalist ethics of aggregate pleasures over pains that justified slavery, as Calhoun believed,[52] by supposing that, whatever its pains, it caused a greatest net aggregate of utility over all; thus understood, utilitarianism was an ideology that rendered invisible to criticism the incommensurable moral evil that slavery was.[53] For Parker, utilitarianism was yet another kind of objectifying tendency. In effect, all the available imper-

50. See Theodore Parker, "The Transient and Permanent in Christianity," in Theodore Parker, *The Transient and Permanent in Christianity*, ed. George Willis Cooke (Boston: American Unitarian Association, 1908).

For commentary on Parker's life and thought, see Henry Steele Commager, *Theodore Parker* (Boston: Little, Brown, 1936); John Edward Dirks, *The Critical Theology of Theodore Parker* (New York: Columbia University Press, 1948). For other examples of abolitionist Bible interpretation, see Weld, *The Bible against Slavery;* Moses Stuart, *Conscience and the Constitution* (1850; New York: Negro Universities Press, 1969); Francis Wayland, *The Elements of Moral Science* (Cambridge: Harvard University Press, Belknap Press, 1963), especially 192–96, 386–90.

51. Theodore Parker, "Transcendentalism," in Theodore Parker, *The World of Matter and the Spirit of Man* (Boston: American Unitarian Association, 1907), 23.

52. On Calhoun's utilitarianism, see Richards, *Conscience and the Constitution*, 34–35.

53. Parker, "Transcendentalism," 12.

sonalist justifications for slavery were themselves hostage to the politically enforced epistemology of proslavery, distorting or degrading impartial ethical assessment of the institution.

Parker clearly followed his teacher Channing's argument that the
ethical consideration of slavery should not focus on external facts like
race but on the internal moral powers of all persons,[54] powers that gave
rise to "the great political idea of America, the idea of the Declaration
of Independence,"[55] the idea of universal human rights. Ethics, on this
view, turned on the moral capacities people have, however degraded
by tyranny and oppression. Accordingly, both Parker and Channing
found no reason whatsoever in the actual situation of blacks under
American slavery to justify the institution from the required contractualist point of view of ethical impartiality. The familiar proslavery arguments standardly pointed out the actual situation of American slaves—
their apparent happiness and docility, the satisfaction of their material
and welfare interests by adequate food, housing, and care, and the
like.[56] But these facts could have no more weight, from a contractualist
perspective, than the comparable arguments should have in the case
of populations historically subjugated by religious or political tyrannies
based on a hierarchical order of natural authority. In all these cases,
a politically entrenched conception of truth had been permitted unreasonably to subjugate persons to the terms of the conception and then
justified its demands in terms of the consequences of the subjugation.

The principle of toleration was central to the abolitionist criticism
of slavery at several levels. As we saw earlier, abolitionists like Weld
and Channing objected to the way in which American slavery had deprived slaves of the most elementary requirements of equal respect
for their moral powers, including abridgment of the inalienable right
to conscience—the formation of their own religious groups and the
opportunities to learn to read and write in the exercise of their own
moral powers. But the abolitionist political criticism cut deeper; the
very structure of authority in Southern life had come to depend on
what the argument for toleration forbade, namely, the political enforcement on society at large of a self-consciously sectarian proslavery
conception of religious and political truth.

In the attempt to defend slavery against abolitionist criticism, the
South had successfully forbade any form of abolitionist advocacy in

54. Channing, *Slavery*, 691.

55. Parker, "Transcendentalism," 26.

56. See, in general, Drew Gilpin Faust, ed., *The Ideology of Slavery* (Baton Rouge: Louisiana State University Press, 1981); Eric L. McKitrick, ed., *Slavery Defended* (Englewood
Cliffs, N.J.: Prentice-Hall, 1963).

the South, pressured the North to discourage any such advocacy there, and in the 1840s undertook to limit congressional discussion of the flood of abolitionist petitions sent there.[57] This resulted not only in the unpopularity of abolitionism both in the South and North but in the removal of slavery from public discussion by either of the great political parties (Democratic and Whig), each of which depended on retaining support in both the South and North. This silencing of reasonable public discussion and debate on the greatest issue of moral conscience of the age led to the debasement of both public morality and constitutional interpretation that the argument for toleration had long identified as one of the greatest evils of the enforcement of sectarian views of normative truth.

The theory of toleration supplied the internal ideals of the supremacy of critical conscience that powered the abolitionist project as well as a diagnosis of the underlying political and constitutional problem. American constitutionalism, ostensibly based on the argument for toleration, had betrayed its own central ideals by allowing a politically entrenched sectarian conception of the religious and political legitimacy of slavery to be the measure of legitimate political debate about this issue. The consequence was what the argument for toleration would lead one to expect: the debasement of public reason about the political morality of slavery and about issues of constitutional interpretation relating to slavery. In the South, the paradox of intolerance ran amok—reasonable doubts about slavery were brutally suppressed, and the politics of group loyalty displaced these doubts into increasingly irrationalist pride and violence that culminated in an unjust and illegitimate civil war.

Political abolitionists, like Theodore Parker and the founders of the Republican Party, developed a unified explanatory theory to explain the force of this debasement: a slave power conspiracy that permeated the fabric of American political life.[58] Abolitionists brilliantly analyzed the political pathology of Southern pride and violence and Northern indifference and cowardice because they clearly saw how they were

57. The following contain excellent general treatments of this period: Russel B. Nye, *Fettered Freedom: Civil Liberties and the Slavery Controversy, 1830–1860* (East Lansing: Michigan State College Press, 1949); Clement Eaton, *The Freedom-of-Thought Struggle in the Old South* (New York: Harper & Row, 1940); William Lee Miller, *Arguing about Slavery: The Great Battle in the United States Congress* (New York: Knopf, 1996).

58. See, in general, Theodore Parker, *The Slave Power,* ed. James K. Hosmer (Boston: American Unitarian Association, n.d.); David Brion Davis, *The Slave Power Conspiracy and the Paranoid Style* (Baton Rouge: Louisiana State University Press, 1969); William E. Geinapp, *The Origins of the Republican Party, 1852–1956* (New York: Oxford University Press, 1987), 353–65.

rooted in an irrationalist intolerance that American constitutional institutions and traditions proved unable to contain. In so doing, they articulated a broader defense of human rights that was not hostage to the
abolition issue alone.

In summary, the abolitionists viewed slavery as an intrinsic moral
evil in itself because it unjustly deprived the slaves of their inalienable
human rights; the deprivation of such rights required a heavy burden
of justification in light of public reasons not themselves hostage to the
institution under examination. Such reasons not only were not and
could not be given, but the rights of conscience and free speech of all
were abridged in order to halt serious and morally independent public
discussion of the evils of slavery and the merits of abolition in terms
not hostage to the dominant slave oligarchy of the South and its commercial allies in the North. The evils of slavery and repression of conscience and speech were not morally or politically independent but,
from the perspective of the argument for toleration, were integrally
linked. The argument identified how the deprivation of basic rights was
illegitimately justified by sectarian arguments hostage to the politically
entrenched epistemology under examination. In similar fashion, the
rights of Northern free labor in the territories were abridged on the
ground of similarly factionalized political and constitutional arguments.

In effect, no rights were safe once some rights were unsafe. Abolitionists crucially helped forge public argument, grounded in the argument for toleration, that explained how and why the defense of slavery
had required the deprivation of the human rights of nonslaves—not
only free blacks but the rights of whites to conscience and free speech
and their right morally to limit the spread of slavery to the extent permitted by constitutional guarantees. In the light of the radical turn of
proslavery thought against the very principles of human rights,[59] political abolitionists could cogently rest their case on the broad foundation
of the defense of the principle of human rights of conscience and free
labor of both whites and blacks.[60] Under the impact of abolitionist
moral and political criticism, the issue of slavery had become the issue
of the principle of human rights for all persons.

59. See, for example, George Fitzhugh, *Cannibals All!* (1857; Cambridge: Harvard University Press, 1960). Fitzhugh's views evidently shocked Lincoln into the realization that the
South was now undertaking an attack on the very idea of human rights. This was an attack
that required a forceful response. See William H. Herndon and Jesse W. Weik, *Life of Lincoln*
(New York: Da Capo, 1983), 297–98.

60. See, in general, Eric Foner, *Free Soil, Free Labor, Free Men: The Ideology of the
Republican Party before the Civil War* (New York: Oxford University Press, 1970).

THE POLITICAL EVIL OF RACISM

If the general focus of the abolitionist movement in general was the criticism and abolition of slavery, a much smaller group of abolitionists argued that the evil underlying slavery was American racism. The argument for toleration was central to this claim and to its underlying political analysis of the evil of racism.

The key to this abolitionist position was their very unpopular attack on the colonization movement (the idea, advocated by Jefferson among others (including Lincoln),[61] that abolition of slavery would be followed by colonization of freedmen abroad). Garrison prominently attacked colonization because it expressed and reinforced "those unchristian prejudices which have so long been cherished against a sable complexion" taking blacks to be "a distinct and inferior caste"[62]—what Lowell called "a depraved and unchristian public opinion."[63] Abolitionists charged that the American conscience was attempting to assuage its guilt about the evil of slavery by advocating a policy (abolition, then colonization) that rested on the more fundamental evil of racism.

The most perceptive and probing abolitionist analysis of the moral evil of racial prejudice and its role in American politics was Lydia Maria Child's *An Appeal in Favor of Americans Called Africans*.[64] Child offered the most elaborate abolitionist criticism of the common American racist assumption of the inferiority of blacks. Following Montesquieu, she urged "that the present degraded condition of that unfortunate race is produced by artificial causes, not by the laws of nature" (148). The evil of racial prejudice was to make of the product of unjust institutions, subject to criticism and reform, "a fixed and unalterable law of our nature, which cannot possibly be changed" (133).

---

61. See Jefferson, *Notes on the State of Virginia*, 135–36. On Lincoln's long-standing advocacy of plans for emancipation and colonization of African Americans abroad (throughout his political life until as late as 1864), see David Herbert Donald, *Lincoln* (New York: Simon & Schuster, 1995), 136–37, 166–67, 343–44, 346–48, 396–97, 560–61 (abortively proposing compensated emancipation plan to his cabinet in 1864).

62. William Lloyd Garrison, *Thoughts on African Colonization* (1832; New York: Arno Press and The New York Times, 1968), 21. See also William Jay, *Inquiry into the Character and Tendency of the American Colonization, and American Anti-Slavery Societies*, in William Jay, *Miscellaneous Writings on Slavery* (1835; New York: Negro Universities Press, 1968), 7–206; James G. Birney, *Letter on Colonization Addressed to the Rev. Thornton J. Mills, Corresponding Secretary of the Kentucky Colonization Society* (New York, 1834).

63. James Russell Lowell, "The Prejudice of Color," in *The Antislavery Papers of James Russell Lowell* (Boston: Houghton Mifflin, 1902), 1:19.

64. Lydia Maria Child, *An Appeal in Favor of Americans Called Africans* (1833; New York: Arno Press and The New York Times, 1968).

In truth, "[w]e made slavery, and slavery makes the prejudice" (134). Correspondingly, the alleged inferior capacities of blacks were themselves the product of unjust cultural patterns and could not justify unequal treatment:

> [T]he wrongs of the oppressed have been converted into an argument against them. We first debase the nature of man by making him a slave, and then very coolly tell him that he must always remain a slave because he does not know how to use freedom. We first crush people to the earth, and then claim the right of trampling on them for ever, because they are prostrate.[65]

The abolition of slavery in the North did not, Child argued, exempt the North from her criticism. The North practiced various discriminations against blacks (including laws requiring segregation and forbidding intermarriage, schooling, voting, travel, and the like), inflicting unjust racial prejudice. Her cogent criticism of antimiscegenation laws as part of an unjustly degrading cultural pattern of discriminations was, in her historical context, remarkable ("the government ought not to be invested with power to control the affections, any more than the consciences of citizens" [196]). And, anticipating de Tocqueville,[66] Child condemned the particular virulence of Northern racism: "The planter is often attached to his negroes, and lavishes caresses and kind words upon them, as he would on a favorite hound: but our coldhearted, ignoble prejudice admits of no exception—no intermission" (195). Comparing the strength of racial prejudice in America with that in other countries (including countries that retained slavery), Child concluded: "no other people on earth indulge so strong a prejudice with regard to color, as we do" (208).

The abolitionists' quite modern critical insight into the cultural roots of racism (its essential confusion of culture with nature[67]) was integral to their criticism of slavery on the basis of the argument of toleration. They were committed to the right of radical Protestant moral conscience, and they criticized slavery's dependence on the abridgment of the right to conscience, both of slaves and of anyone who would criticize the institution. They understood, in a way in which no other Americans of their generation did, the extent to which the political legitimation of slavery in Protestant America depended on and *indeed compelled* racist assumptions: blacks were, in their nature, what Augustinian intolerance supposed could be only the product of a culpable defect in will, namely, blind heretics; the 1834 Synod of South Carolina

65. Ibid. 169. See also ibid., 11, 66, 133–34.
66. See de Tocqueville, *Democracy in America*, 1:373, 390–91.
67. See, for example, Pierre L. van den Berghe, *Race and Racism* (New York: John Wiley & Sons, 1967), 11.

described blacks in exactly such terms: "that heathen of this country, [who] will bear comparison with the heathen of any part of the world."[68] On the abolitionist view, racism was toleration's evil genius of unreason, arising and sometimes flourishing in reaction to what appear to be the greatest achievements of political reason (for example, a constitution committed to universal toleration).

The abolitionist insight captured an important truth about the origins of slavery in colonial America and perhaps a deeper truth about the enduring cultural roots of American racism and its modern European analogue, anti-Semitism. The point about origins was the early historical justification of slavery on the ground that blacks, like the Amerindians, were heathen non-Christians like Jews,[69] a viewpoint that was perhaps an outgrowth of the Spanish and Portuguese association of blacks with the dangerous infidelity of the Moor or the Jew[70] and the putative legitimacy of enslavement of infidels.[71] Shakespeare's *Othello* certainly supports an English conflation of blacks and Moors and suggests corresponding anxieties and fears centering on race and sex.[72] Desdemona's father, Brabantio, who had welcomed Othello into his house, is easily persuaded by Iago that the marriage, which violated antimiscegenation conventions, was "against all rules of nature,"[73] which suggests prejudice easily rationalized as natural group boundaries not to be breached. Such a "folk bias"[74] against blacks thus probably antedated slavery in Britain's American colonies and hardened into more virulent racism under the impact of the special harshness of

68. Cited in Theodore Parker, "A Letter on Slavery," Theodore Parker, *The Slave Power*, ed. James K. Hosmer (Boston: American Unitarian Association, n.d.), 75.

69. See Winthrop D. Jordan, *White over Black: American Attitudes toward the Negro, 1550–1812* (New York: W. W. Norton, 1977), 56, 65, 91–98; , Edmund S. Morgan, *American Slavery American Freedom* (New York: W.W. Norton, 1975), 328–32; Alden T. Vaughan, *Roots of American Racism: Essays on the Colonial Experience* (New York: Oxford University Press, 1995), 162–65; on the express analogy of the Amerindians and the Jews, see ibid., 49–57; Fernando Cervantes, *The Devil in the New World: The Impact of Diabolism in New Spain* (New Haven: Yale University Press, 1994), 39. On the Spanish struggles over the moral status of Amerindians, see Anthony Pagden, *The Fall of Nature Man: The American Indians and the Origins of Comparative Ethnology* (Cambridge: Cambridge University Press, 1982). For the view that Jews are the natural slaves of Christians, see Gavin I. Langmuir, *History, Religion, and Antisemitism* (Berkeley and Los Angeles: University of California Press, 1990), 294–97, 345–46.

70. See David Brion Davis, *The Problem of Slavery in Western Culture* (Ithaca: Cornell University Press, 1976), 170, 195, 207–8, 214, 281.

71. See ibid., 246–47, 473.

72. See Winthrop D. Jordan, *White over Black*, 37–38.

73. See *Othello*, ed. W. J. Craig (London: Oxford University Press, 1966), 1.3.101.

74. See Carl N. Degler, *Out of Our Past: The Forces That Shaped Modern America*, 3d ed. (New York: Harper and Row, 1984), 30.

American slavery. If Locke could so misinterpret his own views to justify black slavery in the Carolinas, less self-critical men could have found it all too natural to legitimize the permanent enslavement of blacks, even after their religious conversion, on racist assumptions. Spanish anti-Semitism may have taken a self-consciously racist turn much earlier than previously supposed (so that conversion to Christianity, however freely undertaken, could not expunge the putative racial taint of the blood),[75] and black racism may share a similar early transmogrification of religious into racial prejudice. In effect, blacks so lacked moral capacity that they were, as it were, permanent heathens and thus permanently exiled from a political community whose condition of unity was respect for the moral powers fundamental to the principle of toleration.

The abolitionist theory of racism offers a cultural analysis both of how this was done and how it was sustained. American racism arose reactively as a way of justifying cultural boundaries of moral and political community—ostensibly universalistic in their terms—that had already excluded a class of persons from the community. Slavery was such an excluding institution, and it was historically based on a folk bias against Africans that reacted to their unfamiliar culture for which color became a kind of proxy. A public culture, based on the principle of toleration, is and should be open to all persons on fair terms of respect for basic human rights, including, as Weld and Channing made clear, rights to freedom of conscience, speech, intimate life, work, and the like. American slavery systematically abridged all these rights, indeed disrupted and intolerantly degraded the culture (including the family life) of African American slaves. The peculiarly onerous conditions of American slavery (prohibitions on reading and writing, on religious self-organization, and on marriage and family life, and limitations and eventual prohibitions on manumission)[76] deprived black slaves of any of the rights and opportunities that the public culture made available to others; in particular, black Americans were deprived of the

75. See B. Netanyahu, *The Origins of the Inquisition in Fifteenth Century Spain* (New York: Random House, 1995), 381–82, 980–83.

76. On the special features of American slavery, in contrast to slavery elsewhere, see Stanley M. Elkins, *Slavery*, 3d ed. (Chicago: University of Chicago Press, 1976); Kenneth M. Stampp, *The Peculiar Institution* (New York: Vintage, 1956); Eugene D. Genovese, *The World the Slaveholders Made* (Middletown, Conn.: Wesleyan University Press, 1988); John W. Blassingame, *The Slave Community*, 2d ed. (New York: Oxford University Press, 1979); Carl N. Degler, *Neither Black Nor White* (Madison: University of Wisconsin Press, 1986); Peter Kolchin, *Unfree Labor: American Slavery and Russian Serfdom* (Cambridge: Harvard University Press, 1987); Peter Kolchin, *American Slavery, 1619–1877* (New York: Hill and Wang, 1993).

respect for their creative moral powers of rational and reasonable freedom in public and private life. The nature of American slavery and the associated forms of racial discrimination against free blacks both in the South and North had socially produced the image of black incapacity that ostensibly justified their permanent heathen status (outside the community capable of Christian moral freedom).

For the antiracist abolitionists, consistent with the argument for toleration, slavery and discrimination were forms of religious, social, economic, and political persecution motivated by a politically entrenched conception of black incapacity. That conception enforced its own vision of truth against both the standards of reasonable inquiry and the reasonable capacities of both blacks and whites that might challenge the conception. A conception of political unity, subject to reasonable doubt as to its basis and merits, had unreasonably resolved its doubts, consistent with the paradox of intolerance, in the irrationalist racist certitudes of group solidarity on the basis of unjust group subjugation.

Black Americans were the scapegoats of Southern self-doubt in the same way European Jews had been the victims of Christian doubt. Frederick Douglass, the leading black abolitionist of the age, stated the antiracist abolitionist analysis with a classical clarity:

> Ignorance and depravity, and the inability to rise from degradation to civilization and respectability, are the most usual allegations against the oppressed. The evils most fostered by slavery and oppression are precisely those which slaveholders and oppressors would transfer from their system to the inherent character of their victims. Thus the very crimes of slavery become slavery's best defence. By making the enslaved a character fit only for slavery, they excuse themselves for refusing to make the slave a freeman.[77]

The abolitionists thought the political evil of racism in America was more fundamental an evil than slavery itself. It was the political evil in terms of which Americans justified slavery; and its evils, if unrecognized and unremedied, would corrupt abolition by means of the illegitimate construction of the boundaries of moral and political community on terms that excluded blacks (as colonization had).

Jefferson's treatment of the advocacy of slavery in *Notes on the State of Virginia* illustrates their point. Jefferson powerfully urged the depravity and injustice of slavery as an institution, its degradation of the children of slaveowners into self-indulged tyrants in mimesis of their parents, and its corruption of republican morality. He concluded: "with what execration should the statesman be loaded, who permitting one

---

77. Frederick Douglass, "The Claims of the Negro Ethnologically Considered," in *The Life and Writings of Frederick Douglass,* ed. Philip S. Foner (New York: International Publishers, 1975), 2:295.

60   CHAPTER TWO

half the citizens thus to trample on the rights of the other, transforms
those into despots, and these into enemies, destroys the morals of the
one part, and the amor patriae of the other."⁷⁸ Nonetheless, Jefferson
advocated emancipation with colonization abroad.

Posing the query, "[w]hy not retain and incorporate the blacks into
the state . . . ?" (138) Jefferson first conceded the force of "[d]eep
rooted prejudices entertained by the whites." Then, he rather superfi-
cially reviewed other features "physical and moral" of blacks essentially
observed by him under the conditions of slavery—hardly the appropriate standard of comparison for an impartial assessment. For all his
tentativeness about his conclusions about race differences ("I advance
it therefore as a suspicion only . . . ," [143]), the force of the account
was driven by a "geyser of libidinal energy,"⁷⁹ focusing on black sexuality; this account stood "[u]ntil well into the nineteenth century . . . as
the strongest suggestion of inferiority expressed by any native American."⁸⁰ The argument is remarkable for its pseudo-scientific, assured
tone with little of the doubt that another Virginian, St. George Tucker,
confessed to feeling about similar conclusions (based, as seemed to
him likely, on "[e]arly prejudices" that "render an inhabitant of a country where negroe slavery prevails, an improper umpire between them
[Hume vs. Beattie on race differences])."⁸¹

Both Jefferson and Tucker did argue for the abolition of slavery in
Virginia, but the abolitionist point against them was that their failure to
take racism seriously as a political evil subverted ostensibly abolitionist
arguments into a kind of justification for the evil that in fact sustained
the institution. Jefferson is thus not only a central figure in the history
of scientific racism,⁸² but his arguments about race were soon to be
elaborated by Southern proslavery apologists into a full-scale justification of black slavery itself.

78. Thomas Jefferson, *Notes on the State of Virginia*, 162–63.
79. Jordan, *White over Black*, 458.
80. Ibid., 455.
81. St. George Tucker, *Blackstone's Commentaries*, "On the State of Slavery in Virginia,"
75, note H. Tucker, however, agrees with Jefferson's conclusions about colonization, citing
his discussion at some length (74–75 n). For Hume's empirical argument for race differences,
see David Hume, "Of National Character," in *Essays Moral Political and Literary*, ed. Eugene
F. Miller (1777; Indianapolis: Liberty Classics, 1987), 208 n. 10; for James Beattie's attack
on Hume's argument, see James Beattie, *An Essay on the Nature and Immutability of Truth*,
ed. Lewis White Beck (1770; New York: Garland Publishing, 1983), 479–84.
82. See, for general treatments of the topic, Jordan, *White over Black*; George M. Fredrickson, *The Black Image in the White Mind: The Debate on Afro-American Character and
Destiny, 1817–1914* (Middletown, Conn.: Wesleyan University Press, 1971); Thomas F.
Goossett, *Race: The History of an Idea in America* (New York: Schocken Books, 1965); Reginald Horsman, *Race and Manifest Destiny: The Origins of American Racial Anglo-Saxonism*

The abolitionists were familiar with these antebellum arguments of the infant American "science" of ethnology that pointed to alleged physical differences (e.g., brain size) between blacks and whites to argue for differences in capacity.[83] Ethnology appealed to the Protestant respect for experience and scientific method, and was aggressively cultivated and used by Southerners to suggest that racist assumptions were not unreasonable in the way that abolitionists had suggested.[84] But even in the relatively incoherent state of the human sciences in this period, abolitionists like James Russell Lowell,[85] Frederick Douglass,[86] and Charles Sumner[87] challenged the validity of the general approach, questioning its interpretation of data, its omission of other evidence, and its failure to incorporate moral ideas[88] and the importance of culture in the human sciences.[89]

The very ease and certitude with which proslavery apologists adopted this ostensibly scientific view suggest the increasingly polemical nature of Southern thought, which appeared no longer able to sustain even a Jefferson's gesture of tentativeness or a Tucker's doubts about impartiality. Some Southerners notably could entertain such doubts, but they were often on the verge of moral revolt against and self-imposed exile from Southern culture.

Moncure Conway, born into a Virginia slave-owning family, was a notable example. Conway had always believed blacks were inferior, but was searching for ways to justify his position. When Agassiz's new theory on race differences appeared, Conway enthusiastically embraced it, giving a public lecture and writing an (unpublished) essay in support of it:

> Something, however, perhaps "the dumb answers of the coloured servants moving about the house, cheerfully yielding . . . unrequited services," soon

(Cambridge: Harvard University Press, 1981). On Jefferson in particular, see Paul Finkelman, *Slavery and the Founders: Race and Liberty in the Age of Jefferson* (Armonk, N.Y.: M. E. Sharpe, 1996), 105–67.

83. For a good general study, see William Stanton, *The Leopard's Spots: Scientific Attitudes toward Race in America, 1815–59* (Chicago: University of Chicago Press, 1960).

84. Ibid.

85. See Lowell, "Ethnology," *Anti-Slavery Papers of James Russell Lowell*, 2:26–32.

86. See Frederick Douglass, "The Claims of the Negro Ethnologically Considered," in *The Life and Writings of Frederick Douglass*, ed. Philip S. Foner (New York: International Publishers, 1975), 2:289–309.

87. See Charles Sumner, "The Question of Caste," in *Charles Sumner: His Complete Works* (New York: Negro Universities Press, 1969), 17:131–83.

88. See Douglass, "The Claims of the Negro Ethnologically Considered," 2:292, 2:307–8; Sumner, "The Question of Caste," 17:138–39.

89. See, especially, Douglass, "The Claims of the Negro Ethnologically Considered," 2:304–6.

brought about a reaction which proved to be "the moral crisis" of his life. Conway was shocked by "the ease with which I could consign a whole race to degradation." . . . The reaction constituted a religious conversion of the eighteenth-century variety, now extinct: "an overwhelming sense of my own inferiority came upon me" and "left me with a determination to devote my life to the elevation and welfare of my fellow-beings, white and black." Thus began Conway's long career in the antislavery movement.[90]

Conway had been reading Ralph Waldo Emerson and was much struck by his emphasis on transcendental moral conscience self-reliantly pursued in criticism of traditional culture and values.[91] His awakening interest in the primacy of ethical impartiality led Conway to experience a reasonable doubt—indeed, a piercing sense of guilt—that neither his polemical culture nor its hard science of ethnology could support or sustain.

Like Conway, the Grimke sisters were from a Southern slave-owning family, and they experienced a similarly haunting sense of guilt that led them into self-exile from the South. Their journey into moral self-discovery and their experience of painful moral growth led to their insight that women like themselves, exercising free moral personality, could find in their own subjugation an oppression similar to that of blacks. They used that personal experience to achieve an ethical impartiality possessed of critical moral insights into the interlinked evils of slavery, racism, the subjection of women, and sexism. Their background and their story begin the narrative of abolitionist feminism.

90. See William Stanton, *The Leopard's Spots*, 111. See also Peter F. Walker, *Moral Choices: Memory, Desire, and Imagination in Nineteenth-Century American Abolition* (Baton Rouge: Louisiana State University Press, 1978), 58–62.

91. See John d'Entremont, *Southern Emancipator: Moncure Conway, The American Years, 1832–1865* (New York: Oxford University Press, 1987), 43–56. On Emerson's abolitionism, see, in general, Len Gougeon, *Virtue's Hero: Emerson, Antislavery, and Reform* (Athens: University of Georgia Press, 1990).

3 Abolitionist Feminism

The distinctive originality of abolitionist feminism may be understood by way of its historical context in related views (in particular, those of Mary Wollstonecraft and Frances Wright), the dominant views of women's roles (notably expressed by Catharine Beecher) that it criticized, and in its roots (as stated by Lydia Maria Child). Against this background, abolitionist feminism was developed by the Grimke sisters and later distinctively elaborated by Lucretia Mott and Elizabeth Stanton and by black women (and ex-slaves) like Sojourner Truth and Harriet Jacobs.

The Feminist Interpretation of Rights-Based Republicanism: Wollstonecraft and Wright

The theory and practice of rights-based republican constitutionalism focused on securing respect for inalienable human rights (like the right to conscience) in the terms required by the argument for toleration. Theocratically Puritan Massachusetts in the seventeenth century certainly did not accept the argument for toleration as Weld, Channing, and Parker would understand it in the nineteenth century, but the role that reasonable conscience played in Puritan thought even at that time[1] was embraced by Anne Hutchinson; it served as the ground for her

---

1. See Perry Miller, *The New England Mind: the Seventeenth Century* (Cambridge: Harvard University Press, 1939), 181–206.

right to speak her mind on ultimate spiritual questions and to make claims that the Puritan religio-political establishment interpreted as heretical, such as her claims of equality with men (including the right to the priesthood).[2] In the late eighteenth century, the struggles to establish rights-based forms of republican constitutionalism in the wake of the revolutions in America and France prominently included successful arguments, by Jefferson and Madison among others, to constitutionalize the argument for toleration in the guarantees of religious liberty in the First Amendment of the American Bill of Rights,[3] and thus plausibly supported arguments analogous to those earlier made by Anne Hutchinson. Leading philosophers of rights-based republican constitutionalism, like Rousseau and Kant, expressly disowned such arguments in favor of a more traditional conception of women's roles.[4] Mary Wollstonecraft and Frances Wright, however, gave strikingly feminist interpretations to the rights-based principles of republican constitutionalism.

Wollstonecraft's companion political essays (*A Vindication of the Rights of Men*[5] (1790) and *A Vindication of the Rights of Woman*[6] [1792]) were provoked by Burke's attack on the rights-based republican constitutionalism of her teacher, Richard Price, and in particular, Price's defense of what he took to be the rights-based principles of the French Revolution.[7] Price had earlier prominently defended the American Revolution (as had Burke for different reasons[8]) on the

2. For an illuminating recent exploration of both the nature of Hutchinson's rather limited claims and the violent rejection of them by political and religious authorities, see Mary Beth Norton, *Founding Mothers and Fathers: Gendered Power and the Forming of American Society* (New York: Knopf, 1996), 359–99.

3. For fuller discussion, see Richards, *Toleration and the Constitution*, 104–21.

4. Ibid., 180–83. For stark statements of Kant's denial to women of basic moral and intellectual competences, see Immanuel Kant, *Observations on the Feeling of the Beautiful and Sublime*, ed. John T. Goldthwait (Berkeley and Los Angeles: University of California Press, 1965), 78–79, 81, 86, 95; for comparable statements of race differences, see ibid., 110–13.

5. Mary Wollstonecraft, "A Vindication of the Rights of Men," in *The Works of Mary Wollstonecraft*, ed. Janet Todd and Marilyn Butler (1790; New York: New York University Press, 1989), 5:5–60.

6. Mary Wollstonecraft, "A Vindication of the Rights of Women," in *The Works of Mary Wollstonecraft*, ed. Janet Todd and Marilyn Butler (1790; New York: New York University Press, 1989), 5:65–266.

7. See Richard Price, "A Discourse on the Love of our Country," in *Richard Price: Political Writings*, ed. D. O. Thomas (1789; Cambridge: Cambridge University Press, 1991), 176–96; Edmund Burke, *Reflections on the Revolution in France*, in *Burke's Politics*, ed. Ross J. S. Hoffman & Paul Levack (1790; New York: Knopf, 1959), 277–400. For commentary, see Virginia Sapiro, *A Vindication of Political Virtue: The Political Theory of Mary Wollstonecraft* (Chicago: University of Chicago Press, 1992), 12–13, 186–222.

8. For Burke's reasons, see the writings excerpted in *Burke's Politics*, 46–112.

ground that it had led to the more principled institution of the Lockean argument for toleration than existed even in Great Britain, and was thus a constitutional model for the world.[9] In the earlier essay, Wollstonecraft defended Price's theory of basic human rights as "the birthright of man" (9, 14, 43) and appealed crucially, contra Burke's emphasis on traditions, to the need for a reasonably impartial standpoint, consistent with the argument for toleration, from which morally corrupt traditions might be assessed and criticized (19–20, 31–33). From such a standpoint, the traditional treatment of women reflected more the morally corrupt "laxity of morals [of the] libertine imagination than the cold arguments of reason, that give no sex to virtue" (46), and the political establishment of a religion might rest on as morally corrupt and unjust a tradition as institutions of slavery or caste systems (49–51). Wollstonecraft's longer and more substantial second essay took the argument for toleration that the earlier essay only applied to women incidentally and innovatively focused it on the condition of women.

Wollstonecraft built upon the expansive interpretation of the Lockean argument for toleration found in Richard Price's works,[10] including protection of all conscientious opinions (religious or irreligious) except when they supported overt acts of secular harm.[11] Price had condemned established churches[12] and inadequately representative constitutions (like those of Great Britain) that unreasonably entrenched the political authority of "slavish governments and slavish hierarchies."[13] In "Two Tracts on Civil Liberty, the War with America, and the Debts and Finances of the Kingdom," Price argued that such condemnations as slavery required the abridgment of inalienable rights that no authority may legitimately touch or compromise:

> As no people can lawfully surrender their religious liberty by giving up their right of judging for themselves in religion, or by allowing any human beings to prescribe to them what faith they shall embrace, or what mode of worship they shall practise, so neither can any civil societies lawfully surrender their civil liberty by giving up to any extraneous jurisdiction their power of legislating for themselves and disposing their property. (33)

9. See Richard Price, "Observations on the Importance of the American Revolution," in in *Price: Political Writings*, ed. D. O. Thomas (1785; Cambridge: Cambridge University Press, 1991), 130–42.

10. For Price's appeal to Locke, see Price, "Two Tracts on Civil Liberty, the War with America, and the Debts and Finances of the Kingdom: with a General Introduction and Supplement" (1778), in *Price: Political Writings*, 20, 81–82, 87, 97.

11. See Price, "The Importance of the American Revolution," in *Price: Political Writings*, 125–30.

12. Ibid., 130–37; "The Evidence for a Future Period of Improvement in the State of Mankind" (1787), in *Price: Political Writings*, 160.

13. Price, "The Importance of the American Revolution," 119.

Respect for these inalienable rights protected the powers of moral personality for free exercise of our reason (90) and for "self-direction, or self-government" (22); their abridgment was slavery because the exercise of these powers became subject to the will of others. Price described such abridgment as an infliction of dehumanization: "[W]ithout religious and civil liberty, he is a poor and abject animal, without rights, without property, and without a conscience, bending his neck to the yoke, and crouching to the will of every silly creature who has the insolence to pretend to authority over him" (23). The institutions that inflicted such slavery (whether established churches or unrepresentative constitutions) rested on "a love of power inherent in human nature" (47) that "intoxicates" (83) and that fundamentally "corrupts" the competence "of a free people" to maintain "a constant and suspicious vigilance."[14] The American revolutionaries thus properly took up arms against their unjust "state of subordination to us" (36), for against any such abridgment of basic rights "people have a right to emancipate themselves as soon as they can" (89). However, Price, echoing Locke, exempted from this analysis any "subordination and dependence, which nature has established and which must have arisen among mankind whether civil government had been instituted or not" (82).[15]

The startling originality of Wollstonecraft's second essay, *A Vindication of the Rights of Woman*, is the way in which she subverted the traditional appeal to natural subordination as applied to women by deploying all the terms of criticism Price had already mustered in service of his attacks on established churches and unrepresentative constitutions. As one would expect in such an elaboration of Price's interpretation of the argument for toleration, the moral core of Wollstonecraft's argument was an appeal for respect for the inalienable right to conscience of women so that "freedom strengthen[s] her reason till she comprehend her duty, and see in what manner it is connected with her real good."[16] "Who made man the exclusive judge, if woman partake with him the gift of reason?" (67) Is not this "[a]bsolute, uncontroverted authority [of men over the religious lives of women] a direct and exclusive appropriation of reason?" (157) From the perspective of the argument for toleration, nothing could be more dehumanizing than abridgment of the right to conscience. Wollstonecraft made her case for "the rights of woman" on this basis in forceful terms she adapted from Price. Women, by virtue of their moral subjugation to men's ap-

14. See Price, "A Fast Sermon" (1781), in *Price: Political Writings*, 109.
15. Cf. ibid., 88.
16. See Wollstonecraft, *Vindication of the Rights of Woman*, 66.

propriation of reason, "may be convenient slaves, but slavery will have its constant effect degrading the master and the abject dependent" (68). Condemnation of the subjection of woman as slavery pervades the second essay.[17]

To make her case against the traditional view of the natural subordination of women, Wollstonecraft explored analogies between the unjustly enforceable political epistemologies of religious and political hierarchies, condemned by Price on the ground of the argument for toleration, and those traditionally enforced against women (as the alleged ground for their natural subordination). Such religious and political epistemologies were unjustly enforceable through law because they confined standards of assessment to a politically entrenched sectarian measure not reasonably justifiable at large and because such standards were applied to deny that persons were even capable of such reasonable argument in private and public life. Wollstonecraft argued that both injustices had been inflicted on women. Standards of politically enforceable argument bearing on gender roles had been unjustly confined to the measure of an unquestioned and unquestionable gender hierarchy, which, like all such unjust hierarchies, depended on the morally corrupt failure to allow reasonable testing at large of its sectarian claims (81–87). Indeed, the enforceable political epistemology had denied the very capacity of women, as persons, to originate moral reasoning, and thus to possess souls capable of reasonable self-government (73–74, 88, 129). Both these injustices should be condemned, Wollstonecraft argued, for the same reasons of principle that the argument for toleration condemned the enforcement at large of the political epistemologies supporting religious intolerance or political despotism. If Bible interpretation could not, as Locke argued, be reasonably enforced at large to support absolute monarchy, the authority of the Bible could not similarly justify the subjection of women (95, 148–49, 224). The authority of absolute monarchs was no more reasonably based in ability than claims of men over women (106); "[t]he *divine right* of husbands" was no more defensible than "the divine right of kings" (110). In both cases, illegitimately entrenched political power corruptly rationalized its claims by denying the very competence of persons reasonably to originate and test claims to authority over them (110–11, 113, 114, 120, 127–29, 224). In the case of women, not only was physical strength unreasonably confused with moral personality (74, 108), but women's very "power [of reason]" had been "denied to

17. See, for example, ibid., 91, 101, 105, 112, 113, 116, 145, 161, 182, 215, 222, 236, 239.

women" (123) as "either a slave, or a despot" each of which "equally retards the progress of reason" (123).

Some of Wollstonecraft's most eloquent passages explored these two dimensions of the dehumanization of women, each of which mirrored, in her view, the denial of women's reasonable nature, as if "she was born only to procreate and rot" (132) or "created to be the toy of man, his rattle" (102) or "spaniel" (152); "[c]onfined . . . in cages like the feathered race, they [women] have nothing to do but to plume themselves, and stalk with mock majesty from perch to perch" (125). On the one hand, women were thus slavishly dependent on men's reasons for taking an interest in them; on the other, "[t]he passions of men have . . . placed women on thrones," which Wollstonecraft analogized to the corruptions of "hereditary power" that "chokes the affections and nips reason in the bud" (125). Such unreasonable power "produces a propensity to tyrannize" (77),[18] which undermines the reasonable powers of women in conducting their lives as lovers and friends, as mothers, or as single women.

Tyrants, by virtue of the corruptively unjust political epistemology that sustains their unreasonable powers, "see things through a false medium" (111). The failure to understand that sexual love "from its nature, must be transitory" (98) disables women and men from forming what can endure, companionate friendships based on reason (98–100, 119, 141–43, 173, 188–90). Chastity in women is thus unreasonably emphasized (206–7, 258), prostitution too harshly judged (140–41), and men subjected to a more lenient, unjust double standard (207–10).[19] Conflicts between being a wife and mother[20] or mother and daughter (118) are not acknowledged, nor are women's powers of reason (as opposed to parroting conventions as "slaves of prejudices" [182]) which disables them from achieving morally responsible agency in understanding and discharging the moral duties of family life (133–37, 220, 250, 261–63). Finally, an unreasonable interpretation of the value of marriage failed to make appropriate room for the reasonable dignity of a single life (101, 132, 217), including the right to earn an independent living (218–19, 237) and even, Wollstonecraft suggested, an associated right to political representation (217).

Such slavery and its mirror image, tyranny, were unjust abridgments of our basic inalienable rights, on the grounds of which women justly

18. See also ibid., 109, 116–17, 125, 135, 226.
19. Cf. ibid., 199–200, 265.
20. Wollstonecraft observed, "the neglected wife is, in general, the best mother." Ibid., 99.

could claim emancipation (113, 145). For Wollstonecraft, such emancipation must demand respect for women's morally independent free exercise of the right to conscience (104, 105, 118, 156–57), and thus their reasonable interpretation and construction of the common moral principles to which all persons are subject (104, 120). Such respect for women's moral powers would, Wollstonecraft argued, undermine "the existence of sexual virtues [applicable only to women], not excepting modesty" (120), a theme later echoed, as we shall see, by the Grimke sisters.

Against the background of the kinds of epistemological injuries from which women had suffered, both Wollstonecraft's criticisms and constructive proposals centered on education. In particular, Wollstonecraft savagely attacked Rousseau's educational reinforcement of the slavery and tyranny of women (90–91, 94, 96, 108–9, 110–11, 131, 147–62), and, invoking Locke, called for a republican education in rational freedom for women (226, 236), including coeducational public education (237–50).

Wollstonecraft acknowledged and struggled to answer the criticism that her views called for "masculine women" (74) not by questioning gender conventions in general, but one in particular (namely, that reasoning must be masculine). If that was all the criticism meant, Wollstonecraft embraced it, wishing that women "may every day grow more and more masculine" (74). But if Wollstonecraft was willing to call for women who were more masculine in this way, she carried her analysis no further—ultimately disavowing, for example, the suggestion of military service on the basis of conventional gender roles (216). She quite uncritically invoked conventional gender stereotypes in the criticism of effeminate men (male homosexuals in particular, who, strikingly, she associated with rampant unchastity in men) (208, 216, 230). In effect, Wollstonecraft acquiesced in the unjustly stereotypical sexualization of homosexual men (as prostitutes) that she criticized as a proper view of sexually active heterosexual women.

Nonetheless, Wollstonecraft quite remarkably identified and explored, on grounds of the argument for toleration, not only the injustice of the subjection of women, but the underlying cultural evil of giving unreasonable political weight to "the privileges of rank and sex" in place of "the privileges of humanity" (220.) The evil, which we today call sexism, was, for Wollstonecraft, "subversive of the birth-right of man, the right of acting according to the direction of his own reason" (225). Being fundamentally unreasonable, sexism was described by Wollstonecraft as expressing prejudice, indeed making both men and women "all their lives the slaves of prejudices" (182). Wollstonecraft analogized the irrationalist grounds of such sexism to those of the evil we call racism:

> Why subject her to propriety—blind propriety, if she be capable of acting from a nobler spring, if she be an heir of immortality? Is sugar always to be produced by vital blood? Is one half of the human species, like the poor African slaves, to be subject to prejudices that brutalize them, when principles would be a surer guide, only to sweeten the cup of man? Is not this indirectly to deny woman reason? for a gift is a mockery, if it be unfit for use. (215)

Wollstonecraft was undoubtedly influential on emergent American feminist thought,[21] but her influence was infrequently acknowledged by nineteenth-century American feminists except by more radical and outspoken advocates like Margaret Fuller[22] and Lucretia Mott.[23] Even while insisting on Wollstonecraft's importance to American feminism, Mott noted that "[h]er name was cast out as evil" (like other moral prophets like Jesus); Fuller accurately diagnosed the problematics of Wollstonecraft for Americans not in her work but in her life[24] as it had been frankly told by her husband, William Godwin.[25] Godwin published his *Memoirs of the Author of A Vindication of the Rights of Woman* one year after his wife died giving birth to her daughter (whom we now know as Mary Shelley).[26] The events of the narrative included Wollstonecraft's passion for a woman (Frances Blood) (19),[27] her passionate though abortive love for a married man (the painter Henry Fuseli) and her love affair with Gilbert Imlay (resulting in a child born out of wedlock) (85–92, 97–99), her suicide attempt when the affair ended (127, 132–35, 146), and her love affair with Godwin (and resulting pregnancy whereupon they married) (148–58). Further, God-

21. The important influence of Lucretia Mott in shaping the feminist theory and practice of Elizabeth Stanton included, as Stanton made clear, Mott's 1840 conversations in London with Stanton about the work of "Mary Wollstonecraft, though . . . tabooed by orthodox teachers." See Anna Hallowell, *James and Lucretia Mott Life and Letters* (Boston: Houghton, Mifflin, 1884), 186.

22. See S. Margaret Fuller, *Woman in the Nineteenth Century*, ed. Madeleine B. Stern (1845; Columbia: University of South Carolina Press, 1980), 62–63, 66.

23. See Lucretia Mott, "No Greater Joy Than to See These Children Walking in the Anti-Slavery Path" (speech delivered on 3–4 December 1863), in *Lucretia Mott: Her Complete Speeches and Sermons*, ed. Dana Greene (New York: Edwin Mellen Press, 1980), 270.

24. See Fuller, *Women in the Nineteenth Century*, 62.

25. Ibid., 66.

26. See William Godwin, *Memoirs of the Author of a Vindication of the Rights of Woman* (London: J. Johnson, 1798).

27. Godwin calls Wollstonecraft's love for Frances Blood the "ruling passion of her mind." See also ibid., 21, 46, 109.

win made quite clear that, for Wollstonecraft, passionate sexual love between men and women was "the principal solace of human life" (91), was indeed "sacred" (106), and was to be pursued "with perfect fidelity to that affection when it existed" (92) whether the couple was married or not (for only sex without love was forbidden by virtue [92][28]). From the perspective of mainstream nineteenth-century America, Wollstonecraft's work and life accordingly stood for the unacceptable principle of free love, and most forms of nineteenth-century feminism would distance themselves from acknowledging any such principle. I shall call this reactionary response, when it shall later occur, the "Wollstonecraft repudiation," marking a central and continuing normative struggle for moral identity within American feminism.

Frances Wright's impact on American abolitionist theory and practice (including the abolitionist feminists) was not derived from the substantive originality of her arguments, which were largely adapted from Wollstonecraft and others (Robert Owen and his son, Robert Dale Owen).[29] Rather, her influence sprung from her public role: her reform efforts at abolitionist experiments like Nashoba and others (93–133) and, starting in 1828, her unusual career as a popular lecturer (134–60). Wright's notoriously unconventional views on various questions included arguments for racial amalgamation (127–29) and free love (115–27), the indictment of marriage as the enslavement of women (157–58), and advocacy of birth control (158–59). Wright also presented a startlingly anticlerical interpretation of the argument for toleration, condemning the political power of the American clergy and the sectarian theology it illegitimately enforced through law.[30] She urged Americans to use their own public reason consistent with the principle of "free inquiry" (21) to think about justice and the common good, and to acknowledge on that basis the justice of claims for equal rights for women (20–21, 24, 29–32, 211, 217) and universal education for all (136). Importantly, Wright used the argument for toleration as the background for a proper understanding of the Declaration of Independence and the role appeal to inalienable human rights should play in the interpretation of American constitutional institutions (206–11).

28. "She conceived that true virtue would prescribe the most entire celibacy, exclusively of affection, and the most perfect fidelity to the affection when it existed." Ibid.

29. See William Randall Waterman, *Frances Wright* (New York: Columbia University Press, 1924).

30. See Frances Wright D'Arusmont, *Course of Public Lectures*, in *Life, Letters and Lectures 1834/1844* (1834; New York: Arno Press, 1972), 16–17, 42–48, 60–71, 73. *Course of Public Lectures* was originally published 1834; *Supplement Course of Lectures*, in 1834; *Biography, Notes, and Political Letters of Frances Wright D'Arusmont*, in 1844).

Wright's greatest contributions to subsequent abolitionist advocacy were here public lectures, both in the their substance and in the novelty of her performance as a female public speaker. She spoke widely to secular, mixed audiences about matters of justice and the public good. If, as Wright elsewhere argued, "[t]he first master measure employed for the more certain enslavement of the species was the subjugation of woman in her body and her soul" (16), breaking the convention of women's silence in public space was the best argument that could be made for the inalienable rights of women, including, as Wollstonecraft had made so clear, claims to the right to conscience. Walt Whitman, himself struggling for voice, was deeply moved when he heard one of Wright's public lectures in New York in 1829: "I never felt so glowingly toward any other woman. She possessed herself of my body and soul."[31] Wright also was a model for comparable abolitionist public speeches by an African American woman, Maria Stewart, in 1832[32] and, somewhat later (as we shall see), for the Grimke sisters.

Strikingly, an American religious leader, Lyman Beecher, recognized Frances Wright as the fundamental challenge to his authority that she certainly claimed to be. In his sermons on "Political Atheism," Beecher condemned "the female apostle of atheistic liberty"[33] who had recently given highly popular lectures in Boston. Such theories of infidelity in America and France "extend to the modification of the religious, civil, and social state of man—contemplating nothing less than the abolition of marriage and the family state, separate property, civil government, and all sense of accountability."[34] Beecher's daughter, Catharine, would articulate a conception of women's role that would critically resist such infidelity, including the later advocacy of the Grimke sisters.

CATHARINE BEECHER ON REPUBLICAN WOMANHOOD

To answer the feminist rights-based republicanism of Wollstonecraft and Wright, republican America needed an alternative conception of woman's place that better defended the traditional role of women, and

31. Reynolds, *Walt Whitman's America*, 56.
32. For pertinent commentary and primary sources, see Bert James Loewenberg and Ruth Bogin, eds., *Black Women in Nineteenth-Century American Life* (University Park and London: The Pennsylvania State University Press, 1976), 183–200; on the hostile reaction to Stewart's public advocacy, see Suzanne M. Marilley, *Woman Suffrage and the Origins of Liberal Feminism in the United States, 1820–1920* (Cambridge: Harvard University Press, 1996), 32–34.
33. Waterman, *Frances Wright*, 179.
34. Ibid., 185.

was demonstrably consistent with the normative premises of American constitutionalism. Mary Wollstonecraft's "own life story, once it was available in Godwin's memoir, could . . . be used to link political feminism to aggressive sexuality"; Wollstonecraft was thus condemned by Timothy Dwight, among others, as "a manly woman," "a strumpet."[35] The conception of republican motherhood proved less threatening to conventional gender roles and yet framed the issue in a way apparently consistent with American republicanism.[36] Catharine Beecher popularly elaborated such a conception for nineteenth-century America; it was more consistent with America's common sense of gender roles, or, at least, less threatening to conventional common sense than the easily parodied and dismissed views of Wollstonecraft and Wright.[37]

But if Beecher's views were less threatening to Americans, they were by no means complacent or uncritical. In some respects, they went further that those of any women of her age both in defending the dignity and value of a single life for women and in defending a quite important role for women in moral reform, thereby having a profound consequence in legitimating an increasingly public role for American women in the nineteenth century.[38] Beecher's views were thus a moral world apart from proslavery Southern theorists like George Fitzhugh or Louisa McCord. Fitzhugh repudiated the basic Protestant and Jeffersonian rights to conscience and free speech[39] and defended slavery and women's subordination as indispensable bastions against abolitionist "total overthrow of the Family and all other existing social, moral, religious and governmental institutions";[40] McCord condemned the appeal to equal human rights in the Declaration of Independence as a "mischievous fallacy,"[41] excoriating any criticism of women's role as, in the overheated rhetoric characteristic of proslavery antifeminist thought, "contrary to Nature,"[42] "a piece with negro eman-

35. See Linda K. Kerber, *Women of the Republic: Intellect and Ideology in Revolutionary America* (New York: W. W. Norton, 1980), 282.

36. Ibid., 228–31, 283–88.

37. The authoritative study of Catharine Beecher remains Kathryn Kish Sklar, *Catharine Beecher: A Study in American Domesticity* (New Haven: Yale University Press, 1973).

38. See, for a useful study, Barbara Leslie Epstein, *The Politics of Domesticity: Women, Evangelism and Temperance in Nineteenth-Century America* (Middletown, Conn.: Wesleyan University Press, 1981).

39. See George Fitzhugh, *Cannibals All! or, Slaves without Masters*, ed. C. Vann Woodward (Cambridge: Harvard University Press, Belknap Press, 1960), 53–54, 130–38, 260–61.

40. Ibid., 198; see also ibid., 190–98, 204–6, 213–16.

41. See Louisa McCord, "Diversity of the Races: Its Bearing upon Negro Slavery," *Southern Quarterly Review* 19 (April 1851): 403.

42. See Louisa McCord, "Enfranchisement of Woman," *Southern Quarterly Review* 21 (April 1852): 325.

cipation" (327) and the work of "moral monsters" (327) and "traitors of her own sex" who would hurl women "from the high pedestal where God has placed" them (340), "the guardian angel[s] of those she loves" (325). Beecher certainly criticized abolitionist advocacy and the abolitionist feminists, and she self-consciously used expressly utilitarian arguments that resembled those used by Calhoun[43] in his rights-skeptical attacks, echoed by Fitzhugh and McCord, on the Declaration of Independence, but she never interpreted her utilitarianism as an attack on equality in general or the Declaration of Independence in particular. She accepted the abolitionist moral judgment of the basic wrongness of slavery and its inconsistency with defensible American values of equality that she expressly endorsed.[44] Within this framework, Beecher struggled to articulate a normative view of women and their roles self-consciously consistent with American republican values.

Beecher thus opened her popular book, *A Treatise on Domestic Economy*,[45] by endorsing the "great maxim, which is the basis of all our civil and political institutions," namely, our equality and our equal entitlement to life, liberty, and the pursuit of happiness (1). Women, Beecher argued, accordingly have an equal interest with men in our democratic institutions, and "no domestic, civil, or political, institution, is right, that sacrifices her interest to promote those of the other sex" (4). Importantly, Beecher expressly gave the test of political rightness a utilitarian interpretation: "to be determined, not with reference to the wishes and interests of a few, but solely with reference to the good of all" (2). Are American women's "duties of subordination" (2) consistent with this test of rightness? Beecher concluded, on the basis of de Tocqueville's observations on American women (4–9, 10–12, 23–24, 131), that the gender-defined dependence of women in the United States, in contrast to such differentiation elsewhere, met this test because the circumstances of American women's confinement in domestic life (eliciting respect for their intelligence and virtue) put them "in a loftier position" (8) than elsewhere. Indeed, de Tocqueville ascribed American prosperity and strength *"to the superiority of their women"* (9). Beecher interpreted de Tocqueville as showing that the subordination of American women not only best advanced the public good, but treated them "as of equal value" by virtue of the compensating disad-

---

43. For commentary, see Richards, *Conscience and the Constitution*, 34.

44. See, in general, Catharine Beecher, "Essay on Slavery and Abolitionism, with Reference to the Duty of American Females" (Philadelphia: H. Perkins, Boston: Perkins & Marvin, 1837).

45. Catharine Beecher, *A Treatise on Domestic Economy*, ed. Kathryn Kish Sklar (1841; New York: Schocken Books, 1977).

vantages and advantages of their domestically confined lives: "In civil
and political affairs, American women take no interest or concern, except so far as they sympathize with their family and personal friends;
but in all cases, in which they do feel a concern, their opinions and
feelings have a consideration, equal, or even superior, to that of the
other sex" (9).

In particular, Beecher made her argument for advantage in terms
of women's moral superiority: "In matters pertaining to the education
of their children, in the selection and support of a clergyman, in all
benevolent enterprises, and in all questions relating to morals and
manners, they have a superior influence" (9). Thus the compensating
advantages were by no means limited to the upbringing of children,
but included the role of shaping American religious and moral life,
including the work of moral reform.

Beecher's own remarkable life (as well as those of her remarkable
sisters, Harriet Beecher Stowe and Isabella Beecher Hooker[46]) illustrates her elastic interpretation of the domesticity of American women,
for it was an enormously important public life that shaped nineteenth-
century American culture. Beecher, who never married, earned her
own living as a teacher, advocate of women's education, and prodigious
writer,[47] and eventually even sought to usurp the traditionally masculine province of her father, Lyman Beecher, and her influential
brother, Henry Ward Beecher, by publishing works on theology, moral
philosophy, and Bible interpretation.[48] Presumably, Beecher would
have rejected a role for women as clergymen as a modern form of the
heresy of Anne Hutchinson; nonetheless, her elastic interpretation of
the morally superior life of women (not only selecting and supporting
clergymen, but "in all questions relating to morals and manners") en-
compassed the scholarly ambitions and achievements of a clergyman—
and a distinguished clergyman at that. In short, Beecher's interpretation of women's roles had an implicitly critical and reformist edge that
stood in sharp contrast to the antifeminist diatribes of Southern proslavery thinkers. Women, she insisted, not only had no obligation to
marry,[49] but "[t]he ability to secure an independent livelihood and hon-

46. See, for an excellent comparative treatment of the three sisters, Jeanne Boydston,
Mary Kelley, and Anne Margolis, *The Limits of Sisterhood: The Beecher Sisters on Women's
Rights and Woman's Sphere* (Chapel Hill: University of North Carolina Press, 1988).

47. See, in general, Kathryn Kish Sklar, *Catharine Beecher*.

48. See Catharine E. Beecher, *Common Sense Applied to Religion; or, The Bible and the
People* (New York: Harper & Bros., 1857); id., *An Appeal to the People in Behalf of Their
Rights as Authorized Interpreters of the Bible* (New York: Harper & Bros., 1860).

49. See Catharine E. Beecher, *The True Remedy for the Wrongs of Women* (Boston:
Phillips, Sampson, 1851), 227.

orable employ suited to her education and capacities, are the only true foundation of the social elevation of woman, even in the very highest classes of society."[50] Indeed, for women in Protestant America who chose not to marry, Beecher urged adapting Catholic models (the role of nuns) that would give American women a more humane range of life choices beyond conventional marriage or dependent spinsterhood.[51]

Beecher dissented, however, from much of nineteenth-century feminist theory and practice. Although she was a leading advocate of women's education, she resisted co-education on the ground of women's distinctive domestic roles[52] and condemned "unwomanly employments"[53] (in contrast to more appropriate vocations like teaching[54]). Her support for woman's suffrage was highly qualified, turning on whether a woman had achieved sufficient economic independence to be given the vote.[55] Her condemnation of free love was unequivocal.[56]

Her criticism of the abolitionist feminists arose not from their abolitionist views or even their writing about them, but from their speaking about their views in public. (Both Beecher and her sister, Harriet, were prodigious authors of books, but not public speakers.[57]) Beecher associated such public speech to mixed audiences with its historical precedent, the popular lectures of Frances Wright, who was an advocate of atheism and free love and thus an "offensive and indecorous" public woman (analogizing such advocacy to "the dancing of an actress," a kind of prostitution).[58] The Grimke sisters, as we shall see, were neither atheists nor advocates of free love. Nonetheless, Beecher impugned their public speeches (including, by implication, those of Maria Stewart as well), because such speeches by women were made on self-

50. See ibid., 59.

51. See Catharine E. Beecher, *The Evils Suffered by American Women and American Children: The Cause and the Remedy* (New York: Harper & Bros., 1846), 30–33; id., *The Duty of American Women to Their Country* (New York: Harper & Bros., 1845), 122; *Woman Suffrage and Woman's Profession* (Hartford: Brown and Gross, 1871), 116–17. On the background changes in the roles of American women under the pressure of urbanization during much of this period, see Barbara J. Berg, *The Remembered Gate: Origins of American Feminism The Woman and the City, 1800–1860* (New York: Oxford University Press, 1978).

52. See Beecher, *Woman Suffrage and Woman's Profession*, 20–21, 29, 35–36, 49, 69, 88.

53. Ibid., 47.

54. See Beecher, *The Duty of American Women to Their Country*, 64.

55. Ibid., 205.

56. Ibid., 3, 185.

57. On Harriet Beecher Stowe's refusal to speak in public until fairly late in her life, see Joan D. Hedrick, *Harriet Beecher Stowe: A Life* (New York: Oxford University Press, 1994), 228–29, 238, 384.

58. See Beecher, *Essay on Slavery and Abolitionism*, 121.

consciously rights-based grounds, as they surely were in the case of the Grimke sisters. This manner of making arguments was, for Beecher, flatly inconsistent with the moral superiority that justified women's subordination:

> All the sacred protection of religion, all the generous promptings of chivalry, all the poetry of romantic gallantry, depend upon woman's retaining her place as dependent and defenceless, and making no claims, and maintaining no right but what are the gifts of honour, rectitude, and love.[59]

Beecher, so otherwise critical of woman's roles, regarded this role, "the office of a mediator, and an advocate of peace,"[60] as "immutable,"[61] and inconsistent with the rights-based nature of the claims the Grimke sisters were making in public not only on behalf of the slaves but of themselves as women.

The operative value of woman's superior morality was, for Beecher, "self-denying benevolence."[62] In her most extended explorations of this moral philosophy, Beecher associated its demands with the "law of sacrifice" required by utilitarian aggregation, "requiring the greatest possible good with the least possible evil"[63] (in terms of which Beecher expressly defined the idea of a right act[64]). Habits of subordination, like those inculcated in women, constituted a superior morality because they required "habits of self-control and self-denial, induced by long practice, [that] so far as experience shows, could never be secured by any other method."[65] Women were thus morally superior because the terms of their subordination rendered them more capable of the crucifixions required by a selfless universal love, "[t]he grand law of God, as learned by experience, . . . that every mind must *sacrifice* the lesser for the greater good in gratifying its own desires."[66] Since such utilitarian demands for self-sacrifice constituted the common sense morality in terms of which the Bible was alone properly interpreted, women should, Beecher argued, play a central role as Bible interpreters[67] and, for that reason, in moral reform. But moral reform, within this framework of self-sacrifice, must be reform for others; it was the

59. Ibid., 101–2.
60. Ibid., 128.
61. Ibid., 98.
62. See Beecher, *A Treatise on Domestic Economy*, 158.
63. See Beecher, *An Appeal to the People in Behalf of Their Rights,* 66.
64. Ibid., 138–39. For similar statements, see Beecher, *Common Sense Applied to Religion*, 36–37, 51, 139–48; and for further statements of "the *law* of SACRIFICE," see ibid., 45, 220.
65. See Beecher, *An Appeal to the People in Behalf of Their Rights,* 89.
66. Ibid., 145–46.
67. Ibid., 352–58.

rationale "that moved the timid Mrs. Bird in [Harriet Beecher Stowe's] *Uncle Tom's Cabin.* Women could act and speak—but only for others."[68]

Certainly, the Grimkes sacrificed as much for their sense of justice as Catharine Beecher had, and were as central as she to the nineteenth-century tradition of American moral reform. But the issue between Beecher and the Grimkes was not the legitimacy of women sacrificing themselves to advance justice and the public good, but the theory and practice of the political and constitutional morality that women legitimately might bring to bear on American public culture and politics. Beecher advocated a sacrifice of self in service of the impersonal sum of the utilitarian greatest good in the world. She likened the role of women in moral reform to the loss of self in some forms of love, particularly the love that Beecher thought best exemplified this superior morality: "that of *the mother,* that most perfect illustration of self-sacrificing love."[69] From this aggregative utilitarian perspective, arguments of human rights, which claimed to rest (as Theodore Parker argued, see chapter 2), on principles of distributive justice more weighty than utilitarian considerations, lacked reasonable weight; as Beecher put the point, "neither man nor woman has any right to anything which is contrary to the *best* good of society."[70] The Grimkes' theory and practice of moral reform emphasized the demands of personal integrity in political morality, calling not for the loss of self but the deepened understanding of the reasonable claims of moral personality, first for the rights of others and then, on the same grounds of principle, for one's own rights. Women, they came to recognize, must speak not just for others, but for themselves. Their struggle for morally responsible agency against the gendered conventions of self-sacrifice that Catharine Beecher defended began in antiracist abolitionism.

LYDIA MARIA CHILD ON WOMEN

To measure how far the Grimkes carried their analysis, we must examine the perspective from which they started: the radical abolitionist criticism of colonization and the racial prejudice it assumed. Lydia Maria Child's brilliant statement and development of this perspective was both influenced by and influential upon the Grimkes.

In her later book, *A History of the Condition of Women, in Various*

68. See Hedrick, *Harriet Beecher Stowe: A Life,* 228.
69. See Beecher, *Common Sense Applied to Religion,* 208.
70. See Beecher, *Woman Suffrage and Woman's Profession,* 205.

Ages and Nations,[71] Child's approach was self-consciously historical, factual, and comparative. Indeed, she prefaced her argument with a disclaimer: "This volume is not an essay upon woman's rights, or a philosophical investigation of what is or ought to be the relation of the sexes. . . . I have simply endeavored to give an accurate history of the condition of women, in language sufficiently concise for popular use" (1:iii). Nevertheless, Child's treatment of the comparative status of women was edged with critical observations drawing analogies between her earlier insights into American slavery and racism and the treatment of women. In China, she observed, "[m]en consider their wives as an inferior race, and sell them when they please" (1:137), and Islamic cultures "regard women as a very inferior race, created to serve them with unconditional submission" (1:238). Of the Islamic arguments urged in support of the treatment of women, Child exclaimed: "Precisely the same arguments for abusing the defenceless are urged by Christian slave-owners!" (1:238) As one would expect from so acute an analyst of American slavery and racism, Child pointed out the "dimness of moral perception, and the obtuseness of moral feeling" (2:214–15) that the institution of slavery inflicted on slave-owners (both men and women) about the maltreatment of women held in slavery. Indeed, the testimony of the Grimke sisters, among others, was urged in support of this claim (2:215–16).

Child did not, however, press the moral analysis implicit in these observations very far. Her comparisons were drawn mainly to emphasize the normatively superior attitudes of the Christian West:

> The Mohammedan religion, which debases woman into a machine, and regards love as a merely sensual passion, was introduced into the East about the same time that chivalry arose in the West, to exalt women into deities, and chasten passion with the purity of sentiment.[72]

On balance, "Christianity . . . has done so much for women" (2:210). Child affirmed the moral and intellectual equality of women. The Grimke sisters acknowledged her as an abolitionist essentially sympathetic to their feminist position,[73] and Sarah Grimke explicitly used

---

71. See Lydia Maria Child, *The History of the Condition of Women, in Various Ages and Nations*, 2 vols. (Boston: Otis, Broaders & Co., 1838).

72. Ibid., 2:120. For Child's views on the paradoxical character of the religious idealization of the Christian romantic love tradition with its celebration of celibacy, see ibid., 2:109–11, 2:116.

73. Angelina E. Grimke to Jane Smith, 20 May 1837, *The Public Years of Sarah and Angelina Grimke: Selected Writings, 1835–1839*, ed. Larry Ceplair (New York: Columbia University Press, 1989), 133; but cf. ibid., 131 (Child's motion that Angelina's already adopted "province of women" motion be reconsidered).

Child's book in her most extended articulation of abolitionist feminism.[74] Child, however, defended the equality of women while endorsing the dominant ideology of separate spheres:

> Many silly things have been written, and are now written concerning the equality of the sexes; but that true and perfect companionship, which gives both man and woman complete freedom in their places, without a restless desire to go out of them, is as yet imperfectly understood. The time will come, when it will be seen that the moral and intellectual condition of woman must be, and ought to be, in exact correspondence with that of man, not only in its general aspect, but in its individual manifestations; and then it will be perceived that all this discussion and relative superiority, is as idle as a controversy to determine which is most important to the world, the light of the sun, or the warmth of the sun (2:211).[75]

Child's views on gender roles at this time may have been closer to those of Catharine Beecher than to the Grimkes, particularly her acceptance of conventional demands for feminine self-sacrifice found, for example, in her childless marriage to her quite improvident and problematic husband.[76] Thus Child sharply criticized the model for women presented by Frances Wright and, earlier, Mary Wollstonecraft,[77] though her views on free love apparently shifted later in life in view of her life experience (including her self-supporting work as a journalist and separation from her husband) and her friendship while in New York City with Margaret Fuller (231, 325–29, 412, 546–47). And, as Beecher had done, she sharply distinguished women's writing (which she did prodigiously) from speaking in public (which she did not) (215). She collaborated closely with and largely supported the Grimke sisters during the period of their activism (242–48), but consistent with her views on feminine self-sacrifice, she resisted the Grimkes' gentle rebukes that she focused her attention only on the claims of

74. See Sarah M. Grimke, *Letters on the Equality of the Sexes and the Condition of Woman*, in *The Public Years of Sarah and Angelina Grimke: Selected Writings, 1835–1839*, ed. Larry Ceplair (New York: Columbia University Press, 1989), 204n, 210.

75. For Maria Child's later development of a similar position, see Letter 34, "Woman's Rights," in Maria Child, *Letters from New York* (London: Richard Bentley, 1843), 261–70. While Child criticizes injustices in traditional conceptions of women's roles and urges less separation between men and women, she repudiates "those who maintain there is no sex in souls" (267) in connection with claims of women to serve in the military, a claim "usually . . . urged by those of infidel tendencies" (269).

76. For a sensitive and probing recent treatment of these and related issues, see Carolyn L. Karcher, *The First Woman in the Republic: A Cultural Biography of Lydia Maria Child* (Durham: Duke University Press, 1994); see also Deborah Pickman Clifford, *Crusader for Freedom: A Life of Lydia Maria Child* (Boston: Beacon Press, 1992).

77. See Karcher, *The First Woman in the Republic*, 118–19, 216, 235–36.

slaves rather than those of women. Child took the view: "In toiling for the freedom of others, we shall find our own" (247).

Child's later views always gave pride of place to her antiracist abolitionism, but with growing acknowledgment of its connections, as a matter of principle, to claims for the rights of women. In 1839, Child had argued strategically that antiracist abolitionist women prudently might avoid the subject of women's rights in order to emphasize the rights of African Americans; but, when a man advised her "to withdraw from a society or convention, or not to act there according to the dictates of my conscience," Child found herself standing on an uncompromisable and self-defining issue of principle: "I am constrained to reply, 'Thou canst not touch the freedom of my soul. I deem that I have duties to perform here. I make no onset upon your opinions and prejudices, but my moral responsibility lies between God and my own conscience'" (261). In 1843, Child wrote that the case for women's rights rested on women's equal right to conscience: "Are we not all immortal beings? Is not each one responsible for himself and herself?"[78] In 1855 Child would, like Catharine Beecher, publish the kind of massive study and distillation of comparative religious and moral ideas that challenged the traditional province of clergymen in America, because, for Child, her right to conscience demanded that she address these issues on equal terms.[79] Finally, in 1860, Child undertook to give assistance to Harriet Jacobs (assistance Harriet Beecher Stowe had rather arrogantly declined to give[80]) in preparing for publication *Incidents in the Life of a Slave Girl*,[81] a classic work, as we shall see, in the later development of abolitionist feminism.[82] Child cumulatively discovered in her own moral experience as an antiracist abolitionist the basic case for the rights of women—rights she herself brilliantly exercised throughout her remarkable life. She had first heard the case for abolitionist feminism stated, in its most principled form, by the Grimke sisters.

ABOLITIONIST FEMINISM: THE GRIMKE SISTERS

Until her early death in 1834, the Philadelphia poet and essayist Elizabeth Chandler made the point that women had a special contribution

78. Child, *Letters from New York*, 266.

79. See Lydia Maria Child, *The Progress of Religious Ideas through Successive Ages*, 3 vols. (New York: C. S. Francis, 1855).

80. For discussion of Stowe's insensitive, even arrogant treatment of the request, see Hedrick, *Harriet Beecher Stowe*, 248–49.

81. See Harriet A. Jacobs, *Incidents in the Life of a Slave Girl*, ed. Jean Fagan Yellin (1861; Cambridge: Harvard University Press, 1987).

82. See Karcher, *The First Woman in the Republic*, 435–37.

to make to the abolitionist movement.[83] She pointed to women's moral experience as wives and mothers and the role such experience could and should play in making clear to American public opinion the appalling injuries American slavery inflicted on basic human rights to family life. Chandler thus asked American women to imagine the experience of a mother whose child had been sold away from her, and to respond accordingly:

> Think of the frantic mother,
> Lamenting for her child,
> Till falling lashes smother
> Her cries of anguish wild!
> Think of the prayers ascending,
> Yet shriek'd, alas! in vain,
> When heart from heart is rending
> Ne'er to be join'd again.
> Shall we behold, unheeding,
> Life's holiest feelings crush'd—
> When a woman's heart is bleeding,
> Shall a woman's voice be hush'd.[84]

Her influential short essay, "Mental Metempsychosis," used the image of the soul at death moving to another body as a metaphor for the reader "to imagine themselves for a few moments in his [the slave's] very circumstances, to enter into his feelings, comprehend all his wretchedness, transform themselves mentally into his very self." One central example vividly appealed to woman's moral experience:

> Let them feel the heart-brokenness of being separated from all they love— take the long last glance at all that is dear to them, and while the brain is reeling, and the hot brow throbbing with agony, know that their sufferings excite only the heartless jest, or the brutal curses . . . let them enter into the desolateness of that moment; stand alone and forsaken in the world; without religion, without a friend in earth or heaven, to whom they may turn for consolation in their hour of trial. . . .[85]

Consistent with Chandler's appeal to the role of woman's moral imagination in advancing the abolitionist movement, Moncure Conway

83. She did so in her columns in the early abolitionist newspaper, Benjamin Lundy's *The Genius of Universal Emancipation.* See Jean Fagan Yellin, *Women and Sisters: The Antislavery Feminists in American Culture* (New Haven: Yale University Press, 1989), 12–13.

84. Excerpts from Elizabeth Chandler's poem, "Think of Our Country's Glory," in Benjamin Lundy, *The Poetical Works of Elizabeth Margaret Chandler* (Philadelphia: Lemuel Howell, 1836), 64.

85. See Elizabeth Margaret Chandler, *Essays, Philanthropic and Moral, Principally Relating to the Abolition of Slavery in America* (Philadelphia: T. E. Chapman, 1845), 117–18.

(the abolitionist self-exile from the polemically entrenched proslavery culture of the South [chapter 2]) thought of women as having a superior moral sense[86] and an intuition about moral personality uncorrupted by intellectual constructions (e.g., ethnology and the like). Harriet Beecher Stowe adopted this view in *Uncle Tom's Cabin,* appealing often to women's experience as wives and mothers, or more simply, to heart over head[87] (the latter exemplified by proslavery interpretations of the Bible[88]). Conway and Stowe emphasized the role that woman's moral experience could and should play in asserting the primacy of impartial ethical thought independent of the dominant political epistemologies that, on the model of religious persecution, rationalized unjustly entrenched political power.[89]

Angelina and Sarah Grimke gave this kind of appeal a deeper basis in common principles that condemned both racism and sexism.[90] Their views self-consciously stated the case for abolitionist feminism that would later be elaborated by Lucretia Mott and Elizabeth Stanton to form an independent women's movement, as well as by ex-slaves like Sojourner Truth and Harriet Jacobs to sharpen the abolitionist feminist analysis of the common roots of American racism and sexism.

Sarah and Angelina Grimke, like Conway, were born and bred in a leading South Carolina slave-holding family, but they felt it to be morally imperative to leave the South, expressing an independent moral conscience critical of slavery as an institution in general and their own family's commitment to the institution in particular. Both initially gravitated to a Quaker expression of their antislavery views, settling in Philadelphia; but eventually, their growing moral independence led them beyond the confines of Quaker propriety into more radical forms of antislavery activism. The negative Northern response to such activism prompted both women to fundamental reflections

86. See John d'Entremont, *Southern Emancipator,* 18–19, 62–63.

87. See Harriet Beecher Stowe, *Uncle Tom's Cabin or, Life among the Lowly,* ed. Ann Douglas (1852; New York: Penguin, 1981), 153, 210, 437. See also Harriet Beecher Stowe, *The Key to Uncle Tom's Cabin* (1854; Salem, N.H.: Ayer Company, 1987).

88. See Stowe, *Uncle Tom's Cabin,* 183, 184, 200, 279, 508; see Stowe, *The Key to Uncle Tom's Cabin,* 460–73.

89. See Stowe, *The Key to Uncle Tom's Cabin,* 401–2, that identifies the analogy between proslavery thought and religious persecution.

90. The best general study is Gerda Lerner, *The Grimke Sisters from South Carolina: Pioneers for Woman's Rights and Abolition* (New York: Schocken Books, 1971). See also Jean Fagan Yellis, *Women and Sisters;* Blanche Glassman Hersh, *The Slavery of Sex: Feminist-Abolitionists in America* (Urbana: University of Illinois Press, 1978); Keith E. Melder, *Beginnings of Sisterhood: The American Woman's Rights Movement, 1800–1850* (New York: Schocken, 1977); Katharine Du Pre Lumpkin, *The Emancipation of Angelina Grimke* (Chapel Hill: University of North Carolina Press, 1974).

about the analogy between race and gender as the objects of immoral prejudice. The Grimke sisters objected, like Child, not only to American slavery but to its underlying moral pathology, American racism, what Angelina called "the monster Prejudice"[91] or "that American Juggernaut, Prejudice."[92] No abolitionist of their generation carried the analysis further.

The extraordinary power of their analysis grew from the intimate knowledge that they, as children of a slave-owning family, brought to it; no aspect of that knowledge more shocked their Northern audiences than their testimony of the tyrannies of women slaveowners (21–23). The public image of the character of Southern women, "their gentleness and love, . . . suavity," was, on their testimony, "the paint and the varnish of hypocrisy, the fashionable polish of a heartless superficiality" (22). The place of Southern women upon what proslavery advocate Louisa McCord had called "the high pedestal where God has placed her"[93] was, as proslavery thought had insisted,[94] the rationale of the polemically repressive culture that sustained and idealized Southern slavery. The Grimke sisters made clear that the required abolitionist criticism of that culture must extend to the role the pedestal and its ideology of spheres of gender played in the obfuscation and rationalization of such appalling injustices. The Grimkes thus began serious American criticism of the interlinked bases for the political evils of racism and sexism.

Strikingly, Angelina Grimke's first important published antislavery works were, by their terms, addressed to Southern[95] and Northern[96] women and aimed at the moral force she took women in American society to possess.[97] She thus formulated moral arguments in terms of rights central to women's moral experience as mothers, asking women critically to extend such rights on fair terms to all:

> I appeal to you, my friends, as mothers; Are you willing to enslave *your* children? You start back with horror and indignation at such a question. But why, if slavery is *no wrong* to those upon whom it is imposed? . . . Do you not perceive that as soon as this golden rule of action is applied to *yourselves*

91. See Grimke, *Letters to Catharine E. Beecher*, 167.
92. See Angelina Grimke, *Appeal to the Women of the Nominally Free States* (New York: William S. Dorr, 1837), 43.
93. Louisa McCord, "Enfranchisement of Woman," *Southern Quarterly Review* 21 (April 1852): 340.
94. See Fitzhugh, *Cannibals All!* 190–98.
95. See Grimke, *Appeal to the Christian Women of the South*, in *The Public Years*, 36–79.
96. Grimke, *Appeal to the Women of the Nominally Free States*.
97. Grimke, *Appeal to the Christian Women of the South*, 54–55, 64–67.

that you involuntarily shrink from the test; as soon as *your* actions are weighed in *this* balance of the sanctuary that *you are found wanting.*[98]

Grimke formulated four principles progressively to guide women's reflections on and responses to such questions: study of the subject of slavery, conscientious prayerful ethical self-examination, public speech, and public action.[99] In her correspondence she called this unity of self-critical and mutually testing thought, speech, and action "pure *practical* christianity."[100]

Like Conway and Stowe, Grimke identified moral argument not with the rationalizing intellectual constructions of proslavery thought, but with an authentic morality of the heart centering on the demands of creative moral personality.[101] Both Angelina and Sarah associated these demands for creative moral freedom and responsibility with the Biblical idea that humankind was made in God's image,[102] and believed that critical demands of moral impartiality were sometimes more accessible to women than men (for example, to women like the Grimke sisters in virtue of critical reflections on their experience of the effects of slavery and racism on Southern women). It is for this reason that the Grimkes' testimony of the tyrannies of Southern slave-owning women so shocked Northerners: They were tyrannies rooted, as Sarah Grimke pointedly put it, in "the vacuity of mind, the heartlessness, the frivolity"[103] of the Southern woman's culture the Grimkes knew at first hand. Sarah could thus write autobiographically of the culture that made such moral heartlessness possible:

> During the early part of my life, my lot was cast among the butterflies of the *fashionable* world; and of this class of women, I am constrained to say, both from experience and observation, that their education is miserably deficient; that they are taught to regard marriage as the one thing needful, the only avenue to distinction; hence to attract the notice and win the attentions of men, by their external charms, is the chief business of fashionable girls.[104]

98. Ibid., 51.
99. Ibid., 55–57.
100. Angelina E. Grimke to Theodore Dwight Weld and John Greenleaf Whittier, 20 August 1837, in *The Public Years of Sarah and Angelina Grimke: Selected Writings, 1835–1839*, ed. Larry Ceplair (New York: Columbia University Press, 1989), 284.
101. For Angelina Grimke's later development of this theme, see Angelina E. Grimke, *Letters to Catharine E. Beecher*, in *The Public Years*, 148, 179, 200, 203.
102. See Angelina Grimke, *Appeal to the Women of the Nominally Free States*, 7; Sarah M. Grimke, *An Epistle to the Clergy of the Southern States*, in *The Public Years*, 93.
103. See Sarah M. Grimke, *Letters on the Equality of the Sexes and the Condition of Woman*, in *The Public Years*, 220.
104. Ibid., 220.

Elsewhere Sarah anatomized related features of Southern life, in particular, the brutal suppression of dissenting free thought, speech and action by the dominant proslavery orthodoxy: "there is a diversity of opinion among them in reference to slavery and the REIGN OF TERROR alone suppresses the free expression of sentiment."[105] In effect, Southern culture deprived women as well as men of all of Angelina Grimke's four principles of ethical action: critical study, self-examination, speech, and action.

The Grimkes brought to their analysis of the evils of slavery and racism critical demands defined, like Child, by the argument for toleration, only now very much interpreted through their experience as Southern women themselves struggling for the moral independence the argument requires. All their thought and action throughout their relatively brief public careers as antislavery activists centered on the critical abolitionist idea, found also, as we have seen, in Weld and Channing (chapter 2), that the murderous opposition to abolitionist analysis and advocacy was a form of illegitimate sectarian religious persecution. In the letter to Garrison that initiated her public career as an antislavery advocate, Angelina characterized the anti-abolitionist mobs in this way: "Religious persecution always begins with mobs."[106] The abolitionists' appeals to conscience were, on Angelina's view, in the great tradition of Protestant reformers and subject, like them, to politically illegitimate persecution by an orthodoxy threatened by their challenge.[107]

In *An Epistle to the Clergy of the Southern States*,[108] Sarah Grimke made her case against American slavery and racism in clear terms of the argument for toleration. Identifying her role with that of the Biblical prophets challenging corrupt politicians (91–92, 108),[109] Grimke founded her analysis on the rational and reasonable powers of persons (made in God's image of creative moral freedom) and on the respect owed persons as originators of claims to inalienable human rights— to be treated as persons, not as things or as machines (92–93, 96). American institutions of slavery blatantly violated such respect, depriving blacks held in slavery of their inalienable rights to conscience,

---

105. See Sarah M. Grimke, *An Epistle to the Clergy of the Southern States*, 112.

106. Angelina E. Grimke to William Lloyd Garrison, 30 August 1835, in *The Public Years*, 26.

107. See Angelina E. Grimke, *Appeal to the Christian Women of the South*, 59–60, 72, 76; *Letters to Catharine E. Beecher*, 161–62, 176, 179.

108. See Sarah M. Grimke, *An Epistle to the Clergy of the Southern States*, 90–115.

109. For Angelina Grimke's similar appeals, see Angelina E. Grimke, *Letters to Catharine E. Beecher*, 170, 174–75.

speech, work, family life, and the like (105–8); American racism, in turn, unjustly ascribed a degraded nature to persons, as permanent heathens, on the basis of systematic denials of rights essential to reasonable moral freedom (104–5, 112, 114). At the root of these evils lay an entrenched epistemology that, consistent with the paradox of intolerance, refused to permit reasonable debate about the abolition of the institution when such debate, in light of the success of British emancipation in the West Indies, was most needed (113–14). Grimke referred to a political "reign of terror" (112) that deprived the South of the reasonable scope of constitutional guarantees of freedom of conscience, thought, and action regarding the abolition of slavery; in effect, no serious public dissent to the dominant political epistemology was permissible, freezing public debate to the sectarian terms of the dominant orthodoxy. Grimke argued along lines similar to Madison's theory of faction[110] that the roots of such politically illegitimate repression lay in the corruptions of group-based political power; its worst ravages were on the life of the mind and of the heart:

> The lust of dominion inevitably produces hardness of heart, because the state of mind which craves unlimited power, such as slavery confers, involves a desire to use that power, and although I know there are exceptions to the exercise of barbarity on the bodies of slaves, I maintain that there *can be no exceptions* to the exercise of the most soul-withering cruelty on the *minds* of the enslaved. (112)

In effect, the Protestant South now enforced an Inquisition worse than any it reasonably condemned in Europe:

> Perhaps all of you would shrink with horror from a proposal to revive the Inquisition and give to Catholic superstition the power to enforce in this country its wicked system of bigotry and despotism. But I believe if all the horrors of the Inquisition and all the cruelty and oppression exercised by the Church of Rome, could be fully and fairly brought to view and compared with the details of slavery in the United States, the abominations of Catholicism would not surpass those of slavery, while the victims of the latter are ten fold more numerous. (112)

Grimke ended her analysis with an appeal to the special responsibility of the Protestant Christian churches of the South, who were historical exponents of the argument for toleration, urging them not to support "this heart-breaking, this soul-destroying system" (114). In effect, proslavery political epistemology had complicitously corrupted the role of religion, consistent with the argument for toleration, as one of the

110. For fuller elaboration, see David A. J. Richards, *Foundations of American Constitutionalism* (New York: Oxford University Press, 1989), 32–39.

agents of morally independent thought and protest. In this political, religious, and moral vacuum, Grimke, a Southern woman self-exiled to the North, appealed to the special need of the South to hearken to its outcasts, for "the weak things of the world . . . confound the things that are mighty" (115).

To this point, the abolitionist arguments of Angelina and Sarah Grimke worked within the general framework of abolitionist criticism of slavery and racism earlier discussed. Their great novelty and arresting appeal for the Northern public mind were both the evident moral and intellectual courage they displayed in making them and the moving personal testimony they, children of a slave-owning family, brought to those arguments. Their arguments evolved into the strikingly original abolitionist feminism that they pioneered in self-conscious response to criticisms of them in the North both for the substance of their abolitionist arguments (in particular, their antiracism) and for their growing willingness to speak in public (like Frances Wright and Maria Stewart before them) regarding these matters to audiences of both men and women. Angelina Grimke was, evidently, a particularly powerful public speaker, and her speeches to sometimes tumultuously antagonistic mixed audiences of men and women explicitly challenged Northern complacency about slavery and implicitly its ideology of separate gender spheres and roles.[111]

Two criticisms were particularly important in prodding the sisters into the abolitionist feminism most extensively defended in Sarah Grimke's *Letters on the Equality of the Sexes, and the Condition of Women.*[112] First, Catharine Beecher published her earlier discussed *Essay on Slavery and Abolitionism* explicitly "Addressed to Miss A. D. Grimke," criticizing, *inter alia*, the Grimkes for their public speeches. Second, Congregational ministers belonging to the General Association of Massachusetts authorized Reverend Nehemiah Adams of Boston to pen an attack on, *inter alia*, women abolitionist agents; it was both read from the pulpits and printed in the *New England Spectator.*[113] Rev. Adams argued that the "power of woman is in her dependence," her need for protection; her role as "a public reformer" challenged this protected role "and her character becomes unnatural."[114]

111. For a good historical narrative of these events, see Lerner, *The Grimke Sisters from South Carolina,* 146–242.

112. See Sarah M. Grimke, *Letters on the Equality of the Sexes and the Condition of Woman,* in *The Public Years,* 204–72.

113. For discussion and commentary on these points, see Larry Ceplair, ed., *The Public Years,* 139.

114. The pastoral letter is reprinted in Sarah Grimke's *Letters on the Equality of the Sexes, and the Condition of Woman,* in *The Public Years,* 211.

The letter was clearly publicly understood to be directed against the Grimke sisters and they certainly so understood it.

In making their abolitionist arguments, the Grimkes had heretofore focused on what they knew best, the repressive proslavery political orthodoxy of the South. They were self-exiles from that culture in order to think, speak, and act the antislavery beliefs that formed the core of their sense of themselves as morally responsible agents. That exile caused them and their families great pain, all the more so when it became irrevocable after publication of views in the North that debarred, under threat of violence, return to their families.[115] Their moral pilgrimage did not end, however, either with their move to Philadelphia or their espousal of the most antislavery of American religions, Quakerism.[116] They bridled at the exclusiveness of the church and its insistence on forms of control and surveillance particularly of its female members.[117] Angelina's form of public antislavery activism was discountenanced by her church; and her response, after further painful reflection, was that her growing sense of moral responsibility and individuality required her to break with her church. She articulated her decision in terms of emancipation:

I have borne them as long as I possibly could with peace of mind, & now that my Master has burst my fetters & set me free, I never expect to suffer myself to be manacled again. I never before was in bondage to any man, & I believ [sic] it is realy [sic] sinful to be influenced by any human authority, as to forget our individual responsibility to Him whose we are & whom we ought to serv [sic], independent of the opinion of man.[118]

In effect, both Angelina and Sarah's moral needs could no longer be sustained by any form of authority less than their own increasingly free and reasonable minds.

Abolitionist feminism arose when the Grimkes' increasingly demanding moral independence was confronted not by proslavery Southern intolerance (from which they fled) or Quaker constraints (which they burst), but by the Northern political culture of separate gender spheres, which would have silenced their speaking in their own voice in the public space that was conventionally defined as that of men alone. As we earlier saw, Catharine Beecher did not object to women's

115. See Lerner, *The Grimke Sisters from South Carolina*, 147.
116. For a good study focusing on the central role of Quaker women both in abolitionism and feminism, see Margaret Hope Bacon, *Mothers of Feminism: The Story of Quaker Women in America* (San Francisco: Harper & Row, 1989).
117. See, for example, Angelina E. Grimke to Sarah M. Grimke, 14 August 1836, in *The Public Years*, 79–80; and Letter of Angelina E. Grimke to Jane Smith, ibid., 81–82.
118. Ibid., 82.

writing about issues of moral reform (she herself prolifically wrote on such issues), because such advocacy, when done in the proper style and on the proper basis, was consistent with women's moral place "[i]n the nursery"; not "the taunting rebuke, or even the fair and deserved reproof of equals," "[b]ut the voice of maternal love, or even the gentle remonstrances of an elder sister."[119] Women were, for Beecher, morally superior precisely because their "immutable" station[120] rendered them more capable of the role self-sacrifice required in utilitarian aggregation for the good of others. Beecher certainly knew that Angelina Grimke (whom she had met amiably when Grimke, who was considering training for a teaching career, visited her Hartford Female Seminary in 1831[121]) was no radical advocate of free love like Frances Wright, as Beecher later suggested (thereby drawing on the polemical power of the Wollstonecraft repudiation).[122] Beecher interpreted Grimke as asserting the same role for women as Wright had claimed, speaking in public in a morally independent mode and on the basis of one's own human rights. Grimke's claims thus were in a style and on a basis that repudiated what Beecher took to be the distinctive moral superiority of women; any fall from such superiority was thus interpreted by her as a degradation analogous to loose morals.

Angelina Grimke saw that, if Beecher's claim were accepted by women, "then may *we* well be termed 'the white slaves of the North'— for, like our brethren in bonds, we must seal our lips in silence and despair."[123] Grimke recognized in the common wrong to blacks and women a ground of common moral indignation and sympathy: "Women ought to feel a peculiar sympathy in the colored man's wrongs, for like him *she* has been accused of mental inferiority, and denied the privileges of a liberal education."[124] The common principle at issue was "the broad ground of *human rights* and human responsibilities . . . , the principle of moral being, [namely,] *All moral beings have essentially the same rights and the same duties*, whether they be male or female."[125] As she put the point in her correspondence, "I feel as if it is not the cause of the slave only which we plead, but the cause of woman as a responsible moral being."[126]

119. See Beecher, *Essay on Slavery and Abolitionism*, 54–55.
120. Ibid., 98.
121. See Sklar, *Catharine Beecher*, 98–100.
122. See Beecher, *Essay on Slavery and Abolitionism*, 120–21.
123. See Angelina Grimke, *Appeal to the Women of the Nominally Free States*, 13.
124. Ibid., 36.
125. Ibid., 19.
126. See Letter of Angelina E. Grimke to Jane Smith, in *The Public Years*, 142.

The Grimkes had struggled to moral independence through the dis-
locations of exiles from home and family and later from a protective
church, and now through forging a new role of public moral responsibility for women in the face of bitter criticism and disdain, some of it
from more conventional fellow women like Catharine Beecher. This
last confrontation compelled them to examine and defend the presup-
positions of their journey as part of a larger struggle for human rights
in terms of the argument for toleration. As we have seen, the claim
for one's inalienable human rights arises as a challenge to a dominant
political epistemology that illegitimately entrenches a political hierarchy of order and submission. The Grimkes came to see the ideology
of separate gender roles as such an illegitimate hierarchy, defining
women as such in terms of gender roles deferential to masculine guid-
ance on basic issues of conscience inconsistent with morally independent thought, speech, and action. Angelina Grimke saw and articulated
the larger point exactly: "No station or character can destroy individual
responsibility, in the matter of reproving sin."[127] Inalienable rights, qua
inalienable, cannot legitimately be varied or conferred by human law
or convention; women's "*rights* are an integral part of her moral being;
they cannot be withdrawn; they must live with her forever,"[128] "as a
moral, an *intellectual,* an accountable being."[129] "If [such rights are]
not [recognized], they [women] are mere slaves, known only through
their masters."[130]

Angelina Grimke articulated her fullest version of abolitionist feminism in the relatively brief letter XII of her *Letters to Catharine E.
Beecher,*[131] referring the reader to Sarah Grimke's more extensive discussion of these issues (198).[132] She started from the role that her abolitionist criticisms of slavery and racism played in the development of
her feminism. Implicitly repudiating Beecher's utilitarian valuation of
women's superiority in terms of self-sacrifice of one's own claims for
others, Grimke argued that only after making claims for universal human rights in her own voice was she morally empowered to understand
and articulate principles that best condemned the evils of racism and
sexism. Such claims necessarily repudiated a role for women that irre-

127. See Angelina E. Grimke, *Letters to Catharine E. Beecher,* in *The Public Years,* 180.
128. Ibid., 191.
129. See Angelina E. Grimke, *An Appeal to the Women of the Nominally Free States,*
67.
130. See Angelina E. Grimke, *Letters to Catharine E. Beecher,* in *The Public Years,* 194.
131. Ibid., 194–98.
132. The reference is to Sarah M. Grimke's *Letters on the Equality of the Sexes and the
Condition of Woman,* in *The Public Years,* 204–72.

sponsibly idealized their disempowerment as full moral persons and agents. Long before our contemporary feminist program (the personal is the political) become fashionable, Grimke saw that her personal struggle for moral independence legitimately advanced, in the way Beecher denied, the larger political struggle for the human rights of all:

> The investigation of the rights of the slave has led me to a better understanding of my own. I have found the Anti-Slavery cause to be the high school of morals in our land—the school in which *human rights* are more fully investigated, and better understood and taught, than in any other. Here a great fundamental principle is uplifted and illuminated, and from this central light, rays innumerable stream all around. Human beings have *rights*, because they are *moral* beings; the rights of *all* men grow out of their moral nature; and as all men have the same moral nature, they have essentially the same rights. (194)

From this perspective, men and women stood, like people of different races, "on the same platform of human rights" (196). Since our common and equal moral nature regulated our physical nature, "the *mere circumstance of sex* does not give to man higher rights and responsibilities, than to woman" (194). Rather,

> When human beings are regarded as *moral* beings, *sex,* instead of being enthroned upon the summit, administering upon rights and responsibilities, sinks into insignificance and nothingness. My doctrine then is, that whatever it is morally right for man to do, it is morally right for woman to do. Our duties originate, not from difference of sex, but from the diversity of our relations in life, the various gifts and talents committed to our care, and the different eras in which we live. (195)

As one would expect in light of her courageous struggle to moral independence, Angelina Grimke's abolitionist feminism critically expressed indignation at what we would call a sexist culture that "has robbed woman of essential rights, the right to think and speak and act on all great moral questions" (195). Viewing ethical responsibility in terms of four principles (study, conscientious self-reflection, speech, and action), her confrontation with Northern sexism led her to see that these principles were not only a threat for both men and women of the South from its increasingly polemical and intolerant proslavery political culture (including its conception of gender roles), but for all American women from a comparably polemical and intolerant sexist culture of separate gender roles.

Angelina and Sarah Grimke eloquently testified to the injuries that American slavery and racism had unjustly inflicted on the very minds and hearts of its perpetrators and its victims; their searing portraits of the tyrannies of Southern women bespoke the former, and their memorialization of the degradation of the slaves to illiterate permanent heathens the latter. Their confrontation with American sexism prodded them to think more deeply than any American of their generation or indeed long after about the roots of the opposition they had always faced, first as Southern women and later as expatriate women in the North, from other women as well as men. If slavery and racism were, as Sarah Grimke had described them, "this heart-breaking, this soul-destroying system,"[133] so too, on examination, was sexism, particularly in view of its blatant contempt for the self-originating moral capacities through which persons both rationally order their own ends and reasonably regulate that pursuit. The failure to respect what Angelina Grimke called "the fundamental principle of moral being" (195) discredits the conventional morality that expressed such contempt, "the antichristian doctrine of masculine and feminine virtues" (195). Such conventional morality, despite its empty romantic rhetoric of idealized women and chivalric men, "has nevertheless been the means of sinking her from an *end* into a mere *means*— . . . of destroying her individuality, and rights, and responsibilities" (196).

Angelina Grimke had always discussed questions of ethics as matters of ethical responsibility and duty (for example, the duty to abolish slavery immediately), distinguishing such questions from consequentialist expediency (176–77, 192).[134] Having articulated the incommensurable moral evil of slavery and racism, their confrontation with the ideology of gender spheres led the Grimkes to see that sexism inflicted exactly the same profound moral evil, denying to women the very propriety of exercising the moral powers through which persons are dignified as responsible and accountable moral agents. This fundamental moral wrong was, Angelina briefly suggested, inflicted through an entrenched culture that illegitimately deprived women of their proper morally creative role both in religion and in politics. Even the Quakers, she observed, "allowed [women] no voice in framing the Discipline by which she is to be governed" (197). Both forms of spiritual disempowerment must be addressed: "If Ecclesiastical and Civil government are ordained of God, *then* I contend that woman has just as much right to sit in solemn counsel in Conventions, Conferences, Associations and General Assemblies, as man—just as much right to sit upon the throne of England, or in the Presidential chair of the United States" (197). Of the two forms of disempowerment, the religious was the more fun-

133. See Sarah M. Grimke, *An Epistle to the Clergy of the Southern States,* 114.
134. See also Angelina E. Grimke, *Appeal to the Christian Women of the South,* in *The Public Years,* 58, 64.

damental, because of its closeness to the sources of ethical responsibility: "until this principle of equality is recognised and embodied in
practice, the church can do nothing effectual for the permanent
reformation of the world" (197).

Both Angelina and Sarah Grimke were, by the American measure of
their time, quite religiously heterodox, but their moral independence
centered, like that of most Americans of their time, on Bible interpretation. They therefore naturally thought that the institutional failure of
American religions to embody the principle of equality in their practice
(including, of course, a central role for women as scholars, preachers,
and teachers) was the consequence of the failure of American religion
adequately to understand the central place of the principle of equality
in ethics and in reasonable Bible interpretation. This was the main
argument of the Grimkes' central contribution to abolitionist feminism, Sarah Grimke's *Letters on the Equality of the Sexes and the Condition of Woman.*[135]

Sarah Grimke's argument centered, first, on making her case that
the dominant Biblical interpretations of normatively influential texts
of the Hebrew Bible and the New Testament wrongly ascribed to them
the moral ideology of separate spheres and the inferiority of women
and, second, on showing how this had happened. Both aspects of her
position brilliantly elaborated the argument for toleration to the ends
of feminist liberation. The dominant misogyny of Bible interpretation
assumed, on examination, a wholly corrupt and illegitimate political
epistemology that unreasonably entrenched a masculine hierarchy of
power and privilege over women (including masculine monopoly of
Bible interpretation); this corrupt epistemology narrowed the terms
of debate to the cramped measure of masculine self-protection and
for this illegitimate reason excluded women from reasonable participation in its dialogue.

Grimke's substantive exercises in Bible interpretation applied a normative conviction that she took to be central to the entire narrative
and, thus understood, to be reasonably supported by the narrative,
namely, that all persons, made in the image of God, have the creative
powers of "a moral and responsible being" (205). As such, each person
was ultimately ethically responsible for one's self and accountable as
such directly to God and to no other person. In the light of this normative perspective, Grimke's substantive exercises in Bible interpretation
had two strategies: first, to show that the texts most commonly urged

135. See Sarah M. Grimke, *Letters on the Equality of the Sexes and the Condition of Woman,* in *The Public Years.*

as supporting women's moral inferiority did not reasonably require that reading; and second, to point to the often ignored texts that support women's equality as creative moral agents. As regards the former, two texts were central: the Adam and Eve narrative and the epistles of St. Paul.

Grimke's reading of the Adam and Eve narrative argued that it cannot reasonably be interpreted to justify women's inferiority as God's punishment for the Fall. In fact, both Adam and Eve shared equal moral fault in the Fall; certainly, "Adam's ready acquiescence with his wife's proposal, does not savor much of that superiority in *strength of mind,* which is arrogated by man" (208). Adam and Eve were punished by the loss of Paradise, but that punishment did not change their natures as equal morally accountable agents (206). Properly understood, God's statement, "Thou wilt be subject unto thy husband, and he will rule over thee," (206) was a prophecy of man's corrupt subjection of women, not a normative command for such subjection. The contrary view reflected the failure of male Bible interpreters to note the ambiguity of the pertinent Hebrew word for "will" (between the normative "shall" and the predictive "will"), a failure Grimke explained in terms of "translators . . . accustomed to exercise lordship over their wives, and seeing only through the medium of a perverted judgment" (207). Grimke's hermeneutic principle was that, among two readings of an ambiguous text, the one should be preferred that better coheres with the basic normative purposes of the text as a whole—in this case, the primary ethical principle that all persons are equal moral agents. The prophetic interpretation of the text better accorded with this principle since all persons retained this status, albeit some of them exercised it wrongly to the disadvantage of others.

Grimke appealed to this hermeneutic principle in repudiating the misogynist interpretation traditionally assigned to various passages in Paul's epistles (241–57, 266–67), for example, "Wives submit yourselves unto your own husbands as unto the Lord" (244). For Grimke, the traditional reading cannot be believed because it conflicted with the primary ethical principle of the Bible, the equality of all persons: "Now I must understand the sacred Scriptures as harmonizing with themselves, or I cannot receive them as the word of God" (245). Other reasonable readings were available that interpreted such passages without compromising this principle. Such passages might, for example, be contextualized to a specific historical circumstance (converted Christian women married to unconverted men) urging women in those circumstances patiently to bear evil (244–45). This interpretation granted that husbands had no right to oppress women, but insisted that the response to such evil not appeal to what Grimke took to be un-Christian principles of violent resistance.

Grimke's affirmative interpretive case, as had her sister's,[136] relied heavily on the role of powerfully active female prophets in the Hebrew Bible[137] and the comparably important role played by women as preachers in early Christianity (250–57). Grimke's argument was very much in the radical Protestant spirit of the argument for toleration as it had been earlier interpreted by Bayle and Locke against the Augustinian tradition of intolerance.[138] Bayle and Locke had there argued that the Augustinian tradition (dominant in their period in both Catholic and Protestant thought and practice) illegitimately enforced on society at large a corrupt political epistemology that narrowed both the scope of discussion and of participants therein to the measure of the entrenched interests of a dominant political and religious hierarchy; both Bayle and Locke argued as religious Protestants who claimed that this enforced political epistemology included a corrupt tradition of Bible interpretation that betrayed the humane tolerance central to pre-Augustinian Christianity.[139] Sarah Grimke's central claim was that the dominant Christian tradition endorsing the subjection of women was similarly illegitimate, giving rise to an unreasonable genre of Bible interpretation that betrayed early Christianity's treatment of women as the moral and spiritual equals of men, a view strikingly taken to similar effect today by, among others, Elaine Pagels.[140]

Grimke indicted the unreasonable exclusion of women from the Christian ministry and all the consequences this exclusion inevitably had for the development of a corrupt tradition of misogynist Bible interpretation:

> It is manifest, that if women were permitted to be ministers of the gospel, as they unquestionably were in the primitive ages of the Christian church, it would interfere materially with the present organized system of spiritual power and ecclesiastical authority, which is now vested solely in the hands of men. (266)

136. See, for example, Angelina E. Grimke, *Appeal to the Christian Women of the South*, 60–61, 65–66; "Motion of Angelina E. Grimke," *Proceedings of the Anti-Slavery Convention of American Women, Held in the City of New York, May 9th, 10th, 11th, and 12th, 1837*, in *The Public Years*, 110; *Letters to Catharine E. Beecher*, 189–90.

137. See Sarah M. Grimke, *Letters on the Equality of the Sexes and the Condition of Women*, in *The Public Years*, 246–50.

138. For further discussion, see David A. J. Richards, *Toleration and the Constitution* (New York: Oxford University Press, 1986), 89–98.

139. On tolerance in early Christianity, see Richards, *Toleration and the Constitution*, 85–86.

140. See, in general, Elaine Pagels, *Adam, Eve, and the Serpent* (New York: Random House, 1988).

She based her argument on the political illegitimacy of this exclusion of women not only on the usual grounds urged by Bayle and Locke (the failure to respect the rights of persons to conscience, speech, and the like), but on further grounds specific to the qualitatively grave deprivation of rights associated with the traditional political and religious treatment of women.

For Sarah Grimke, consistent with Angelina's similar arguments, the essential issue of political illegitimacy was posed in terms of a morally precise analogy between the rights-based subjection of women and slavery. Her arguments included both diachronic and synchronic claims.

Diachronically, Grimke argued very much along the lines of Gerda Lerner's recent exploration of similar historical themes[141] that women's subjugation was the historically generative pattern for slavery. Dating this subjugation from the fall of Adam and Eve, Grimke claimed that "[t]he lust of dominion was probably the first effect of the fall; and as there was no other intelligent being over whom to exercise it, woman was the first victim of this unhallowed passion . . . Here we see the origin of that Upas of slavery, which sprang up immediately after the fall, and has spread its pestilential branches over the whole face of the known world" (209).[142] The nerve of the issue of enslavement was "to regard woman as property, and hence we find them sold to those, who wished to marry them, as far as appears, without any regard to those sacred rights which belong to woman, as well as to man in the choice of a companion" (210). Women, objectified as property, are thus not only exchanged as slaves, but were the model for the institution of slavery as such (later generalized to include men as well).[143]

Synchronically, Grimke argued that the illegitimacy of the contemporary deprivations of rights of women was based on the same grounds as slavery as an institution. She pointed to the systematic unity among the deprivations of rights to which women, like slaves, were subject: voting rights, rights to bring legal actions against her master-husband, freedom from chastisement, liberty of religious and moral conscience, and work and property rights (231–35). Such laws "approximate too nearly to the laws enacted by slaveholders for the government of their

141. See Gerda Lerner, *The Creation of Patriarchy* (New York: Oxford University Press, 1986), 76, 99. See also Gerda Lerner, *The Creation of Feminist Consciousness: From the Middle Ages to 1870* (New York: Oxford University Press, 1993).

142. For later appeal to this idea, see ibid., 263.

143. See, in general, Lerner, *The Creation of Patriarchy.*

slaves" (236) and were illegitimate for the same reason: the failure to take seriously women as persons with inalienable rights of moral agency and self-government. Such unjust denials of the central rights of moral agency led to a cultural construction of woman's roles that "have a tendency to lessen them in their own estimation as moral and responsible beings, . . . teaching them practically the fatal lesson to look upon man for protection and indulgence" (236–37). This debasing insult to "self-respect" (223) was, in turn, extended to the devaluation of women's work (222). Grimke, like her sister a probing critic of American racism as the root of American slavery, generalized that argument to criticize sexism as the unjustifiable basis of the subjection of women.

The brilliance of Grimke's analysis of these matters was, I believe, to anatomize the common indignity to women and the slave on what she, like her sister, called "the same platform of human rights" (239, 259).[144] The core of this common indignity was its debasement of the essential culture-creating moral powers of conscience, free speech, association, and work through which persons reasonably understand their ethical responsibilities and the meaning of their lives. In particular, Grimke argued that such contempt for women's moral autonomy—reflected, *inter alia,* in corrupt traditions of male-dominated Bible interpretation—had deprived them of the resources of coming to know, understand, and act on a reasonable understanding of their ethical rights and responsibilities as persons.[145] From the perspective of this corrupt moral culture, women, like slaves, were "a kind of machinery" (221), defined in terms of meeting masculine interests in their own physical needs and comforts (216–19). The distinctively woman's sphere thus defined "destroy[s] her character as a rational creature," resulting in "the vacuity of mind, the heartlessness, the frivolity which is the necessary result of this false and debasing estimate of women" (220). The nerve of the problem was a woman's intellectual and moral "servitude" when "she permits her husband to be her conscience-keeper" (239).[146] In effect, women lived in a heretically idolatrous worship of men (241).[147]

Under Grimke's analysis, both the enslavement of blacks (and its associated racism) and the subjection of women (and its associated

144. Cf. Angelina E. Grimke, *Letters to Catharine E. Beecher,* 196.
145. See Sarah M. Grimke, *Letters on the Equality of the Sexes and the Condition of Woman,* 213, 214, 216, 237, 241, 243, 245, 248, 258–59, 260, 265–67.
146. See also ibid., 262.
147. See also ibid., 258–59.

sexism) instantiated a common radical moral evil, the politically illegitimate failure to regard a whole class of persons as bearers of human
rights and their debasement to a servile status on that basis; both cases
exemplified the evil of "moral slavery." Such moral slavery turned on
three related kinds of radical evil: the denial of rights of conscience
and free speech; the denial of associational liberty, including intimate
life, on fair terms of equal respect; and the denial of the right to work.
The radical abolitionist analysis of the evils of slavery and racism made
these same points, but Grimke elaborated these points to the situation
of women. Women's unjust servile status, for Grimke, thus resulted
from the servitude of her moral life (an insult to rights of conscience
and free speech) and of her personal and public life (an insult to rights
of associational liberty and of work). Grimke had, as we have seen,
anatomized the diachronic background of the servile status as women
in terms of regarding "woman as property" to be effectively sold accordingly "without any regard to those sacred rights which belong to
women, as well as to man in the choice of a companion" (210). This
historical indignity set the stage for the contemporary objectification
of women in terms of their sexuality and the relationship of that sexuality to men's interests (216–19). A corrupt moral culture, guilty of such
objectification, deprived women of any of the rights of associational
liberty (including not associating with men) inconsistent with such objectification.

Moral slavery, thus understood, deadened moral sensibility and responsibility, and Grimke, anticipating later critics of both racism and
sexism, indicted it most severely on these grounds. Grimke sensitively
articulated the ways in which a sexist moral culture, because it silenced
the voice of woman's moral autonomy, distorted consciousness to its
conventional demands. Grimke made the same point about the injuries
of sexism that W. E. B. Du Bois was later to make of those of racism—

a world which yields him [a black person] no true self-consciousness, but
only lets him see himself through the revelation of the other world. It is a
peculiar sensation, this double-consciousness, this sense of always looking at
one's self through the eyes of others, of measuring one's soul by the tape of
a world that looks on in amused contempt and pity. One ever feels his two-
ness,—an American, a Negro; two souls, two thoughts, two unreconciled
strivings, two warring ideals in one dark body, whose dogged strength alone
keeps it from being torn asunder.[148]

148. See W. E. B. Du Bois, *The Souls of Black Folk*, in *W. E. B. Du Bois: Writings*, ed.
Nathan Huggins (New York: The Library of America, 1986), 364–65.

Grimke spoke piercingly of the obverse side of women's idolatry of men, namely, their "love to be idolized" (263). Not properly the master of herself, the corrupt sexist culture

> makes our case too hard, and compels us to be double minded, and unstable in our ways. Deception gives a mortal stab to moral rectitude. The moment we admit the idea, that we may do evil that good may come, we lose our self-respect, and adopt policy as our rule, instead of righteousness. . . . It is of unspeakable importance to woman, to the world, that she should disenthral her mind of the opinion which spell-binds her as by sorcery, that she is to look to man as the regulator of her actions, the prescriber of the sphere in which she is to move. (263)

Such colonialization of consciousness—common to both the evils of racism and sexism—was the consequence of the illegitimate exclusion of groups from a public culture ostensibly based on respect for human rights.[149] The Grimkes had been astute critics of the racist public culture that thus excluded black Americans from its terms, and the brilliance of their abolitionist feminism was their comparable criticism of the sexist public culture that would silence them and any women who would address the public culture on terms of equal respect for their basic rights of conscience, speech, association, and work. Angelina and Sarah Grimke achieved the degree of moral independence they did through their growing demands to be taken seriously as both religious and moral thinkers and actors on a par with men. It is for this reason that the fullest development of their abolitionist feminism was so preoccupied, as we have seen, with what for the Grimkes were interconnected questions: the sexist corruption of both Bible interpretation and ethics. Their plea was for nothing less than "a great work of public reformation" (216) that would fairly extend the argument for toleration, in the spirit of the Renaissance and the Protestant Reformation, not only to slavery and racism but to the subjection of women and sexism and all ancillary evils.

The Grimkes' ultimate recognition was that their abolitionism and their feminism rested, for reasons we have now examined, on "the same platform of human rights" (239); a common evil (degradation of bearers of human rights to a servile status) required a comparable remedy. Abolitionist argument, consistently pursued in a principled way, condemned both the slavery of blacks and of women and of racism and sexism on the ground of respect for human rights.

The Grimkes effectively retired from public life after Angelina's

---

149. For further development of this theme, see Richards, *Conscience and the Constitution,* chap. 5.

marriage to Theodore Weld on May 14, 1838. Like Maria Stewart before them, they had been the targets of severe criticism and, under the strain of such unjust treatment, left the public sphere.[150] (Angelina, who had borne the brunt of public utterance, broke under the strain in May 1838 and did not lecture again for many years.[151]) Both Sarah and Angelina assumed that their feminist principles would now be tested in private life as they had earlier been in public life. Sarah Grimke had thus written of the corrupt "fear of being thought unfeminine" (260) as a deterrent to the exercise of woman's moral independence, when, in fact, such independence would, if anything, make women better mothers (221–22). Her sister's marriage to Weld would be a test of this proposition; in correspondence at this time, Angelina took this to be the challenge she and her sister (who joined her household) would have to meet: "we are *thus* doing *as much* for the cause of woman as we did by public speaking."[152] Neither may have been well prepared for "the all-consuming tasks of housekeeping and child-rearing on a poverty-level income—tasks for which the Grimkes' upbringing as southern ladies had ill-prepared them"[153]—and Angelina also suffered from invalidism associated with painful conditions probably arising from her pregnancies.[154] In addition, the 1840 schism in the abolitionist movement put Weld and the Grimkes in the position of making a "decision between those who favored woman's rights and rejected political action and those who enthusiastically endorsed political action and excluded women from participation in it. To them, the split was a personal disaster. All they could do was temporarily withdraw from activity, rather than engage in a bitter and hopeless 'family feud.'"[155]

After their retirement, the Grimke sisters importantly assisted Weld in assembling the materials, including their own antislavery testimonies as members of a Southern slave-owning family, for his highly influential *American Slavery As It Is*.[156] And Weld himself prominently

150. For an illuminating comparative discussion of Stewart and the Grimkes, see Suzanne M. Marilley, *Woman Suffrage and the Origins of Liberal Feminism in the United States, 1820–1920*, 32–36.

151. Ibid., 35.

152. Angelina E. Grimke to Anne Warren Weston, 15 July 1838, ibid., 326; see Grimke to Anne Warren Weston, 330.

153. See Karcher, *The First Woman in the Republic*, 248.

154. See Lerner, *The Grimke Sisters from South Carolina*, 289–90.

155. Ibid., 288.

156. See Theodore Weld, *American Slavery As It Is* (1839; New York: Arno Press and the New York Times, 1968). For commentary on the collaboration between the Grimke sisters

assisted John Quincy Adams in his political abolitionist resistance to
the gag rule in the House of Representatives (the rule sought to stem
the tide of antislavery petitions that had, increasingly throughout the
1830s, been sent by abolitionist women, including the Grimke sisters).[157] Adams's resistance to the gag rule on free speech grounds crystallized the public argument linking the right of free speech to the
antislavery rights claimed by the abolitionist movement, which advanced the growing successes of political abolitionism that culminated
in the political victory of the Republican Party in 1860.[158] But, the
Grimke sisters would not again undertake an activist public role in
their own voice until the Civil War.[159] The abolitionist feminist mantle
passed to others.

The enduring public legacy of the Grimke sisters was the leading
public argument for the links of principle between abolitionism and
feminism. Their distinctive legacy (resting on common antiracist and
antisexist principles) was carried on by, among others,[160] Lucretia Mott
and Elizabeth Stanton, who began an independent feminist movement
in the United States.

ABOLITIONIST FEMINISM: LUCRETIA MOTT
AND ELIZABETH STANTON

The political tenor of the age was not hospitable to the Grimkes' conception of abolitionist feminism. Feminism was more controversial
than abolitionism; even Theodore Weld thought it politically unwise
to press, as the Grimkes had, their feminist arguments of principle
(with which he agreed) at the expense of abolitionist advocacy.[161] The
breaking point came, shortly after the Grimkes' retirement, at the
World Anti-Slavery Convention in London in the summer of 1840.

The American delegation included a number of women, but despite
the strong objection of some American leaders, the convention ruled,

and Weld, see William Lee Miller, *Arguing about Slavery: The Great Battle in the United
States Congress* (New York: Knopf, 1996), 325–33.

157. On the important role of women in the petition movement, see Miller, *Arguing
about Slavery*, 110–11, 311–23, 366–67.

158. On the central role of John Quincy Adams in this struggle and its important consequences for political abolitionism, see, in general, Miller, *Arguing about Slavery*.

159. See Lerner, *The Grimke Sisters from South Carolina*, 340–68.

160. For accounts of other important figures, see Dorothy Sterling, *Ahead of Her Time:
Abby Kelley and the Politics of Antislavery* (New York: W. W. Norton, 1991); Andrea Moore
Kerr, *Lucy Stone: Speaking Out for Equality* (New Brunswick, N.J.: Rutgers University Press,
1992).

161. See Lerner, *The Grimke Sisters from South Carolina*, 200–203.

after vigorous debate, that only male delegates could be seated. Among the women compelled to sit passively in the galleries were Lucretia Mott and the young wife of an antislavery leader, Elizabeth Cady Stanton. Mott and Stanton began in London discussions about their common sense of indignation; and Mott in particular, drawing upon the work of the Grimke sisters (notably, Sarah Grimke's recent book on the rights of women[162]), made the case for women's rights to Stanton, as Stanton would later comment, "like an added sun in the heavens, lighting the darkest recesses and chasing every shadow away."[163] Mott and Stanton concurred on the need for an independent statement of feminist principles that eventually culminated in the Seneca Falls Convention of 1848, which is usually taken to mark the emergence of an independent woman's rights movement in the United States.[164] The basis for their collaboration was, as we shall see, abolitionist feminism.

The abolitionist feminism of Lucretia Mott was grounded in her interpretation of Hicksite Quakerism, which had separated from the Orthodox group (the group joined, then challenged and left by the Grimke sisters).[165] As a recent history of George Fox, the founder of Quakerism, notes, "[I]mplying that women's opinions merited consideration [had been] more than enough to label Fox a threat to established religion."[166] Hicksite Quakerism, which also influenced Walt Whitman,[167] carried this traditional Quaker policy one step further, allowing Hicksite women like Mott greater independence, "initiating actions and undertaking concerns without waiting for the approval of the men," the pattern still assumed by Orthodox Quakers.[168] Hicksite

162. See Frederick B. Tolles, *Slavery and "The Woman Question": Lucretia Mott's Diary of Her Visit to Great Britain to Attend the World's Anti-Slavery Convention of 1840* (Haverford, Pa.: Friends' Historical Association, 1952), 58, 66.

163. See Elizabeth Cady Stanton, Susan B. Anthony, and Matilda Joslyn Gage, *History of Woman Suffrage* (1881; Salem, N.H.: Ayer Company, 1985), 1:419.

164. For a fascinating narrative by participants, see ibid., 1:50–87. Good secondary sources on these and later developments include Eleanor Flexner, *Century of Struggle: The Woman's Rights Movement in the United States* rev. ed. (Cambridge: Harvard University Press, Belknap Press, 1975); Aileen S. Kraditor, *The Ideas of the Woman Suffrage Movement, 1890–1920* (New York: Columbia University Press, 1965); Ellen Carol DuBois, *Feminism and Suffrage: The Emergence of an Independent Women's Movement in America, 1848–1869* (Ithaca: Cornell University Press, 1978).

165. See Margaret Hope Bacon, *Mothers of Feminism: The Story of Quaker Women in America* (San Francisco: Harper & Row, 1986), 92–93, 104–15.

166. See H. Larry Ingle, *First among Friends: George Fox and the Creation of Quakerism* (New York: Oxford University Press, 1994), 63.

167. For Whitman's tribute to Elias Hicks, see Walt Whitman, "Elias Hicks, Notes (Such as They Are)," in *Walt Whitman: Complete Poetry and Collected Prose,* ed. Justin Kaplan (New York: Library of America, 1982), 1221–44.

168. See Bacon, *Mothers of Feminism,* 93.

Quaker women brought this emancipation powerfully to bear on the movement for women's rights; Lucretia Mott, Susan B. Anthony, Florence Kelley, and Alice Paul were all Hicksite Quakers.[169]

Lucretia Mott was able to claim and to exercise, as a Hicksite Quaker, the right to be a minister[170] in the way and to the effect that Sarah Grimke had defended if the argument for toleration was fairly to be applied to condemn not only slavery and racism (as antiracist abolitionists had argued) but the subjection of women and sexism as well. In particular, Mott concurred with Grimke's views about the illegitimate role that misogynist Bible interpretation had played in the unjust rationalization of the subjection of women (on the basis of St. Paul,[171] or of mistranslations [28, 133, 216–17]) analogous to the similar proslavery interpretive abuses of the Bible.[172] Mott took to be fundamental the basic human right of conscience and "toleration without limit" (239),[173] which would allow full and fair expression of the "principle in the human mind which renders all men essentially equal" (327), "this inward principle as the all sufficient teacher" (353). Consistent with the argument for toleration, Mott called for less political dependence on sectarian interpretations of the Bible as the measure of a reasonable public understanding of basic rights and responsibilities.[174] American women were, in Mott's view, altogether too dependent on the views of sectarian, male ministers (242, 258); like Harriet Beecher Stowe (197, 222), they should claim the full and morally independent exercise of their own moral faculties (203) and rely on their own moral judgments of public reason not only in the area of feminist abolitionism but all areas (139, 276–77, 304) (for example, making arguments against Sunday closing laws (131) and capital punishment [176]). To allow proper scope for such exercise of women's reasonable moral powers, Mott underscored the necessity of a robust principle of free speech to guarantee that a polemically entrenched, sectarian political epistemology not be politically enforceable at large,[175] but be freely open to skeptical scrutiny and debate (280, 360). Otherwise, such a sectarian orthodoxy would be both the measure of legitimate debate and of those who may participate in such debate, repressing (consistent

---

169. Ibid., 93.

170. For Mott's insistence on this point, see Dana Greene, ed., *Lucretia Mott: Her Complete Speeches and Sermons* (New York: Edwin Mellen Press, 1980), 203–4, 214–15, 217.

171. Ibid., 26–27, 146–47, 208–9, 216–17, 229–30, 360.

172. Ibid., 123, 125, 132–33, 168–69, 176–77, 214–17, 239–40, 322.

173. See also ibid., 319–20.

174. Ibid., 59, 61, 111–12, 123–34, 217, 321–22, 338, 359–60.

175. Ibid., 42–43, 45, 54–56, 132–33, 144, 195–96, 204.

with the paradox of intolerance) the discourse and the voices most needed to bring public reason to bear on politics. Like racism, the sexist devaluation of women's moral capacities was a repressive orthodoxy that assumed the same vicious circle (132–33, 265).

In her important "Discourse on Women,"[176] Mott took as her starting point the role that woman's moral experience had played in enabling people, as she earlier observed, to "put our own souls in their souls' stead, who are in slavery" (30),[177] and offered the generalization that the reasonable elaboration of the argument for toleration to include women would legitimate a powerful role for women in moral reform (147–48). Mott cited and endorsed Catharine Beecher's similar views on women's role in moral reform (149–50, 175, 231–32), but her argument, unlike Beecher's appeal to utilitarian self-sacrifice, claimed the "right . . . to be acknowledged a moral, responsible being" (154); acknowledgment of that right would make possible a more reasonable public discourse about justice and the public good, including the justice of women's claims to rights to work (159–62). Accordingly, Mott did not appeal to utilitarianism or indeed to the Bible as the moral basis for such arguments; rather, she looked to E. P. Hurlbut's anti-utilitarian, secular theory of universal human rights and women's rights (158, 212)[178] just as she elsewhere appealed to such secular rights-based views of the American antebellum philosopher, William Ellery Channing.[179]

Mott repeatedly drew the analogy between the treatment of African Americans and women in terms of moral slavery. On proper analysis, the traditional view of women was "servitude" because "[s]he has been subject to the disabilities and restrictions, with which her progress has been embarrassed, that she has become enervated, her mind to some extent paralysed; and, like those still more degraded by personal bondage, she hugs her chains."[180] Sometimes, Mott offered the analogy to clarify a particular context, like women's lack of rights in marriage (157) (including lack of rights of property and physical security [159]) or lack of rights to the ministry (219). She made clear that the "enslavement [of women was] not equal to the degradation of the poor black

176. Ibid., 143–62 (originally published in 1850).

177. See also ibid., 89, 188.

178. See E. P. Hurlbut, *Essays on Human Rights and Their Political Guaranties* (New York: Greeley & McElrath, 1845). Hurlbut rejects Bentham's utilitarian rights-skepticism as "a giant groping in darkness" (14); for Hurlbut's endorsement of arguments for the rights of women, see ibid., 144–72, including the right to vote, ibid., 112–23.

179. Ibid., 45, 101, 105, 151, 307, 363; for criticism of some of Channing's views on women, see ibid., 205, 297.

180. See Greene, ed., *Lucretia Mott: Her Complete Speeches and Sermons*, 155.

slaves" (268), but her fundamental ground for drawing the analogy was the common rights-denying evil underlying "the prejudice" (265) of race and gender, namely, the thesis of the common moral slavery of blacks and women.

Moral slavery, as the Grimke sisters formulated it, described the indignity of degrading a whole class of persons from their status as bearers of human rights (including the basic rights of conscience, speech, association, and work) on grounds of incapacity that depended on the vicious circle of the traditional abridgment of such rights for the benefit of another group illegitimately in control. Mott made the point of moral slavery by focusing on its focal dependence on the unjust abridgment of basic rights of responsible moral agency and deliberation, so that the deprived group was made "the mere slave of social custom, the unreasoning victim of conventional cruelty" (204). Such abridgment of free exercise of one's reasonable moral powers over one's convictions, speech, associations, and work dehumanized moral personality into the mere object of another's interests, and was sustained by unjust traditions of moral slavery. Such traditions morally enslaved because they rested on cultural dehumanization that disabled its victims from engaging in reasonable criticism, debate, dissent, and refusal.[181] For this reason, contentment of the moral slave with his situation "only proves the depth of his degradation" (233).

The abolitionist feminism of Lucretia Mott, like that of the Grimke sisters, drew upon and elaborated strands of Garrisonian abolitionism, including its sympathy with women's rights,[182] its focus on criticizing the corrupt moral conscience of Americans, its self-consciously apolitical character (including advocacy of not voting[183]), its repudiation of the United States Constitution as "a covenant with death and an agreement with hell,"[184] and indeed its moral anarchism (repudiating any

181. For developments of this point, see ibid., 204, 213, 215, 222, 232–33, 265, 268–69, 287–88.

182. For an important treatment of the role of Garrison in American abolitionism, see Aileen S. Kraditor, *Means and Ends in American Abolitionism: Garrison and His Critics on Strategy and Tactics, 1834–1850* (New York: Pantheon, 1969). For the sympathy and advocacy of Garrison and Wendell Phillips for women's rights, see Archibald H. Grimke, *William Lloyd Garrison: The Abolitionist* (1891; New York: Negro Universities Press, 1969); Wendell Phillips, "Woman's Rights," in Wendell Phillips, *Speeches, Lectures, and Letters* (1851; Boston: Lothrop, Lee, & Shepard, 1891), 11–34; id., "Suffrage for Woman," in Wendell Phillips, *Speeches on Rights of Women* (1861; Philadelphia: A. J. Ferris, 1898).

183. See Wendell Phillips, *Can Abolitionists Vote or Take Office under the United States Constitution?* (New York: American Anti-Slavery Society, 1845).

184. See Wendell Phillips Garrison and Francis Jackson Garrison, *William Lloyd Garrison, 1805–1879* (New York: Century Co., 1889), 3:88.

kind of force, and thus the legitimacy of the state, in favor of appeals to free and informed conscience).[185] This latter doctrine of nonresistance was clearly assumed as part of her Quakerism by Mott[186] and by the Grimke sisters during their activist period at the end of which Theodore Weld's objections led them to express doubts.[187] Garrison's authorship in 1833 of the Declaration of Sentiments of the American Anti-Slavery Convention illustrated the force of the doctrine. On the one hand, Garrison condemned slavery as inconsistent with the Lockean rights-based political theory of the Declaration of Independence, but he denied what the earlier Declaration endorsed, namely, the legitimacy of revolutionary force or force of any kind in order to enforce one's human rights: "Ours shall be . . . the opposition of moral purity to moral corruption . . . the abolition of slavery by the spirit of repentance." The abolitionist movement was only to make arguments appealing to the conscience of other Americans; all else were "carnal weapons" and therefore illegitimate.[188] Within this Garrisonian framework, the abolitionist feminism of the Grimkes and Lucretia Mott expanded and deepened the Garrisonian rights-based criticism of American conventional attitudes on matters of race and gender, but its claims of abridgment of basic rights would not justify the use of force. To this point in its development, abolitionist feminism was, like Garrisonian abolitionism, a moral movement, not a political or constitutional one.

The monumental importance of Elizabeth Stanton to American feminism in general and abolitionist feminism in particular comes not only from her significant contributions to the moral claims of abolitionist feminism, but her insistence that its moral theory (the rights-based argument for toleration) was the basic political theory of American political and constitutional institutions and thus the just grounds for both political action and constitutional interpretation. I deal here with Stanton's antebellum role in the forging of abolitionist feminism as a political and constitutional as well as moral movement, turning in the next chapter to her more tragic role as a leader in the rather racist

185. For a good study, see Lewis Perry, *Radical Abolitionism: Anarchy and the Government of God in Antislavery Thought* (Ithaca: Cornell University Press, 1973).

186. See Greene, ed., *Lucretia Mott: Her Complete Speeches and Sermons*, 261–62.

187. For endorsement of the doctrine, see Gilbert H. Barnes and Dwight L. Dumond, *Letters of Theodore Dwight Weld, Angelina Grimke Weld, and Sarah Grimke, 1822–1844* (Gloucester, Mass.: Peter Smith, 1965), 1:377–78, 408, 422, 480–81; for Weld's doubts, see ibid., 2:513–14; for the apparent subsequent doubts of the Grimke sisters, see ibid., 2:856.

188. See William Lloyd Garrison, *Declaration of Sentiments of the American Anti-Slavery Society*, in *Selections from the Writings and Speeches of William Lloyd Garrison* (Boston: R. F. Wallcut, 1852), 67.

reaction to antifeminist interpretations of the Reconstruction Amendments and in the related compromises of principle that framed the
growing political success of suffrage feminism.

Stanton's abolitionist feminist thought was not based on Garrisonian
moral anarchism, but on a Lockean rights-based theory of political legitimacy along the lines advanced by Theodore Parker as a defense of
political abolitionism[189] and by E. P. Hurlbut to test the legitimacy of
political power.[190] Both Parker and Hurlbut expressly rejected utilitarianism because it failed to take seriously the proper normative weight
to be accorded respect for human rights,[191] and had questioned the
political legitimacy of depriving women of basic rights. E. P. Hurlbut
made arguments for the rights of women, including the right to vote,[192]
on the basis of the inalienable right of all persons to protection of the
basic moral powers and propensities common to all persons.[193]

Parker had applied his quest for ethical impartiality to recognizing
and enforcing universal human rights not only to antislavery interpretations of both the Bible and the Constitution, but to comparable interpretations that human rights are "as unalienable in a woman as in a
man."[194] He directed his rights-based criticism at what his larger defense of the argument for toleration would lead one to expect, namely,
that the failure to acknowledge women's human rights to be a lawyer
or a minister unjustly entrenched a sectarian ideology of gender roles
and thus unreasonably distorted the interpretation of both legal and
religious texts (16–17). In the case of Bible interpretation, such injustice led to interpretations that leave "us nothing feminine in the character of God" (17); "and a State without her equal political action, is

189. On Parker's significant influence on Stanton's thought, see Elisabeth Griffith, *In Her Own Right: The Life of Elizabeth Cady Stanton* (New York: Oxford University Press, 1984), 45–46, 54; Elizabeth Cady Stanton, *Eighty Years and More (1815–1897)* (London: T. Fisher Unwin, 1898), 132–34.

190. See E. P. Hurlbut, *Essays on Human Rights and Their Political Guaranties* (New York: Greeley & McElrath, 1845); on the influence on Stanton, see Stanton, *Eighty Years and More,* 197–98.

191. See Theodore Parker, "Transcendentalism," in Theodore Parker, *The World of Mat-ter and the Spirit of Man,* ed. George Willis Cooke (Boston: American Unitarian Association, 1907), 23; for commentary on this point, see Richards, *Conscience and the Constitution,* 76–77. For Hurlbut's rejection of Bentham for this reason, see Hurlbut, *Essays on Human Rights and Their Political Guaranties,* 13–14.

192. On the right to vote, see Hurlbut, *Essays on Human Rights and Their Guaranties,* 112–23; on other rights of women, see ibid., 144–72.

193. Ibid., 25–27, 37, 108, 116–17, 161–62, 165, 169.

194. See Theodore Parker, *The Public Function of Woman* (London: John Chapman, 1855), 13. The essay was sufficiently important to Stanton to be reprinted, in part, in Stanton et al., *History of Woman Suffrage,* 1:277–82.

almost as bad—is very much what a house would be without a mother, wife, sister, or friend" (20). Both in religion and law, such injustice deprived us of "moral feeling, affectional feeling, religious feeling, far in advance of man" (22).[195]

Stanton made the case for abolitionist feminism in terms of the legitimacy of translating its central claims of moral slavery into political and constitutional demands defined by the role this anti-utilitarian, rights-based political theory of toleration played in American revolutionary constitutionalism (as reflected in the Declaration of Independence).[196] As early as 1848 at the Seneca Falls Convention, Stanton's distinctive position had evident impact. Of the five women who organized the meeting (including Lucretia Mott), all but Stanton were Garrisonian abolitionists and liberal Quakers.[197] Stanton prepared the central document for the convention, entitled "A Declaration of Sentiments," a phrase borrowed from Garrison's earlier described covenant of the American Anti-Slavery Association. Stanton and Garrison framed their respective arguments around the Declaration of Independence, but Garrison referred only to Jefferson's great normative appeals to equality and endowment with inalienable rights and expressly disowned the use of such appeals to make revolutionary demands. Remarkably, Stanton's document carefully adapted and extensively repeated much of the language of the Declaration of Independence and affirmed its revolutionary grounds: "Whenever any form of government becomes destructive of these ends, it is the right of those who suffer from it to refuse allegiance to it, and to insist upon the institution of a new government."[198] For Stanton, abolitionist feminism appealed directly and uncompromisingly to the tests of Lockean political legitimacy (respect for inalienable human rights) of American revolutionary constitutionalism.

The grounds listed and resolutions proposed at Seneca Falls were a compendium of claims, central to abolitionist feminism, that women as a class had on inadequate grounds been deprived of basic human

195. Parker claims, however, that women have weaker intellects than men because "he has the bigger brain." Ibid., 22.

196. For Stanton's criticism of Bentham for his failure to recognize, indeed his repudiation of, inalienable human rights, see Beth M. Waggenspack, *The Search for Self-Sovereignty: The Oratory of Elizabeth Cady Stanton* (Westport, Conn.: Greenwood Press, 1989), 111. For good statements of Stanton's rights-based political theory, see Elizabeth B. Clark, "Self-Ownership and the Political Theory of Elizabeth Cady Stanton," *Connecticut Law Review* 21 (1989): 905; id., "The Politics of God and the Woman's Vote: Religion in the American Suffrage Movement, 1848–1895" (Ph.D. diss., Princeton University, 1989).

197. See Griffith, *In Her Own Right*, 51.

198. See Stanton et al., *History of Woman Suffrage*, 1:70.

rights to conscience, speech, association, and work. The resolutions thus included several that deployed the Grimkes' and Mott's conception of women's moral slavery: women's failure to understand and protest "their degradation" and "the corrupt customs and a perverted application of the Scriptures" (1:72) on which such degradation rested. Other resolutions, drawing on the same conception, expressly condemned the failure to allow women's rights of free speech both in religious and secular assemblies (with an implicit reference to Catharine Beecher's criticism of the Grimke sisters, the resolutions note "the objection of indelicacy and impropriety" when no objection was taken to "her appearance on the stage, in the concert, or in feats of the circus"). Another resolution took objection to the double standard in matters of "virtue, delicacy, and refinement," demanding that "the same transgressions . . . be visited with equal severity on man and woman." Among the objects of rights-based protest were, consistent with Mott's thought,[199] abridgment of basic rights to employment (including teaching theology, medicine, or law),[200] to be a minister, and to higher education. The unjust ground for such abridgment was "a false public sentiment by giving to the world a different code of morals for men and women" (usurping "the prerogative of Jehovah himself, claiming it as his right to assign for her a sphere of action, when that belongs to her conscience and to her God"). Such a false public morality corruptly aimed "to destroy her confidence in her [woman's] own powers, to lessen her self-respect, and to make her willing to lead a dependent and abject life" (1:71).

The grounds went on to encompass a new right and interpretations of old rights that reflected Stanton's distinctive contribution to abolitionism feminism. The new right was expressly political and aligned abolitionist feminism with political abolitionism. Stanton thus listed as the first grievance having "never permitted her to exercise her inalienable right to the elective franchise . . . this first right of a citizen" "thereby leaving her without representation in the halls of legislation." Over the objections of both Lucretia Mott and her husband Edward Stanton, Stanton insisted on proposing as well a resolution invoking "the duty of the women of this country to secure to themselves their

---

199. See Lucretia Mott, "Discourse on Woman" in *Lucretia Mott: Her Complete Speeches and Sermons*, ed. Dana Greene (New York: Edwin Mellen Press, 1980), 158–62. Indeed, at the last session, Mott offered and spoke to a resolution calling "for the overthrow of the monopoly of the pulpit, and for the securing to woman an equal participation with men in the various trades, professions, and commerce." Stanton et al., *History of Woman Suffrage*, 1:73.

200. Ibid., 71.

sacred right to the elective franchise" (1:72).[201] It was the only resolution not adopted unanimously, passing by a narrow vote with the strong advocacy of Stanton and Frederick Douglass (1:73).

The distinctive interpretation of old rights was the construal Stanton gave to abridgment of basic rights of intimate association (marriage and divorce), an issue on which she was to insist throughout her life, sometimes in quite unconventional, even radical ways. Her passionate interest in these questions arose from her personal experience as a wife and mother, her growing indignation at the larger plight of women this experience reflected, and her transformation of this indignation into an important interpretation and articulation of the rights-based principles of abolitionist feminism.

There is no doubt that the immediate impetus to Stanton's increasingly activist stance on abolitionist feminism was her experience of married life after her family moved from Boston to Seneca Falls. In her autobiography, she described her dark mood:

> I suffered with mental hunger, which, like an empty stomach, is very depressing. I had books, but no stimulating companionship. . . . Cleanliness, order, the love of the beautiful and artistic, all faded away in the struggle to accomplish what was absolutely necessary from hour to hour. . . . I now fully understood the practical difficulties most women had to contend with in this isolated household, and the impossibility of woman's best development if in contact, the chief part of her life, with servants and children. . . . The general discontent I felt with woman's portion as wife, mother, housekeeper, physician, and spiritual guide, the chaotic conditions into which everything fell without her constant supervision, and the wearied, anxious look of the majority of women impressed me with a strong feeling that some active measure should be taken to remedy the wrongs of society in general, and of women in particular. My experience at the World's Antislavery convention, all I had read of the legal status of women, and the oppression I saw everywhere, together swept across my soul, intensified now by many personal experiences. It seemed as if all the elements had conspired to impel me to some outward step. I could not see what to do or where to begin—my only thought was a public meeting for protest and discussion.[202]

It was in this mood that Stanton met with her old friend and mentor, Lucretia Mott, and the other Quaker women at Seneca Falls; and it was Stanton's rights-based rage (interpreting the personal as the political) that was the catalyst: "I poured out, that day, the torrent of my long-accumulating discontent, with such vehemence and indignation

---

201. On Mott's and Henry Stanton's opposition, see Elisabeth Griffith, *In Her Own Right*, 54–55.

202. See Stanton, *Eighty Years and More*, 147–48.

that I stirred myself, as well as the rest of the party, to do and dare anything."[203]

After listing four grounds for grievance dealing with political rights, Stanton went on to enumerate five others, all of which dealt with injustices in the law of marriage and divorce. If the Grimke sisters had repudiated Catharine Beecher's dogma that women's moral reforms must impersonally advance the interests of others (never one's own), Stanton carried their rights-based project one step further into women's personal lives. Women must claim not only rights of conscience, free speech, and work, but also must fairly lay claim to their intimate lives on terms of justice. Stanton thus challenged the loss of women's legal individuality in marriage,[204] her loss of property and income rights, lack of criminal responsibility and subjection to her husband's control (including "chastisement" [1:71]), a law of divorce and custody "wholly regardless of the happiness of women" and "going upon the false supposition of the supremacy of man, and giving all power into his hands," and the subjection of single women to taxation "when her property can be made profitable to it" (1:71).

Finally, Stanton's political philosophy that women were not appendages, but independent sources and claimants of basic human rights, framed the first three Seneca Falls resolutions:

> *Resolved,* That such laws as conflict, in any way, with the true and substantial happiness of woman, are contrary to the great precept of nature and of not validity.
>
> *Resolved,* That all laws which prevent woman from occupying such a station in society as her conscience shall dictate, or which place her in a position inferior to that of man, are contrary to the great precept of nature, and therefore of no force or authority.
>
> *Resolved,* That woman is man's equal—was intended to be so by the Creation, and the highest good of the race demands that she should be recognized as such. (1:72)

Stanton's feminist activism in the remaining antebellum period focused on divorce reform.[205] Two addresses to the New York legislature, in 1854 and in 1860, reflect the development of her thought and growing influence.

In the 1854 address,[206] Stanton described women's situation as

---

203. Ibid., 148.

204. See Stanton et al., *History of Woman Suffrage,* 1:70: "He has made her, if married, in the eye of the law, civilly dead."

205. See Griffith, *In Her Own Right,* 86–107.

206. See Elizabeth Cady Stanton, "Address to the Joint Judiciary Committee, New York Legislature, 1854," in Waggenspack, *The Search for Self-Sovereignty,* 97–109.

woman, wife, widow, and mother: women "are persons; native, free-born citizens; property-holders, tax-payers" (97), yet they lacked the rights of citizens, such as voting, holding office, trial by peers, and equal treatment under the criminal law. The marriage contract should be treated like civil contracts, outlining obligations and allowing suits for breach. Once married, married women should be protected from abuse from and the insolvency of husbands, which required that married women have the right to inherit and earn money; voting rights would enable women to protect their property. As widows, women needed fair inheritance and tax laws and the right to serve as executors of their husband's will. As mothers, women needed to share custody rights over children, so that husbands could not dispose of them (for example, as apprentices) without consent of the mother. Women also needed education to be good mothers and protection against drunk husbands. To make her case against the unjust subordination of women, Stanton pressed the Southern analogy central to the abolitionist feminist argument of moral slavery: "It is impossible to make the Southern planter believe that his slave feels and reasons just as he does—that injustice and subjection are as galling as to him—that the degradation of living by the will of another, the mere dependent on his caprice, at the mercy of his passions, is a[s] keenly felt by him as his master. . . . Here gentlemen, is our difficulty" (106).[207] In conclusion, Stanton made her case "simply on the ground that their rights of every human being are the same and identical" (107).

Stanton had met Susan B. Anthony in 1851, forming a friendship and feminist collaboration that would last 50 years.[208] Stanton, Anthony, and others had petitioned the New York legislature to further enlarge the scope of the Married Women's Property Act, passed in 1848, to include, *inter alia,* the right of married women to hold property, to carry on any trade or service, to use their earnings, to have joint custody of child, and the like. Stanton spoke in support of the amendments in her second 1860 address to the New York legislature.

Stanton's 1860 address[209] directly compared woman's legal status to that of the slave, demanding that women be treated as citizens rather than as slaves. This demand rested on "natural rights as inalienable to civilization as are the rights of air and motion to the savage in the wilderness" (111). Stanton elaborated analogies between both Ameri-

207. See ibid., 106.

208. See Griffith, *In Her Own Right,* 82–83.

209. See Stanton, "Address to the New York State Legislature, 1860," in Beth M. Waggenspack, *The Search for Self-Sovereignty,* 111–18.

can slavery and the subjection of women and between "[t]he prejudice against color [and] against sex" (113). Abridgment of the basic rights of women paralleled those of American slaves, including rights to: an independent name, earnings one can call one's own, control of one's children, independent legal existence, and locomotion and bodily security (112–13). Indeed, "the refinements of degradation" of women "are worse [than American slavery], by just so far as woman, from her social position, refinement, and education, is on a more equal ground with the oppressor" (112). Prejudice against blacks and women were "produced by the same cause, and manifested very much in the same way. The negro's skin and the woman's sex are both *prima facie* evidence that they were intended to be in subjection to the white Saxon man" (113). Women, Stanton granted, were accorded social privileges ("to sit at the same table and eat with the white man" [113]) not accorded free blacks, but free blacks were accorded basic civil rights (to own property, to vote, and to be ministers) not granted women. By the degree to which civil rights were more important than social privileges, "it is evident that the prejudice against sex is more deeply rooted and unreasonably maintained than that against color" (113). Anticipating the usual objection of separate spheres to woman's engaging in public life, Stanton retorted:

> But, say you, we would not have woman exposed to the grossness and vulgarity of public life, or encounter what she must at the polls. When you talk, gentlemen, of sheltering woman from the rough winds and revolting scenes of real life, you must be either talking for effect, or wholly ignorant of what the facts of life are. The man, whatever he is, is known to the woman. She is the companion not only of the accomplished statesman, the orator, and the scholar, but the vile, vulgar, brutal man has his mother, his wife, his sister, his daughter . . . and if a man shows out what he is anywhere, it is at his own hearthstone. . . . Gentlemen, such scenes as woman has witnessed at her own fireside, where no eye save Omnipotence could pity, no strong arm could help, can never be realized at the polls, never equaled elsewhere, this side the bottomless pit. (114)

Stanton also answered the objection that a majority of women did not call for legal reform by denying the issue was one for majority rule: "if there is but one woman in this State who feels the injustice of her position, she should not be denied her inalienable rights" (115).

Stanton called her address: "A Slave's Appeal." The legislation passed the New York legislature the next day.[210]

210. See Griffith, *In Her Own Right,* 101.

ABOLITIONIST FEMINISM: SOJOURNER TRUTH AND HARRIET JACOBS

Elizabeth Stanton drew on and elaborated the normative conception of moral slavery of abolitionist feminism. Two ex-slaves, Sojourner Truth and Harriet Jacobs, forged out of their moral experience yet another interpretive deepening of this conception, in particular, its analysis of the interlinked evils of racism and sexism.[211] Truth took up and advanced the Grimkes' analysis of the part played by gender roles in the political epistemology of racism; Jacobs also advanced that analysis and further developed Lydia Maria Child's suggestion that the abridgment of rights of autonomy in intimate life (reflected in antimiscegenation laws) was a constitutive component of American racism.

The life of Sojourner Truth, as she chronicled in *Narrative*,[212] is a remarkable tale of the abolitionist feminist quest for discovering and exploring morally independent voice and identity and the power of that quest for moral and political growth in American public life. *Narrative* traces the transformation of a Northern slave child, Isabella, into Sojourner Truth, who by the 1840s had become an abolitionist and an important speaker in the revival movement sweeping the Northeast.[213] Truth had discovered her moral voice by asserting the right of preaching, as an itinerant millennialist minister, that so many abolitionist feminists had regarded as a central human right abridged by moral slavery. Truth's millennial quest had led her into disastrous associations, as when she joined the commune of Robert Matthias, a New York City mystic and madman (later he would be tried for fraud and murder) obsessed by the need for patriarchal controls over "meek Christian devils and their disobedient women."[214] Truth, however, learned from such mistakes; once having recognized Matthias's patriarchal misogyny as a delusion, she embarked in 1843 on her own quest to originate moral "claims of human brotherhood,"[215] "her name no longer Isabella,

211. For an important investigation of their contribution, see Yellin, *Women and Sisters*, 77–96. For a useful study of other black abolitionist women, see Shirley J. Yee, *Black Women Abolitionists: A Study in Activism, 1828–1860* (Knoxville: University of Tennessee Press, 1992). See also Benjamin Quarles, *Black Abolitionists* (London: Oxford University Press, 1969).

212. See Jeffrey C. Stewart, ed., *Narrative of Sojourner Truth* (1850; New York: Oxford University Press, 1991).

213. For useful commentary, see Jeffrey C. Stewart, "Introduction," in Jeffrey C. Stewart, ed., *Narrative of Sojourner Truth*, xxxiii–xlvi.

214. See Paul E. Johnson and Sean Wilentz, *The Kingdom of Matthias* (New York: Oxford University Press, 1994), 94.

215. Stewart, *Narrative of Sojourner Truth*, 99.

but SOJOURNER."[216] She became what Matthias despised: a morally independent woman, indeed, an abolitionist feminist.

As a black illiterate ex-slave woman, Truth forged her moral independence as an outsider from the conventions of the woman's sphere rationalized by Catharine Beecher, preaching in public to mixed religious and secular audiences in precisely the way that Beecher condemned in the Grimke sisters. This moral independence enabled Truth to muster her extraordinary defense of white feminist women against hostile white ministers at the 1851 Akron Women's Rights Convention; the ministers, spouting biblical strictures against women participating in public life, were trying to take over the meeting. In Frances Gage's influential record of that meeting,[217] many of the white women in attendance pressed her, as president, not to permit Sojourner Truth to speak for fear of tainting the feminist cause with abolitionism. But most of these women, shaped by the powerful gender conventions of the day, would not themselves speak in support of women's rights against the many men who aggressively spoke against the cause. Sojourner Truth had no such inhibitions, and when Gage called on her to speak, she aggressively questioned the racialized conventions of gender to which the ministers appealed:

"Wall, chilern, whar dar is so much racket dar must be somethin' out o' kilter. I tink dat 'twixt de neggers of de Souf and de womin at de Norf, all talk' 'bout rights, de white men will be in a fix pretty soon. But what's all dis here talkin' 'bout?

"Dat men ober dar say dat womin needs to be helped into carriages, and lifted ober ditches, and to hab de best place everywhar. Nobody eber helps me into carriages, or ober mud-puddles, or gibs me any best place!" And raising herself to her full height, and her voice to a pitch like rolling thunder, she asked, "And a'n't I a woman? Look at me! Look at my arm! (and she bared her right arm to the shoulder, showing her tremendous muscular power). I have ploughed, and planted, and gathered in barns, and no man could head me! And a'n't I a woman? I could work as much and eat as much as a man—when I could get it—and bear de lash as well! And a'n't I a woman? I have borne thirteen chilern, and seen 'em mos' all sold off to slavery, and when I cried out with my mother's grief, none but Jesus heard me. And a'n't I a woman?

"Den dey talks 'bout dis ting in de head; what dis dey call it?" ("Intellect,"

216. Ibid., 100.

217. See "Reminiscences by Frances D. Gage: Sojourner Truth," in Stanton et al., *History of Woman Suffrage*, 1:115–17. For an argument, in my judgment ultimately not convincing, that Gage's version is less accurate than another version of her speech, see Nell Irvin Painter, *Sojourner Truth: A Life, A Symbol* (New York: W. W. Norton, 1996), 125–26, 164–69, 171, 281–87; for cogent criticism, see Michael P. Johnson, "Twisted Truth," *The New Republic*, 4 November 1996, 37–41.

whispered some one near.) "Dat's it, honey. What's dat got to do wid womin's rights or nigger's rights? If my cup won't hold but a pint, and yours holds a quart, wouldn't ye be mean not to let me have my little half-measure full?" And she pointed her significant finger, and sent a keen glance at the minister who had made the argument. The cheering was long and loud.[218]

Sojourner Truth breached the wall between issues of gender and of race that fearful white women at the 1851 meeting anxiously insisted on maintaining. If the central claim of abolitionist feminism was to advance understanding of the rights-denying evils of racism and sexism by analyzing them as resting on common indignities of moral slavery, Truth's elaboration of abolitionist feminism confirmed the moral fertility of this approach. Truth's argument brought to critical consciousness and debunked, in her own incomparable moral voice, the racialized conception of gender that was uncritically accepted by her audience. If the white ministers' conception of gender clearly did not fit the experience of black women, it reflected a critically defective conception of women as such: a conception flawed by an unreasonable mythological idealization that, on Truth's analysis, unjustly created rather than reflected the frailty or incompetence of white women and the strength to bear multiple adversities of black women. In both cases, such mythological idealization was at the core of an unjustly enforceable political epistemology, self-blinding its proponents to injustice thus inflicted on both women and blacks. Truth insisted not only on making clear its false factual premises, but its failure to take seriously some of the worst injustices of American slavery (insisting, as she did, on the moral atrocities of forced physical labor, beatings, and the sale of children). Finally, Truth underscored the common moral grounds of human rights (of claims by blacks and women), resting, as they do, on minimal powers of moral personality that all persons enjoy.

Sojourner Truth deepened abolitionism feminism, but left one topic unexamined. She never discussed sexuality. The subject was, however, brilliantly raised and explored by Harriet Jacobs in her slave narrative, *Incidents in the Life of a Slave Girl*.[219]

No criticism of slavery and racism was more stinging to Americans than any discussion of underlying issues of sexuality. Lydia Maria Child had, as we have seen, crucially identified antimiscegenation laws as part of her larger indictment of the unjust cultural construction of

218. Stanton et al., *History of Woman Suffrage*, 1:116.
219. See Harriet A. Jacobs, *Incidents in the Life of a Slave Girl*, ed. Jean Fagan Yellin (1861; Cambridge: Harvard University Press, 1987). For important commentaries, see Deborah M. Garfield and Rafia Zafar, eds., *Harriet Jacobs and Incidents in the Life of a Slave Girl* (Cambridge: Cambridge University Press, 1996).

Northern racism; at the apex of her literary fame, her outspoken truth to inner conviction so fundamentally challenged unspoken premises of America's culturally embedded racism that she lost friends and readers alike, and indeed suffered boycotts of her work that reduced her "income to a pittance."[220] And no aspect of Northern novelistic treatments of Southern slavery more provoked always intemperate proslavery advocates than treatment of the sexual exploitation by white men of black woman under slavery and the resulting place of the mulatto (including sexually valued mulatto women) in Southern culture. Louisa McCord thus exploded at Harriet Beecher Stowe's treatment of these issues in *Uncle Tom's Cabin* as "the most revolting at once to decency, truth, and probability," put "nauseously forward."[221] McCord's idealization of slavery drew upon values of intimate life: "the slave [as] almost a part of himself, a dependant to live and die with" (108), "relations of life, the nearest, the dearest" (111), a way of life that, echoing Calhoun's utilitarian rationale for slavery, "brings the greatest sum of good to the greatest number" (119). Dealing with the rampant sexual exploitation of black women outraged a mythology of race relations under slavery as "all of a softening character" (111).

The arresting importance of Harriet Jacobs's contribution to abolitionist feminism was her finding and articulating the moral voice to speak to white women (highly cognizant, as she was, of the differences in viewpoint of white and black women) from within the experience of a Southern ex-slave, black woman about the pivotal role abridgment of basic human rights of intimate association played in the dehumanization of African Americans. Lydia Maria Child certainly had earlier touched on these issues when she condemned Northern antimiscegenation laws (like that in Massachusetts) in terms of an illegitimate assertion of political power over an inalienable human right of choice in matters of love as fundamental to our moral powers as the choice or religion or religious identity: "the government ought not to be invested with power to control the affections, any more than the consciences of citizens. A man has at least as good a right to choose his wife, as he has to choose his religion."[222] In her 1839 petition to the Massachusetts legislature to repeal its law, Child similarly condemned the law "as obviously a violation of the great principles of freedom, on which our institutions rest, as a law prohibiting marriages between Catholics and

220. See Karcher, *The First Woman in the Republic*, 192; for further discussion, see ibid., 182–83, 191–92.
221. Louisa McCord, "Uncle Tom's Cabin," *Southern Quarterly Review*, n.s., 13 (January 1853), 104.
222. Child, *An Appeal in Favor of Americans Called Africans*, 196.

Protestants—and more absurd—inasmuch as religious opinions have a more important bearing on character and happiness, than gradations of complexion."[223] Such an abridgment of the basic human right to intimate life was, Child suggested, as dehumanizing an indignity to blacks as comparable restrictions were to Jews, an analogy between racism and anti-Semitism that Child, like Weld and Channing and other abolitionists (chapter 2), expressly made.[224] For Child, the issue of principle was the illegitimacy of any such coercion of the right of choice in intimate life (whether for or against such intimacy). She understandably assisted Harriet Jacobs in preparing her slave narrative for publication (including acting as its editor)[225] because she found in it a remarkable deepening of her earlier analysis of the dehumanizing consequences of such illegitimate coercion of intimate life, only here spoken in the morally authentic voice of a Southern ex-slave woman about coercion to engage in unwanted sexual relations.

Leading abolitionist thinkers like Weld and Channing as well as Elizabeth Chandler had prominently mentioned abridgment of basic human rights to family life as important aspects of the rights-denying evil of American slavery (including lack of recognition of marriage or control over children, and selling family members away from one another). And the Grimke sisters had afforded piercing insights into the role played by Southern white women in cruelly sustaining the injustice of slavery. Harriet Jacobs spoke, however, with the moral authority of an ex-slave who had found morally independent voice; she raised unspoken and unspeakable matters of sexual exploitation under slavery and thus brought to consciousness and public discussion and debate the morally corrupt American political epistemology of race and gender that had long been permitted unjustly to silence such debate. Harriet Jacobs took as her objective bringing these issues to public debate: "to arouse the women of the North to a realizing sense of the condition of two millions of women at the South, still in bondage, suffering what I suffered, and most of them far worse" (1). Lydia Maria Child in her introduction frontally addressed accusations "of indecorum for presenting these pages to the public" (3) by observing that "[t]his peculiar phase of Slavery has generally been kept veiled" and that "the public ought to be made acquainted with its monstrous features," and "will-

223. See Milton Meltzer and Patricia G. Holland, eds., *Lydia Maria Child Selected Letters, 1817–1880* (Amherst: University of Massachusetts Press, 1982), 111.
224. See Meltzer and Holland, *Lydia Maria Child Selected Letters*, 483.
225. For fuller discussion, see Jean Fagan Yellin, "Introduction" to Harriet A. Jacobs, *Incidents in the Life of a Slave Girl*, ed. Jean Fagan Yellin (1861; Cambridge: Harvard University Press, 1987), xviii–xxv.

ingly [undertaking] the responsibility of presenting them with the veil withdrawn" (4).

The slave narrative of Harriet Jacobs told the story, under the pseudonym Linda Brent, of the indignities she suffered under slavery, her moral revolt against them (leading to her hiding for seven years in a small garret), and her eventual escape North to freedom. Jacobs's narrative has been carefully studied by literary critics as the contribution it was to the literary reconstruction of African American womanhood.[226] My interest in the narrative is in the way it explored in various dimensions the centrality of the abridgment of the basic human right of intimate life to the dehumanization of Linda Brent both as an African American and as a woman.[227] Three dimensions of such abridgment are worthy of note: (1) the frustration of Brent's choice of a black husband, (2) the demand of her white, married master, Dr. Flint, that she become his mistress, and her resistance to this demand by seeking the protection of a white lover, with whom she had several children, and (3) her struggle to assert control over her children against laws and practices that deprived her of such control. All these struggles centered on Linda Brent's resistance to the unwanted sexual advances of her master, Dr. Flint.

Brent's first struggle with Dr. Flint was over his refusal to allow her to marry the free black man she loved and who loved her. Brent "loved him with all the ardor of a young girl's first love" (37), and she struggled to realize "this love-dream" (38). Dr. Flint categorically refused to acknowledge her love or right to love, indeed struck her in rage and threatened killing her when she stated her love (39–40). Flint refused to sell Brent to her lover, and she knew their love was impossible: "the lamp of hope had gone out" (42); she despaired of the human need for "something to love" (42). Flint "had blighted the prospects of my youth, and made my life a desert" (52).

Brent's second struggle was against Flint's demand that she become his mistress. Jacobs described the world of the fifteen-year-old, slave girl as being "reared in an atmosphere of licentiousness and fear" (51), "that cage of obscene birds" (52), one in which "[w]omen are considered of no value, unless they continually increase their owner's stock. They are put on a par with animals" (49). Brent struggled against this background as it was embodied for her in Dr. Flint's attempt to reduce

226. See, for example, Hazel V. Carby, *Reconstructing Womanhood: The Emergence of the Afro-American Woman Novelist* (New York: Oxford University Press, 1987), 47–61.
227. Cf. Yellin, *Women and Sisters*, 77–96.

her to its terms, to serve his sexual and reproductive aims as a man and slave master. "[L]iberty," Jacobs wrote, "is more valuable than life," which she defined as people coming "to understand their own capabilities, and exert themselves to become men and women" (43). For Linda Brent, liberty had come to mean freedom to love on her own self-authenticating terms, which were certainly not the dehumanizing terms of Dr. Flint, who had frustrated the great love of her youth. To resist Flint on her own moral terms was to resist her dehumanization, to assert her right, as a person, to love. Brent's moral terms were, Jacobs insisted, not unreasonably those of a young black woman "prematurely knowing, concerning the evil ways of the world" (54). They were certainly not the terms of sexuality of white women of the North "whose purity has been sheltered from childhood, who have been free to choose the objects of [their] affections, whose homes are protected by law" (54). Brent acted "with deliberate calculation" (54) reasonably to defend herself against Dr. Flint's demands on moral terms that would dignify her right of choice in matters of love. In order to protect herself from Dr. Flint and the children she might have had with him (who would be "owned by my old tyrant" [55]), she sought protection and love (a "tender feeling crept into my heart" [54]) in a liaison with an unmarried white man, Mr. Sands, "a man of more generosity and feeling than my master" (55) who would, Brent expected, eventually buy her freedom. In a world of limited choices, Jacobs defended her choice as the girl Linda Brent in terms of a not unreasonable way to retain self-respect: "It seems less degrading to give one's self, than to submit to compulsion. There is something akin to freedom in having a lover who has no control over you, except that which he gains by kindness and attachment" (55). Jacobs acknowledged: "I know I did wrong. . . . Still, in looking back, calmly, on the events of my life, I feel that the slave woman ought not to be judged by the same standard as others" (56).

Brent's third struggle with Dr. Flint was over the children she had with Mr. Sands. The children were the property of Dr. Flint, who refused to sell Linda or the children to freedom. To resist such claims over her, Linda contemplated escape, but she would not escape alone: "it was more for my helpless children than for myself that I longed for freedom" (89); "my life was bound up in my children" (101). The event that decided Linda for escape was learning that Dr. Flint intended to bring her children to the plantation "to be 'broke in'" (94). To obviate this, Linda escaped from Dr. Flint, who thereafter sold her children to Mr. Sands, who restored them to Linda's grandmother. Linda remained hidden in a garret in her grandmother's house for seven years, where she could see her children. Eventually, she escaped North, where she was reunited with her children in freedom.

The struggle of Harriet Jacobs centered on her claims as a person for the right to love and her resistance to a tyrant's denial of this right. When she came to leave her garret after seven years, she reflected on the loves and hopes for love that framed and sustained her moral struggle in that home: "where I had been sheltered so long by the dear old grandmother; where I had dreamed my first young dream of love; and where, after that had faded away, my children came to twine themselves so closely around my desolate heart" (155). Her narrative tells a story moving from slavery to freedom not only literally but as a humanizing narrative of a struggle from dehumanizing moral slavery, in the abolitionist feminist sense, to moral freedom. It is the narrative of both a woman and a black, and it eloquently suggests elements of moral slavery common to both, in particular, the dehumanizing significance of the abridgment of the self-authenticating human right to love on one's own moral terms, not on the sexualized or reproductive terms that make one solely the instrument of the interests of others.

Jacobs's narrative dealt frankly with issues of sexuality as they arose under slavery and the racist conception of gender that sustained it in ways that more recent studies have confirmed.[228] Black and white women under slavery were not only, as Sojourner Truth argued, subjected to different standards of frailty versus strength, but to different standards of sexuality. Jacobs did not argue that white standards of sexuality were wrong; indeed, as we have seen, she conceded that Brent's violation of them was wrong. But, she did argue, as Lincoln had argued about slavery,[229] that her conduct though wrong was not, in light of the injustices of her situation, reasonably held culpable: "the slave woman ought not to be judged by the same standard as others" (56). Jacobs thus found a way to address the ethical imagination of

---

228. See, for example, Deborah Gray White, *Ar'n't I a Woman? Female Slaves in the Plantation South* (New York: W. W. Norton, 1985). For related studies, see Anne Firor Scott, *The Southern Lady: From Pedestal to Politics, 1830–1930* (Chicago: University of Chicago Press, 1970); Elizabeth Fox-Genovese, *Within the Plantation Household: Black and White Women in the Old South* (Chapel Hill: University of North Carolina Press, 1988); Jean E. Friedman, *The Enclosed Garden: Women and Community in the Evangelical South, 1830–1900* (Chapel Hill: University of North Carolina Press, 1985); Drew Gilpin Faust, *Mothers of Invention: Women of the Slaveholding South in the American Civil War* (Chapel Hill: University of North Carolina Press, 1996); Brenda E. Stevenson, *Life in Black and White: Family and Community in the Slave South* (New York: Oxford University Press, 1996).

229. For fuller discussion, see Richards, *Conscience and the Constitution*, 26n., 62, 110–11.

white women, while remaining quite self-conscious of the differences in viewpoint of white and black women and about the special subordination experienced by black women. As she observed elsewhere, "[s]lavery is terrible for men; but is far more terrible for women" (77). She had in mind the sexual tyranny of Dr. Flint, the struggle against which defined the moral meaning, the remarkable integrity, of her life.

That her argument may have a wider significance than Jacobs herself claimed for it is suggested by her treatment of white woman slaveowners. The Grimke sisters had probed this issue from their own perspective as former slaveowners; Jacobs examined the role of slaveowning women from the perspective of the slave. Her portrait of Dr. Flint's wife explored "her constant suspicion and malevolence" (31). Herself pridefully virtuous on her idealized pedestal of Southern womanhood, Mrs. Flint denied any virtue to a woman slave; indeed, "[i]t is deemed a crime in her to wish to be virtuous" (31). The basis of marriage in a slaveholding family was hypocrisy and denial, treating white women contemptuously as pets on a very tight leash: "[t]he secrets of slavery are concealed like those of the Inquisition" (35). Echoing similar observations of Sarah Grimke, Jacobs had pointed to Southern institutions of political terror that silenced reasonable debate and discussion of issues of justice and the public good (63–67), such as any acknowledgment of the sexual exploitation incident to American slavery. To Brent's certain knowledge, Dr. Flint was "the father of eleven slaves" (35), but the reality was known and not known; as Mrs. Chesnut confided to her diary: "every lady tells you who is the father of all the Mulatto children in every body's household, but those in her own, she seems to think drop from the clouds or pretends so to think."[230] Indeed, slave women, themselves victimized by slaveowners like Dr. Flint, were jealously attacked and denigrated by slave-owning wives like Mrs. Flint. White slaveholding women themselves sustained this mythology by falsely idealizing their virtue and denigrating that of slaves, whose unjust situation, on Jacobs's view, made such virtue unreasonably difficult; thus, "this bad institution [slavery] deadens the moral sense, even in white women, to a fearful extent" (36). On Jacobs's analysis, white women as slaveowners wielded unjust power on the basis of race and white womanhood, suggesting a racialized conception of gender common to the injustice of American racism and sexism. Thus, Jacobs laid the foundation for later antiracist and antisexist analysis of the role that an unjustly enforceable sectarian political

230. See C. Vann Woodward and Elisabeth Muhlenfeld, *The Private Mary Chesnut: The Unpublished Civil War Diaries* (New York: Oxford University Press, 1984), 42.

epistemology of race and gender, based on abridgment of basic human rights, played in the dehumanization not only of black but of white women as well. Her work suggests that analogies between race and gender risk omitting black women, and that the normative and explanatory power of a conception of moral slavery (of the sort developed in this book) is the way in which it is structurally attentive to this problem (insisting, as it does, on the role of an unjustly racialized conception of gender in the common evils of racism and sexism).

4   Suffrage Feminism: Struggle, Triumph, Collapse

A bolitionist feminism, as we have so far studied it, was a reasonably coherent and, for its time, radical movement of public criticism of American slavery, racism, the subjection of women, and sexism. Its critical moral resources included the theory of moral slavery that its proponents developed as a common basis for the criticism of all these institutions and practices. To the extent there was an important division among abolitionist feminists in the antebellum period, it was between Garrisonian moral abolitionists like Lucretia Mott and political abolitionists like Elizabeth Stanton. But the difference was muted during the antebellum period; both moral and political abolitionists largely concurred on the Declaration of Sentiments and resolutions of the Seneca Falls Convention of 1848. Only Stanton's resolution calling for voting rights was the subject of any disagreement, and it was approved by a small majority. We turn now to the Civil War and Reconstruction Amendments and the associated crisis of internal divisions within abolitionist feminism leading to suffrage feminism, the eventual victory of suffrage feminism (after its repudiation of much of abolitionist feminism), and the collapse of feminism as a seriously rights-based reform movement until the rebirth of second wave feminism in the 1960s (the subject of the next chapter). The main feature of our study will be an interpretation of deep internal flaws within suffrage feminism that explain both its political success and its critical moral failures, specifically, its abandonment of core elements of abolitionist feminism, such as its commitment to the argument for toleration, and associated concerns with antiracism and protection of basic rights like rights of intimate association.

A radical movement like abolitionist feminism understandably remained reasonably cohesive during a period when women suffered under many disadvantages as public, let alone political actors (lacking, as they did, not only firm guarantees of basic rights, but voting rights and economic independence). Some progress was made on the distinctively feminist agenda of abolitionist feminists (for example, the success of Stanton and Anthony in 1860, with the nation on the verge of civil war, in securing amendments enlarging the scope of New York's Married Women's Property Act), but most of the agenda, as stated in the resolutions of the Seneca Falls Convention, was, by the political common sense of the day, still radical. Political abolitionists, always happy to have the support of abolitionist feminists when they needed it, saw no political need to reciprocate, and some political danger in reciprocating. The increasing success of political abolitionism was a tribute to this strategy, which included marginalizing both the antiracist and antisexist strands of abolitionist feminist argument. The growth and political success in 1860 of the Republican Party turned on the way it forged an American public opinion that linked the rights of free speech and free labor of white Americans and the antislavery rights underlying abolitionism.[1] Such antislavery rights, as Lincoln himself made clear in the Lincoln-Douglas debates of 1858,[2] did not question, but impliedly endorsed the widespread American racist assumption that African Americans, when emancipated, should not join the political community on equal terms. A political movement whose success depended on endorsing racism would hardly endanger its ap-

1. See, for example, William E. Gienapp, *The Origins of the Republican Party, 1852–1856* (New York: Oxford University Press, 1987); Eric Foner, *Free Soil, Free Labor: The Ideology of the Republican Party before the Civil War* (New York: Oxford University Press, 1970).

2. Lincoln thought it important to refute Justice Taney's interpretation in *Dred Scott* that the Declaration of Independence could not be reasonably interpreted to apply to blacks. See Abraham Lincoln, Fifth Joint Debate, Galesburg, 7 October 1858, in Robert W. Johannsen, *The Lincoln-Douglas Debates of 1858* (New York: Oxford University Press, 1965), 219–20; ibid., Seventh Joint Debate, Alton, 15 October 1858, 304. But he stated Taney's views excluding African Americans from citizenship "without making any complaint of it at all." See ibid., 302. Lincoln knew that Taney's history on this point was wrong as well, but made little of it because he agreed with its normative recommendation. Though states had constitutional power to make blacks citizens of the state and of the nation, "I should be opposed to the exercise of it." See ibid., Fourth Joint Debate, Charleston, 18 September 1858, in 198. Taney offered a racial conception of American national identity as constitutionally compelled, Lincoln as permitted and desirable.

peal by questioning what seemed even more unquestioned and unquestionable, namely, American sexism.[3]

Antebellum common sense was, however, not the measure of America's sense of its moral and constitutional responsibilities in the wake of the Civil War. The Civil War had been fought originally by the North to defend the Union against the moral and constitutional illegitimacy of southern secession[4] and not to secure the abolition of slavery; Lincoln himself insisted on this very point in his 1862 letter to Horace Greeley.[5] But as the Civil War wore on, the kinds of terrible human losses that the conflict required called for a moral justification more able and worthy to sustain the will and morale of the North.[6]

Lincoln, after various attempts to secure some form of voluntary compensated abolition with colonization of freedmen abroad, came to regard immediate uncompensated emancipation as necessary to win the war. He defended the Emancipation Proclamation in such terms; it had stimulated the presence of blacks (both free and slave) in the Union armies, and that presence was important to the increasingly successful war effort.[7] By the end of the war, most slaves had been effectively emancipated, and Lincoln recognized that only the constitutional abolition of slavery would and did give the war an enduring moral and constitutional meaning.[8] The Civil War was to be regarded as a revolutionary battle for human rights, and the constitutional abolition of slavery must be the symbol of that moral achievement.

3. Consistent with this way of thinking and probative of its conventionality, Horace Bushnell argued that the entirely proper case for the abolition of slavery should not and did not apply to reforms, like feminism, "that go against nature." See Horace Bushnell, *Woman Suffrage; The Reform against Nature* (New York: Charles Scribner and Co., 1869), 30.

4. See Abraham Lincoln, "First Inaugural Address," 4 March 1861, in *Abraham Lincoln: Speeches and Writings*, ed. Don E. Fehrenbacher (New York: Library of America, 1989), 2: 215–24.

5. See Lincoln to Horace Greeley, 22 August 1862, in *Speeches and Writings*, 2:357–58. "I would save the Union. I would save it the shortest way under the Constitution. . . . If I could save the Union without freeing *any* slave I would do it, and if I could save it by freeing *all* the slaves I would do it; and if I could save it by freeing some and leaving others alone I would also do that." Ibid., 358.

6. See, for example, Lewis Tappan, "The War, Its Cause and Remedy: Immediate Emancipation: The Only Wise and Safe Mode," in *Union Pamphlets of the Civil War, 1861–1865*, ed. Frank Freidel (New York, 1861; Cambridge: Harvard University Press, Belknap Press, 1967), 102–17; Orestes Augustus Brownson, "Brownson on the Rebellion" (St. Louis, 1861), ibid., 128–65.

7. See Lincoln to James C. Conkling, 26 August 1863, *Speeches and Writings*, 2: 495–99.

8. See Abraham Lincoln, "Annual Message to Congress," 6 December 1864, in *Speeches and Writings*, 2:657–58; "Second Inaugural Address," 4 May 1865, ibid., 2:686–87.

The Civil War has been termed the Second American Revolution and, like the first American Revolution, it was a revolution over constitutional and moral ideals. It required, like its predecessor, a constitutional order that would conserve its astonishing accomplishments in a legacy of principle for posterity. Prior to the Civil War, a widely recognized sharp distinction was made between the question of the abstract requirements of justice (namely, that slavery was morally wrong, and should not exist) and the question of the morally tolerable and reasonable burdens that could be imposed on the South to abolish slavery. On this view, the institution of slavery had been foisted on the South by history; it had not been adopted by the present generation, many of whom would not have adopted it if adoption had been an open question.[9]

After the Civil War, the distinction between these questions had been subverted by new moral realities. The slaves had been emancipated and, more importantly from the vantage of the emerging conception of Union moral identity, many of them had fought well and nobly in a civil war to save the Union. In response to objections to his emancipation policy, Lincoln made quite clear the new moral weights black and white Americans now deserved in light of the great moral testing that was this civil war over national identity:

> You say you will not fight to free negroes. Some of them seem willing to fight for you. . . . If they stake their lives for us, they must be prompted by the strongest motive—even the promise of freedom. And the promise being made, must be kept. . . . Peace does not appear so distant as it did. I hope it will come soon, and come to stay . . . then, there will be some black men who can remember that, with silent tongue, and clenched teeth, and steady eye, and well-poised bayonet, they have helped mankind on to this great consummation; while, I fear, there will be some white ones, unable to forget that, with malignant heart, and deceitful speech, they have strove to hinder it.[10]

The injustice of slavery was no longer an abstract question. The public conscience of the nation was, for the first time in our constitutional history, alive to the claims of black Americans and no longer reasonably bound to the demands of the South. Now, in light of the de facto wreckage of American slavery, the demands of justice required action. America faced in 1865 the question of how the terms of political community and national unity and identity were to be understood in the light of the antebellum debates, the Civil War, and the emancipation

9. Lincoln embraced this point in 1854. See Abraham Lincoln, "Speech on Kansas-Nebraska Act," 16 October 1854, *Speeches and Writings*, 2:316.
10. Lincoln to James C. Conkling, 26 August 1863, ibid., 2:498–99.

of the millions of blacks that had been held in slavery in the South.

The antebellum mainstream understanding was reasonably clear, and clearly racist. Chief Justice Roger Taney had given an authoritative interpretation of American national identity in *Dred Scott v. Sanford.* Blacks were "beings of an inferior order, and altogether unfit to associate with the white race, either in social or political relations; and so far inferior, that they had no rights which the white man was bound to respect; . . . "[11] Blacks accordingly could not be citizens (404–5). Correspondingly, Taney argued that the words of the Declaration of Independence ("all men are created equal [and] endowed with certain unalienable rights") "were not intended" to include "the enslaved African race" (410). Both of Taney's originalist claims were historically doubtful: the dissent noted that blacks had voted in states at the time of the 1787 Convention (572–74, 576) and that the Declaration of Independence, understood as a statement of long-term ambition and aspiration, could reasonably be taken to mean what it said (574–75).[12] Lincoln knew both these claims were false, but, as we saw earlier, agreed with Taney that African Americans should not, after emancipation, be included in the American community on equal terms.

This antebellum world of racist complacency was shattered by the Civil War and could not be a reasonable guide to the reconstruction of American constitutionalism in its wake. Northern public opinion was in a state of volatile flux on fundamental questions like racism and its place in American public life in a way it had never been before. The abolitionist movement, including even notorious antiracist and antisexist radical disunionist abolitionists like William Lloyd Garrison and Wendell Phillips (let alone the black abolitionist Frederick Douglass), had become leaders of a northern public opinion increasingly favorable to both abolition by constitutional amendment and some steps to include African Americans in the constitutional community on equal terms (thus, questioning American racism).[13] Abolitionist feminists understandably sensed new possibilities in this volatile political environment and brought their energies to bear on shaping its

11. See *Dred Scott v. Sanford,* 60 U.S. (19 How.) 393, 407 (1857).

12. But see, for a discussion of the conflicting Founders' denotations in the North and South, Paul Finkelman, "The Constitution and the Intentions of the Framers: The Limits of Historical Analysis," *University of Pittsburgh Law Review* 50 (1989): 349, 392–93. Finkelman questions whether such narrow originalism was in any case the appropriate interpretive attitude to be taken in *Dred Scott.* Id. at 393–94.

13. See James M. McPherson, *The Struggle for Equality: Abolitionists and the Negro in the Civil War and Reconstruction* (Princeton: Princeton University Press, 1964), 34–36, 260–62, 266, 268–72, 285.

moral direction to question, on the same platform of human rights, American racism and sexism. If Americans could reexamine so fundamental an assumption of their historical common life as racism on grounds of human rights, why not sexism as well?

No abolitionist feminist was more alive to these possibilities than the leading antebellum political abolitionist feminist, Elizabeth Stanton; no abolitionist feminist had higher hopes or experienced more poignant despair upon disappointment than she. We need to understand both if we are to make interpretive sense of the tragic collapse of abolitionist into suffrage feminism and its long-term deleterious consequences for American feminism as a seriously principled rights-based movement.

The growing public appeal of the Republican Party was a triumph for political abolitionism, and Stanton understandably took this achievement as a challenge to shape political abolitionism in an abolitionist feminist direction. In May, 1860, six months after John Brown's raid on Harper's Ferry, Stanton addressed the annual meeting of the Garrisonian American Anti-Slavery Society and clearly interpreted the case for the abolition of slavery as one applicable to both race and gender.[14] Stanton recalled the roles of both Garrison and Phillips in challenging the exclusion of women from the World Anti-Slavery Convention in London in 1840, and their later elaboration of abolitionist principles to include both blacks and women (80–81). The mission of the abolitionist movement, accordingly, "is not to the African slave alone, but to the slaves of custom, creed, and sex, as well" (81). She argued that since the abolitionist movement rested on a moral judgment (namely, the incommensurable wrong of slavery), women had understandably come to play a central role in that movement, for they can better empathetically make the relevant moral judgment, turning, as it does, on "the feelings of those who are born to contempt, to inferiority, to degradation" (83). White men, Stanton opined, can "take only an objective view" of "the general features of that infernal system" (82–83); because such men are "a privileged class" (83), they find it more difficult to make moral judgments that turn on the degradation central to moral slavery. In contrast, "woman [is] more fully identified with the slave than man can possibly be," for she, sharing his moral slavery, "can take the subjective view" (83), that is, understand from within her own moral experience the kinds of degradation of moral personal-

14. See Elizabeth Stanton, "Speech to the Anniversary of the American Anti-Slavery Society," in *The Elizabeth Cady Stanton–Susan B. Anthony Reader: Correspondence, Writings, Speeches,* ed. Ellen Carol DuBois, rev. ed. (Boston: Northeastern University Press, 1992), 79–85.

ity central to the wrongness of slavery. Blacks and women share a common rights-denying indignity:

> There is a Procrustean bedstead ever ready for them, body and soul, and all mankind stand on the alert to restrain their impulses, check their aspirations, fetter their limbs, lest, in their freedom and strength, in their full development, they should take an even platform with proud man himself. . . . The badge of degradation is the skin and sex. (83)

Stanton focused, in particular, on the degradation of black women under slavery in various rights-denying dimensions:

> [They are] raised for the purposes of lust . . . sold on the auction-block. . . . For them there is no Sabbath, no Jesus, no Heaven, no hope, no holy mission of wife and mother, no privacy of home, nothing sacred to look for. . . . And these are the daughters and sisters of the first men in the Southern states . . . selling their own flesh on the auction-block. (84)

Jacobs could not have put it better. By the end of Stanton's speech, her emphasis on the sexual abuse and mental crippling of women under slavery left it unclear whether she was talking about black women or white. Consistent with the abolitionist feminist theory of moral slavery, her audience could plausibly have taken her to mean both.

Elizabeth Cady Stanton and Susan B. Anthony saw the Civil War in different lights. Anthony, a Quaker pacifist, opposed the war in principle, but she also thought it would interrupt and reverse the progress that had been made in women's rights. Stanton, a political abolitionist, saw women's activism in support of a just war as an opportunity. If women supported the war, such contributions would be rewarded with equal rights, including suffrage.[15] Stanton's hopeful prophecy may have proved false in her circumstances, but it was by no means an argument without principled appeal and even force (for example, in the circumstances of World War I, war work by American women was appealed to by President Wilson in urging Congress to ratify the Nineteenth Amendment[16]). As a matter of strategy, Stanton accordingly was willing not to press the issue of women's rights, but to support the war and emancipation; Anthony doubted that such activism, however otherwise justified, would be rewarded in the way Stanton supposed. While Stanton and Anthony disagreed on this strategic judgment, they were, as abolitionists, allied on the war work appropriate to women, namely, to push for emancipation in the political arena.[17]

15. See Elisabeth Griffith, *In Her Own Right: The Life of Elizabeth Cady Stanton* (New York: Oxford University Press, 1984), 109–10.
16. See Eleanor Flexner, *Centuries of Struggle: The Woman's Rights Movement in the United States*, rev. ed. (1959; Cambridge: Harvard University Press, Belknap Press, 1975), 321–22.
17. See Griffith, *In Her Own Right*, 110–12.

Stanton and Anthony decided to create a political organization for Northern women.[18] In March 1863, their "An Appeal to the Women of the Republic" issued a call to "determine the final settlement of the war."[19] At a gathering of interested women in New York City in May 1863, the meeting decided to collect one million petition signatures in support of the Thirteenth Amendment that would constitutionally guarantee the freedom of American slaves. Stanton's thinking about moral slavery was in evidence in the resolution narrowly adopted by the meeting: "There never can be a true peace in this republic until the civil and political rights of all citizens of African descent and all women are practically established."[20] After a two-day meeting, Stanton was elected president of the newly formed National Woman's Loyal League (among others, Angelina Grimke Weld was a member). By the time it disbanded in August 1864, the Loyal League had gathered an unprecedented four hundred thousand signatures in support of the Thirteenth Amendment. Senators Sumner and Henry Wilson assured the League that their petition campaign had crucially assisted the struggle to secure congressional passage of the Thirteenth Amendment, which was ratified in 1865.[21]

The Reconstruction Amendments are best understood both historically and constitutionally as a set of ramifying principles all interpretive of the central judgment of political morality at the heart of the abolitionist movement, namely, the fundamental moral wrongness of slavery because it abridges fundamental human rights.[22] On this view, the Thirteenth Amendment's abolition of slavery and involuntary servitude were not merely negative prohibitions on certain institutions and practices. The amendment also affirmed the constitutionally enforceable judgment of political morality that made sense of these prohibitions, namely, a judgment about the substance, nature, and weight of the inalienable human rights of all persons subject to political power in the United States.[23] Abolitionist feminists played the central public role

18. I draw here upon accounts of these events in Flexner, *Century of Struggle*, 108–12; McPherson, *The Struggle for Equality*, 125–27; Griffith, *In Her Own Right*, 111–13.

19. See Griffith, *In Her Own Right*, 112.

20. Ibid., 112.

21. See McPherson, *The Struggle for Equality*, 125–27.

22. For historical support for this view, see Jacobus tenBroek, *Equal under Law* (New York: Collier, 1965); Harold M. Hyman, *A More Perfect Union: The Impact of the Civil War and Reconstruction on the Constitution* (New York: Knopf, 1973); Harold M. Hyman and William M. Wiecek, *Equal Justice under Law: Constitutional Development, 1835–1975* (New York: Harper & Row, 1982).

23. See, in general, George H. Hoemann, *What Hath God Wrought: The Embodiment of Freedom in the Thirteenth Amendment* (New York: Garland Publishing, Inc., 1987).

they did in securing support for and ratification of the Thirteenth Amendment because they interpreted this moral judgment, as both their theory and practice made repeatedly clear, in light of their conception of moral slavery. The background of the Reconstruction Amendments in antebellum debate, including radical abolitionist moral and constitutional theory, suggests good reasons in support of their interpretive conviction.

Lincoln's famous 1864 letter on the wrongness of slavery memorialized for the nation moral views central to the public mind deliberating on the constitutional abolition of slavery. One sentence in that letter, echoing a similar passage in Channing's great essay,[24] was conspicuously cited by proponents of the Thirteenth Amendment in the Congressional debates: "If slavery is not wrong, nothing is wrong." Lincoln referred to the antislavery views thus expressed as "my primary abstract judgment on the moral question of slavery," and members of Congress thought of it similarly as expressing a "philosophical truth."[25]

That abstract truth was a natural moral judgment about the origination of natural rights in moral personality and the weight such claims should enjoy in legitimate political argument. It was a truth central to American revolutionary constitutionalism: "Did not our fathers declare that [certain] rights were inalienable?"[26] Democratically legitimate power cannot for this reason include the "right of one people to enslave another people to whom nature has given equal rights of freedom."[27] Such distortions of legitimate democracy were "conceived more than thirty years ago, and John C. Calhoun was present at its conception."[28] Its basis was "tyrannic and despotic power" of the sort "exercised abroad for the purpose of restricting liberty of opinion . . . where, . . .

24. "Is there any moral truth more deeply rooted in us, than that such a degradation [slavery] would be an infinite wrong? And, if this impression be a delusion, on what single moral conviction can we rely?" William Ellery Channing, *Slavery*, in *The Works of William E. Channing* (1836; New York: Burt Franklin 1970), 692–93.

25. Lincoln to Albert G. Hodges, 4 April 1864, *Speeches and Writings*, 2:585. For citations to this statement by Lincoln, see Representative Ashley, *Congressional Globe*, 38th Congress, 2d sess., 1864–65, January 6, 1865, 138: "Mr. Speaker, *'If slavery is not wrong, nothing is wrong.'* Thus simply and truthfully has spoken our worthy Chief Magistrate." See also Representative Smith, ibid., January 12, 1865, 237: "Mr. Speaker, in my judgment there never was a sounder or a more philosophical truth communicated by any man than that of the President of the United States, when he wrote to Colonel Hodges, of Frankfort, Kentucky, that 'if slavery is not wrong, nothing is wrong.'"

26. See Representative Farnsworth, *The Congressional Globe*, 38th Congress, 2d sess. 1864–65, January 10, 1865, 200.

27. See Representative Davis, *The Congressional Globe*, 38th Congress, 2d sess. 1864–65, January 7, 1865, 154.

28. Ibid.

the despotism of Church and State attempted to control the minds of men."[29]

The abstract moral judgment underlying the Thirteenth Amendment expressed the truth, following Locke, that persons have inalienable human rights; the legitimacy of political power must be tested against respect for such rights, and revolution is justified against forms of political power that fail to respect such rights. Locke's argument for human rights and associated limits on political power must be construed within the structure of his seminal defense of an inalienable right to conscience (chapter 2); his argument for toleration called for skepticism about the uses of political power to self-entrench hierarchies of "natural" privilege that deprived persons of their reasonable moral freedom as democratic equals. All these elements of Lockean skepticism were crucially in play in the most philosophically elaborate defense of the Thirteenth Amendment, that made by Representative James Wilson introducing the amendment on the floor of the House of Representatives on March 19, 1864.[30]

Wilson began and ended his address by appealing to the great change in American public opinion stimulated by the Civil War: a "public opinion now existing in this country in opposition to this power [that] is the result of slavery overleaping itself, rather than of the determination of freemen to form it" (1199). The Civil War "awakened to its true and real life the moral sense of the nation" (1200), a sense that had lain dormant for "half a century . . . when slavery controlled the national mind" (1201). What we, in contrast to the Founders, have learned both from the antebellum controversies and from the Civil War is the imperative moral need for revolutionary political action against slavery: "We see that the death [of slavery] can only be accomplished by an executioner. Slavery will not kill itself" (1203).

The nation, in fighting a just civil war now seen to be essentially against slavery, had recovered, as a people, the revolutionary political morality of the American Revolution that justified war on grounds of defending human rights (1203). The task now was to forge a constitutionalism that would memorialize and give adequate institutional expression to "the grand volcanic action that is upheaving the great moral ideas which underlie the Republic" (1203). The right to revolution was, in Lockean political theory, centrally linked to the right to conscience because only the required guarantees for the moral independence of

---

29. Ibid., 155 (citing examples of Holland, Spain, and Britain).

30. See Representative James Wilson, *Congressional Globe*, 38th Congress, 1st Sess, March 19, 1864, 1199–1206.

critical conscience would enable it to make the kinds of judgments on the basis of which the right to revolution might legitimately be asserted; as Locke put the point, "I my self can only be Judge in my own Conscience."[31] The abridgment by the state of the rights to conscience and free speech would allow it illegitimately to determine what counted as valid or proper criticism of the state or, even worse, to set the critical intellectual and ethical standards of public reason. In effect, dominant political powers would self-entrench an epistemology that would immunize its powers from the kind of independent critical assessment required by the tests in terms of which the legitimacy of any political power should be assessed, namely, respect for rights and pursuit of the public interest. Thus the right to revolution might be claimed for the abridgment of the right to conscience.

The normative heart of Wilson's argument of revolutionary justification for the Civil War was thus put in terms of the illegitimate abridgment of the inalienable rights of conscience, free speech, and assembly (1202). From the contractualist perspective of Lockean political theory that Wilson assumed, the abridgment of such rights—at the very core of the inalienable human rights that government was instituted to secure—deprived political power of legitimacy, and justified the right to revolution in order to secure those rights in a form of constitutionalism that would, at a minimum, better protect them. Americans in 1864–65 were thus, on grounds of abstract natural right, at least as well justified as the American revolutionaries of 1776 in rejecting the illegitimate political claims made on behalf of the Southern slave power, revolting against such power, and forging new constitutional forms adequate to their just grievances.

The abstract normative judgment of the intrinsic wrongness of slavery, premised on rights-based premises of American revolutionary constitutionalism, reflected and drew upon the most radical forms of antebellum abolitionist moral and constitutional theory. The moral theory was as much antiracist as antislavery, contemplating, as the Reconstruction Amendments clearly did, full inclusion of African Americans in the American community on terms of equality. However, unlike some radical abolitionists (like Garrison), the speech of Wilson and others in the Reconstruction Congress supported the constitutional rebirth of American revolutionary constitutionalism in the terms of political abolitionism, not moral pacifism. The Civil War was to be justified as a rights-based use of legitimate coercion, and the constitutional

31. See Locke, *Second Treatise of Government,* 300 (sec. 21); see also 398 (sec. 168), 422–23 (sec. 209), 445 (sec. 242). For commentary, see Richards, *Foundations,* 78–97.

amendments under discussion were to assure the central role of re-spect for inalienable human rights as constitutionally enforceable tests for valid laws. The form of antebellum political abolitionism closest to the mission and purposes of the amendments under discussion was one of the most radical forms of abolitionist constitutional theory: radical constitutional antislavery.[32] Radical constitutional antislavery inter-preted the antebellum Constitution to forbid slavery both at the na-tional and state levels (moderate constitutional antislavery, in contrast, applied the prohibition only at the national, not the state levels[33]). It did so by construing any text apparently to the contrary strictly in favor of natural rights, and by ignoring contrary history as irrelevant in light of the text thus interpreted. Whatever the implausibility of radical constitutional antislavery as a way of interpreting the antebellum Con-stitution, the centrality it accorded rights-based political theory in constitutional interpretation fit the context and ambitions of the Reconstruction Amendments in a way its interpretation of antebellum constitutionalism did not.[34] Both the text and history of the Reconstruc-tion Amendments interpretively call for arguments about the nature and weight of inalienable human rights to play a central role in the constitutional interpretation of the legitimacy of political power.

Appeal to such arguments challenges, just as the relevant forms of radical abolitionism certainly did, conventional and historically rooted institutions like Southern chattel slavery and racism. As the antebellum radical abolitionist constitutionalist Joel Tiffany put the point, "to admit the right of the people to establish a government destructive of the rights of man, is to deny the *inalienability* of those rights, which is to deny the authority of the people to establish a government in defense of them";[35] accordingly, for Tiffany, both slavery and the racist exclusion of free blacks from the rights of citizens were illegitimate failures to extend to all who share the benefits and burdens of Ameri-can social co-operation "equal protection"[36] of basic human rights.[37] The measure of such rights, as tests of constitutional legitimacy, could not be what may have been the actual intentions of the American peo-ple in 1787 (for that might legitimate both slavery and racism), but

32. For fuller discussion of the main proponents of the view, see Richards, *Conscience and the Constitution,* 97–104.
33. Ibid., 95–97; see also ibid., 42–57.
34. Ibid., 134–48.
35. See Joel Tiffany, *A Treatise on the Unconstitutionality of American Slavery* (1849; Miami: Mnemosyne, 1969), 43.
36. Ibid., 87.
37. For Tiffany's arguments against slavery, see ibid., 23–32; for including blacks as citi-zens, see ibid., 92–97.

Lysander Spooner's insistence on "[t]he abstract intentions, or meaning, of the [rights-based] instrument itself."[38] To assess political power in this way was to test it against abstract rights-based principles that might challenge the legitimacy of quite widespread normative convictions that undermined respect for human rights; William Hosmer, echoing Channing and anticipating Lincoln, appealed to such higher law principles in 1852 to challenge racist tolerance of slavery: "[t]here either is no wrong, or slavery is wrong."[39] Once political power is subject to such demanding tests, arguments of principle might extend beyond the illegitimacy of chattel slavery and racism to include even more conventionally and historically rooted institutions and practices. In 1845, E. P. Hurlbut challenged, on such political abolitionist rights-based grounds, those American laws relating to women as inconsistent with proper respect for their inalienable human rights.[40]

Elizabeth Stanton was, as we have observed, remarkable among leading abolitionist feminists for her political abolitionism. Consistent with these convictions, she distinctively framed the 1848 Declaration of Sentiments of the Seneca Falls Convention in the terms of the rights-based revolutionary constitutionalism of the Declaration of Independence. Such convictions reasonably led Stanton, more than any abolitionist feminist of her generation (many of whom were Garrisonian pacifists), to embrace the rebirth of revolutionary constitutionalism in the Thirteenth Amendment as powerfully in service of abolitionism feminism. If such rebirth drew upon the rights-based principles of the most radical forms of antebellum abolitionist moral and constitutional theory, those principles applied (and indeed had been applied by radical abolitionists, including the abolitionist feminists) to condemn not only slavery and racism, but the subjection of women and sexism. The arguments of text and history that called for an appeal to abstract arguments of human rights in condemning slavery and racism surely should, on the same platform of human rights, embrace the aims of abolitionist feminism as well (including its central theory of moral slavery).

Stanton surely recognized that many of her contemporaries would not agree that abolitionist feminism afforded the best interpretation of the prohibition of slavery and involuntary servitude in the Thirteenth

38. See Lysander Spooner, *The Unconstitutionality of Slavery* (New York: Burt Franklin, 1860), 223.

39. See William Hosmer, *The Higher Law in Its Relations to Civil Government* (Auburn: Derby & Miller, 1852), 124.

40. See E. P. Hurlbut, *Essays on Human Rights and Their Political Guaranties*, 112–23, 145–72.

Amendment, or related constitutional amendments that might later be proposed and ratified. One Congressional proponent of the amendment thus enumerated basic inalienable rights to include "a man's right to himself, to his wife and children,"[41] a suggestion of natural property rights in one's wife that Stanton would surely have repudiated as inconsistent with women's moral personality as an independent source of claims of rights. What was important for Stanton was not that most people agreed with her interpretation in 1865, but that such an interpretation could reasonably be urged by abolitionist feminists as the most principled reading of such constitutional guarantees; this would afford solid constitutional support for continuing advocacy that might over time have as much impact on American public opinion about issues of women's rights as such antebellum abolitionist advocacy, on much less powerful historical and textual constitutional grounds, had had in moving the nation in an abolitionist direction. What Stanton found intolerable was the introduction into the *texts* of any proposed constitutional amendments of language that expressly excluded women from its terms.

The Thirteenth Amendment had been enthusiastically supported by Stanton and Anthony because its text and background were consistent with an abolitionist feminist interpretation. Both were stung with indignation when they learned that the Fourteenth Amendment would use, in section 2, the word "male" three times, associating voting rights with gender; with the word "male" thus placed, it might require another constitutional amendment to enfranchise women.[42] Stanton and Anthony organized a petition drive to oppose the amendment in its current form, but collected less than 3 percent of the number who had favored the Thirteenth Amendment (124–25). On similar grounds, they also later abortively opposed the Fifteenth Amendment, because it extended voting rights only to black men (134).

Stanton's unsuccessful opposition included elitist, nativist, impliedly racist appeals pointing to the enfranchisement of "all the lower stratas of manhood . . . , moulding to their untutored will the institutions of a mighty continent"[43] and quite explicitly racist appeals to white woman's fears of black male sexuality, querying from this perspective: "[h]ave

41. See Representative Farnsworth, *Congressional Globe*, 38th Cong., 2d sess., January 10, 1865, 200.

42. See Griffith, *In Her Own Right*, 123.

43. See Elizabeth Stanton, "Who Are Our Friends?" in *The Woman Movement: Feminism in the United States and England*, ed., William L. O'Neill (1868; Chicago: Quadrangle, 1969), 116.

Saxon women no wrongs to right, and will they be better protected when negroes are their rulers?"[44] Stanton and Anthony broke not only with former radical abolitionist allies like Wendell Phillips[45] and Gerrit Smith[46] over this issue, but with leading abolitionist feminists like Lucy Stone,[47] Abby Kelley,[48] and, notably, Frederick Douglass (who had been Stanton's ally since Seneca Falls);[49] Lucretia Mott was appalled at Stanton's racist appeals.[50] Stanton ultimately rested her case on reminding her former radical abolitionist allies what had been fundamental to their radicalism, the appeal, on grounds of principle, to "our great American idea . . . 'individual rights.' "[51] If the Reconstruction Amendments could constitutionalize the antiracist strand of radical abolitionist thought, why not, on the same grounds of principle, the antisexist strand?

To understand the lack of support for Stanton's position, we need to keep in mind that the growing moral appeal of the antiracist strand of radical abolitionism derived from the significant role that African American troops played in the Union army in the Civil War.[52] If African Americans could fight and die for the Union cause, it seemed elementary justice, as Lincoln acknowledged,[53] to extend to them the rights and benefits of citizenship. In contrast, abolitionist feminist thinkers (Stanton excepted) tended to be pacifist; they certainly did not imagine, let alone legitimate any just role for women in military force. Horace Greeley challenged Stanton's plea for women's suffrage in precisely such terms; her flippant retort ("We are ready to fight, Sir, just as you did in the late war, by sending our substitute"[54]) evaded the issue of the unjustly gendered character of military service. Stanton apparently believed that the service women rendered in support of the Civil War would lead their claims for equality to be taken seriously

44. See Elizabeth Stanton, "Gerrit Smith on Petitions," in *The Elizabeth Cady Stanton– Susan B. Anthony Reader: Correspondence, Writings, Speeches,* ed. Ellen Carol DuBois, rev. ed. (Boston: Northeastern University Press, 1992), 122–23.

45. See Griffith, *In Her Own Right,* 123.

46. Ibid., 132–33.

47. See Andrea Moore Kerr, *Lucy Stone: Speaking Out for Equality* (New Brunswick, N.J.: Rutgers University Press, 1992), 129–42.

48. See Dorothy Sterling, *Ahead of Her Time: Abby Kelley and the Politics of Antislavery* (New York: W. W. Norton, 1991), 351–55.

49. See Griffith, *In Her Own Right,* 134.

50. Ibid., 124.

51. See Elizabeth Cady Stanton, "Who Are Our Friends?" ibid., 117.

52. See McPherson, *The Struggle for Equality,* 192–220.

53. See, for example, Donald, *Lincoln,* 430, 456–57, 526–27; cf. ibid., 556.

54. Griffith, *In Her Own Right,* 127.

when the conflict ended; but such service could not be deemed of comparable moral weight to military service without much more argument than Stanton was able or willing to supply.[55]

Stanton, who certainly did not have the deep understanding of American racism of Lydia Maria Child or the Grimke sisters,[56] clearly overestimated the degree to which the Reconstruction Amendments did constitutionalize radical abolitionist antiracism. The Reconstruction Congress may have condemned certain expressions of racial prejudice through law,[57] but apparently the dominant view did not extend such condemnation to state-sponsored racial segregation[58] or to anti-miscegenation laws.[59] This was certainly not the antiracism of Lydia Maria Child. If the Reconstruction Amendments were drawing only on the less radical aspects of abolitionist antiracist moral and political thought, their failure to draw upon one of their most radical strands (abolitionist feminism) may appear much less unprincipled than Stanton supposed.

Stanton would have made a wholly compelling moral point against her antebellum radical abolitionist allies if she had truly based her argument with them on their failure responsibly to address these issues on the same platform of human rights as the abolitionist feminist criticism of slavery, racism, the subjection of women, and sexism. But, while she decorated some of her argument in these terms, the argument she made effectively and tragically subverted the perspective of universal human rights by posing the case for women's rights, as we have seen, on terms "simultaneously more gender-based and more elitist and racist."[60] In such terms, Stanton set the stage for the tragic trajectory from the principled character of abolitionism feminism to the fundamentally flawed compromises of principle undertaken in the struggle and eventual victory of suffrage feminism.

Abolitionist feminism, which had remained a powerfully cohesive force in American public life when it supported the Thirteenth Amendment, fell into intramural disarray in the wake of the disagreements over the remaining Reconstruction Amendments. Such dis-

55. For recent such arguments, see, for example, Nancy Loring Goldman, *Female Soldiers—Combatants or Noncombatants?* (Westport, Conn.: Greenwood Press, 1982); Jean Bethke Elshtain, *Women and War* (New York: Basic Books, 1987).

56. Griffith, *In Her Own Right,* 111.

57. See William E. Nelson, *The Fourteenth Amendment: From Political Principle to Judicial Doctrine* (Cambridge: Harvard University Press, 1988), 124.

58. Ibid., 133–36.

59. Ibid., 133.

60. See Ellen Carol DuBois, "Introduction to the Revised Edition," in *The Elizabeth Cady Stanton-Susan B. Anthony Reader,* xvi.

agreements gave rise in 1869 to two rather antagonistic women's suffrage groups, the National Woman Suffrage Association (led by Stanton and Anthony) and the American Woman Suffrage Association (led by Lucy Stone).[61] It was not until 1890 that the groups merged into the National American Woman Suffrage Association.[62]

The story of suffrage feminism, ending in ratification of the Nineteenth Amendment in 1920, has been well told by historians.[63] My interest in that story is the interpretive investigation of the compromises of abolitionist feminist principle that led to the growing political success of that movement. Such compromises crippled the moral promise abolitionist feminism once held for American public life, and rendered the victory of suffrage feminism morally vacuous. The political struggle and victory of suffrage feminism exacted this tragic moral price in ways well worth careful interpretive study. I focus here on three ways in which suffrage feminism disowned or diluted aspects of the ways in which abolitionist feminism had elaborated the argument for toleration: first, the dilution of the appeal to universal human rights to a highly sectarian conception of women's maternal role (reflecting the political alliance of suffrage feminism with the temperance and purity movements); second, the impact of the Wollstonecraft repudiation of free love on the denial of central human rights of associational liberty; and third, the increasingly powerful use of a racialized conception of gender that reinforced rather than challenged American racism.

FROM UNIVERSAL TOLERATION TO ORGANIZED MOTHER LOVE

Abolitionist feminism was a distinctive elaboration of the argument for toleration, applied by abolitionists to condemn slavery and racism, to discredit as well the subjection of women and sexism on the same platform of human rights. The structure of that argument emerged from

61. For fuller discussion of their disagreements, see Griffith, *In Her Own Right*, 137–41.

62. See ibid., 196–200.

63. See, for example, Ellen Carol DuBois, *Feminism and Suffrage: The Emergence of an Independent Women's Movement in America, 1848–1869* (Ithaca: Cornell University Press, 1978); Eleanor Flexner, *Centuries of Struggle: The Woman's Rights Movement in the United States*, rev. ed. (1959; Cambridge: Harvard University Press, Belknap Press, 1975); William L. O'Neill, *Everyone Was Brave: The Rise and Fall of Feminism in America* (Chicago: Quadrangle Books, 1969); Suzanne M. Marilley, *Woman Suffrage and the Origins of Liberal Feminism in the United States, 1820–1920* (Cambridge: Harvard University Press, 1996); Sara Hunter Graham, *Woman Suffrage and the New Democracy* (New Haven: Yale University Press, 1996).

the constructive, empowering moral experience of women like the Grimke sisters who, in demanding to think and speak in their own voice in independent moral criticism of a repressive Southern culture of slavery and racism, confronted and challenged in the same way and on the same grounds the repressive culture of the subjection of women and sexism in the North. The distinctive object of abolitionist feminist criticism was the conventional conception of gender roles urged against the Grimkes by Catharine Beecher. That conception sharply limited the scope of legitimate free exercise by women of basic rights of conscience, speech, association, and work. Such limitations were, for the abolitionist feminists, wrong on the same grounds the comparable restrictions on basic liberties of African Americans were wrong: they deprived whole classes of persons of respect for basic human rights on the basis of dehumanizing assumptions that themselves depended, in a moral vicious circle, on failures to extend to the stigmatized group any fair respect for their basic rights. Such failures were rationalized in terms of a politically entrenched and enforceable political epistemology of race and gender that limited debate on these questions to the sectarian terms of the political orthodoxy; those terms included denial of basic rights to whole classes of persons, thus failing to accord them respect for their moral personalities as bearers of such rights. Subjugated groups were thus denied the basic rights of conscience, speech, association, and work that would enable them reasonably to contest the force of the dominant orthodoxy. The abolitionist feminist theory of this rights-based wrong was moral slavery, an analysis whose terms (drawing an analogy between the slavery of African Americans and women) were prominently used by John Stuart Mill in his 1869 essay, *The Subjection of Women*,[64] an argument that American abolitionist feminists (who had invented the analysis) understandably acclaimed.[65]

The moral power of the abolitionist feminist analysis was to articulate common, interlinked grounds of injustice for both racism and sexism. The evils of racism and sexism could, on this analysis, neither be understood nor remedied without addressing both. The Grimke sisters

64. See John Stuart Mill, *The Subjection of Women*, in John Stuart Mill and Harriet Taylor Mill, *Essays on Sex Equality*, ed. Alice S. Rossi (Chicago: University of Chicago Press, 1970), 125–242.

65. Sarah Grimke was so impressed with it that at the age of seventy-nine, she "trudged up and down the country side, circulating and selling 150 copies." See Gerda Lerner, *The Grimke Sisters from South Carolina*, 366. For Mill's close identification with the feminism of Stanton and Mott, see his December 11, 1869 letter reprinted in Elizabeth Cady Stanton, Susan B. Anthony, and Matilda Joslyn Gage, eds., *History of Woman Suffrage, 1861–1876* (New York: Fowler & Wells, 1882), 2:419.

and Harriet Jacobs made this point by probing the role that Southern women on their idealized pedestal played in the Southern interlinked political epistemologies of race and gender; similarly, Sojourner Truth had critically exposed the role of a racialized normative conception of gender in the repression of women, black and white, a theme Jacobs powerfully elaborated in the realm of sexuality. Failure to extend such analysis to both race and gender would threaten the analysis of either, an idea that requires further exploration in light of the argument for toleration.

The argument for toleration is an argument of principle that extends to all persons, on universalistic terms, respect for basic human rights and expresses skepticism about the enforcement at large of sectarian political orthodoxies that self-entrench their political power by the abridgment of such basic rights. A constitutional order that ostensibly accepts the argument for toleration (like the United States) offers a vivid example of the devastating consequences of failures to extend the argument on fair terms. Precisely the patterns of unjust subjugation (American slavery and racism) that most reasonably required public debate and criticism were most uncritically accepted and most repressively enforced against dissenting voice, or even the possibility of such dissenting voices. I earlier marked this phenomenon (chapter 2) in terms of a paradox of intolerance familiar from the study of religious persecution in general and Western anti-Semitism in particular. Certain issues of the dominant religious orthodoxy (for example, the doctrine of transubstantiation) were reasonably subject to doubt and discussion; but, paradoxically, the embattled sectarian orthodoxy, at war with its own doubts (even warring on doubt itself), repressed the reasonable debate its tradition most needed; to do so, it subjugated dissenters to the dominant orthodoxy on terms that exposed them to irrationalist stereotypes and rationalized atrocity. In effect, dissenters were unjustly sacrificed as scapegoats to repress orthodoxy's doubts. In the same way, American doubts about entrenched institutions of slavery and racism, understandably based on the place of the argument for toleration in basic constitutional institutions, were not subject to the reasonable discussion and debate they needed; rather, the polemical epistemology of proslavery warred on even the possibility of doubt, subjugating African Americans in ways that exposed them to irrationalist, dehumanizing stereotypes and rationalized fundamental injustices. The failure to extend the argument for toleration on fair terms was not, then, a minor mistake without significant consequences; it legitimated the worst abridgments of human rights within a framework that paid ostensible tribute to its respect for such rights.

Abolitionist feminism generalized this insight to encompass racism and sexism. Both American racism and sexism arose and thrived in the virulent forms they did because, against the background of a constitution committed to the argument for toleration, they rested on such unjust abridgments of basic human rights and politically entrenched sectarian orthodoxies that rationalized such abridgments; and the same kind of consequences would follow if either rights-based evil were addressed without taking into account the other. From this perspective, the earlier mentioned dominant view of the Reconstruction Congress that constitutional prohibitions on state-sponsored racism would not condemn state-supported racial segregation or antimiscegenation laws was of a piece with their failure to take seriously sexism as a rights-denying prejudice (like racism) and thus the role that an unjustly racialized conception of gender played in American racism. Such a seriously defective understanding of the application of the argument of toleration to race and gender, even in a body so committed to the rebirth of American revolutionary constitutionalism as the Reconstruction Congress, did not bode well for the intelligence and will of national leaders in later more complacent and accommodating periods like the Gilded Age to enforce rights-based constitutional principles. In fact, as we shall see, they did nothing of the sort: America in the late nineteenth and early twentieth centuries may have become a more racist nation than ever before.[66] Similar consequences of a fundamentally flawed application of basic principles flowed from the growing tendency of suffrage feminism to compromise the rights-based principles of abolitionist feminism: suffrage feminism not only aggravated sexism but worsened American racism.

The historical dynamic over time of suffrage feminism, whatever the intentions of its early abolitionist feminist leaders, was to narrow rigidly the public issue of women's rights to one issue, and one issue alone: votes for women. The issue of votes for women had never been central to abolitionist feminism, which focused on larger questions of indignities to basic rights like conscience, speech, association, and work on inadequate sectarian grounds; Stanton included the issue of voting rights over objections among the resolutions at Seneca Falls in 1848, and it was the only resolution not approved unanimously (passing by a small majority). While the suffrage feminism of Stanton and Anthony insisted on the continuing centrality of this larger program (including

66. See C. Vann Woodward, *Reunion and Reaction: The Compromise of 1877 and the End of Reconstruction* (New York: Oxford University Press, 1966); *The Strange Career of Jim Crow,* 3d ed. (New York: Oxford University Press, 1974); and *Origins of the New South, 1877–1913* (Baton Rouge: Louisiana State University Press, 1971).

controversial issues like divorce reform), that of Lucy Stone did not.[67] The dynamics of suffrage feminism after the merger of the two rival organizations in 1890 and Stanton's withdrawal from active participation diluted the aims of abolitionist feminism to the vanishing point. Susan B. Anthony, in order to broaden the appeal of suffrage feminism, aligned the suffrage group with another even more powerful women's movement, Frances Willard's Woman's Christian Temperance Union (WCTU).[68] That alignment brought with it a reorientation of suffrage feminism in terms of a normative conception of gender roles that had traditionally been at war with abolitionist feminism. In particular, Catharine Beecher's view of women's roles became the operative normative ideology of suffrage feminism just as it had long been that of the temperance movement.

Beecher had defended a normative conception of women's proper role in terms of the utilitarian value of women's training in self-sacrifice as mothers for their children, and derived from that conception a surprisingly activist public role for unmarried women like herself as teachers and writers on subjects relating to advancing women's competence at being better wives and mothers. Beecher drew the line at abolitionist feminist activism like that of the Grimke sisters or of Stanton's suffrage feminism because both their forms of activism (speaking in public to mixed audiences) and grounds (demands for human rights) departed too radically from the maternal, self-abnegating model of gentle suasion that Beecher thought to be central to women's utilitarian moral superiority. Such moral superiority expressed, for Beecher, basically gendered moral values available only to women of the sort that abolitionist feminists, appealing to universal moral principles applicable to all persons alike, centrally criticized.

Beecher defended her normative conception on ostensibly secular utilitarian grounds, but it was informed as well by a religiously-based ideal calling, on the model of Jesus of Nazareth, for the sacrifice of basic interests for the good of others. It is one thing to admire the pursuit of such ideals, and quite another to demand such pursuit, as Beecher did, as the only legitimate role for women. Such a demand (of women only) does not appear to be what even a secular utilitarianism would require. Beecher's apparently utilitarian argument assumed, as its controlling background, uncritical sectarian ideals of womanhood that were conventional in her society, not secular considerations impersonally pursued.

67. For the contrast, see Griffith, *In Her Own Right*, 140.
68. Ibid., 192–94.

The sectarian character of this normative conception was made quite clear by the important theologian, Horace Bushnell, in his 1869 diatribe against woman's suffrage entitled, *Women's Suffrage: The Reform against Nature.*[69] Bushnell, a Congregationalist minister in the tradition of Jonathan Edwards, had earlier reinterpreted traditional Calvinist doctrines to justify parental upbringing in Christianity ("Christian nurture") against the "overdone . . . individualism"[70] of the age.[71] The organic unity of the family turned on the role of the father in family government, only properly regarded "as a viceregent authority, set up by God, and ruling in his place" (271). Women's role (as mother) in this organic conception was, like Beecher's comparable theory, subordinate to men's (276), but reflective of an aspect of the deity (which she embodies), "a kind of nursing Providence" (271).

Bushnell's book combined detailed domestic advice with theology in a more blatantly sectarian style than Beecher allowed herself in her many books on the proper conduct of domestic life;[72] but their views amounted to the same thing. They both were skeptical about the kind of activism by women they associated with women's suffrage. In his attack on women's suffrage Bushnell certainly granted that women could, consistent with their proper roles as nurturing mother, perform many public roles, such as being doctors (but not litigators) (18–21) and preachers (but not administrators) (22–26, 113, 121, 181–82). Women and men were "two species" (51), the one covertly domestic, the other forcefully governmental (52, 54). Though properly subordinate to men, women were morally superior (57) because their maternal selflessness made them a closer approximation to the divinely self-sacrificing goodness of Jesus (63, 96–97, 99, 142, 171–72). But women could not, consistent with their morally superior nature, undertake governmental functions that required "a self-centered, governing, driving-engine character" (166). The proposal of woman's suffrage was, therefore, "a . . . radical revolt against nature" (56) like "manly women" or "womanly men" (109) or "[t]he claim of a beard" (56).

69. See Bushnell, *Women's Suffrage.*

70. See Horace Bushnell, *Christian Nurture,* ed. Luther A. Weigle (1861; New Haven: Yale University Press, 1916), 183. See also the earlier Horace Bushnell, *Views of Christian Nurture and of Subjects Adjacent Thereto (1847),* ed. Philip B. Eppard (New York: Delmar, 1975).

71. On Bushnell's background and importance, see Barbara M. Cross, *Horace Bushnell: Minister to a Changing America* (Chicago: University of Chicago Press, 1958); Theodore T. Munger, *Horace Bushnell: Preacher and Theologian* (Boston: Houghton, Mifflin, 1899); H. Shelton Smith, ed., *Horace Bushnell* (New York: Oxford University Press, 1965).

72. See, in general, Sklar, *Catharine Beecher.*

Both Beecher and Bushnell waged sectarian religious war on the idea of basic rights claimed by and for women and, in particular, the idea of such rights asserted by and for women in the family. To make their point, they focused on one aspect of women's lives, the relationship of women as mothers to their dependent and vulnerable young children, and characterized that relationship in terms of a superior morality in which women approximated more closely to the self-sacrificing ideal of the life of Jesus (63). They described the alleged superior moral value of the relationship not from the perspective of women, but from the perspective of the powerful feelings ("the remembrances of their almost divine motherhood" [172]) that children, as adults, have about the relationship to their mothers, who have "such ineradicable, inexpugnable possession of the life of sons and daughters" (171). This is romantic idealization in the tradition of romantic love whose appeal here assumes undoubtedly profound and widespread human experiences and feelings of stages of one's life when ego boundaries barely exist (if they exist at all) and one's experience is symbiotically one with one's primary care taker (usually, one's mother), the stage psychoanalysts call primary love.[73] From within such intense feelings, one's mother may barely exist as an independent person but as an intense fantasy of almost religious devotion; such feelings may be the basis of one's worship, as Catholic medieval spirituality apparently did, of Jesus as mother,[74] or, as nineteenth-century Protestant Americans like Beecher and Bushnell did, of one's mother as Jesus.[75]

From the perspective of the argument for toleration, feelings of romantic love, colored by sectarian religious idealization, hardly rise to the level of an argument of public reason of the sort required to justify abridgment of basic human rights. Arguments of public reason do, of course, apply to the structure of family life, including the relationship between spouses and the appropriate relationship of parents to their children.[76] However, the Beecher-Bushnell argument, if it can

73. For an important treatment, see Michael Balint, *Primary Love and Psycho-Analytic Technique* (New York: Liveright, 1965), especially the articles by Michael Balint, 74–90 and 109–35, and by Alice Balint, 91–108. On the religious force of the romantic love tradition in nineteenth-century America, see Karen Lystra, *Searching the Heart: Woman, Men, and Romantic Love in Nineteenth-Century America* (New York: Oxford University Press, 1989).

74. See, for example, Caroline Walker Bynum, *Jesus as Mother: Studies in the Spirituality of the High Middle Ages* (Berkeley and Los Angeles: University of California Press, 1982).

75. On the background of this American development, see Ann Douglas, *The Feminization of American Culture* (New York: Knopf, 1977).

76. See, for example, Susan Moller Okin, *Justice, Gender, and the Family* (New York: Basic Books, 1989).

be called that, does not critically rest on the relevant features of these relationships (the liberties, opportunities, resources) to which public reasons of justice must and do attend. Nor does it bring any realism or sense of justice to women's perspectives, as persons, on their role as mothers. Rather, it looks on mothering as romantic fantasy, not as an exercise of practical reason and intelligence, or emphasizes the crippling character (for mothers and children) of what Adrienne Rich observed and criticized in the "maternal altruism . . . universally approved and supported in women."[77] Beecher and Bushnell offer a highly sectarian political epistemology of rigidly stereotypical gender roles whose force reflects chimerical fantasies like those Langmuir studied in anti-Semitism (chapter 2). Intense feelings of identification, in which ego boundaries are barely drawn, dissolve mothers, as persons, into intrapsychic idealized images of religious devotion; fantasies, which repudiate the minimal moral requirements of respect for the separateness of persons, are made the measure of a higher "morality." Finally, these essentially amoral chimeria are to stand judgment over the ethical demands of equal respect for persons.

Such politically entrenched fantasies drew their reactionary point and power not only from their starkly antifeminist uses in the North (Beecher and Bushnell) but their interlinked proslavery, racist, and antifeminist uses in the South in, among others, earlier discussed works of George Fitzhugh and Louisa McCord. Both Fitzhugh and McCord condemned abolitionists for attacking the family,[78] associating slavery and the subjection of women with "relations of life, the nearest, the dearest."[79] The thought was that under Southern slavery blacks were, like white women on their idealized pedestal, thought of and cared for as "almost a part of himself, a dependant to live and die with."[80] In both the Northern and Southern cases, the embattled dominant political orthodoxy polemically inverted reality to the measure of its sectarian vision precisely when subjected to reasonable doubts about the justice of its factual and normative premises. African Americans and women were dissolved into fantasies or intimately romantic parts of oneself that one may defend against critics as literally unjust aggressions on one's self. Arguments for justice, in this polemically irrationalist world,

77. See Adrienne Rich, *Of Woman Born: Motherhood as Experience and Institution,* 10th anniversary ed. (1976; New York: W. W. Norton, 1986), 213.
78. See George Fitzhugh, *Cannibals All!* 190–98, 204–6, 213–16.
79. See McCord, "Uncle Tom's Cabin," 111; id., "Enfranchisement of Woman."
80. See McCord, "Uncle Tom's Cabin," 108.

become invasions of privacy; ethical demands, an inferior morality (if a morality at all); claims for human rights, unnatural acts.

Beecher developed her normative conception of gender in explicit opposition to abolitionist feminism, and opposed the general claims of suffrage feminism;[81] Bushnell developed his theology of gender in explicit opposition to the suffrage movement. The interest of Frances Willard to our study is that, starting from a Beecher-Bushnell normative conception, she nonetheless came to defend suffrage feminism, albeit not on the terms or grounds of Elizabeth Stanton. The difference between Willard and Stanton and the increasing dominance of Willard's views mark the decisive shift of suffrage feminism away from rights-based abolitionist feminism.[82]

Frances Willard worked very much within the framework of Catharine Beecher's interpretation of women's roles, including the role Beecher accorded unmarried women (Willard, like Beecher, did not marry) as moral teachers;[83] this moral teaching was, for both reformers, decidedly utilitarian: rights, in particular, always should yield to social advantage.[84] Like Beecher, Willard grounded women's role as moral teacher and reformer in the mother-child relationship; the slogan of the WCTU was "organized mother love."[85] Willard assumed the sectarian religious interpretation accorded this role (as morally superior) by Beecher and Bushnell, centering her reform efforts in the protection "of home's inmost sanctuary, where Madonna and Child are evermore enshrined."[86] The religious vocabulary (Madonna and child) was not accidental: Willard interpreted women's higher morality in terms of idealizing fantasies and feelings of maternal identification. (She was, in fact, devoted to her mother, and her mother to her, throughout their lives largely spent together.[87]) Willard took this politically appealing sectarian epistemology, enforcing as it did the conventionally domestic

81. Beecher accepted the case for suffrage only when a woman satisfied property qualification requirements. See Beecher, *Woman Suffrage and Woman's Profession*, 205.

82. For an excellent comparison of Stanton and Willard, see Elizabeth B. Clark, "The Politics of God and the Woman's Vote: Religion in the American Suffrage Movement, 1848–1895" (Ph.D. diss., Princeton University, 1989).

83. See, in general, Ruth Bordin, *Frances Willard: A Biography* (Chapel Hill: University of North Carolina Press, 1986).

84. For Willard on this point, see Clark, "The Politics of God and the Woman's Vote," 286–87, 292–93.

85. Ibid., 224.

86. See Frances E. Willard, *Glimpses of Fifty Years: The Autobiography of An American Woman* (Chicago: H. J. Smith, 1889), 610.

87. See, in general, Bordin, *Frances Willard*. On Willard's intense homosocial relationships to other women, see ibid., 44–47, 90–93, 198–200.

women's ideology of the day,[88] as axiomatic;[89] she brought her considerable political skills opportunistically to bear on forging organizations
of women around issues that would bring into public life what she took
to be their higher maternalist morality.[90] In an age when the role of
minister was not open to women in mainstream American churches,
she forged leadership roles for women in the WCTU (12, 26, 113) in
close collaboration with the Protestant churches (29, 41).

Temperance was a natural place for Willard to start her organizational efforts among American women. The temperance movement
had developed in the antebellum period in response to a social evil of
alcohol abuse that was both real and widespread; antebellum temperance efforts, usually voluntary (experiments with prohibition were repealed), apparently substantially lowered use of alcohol (5–6).[91] Lyman
Beecher, Catharine's father, had during the antebellum period excori-
ated Garrisonian abolitionism,[92] but passionately supported the most
radical form of temperance, prohibition, on the ground that intemperance was not only an evil like the slave trade,[93] but worse than slavery.[94]
Temperance, unlike radical abolitionism and feminism, was during this
period a mainstream reform movement.[95] The production and use of
alcohol increased rapidly during and after the Civil War, leading to
growing rates of alcohol abuse as a largely male prerogative in saloons;
women were often abused by such drunken husbands, a fact underscored by Susan B. Anthony in 1875.[96] Willard naturally identified temperance, a much more conventionally appealing movement than abolitionist feminism, as a politically attractive issue around which women
might organize on two grounds. First, drinking, a male-defined public

88. See, in general, Ruth Bordin, *Woman and Temperance: The Quest for Power and
Liberty, 1873–1900* (New Brunswick, N.J.: Rutgers University Press, 1990); Barbara Leslie
Epstein, *The Politics of Domesticity: Women, Evangelism and Temperance in Nineteenth-
Century America* (Middletown, Conn.: Wesleyan University Press, 1981).

89. For a good discussion of the centrality of identification with mothers to the temperance movement, see Ian R. Tyrrell, *Woman's World Woman's Empire: The Women's Christian Temperance Union in International Perspective, 1800–1930* (Chapel Hill: University of
North Carolina Press, 1991), 125–29.

90. See Bordin, *Woman and Temperance,* 46.

91. For important studies, see Ian R. Tyrrell, *Sobering Up: From Temperance to Prohibition in Antebellum America, 1800–1860* (Westport, Conn.: Greenwood Press, 1979); Jed Dannenbaum, *Drink and Disorder: Temperance Reform in Cincinnati from the Washingtonian
Revival to the WCTU* (Urbana: University of Illinois Press, 1984).

92. See Robert H. Abzug, *Cosmos Crumbling: American Reform and the Religious Imagination* (New York: Oxford University Press, 1994), 180.

93. Ibid., 88–89.

94. Ibid., 139–40.

95. Ibid., 127.

96. See Bordin, *Woman and Temperance,* 6–7.

activity outside the home, would be a natural subject for criticism from
the perspective of women's domestically situated higher morality; and
second, the consequences of alcohol abuse were borne by women in
the home. Women could naturally organize around this issue as a way
of protecting the home.[97]

Willard, however, invested this issue, as had Lyman Beecher before
her, with a specifically nativist Protestant evangelical perfectionism,
which demanded "a religion of the body" based on "Christ's whole-
some, practical, yet blessedly spiritual religion of the soul."[98] Such sectarian demands required not merely the voluntary organizations or
state education and regulations that would sensibly reduce alcohol
abuse and encourage temperate uses of liquor (as had happened in
the antebellum period), but something (prohibition) such secular ends
not only did not justify, but might condemn (to the extent such laws, on
balance, inflicted more secular harm than good).[99] In a constitutional
democracy committed to the argument for toleration, such prohibitionist laws, having only a sectarian basis, should, as John Stuart Mill
argued against comparable laws in Britain, at least raise serious questions as inadequately justified violations of the rights of consumers.[100]
Willard evaded taking such arguments seriously[101] for the same reason
she once opposed the role of Stanton and Anthony in the suffrage
movement:[102] namely, she opposed arguments of universal human
rights that would critically threaten the political legitimacy of sectarian
appeals to the higher morality of women's duties and roles.[103] Willard
inferred the sectarian (as opposed to the secular) component of the
WCTU's temperance advocacy from the political epistemology of gen-

97. Ibid., 57–58.

98. See Frances E. Willard, *Woman and Temperance* (1883; New York: Arno Press,
1972), 42.

99. For development of this theme, see David A. J. Richards, "Drug Use and the Rights
of the Person: A Moral Argument for the Decriminalization of Certain Forms of Drug Use,"
Rutgers L. Rev. 22 (1981): 607, reprinted in David A. J. Richards, *Sex, Drugs, Death and
the Law: An Essay on Human Rights and Overcriminalization* (Totowa, N.J.: Rowman and
Littlefield, 1982), 157–212.

100. For Mill's arguments, see Ross Evans Paulson, *Women's Suffrage and Prohibition:
A Comparative Study of Equality and Social Control* (Glenview, Ill.: Scott, Foresman, 1973),
80–82.

101. Remarkably, Willard acknowledged that many people could use alcohol with no ill
effects. See Bordin, *Woman and Temperance,* 99. She evades even thinking about the natural
inference from this admission: that a less restrictive, more regulatory approach than prohibitionism might better respect these people's interests while responsibly taking measures to
minimize harms others might otherwise suffer from alcohol abuse.

102. See Bordin, *Woman and Temperance,* 43.

103. Ibid., 119; Clark, "The Politics of God and the Woman's Vote," 286–87, 292–93.

der that she took to be axiomatic; on this basis, she pressed prohibitionism, as opposed to quite legitimate educational and regulatory concerns in lowering the harms incident to public consumption of alcohol largely by men. From this politically entrenched perspective, women's higher morality self-immunized itself from scrutiny in terms of independent ethical standards that fairly assessed the balance of secular harms. Conventional gender roles, shaped as they were by highly contingent cultural factors (separating the idealized private from the corrupt public), were thus reinforced, indeed idealized. In this polemically inverted and insular world, the protection of one's maternally identified self served to rationalize aggression against the rights of others, especially the racial minorities, working classes, and immigrant groups who reasonably rejected sectarian Protestant perfectionism as the measure of a well-lived life.[104]

Willard's political genius at organization made the WCTU the largest and most effective woman's organization of her time.[105] Her political skills and organizational achievement advanced a wider public role for women in service of an alleged higher morality. She thus elaborated the moral sphere of woman's activism further than Catharine Beecher had, and, as a good politician does, sought wider coalitions that might further enhance such activism in furtherance of women's moral superiority (as a kind of "policy entrepreneur"[106]). She thus embraced issues and causes that, in her judgment, suitably cohered with this ambition, including the ordination of women,[107] social purity,[108] prison reform,[109] socialism (209–10), and woman's suffrage (97–105). In contrast to Beecher and Bushnell, Willard saw woman's suffrage as a way of advancing the normative conception of woman's role that she shared with them; it was, from her perspective, simply another means of securing home protection (100). Willard insisted, however, that the case for women's suffrage did not rest on natural rights, but on utilitarian grounds of advancing woman's moral superiority (97–99, 119–20).[110] Her political and organizational skills widened the support for woman's suffrage, but on grounds that reframed the movement decisively away from its founding vision in abolitionist feminism (119–20).

104. See Epstein, *The Politics of Domesticity*, 90, 99, 101, 110, 114.

105. See Bordin, *Woman and Temperance*, 4, 52, 72, 94, 140.

106. See Suzanne M. Marilley, *Woman Suffrage and the Origins of Liberal Feminism in the United States, 1820–1920*, 126; see also Bordin, *Frances Willard*, 186–89.

107. See Bordin, *Frances Willard*, 117, 160–63, 167–68.

108. Ibid.,131–33, 236–37.

109. See Bordin, *Woman and Temperance*, 99–100.

110. On Willard's utilitarian skepticism about rights, see Clark, "The Politics of God and the Woman's Vote," 286–87, 292–93.

Susan B. Anthony had been an early temperance advocate (founding, in 1852, the first women's temperance group [5]), but she did not support prohibition.[111] Anthony had, however, been friends with Willard since 1875; when Stanton later became less active, Anthony allied with Willard to further engage the WCTU's support of women's suffrage. In return, suffragists would quietly support prohibition, Sunday closing laws, and the appeal to righteousness as a ground for voting.[112] In effect, Anthony adopted a conservative strategy of suffrage-first based on a religious alliance. This shift made possible the National-American merger in 1890. The suffrage movement was now decisively aligned with the sectarian ideology of gender roles of Catharine Beecher.

Stanton did not agree with Anthony's strategy, but, unable to win against her (Anthony enjoyed the support of the majority of National members), Stanton chose not to fight.[113] While Stanton was elected president of the merged National American Woman Suffrage Association in 1890, the conservative views of the dominant majority shut her out and she did not actively participate in the organization.[114]

In 1892, Stanton delivered the definitive statement of her abolitionist feminism, "The Solitude of Self."[115] She uncompromisingly reaffirmed the case for the rights of women in the argument for toleration, based on "the individuality of each human soul—our Protestant idea, the right of individual conscience and judgment—our republican idea, equal citizenship."[116] Against the background of Willard's ideology of utilitarian, person-dissolving, social maternalism, Stanton insisted on a woman's rights to moral independence as a person:

> The strongest reason for giving woman all the opportunities for higher education, for the full development of her faculties, her forces of mind and body; for giving her the most enlarged freedom of thought and action; a complete emancipation from all forms of bondage, of custom, dependence, superstition; from all the crippling influences of fear; is the solitude and personal responsibility of her own individual life. The strongest reason why we ask for woman a voice in the government under which she lives; in the religion she is asked to believe; equality in social life, where she is the chief factor; a place in the trades and professions, where she may earn her bread, is be-

---

111. See Bordin, *Frances Willard,* 99–100.
112. See Griffith, *In Her Own Right,* 194.
113. Ibid., 194–95.
114. Ibid., 199–200.
115. See Elizabeth Cady Stanton, "The Solitude of Self," in Beth M. Waggenspack, *The Search for Self-Sovereignty: The Oratory of Elizabeth Cady Stanton* (Westport, Conn.: Greenwood Press, 1989), 159–67.
116. Ibid., 159.

cause of her birthright to self-sovereignty; because, as an individual, she must rely on herself. No matter how much women prefer to lean, to be protected and supported, nor how much men desire to have them do so, they must make the voyage of life alone, and for safety in an emergency they must know something of the laws of navigation. . . . It matters not whether the solitary voyager is man or woman.[117]

Stanton's concern for women's "emancipation from all forms of bondage, of custom, dependence, superstition" culminated in her publication of *The Woman's Bible* in 1895.[118] Stanton acknowledged that her interest in Bible interpretation arose from clerical uses of appeals to the Bible against both the antislavery and women's suffrage movements (8–9). Arguing very much in the spirit of Theodore Parker's rights-based approaches to biblical and constitutional interpretation, Stanton's project, following the comparable efforts of Sarah Grimke, was to question not so much the authority of the Bible, but the misogynist patterns of male Bible interpretation that, she argued, could be reasonably challenged (10–11). She analyzed those biblical texts crucially bearing on women's role. Again following Parker, she suggested a feminine element in God (14–15), interpreting creation in the image of God in terms of "[t]he Heavenly Mother and Father" (21). *The Woman's Bible* was a sensational bestseller—and a scandal to the increasingly conservative suffrage movement.[119] Their reaction suggests how far suffrage feminism now had departed from its abolitionist feminist roots.

Younger suffragists, under the leadership of Carrie Chapman Catt, planned to condemn both the book and its author at the 1896 meeting of the National American. At the meeting, a resolution was proposed affirming the nonsectarian character of the association and that it "has no official connection with the so-called *Woman's Bible,* or any theological association."[120] After an hour's fierce debate, Anthony herself stepped down from the chair, defending both the author and her right of free speech:

Who can tell now whether these commentaries may not prove a great help to woman's emancipation from old superstitions which have barred the way? Lucretia Mott at first thought Mrs. Stanton had injured the cause of all women's other rights by insisting upon the demand for suffrage, but she had sense enough not to bring in a resolution against it. In 1860 when Mrs. Stanton made a speech before the New York legislature in favor of a bill making

117. Ibid., 160.
118. See Elizabeth Cady Stanton, *The Woman's Bible* (New York: European Publishing Company, 1895).
119. See Griffith, *In Her Own Right,* 210–12.
120. Ibid., 212.

drunkenness a ground for divorce, there was a general cry among the friends
the she had killed the woman's cause. I shall be pained beyond expression
if the delegates are so narrow and illiberal as to adopt this resolution. You
would better not begin resolving against individual action or you will find
no limit. This year it is Mrs. Stanton; next year it may be I or one of yourselves
who may be the victim.[121]

The censure resolution passed, 53–41. Carrie Chapman Catt was to
succeed Susan B. Anthony as president of the National American in
1900.[122] The conservative trajectory of suffrage feminism, based on its
alliance with the WCTU, was set, leading to ratification of the Eighteenth Amendment (prohibiting manufacture or sale of intoxicants) in
1919 and of the Nineteenth Amendment (extending the vote to
women) in 1920. The amendments had a common basis in the anti-
abolitionist feminist ideology of Catharine Beecher.

SUFFRAGE FEMINISM AND THE ATTACK ON FREE LOVE

The theory of moral slavery, central to abolitionist feminism, identified
the abridgment of basic human rights as constitutive features in the
dehumanization of a whole class of persons on inadequate sectarian
grounds. As leading abolitionist thinkers like Weld and Channing made
clear, one such basic human right was the right to intimate life, which
was conspicuously and flagrantly abridged for African American slaves,
who were denied the right to marry and the right to custody of their
children. The poems and essays of Elizabeth Chandler prominently
brought women's moral experience to bear on such atrocities, and abolitionist feminists ranging from the Grimke sisters to Harriet Jacobs
had explored the pivotal role abridgment of such basic human rights
played in the dehumanization of African Americans. When Lydia Maria Child offered her important antiracist criticism of the Massachusetts antimiscegenation law, she identified the inalienable human right
at stake as the "power to control the affections, any more than the
consciences of citizens,"[123] "a connexion which, above all others, ought
to be left to private conscience and individual choice."[124]

I will now turn to the further elaboration of this argument for a
basic human right—the right to love—in the wake of the Civil War.
The focus will be on such a rights-based challenge to conventional
marriage (by, among others, Elizabeth Stanton, Victoria Woodhull,

---

121. Ibid., 212–13.
122. See Flexner, *Century of Struggle*, 245–46.
123. See Child, *An Appeal in Favor of that Class of Americans Called Africans*, 196.
124. See Milton Melzer et al., eds., *Lydia Maria Child Selected Letters*, 110.

Stephen Pearl Andrews, Ezra Heywood, and, in a different form, Lysander Spooner); the sharp repudiation of that argument by increasingly conservative suffragists and their allies (including the purity and antipolygamy movements); the resulting political war on contraception, abortion, and prostitution; and the censorship of serious discussion of these matters when both Emma Goldman and Margaret Sanger sought to raise them in the years leading up to the ratification of the Nineteenth Amendment. The voice of rights-based abolitionist feminism on issues central to the emancipation of women was decisively silenced largely by conservative suffragists and their allies en route to their morally problematic prohibitionist victory in 1919 and their morally vacuous suffrage victory in 1920.

The argument for free love was associated in the antebellum period with Mary Wollstonecraft and Frances Wright, and was largely repudiated as much for the way of life as for the arguments of its proponents. In particular, Mary Wollstonecraft, a towering figure in the development of rights-based feminism, could not be acknowledged as such because Godwin's memoir frankly exposed a life of premarital affairs, pregnancies, and suicide attempts that shocked conventional morality. Godwin emphasized that Wollstonecraft firmly believed in sexual fidelity when in love, and Wollstonecraft herself defended long-term relationships when based on rationally-based friendship and mutual affection. These points hardly assuaged American horror at Wollstonecraft's theory and practice of successive changes in sexual love objects and her flat and antiromantic acknowledgment that sexual love in women (as in men) was in its nature quite short-lived. American attitudes to sexual love in the nineteenth century were nothing if not highly (even religiously) idealized and romantic;[125] as Harriet Beecher Stowe wrote to her husband Calvin about her "almost insane love" before they married, "I loved you as I now love God."[126] Such religiously idealized sentiments were outraged by Wollstonecraft's sadly quotidian and deflationary picture of marriage as, at best, mutual lust followed by a coolly rational friendship.

To forestall such objections, any plausible American defense of a basic right to love had to situate its argument in the role of sexual love as a romantically imaginative expression and sharing of moral personality with the beloved.[127] Lydia Maria Child, when she prefigured later arguments for this right, thus grounded it on an inalienable right to

125. For an important study on this point, see Lystra, *Searching the Heart*, 237–58.
126. Nancy F. Cott, "Passionlessness: An Interpretation of Victorian Sexual Ideology, 1790–1850," *Signs* 4, no. 2 (winter 1978): 234.
127. See Lystra, *Searching the Heart*, 75–77, 80–83.

feel and act on affections that she associated with the inalienable right to conscience: for nineteenth-century Americans, love, like religion, was a central expression and authentication of one's free moral personality fulfilled in tender and caring relationship to the value placed on other personalities.[128] Thus understood, an argument for a right to love might take its place among other basic human rights, securing to all persons appropriate respect for so basic a right.

Abolitionist feminism, which distinctively placed such emphasis on the unjust abridgment of women's basic rights to conscience and speech, could reasonably be elaborated as well to criticize the unjust abridgment of women's rights to free moral personality in intimate life. As we have seen (chapters 2 and 3), Elizabeth Stanton had controversially pressed such arguments in the antebellum period in service of reforms of marriage and divorce; she continued to do so, equally controversially among fellow suffragists, after the Civil War. In 1869, Stanton thus publicly embraced the right to free love as the ground for securing to women the right to divorce, "freedom from all unnecessary entanglements of concessions, freedom from binding obligations involving impossibilities, freedom to repair mistakes."[129] Denying that free love meant promiscuity, Stanton adduced Mary Wollstonecraft as an example that "true free lovers are among the most progressive, the most virtuous of women and of men."[130] Marriage, unless reformed consistent with respect for this right, was slavery, and thus such reform "is the same issue as that of immediate or gradual emancipation in the slavery question."[131] Abolitionist feminist arguments for women's suffrage "mean logically . . . that the next logical equality and next freedom is in a word 'free love.' "[132]

Unfortunately, the argument for free love in this period became tainted by one of the great scandals of the era, the Beecher-Tilton affair,[133] and the role played in that affair of certainly the most notorious advocate of free love of that time, Victoria Woodhull.[134] Woodhull

128. On the pervasive analogy between love and religion, see Lystra, *Searching the Heart*, 237–58.

129. See Elizabeth Stanton, "Speech of Marriage and Divorce, 1869," *The Search for Self-Sovereignty*, 122. The speech is also reprinted, here dated 1870, in Ellen DuBois, "On Labor and Free Love: Two Unpublished Speeches of Elizabeth Cady Stanton," *Signs* 2, no. 1 (1975), 265–68.

130. Ibid., 123.

131. Ibid.

132. Ibid., 124.

133. See Altina L. Waller, *Reverend Beecher and Mrs. Tilton: Sex and Class in Victorian America* (Amherst: University of Massachusetts Press, 1982).

134. See, in general, Johanna Johnston, *Mrs. Satan: The Incredible Saga of Victoria C. Woodhull* (New York: G. P. Putnam's Sons, 1967); Lois Beachy Underhill, *The Woman Who*

had a sordid past before she came to national attention. One of ten children in a flamboyant family that staged a traveling road show, Woodhull played a psychic healer. Married at fifteen to a physician and drunkard, Canning Woodhull, they had two children before the couple separated. Victoria returned to her family, specializing with her sister, Tennessee, in spiritualism.[135] After the Civil War, Woodhull married her lover, Dr. Blood, but kept her first husband's name. Following a vision, Victoria brought her extended family to New York City in 1868; there the recent widower, Cornelius Vanderbilt, was smitten by Tennessee and established the sisters as financial speculators and stock brokers. Vanderbilt leaked information to them, making them financially successful. In 1870, Woodhull declared herself a candidate for president of the United States, and published with her sister *Woodhull and Claflin's Weekly.* More strident and extreme, though better financed, than Stanton and Anthony's short-lived *Revolution,*[136] the *Weekly* advocated free love, short skirts, and legalized prostitution; it also printed the first translation of the Communist Manifesto in America. Woodhull practiced as well as preached free love, having various love affairs. Her domestic arrangements included living with both her first and second husbands.[137] The Wollstonecraft repudiation was to apply, *a fortiori,* to Woodhull; her publicly notorious arguments for free love in particular were read in light of the scandals of her life, and were easily discredited (Stanton notwithstanding) for that reason. We need first to understand her arguments, and then the scandals that discredited them.

Woodhull played an important public role in the early suffrage movement. On her own, she presented a suffrage petition to Congress in December 1870 and had been invited to testify before the House Judiciary Committee in January. Her hearing was scheduled on the same day as the opening session of the National Association convention being held in Washington, D.C. (its leaders were Isabella Beecher Hooker, the sister of Catharine Beecher and Harriet Beecher Stowe, and Susan B. Anthony). Hooker and Anthony interrupted their proceedings to attend Woodhull's testimony. Both were impressed with

Ran for President: The Many Lives of Victoria Woodhull (Bridgehampton, N.Y.: Bridge Works Publishing Co., 1995).

135. For an important study of the connections between spiritualism and woman's rights in nineteenth-century America, see Ann Braude, *Radical Spirits: Spiritualism and Women's Rights in Nineteenth-Century America* (Boston: Beacon Press, 1989).

136. *Revolution* survived only two-and-a-half years. See Griffith, *In Her Own Right,* 131–33, 148–49.

137. See, in general, Johnston, *Mrs. Satan;* Griffith, *In Her Own Right,* 148–49.

her intelligence and beauty, and invited her to attend their convention, joining them on the platform. Woodhull argued before the committee and the convention that a woman suffrage amendment was otiose. Using an argument Stanton had made the year earlier (interpreting the text, consistent with radical abolitionist constitutionalism, to enforce the best reading of human rights),[138] she claimed that the Fourteenth Amendment already gave women the right to vote and run for political office.[139] Woodhull's cogent presentation of Stanton's case was well received, and led suffragists for several years to pursue this line of argument rather than the federal amendment route.[140] On the basis of this argument, Woodhull ran for president in the 1872 election.[141]

Woodhull made the case for the principle of free love in a speech delivered in 1871.[142] Consistent with the abolitionist feminist approach earlier discussed, Woodhull grounded her argument in the idea of inalienable human rights appealed to by the Declaration of Independence, a normative ideal that rendered each person "self-owned" (6). Echoing Lydia Maria Child, Woodhull argued that "[g]overnments might just as well assume to determine how people shall exercise their right to *think* or to say that they shall not think at all, as to assume to determine that they shall not love, or how they may love, or that they shall love" (16). The state owed each person protection "in the *free* exercise of his or her *right* to love" (16), "an *inalienable, constitutional, and natural* right" (23) as basic to moral personality as the right to conscience (40), indeed, an aspect of it ("Free Love will be an integral part of the religion of the future" [23]). Woodhull used the right as the basis for the criticism of the economic imperatives that compelled women of her age to marry as "legalized prostitution" (17);[143] conventional women thus have no "right to . . . sit in judgment over our unfortunate sisters" (32). Marriage institutions, which violated this right, were "slavery" (29, 35–36); enslaved women had a right to emancipation (37–38).

138. See Griffith, *In Her Own Right*, 125–26, 136, 147–48.

139. See *Congressional Reports on Woman Suffrage*, in *The Victoria Woodhull Reader*, ed., Madeleine B. Stern (Weston, Mass.: M & S Press, 1974), 40–112. See also Victoria Woodhull, "A Lecture on Constitutional Equality" (delivered 1871), ibid., 3–33; Tennie C. Claflin, *Constitutional Equality a Right of Woman* (New York: Woodhull, Claflin & Co., 1871).

140. See, for example, Susan B. Anthony, "Constitutional Argument," 1872, in *The Elizabeth Cady Stanton—Susan B. Anthony Reader*, 152–65.

141. See Griffith, *In Her Own Right*, 151–52.

142. See Victoria Woodhull, "A Speech on The Principles of Social Freedom" (New York: Woodhull, Claflin, & Co., 1871), in *The Victoria Woodhull Reader*, 3–43.

143. Cf. ibid., 34–35.

Woodhull's argument for free love was ghostwritten by her then-intellectual mentor, Stephen Pearl Andrews.[144] (Andrews's views also shaped those of Elizabeth Stanton on free love, marriage, and divorce.[145]) Andrews developed and published his path-breaking arguments for a basic moral, political, and constitutional principle of free love in the antebellum period, drawing upon radical abolitionist arguments in general and the abolitionist feminist theory of moral slavery in particular.[146] While clearly influenced by Fourier,[147] Andrews's innovation was to make the case for free love in terms of a principled elaboration of the argument for toleration, while drawing on the religiously idealized American conception of romantic love that would alone give the argument any appeal in America.[148] "Freedom of the Affections" (106), as an inalienable human right, had the same basis as the other such rights of conscience (86, 108), thought (89), speech (66), association (32–33), and of action expressive of these rights (89). Respect for such an inalienable human right (95, 107) should be accorded the same scope as other such rights like religious liberty, namely, free exercise of the right *"provided* he assails nobody else's Liberty, or Life, or Property"* (108). Within the just scope of such rights, persons must "judge for themselves what is moral, and proper, and right for them to do or abstain from doing" (107). For the same reason that the state may not judge what it is religious for a person to believe, it may not make or enforce judgments in the sexual arena:

> for me to aid in sending you or another man to prison for Fornication, or Bigamy, or Polygamy, or a woman for wearing male attire, and the like, is just as gross an outrage in kind, upon Human Rights, as it would be to aid in burning you at Smithfield for Protestantism or Papacy, or at Geneva for discarding the doctrine of the Trinity. (107)

Women were owed respect for this basic right on equal terms with men as a condition of their normative self-ownership (65, 67, 69, 95–96, 119). Failure to accord them respect for this right in conventional

---

144. See Johnston, *Mrs. Satan,* 65–66; Madeleine B. Stern, *The Pantarch: A Biography of Stephen Pearl Andrews* (Austin: University of Texas Press, 1968), 116–21.

145. See Clark, "The Politics of God and the Woman's Vote," 94–97, 123, 125, 133–45, 176–99, 270–71.

146. See Henry James, Horace Greeley, and Stephen Pearl Andrews, *Love, Marriage, and Divorce* (1853; New York: Source Book Press, 1972).

147. For acknowledgment of the influence, see ibid., 17–18, 35, 62, 76, 127. See Jonathan Beecher and Richard Bienvenu, *The Utopian Vision of Charles Fourier* (Boston: Beacon Press, 1971); Jonathan Beecher, *Charles Fourier: The Visionary and His World* (Berkeley and Los Angeles: University of California Press, 1986).

148. Andrews thus invoked the Protestant principle as central to his argument. James, Greeley, and Andrews, *Love, Marriage, and Divorce,* 11–14, 62, 68.

marriage was moral slavery (10, 31, 35, 67), and made of marriage a kind of prostitution (29). Securing respect for this right would guarantee the only form of love that could reasonably be called romantic and therefore pure (28), and was, Andrews suggested, the most fundamental right owed women as a matter of basic justice (96).

Neither the power of Andrews's argument (including its use of the American conception of romantic love) nor Woodhull's beauty and eloquence in making it could shift a public opinion that interpreted the argument against the background of the national scandal that shortly erupted around Woodhull. Woodhull was arrested in 1872 on a federal obscenity charge brought by Anthony Comstock for a defense she had published of her living arrangements that included a revelation of an extramarital love affair of a leading preacher of the age.[149] Woodhull defended her arrangements as a legitimate exercise of her right to love, for which she made no apology. In contrast, she now publicly pointed to the moral hypocrisy shown by a leading preacher of the age (Henry Ward Beecher, brother of Catharine Beecher as well as Harriet Beecher Stowe and Isabella Hooker), who privately accepted the right to free love (having had an affair with Elizabeth Tilton, wife of Beecher's protégé, Theodore Tilton), but refused to defend it in public.[150] Woodhull named Elizabeth Stanton as the source of her story, and publicly demanded a confession of adultery by Beecher. (In fact, Woodhull herself had had an affair with Theodore Tilton[151] and probably with Henry Ward Beecher as well.[152])

Woodhull's accusations were true, but she had underestimated Henry Ward Beecher's egotism and influence and the capacity of ideologically self-deceiving Americans to blink reality (including his influential sisters Catharine and Harriet, though not Isabella[153]) in order to hold men and women to a double-standard of sexual morality. Beecher was tried twice, first, by a church board he appointed (that acquitted him); second, by a civil court (the jury was unable to reach a verdict).

149. For fuller discussion, see Johnson, *Mrs. Satan*, 156–92; Underhill, *The Woman Who Ran for President*, 220–46.

150. On Woodhull's concern at Beecher's belief in free love but refusal publicly to acknowledge his belief, see Johnston, *Mrs. Satan*, 173; Walker, *Reverend Beecher and Mrs. Tilton*, 93, 112–13, 136.

151. See Johnston, *Mrs. Satan*, 112–19.

152. Ibid., 124–25.

153. On Harriet Beecher Stowe's hostility to Woodhull, including a fictionalized portrait of her in her novel, *My Wife and I*, and her passionate defense of her brother's innocence, see Hedrick, *Harriet Beecher Stowe*, 371–79; on Catharine Beecher's hostility, see ibid., 375. On Isabella Beecher Hooker's skepticism about her brother's conduct and defense of Woodhull's right of free speech, see Boydston, *The Limits of Sisterhood*, 292–327.

Beecher had dismissed Woodhull and her sister as "two prostitutes,"[154] and they were vilified by his supporters in the press and in public (eventually going to Britain where they married wealthy men and adopted conservative life styles). Beecher, frightened by what Stanton knew (she never denied Woodhull's story), launched a campaign against her and Anthony as advocates of free love. Stanton, in fact, accepted the principle of free love as a legitimate one when grounded in romantic love and monogamy.[155] Stanton, disgusted at Beecher's moral duplicity, published her own account of the events, and was the only public figure to criticize the two jury verdicts.[156]

The principle of free love, as a crucial component of feminist civil liberties, was also forthrightly defended during this period by Ezra H. Heywood.[157] Heywood made his argument, like Andrews and Woodhull, in terms of the principled elaboration of "the right of private judgment, which is conceded in politics and religion . . . to domestic life."[158] Abridgments of so basic a right could no more be legitimately justified on sectarian grounds than abridgment of any other such basic right; "priests and magistrates [should not] supervise the sexual organs of citizens any more than the brain and stomach."[159] A universal human right, founded in the Declaration of Independence, "is now legitimately claimed in behalf of sexual self-government."[160] In particular, each woman has "a right to herself,"[161] including emancipation from the moral slavery that conventional marriage now imposed on her.[162]

And the important antebellum radical abolitionist constitutionalist, Lysander Spooner, made a more general argument in 1875 suggesting limits of rights-based principle to the intrusion of criminal law into a number of areas.[163] Spooner's essay articulated a general right to experience, acquire knowledge, and learn from mistakes, central to respect

154. See Griffith, *In Her Own Right,* 157.
155. Ibid.
156. Ibid., 158.
157. See Ezra H. Heywood, *Cupid's Yokes* (originally published, 1874), in *The Collected Works of Ezra H. Heywood,* ed. Martin Blatt (Weston, Mass.: M & S Press, 1985); id., *Uncivil Liberty* (Princeton, Mass.: Cooperative Publishing Co., 1871), ibid. For useful commentary on the free love movement in general and Heywood's role in particular, see John C. Spurlock, *Free Love: Marriage and Middle-Class Radicalism in America, 1825–1860* (New York: New York University Press, 1988).
158. See Heywood, *Cupid's Yokes,* 22.
159. Ibid.
160. Ibid., 23.
161. See Heywood, *Uncivil Liberty,* 16.
162. Ibid., 20–21.
163. See Lysander Spooner, *Vices Are Not Crimes: A Vindication of Moral Liberty* (1875; Cupertino, Cal.: Tanstaafl, 1977).

for a free person (4–5, 15, 32–33), and the inadequacy of abridgment of this right either on paternalistic (17) or sectarian theological grounds (18). Spooner's essay was published as part of an effort to resist arguments, like those of the WCTU, for liquor prohibition (xiii–ix), but he noted that it would condemn as well criminalization of sexual crimes like prostitution (17) and fornication (22–23).

Suffrage feminism, particularly after its alliance with the WCTU, increasingly resisted both the general form of Spooner's argument and, in the wake of the Woodhull scandal, the specific application of the argument by Heywood and others to a right of free love alleged to be central to women's rights. Indeed, the increasingly repressive moral temper of the nation was reflected in the unsuccessful federal obscenity prosecution brought by Anthony Comstock against Woodhull[164] and the recurrent prosecutions against Heywood for publication of his free love essays, two of which led to convictions. Although the first was presidentially pardoned, the second conviction resulted in a punishment of two years at hard labor; Heywood lived only one year after his release in 1892.[165] Free love advocate Lois Waisbrooker was also repeatedly arrested for her publications both under the federal obscenity law and comparable state laws, culminating in her prosecution at the age of seventy-six for the publication of her article, "The Awful Fate of Fallen Women," which a Washington state court judged obscene in 1902.[166]

Harriet Beecher Stowe, who had converted to suffrage feminism by 1869,[167] nonetheless demonized Woodhull in a way she had never attacked proslavery apologists, even at the height of her most passionate indignation (377). If the Comstock Law and related state laws were silencing Heywood and others by criminal sanctions, Stowe was doing so in the court of public opinion by her forceful Wollstonecraft repudiation of Woodhull and her ilk (378–79). Stowe made her point by defending her brother, who was in fact a moral and sexual hypocrite in the very way Woodhull had charged, "as a sexless angel" (377). Stowe's defense bespoke the repressive ideological power of the conception of gender roles (women's higher morality) increasingly salient, as we have seen, in suffrage feminism. Men and women were to be held to the same standard, but one "holding men to a standard even more virtuous than that of the Victorian woman" (377). Stowe affirmed such

164. The charge was eventually dismissed. See Johnston, *Mrs. Satan,* 160–64, 183, 196.
165. See Spurlock, *Free Love,* 226–29.
166. See Braude, *Radical Spirits,* 139–40.
167. Joan D. Hedrick, *Harriet Beecher Stowe: A Life* (New York: Oxford University Press, 1994), 358–62.

unreasonable standards in response to the first publicly serious argument of a human right to love specifically urged by and on behalf of women in the United States. Precisely at the time when the traditional orthodoxy of women's general roles had been subjected to reasonable doubt, Stowe polemically demanded that all discourse conform to the orthodoxy, repressing the arguments and claimants the public most reasonably needed to hear. The Wollstonecraft repudiation thus worked the worst ravages of the paradox of intolerance on American feminism: exactly the discourse most reasonably needed to challenge unjust gender roles was repressed, and an insular and parochial epistemology of gender roles distorted political reality to its own unjust terms. A man, who was a moral and sexual hypocrite, became a sexless angel; a dissenting woman, who fairly subjected his hypocritical conduct to criticism, was demonized as a "witch" (377) or, in the terms used by Henry Ward Beecher of Woodhull and her sister, "two prostitutes."[168] As the terms of insult indicate, prostitutes were to be the primary scapegoats of this ideologically embattled repression of reasonable doubt and discussion.

The purity movement was an ideological outgrowth of temperance that powerfully enforced this repressive political ideology at large, including its impact on suffrage feminism. The idea of purity was historically allied to temperance;[169] prohibitionist attitudes toward liquor were thus naturally extended to prostitution, which was understood as sexual intemperance.[170] Liquor consumption was associated with loss of inhibitions, including sexual restraints. Frances Willard captured the worry of temperance women when she spoke of "intemperance and impurity" as "iniquity's Siamese Twins."[171] The worry, however, cut deeper: impurity reflected "pollution beliefs in which certain practices were prohibited because they obscured the clarity of the division between evil and good."[172] Among these was sex not for the purpose of procreation (long a matter of concern to Christian morality) and sex that was not an expression of religiously idealized romantic love. Americans in the nineteenth century did not use purity to refer to the asexual or passionless;[173] both men and women could regard their sex-

168. Griffith, In Her Own Right, 157.

169. See David J. Pivar, Purity Crusade: Sexual Morality and Social Control, 1868–1900 (Westport, Conn.: Greenwood Press, 1973), 33, 81, 99.

170. Ibid., 100.

171. Tyrrell, Woman's World Woman's Empire, 192.

172. Ibid.

173. See, in general, Lystra, Searching the Heart; but cf. Nancy F. Cott, "Passionlessness: An Interpretation of Victorian Sexual Ideology, 1790–1850," Signs 4, no. 2 (winter, 1978), 219–36; and for Britain, see Michael Mason, The Making of Victorian Sexuality (Oxford:

ual relations as pure (including premarital relations) if they were sexually legitimate, and one ground for such legitimacy was its romanticism,[174] often religiously idealized.[175] Frances Willard would thus effectively describe women's purity in marriage not as asexuality, but as a sexual life in which she has "undoubted custody of herself," including Willard's euphemism for the timing and quality of sexual relations (determining "the frequency of the investiture of life with form and of love with immortality"[176]).

The prohibition of prostitution became an obsession of the purity movement because its very existence blurred the line the movement wanted to draw between legitimate and illegitimate sexual relations. In the antebellum period, when abolitionist feminists like Lydia Maria Child and the Grimke sisters were exploring their common ground with the slave and the black, they identified and explored their common grounds as well with women prisoners and prostitutes, each, as Child put it, within "a hair's breadth" of being the other.[177] Women, under the impact of the theory of moral slavery of abolitionist feminism, confronted "the enslaving ethos of the woman-belle ideal."[178] The Grimke sisters, Harriet Jacobs, and Sojourner Truth had underscored the unjust force this ideal played in sustaining not only slavery but racism and sexism more generally. Not only were black women, on the basis of a racialized conception of the ideal, not regarded as women, but any woman who seriously demanded basic human rights was similarly condemned, and in a way no man was for his demand of such rights on equal terms. The abolitionist feminist challenge was at its core a critique of this ethical double standard, identifying the role that the woman-belle ideal unjustly played in degrading women from their status as bearers of universal human rights. The injustice of the treatment of prostitutes was, from this perspective, yet another instance and example of this injustice from which all women (as sisters) suffered. Their treatment rested on the unjust double standard of the belle-femme ideal, which did not regard prostitutes as women. Prostitution was thus a natural symbol for this wider injustice.[179]

Oxford University Press, 1994); *The Making of Victorian Sexual Attitudes* (Oxford: Oxford University Press, 1994).

174. See Lystra, *Searching the Heart*, 75–77, 80, 83.

175. Ibid., 237–58.

176. See Willard, *Glimpses of Fifty Years*, 614.

177. See Barbara J. Berg, *The Remembered Gate: The Origins of American Feminism: The Woman and the City, 1800–1860* (New York: Oxford University Press, 1978), 219; see also ibid., 219–22.

178. Ibid., 174.

179. Ibid., 179–80, 207, 219–22.

This charitable and rights-based approach to prostitution was the ground for Judith Butler's successful opposition in the late 1860s to the introduction of the licensing of prostitution into Great Britain.[180] Butler's advocacy importantly built upon and elaborated the opposition of prostitutes themselves to the forms of police control over women's sexuality contemplated by the Contagious Diseases Acts;[181] indeed, she encouraged prostitutes to organize to resist the act (138). Butler thus underscored the lack of legal safeguards of the basic rights of women under the system (93) and worked within a framework that accepted the right of these women to control their persons (117, 137). Consistent with this position, Butler opposed attempts to repress prostitution itself through criminalization (140–41, 146–47). Indeed, in 1897 Butler warned against "the soundness of principle of those engaged in social purity work" which, while discoursing in public "of the divinity of womanhood [was] yet . . . ready to accept and endorse any account of coercive and degrading treatment of their fellow creatures, in the fatuous belief that you can oblige human beings to be moral by force" (252).

Butler's opposition to licensing was influential in the United States, but her warnings about a repressive social purity movement went unheeded.[182] Under the leadership of Frances Willard and the WCTU,[183] the evil of prostitution was redefined "as sexual intemperance"[184] and thus subject to the same prohibitionism advocated for alcohol; it was, in fact, no better justified on secular grounds.[185] The rights-based approach of antebellum abolitionist feminists to prostitution was repudiated, indeed warred upon. In a particularly vivid example of the political irrationalism wrought by the paradox of intolerance, a conspicuously sectarian view of woman's higher morality repressively enforced its claims at large on the basis of an ostensible attack on the double standard when its own normative stance (woman's higher morality) expressed and reinforced precisely the ethical double standard that it

180. See, in general, Judith R. Walkowitz, *Prostitution and Victorian Society: Woman, Class, and the State* (Cambridge: Cambridge University Press, 1980); Barbara Caine, *Victorian Feminists* (Oxford: Oxford University Press, 1992), 151–95; Sheila Jeffreys, ed., *The Sexuality Debates* (New York: Routledge & Kegan Paul 1987), 111–89.

181. See Walkowitz, *Prostitution and Victorian Society*, 8–9, 128; on the strong female subculture during this period, see ibid., 25–26.

182. See Pivar, *Purity Crusade*, 65–66, 87, 111.

183. Ibid., 117, 174–75.

184. Ibid., 100.

185. See David A. J. Richards, "Commercial Sex and the Rights of the Person: A Moral Argument for the Decriminalization of Prostitution," *University of Pennsylvania Law Review* 127 (1979): 1195, reprinted in part in Richards, *Sex, Drugs, Death and the Law*, 84–153.

had been the aim of abolitionist feminism to expose and criticize. Where abolitionist feminism underscored the moral continuities among all the injustices experienced by women (including prostitutes), increasingly conservative suffragists, like Willard, drew a Manichean line between the idealized experience of organized mother-love and the depraved conduct of other women, of which an example must be made.

Willard's leadership gave political expression to a movement of repressive suffrage feminism endorsed as well by Harriet Beecher Stowe, and the prostitute was its scapegoat. Its normative attitude was centrally shaped by its reactionary opposition to and repression of abolitionist feminism as a theory and practice of feminist emancipation on grounds of universal human rights.

As we have seen, antebellum abolitionist feminism was largely a form of moral criticism within radical moral abolitionism. It was only in the wake of the triumph of political abolitionism in Lincoln's 1860 election, the Civil War, and the growing public appeal of radical moral abolitionism as the background of the Reconstruction Amendments that abolitionist feminism would arrive at center stage as a credible form of political abolitionism. Abolitionist feminism called, however, for a rights-based criticism of the theory of gender roles endorsed by Catharine Beecher, Horace Bushnell, and Frances Willard in terms of abridgment of at least four areas of human rights: conscience, speech, intimate association, and work. Its theory of moral slavery argued that abridgment of basic human rights in all four areas on inadequate sectarian grounds unjustly dehumanized both African Americans and women. Basic rights of conscience had thus been abridged by imposing on women a normative conception of gender roles based on a misogynist interpretation of basic religious and other cultural texts in which women had never been permitted to participate as scholars, teachers, and ministers on equal terms. To accomplish this, central rights of free speech (and ancillary rights of education) had not been fairly extended to women on equal terms, as the experience of the Grimke sisters dramatically attested. Rights of intimate association had not been extended to women on equal terms because the terms of marriage (including custody of children) were fundamentally unfair. Finally, women had not been extended their basic rights to work and the economic independence to which exercise of that right would lead.

Such abolitionist feminist criticisms subjected the theory and practice of American gender roles as they were conventionally understood to reasonable doubt on the basis of fundamental conceptions of rights-based American political and constitutional morality (that had been saliently reaffirmed in the texts of the Reconstruction Amendments). In particular, the analysis raised questions about previously unquestionable matters, destabilizing a normative conception of women as essentially centered in private, intimate family relations. If women had been unjustly deprived of basic human rights as the abolitionist feminist theory of moral slavery alleged, then fundamental questions about the traditional normative conception had to be raised. The unjust political power of sectarian religious beliefs over their lives had to be contested by their own increasingly morally independent minds and in their own public voices as the Grimke sisters, Lucretia Mott, and Elizabeth Stanton had insisted; marriage and divorce would have to be reexamined and reformed, as Stanton urged, on terms of justice; an economic structure of work, which deprived women of their fair rights to work, would be contested and its opportunities competitively made available to women, as Mott argued.

If abolitionist feminism arose as a principled elaboration of the argument for toleration on the same platform of human rights, repressive suffrage feminism sought sharply to truncate the force of this argument by the enforcement at large of precisely the sectarian political epistemology of traditional gender roles about which abolitionist feminism had raised reasonable doubts. Consistent with the paradox of toleration, the traditional orthodoxy polemically enforced its sectarian claims in the areas under challenge by abolitionist feminism. Its normative measure was sectarian religion; the scope of debate was limited to the terms of the orthodoxy, repressing dissenters through obscenity prosecutions, censure (as with Stanton's *Woman's Bible*), and the like; women's traditional role in the family was the source of a politically enforceable higher morality that was to stand judgment over the ethics of human rights (rather than conversely); women's idealized moral role rendered them superior to the competitive world of work.

No person was a better scapegoat for this repressive ideology than Victoria Woodhull's theory and practice of free love and its conflation in the public mind with prostitution. Woodhull defied the ideology at each of its reactionary points: she not only challenged the role of traditional religion in politics, but spoke in her own morally independent public voice; she criticized women's role in the family as inconsistent with the human right to love, condemned marriage as legalized prostitution, lived and justified living on the basis of free love, and took objection to hypocrites like Henry Ward Beecher who lived but would not justify free love; and she worked as a successful stockbroker. Free love, on the view of some of its advocates (Stanton), had nothing to do with promiscuity, still less with commercial sex. But, the repressive ideology of gender roles was not interested in entertaining such distinctions, but giving effect to an embattled political ideology of gender roles. To do so, the political epistemology of gender, concerned to maintain conventional norms of good and bad women, ferociously attacked the role for women that Woodhull offered. Nineteenth-century condemnation of prostitutes crudely could include all sexually active women outside marriage,[186] or women who engaged in sexual intercourse not for propagation[187] or, most generally, women who misused any power or function;[188] the condemnation reflected as well opposition to sexual autonomy and economic independence in women[189] in circumstances of growing urban anonymity and commercialism.[190] Woodhull disagreed with these grounds or forms of condemnation. Indeed, her theory and practice of free love and feminism would wholly destigmatize women for love affairs outside marriage, for loving without propagation, and for being sexually and economically independent; she also pressed the argument for free love beyond Stanton to question legal and even abusive moral condemnation of women who engaged in commercial sex on the ground that they were within their rights and the condemnation rested on "an assumed right to thus sit in judgment over our unfortunate sisters,"[191] that is, questioning whether there was a defensible moral line of principle between their situations and that of many conventional women who marry.

The polemical force of the purity leagues arose as a political reaction to this kind of challenge to traditional gender roles, aiming to condemn and indeed abolish the evil of prostitution in order to quash the very idea of the legitimacy of Woodhull's theory and practice (particularly her suggestion that traditional marriage was not only moral slavery[192] but legalized prostitution).[193] Purity occupied the space of a politically enforced pollution ritual meant to reaffirm traditional certainties about good and evil that were, in fact, very much in reasonable doubt; from its perspective, the prostitute's "life style, attitudes, and behavior were

186. See Christine Stansell, *City of Women: Sex and Class in New York, 1789–1860* (New York: Knopf, 1986), 175.

187. See Pivar, *Purity Crusade*, 35.

188. Ibid.

189. Ibid., 190–91.

190. See Ruth Rosen, *The Lost Sisterhood: Prostitution in America, 1900–1918* (Baltimore: Johns Hopkins University Press, 1982), 40–41.

191. Woodhull, "A Speech on the Principles of Social Freedom," 32.

192. Ibid., 29, 35–36.

193. Ibid., 17, 34–35.

ominous signs of change in the feminine ideal, which would ultimately influence all women,"[194] and the reactionary defense of the threatened ideal saw abolitionist condemnation of prostitution as the dike against the flood of disastrous changes it feared. To achieve its abolitionist ends, as it successfully did in the early twentieth century,[195] the purity movement symbolically transformed prostitution, which had been a metaphor for the situation of all women in the antebellum era and thus for appropriate charity and sisterhood,[196] into an evil radically discontinuous from the experience of conventional women. Where abolitionist feminists had developed a general theory of moral slavery for all women, purity advocates tendentiously used prostitution as a "master symbol"[197] that inverted the general theory of moral slavery, ascribing such slavery only to prostitution on grounds that were, in fact, quite dubious and known to be dubious (ascribing prostitution to economic necessity,[198] to exploitation of immigrants,[199] to force and kidnapping,[200] and the like). In effect, the sectarian normative conception of gender roles, which abolitionist feminism subjected to such profound rights-based criticism on the basis of the argument for toleration, was not just immunized from the reasonable public criticism and debate it needed, but was in fact idealized as the source of a higher morality that was politically enforceable at large as the sole measure of legitimate discussion of issues of gender. On this basis, prostitutes were demonized as not women and treated as barely persons, and the ideology repressed reactively the speakers and speech, grounded in abolitionist feminism, that raised the larger questions of principle about patterns of injustice that were intractably rooted in conventional gen-

194. See Mark Thomas Connelly, *The Response to Prostitution in the Progressive Era* (Chapel Hill: University of North Carolina Press, 1980), 47.

195. For useful studies of this era, see Mark Thomas Connelly, *The Response to Prostitution in the Progressive Era;* Ruth Rosen, *The Lost Sisterhood: Prostitution in America, 1900–1918* (Baltimore: The Johns Hopkins University Press, 1982); Barbara Meil Hobson, *Uneasy Virtue: The Politics of Prostitution and the American Reform Tradition* (Chicago: University of Chicago Press, 1990); Timothy J. Gilfoyle, *City of Eros: New York City, Prostitution, and the Commercialization of Sex, 1790–1920* (New York: W. W. Norton, 1992). For background, see Pivar, *Purity Crusade.*

196. See Rosen, *Lost Sisterhood,* 8–9.

197. See Connelly, *Response to Prostitution,* 6.

198. On the contemporary lack of support for the economic deprivation theory of prostitution, see Connelly, *Response to Prostitution,* 33–34; Rosen, *Lost Sisterhood,* 137–68.

199. Contemporary studies showed that immigrants were, in fact, underrepresented in the prostitute population; see Connelly, *Response to Prostitution,* 62–64; Rosen, *Lost Sisterhood,* 140–41.

200. On the lack of support for the claims made for white slavery as the cause of American prostitution, see Connelly, *Response to Prostitution,* 124–35; Rosen, *Lost Sisterhood,* 112–35.

der roles. Conventional gender roles became an unquestioned and un-questionable national political religion, and suffrage feminism was its minister.

Another politically successful nineteenth-century reform move-ment, antipolygamy, further reinforced this result.[201] The antipolygamy movement was wholly successful in mobilizing American public opin-ion, the newly formed Republican Party (whose 1856 party platform condemned slavery and polygamy as "the twin relics of barbarism"[202]) and, in the wake of the Civil War, the Congress and Supreme Court to end Mormon polygamy. The condemnation of Mormon polygamy rested not only on its alleged constitutional violation of church-state separation (in view of the political power of the Mormon Church in Utah),[203] but on the secular role monogamy was alleged to play in American conceptions of democracy and human rights. Francis Lieber explained in his *Political Ethics*,[204] an important antebellum work of constitutional theory, that polygamy, in contrast to monogamy, was problematic because it endorsed "the patriarchal principle . . . which, when applied to large communities, fetters the people in stationary despotism."[205] Lieber called for respect for universal human rights in appropriate constitutional guarantees, and certainly believed that the progress of American civilization was tied to the advancement of women in the style endorsed by a Catharine Beecher. However, he was no advocate of suffrage for women or, for that matter, of any public duties, like those acknowledged by abolitionist feminists, inconsistent with women's private "sacred duties" of wifely and motherly care.[206] Support for antipolygamy centrally came from such men and women committed to Catharine Beecher's normative conception of women's roles. Frances Willard was thus a passionate antipolygamist, urging that "the Book of Mormon be burned in the fierce blaze of Christian man-hood's indignation and woman's righteous wrath [restoring] woman her lost inheritance, 'the equality of equals', [the Gospel's] beloved Home Religion in every Home."[207] Support for antipolygamy, if any-

201. My analysis of the movement and its effects on American life and thought depends on the important work of Sarah Barringer Gordon. See, in general, Sarah B. Gordon, *"The Twin Relic of Barbarism": A Legal History of Anti-Polygamy in Nineteenth-Century America,* Ph. D. diss., Princeton University History Department (June 1995).

202. Ibid., 113.

203. Ibid., 100–102.

204. See Francis Lieber, *Manual of Political Ethics,* 2 vols. (Boston: Little, Brown, 1838–39).

205. Ibid., 2:9.

206. Ibid., 2:124–25.

207. See Gordon, *The Twin Relic of Barbarism,* 109.

thing, endorsed conventional American gender roles (including monogamy) as ideals, and, as such, was appealing to women like Willard
whose views idealized American gender roles and resisted the rights-
based criticism of such roles offered by abolitionist feminists.[208] To this
extent, the success of antipolygamy reinforced this idealization, further
suppressing the critical questions raised by Stanton (let alone Woodhull) about the injustices of American marriage.[209] Polygamy became a
trope for divorce; the success of antipolygamy thus naturally reinforced
opposition to divorce reform.[210]

By the beginning of the twentieth century, nearing its constitutional
victory in 1920, suffrage feminism was decisively now the instrument
of the repressive conception of gender roles that we have now studied
at some length. Suffrage feminism was no longer the solution to American sexism; it had become part of the problem. The consequences were
catastrophic for the pioneering feminists of this period, like Emma
Goldman and Margaret Sanger, who not only made forms of the free
love argument, but interpreted it to extend to basic rights like contraception, abortion, and even consensual homosexuality.

There was evidently in nineteenth-century America a lively practice
among American women of both use of various contraceptive techniques and contraceptives and of abortion services, but practice was
supported by little self-conscious public theory or argument.[211] The
books of Robert Dale Owen and Charles Knowlton made the discussion of reproductive control a more public matter in the 1830s.[212]
Knowlton, however, suffered several obscenity prosecutions; two resulted in convictions (one leading to three months at hard labor), another in hung juries.[213] In this environment, even leading advocates of
free love like Victoria Woodhull and Ezra Heywood expressly condemned contraception.[214]

The importance of Emma Goldman and Margaret Sanger was to
interpret the principle of free love, as we have so far studied it, to

208. Abolitionist feminists, like Susan B. Anthony, did find polygamy highly distasteful,
but asked for sympathy for polygamists. See Gordon, *The Twin Relic of Barbarism*, 434.
209. Ibid., 450–51.
210. See Gordon, *The Twin Relic of Barbarism*, 214–15, 247–48. For Horace Bushnell,
antipolygamy reenforced the case for antisuffrage; see ibid., 216.
211. For important studies, see Linda Gordon, *Woman's Body, Woman's Right: A Social
History of Birth Control in America* (Harmondsworth: Penguin, 1976); Janet Farrell Brodie,
Contraception and Abortion in 19th-Century America (Ithaca: Cornell University Press,
1994).
212. See Brodie, *Contraception and Abortion*, 89–106.
213. Ibid., 95–96.
214. See Gordon, *Woman's Body*, 97, 101–3.

encompass contraception and much else. Of the two women, Goldman offered the more profound rights-based interpretation of the principle, but Sanger, because of her strategically narrower focus (on contraception), had the more enduring impact on American culture and law. Both endured criminal prosecutions for their advocacy of free love; Goldman, who had immigrated to the United States from Russia in 1885, was ultimately deported in 1919.[215]

Goldman's remarkable moral voice, more than any other of her generation, indicted the state of suffrage feminism (in particular, its support of the purity movement) from the perspective of a rights-based feminism self-consciously aligned with the Garrisonian moral abolitionism that gave rise to abolitionist feminism.[216] Goldman's anarchism, like Garrison's, affirmed the primacy of a rights-based moral discourse grounded in "the sovereignty of the individual" (67) and the argument for toleration (using the analogy of the Reformation) (74–75), which empowered persons to claim their basic rights of moral personality against the unjust political orthodoxies that traditionally stifled and silenced them.[217] Goldman opposed electoral politics not only because it was ineffective in securing people's rights (62–63), but because it demoralized the moral competence of persons to come to know and demand their rights as free people (64). Her indictment of suffrage feminism was expressed in her two essays, "Woman Suffrage" (195–211) and "The Tragedy of Woman's Emancipation" (213–25). The obsession with securing suffrage, she argued, with all the political compromises of principle that struggle required, had rendered suffrage feminism not only morally vacuous (because it was not rights-based) but, in fact, aggressively hostile to realizing the rights of women. Suffrage feminists were not criticizing the sectarian ideologies that traditionally crippled the capacity of women to come to know and demand their human rights; rather, through their political deals with the WCTU, the purity movement, and Anthony Comstock, they were themselves the enforcers of such ideologies (170), "strengthening the omnipotence of the very Gods that woman has served from time immemorial" (52). In fact, the right to vote has a very different normative status, Goldman argued, than the more fundamental human rights of

215. For a good general study, see Richard Drinnon, *Rebel in Paradise: A Biography of Emma Goldman* (Chicago: University of Chicago Press, 1961).

216. For Goldman's identification with Garrison, see Emma Goldman, *Anarchism and Other Essays,* ed. Richard Drinnon (1969; New York: Dover, 1969), 76.

217. For further development of this point (the foundation of Goldman's anarchism on the demand for the right to conscience central to the argument for toleration), see Drinnon, *Rebel in Paradise,* 105–11.

the person: it is not a right in the latter sense at all, but at best an instrument by which such more basic rights may be secured (197–99). The tragedy of suffrage feminism was its obsession with an amoral means at the expense of betraying its only defensible moral ends.

The crux of this tragedy was suffrage feminism's Wollstonecraft repudiation of women's basic human right to love. Goldman grounded this right in the source of all human rights, the self-originating claims of one's moral personality. To understand herself as a bearer of human rights, a woman must assert "herself as a personality, and not as a sex commodity" (211), which includes "refusing the right to anyone over her body; by refusing to bear children, unless she wants them; by refusing to be a servant to God, the State, society, the husband, the family, etc., by making her life simpler, but deeper and richer" (211). Against the background of a conspicuously unjust conscription of women's soul and body for the sexual and reproductive uses of others, "the most vital right is the right to love and be loved" (224) on one's own terms as a woman, to "listen to the voice of her nature" (222), and bravely "to acknowledge that the voice of love is calling, wildly beating against their breasts, demanding to be heard, to be satisfied" (222). Echoing the abolitionist feminist theory of moral slavery, Goldman underscored how "truly enslaved" women are by their "own silly notions and traditions" (208), and that "[s]uffrage can not ameliorate that sad fact; it can only accentuate it, as indeed it does" (208). To truly emancipate themselves from such moral slavery, women must be guaranteed the moral, educational, and personal resources to defy the "internal tyrants, whether they be in the form of public opinion or what will mother say, or brother, father, aunt, or relative of any sort; what will Mrs. Grundy, Mr. Comstock, the employer, the Board of Education say? All these busybodies, jailers of the human spirit" (221).

The abolitionist war against prostitution had recently been defended by Jane Addams on the basis of the need for state-imposed curbs to realize "chastity and self-restraint"[218] in the anonymity and temptations urban environments (206, 212)[219] particularly offered immigrants (28–30); Addams had endorsed the common abolitionist case for liquor and prostitution (112, 188), the purity movement's analogy of prostitution to slavery (3–13, 197), and the role of female suffrage

218. See Jane Addams, *A New Conscience and an Ancient Evil* (New York: Macmillan, 1913), 190, 210–11.
219. The very secrecy of urban life now required, Addams argued, more state controls to secure chastity. Ibid. Addams was particularly concerned by the temptations (or opportunities) now open to working women living alone (outside the control of their families) in such environments.Ibid., 28–31, 55–9, 64–71, 72–73, 77, 79, 89–90, 143.

in securing these aims (191–98). Goldman responded with several important essays, including "The Traffic in Women."[220] Very much in the spirit of antebellum abolitionist feminists and of Victoria Woodhull, Goldman insisted that prostitution be regarded as raising an issue (treating women exclusively as a sex object and economically bargaining for them on that basis) central to the moral subjugation of all women, including conventionally married women (20, 24–27). Addam's abolitionism evaded the deeper issue of moral slavery and, Goldman argued, perversely reinforced it by ascribing to prostitution an evil wholly discontinuous with the experience of other women on grounds that would not bear examination. In fact, "it is merely a question of degree whether [a woman] sells herself to one man, in or out of marriage, or to many men" (179). The abolitionist case made, by Addams and others, used both distortions of fact and of value. Overwrought factual distortions included ascribing American prostitution to immigrants and coercive white slavery (189–93) as well as, monocausally, to economic factors (184). These distortions, in turn, reflected a sectarian conception of value ("a perverted conception of morality" (25) whose unjust political enforcement very much entrenched the interests of a politician like "the future Napoleon of America, Theodore Roosevelt" [29]);[221] that conception rested and indeed legitimated the abridgment of human rights, in particular, the denial to women in general of their human right to sexual autonomy, including their right to love on their own terms. This conception kept women "in absolute ignorance of the meaning and importance of sex" rendering "the entire life and nature of the girl . . . thwarted and crippled" (24). And deviation from this repressive and unjustly defined gender role led to the stigmatization of a girl who sought love before marriage or outside marriage as a fallen woman and thus a prostitute, in effect, unjustly creating the status that it now would further condemn (185–88). The consequence of such an unjust enforcement through law of a sectarian ideal of puritanical gender roles was "the perversion of the significance and functions of the human body, especially in regard to woman" (171). Suffragist women, like Addams, thus forged a deeply flawed conception of the emancipation of women: one calling for "a dignified, proper appearance, while the inner life is growing empty and dead," "a com-

---

220. See, in general, Emma Goldman, *Anarchism and Other Essays,* including "The Traffic in Women," pp. 177–94.

221. On the important role of Theodore Roosevelt in reenforcing both sexist and racist conceptions of gender roles during this era, see Gail Bederman, *Manliness and Civilization: A Cultural History of Gender and Race in the United States, 1880–1917* (Chicago: University of Chicago Press, 1995), 177–215.

pulsory vestal, before whom life, with its great clarifying sorrows and its deep, entrancing joys, rolls on without touching or gripping her soul" (217).

In contrast, Goldman argued, a rights-based feminism condemned the abolitionism of both the purity movement (173–74) and the WCTU (175) and the suffrage feminism that now supinely served these movements on the shallow populist grounds that these issues provided an opposition that politically united feminists (195–225).[222] Goldman thus offered a compelling internal criticism of the abusive use of the theory of moral slavery against commercial sex as such. Properly understood in terms of its abolitionist feminist origins, the theory required skeptical scrutiny of the unjust weight traditional conceptions of gender roles played in the abridgment of basic human rights. The theory was wrongly applied by Addams and others to condemn commercial sexual work as such since the condemnation itself rested on an uncritical conception of gender roles (idealizing narrowly defined, mandatory sexual, social, and economic roles dependent on men in family life) and, on that ground, abridged basic human rights. Any principled application and elaboration of the theory of moral slavery must, Goldman suggests, take seriously both its critical demands: first, a reasonable understanding of the basic human rights owed all persons, and, second, the structurally unjust grounds on which such rights were denied to a whole class of persons. The principled agenda of such normative criticism must include protections of the rights of conscience and speech of a Mary Wollstonecraft and Oscar Wilde (168) against the unjust political repression led by an Anthony Comstock (169–70, 174). (Roger Baldwin, the founder of the ACLU, admired, assisted, and learned from Goldman in her insistence on organizing to protect basic civil liberties.[223]) It must address, as Elizabeth Stanton and Edward Carpenter more recently had urged (229), basic injustices not only in marriage as an institution but in lack of economic opportunities that deprived women of economic independence (227–39). Finally and crucially, it must address the rights-based principle of free love, which Goldman interpreted as capaciously as Woodhull (condemning the prohibitionism of the purity movement). Goldman not only defended the principle (on this ground condemning the prohibitionism of commercial sex of the purity leagues), but clearly pioneered its application

222. On the power of antiprostitution as an issue that united suffrage feminists, see Suzanne M. Marilley, *Woman Suffrage and the Origins of Liberal Feminism in the United States, 1820–1920*, 185–86, 202–4.

223. See Drinnon, *Rebel in Paradise*, 140–41.

to the right to contraceptives (172).[224] She also suggested that it might apply to abortion (172–73), and evidently defended in speeches and elsewhere its application to consensual homosexuality.[225] On the last point, Goldman condemned the trial of Wilde, cited a leading British advocate of the rights of homosexuals, Edward Carpenter,[226] and enthusiastically claimed Walt Whitman as an influence on her views on free love.[227]

Goldman's life was at least as sexually radical as Victoria Woodhull's, and her political life more so.[228] She was neither a politician nor interested in politics, for which she had a rights-based contempt worthy of Garrison. The entire point of her anarchism was, very much like antebellum radical moral abolitionism, to confront the American public mind in general and American suffrage feminism in particular with basic issues of conscience rooted in the argument for toleration. She, more than any feminist of her generation, spoke in the authentic ethical voice of antebellum abolitionist feminism, and, in that voice, cogently indicted suffrage feminism for the shrunken and decrepit thing it had made of its rights-based heritage (reflected in the perverse, rights-denying interpretation it gave the idea of moral slavery).

Goldman's critique of suffrage feminism must caution us to insist on the full critical normative demands of the theory of moral slavery, including its application to cultural roles uncritically accepted as the irrationalist basis for a reasonable understanding of basic human rights. In particular, Goldman's critique suggests the pivotal importance of insisting, in the spirit of abolitionist feminism, on the principled elaboration of their central normative insight on the platform of human

224. For Goldman's crucial work to defend this right, see Drinnon, *Rebel in Paradise,* 165–72.

225. See Alix Shulman, "The Most Dangerous Woman in the World," in Emma Goldman, *The Traffic in Women and Other Essays on Feminism* (New York: Times Change Press, 1970), 13; Bonnie Haaland, *Emma Goldman: Sexuality and the Impurity of the State* (Montreal: Black Rose Books, 1993), 164–76; Jonathan Ned Katz, *Gay American History: Lesbians and Gay Men in the U.S.A.* (New York: Meridian, 1992), 376–80, 530–38.

226. For Goldman's amused comments on her later meeting with Carpenter and his domestic arrangements with his lover, see Richard and Anna Maria Drinnon, *Nowhere at Home: Letters from Exile of Emma Goldman and Alexander Berkman* (New York: Schocken, 1975), 127–28.

227. See Drinnon, *Rebel in Paradise,* 160–62. For Goldman's own later comments on the importance of Whitman's homosexuality to his greatness as a poet and rebel, see Richard Drinnon and Anna Maria Drinnon, eds., *Nowhere at Home,* 140–41.

228. On Goldman's personal life, see, in general, Drinnon, *Rebel in Paradise.* With respect to her political radicalism, I have in mind her complicity with the attempt of Alexander Berkman, her lover at the time, to murder Henry Frick. Ibid., 41–54.

rights. Suffrage feminism betrayed this project when, for short-term political gain, it abandoned this normative foundation, in effect, scapegoating one class of women (prostitutes) as the condition of the legitimacy of all others. Such scapegoating (whether of other women or, as we shall shortly see, other races) must be condemned by any principled understanding of the normative foundations of moral slavery. We can perhaps understand the political temptations that led to the normative perversity that Goldman properly identified and condemned (privileging conventional gender roles as the basis for a sense of political solidarity and action to achieve the aims of suffrage feminism). But, such perhaps understandable short-term coalitions, when thus based on structural injustice, ultimately reinforce injustice. Indeed, the very basis for injustice (traditional gender roles) becomes, perversely, the ostensible measure of justice. It confirms the power of such blinding moral myopia (exemplifying yet again the irrationalist repressive political force of the paradox of intolerance) that it could use the theory of moral slavery thus better to enslave. The lesson for us must be to insist on the full critical demands of the theory at all levels, including close scrutiny of the role uncritical cultural stereotypes, unjustly enforced through law, have played (as in suffrage feminism) in compromising the integrity of its demands.

Margaret Sanger's early public career espoused principles quite similar to Goldman's, but she eventually applied them much more narrowly to the issue of women's rights to contraception.[229] Sanger's 1914 monthly journal, the aptly named *The Woman Rebel,* offered a theory of woman's moral slavery by unjustly politically enforced sectarian conventions of gender in marriage and elsewhere that was quite as radical as Goldman's,[230] and similarly founded on a basic human right, namely, that "[a] women's body belongs to herself alone."[231] But, even at this early, rather radical period of her career, Sanger underscored "the importance of our fight for birth control."[232] Sanger was indicted in 1914, in part under the federal anti-obscenity Comstock law, for her publication of *Woman Rebel;* her arrest was followed by that of her husband, who had, in his wife's absence, sold her pamphlet on *Family Limitation* to a Comstock agent. Sanger's response was to go to Europe (her husband was convicted and served a prison term in her absence); here

229. For an excellent general study of Sanger, see Ellen Chesler, *Woman of Valor: Margaret Sanger and the Birth Control Movement in America* (New York: Anchor, 1992).

230. See Alex Baskin, ed., *Woman Rebel* (New York: Archives of Social History, 1976), 16, 20, 40.

231. Ibid., 25.

232. Ibid.,

Havelock Ellis, the important British student and advocate of sexual reform (including decriminalization of homosexuality[233]) became perhaps the closest mentor of her life and, for a period, her lover.[234] Sanger returned to the United States when she saw that confronting such prosecutions might lead to building public support for women's rights to contraceptives. Growing public outrage at her prosecution led to the charges being dropped, but Sanger was criminally convicted in 1916 under New York's Comstock law when she opened a birth control clinic in New York. Her conviction and prison time enormously enhanced her growing reputation.[235] Sanger made an essentially political decision to build gradually a movement centering only on the issue of contraception rights, suppressing not only many of her other more radical views (for example, about a right to sexual variety[236]) but also, in contrast to Goldman's honesty, the facts of her sexually quite unorthodox life style (usually conducted in Europe).[237] Sanger also became antiabortion (changing the views of her *Woman Rebel* days);[238] and her associate in her New York City birth control clinic, Hannah Stone, condemned homosexuality.[239]

Nonetheless, in one of her two most articulate defenses of her position, Sanger's argument opened with a quotation from Whitman[240] and cited the work of Havelock Ellis repeatedly.[241] Sanger made the case for a woman's right to use contraceptives in terms of a more general right of love, expressing "a new conception of sex, not as a merely propagative act, not merely as a biological necessity for the perpetuation of the race, but as a psychic and spiritual avenue of expression";[242] and, like Goldman, she regarded this "natural right of

233. See Havelock Ellis and John Addington Symonds, *Sexual Inversion* (London: Wilson and Macmillan, 1897).

234. See Chesler, *Woman of Valor*, 111–25.

235. Ibid., 102–3, 109, 126–27, 128ff., 138–40, 150–60.

236. Ibid., 96.

237. Ibid., 110, 249, 315.

238. Ibid., 271; but cf. ibid., 300–303.

239. Ibid., 306.

240. See Margaret Sanger, *The Pivot of Civilization* (1922; Elmsford, N.Y.: Maxwell Reprint Co. 1969), 1. See also Margaret Sanger, *Woman and the New Race* (1920; Elmsford, N.Y.: Maxwell Reprint Co., 1969).

241. See Sanger, *The Pivot of Civilization*, 50–51, 78–79, 141–42, 183, 186, 211, 243. Indeed, Ellis wrote the preface to Sanger's *Woman and the New Race*, vii–x.

242. See Sanger, *The Pivot of Civilization*, 140; see also ibid., 211–19, 259. For a similar argument rooted in a basic human right of moral personality and control of one's body, see Sanger, *Woman and the New Race*, 53–56, 59, 68, 94, 193–94, 197, 211; for the new imaginative value placed on sex, see ibid., 108–12, 117, 167–70. Like Goldman, Sanger argued that this right was a more basic right central to the emancipation of women, ibid., 94–95, 210–11, and that marriage, without guarantees of this right, was a kind of prostitution, ibid., 112.

woman to the control of her own body, to self-development and to self-expression"[243] as more fundamental than the right to suffrage,[244] freeing women, as it would, from "[t]he barriers of prurient puritanism."[245] The unjust abridgment of this basic human right had, echoing the abolitionist feminist theory of moral slavery, made of maternity a kind of slavery[246] not a motherhood freely expressive of moral personality but a kind of unjust conscription or compulsion,[247] not a life expressive of "a vigorous, constructive, liberated morality" but the "role . . . of an incubator and little more."[248] Abridgment of such a basic human right required, consistent with the argument for toleration, a compelling secular justification, but there was none in contemporary circumstances. In fact, a highly sectarian normative conception of women, one in which "women have been so degraded that they have been habituated to look upon themselves through the eyes of men,"[249] had been unjustly imposed on women. Such a sectarian normative conception failed to allow women to develop "their own self-consciousness," and thus "the exercise of judgment, reason, or discrimination," "the exercise of self-guidance and intelligent self-direction" of "that inalienable, supreme, pivotal [moral] power"[250] which they, as persons, possess. Only the removal of such "moral taboos" as the measure of public law can "free the individual from the slavery of tradition, [and] remove the chains of fear from men and women. . . . Free, rational and self-ruling personality would then take the place of self-made slaves, who are the victims both of external constraints and the playthings of the uncontrolled forces of their own instincts."[251] The consequence for women would be that, for the first time in human history, they will be accorded the respect due them as persons, including the ultimate human right to be an individual. Woman's ethical role was not set, as Catharine Beecher and her suffrage feminist followers supposed, "by self-sacrifice but by self-development."[252] Respect for

---

243. See Sanger, *Woman and the New Race,* 68.

244. Ibid., 2, 94–95, 210–11.

245. Ibid., 211.

246. See Sanger, *The Pivot of Civilization,* 24–25, 38. See also Sanger, *Woman and the New Race,* 28–29, 45, 53, 55, 59, 64, 70–72, 93, 94, 179, 183.

247. See Sanger, *The Pivot of Civilization,* 28, 30.

248. See Sanger, *Woman and the New Race,* 226.

249. See Sanger, *The Pivot of Civilization,* 209; see also Sanger, *Woman and the New Race,* 98–99, 210.

250. See Sanger, *The Pivot of Civilization,* 209.

251. Ibid., 232.

252. Ibid., 272.

moral personality, which included the human right to love, will awaken "woman's interest in her own fundamental nature," "[f]or in attaining a true individuality of her own she will understand that we are all individuals";[253] Sanger thus held women to what her abolitionist feminist forebears would have called the standards of universal human rights on the platform of human rights. There was, for Sanger, no higher morality than the ethics of respect of persons. The ethical challenge for women was not to idealize a sectarian tradition which in fact degraded them, but to reconstruct themselves and their societies on the terms that would dignify their transformative moral powers as ethically responsible agents and bearers of human rights to construct a more reasonable morality of sex and gender.[254] That, Sanger argued, was "their pivotal function in the creation of a new civilization."[255]

When she tried to express and act on these convictions, Sanger, however, was made to suffer criminal prosecution, conviction, and imprisonment under obscenity laws she condemned as the unjust political repression of women's struggle for basic human rights.[256] Goldman was also arrested, convicted, and imprisoned for public birth control lectures in 1916.[257] Goldman's broader interests led her to oppose conscription to raise troops for America's entry into World War I, and she was prosecuted, convicted, and imprisoned under a federal law for obstruction of the draft in 1917.[258] The government, anxious to be rid of so troublesome a critic, shortly thereafter successfully deported her on the ground she was not and never had been a citizen.[259] One District of Columbia attorney observed: "With Prohibition coming in and Emma Goldman going out, 'twill be a dull country."[260]

The events, as we have seen, were not unconnected. Goldman, the severest critic of suffrage feminism, was deported as an outcast to America at exactly the time suffrage feminism was to achieve its final victories in 1919 and 1920. The price paid was repression of some of the arguments of human rights that feminists and the nation most needed to hear. There were yet further arguments whose repression also rendered the victory of suffrage feminism morally bankrupt.

253. Ibid., 273.
254. See Sanger, *Woman and the New Race*, 167–85.
255. Ibid., 272. For the role of women in creating a new morality of sex, see Sanger, *Woman and the New Race*, 167–86.
256. See Sanger, *Woman and the New Race*, 186–97, 210–25.
257. See Richard Drinnon, *Rebel in Paradise*, 168–69.
258. Ibid., 184–205.
259. Ibid., 206–23.
260. Ibid., 223.

Suffrage Feminism and Racism:
The Critique of Ida Wells-Barnett

As we have seen, abolitionist feminism distinctively developed a common set of principles to condemn not only slavery and racism but the subjection of women and sexism; I have called its governing conception of these common principles the theory of moral slavery. We have now studied the impact of the political compromises of suffrage feminism, which effectively reinforced the rights-abridging normative conception of gender roles by making it the measure of the mission of suffrage feminism. Another related aspect of this declension was the racialized conception of gender that suffrage feminism increasingly idealized. As we have seen, Stanton had herself set the trajectory of this decline when, in arguing against both the Fourteenth and Fifteenth Amendments, she made frankly nativist and racist appeals for solidarity among native-born American whites (men and women) against threats to their rights (like rape) as a reason for extending the franchise to women. We need now to examine further the dimensions of this problem in suffrage feminism as a continuing exploration of yet another aspect of its increasingly idealized conception of gender.

The political dynamic of the problem was set by the need of suffrage feminism to seek ever larger coalitions of women who could be persuaded to organize around the issue of woman suffrage. The alliance with the temperance and purity movements expressed this dynamic with the consequences already discussed. A related alliance was sought regionally between the women of the North (who had founded suffrage feminism on the basis of abolitionist feminism) and of the South (who had traditionally resisted abolitionism in general and abolitionist feminism in particular). The basis for this alliance was increasingly one of racial solidarity—a fundamental compromise of abolitionist feminist principle.[261] The franchise, on this view, should not extend to all men, but only to those who were sufficiently educated and acculturated; blacks and immigrants, who didn't meet this criterion, should not vote; women, who did, should.[262]

The idealization of women as moral superiors lent force to this argument. If women were morally superior in the way Frances Willard and

261. For illuminating discussion of the dynamic, see Aileen S. Kraditor, *The Ideas of the Woman Suffrage Movement, 1890–1920* (New York: Columbia University Press, 1965), xi, 137–38, 163, 173, 199–200; Suzanne M. Marilley, *Woman Suffrage and the Origins of Liberal Feminism in the United States, 1820–1920,* 159–86; William L. O'Neill, *Everyone Was Brave: The Rise and Fall of Feminism in America* (Chicago: Quadrangle Books, 1969), 69–74, 87–88.
262. Kraditor, 32, 40–41, 53, 124ff., 254.

others supposed, then this superiority served as an answer to those men who familiarly resisted woman's suffrage because women could not fight for their country.[263] Men's military prowess might be a sufficient condition of the right to vote, but it was certainly not necessary; women's moral superiority more than adequately supported their right to vote at least on equal terms with men (and perhaps even on superior terms, if one were to press the argument to its full reasonable extent).

But the idealization of gender, when used in this way and in this context, was fundamentally racialized: the argument applied and was understood to apply only to white women. To this extent, the normative weight placed on morally superior gender roles served to reinforce unjust patterns of gender subjugation and racial hierarchy. No better example of the consequences of compromise of basic issues of rights-based principle can be offered: the attempt to privilege gender at the expense of race resulted in an approach that reinforced racism and sexism.

The consequences of such compromises of principle are illustrated in the way the Reconstruction Congress framed and understood the new principles of constitutional law it had introduced into American public law. The problem was not only an inadequate understanding of the rights-denying character of sexism, but of racism as well (for example, the failure to condemn state-imposed racial segregation and anti-miscegenation laws). Congress's failure set the terms of the Supreme Court's equally defective interpretation of the moral promise of the Reconstruction Amendments both in the areas of race and gender. In 1873, the Court seriously blundered in *The Slaughter-House Cases*[264] by torturing the text and ignoring the history and political theory of the Reconstruction Amendments to deny national power to protect basic human rights.[265] This decision set the stage for the Court's 1883 failure in *The Civil Rights Cases*[266] to extend national power to protect basic human rights of African Americans against racism[267] and its appalling 1896 endorsement of state-sponsored racial segregation in *Plessy v. Ferguson*.[268] The Court, so nescient about its constitutional responsibilities in the area of race, invoked the same standards (or lack

263. Ibid., 28, 33, 250–51.

264. See *Slaughter-House Cases*, 83 U.S. (16 Wall.) 36 (1873).

265. For an elaboration of this criticism, see Richards, *Conscience and the Constitution*, 204–17.

266. See *Civil Rights Cases*, 109 U.S. 3 (1883).

267. For further criticism, see Richards, *Conscience and the Constitution*, 176–77.

268. See *Plessy v. Ferguson*, 163 U.S. 537 (1896). For further criticism, see Richards, *Conscience and the Constitution*, 160–70.

of standards) when in 1873, explicitly invoking *The Slaughter-House Cases*, it refused to protect a women's basic right to be a lawyer in *Bradwell v. State*[269] and on the same basis the following year refused to protect a woman's right to vote.[270] Indeed, in his concurring opinion in *Bradwell*, Justice Bradley infamously and uncritically endorsed the conception of gender roles of a Catharine Beecher or Horace Bushnell as the measure of women's constitutional rights, denying on this basis that a married woman could occupy the role of lawyer:

> [T]he civil law, as well as nature herself, has always recognized a wide differ-ence in the respective spheres and destinies of man and woman. Man is, or should be, woman's protector and defender. The natural and proper timidity and delicacy which belongs to the female sex evidently unfits it for many of the occupations of civil life. The constitution of the family organization, which is founded in the divine ordinance, as well as in the nature of things, indicates the domestic sphere as that which properly belongs to the domain and functions of womanhood. The harmony, not to say identity, of interests and views which belong, or should belong, to the family institution is repug-nant to the idea of a woman adopting a distinct and independent career from that of her husband. . . . The paramount destiny and mission of woman are to fulfill the noble and benign offices of wife and mother. This is the law of the Creator.[271]

Suffrage feminism, in light of its tightening alliance with the WCTU and other conservative women's groups, not only failed to offer appro-priate criticisms of these developments, but as we have seen, rein-forced them. The nerve of its moral vacuity, its failure to serve justice for either women or for African Americans, was the mythological ideal-ization of gender in terms of which it understood its mission.

Justice Bradley could not have written as he did if suffrage feminists and their allies had given greater weight than they did to the views of abolitionist feminists like Sojourner Truth and Harriet Jacobs. The whole point of Sojourner Truth's challenge to the white ministers in 1851 who tried to silence activist rights-claiming women as unwomanly was that their appeal to gender was mythologically racialized (black women worked outside the home, engaged in hard physical labor, were often as strong as men, yet also brought up children on their own). Harriet Jacobs wrote with astonishing honesty about the culture of black women's gender roles under slavery in which their sexual degra-dation was the obverse side of the highly idealized romanticism of white women's roles. It was only one step beyond Jacobs to make the

---

269. See *Bradwell v. State*, 83 U.S. (16 Wall.) 130 (1873).
270. See *Minor v. Happersett*, 88 U.S. (21 Wall.) 162 (1874).
271. See *Bradwell*, 83 U.S. at 141.

more general point, as Emma Goldman later did, that the political enforcement of gender roles on the basis of a romantic idealization of white women was sustained by the correlative unjust condemnation and degradation of the women who violated the terms of that idealization. The unjustly dichotomous terms of gender roles were either the purity of the virgin or the corruption of the whore; and the gender roles of white versus black women were then unjustly interpreted in accord with this dichotomy. One injustice thus became the ground for yet another injustice, and their common ideology was the dehumanization of a class of persons (as not bearers of human rights) on mythologically enforced terms of their either unjustly idealized or devalued sexuality. Suffrage feminists and their allies not only failed to press these points that would have kept before the American public mind the common principles that condemned racism and sexism, they perversely promoted the idealization of women in ways that reinforced its power to work injustice both on women and on blacks.

The problem for suffrage feminism was very well posed by the challenge made in the 1890s to one of its most distinguished proponents, Frances Willard, by a black woman, Ida Wells-Barnett. Wells had been born in 1862 in Mississippi, the child of slave parents. Upon the death of her parents in a yellow fever epidemic in 1878, Wells assumed responsibility for her siblings. After attending Shaw University, she taught school to support her family, and moved to Memphis to improve her career opportunities. As early as 1887, Wells found her life work as a journalist and became editor of a Memphis newspaper, the *Free Speech*.[272]

In 1892, when Wells was in Natchez, Mississippi, in connection with her work, three young black businessmen, regarded as too prosperous by white competitors, were lynched in Memphis. Wells knew one of them well, considering him and his family her best friends in Memphis. Wells initially used her newspaper to urge blacks to leave Memphis:

> The city of Memphis has demonstrated that neither character nor standing avails the Negro if he dares to protect himself against the white man or become his rival. There is nothing we can do about the lynching now, as we are out-numbered and without arms. . . . There is therefore only one thing

---

272. See, on these points, Trudier Harris, "Introduction," in *Selected Works of Ida B. Wells-Barnett* ed., Trudier Harris (New York: Oxford University Press, 1991), 3–13; see also Alfreda M. Duster, ed., *Crusade for Justice: The Autobiography of Ida B. Wells* (Chicago: University of Chicago Press, 1970). For an important recent study of these issues that complements my own analysis, see Gail Bederman, *Manliness and Civilization: A Cultural History of Gender and Race in the United States, 1880–1917* (Chicago: University of Chicago Press, 1995); for pertinent analysis, specifically, of Ida B. Wells, see ibid., 45–76.

left that we can do; save our money and leave a town which will neither protect our lives and property, nor give us a fair trial in the courts, but takes us out and murders us in cold blood when accused by white persons.[273]

In response, many black people left Memphis. Members of the white community, in response to the loss of labor and business income, pleaded with Wells to halt the exodus; she refused. Shortly thereafter, further lynchings occurred. Wells originally had believed the conventional wisdom "that although lynching was irregular and contrary to law and order, unreasoning anger over the terrible crime of rape led to the lynching; that perhaps the brute deserved death anyhow and the mob was justified in taking his life" (64). But, Wells had investigated and knew that the Memphis lynchings were of men who committed no crime against white women; rather, lynching was "[a]n excuse to get rid of Negroes who were acquiring wealth and property" (64). She therefore investigated each lynching she heard about, and "stumbled on the amazing record that every case of rape reported in that three months became such only when it became public" (64–65). In fact, the sexual relationship between white woman and black man had been consensual (65). In May 1892, she published an editorial in her newspaper to set out her findings:

> Eight Negroes lynched since last issue of the *Free Speech*. Three were charged with killing white men and five with raping white women. Nobody in this section believes the old thread-bare lie that Negro men assault white women. If Southern white men are not careful they will over-reach themselves and a conclusion will be reached which will be very damaging to the moral reputation of their women. (65–66)

A few days later, the editorial was republished in another newspaper, and an editorial "called on the chivalrous white men of Memphis to do something to avenge this insult to the honor of their women" (66). A committee of citizens met, and a group went to the *Free Speech* office and destroyed its type and furnishings. Her life threatened, Wells, who had left the day before the editorial was published for a vacation in New York, never returned, becoming, like the Grimke sisters before her, an exile from a South too intolerant to respect the right of free speech. She became a journalist for a New York newspaper, the *New York Age*. She initially published a seven-column article on the front page of this newspaper "giving names, dates, and places of many lynchings for alleged rape" (69) and later expanded the article into

273. Duster, *Crusade for Justice,* 52.

her important 1892 work, *Southern Horrors: Lynch Law in All Its Phases.*[274]

Wells had stumbled across "facts of illicit [consensual] association between black men and white women,"[275] "that what the white man of the South practiced as all right for himself, he assumed to be unthinkable in white women" (70). She was convinced that the facts she had discovered put lynching in an entirely new light: it was an irrational expression of the Southern racist "resentment that the Negro was no longer his plaything, his servant, and his source of income" (70). Such racism expressed an unjustly enforced political epistemology of race and gender that dehumanized African Americans as sexually rapacious animals (nonbearers of human rights); it distorted reality to comply with its terms, in particular, repressing by "the cold-blooded savagery of white devils under lynch law" (70) the reasonable exercise by African Americans of the basic human rights that would challenge this orthodoxy. Lynching was the mechanism of this unjust dehumanization; it both polemically denied the exercise of intimate rights of association between black men and white women ("striking terror into the hearts of other Negroes who might be thinking of consorting with willing white women" [71]) and it abridged the basic rights of conscience and speech by which such atrocities might be reasonably understood and protested by African Americans as atrocities (branding us "as moral monsters and despoilers of white womanhood and childhood" thus robbing African Americans of "the friends we had and silence any protests" [71]). Like anti-Semitism, the irrationalist power of the ideology denied reality and imposed crude stereotypes of black sexuality as reality, remaking the consent of white women into purity raped and the consent of black men into rapist violence.

At the root of the racist ideology lay, as Wells came to see, Southern antimiscegenation laws, which

> only operate against the legitimate union of the races; they leave the white man free to seduce all the colored girls he can, but it is death to the colored man who yields to the force and advances of a similar attraction in white women. White men lynch the offending Afro-American, not because he is a despoiler of virtue, but because he succumbs to the smiles of white women.[276]

Lydia Maria Child had certainly made a related point when she earlier condemned Northern antimiscegenation laws for the role they played not only in the denial of the basic human right of love but in constructing the dehumanizing degradation of African Americans as non-bearers of human rights. Wells, through her observation and interpretive skills, deepened Child's analysis by offering a cogent analysis of the double standard that governed interracial sexual relationships outside marriage under a hegemonic racism: white men could acceptably have consensual sexual relations with black women, but white women could not (even imaginably) have consensual sexual relations with black men. Wells thus laid bare, in a way Child had not, the role the unjust idealization of white women played in American racism. White women were thus ascribed by law and convention a sexual virtue that they often lacked; black women, equally unfairly, a sexual vice. Wells wrote from within the experience of a Southern black woman as Harriet Jacobs had earlier written, giving voice to the profound injury such racist mythology inflicted on black women. She wrote "that many a slave woman had fought and died rather than yield to the pressure and temptations to which she was subjected" (44), and that a black woman under such politically entrenched injustice "has suffered as no white woman has ever been called upon to suffer or to understand" (328). Wells would not keep silent if white women's alleged feminism failed to take seriously the unique experience of black women.

Wells's insight into the role that a racialized idealization of gender played in American racism was central to her criticism of white women leaders of suffrage feminism. Wells knew personally and liked Susan B. Anthony, but one of the issues about which they disagreed was the importance of securing the vote for women. Wells doubted, "[k]nowing women as I do, and their petty outlook on life," that "the millennium is going to come when women get the ballot" (230). She was skeptical about the moral idealization of women by suffrage feminism because her research showed the view was not only false, but dangerously ideological in the way she had come so clearly to see in her analysis of lynching.

Though she agreed to disagree with Anthony about the importance of woman suffrage, her confrontation with Frances Willard turned on fundamental matters about which Wells would not compromise. These were matters of conscience about which, like her abolitionist feminist forebears, she had to speak to the wider world. If suffrage feminism meant what Willard took it to mean, it was not worth having.

Wells's antilynching campaign was aimed at arousing public sentiment on behalf of innocent black victims who had had consensual sexual relations with white women. Wells documented many such cases and concluded, "There are thousands of such cases throughout the

South."[277] Her forthright critical analysis of racism included as well a critical analysis of the idealization of white women by the ideology of Frances Willard and the WCTU.

Willard had unequivocally denounced lynchings as a barbaric injustice, but she was ideologically unable to accept "that white women might willingly acquiesce in sexual congress between the races."[278] Wells had become a popular lecturer who was given considerable press attention. She bitterly criticized Willard's condemnation of both lynching and, in the words of a WCTU resolution, "the unspeakable outrages which have so often provoked such lawlessness."[279] Willard, when confronted with the tension between her life-long support of black causes and her ideological idealization of women, had opted for the latter and simply denied the facts that Wells had put before the public: Southern white women simply could not have had the sexual lives that Wells ascribed to them. Indeed, after a tour of the South, Willard had publicly credited what she had been told by "the best white people," namely, "The grogshop is the Negro's center of power. . . . The safety of woman, of childhood, the home, is menaced in a thousand localities at this moment, so that men dare not go beyond the sight of their own roof-tree" (201–2). Willard's ideology of gender roles ignored the facts as Wells had documented them, and, worse, turned victims into aggressors. Willard's antiracism was simply "put on hold" when it conflicted with her ideology. Indeed, the ideological exigencies of the idealization of women led Willard actively to endorse the rationalizing distortions of reality on which lynching rested. Under Wells's withering criticism, Willard's position as a moral reformer, especially in Britain, was compromised (201–2, 216–17, 226–37).[280]

Wells's remarkable analysis probed, in a way never done before, the common roots of American racism and sexism. Many (including apologists for lynching) had observed before Wells "that the Southern people are now and always have been most sensitive concerning the honor of their women—their mothers, wives, sisters, and daughters" (146–47). But Wells gave this fact a new interpretation in terms of the place of an idealizing code of chivalry in an unjustly enforceable political epistemology that dehumanized white women in a degrading ideal-

277. See Wells-Barnett, *Southern Horrors*, 21.

278. See Bordin, *Frances Willard*, 217.

279. See Ida Wells-Barnett, *A Red Record: Tabulated Statistics and Alleged Causes of Lynchings in the United States, 1892–1893–1894* (1895), in *Selected Works of Ida B. Wells-Barnett*, 138–252, 236.

280. For further discussion of the episode from Wells's perspective, see Duster, *Crusade for Justice*, 112–13, 136, 151–52, 201–10; Bordin, *Frances Willard*, 216–18, 221–22.

ization of their sexual virtue and black men and women in the mirror image degradation of their sexual vice. Wells insisted that her defense of the black victims of this code had no purpose "to say one word against the white women of the South" (147). "[I]t is their misfortune" to be treated not as persons, but as tropes in a mythology of chivalry that in fact rationalized "barbarism" (147).

Wells's criticism of Willard suggested that the Southern idealization of women, with its virulently racist consequences, was only a more extreme form of a wider national idealization of women that also advanced racist ends. Willard, like other suffrage feminists of her age, had endorsed the refusal to extend the franchise to "illiterate colored men" at the South (231), and was prepared to blinker reality at precisely the ideological points that sustained the unjust political epistemology of racism in all its forms. The problem of suffrage feminism extended to its treatment of race as well: in both cases, the key to the political power of the rights-denying dehumanization of both women and blacks was an idealization of women that, in the name of a higher morality, immunized itself from any scrutiny in terms of reasonable arguments of basic human rights. Wells's argument suggested that to deal with such interlinked evils, the wisdom of abolitionist feminism (which Wells certainly assumed and elaborated) must be rediscovered before either racism or sexism could be responsibly understood and addressed as rights-denying constitutional evils.

VICTORY AND COLLAPSE

The victory of suffrage feminism in 1920 disappointed the political expectations of the suffrage feminists who had made such compromises of principle to achieve it. As one historian of this period observed:

> [The suffrage feminists] oversold the vote, which meant that both they and the generation that followed them were inevitably disillusioned with public affairs in general. They made too many compromises. . . . Practical politics made these choices essential, but expediency tarnished the moral quality that was the movement's most precious asset in the postsuffrage era. They failed to think seriously about what was to come after the federal amendment was passed. And, perhaps worst of all, in overconcentrating on politics they neglected other areas—economic, social, domestic—that more profoundly governed women's lives.[281]

---

281. See O'Neill, *Everyone Was Brave*, 273–74.

Women, once having the vote, not only did "not hang together, but [did] not even support for public office the best female candidates. Since there was no bloc vote, there was no reason for men to cater to it."[282]

Initially, there were some advances, including the 1921 Sheppard-Towner bill (calling for an annual appropriation of $1,250,000 for educational instruction for the health care of mothers and babies) and congressional approval of the Child Labor Amendment to the Constitution in 1924. Beginning in mid-decade, however, women's political impact fell precipitously, as politicians noted that women failed to vote in the cohesive way that, pre-suffrage, they had feared. The Child Labor Amendment, supported by many woman's groups, failed ratification in the key states of Massachusetts and New York as Catholic bishops joined the opposition against the amendment because it would destroy the sanctity of the home.[283] The low turnout of women at the polls was the first blow to suffragist dreams, followed by the lack of evidence that women voted differently from men (28–29).[284] In fact, the overall decline in voter turnout during the 1920s (for both men and women) reflected a shift in American political culture in which direct participation in mass political culture declined in favor of interest-group politics. As Suzanne La Follette observed in 1926, the misfortune of suffrage feminism was that "it has succeeded in securing political rights for women at the very period when political rights are worth less than they have been at any time since the 18th century" (31).

Before passage of the Nineteenth Amendment, women's political culture had developed through voluntary organizations and women's reform groups; and these forms of organization continued to thrive in the 1920s and 1930s (34–44).[285] During a period when Progressivism was supposedly dead, women's groups like the Consumers League pushed for incremental reform in the social democratic tradition of early twentieth-century settlement workers like Jane Addams.[286] Not all women's groups were equally successful: the new League of

282. Ibid., 268.

283. See William H. Chafe, *The Paradox of Change: American Women in the 20th Century* (New York: Oxford University Press, 1991), 26–28.

284. Ibid., 28–29. See also Nancy E. McGlen and Karen O'Connor, *Women's Rights: The Struggle for Equality in the Nineteenth and Twentieth Centuries* (New York: Praeger, 1983), 82–109.

285. See, in general, Nancy F. Cott, *The Grounding of Modern Feminism* (New Haven: Yale University Press, 1987); Kathryn Kish Sklar, *Florence Kelley and the Nation's Work: The Rise of Women's Political Culture, 1830–1900* (New Haven: Yale University Press, 1995).

286. On Addams, see Sklar, *Florence Kelley and the Nation's Work*, 171–205.

Women Voters had little of the popular appeal of its suffragist predecessor, NAWSA, although it was an overtly political organization. Other groups, more like the indirectly political groups of the Progressive Era, experienced growth, and many of these woman reformers flocked to Washington to manage the New Deal's social welfare institutions (35–36). Eleanor Roosevelt, who had a background working among these reformers (she was active in the Consumers League), became the critical link between them and their impact on and role in her husband's administration (36–42).

Women's greatest political power had been exercised indirectly through voluntary women's organizations based on the perception, which suffrage feminism had fostered, that women had a normatively special sphere of responsibility (42).[287] Despite the suffragists' political disappointment over the Nineteenth Amendment, these groups continued to pursue their separate agenda in the 1920s, quite continuously with the political role of women in the Progressive Era.[288] When large segments of this network moved to Washington with the New Deal, the attainment of the goals of the separate women's organizations was apparently at hand. But, even on their own terms, women's strength as political actors continued to depend on a woman-controlled separatist base. Assimilation into the New Deal bureaucracy (a largely male-controlled structure) weakened their home base and "could well signify the extinction of women's influence, not its triumph" (42).

There was a still deeper problem. Both the suffragist victory of the Nineteenth Amendment and the continuity of most woman's reform groups thereafter significantly reinforced the conventional conception of women's idealized gender roles. Indeed, such an idealized conception was used by suffragists like Frances Willard in ways sometimes quite hostile to any assessment of gender roles (including their role in racism) in light of independent values of human rights; socialist supporters of woman suffrage expressly warred on such values as fatally bourgeois.[289] The legacy of this tradition was a woman's reform movement fatally disunited on central normative issues of woman's emanci-

287. Paula Baker, "The Domestication of Politics: Woman and American Political Society, 1780–1920," *American Historical Review* 89 (June 1984); Suzanne Lebsock, "Across the Great Divide: Women and Politics, 1890–1920," in Louise Tilly and Patricia Gurin, eds., *Women, Politics, and Change in Twentieth-Century America* (New York: Russell Sage Foundation, 1990).

288. See, in general, Cott, *The Grounding of Modern Feminism.*

289. See Mari Jo Buhle, *Woman and American Socialism, 1870–1920* (Urbana: University of Illinois Press, 1981), 218–19.

pation and indeed often self-consciously hostile to assessment of these matters in terms of principles of human rights.[290]

A small group of reformist women, who had as the Woman's Party (formerly the Congressional Union) engaged in more radical tactics than the NAWSA before ratification of the Nineteenth Amendment, proposed in 1923 the Equal Rights Amendment to the Constitution (ERA). The National Woman's Party (NWP), under the leadership of Alice Paul, minimized the value of the suffrage victory on the ground that "women today . . . are still in every way subordinate to men before the law, in the professions, in the church, in industry, and in the home" (48). The NWP pledged itself exclusively to the goal of equality for women in the form of ratification of the ERA. Echoing the abolitionist feminist theory of moral slavery, the NWP believed that women were still enslaved and that only dedication to rights-based equality could guarantee their emancipation.

The League of Women Voters, in contrast to the NWP, tried to serve a broader constituency. League members argued that women had already secured their fundamental rights. Indeed, its president during the 1930s urged that "the well-worn old 'equal rights' slogan [be] reverently and gratefully returned to the suffragists at Seneca Falls. . . . Nearly all discriminations have been removed" (49). The league took as its agenda issues like child labor, wages and working hours, and disarmament as much as legislation concerned with women's rights.

The differences between the groups crystallized over protective legislation. Reformers took pride in having secured enactment of minimum-wage and maximum-hour laws for women; they feared that the NWP's doctrinaire approach to equal rights would abrogate any such legislation. Alice Paul urged that the problem be solved "by raising the standard of protective labor laws for men until they are equal to those already now in existence for . . . women" (50) (suggesting that such protective labor legislation is best understood strategically as a first step to implement women's conceptions of justice, later to be extended on fair terms to men as well). While Paul seemed willing to compromise on this issue, ultimately the groups remained at loggerheads over what both came to regard as a defining issue of feminist principle (50–

290. See Carl N. Degler, *At Odds: Women and the Family in America from the Revolution to the Present* (New York: Oxford University Press, 1980), 326–29, 334, 436–37. For a highly critical recent account of the legacy of suffrage feminism along similar lines, see, in general, Graham, *Woman Suffrage and the New Democracy;* but cf. Marilley, *Woman Suffrage and the Origins of Liberal Feminism in the United States, 1820–1920.*

51). From the NWP's perspective, laws singling out women for special treatment discriminated against women in job opportunities. To support their position, they offered evidence to show that many women lost jobs in industries subject to such requirements (53–55). The reformers responded that differences in physical and psychological makeup prevented women from ever competing on an equal basis with men and that special labor laws were required if women were to be protected from exploitation and given just treatment in their economic lives (55–58). The approach of the reformers was very much "the utilitarian contention that protective laws meant the greatest good to the greatest number of women workers (at least in the short run)" and took it to be axiomatic that the differences between women and men were permanent and required differential treatment.[291] In contrast, the rights-based approach of the NWP was "envisioning the labor market as it might be, trying to ensure women the widest opportunities in that imagined area,"[292] regarded "women's differentiation from men in the law and the labor market [as] a particular, sociohistorical construction, not necessary or inevitable,"[293] and argued that it was unjust to give controlling weight to a sexual division of labor that arose "from archaic social custom, . . . enshrined in employer and employee attitudes, and reified in the law."[294]

Dominant opinion among reform-minded women resisted the approach of the NWP because they largely accepted the more conventional conception of gender roles that the suffrage and related movements had, as we have seen, uncritically assumed and reinforced.[295] More radical rethinking of gender roles, including the role of love and motherhood, had been urged by Caroline Dall in her 1867 plea for economic opportunities for women, *The College, the Market, and the Court*,[296] and by Charlotte Perkins Gilman in her 1898 argument for the importance of the economic independence of women, *Women and Economics*.[297] Even Gilman, however, had interpreted her progressive

291. See Cott, *The Grounding of Modern Feminism*, 136, 138.

292. Ibid., 136.

293. Ibid., 138.

294. Ibid., 138–39.

295. See Degler, *At Odds*, 401–5. See also Kristi Andersen, *After Suffrage: Woman in Partisan and Electoral Politics before the New Deal* (Chicago: University of Chicago Press, 1996); Gwendolyn Mink, *The Wages of Motherhood: Inequality in the Welfare State, 1917–1942* (Ithaca: Cornell University Press, 1995).

296. See Caroline H. Dall, *The College, the Market, and the Court* (Boston: Lee and Shepard, 1867). For her criticism of women's dying for love, see ibid., 125–26.

297. See Charlotte Perkins Gilman, *Women and Economics: A Study of the Economic Relation Between Men and Women as a Factor in Social Evolution*, ed. Carl N. Degler (1898;

feminism in ways that reinforced the dominant racist stereotypes that Ida Wells-Barnett had contested.[298] In this uncritical environment, suffrage feminism suppressed critical thinking about the rights-based aims of feminism, including rights of economic independence. Its obsession with political rights blunted any clear thought about the more important human rights of women that had not yet been addressed. As Nancy Cott has cogently observed:

> The right of suffrage based on the concept of individual independence—meaning individual ownership of one's labor power—was still, in 1920, self-contradictory for wives. Reversing the sequence of liberal theory that predicated the vote on having an independent stake in society, wives gained political independence—if the ballot can be so called—while still lacking the clear legal right to economic independence.[299]

Progressive thought also took traditional gender roles as axiomatic in ways that uncritically assumed and enforced the political epistemology of gender announced by Justice Bradley in *Bradwell* in 1873. Louis Brandeis, for example, successfully argued to the Supreme Court in *Muller v. Oregon*[300] that women should be accorded special protections in maximum-hours laws on the basis of fundamental gender differences. In accepting his argument in 1908, the Court noted that "history discloses the fact that woman has always been dependent upon man" and thus must be protected as "minors."[301] In particular, "from the viewpoint of the effort to maintain an independent position in life, she is not upon an equality [but] properly placed in a class by herself, and legislation for her protection may be sustained"[302] on the basis of "the inherent difference between the two sexes, and in the different functions in life which they perform."[303] The crucial gender differences were "her physical structure and a proper discharge of her maternal functions—having in view not merely her own health, but the well-being of the race" which "justify legislation to protect her from the greed as well as the passion of man."[304] Such judicial affirmation of

---

New York: Harper & Row, 1988). On the importance of economic independence to a better conception of motherhood, see ibid., 173, 268–69, 278–80, 292–94. For related arguments, see Olive Schreiner, *Woman and Labour* (London: T. Fisher Unwin, 1911); Ellen Key, *The Renaissance of Motherhood* (1914; New York: Source Book Press, 1970).

298. For illuminating discussion on this point, see Bederman, *Manliness and Civilization,* 121–69.

299. See Cott, *The Grounding of Modern Feminism,* 185.

300. *Muller v. Oregon,* 208 U.S. 412 (1908).

301. Id. at 421.

302. Id. at 422.

303. Id. at 423.

304. Id. at 422.

gender differences was applauded by suffrage feminists for legitimating the conception of gender roles they endorsed.[305] Felix Frankfurter
in 1924 agreed: "Nature made men and women different; the law must
accommodate itself to the immutable differences of Nature."[306] Earlier
in 1923, Frankfurter asserted: "Only those who are ignorant of the law
. . . or indifferent to the exacting aspects of women's life can have the
naiveté, or the recklessness, to sum up women's whole position in a
meaningless and mischievous phrase about 'equal rights.' "[307] On the
same basis, Eleanor Roosevelt opposed the ERA.[308] American thought
on gender, even its supposedly most progressive thought, had advanced little beyond Justice Bradley well into the twentieth century.

To illustrate, take *Goesaert v. Cleary*,[309] which was decided in 1948.
Justice Frankfurter, writing for the Court, upheld a Michigan statute
that forbade any women to act as a bartender unless she be "the wife
or daughter of the male owner" of the licensed liquor establishment.[310]
While three dissenting justice briefly criticized the statute's gender
classification as "invidious,"[311] Frankfurter, consistent with the dominant progressive view, argued that since "Michigan may deny to all
women opportunities for bartending," it may also reasonably assume
"that the oversight assured through ownership of a bar by a barmaid's
husband or father minimizes hazards that may confront a barmaid
without such protecting oversight."[312] Despite "the vast changes in the
social and legal position of women . . . [t]he Constitution does not
require legislatures to reflect sociological insight, or shifting social standards, any more than it requires them to keep abreast of the latest
scientific standards."[313] Indeed, as late as 1961, the Court in *Hoyt v.
Florida*[314] unanimously upheld a Florida law providing that no woman
shall be taken for jury service unless she volunteers. The gender classification in question reasonably reflected, Justice Harlan argued (writing for the Court), that "woman is still regarded as the center of home
and family life" and therefore "should be relieved from the civic duty

305. See Marilley, *Woman Suffrage and the Origins of Liberal Feminism in the United States, 1820–1920*, 201–2.
306. Quoted at William Henry Chafe, *The American Woman: Her Changing Social, Economic, and Political Roles, 1920–1970* (New York: Oxford University Press, 1972), 129.
307. Ibid., 124.
308. See Chafe, *The Paradox of Change*, 166.
309. *Goesaert v. Cleary*, 335 U.S. 464 (1948).
310. Id. at 464.
311. Id. at 468 (Rutledge, J., dissenting; joined by Douglas and Murphy, JJ.).
312. Id. at 466.
313. Id. at 465–66.
314. *Hoyt v. Florida*, 368 U.S. 57 (1961).

of jury service unless she herself determines that such service is consistent with her special responsibilities."[315]

In this political environment, not only was rights-based feminism no longer a serious option for many American women, but those for whom it remained an option were now accused of neurotic incapacity, displaying, in the view of Ferdinand Lundberg and Marynia Farnham's 1947 publication, *Modern Women: The Lost Sex*,[316] a symptom of mental illness. Lundberg and Farnham based their analysis on an aggressively reactionary development of the Wollstonecraft repudiation. Mary Wollstonecraft's arguments in *Vindication of the Rights of Woman* were literally reduced to a case history: an unhappy home, rejection by her father, jealousy of a favored elder brother, love affairs to find a mate, feminism to rationalize her neurotic revolt against the family.[317] In fact, Wollstonecraft was a sex-starved female who literally begged to become the slave of any man who would take her in. With the case history as a reference point, any feminist in Wollstonecraft's mode was neurotically at war with her natural gender role of passivity in sexual and reproductive dependence on men, desiring to raise children.[318] The dissatisfaction of modern women was fomented by feminists who wooed them away from their true identity to a quest for masculinity. Both their demasculinizing domination of their sons and employment outside the home were expressions of this neurosis. To restore matters, Lundberg and Farnham proposed a program to curb the influence of masculine women, including a state-sponsored propaganda campaign to boost the family, subsidized psychotherapy for neurotics, cash subsidies to encourage women to have more children, and annual rewards to exceptional mothers. Women had to reclaim the home as the central focus of their existence.[319]

The very terms of Lundberg and Farnham's book suggests, in the face of widening employment opportunities for women during and after World War II,[320] an awakening sense of injustice among American women that raised novel questions about gender roles. If such rights-based feminism was to have any significant claim on the American public conscience as more than a perceived symptom of mental illness,

315. Id. at 62.

316. For discussion see William Henry Chafe, *The American Woman: Her Changing Social, Economic, and Political Roles, 1920–1970* (New York: Oxford University Press, 1972), 202–6.

317. Ibid., 203–4.

318. Ibid., 204–5.

319. Ibid., 205–6.

320. See Chafe, *The Paradox of Change*, 121–34.

it would require women themselves to more aggressively question the justice of conventional gender roles in the fundamental way that abolitionist feminists had called for. As we have seen, mainstream reform women and their progressive allies had largely come to regard that tradition as anachronistic, indeed retrograde. Its reawakening would require a volcanic public rethinking not only of the largely unexamined issues of sexism but of racism as well. Abolitionist feminism would be reborn in the wake of a public rethinking of American racism on grounds of rights-based principle.

5 Second Wave Feminism as Abolitionist Feminism

A bolitionist feminism arose as a distinctive interpretation of the antiracist strand of radical abolitionism, which was in turn very much the normative background for the Reconstruction Amendments. The tragically flawed struggle of suffrage feminism began in a wholly principled argument that the theory of moral slavery was the best interpretation of the meaning of the Thirteenth Amendment and should guide as well both the framing and interpretation of the rights-based principles later amendments would introduce to complement and perfect the abolition of slavery. Suffrage feminism made basic compromises of all these principles, and thus its victory in 1920 was fundamentally flawed, leaving a normative legacy that was, if anything, hostile to the rights-based feminism of its founding in ways I have now explored at some length (chapter 4).

Second wave rights-based feminism arose in the wake of the most profound public criticism and action against American racism since antebellum radical abolitionism, and based its antisexist principles on the same platform of human rights as the antiracist principles that increasingly informed both American public opinion and the constitutional interpretation of the Reconstruction Amendments. My task now is, against the background of our earlier study of both abolitionist and suffrage feminism, to make the best interpretive sense of this remarkable development both in the public conscience of the American people and in the integrity of our constitutional interpretation. Both second wave feminism and the developments in constitutional interpretation that reflect it are, I shall argue, best interpreted as taking up and building upon the theory of moral slavery central to abolitionist feminism.

To make this case, I start with the development of a seriously anti-racist interpretation of the Reconstruction Amendments in the theory and practice of the African American struggle for recognition of their basic constitutional rights, including the civil rights movement; in particular, my argument tries to clarify the ways in which that struggle importantly took up and elaborated strands of antebellum antiracist analysis that we have already examined. Second wave feminism will then be examined as a civil rights movement that, like abolitionist feminism, built upon and expanded these antiracist principles into antisexist principles as well. In light of this argument, I then offer an interpretive account of the constitutional principles both of privacy and equal protection that, in my judgment, are best understood in terms of these antisexist principles.

My account in both areas will be framed by the central role I give in my interpretation to a principled elaboration of the argument for toleration. Such a principled elaboration required both a practice and theory of a certain kind of rights-based struggle based on an appeal to basic inalienable human rights and the closer scrutiny of traditional grounds for abridgment of such rights in terms of the kinds of morally independent standards of public reason that the argument for toleration requires. Thus the antiracist and antisexist struggles powerfully used and sponsored increasingly muscular rights of conscience, speech, intimate life, and work; both struggles subjected traditional grounds for the abridgment of such rights to a more searching and reasonable public examination. In both cases, such rights empowered traditionally subjugated groups (under the theory of moral slavery) to come to understand and to demand their basic rights of moral personality and to engage increasingly in the reasonable public discourse and debate in their own voice that such rights make possible.

ABOLITIONIST ANTIRACISM AS THE MEASURE OF HUMAN AND CONSTITUTIONAL RIGHTS

Reconstruction Amendments: Promise and Betrayal

The antebellum radical-abolitionist criticism of slavery and racism focused on the denial of blacks' basic capacity to be even eligible to bear the rights that were central to the moral identity of the culture: conscience, free speech, intimate personal and family life, free labor, and the like (chapter 2). These rights are, by their nature, culture-creating rights, that is, forms of moral creativity through which people authenticate themselves, the larger meaning of their lives, and the culture of public reason required for exercise of their moral powers as persons. The systematic denial of these rights to any group by the dominant culture condemns that group to cultural death and deformed marginality, or a form of denationalization.[1] The national identity of dominant white America was conditioned on the construction of a negative identity (what an American is not); a culturally defined image of a race-defined people accorded them lower moral status because of alleged underlying moral incapacity. Both Roger Taney and Alexander Stephens thus had argued that white supremacy was constitutive of American constitutional identity.[2]

Under American slavery, the image of blacks as subhuman was constructed from alleged incapacities disqualifying them from basic rights. These included putative incapacities of moral reflection and deliberation (no right to conscience), lack of reasoning skills like literacy (no right of free speech), incapacity for responsible sexual intimacy and moral education of young (lack of privacy rights of sexual autonomy and family integrity), and lack of rational powers for many forms of work calling for independent exercise of rational powers (no right to free labor).[3] The underlying image of incapacity, constructed on the

1. For a related mode of analysis, see Orlando Patterson, *Slavery and Social Death* (Cambridge: Harvard University Press, 1982).

2. Chief Justice Roger Taney gave an authoritative interpretation of American national identity in *Dred Scott:* blacks were "beings of an inferior order, and altogether unfit to associate with the white race, either in social or political relations; and so far inferior, that they have no rights which the white man was bound to respect." See *Dred Scott v. Sanford,* 60 U.S. (19 How.) 393, 407 (1857). Alexander Stephens, vice-president of the Confederacy, argued to similar effect in a speech delivered in Savannah, Georgia on March 21, 1861: "Our new government is founded upon exactly the opposite idea; its foundations are laid, its cornerstone rests upon the great truth, that the negro is not equal to the white man—subordination to the superior race—is his natural and normal condition." Alexander H. Stephens, "Sketch of the Corner-stone Speech," in Henry Cleveland, *Alexander H. Stephens, in Public and Private* (Philadelphia: National Publishing Co., 1866), 721.

3. On these features of American slavery, see Stanley M. Elkins, *Slavery: A Problem in American Institutional and Intellectual Life,* 3d ed. (Chicago: University of Chicago Press, 1976); Kenneth M. Stampp, *The Peculiar Institution: Slavery in the Ante-Bellum South* (New York: Vintage Books, 1956); Eugene D. Genovese, *Roll, Jordan, Roll: The World the Slaves Made* (New York: Vintage Books, 1974); id., *The World the Slaveholders Made: Two Essays in Interpretation* (Middletown, Conn.: Wesleyan University Press, 1988); John W. Blassingame, *The Slave Community: Plantation Life in the Antebellum South,* rev. ed. (New York: Oxford University Press, 1979); Herbert G. Gutman, *The Black Family in Slavery and Freedom, 1750–1925* (New York: Vintage Books, 1976). For a leading proslavery justification of many of these features of the institution, see Thomas R. R. Cobb, *An Inquiry into the Law*

basis of the abridgment of such rights, was then alleged to be the reasonable basis for American slavery. Only in this way could some Americans square their belief in human rights with the forms of total control that American slavery—in contrast to that in Latin America—peculiarly involved (including abridgments of legal rights to religious liberty, free speech, and family life, and restrictions on manumission).[4] A group thus supposed by nature to be unentitled to the basic rights constitutive of American nationality could not, by definition, be part of American nationality.

The radical abolitionist criticism of American racism observed that the same definition of national identity that had rationalized slavery in the South also supported racial discrimination against free blacks both in the South and the North.[5] In the North the alleged inferiority of blacks could not perhaps justify slavery, but it could justify deprivations of rights aimed to exclude blacks from the political community. For example, states forbade blacks from entering[6] and passed various discriminatory measures in voting rights, education, and the like that encouraged free blacks to leave.[7] Abolitionists like Garrison and Lydia

---

of Negro Slavery in the United States of America (1858; New York: Negro Universities Press, 1968).

4. See works cited supra note 3, especially Elkins, Slavery; see also Herbert S. Klein, Slavery in the Americas: A Comparative Study of Virginia and Cuba (Chicago: Elephant Paperbacks, 1989). It remains controversial, however, whether on balance slaves were treated worse in British than Latin America. See, for example, David Brion Davis, "The Continuing Contradiction of Slavery: A Comparison of British America and Latin America," in The Debate over Slavery: Stanley Elkins and His Critics, ed. Ann J. Lane (Urbana: University of Illinois Press, 1971), 111–36; Herbert S. Klein, "Anglicanism, Catholicism, and the Negro Slave," in Debate over Slavery, 137–90. For an important general study, see Carl N. Degler, Neither Black Nor White: Slavery and Race Relations in Brazil and the United States (Madison: University of Wisconsin Press, 1986).

5. On the South, see Ira Berlin, Slaves without Masters: The Free Negro in the Antebellum South (New York: Pantheon Books, 1974). On the North, see Leon F. Litwack, North of Slavery: The Negro in the Free States, 1790–1860 (Chicago: University of Chicago Press, 1961); V. Jacque Voegeli, Free but Not Equal: The Midwest and the Negro during the Civil War (Chicago: University of Chicago Press, 1967). For a balanced account of the improving treatment of blacks in the North prior to the Civil War, see Paul Finkelman, "Prelude to the Fourteenth Amendment: Black Legal Rights in the Antebellum North," Rutgers Law Journal 17 (1986): 415.

6. Three states—Illinois, Indiana, and Oregon—incorporated such anti-immigration provisions in their state constitutions, which were overwhelmingly approved by white state electorates. See Litwack, North of Slavery, 70–74.

7. By 1840, some 93 per cent of Northern free blacks lived in states which either completely or as a practical matter excluded them from the right to vote. See Litwack, North of Slavery, 74–75. Although some white schools admitted blacks especially before 1820, most northern states either excluded them from schools altogether or established racially separate and unequal schools for them. Ibid., 114.

Maria Child saw that the natural expression of this view was the advocacy from Jefferson to Lincoln of abolition on terms of colonization abroad, confirming the basic racist image of the terms of American national identity.[8] The theorists of radical antislavery drew the remedial inference that blacks must be fully included in the terms of a national citizenship that extended equal protection of basic rights to all.

Abolitionist analysis of the corruption of public reason that slavery's defense required pointed out how the nature of the evil to be defended required the deprivation of the basic rights of whites as well as blacks, such as the right to free debate about the evils of slavery and racism. The radical abolitionists—the only consistent advocates of the argument for toleration in antebellum America—were for this reason pathbreaking moral and constitutional dissenters of conscience from and critics of the stifling tyranny of the majority of Jacksonian America. The ethical impulse that motivated abolitionists was the corruption of conscience that slavery and racism, like religious persecution, had worked on the spiritual lives of Americans. To sustain these practices and institutions, proslavery theorists had, consistent with the paradox of intolerance, repressed criticism when it was most needed and instead used decadent standards of argument in the use of history, constitutional analysis, Bible interpretation, and even science. For abolitionists like Garrison and Child, such attitudes could, consistent with respect for human rights, no more legitimately be allowed political expression than religious intolerance with its analogous corruption of public reason.

The original abolitionist aim was the ethical transformation of these public attitudes from their decadent to a more critically informed sense of the requirements of ethical impartiality by making public arguments that would deliberatively persuade and enlighten the public conscience. In response to the brick wall of repression that met them, ethical persuasion remained their overriding aim. The abolitionists' commitment to nonviolence reflected this approach; only very late in the antebellum period did rational despair lead some of them (Theodore Parker and Henry David Thoreau,[9] for example) to support the armed revolution of John Brown. Most abolitionists turned to politics as the best way effectively to make their ethical case, to forge through

8. For Jefferson on colonization, see Richards, *Conscience and the Constitution*, 82, 86, 152; for Lincoln, ibid., 81, 97–98, 110, 152.

9. On Parker, see, in general, Henry Steele Commager, *Theodore Parker* (Boston: Little, Brown, 1936); on Thoreau, see, for a good general treatment on this point, Daniel Walker Howe, "Henry David Thoreau on the Duty of Civil Disobedience," An Inaugural Lecture delivered before the University of Oxford on 21 May 1990 (Oxford: Clarendon Press, 1990).

democratic politics a new moral consensus around sound ethical principles.

The task of the Reconstruction Amendments was not only, however, to set the terms of a desirable ethical transformation of American public opinion. It was also to undertake a rather more difficult task in which its abolitionist forebears had not taken much interest (and some expressly disavowed), namely, to enforce constitutional standards of respect for rights against those who would flout them.[10] The aims of ethical transformation of public attitudes and constitutional enforcement to protect rights at risk were not necessarily coincident at least in the short term. Indeed, one abolitionist, Lydia Maria Child, had prophetically worried, twenty-three years before the Thirteenth Amendment was ratified, about their possible antagonism: "Great political changes may be forced by the pressure of external circumstances, without a corresponding change in the moral sentiment of a nation; but in all such changes, the change is worse than useless; the evil reappears, and usually in a more aggravated form."[11] Those committed to the abolitionist ethical vision would have universally preferred that Americans both in the North and South had been persuaded to assent to the vision that condemned both slavery and racism. Some of them, notably Child herself, believed that such antiracist principles condemned both state-sponsored racial segregation and antimiscegenation laws. But the circumstances of the Reconstruction Amendments were those of a moral chasm in public opinion between the moral revolution the Civil War worked in the North and a counterrevolution in the South of which the freedmen and women were the unjust victims.[12]

The moral revolution in American public opinion in the North worked by the Civil War rendered abolitionist antiracist arguments—the same arguments formerly regarded as so marginally radical in the antebellum period—to be the basic conservative principles of Ameri-

10. The leading criticism of the abolitionists, for not properly preparing the ground for what the Reconstruction Amendments required, is that of Stanley Elkins. Elkins, *Slavery*, 140–206; for response to his criticism, see Aileen S. Kraditor, "A Note on Elkins and the Abolitionists," in *Debate over Slavery*, 87–101. For a good collection of essays that explore the issue, see Martin Duberman, ed., *The Antislavery Vanguard: New Essays on the Abolitionists* (Princeton: Princeton University Press, 1965).

11. Cited in Kraditor, "A Note on Elkins and the Abolitionists," 100–101.

12. See Leon F. Litwack, *Been in the Storm So Long: The Aftermath of Slavery* (New York: Vintage Books, 1979). See also C. Vann Woodward, *The Strange Career of Jim Crow*, 3d ed. (New York: Oxford University Press, 1974); id., *Origins of the New South, 1877–1913* (Baton Rouge, Louisiana State University Press, 1971); and id., *The Future of the Past* (New York: Oxford University Press, 1989).

can revolutionary constitutionalism embodied in the Reconstruction Amendments.[13] The stark contrast of black contribution to the Civil War and Southern efforts to return freedmen to the functional equivalent of slavery enabled the congressional leadership of the Republican Party to move public opinion in the nation—despite a resisting president—to support the central principles of the Reconstruction Amendments.[14] Black Americans were to be included in the American political community on terms of principles guaranteeing them equal protection of their basic human rights for the reasons that antebellum radical abolitionists had advocated.

The constitutional and political problem American faced was a grave one. "[T]he South was united [on racism] as it had not been on slavery."[15] The constitutional abolition of slavery and guarantee of equal rights of citizenship to black Americans were dead letters without some effective constitutional protection of the rights of black Americans against the populist racism that now flourished in the defeated South as the terms of Southern sectional identity. The Reconstruction Amendments stood for an ethical vision of *national* identity based on respect for the human rights of all persons. Southern attempts to perpetuate racist subjugation through law (the Black Codes) were inconsistent with such respect and could not legitimately be allowed expression through public law.

The equal protection clause of the Fourteenth Amendment afforded a nationally applicable constitutional guarantee and enforcement power aimed to protect American citizens against such subjugation.[16] The task now was the novel one, not really anticipated by the abolitionists, of how such guarantees were to be understood, interpreted, and implemented against those who would unconstitutionally abridge the rights of Americans to equal standing before the law, and were not open to reasonable persuasion on the question. If the abolitionists (with their historical mission of persuasion by appeal to conscience) were unprepared for the task before them, the nation at large had even less understanding of what was required to achieve its publicly avowed constitutional aims to rectify the American heritage of

13. See McPherson, *The Struggle for Equality.*

14. For good general studies, see Eric L. McKitrick, *Andrew Johnson and Reconstruction* (New York: Oxford University Press, 1960); Michael Les Benedict, *A Compromise of Principle: Congressional Republicans and Reconstruction, 1863–1869* (New York: W. W. Norton, 1974).

15. C. Vann Woodward, "Emancipations and Reconstructions: A Comparative Study," in C. Vann Woodward, *The Future of the Past* (New York: Oxford University Press, 1989), 166.

16. For further discussion, see Richards, *Conscience and the Constitution,* chap. 4.

both slavery in the South and the cultural construction of racism nationwide.

The principles of the Reconstruction Amendments could probably only have been effectively realized by a continuing national commitment to the ongoing federal enforcement of constitutional rights in the South; such federal programs would have included land distribution and integrated education for the freedmen (of the sort suggested by Thaddeus Stevens in the House[17] and Charles Sumner in the Senate[18]) and active and ongoing federal protection of black voting rights. However, mainstream antebellum abolitionist thought (besides radicals like Stevens and Sumner), was unprepared for the task that Reconstruction would pose,[19] and the rest of the nation was even less prepared. The dominant view in the Reconstruction Congress itself was that the guarantee of equal protection would not condemn state-sponsored racial segregation or antimiscegenation laws, which were views clearly at odds with the antiracism of a Lydia Maria Child. The failure to adequately protect the freedmen exposed them to the hostile environment of the South now committed with redoubled fury to the cultural construction of racism as the irrationalist symbol of Southern sectional unity in defeat. Southern racism now evolved into a politically aggressive racism that the victory of the Union had, if anything, worsened. By 1877, what inadequate congressional and presidential commitment to black rights there was (protecting voting rights and prosecuting the KKK) effectively ceased.[20]

The judiciary, for its part, did little better. I focus here on its misinterpretation of the guarantee of equal protection itself as applied both to state-sponsored racial segregation and antimiscegenation laws, and the nature and grounds of the struggle for public recognition of stronger antiracist principles that the Supreme Court would eventually endorse and use in the constitutional condemnation of both institutions. The theory of illegitimate racist degradation—central to the un-

17. On Stevens's abortive proposals for confiscation and distribution of Southern plantations to the freedman, see Eric Foner, *Reconstruction: America's Unfinished Revolution, 1863–1877* (New York: Harper & Row, 1988), 222, 235–37, 245–46, 308–10.

18. On Sumner's proposals for federally sponsored land distribution and integrated education for the freedmen, see Foner, *Reconstruction*, 236, 308.

19. The key to much abolitionist thought during this period was the guarantee of voting rights to the freedmen (eventually realized through the Fifteenth Amendment), which would, it was hoped, accord them sufficient political power to defend themselves without the need for more extensive federal intervention in the South to protect them. See, in general, McPherson, *The Struggle for Equality*; Benedict, *A Compromise of Principle*.

20. See C. Vann Woodward, *Reunion and Reaction: The Compromise of 1877 and the End of Reconstruction* (New York: Oxford University Press, 1966).

derstanding of equal protection—must be interpreted and applied in light of the circumstances relevant to its terms of reasonable justification of state power. The pivotal interpretive issue should be whether some law or policy by act or omission gives expression to an unreasonable exclusion of black Americans from one of the culture-creating rights central to the American public constitutional culture of equal rights.

One such issue should surely be state-sponsored racial segregation; such segregation perpetuates and reinforces the image of black Americans as outcasts from the common culture of the larger society—an argument Charles Sumner (pointing to the analogy of European anti-Semitism) had forcefully made.[21] Another such issue, as Lydia Maria Child had argued, would be antimiscegenation laws, endorsing as they do the sexual dehumanization of African Americans as incompetent to exercise basic human rights of intimate association. Illegitimate racist degradation is an important component of the cultural intolerance fundamental to the social construction of American racism, in particular, the historical exclusion of the disfavored group from any of the rights of conscience, free speech, family life, and work that have been accorded other persons and the cultural groups with whom they identified. The task of equal protection, construed against that background, must be to refuse public recognition and enforcement of the attitudes of unjust exclusion on the basis of which racist degradation was rationalized. But state-sponsored racial segregation and antimiscegenation laws were precisely so motivated, expressing and legitimating a social construction of isolation and exclusion of the disfavored race-defined people that perpetuated the underlying evil of moral subjugation.[22]

The mission of the Reconstruction Amendments was and should have been the inclusion, on terms of equal rights, of black Americans into the American political community now understood to be a moral community of free and equal citizens, not two nations divided by a

21. See Charles Sumner, "Equality before the Law," in Charles Sumner, *His Complete Works* (New York: Negro Universities Press, 1969), 3:51–100; for the analogy of anti-Semitism, see his discussion of the construction of anti-Semitism on the basis of compulsory segregation in ghettoes, 3:88; see also Charles Sumner, "The Question of Caste," ibid., 17:133–83; on anti-Semitism, see ibid., 17:158. For commentary on Sumner's attacks on racial segregation throughout his career, see David Donald, *Charles Sumner and the Coming of the Civil War* (New York: Alfred A. Knopf, 1960), 180–81; David Donald, *Charles Sumner and the Rights of Man* (New York: Alfred A. Knopf, 1970), 152, 246–47, 298, 422.

22. See, in general, Woodward, *The Strange Career of Jim Crow;* for an interesting comparison of the comparable development of state-sponsored segregation in the United States and South Africa, see George M. Fredrickson, *White Supremacy: A Comparative Study in American and South African History* (Oxford: Oxford University Press, 1981).

culturally constructed chasm of intolerance and subjugation supported by law.[23] In 1896 in *Plessy v. Ferguson*,[24] the Supreme Court held state-sponsored racial discrimination to be consistent with the equal protection clause of the Fourteenth Amendment, one of the more egregious interpretive mistakes in the Court's checkered history. Similarly, in its earlier 1883 decision, *Pace v. Alabama*,[25] the Court held that stronger penalties for interracial, as opposed to intraracial, sexual relations were not racially discriminatory (since both whites and blacks were subject to the same penalty). The Supreme Court in both these opinions itself powerfully advanced the cultural construction of American racism. I begin with *Plessy* and the struggle leading to its overruling, and then turn to *Pace* and its repudiation.

Constitutional Struggle, the Civil Rights Movement, and Abolitionist Antiracism

The interpretive issue in *Plessy* was whether there was a reasonable basis for the racial distinction that the state law used. The Court's decision can be plausibly explained, as Charles Lofgren has recently shown,[26] against the background of the dominant racist social science of the late nineteenth century. I have already noted the importance of the American ethnologists to antebellum proslavery thought (chapter 2).[27] Ethnology was the supposed science of natural race differences; moral capacity was allegedly measured, for example, via physical differences in brain capacity or cephalic indices.[28] These measurements afforded a putatively scientific basis for making the allegedly reasonable judgment that the separation of races was justified. Segregation in transportation (the issue in *Plessy*) might thus discourage forms of social intercourse that would result in degenerative forms of

23. On the continuing power of this cultural construction today, see Andrew Hacker, *Two Nations: Black and White, Separate, Hostile, Unequal* (New York: Charles Scribner's Sons, 1992).

24. *Plessy v. Ferguson*, 163 U.S. 537 (1896).

25. *Pace v. Alabama*, 106 U.S. 583 (1883).

26. See Charles A. Lofgren, *The Plessy Case* (New York: Oxford University Press, 1987).

27. See, in general, William Stanton, *The Leopard's Spots: Scientific Attitudes toward Race in America, 1815–59* (Chicago: University of Chicago Press, 1960).

28. For good general treatments, see Stephen Jay Gould, *The Mismeasure of Man* (New York: W. W. Norton, 1981); Thomas F. Gossett, *Race: The History of an Idea in America* (New York: Schocken Books, 1965); George M. Fredrickson, *The Black Image in the White Mind: The Debate on Afro-American Character and Destiny, 1817–1914* (Middletown, Conn.: Wesleyan University Press, 1971); John S. Haller, Jr., *Outcasts from Evolution: Scientific Attitudes of Racial Inferiority, 1859–1900* (New York: McGraw-Hill Book Company, 1971); Reginald Horsman, *Race and Manifest Destiny: The Origins of American Racial Anglo-Saxonism* (Cambridge: Harvard University Press, 1981).

miscegenation, and segregation in education would reflect race-linked differences in capacity best dealt with in separate schools, as well as usefully discourage social intercourse.

The abolitionists offered plausible objections to the scientific status of American ethnology, and similar objections were available at the time *Plessy* was decided in 1896. For example, Franz Boas had already published his early 1894 paper debunking the weight to be accorded race in the social sciences.[29] It is striking that the putative reasonable basis for *Plessy* was not, in fact, critically stated or discussed in the opinion, but assumed in a rather conclusive manner. Even given the state of the human sciences in the 1890s, the interpretive argument in the decision did not meet the standards of impartial public reason surely due all Americans. Americans had a right to expect more of their highest court than its unquestioning acceptance of controversial scientific judgments hostage to an entrenched political epistemology that protected the increasingly racist character of the American South. One justice (Justice Harlan, a southerner) powerfully made precisely this point in his dissent.

At the time of *Plessy,* Southern blacks had been left by the federal government almost wholly to the mercies of Southern state governments; these governments had (in violation of the spirit of the Fifteenth Amendment) effectively disenfranchised them, deprived them of adequate educational opportunity, and turned a blind eye to the informal forms of terrorism (including lynching) used to intimidate blacks from challenging their subjugated economic, social, and political position.[30] The Supreme Court, abandoning abolitionist ethical impartiality, supinely surrendered any semblance of morally independent critical testing in order to take instruction from bad and politically corrupt science to legitimate the further degradation of this already unconstitutionally victimized group. The consequence was what betrayal of the argument for toleration has taught us to expect. The political identity of the South, like its antebellum predecessor, immunized itself from serious discussion of its greatest evil[31] and constituted its sense of political identity in racist subjugation. Consistent with the paradox of intolerance, such a failure of reason projectively fed on forms of

29. See Franz Boas, "Human Faculty as Determined by Race," in *A Franz Boas Reader: The Shaping of American Anthropology, 1883–1911,* ed. George W. Stocking, Jr. (1894; Chicago: University of Chicago Press, 1974), 221–42.

30. See, in general, Woodward, *Reunion and Reaction: The Compromise of 1877 and the End of Reconstruction;* id., *The Strange Career of Jim Crow;* id., *Origins of the New South, 1877–1913.*

31. See, in general, W. J. Cash, *The Mind of the South* (New York: Vintage Books, 1941).

political irrationalism (myth, factual distortion, deprivation of basic rights of conscience and free speech) based on the racist subjugation of its victims.

The consequences for the nation at large were felt not only in racist aspects of America's increasingly imperialist foreign policy, but in the racist immigration restrictions on Asians and, after World War I, on Southern and Eastern Europeans.[32] If race and culture were in this period so unreasonably confused, it is not surprising that American intolerance, to the extent legitimated by betrayal of constitutional principles, should turn from blacks to non-Christian Asians or Catholic Latins or Jewish Slavs whose cultures appeared, to nativist American Protestant public opinion, so inferior and (equating culture and race) therefore peopled by the racially inferior.

The long road to *Brown v. Board of Education*[33] traced the story of the critical testing and recasting of the assumptions that made *Plessy* possible. The mobilization of a constitutional movement of Americans, black and white, which kept alive the theory and practice of radical abolitionism during a period of resurgent national racism (culminating in patterns of lynching and the Atlanta race riots of 1906 and the Springfield, Illinois riots of 1908), led to the founding of the NAACP in 1910 to challenge such racism in the terms of radical abolitionist antiracism.[34] Frederick Douglass, who had been a central black abolitionist (and abolitionist feminist) in the antebellum period, played a central role in such antiracist resistance until his death (after attending a woman's rights rally) in 1895;[35] Ida Wells-Barnett, as we earlier saw (chapter 4), similarly forged such resistance in the 1890s in her remarkable attack on Southern lynching and the racism it expressed and sustained; Anna Julia Cooper defended a central role for black women in antiracist protest, "stepping from the pedestal of statue-like inactivity in the domestic shrine, and daring to think and move and speak"[36] in her 1892 *A Voice from the South,* and crucially grounded such rights-

32. See, for a good general treatment, John Higham, *Strangers in the Land: Patterns of American Nativism, 1860–1925* (New Brunswick, N.J.: Rutgers University Press, 1988). See also Ronald Takaki, *Iron Cages: Race and Culture in 19th-Century America* (New York: Oxford University Press, 1990).

33. *Brown v. Board of Education,* 347 U.S. 483 (1954) (expressly overruling *Plessy*).

34. For a good general study of this development, see James M. McPherson, *The Abolitionist Legacy: From Reconstruction to the NAACP* (Princeton: Princeton University Press, 1975).

35. See, in general, William S. McFeely, *Frederick Douglass* (New York: W. W. Norton, 1991).

36. See Anna Julia Cooper, *A Voice from the South,* ed. Mary Helen Washington (1892; New York: Oxford University Press, 1988), 121–22.

based protest in an elaboration of the argument for toleration.[37] Abolitionist antiracism (like abolitionist feminism) remained very much alive
as a dissenting interpretive tradition during a deeply racist (and sexist)
period of American history.

That tradition was powerfully deepened and energized by the scholarship and activism of W. E. B. Du Bois. His historical studies challenged the dominant, often racist orthodoxy of the age,[38] and his 1903
The Souls of Black Folk[39] offered a pathbreaking interpretive study of
African American culture and the struggle for self-consciousness under
circumstances of racial oppression[40]—"a world which yields him no
true self-consciousness, but . . . this double-consciousness, this sense
of always looking at one's self through the eyes of others, of measuring
one's soul by the tape of a world that looks on in amused contempt
and pity. One ever feels his two-ness,—an American, a Negro; two
souls, two thoughts, two unreconciled strivings; two warring ideals in
one dark body."[41] The struggle for justice was thus a struggle for self-
respecting identity on terms of justice that would transform both:

> The history of the American Negro is the history of this strife,—this longing
> to attain self-conscious manhood, to merge his double self into a better and
> truer self. In this merging he wishes neither of the older selves to be lost.
> He would not Africanize America, for America has too much to teach the
> world and Africa. He would not bleach his Negro soul in a flood of white
> Americanism, for he knows that Negro blood has a message for the world.
> He simply wishes to make it possible for a man to be both a Negro and an
> American, without being cursed and spit upon by his fellows, without having
> the doors of Opportunity closed roughly in his face.[42]

Du Bois also played a central activist role as Director of Publicity and
Research of the NAACP, editing *The Crisis*. (Wells-Barnett attended

---

37. Ibid., 119–26. For a good anthology including the work of other nineteenth-century
black women often arguing to similar effect, see Bert James Loewenberg and Ruth Bogin,
eds., *Black Women in Nineteenth-Century American Life: Their Words, Their Thoughts,
Their Feelings* (University Park: Pennsylvania State University Press, 1976).

38. See W. E. B. Du Bois, *The Suppression of the African Slave-Trade*, in *W. E. B.
Du Bois*, ed. Nathan Huggins (1896; New York: Library of America, 1986), 3–356; id., *Black
Reconstruction in America, 1860–1880* (1935; New York: Atheneum, 1969).

39. See W. E. B. Du Bois, *The Souls of Black Folk*, in *W. E. B. Du Bois*, ed. Nathan
Huggins (1903; New York: Library of America, 1986), 359–546.

40. See, in general, David Levering Lewis, *W. E. B. Du Bois: Biography of a Race, 1868–
1919* (New York: Henry Holt, 1993); Eric J. Sundquist, *To Wake the Nations: Race in the
Making of American Literature* (Cambridge: Harvard University Press, Belknap Press, 1993),
457–625.

41. Du Bois, *The Souls of Black Folk*, 364–65.

42. Ibid., 365.

the NAACP's biracial founding but withdrew in pique when her name was not included on a Committee of Forty on permanent organization.[43])

The founders of the NAACP believed that existing tactics for black advancement neglected issues of civil and political rights and reflected too moderate a position on economic issues. In addition to conducting lobbying efforts and publicity campaigns, the NAACP soon established a legal redress committee, in which figures like Charles Houston and Thurgood Marshall played central roles in the ultimately successful struggle to repudiate *Plessy* and *Pace*.[44] Such activism was sustained by and also fostered a growing civil rights movement that drew importantly upon both the black churches and colleges and the networks of women's groups.[45] Black Americans in the South and elsewhere asserted and were finally accorded some measure of national protection by the Supreme Court (reversing early decisions to the contrary[46]) in the exercise of their First Amendment rights of protest, criticism, and advocacy.[47] Martin Luther King, a towering figure in the later development of the civil rights movement to support and expand the abolitionist antiracist principle after *Plessy* was overruled,[48] brilliantly used and elaborated the right of conscience and free speech to protest American racism very much in the spirit of Garrisonian nonviolence; he thus appealed, as he did in his classic "Letter from Birmingham City Jail,"[49] for the need for "nonviolent direct action . . . to create such a [moral] crisis and establish such creative tension that a community that has

43. See Lewis, *W. E. B. Du Bois*, 394–97.

44. See Mark V. Tushnet, *The NAACP's Legal Strategy against Segregated Education, 1925–1950* (Chapel Hill: University of North Carolina Press, 1987); *Making Civil Rights Law: Thurgood Marshall and the Supreme Court, 1956–1961* (New York: Oxford University Press, 1994); Genna Rae McNeil, *Groundwork: Charles Hamilton Houston and the Struggle for Civil Rights* (Philadelphia: University of Pennsylvania Press, 1983); Jack Greenberg, *Crusaders in the Courts: How a Dedicated Band of Lawyers Fought for the Civil Rights Revolution* (New York: BasicBooks, 1994).

45. See Evelyn Brooks Higginbotham, *Righteous Discontent: The Women's Movement in the Black Baptist Church, 1880–1920* (Cambridge: Harvard University Press, 1993). See also Aldon D. Morris, *The Origins of the Civil Rights Movement: Black Communities Organizing for Change* (New York: Free Press, 1984).

46. See *Gitlow v. New York*, 268 U.S. 652 (1925) (First Amendment held applicable to states under Fourteenth Amendment).

47. See, in general, Harry Kalven, Jr., *The Negro and the First Amendment* (Chicago: University of Chicago Press, 1965).

48. For a good general study, see Taylor Branch, *Parting the Waters: Martin Luther King and the Civil Rights Movement, 1954–63* (London: Papermac, 1990).

49. See Martin Luther King, "Letter from Birmingham City Jail," in *A Testament of Hope: The Essential Writings of Martin Luther King, Jr.*, ed. James Melvin Washington (1963; New York: Harper & Row, 1986), 289–302.

constantly refused to negotiate is forced to confront the issue."[50] Like Garrisonian radical abolitionists in the antebellum period, King demanded his basic human rights of conscience and speech to engage in reasonable public discourse about basic issues of justice, including criticism of the racist orthodoxy "that degrades human personality" and is therefore "unjust."[51] Now, however, the Supreme Court, in light of the Reconstruction Amendments, extended to the NAACP and King federal constitutional protection of basic free speech rights of public voice and criticism. The consequences were those to be expected by the liberation, on fair terms, of culture-creating moral powers.[52] The racist orthodoxy of *Plessy,* no longer the enforceable measure of acceptable public discourse, was subjected to reasonable debate and criticism in the free exercise of their human rights by the groups previously subjugated. The interpretive foundations of *Plessy* itself could not withstand such reasonable criticism.

The interpretive substance of the argument against *Plessy* made extensive use of forms of social science research, some of it arguably of dubious analytic value for the purpose at hand.[53] But one strand of the argument based on social science reflected a structure of moral argument that built upon antebellum radical abolitionist ethical analysis of these issues.

The eighteenth-century comparative science of human nature, developed by Montesquieu and Hume, viewed human nature as constantly subject to modification from the environment, history, institutional development, and the like. Both had discussed race differences from this perspective. Montesquieu's position was one of ironic skepticism, while Hume departed from the model of a uniform human nature to suggest significant, constitutionally-based race differences inferred from comparative cultural achievements.[54] The Humean sug-

50. Ibid., 291.

51. Ibid., 293.

52. Even under the harsh terms of American slavery, black Americans—though brutally cut off from their native cultures as well as from the rights of American public culture—demonstrated remarkable creativity in giving ethical meaning to their plight, laying the foundations of their later interpretations of the religious and constitutional values of emancipatory freedom that they correctly understood to be at the basis of the public culture around them. See, on the black interpretation of Christian freedom under slavery, Genovese, *Roll, Jordan, Roll,* 159–284; on religious and political freedom under emancipation, see Litwack, *Been in the Storm So Long,* 450–556; on the ideals of religious and constitutional freedom of Martin Luther King, see, in general, Branch, *Parting the Waters.*

53. See Edmond Cahn's trenchant criticism along these lines, "Jurisprudence," *New York University Law Review* 30 (1955): 150.

54. See David Hume, "Of National Characters," in David Hume, *Essays Moral Political and Literary* (Indianapolis: LibertyClassics, 1987), 208 n. 10.

gestion of separate races had an antitheological significance; it was thus condemned, notably by James Beattie,[55] as one aspect of a larger repudiation of a Christian ethics of equality in terms of the Biblical idea of one divine creation of humans. Hume's suggestion was later developed in the nineteenth century into polygenetic theories of human origins by the American ethnologists and others,[56] who thought of their theories as part of the battle of progressive science against reactionary religion.

In the nineteenth century, this artificially drawn contrast was hardened into one between certain approaches to the human sciences and nearly anything else. These approaches, very much under the influence of models of explanation drawn from the physical sciences, assumed that good explanations in the human sciences must be crudely reductive to some physical measure, like brain capacity or cephalic indices. Little attention was paid to culture as an independent explanatory variable, and thus no concern expressed with the interpretive dimension of human personality in general and of our moral powers in particular. To the extent culture was attended to at all, cultural transmission was thought of in Lamarckian terms.[57] The efforts and resulting achievements of one generation were wired into the physical natures of the offspring of that generation. As a result, any cultural advantage that one people might have had was not only peculiarly its own (not necessarily transmissible to other peoples), but a matter of rational pride for all those born into such a people. The cultural advances in question were never accidents of time and circumstances, but products of the achieving will with each generation playing its part in further acts of progressive will building on the achievements of past generations.

These views failed to appreciate what culture is, let alone its explanatory weight in the human sciences. They confused culture with acts of will, misunderstanding the nature of cultural formation and transmission, the role of contingency and good luck in cultural progress, and the complete impropriety of taking credit for such advances just by virtue of being born into such a culture. This whole way of thinking naturally created ethical space for explanations in terms of superior and inferior races as a proxy for the comparison between the remarkable

55. See James Beattie, *An Essay on the Nature and Immutability of Truth* (New York: Garland Publishing, Inc., 1983), 479–84. See also James Beattie, *Elements of Moral Science* (Delmar, N.Y.: Scholars' Facsimiles & Reprints, 1976), 183–223.

56. See Stanton, *The Leopard's Spots;* Fredrickson, *The Black Image in the White Mind;* Haller, *Outcasts from Evolution;* Gossett, *Race: The History of an Idea in America.*

57. See George W. Stocking, Jr., *Race, Culture, and Evolution: Essays in the History of Anthropology* (New York: The Free Press, 1968), 47–48, 124, 234–69.

scientific advances in Western culture in the nineteenth century in contrast to the putative lack of comparable advances nearly everywhere else.[58] If the least such progress appeared to be in African cultures, such peoples must be inferior; and if Egyptian culture clearly had been for some long period advanced and had an important impact on progressive cultures like that of ancient Greece, then Egyptians could not be black.[59]

Assumptions of these sorts explain why the Supreme Court in *Plessy* could be so ethically blind, in the same way proslavery thinkers had been blind, to the ignoble and unjust contempt that its legitimation of the further cultural degradation of blacks inflicted on black Americans. For the *Plessy* Court, race was not morally arbitrary, but a physical fact crucially connected with other physical facts of rational incapacity for which blacks, being from a nonprogressive culture, must be ethically responsible. In contrast, white Americans, taking rational ethical pride in their willed success in sustaining a progressive culture, should take the same pride in their race, and might reasonably protect their achievements from those of another race who were culpably nonprogressive by nature. Race, a physical fact supposed to be causally connected to other physical facts, had been transformed into a trait of character. The highly moralistic mind of nineteenth-century America, once having bought the idea of such transformation, had no difficulty protecting people of good moral character from those who were culpably of unworthy character.

Abolitionist thought had taken the moral insularity of proslavery defenses as an example of the corruption of conscience so common in the history of religious persecution. Modern racism both in America and Europe comparably exemplified one of human nature's more artfully self-deceiving evasions of the moral responsibilities of liberal political culture—illustrated, in *Plessy*, by the way in which the culture's respect for science had been manipulated to serve racist ends. Fundamental public criticism of this view of the human sciences must, by its nature as a form of public reason bearing on constitutional values, reshape constitutional argument.

The pivotal figure in such criticism was a German Jew and immigrant to the United States, Franz Boas, who fundamentally criticized the racial explanations characteristic of both European and American physical anthropology in the late nineteenth century.[60] Boas argued

58. Ibid., 234–69.
59. See, for example, Stanton, *The Leopard's Spots*, 50.
60. See Franz Boas, *The Mind of Primitive Man*, rev. ed. (1911; Westport, Conn.: Greenwood Press, 1983); George W. Stocking, Jr., ed., *A Franz Boas Reader: The Shaping of Ameri-*

that comparative anthropological study did not sustain the explanatory weight placed on race in the human sciences. In fact, more significant variability existed *within* races than *between* races.[61] Many of the human features supposed to be unchangeably physical (like the cephalic index) were responsive to cultural change; Boas had thus shown that the physical traits of recent immigrants to the United States had changed in response to acculturation.[62]

The crucial factor, heretofore missing from the human sciences, was culture; Boas made this point to Du Bois on a visit to Atlanta University, a visit that "had an impact of lasting importance"[63] for Du Bois's interest in black culture and its sources. Cultural formation and transmission could not be understood in terms of the reductive physical models that had heretofore dominated scientific and popular thinking. In particular, Lamarckian explanation—having been discredited by Mendelian genetics in favor of random genetic mutation—was not the modality of cultural transmission, which was not physical at all but irreducibly cultural. One generation born into a progressive culture could take no more credit for an accident of birth than a generation could be reasonably blamed for birth into a less progressive culture. In fact, cultures advance often through accident and good luck and through cultural diffusion of technologies from other cultures. Such diffusion has been an important fact in the history of all human cultures at some point in their histories. No people has been through all points in its history the vehicle of the cultural progress of humankind, nor can any people reasonably suppose itself the unique vehicle of all such progress in the future.[64]

Boas's general contributions to the human sciences were powerfully

can Anthropology, 1883–1911 (Chicago: University of Chicago Press, 1974). For superb commentary, see Stocking, *Race, Culture, and Evolution;* Carl N. Degler, *In Search of Human Nature: The Decline and Revival of Darwinism in American Social Thought* (New York: Oxford University Press, 1991), 61–83. For a useful recent comparative study of comparable such developments in the United States and Britain, see Elazar Barkan, *The Retreat of Scientific Racism: Changing Concepts of Race in Britain and the United States Between the World Wars* (Cambridge: Cambridge University Press, 1992).

    61. See Franz Boas, "Race," in Edwin R. A. Seligman, ed., *Encyclopaedia of the Social Sciences* (New York: Macmillan, 1937), 7:25–36; id., *The Mind of Primitive Man*, 45–59, 179. For commentary, see Stocking, Jr., *Race, Culture, and Evolution*, 192–94.

    62. See Franz Boas, "Changes in Immigrant Body Form," in *A Franz Boas Reader*, 202–14; id., *The Mind of Primitive Man*, 94–96. For commentary, see Stocking, Jr., *Race, Culture, and Evolution*, 175–80.

    63. See Lewis, *W. E. B. Du Bois*, 352; see also ibid., 414, 462.

    64. See, in general, Boas, *The Mind of Primitive Man*. For commentary, see, in general, Stocking, Jr., *Race, Culture, and Evolution*.

elaborated in the area of race by his students Otto Klineberg[65] and Ruth Benedict.[66] They argued that the explanatory role of race in the human sciences was, if anything, even less important than the judicious Boas might have been willing to grant.[67] (Boas's student, Margaret Mead, suggested much the same might be true to some significant extent of gender.[68])

The most important scientific study of the American race problem was conducted by the Swedish social scientist, Gunnar Myrdal, whose monumental *An American Dilemma*[69] brought the new approach to culture powerfully to bear on the plight of American blacks who, from the perspective of the human sciences, now were increasingly well understood as victims of a historically entrenched cultural construction of racism. In effect, the advances in morally independent critical standards of thought and analysis in the human sciences had enabled social scientists to make the same sort of argument that abolitionist theorists of race, like Lydia Maria Child, had made earlier largely on ethical grounds.

Previously, the human sciences had been claimed on the side of race differences against regressive religion and ethics; now, however, developments in the human sciences had cleared away as so much rationalizing self-deception the false dichotomy between science and ethics and revealed the ethically regressive uses to which even science may be put by politically entrenched epistemologies concerned to preserve the politics of race. Such political epistemologies—a modernist expression of essentially sectarian conceptions of religious and moral truth—cannot legitimately be the basis of political enforcement on society at large. Rather, legitimate political power must be based on contractualist impartial standards of reasonable discussion and debate not hostage to entrenched political orthodoxies. An old ethical point— that of the argument for toleration already used by the abolitionists against slavery and racism—was articulated yet again, now used in the service of an argument of public reason against the force that American racism had been permitted to enjoy in the mistaken interpretation of

65. See Otto Klineberg, *Race Differences* (New York: Harper & Brothers, 1935).

66. See Ruth Benedict, *Race: Science and Politics* (New York: The Viking Press, 1945).

67. See, for example, Franz Boas, "Human Faculty as Determined by Race," in *A Franz Boas Reader,* 231, 234, 242; id., *The Mind of Primitive Man,* 230–31.

68. See Degler, *In Search of Human Nature,* 73, 133–37.

69. See Gunnar Myrdal, *An American Dilemma: The Negro Problem and Modern Democracy* 2 vols. (1944; New York: Pantheon Books, 1972). For commentary, see David W. Southern, *Gunnar Myrdal and Black-White Relations: The Use and Abuse of An American Dilemma, 1944–1969* (Baton Rouge: Louisiana State University Press, 1987).

equal protection in cases like *Plessy*. Thus, a contractualist political theory of suspect classification analysis, rooted in the argument for toleration, affords an illuminating account of interpretive mistake and of the nature of the argument of public reason required to rectify that mistake.

This point of public reason was much highlighted in the American public mind by the comparable kind of racism that had flourished in Europe in the relevant period in the form of modern anti-Semitism. As I have elsewhere argued,[70] during this period both American racism and European anti-Semitism evolved into particularly virulent political pathologies under the impact of the respective emancipations of American blacks from slavery and European Jews from various civil disabilities keyed to their religious background. In both cases, the respective emancipations were not carried through by consistent enforcement of guarantees of basic rights (in the United States, in despite of clear constitutional guarantees to that effect).

The characteristic nineteenth-century struggles for national identity led, in consequence, to rather stark examples of the paradox of intolerance in which the exclusion of race-defined cultural minorities from the political community of equal rights became itself the irrationalist basis of national unity. Strikingly similar racist theorists evolved in Europe to sustain anti-Semitism (Houston Chamberlain[71]) and in America to sustain a comparable racism against the supposedly non-Aryan (Madison Grant[72]). American constitutional institutions were, as a consequence, misinterpreted, but nonetheless increasingly were the object of organized black protest and dissent,[73] including the protests we have already mentioned. Certainly, American institutions did not collapse on the scale of the German declension into atavistic totalitarianism and the genocide of five million European Jews.[74] In both cases, however, the underlying irrationalist racist dynamic was strikingly similar: emancipation, inadequate protection of basic rights, and a devas-

70. See Richards, *Conscience and the Constitution,* 156–60. See also my use of this analogy in chapter 8 below.

71. See Houston Stewart Chamberlain, *The Foundations of the Nineteenth Century,* trans. John Lees, 2 vols. (London: John Lane, 1911).

72. See Madison Grant, *The Passing of the Great Race or The Racial Basis of European History* (New York: Charles Scribner's Sons, 1919).

73. For good general studies, see John Hope Franklin and Alfred A. Moss, Jr., *From Slavery to Freedom: A History of Negro Americans,* 6th ed. (New York: Knopf, 1988); Donald G. Nieman, *Promises to Keep: African-Americans and the Constitutional Order, 1776 to the Present* (New York: Oxford University Press, 1991).

74. See Raul Hilberg, *The Destruction of the European Jews* (New York: Holmes & Meier, 1985), 3:1201–20.

tating and humiliating defeat that took the excluded minority as an irrationalist scapegoat.[75]

Boas's important criticism of the role of race in the human sciences had, of course, been motivated as much by his own experience of European anti-Semitism as by American racism; Boas as much forged his own self-respecting identity as a Jew against anti-Semitism as Douglass or Du Bois defined theirs as African Americans against American racism. The subsequent elaboration of his arguments by Klineberg, Benedict, and Myrdal had further raised the standards of public reason to expose the intellectual and ethical fallacies of racism both in America and Europe. In light of such criticism, the constitutional attack on the analytic foundations of *Plessy* began well before World War II in the litigation strategy undertaken by the NAACP to question and subvert the racist principle of separate-but-equal in the area of public segregated education.[76]

But World War II itself, not unlike the Civil War, stimulated the development of much more enlightened public attitudes on racial questions than had prevailed theretofore. Not only did the distinguished military service of African Americans in both wars call for recognition of full citizenship, but the Allied victory in World War II raised corresponding questions about the state of American constitutionalism prior to the war not unlike those raised by the Reconstruction Amendments about antebellum American constitutionalism. The United States successfully fought that war in Europe against a nation that, like the American South in the Civil War, defined its world historic mission in self-consciously racist terms. The political ravages of such racism—both in the unspeakable moral horrors of the Holocaust and in the brutalities the war inflicted on so many others—naturally called for a moral interpretation of that war, again like the Civil War, in terms of the defense of the political culture of universal human rights against its racist antagonists. Following the war, the United States took up a central position on the world stage as an advocate of universal human rights. America was thus naturally pressed to critically examine, both at home and abroad, practices like state-sponsored racial segregation in light of the best interpretation of American ideals of human rights in contemporary circumstances.[77] Thus World War II

75. For related similarities between the United States and South Africa, see George M. Frederickson, *White Supremacy: A Comparative Study in American and South African History* (Oxford: Oxford University Press, 1981).

76. See Tushnet, *The NAACP's Legal Strategy against Segregated Education, 1925–1950.*

77. See Mary L. Dudziak, "Desegregation as a Cold War Imperative," *Stanford Law Review* 41 (1988): 61; Frederickson, *The Black Image in the White Mind,* 330.

played the role in American moral and political thought of a kind of "Third American Revolution" (the Civil War being number two[78]). American ideals of revolutionary constitutionalism were tested against the aggression on human rights of a nation, Nazi Germany, that attacked everything the American constitutional tradition valued in the idea and constitutional institutions of respect for universal human rights.[79] The self-conscious American defense of human rights against the totalitarian ambitions of Nazi Germany required Americans, after the war, to ask if their own constitutionalism was indeed adequate to their ambitions.

In fact, the painful truth was what Boas and others had long argued, namely, that America had betrayed the revolutionary constitutionalism of its Reconstruction Amendments in ways and with consequences strikingly similar to the ways in which Germany had betrayed the promise of universal emancipation. Americans did not, however, have to reconstruct their constitutionalism in order to correct this grievous mistake. Unlike the question that faced the nation in the wake of the Civil War, the problem was not a structural flaw in the very design of American constitutionalism. Rather, the issue was corrigible interpretive mistake: the judiciary had failed to understand and give effect to the moral ambitions fundamental to the Reconstruction Amendments themselves, namely, that the American political community should be a moral community committed to abstract values of human rights available on fair terms of public reason to all persons, not a community based on race.

The focus for such testing of American interpretive practice was, naturally, *Plessy v. Ferguson,* in which the Supreme Court had accepted the exclusion of black Americans from the American community of equal rights. But the intellectual and ethical foundations of *Plessy,* to the extent it ever had such foundations, had collapsed under the weight of the criticism we have already discussed. The idea of natural race differences had been thoroughly discredited as itself the product of a long American history of the unjust cultural construction of racism in the same way that European anti-Semitism had been discredited. The Supreme Court, which in 1896 could rationalize *Plessy* as merely following nature or history, faced in the early 1950s a wholly different space for moral choice that Boasian cultural studies had opened up.

---

78. I develop this thought at greater length in Richards, *Conscience and the Constitution.*

79. See, in general, Hannah Arendt, *The Origins of Totalitarianism* (New York: Harcourt Brace Jovanovich, 1973).

Thurgood Marshall, in his argument to the Supreme Court for the NAACP in *Brown v. Board of Education*,[80] morally dramatized this choice in terms of the blue-eyed innocent African American child indistinguishable in all reasonable respects from other children playing with them and living near them except for the role the Supreme Court would play in legitimating a constructed difference (segregated education) that enforced an irrationalist prejudice backed by a long history of unjust subjugation.[81] The Supreme Court was compelled to face, on behalf of American culture more generally, a stark moral choice *either* to give effect to a culture of dehumanization *or* to refuse any longer to be complicit with such rights-denying evil. Moral responsibility for one's complicity with evil could not be evaded. In effect, Marshall, as an African American, stood before the Court in the full voice of his moral personality as a free person, and asked the Court to accept its responsibility for either degrading him as subhuman or to refuse any longer to degrade any person. It chose the latter, holding unanimously to strike down state-sponsored racial segregation as a violation of the equal protection clause of the Fourteenth Amendment. State-sponsored racial segregation, once uncritically accepted as a reasonable expression of natural race differences, now was construed as itself an unjust construction of an irrationalist dehumanization that excluded citizens from their equal rights as members of the political community, and, as such, unconstitutional.

In 1967 in *Loving v. Virginia*,[82] a similarly unanimous Supreme Court struck down state antimiscegenation laws as unconstitutional. Repeating, as it had in *Brown,* that the dominant interpretive judgments of the Reconstruction Congress could not be dispositive on the exercise by the judiciary of its independent interpretive responsibilities, the Court rejected the equal application theory of *Pace v. Alabama* on the same grounds it had earlier rejected it in 1964 in a decision invalidating a state criminal statute prohibiting cohabitation by interracial married couples.[83] The equal protection clause condemned all state-sponsored sources of invidious racial discrimination and, the Court held, antimiscegenation laws were one such source. Indeed, the only basis for such laws was the constitutionally forbidden aim of white supremacy.

Antimiscegenation laws had come to bear this interpretation as a

---

80. *Brown v. Board of Education*, 347 U.S. 483 (1954).

81. See Anthony G. Amsterdam, "Thurgood Marshall's Image of the Blue-Eyed Child in *Brown*," *New York University Law Review* 68 (1993): 226.

82. *Loving v. Virginia*, 388 U.S. 1 (1967).

83. See *McLaughlin v. Florida*, 379 U.S. 184 (1964).

consequence of the Court's endorsement of the cultural theory of the rights-denying construction of racism first suggested by Lydia Maria Child in 1833 and importantly elaborated by Ida Wells-Barnett in 1892. Child had examined and condemned both American slavery and racism in light of the argument for toleration: basic human rights of the person were abridged on wholly inadequate sectarian grounds that Child, like other radical abolitionists, expressly analogized to religious persecution. Antimiscegenation laws violated the basic human right of intimate association on such inadequate grounds, thus dehumanizing a whole class of persons as subhuman animals unworthy of the forms of equal respect accorded rights-bearing persons. Following Harriet Jacobs, Wells-Barnett elaborated the role of the rights-denying sexual dehumanization of African Americans under slavery and analyzed Southern racism after emancipation on a similar basis sustained, in part, by antimiscegenation laws. The point of such laws was, Wells showed, not only to condemn all interracial marriages (the focus of Child's analysis) but the legitimacy of all sexual relations (marital and otherwise) between white women and black men; illicit relations between white men and black women were, in contrast, if not legal, socially acceptable. The asymmetry rested on the enforcement at large (through antimiscegenation and related laws and practices, including lynching) of a sectarian sexual and romantic idealized mythology of white women and a corresponding devaluation of black women and men as sexually animalistic; illicit sexual relations of white men with black women were consistent with this political epistemology, and thus were tolerable; both licit and illicit consensual relations of black men with white women were not, and thus were ideologically transformed into violent rapes requiring lynching.

W. E. B. Du Bois was, like Frederick Douglass, a life-long feminist; he condemned in related terms the role the idealized image of women (as either virgin or prostitute) played in sustaining not only racism but a sexism that unjustly treated all women:

> The world wants healthy babies and intelligent workers. Today we refuse to allow the combination and force thousands of intelligent workers to go childless at a horrible expenditure of moral force, or we damn them if they break our idiotic conventions. Only at the sacrifice of intelligence and the chance to do their best work can the majority of modern women bear children. This is the damnation of women.
>
> All womanhood is hampered today because the world on which it is emerging is a world that tries to worship both virgins and mothers and in the end despises motherhood and despoils virgins.
>
> The future woman must have a life work an economic independence. She must have knowledge. She must have the right of motherhood at her

discretion. The present mincing horror at free womanhood must pass if we are ever to be rid of the bestiality of free manhood; not by guarding the weak in weakness do we gain strength, but by making weakness free and strong.

The world must choose the free women or the white wraith of the prostitute. Today it wavers between the prostitute and the nun.[84]

American racism, on this analysis, expressed a culturally constructed and sustained racialized sexual mythology of gender (white virgin versus black prostitute), and antimiscegenation laws were unconstitutional because of the role they played unjustly in sustaining this sectarian ideology. Both Jacobs and Wells-Barnett had analyzed this injustice from the perspective of black women who had first-hand experience of its indignities.

James Baldwin, one of the greatest American writers of his generation and a black homosexual, brought the same experienced sense of indignity to bear on his later explorations of American sexual racism.[85] When he traveled in the South, Baldwin wrote "about my unbelieving shock when I realized that I was being groped by one of the most powerful men in one of the states I visited."[86] He wrote searingly of his indignation from his experience as a black man, and what he learned of the way racism fulfilled men's "enormous need to debase other men"[87]:

To be a slave means that one's manhood is engaged in a dubious battle indeed, and this stony fact is not altered by whatever devotion some masters and some slaves may have arrived at in relation to each other. In the case of American slavery, the black man's right to his women, as well as to his children, was simply taken from him and whatever bastards the white man begat on the bodies of black women took their condition from the condition of their mothers: blacks were not the only stallions on the slave-breeding farms! And one of the many results of this loveless, money-making conspiracy was that, in giving the masters every conceivable sexual and commercial license, it also emasculated them of any human responsibility—to their women, to their children, to their wives, to themselves. The results of this blasphemy resound in this country, on every private and public level, until this hour. When the man grabbed my cock, I didn't think of him as a faggot, which, indeed, if having a wife and children, house, cars, and a respectable and powerful standing in that community, mean anything, he wasn't: I

84. See W. E. B. Du Bois, "The Damnation of Women" (1920), in *W. E. B. Du Bois*, 952–53. On the specifically racist use of such an unjust idealization, see ibid., 958: "one thing I shall never forgive, neither in this world nor the world to come: its wanton and continued and persistent insulting of the black womanhood which it sought and seeks to prostitute to its lust."

85. See, in general, David Leeming, *James Baldwin* (New York: Knopf, 1994).

86. See James Baldwin, *No Name in the Street* (New York: Dell, 1972), 61.

87. Ibid., 63.

watched his eyes, thinking with great sorrow, *The unexamined life is not worth living.*[88]

Baldwin made clear the general role that sexual dehumanization played in American racism as such: the mythological reduction of both black women and men to their sexuality on terms that fundamentally denied their moral personalities and their human rights to respect for conscience, speech, work, and, of course, intimate life, including their right to love on terms of respect (a right, for Baldwin, owed all persons, heterosexual or homosexual, male or female, white or nonwhite).[89]

SECOND WAVE FEMINISM AS A CIVIL RIGHTS MOVEMENT

The struggle for recognition of a strong antiracist constitutional principle had implicit within it a criticism of the racialized ideal of gender roles in persistent patterns of American racism. The constitutional repudiation of antimiscegenation laws clearly reflected this criticism. Since the purpose of state-sponsored segregation was importantly to discourage even the possibility of such intimate relations, the unconstitutionality of segregation reflected this critical theme as well. Some of the most important exponents of this criticism had been black women, like Harriet Jacobs and Ida Wells-Barnett, who spoke from within their own moral experience about the indignity this dehumanizing stereotype of black sexuality inflicted on them. The criticism was, in its nature, an assault upon the idealized conception of women in suffrage feminism. For this reason, Ida Wells-Barnett was, as we have seen, at loggerheads with a leading suffrage feminist advocate of this conception, Frances Willard (chapter 4). Activist antiracist black women, like Wells-Barnett and others, were for good reasons skeptical of a feminism rooted in such an ideology, and would continue to be so for a long period.[90] Only a feminism, itself skeptical of this ideology, would have the promise of both advancing antiracist and antisexist principles in an acceptable way and thus engage the moral convictions of black as well as white women.

Second wave feminism arose on such a basis. Betty Friedan's 1963

88. Ibid., 62–63.

89. For Baldwin's frankest first-person treatment of these issues, see James Baldwin, "Here Be Dragons," in James Baldwin, *The Price of the Ticket: Collected Nonfiction, 1948–1985* (New York: St. Martin's, 1985), 677–90; for a much more elliptical, self-hating treatment, see James Baldwin, "The Male Prison," ibid., 101–5.

90. See, for a good general study, Paula Giddings, *When and Where I Enter . . . : The Impact of Black Woman on Race and Sex in America* (New York: William Morrow, 1984). See also bell hooks, *Ain't I a Woman: Black Women and Feminism* (Boston: South End Press, 1981); id., *Feminist Theory: From Margin to Center* (Boston: South End Press, 1984).

The Feminine Mystique[91] struck a responsive chord among American women (more of whom now worked outside the home than before[92]) when she critically addressed both the idealized conception of gender roles and the force it had over women's lives.[93] Citing as precedent Stanton's dissatisfaction with the demands of domesticity (leading to her role in the Seneca Falls Convention),[94] Friedan argued that American women in the post-World War II period experienced a comparable crisis of identity but over contemporary gender roles so impoverished that they "had no name for the problem troubling them" (10). Friedan spoke from her own personal experience of an advanced education that went unused in domestic life (26, 62–63) and of the unjust epistemological power over women's consciousness and lives of the normative conception of gender roles that Farnham and Lundberg invoked as the ground for pathologizing any feminist dissent (37, 107, 139, 169–70). A woman's problematic sense of herself, Friedan argued, was not to be dismissed or trivialized as merely psychologically personal and deviant as perceived through the prism of this normative conception when its political force was so demonstrably unjust. Otherwise, injustice would be the measure of the awakening sense of justice that alone might protest it. Friedan's criticisms of the justice of this normative conception, the feminine mystique, questioned not only its substance (making of femininity an end in itself (38, 40–41) or sex as women's exclusive career [228]), but its sectarian religious force (38, 44, 111, 173) that permitted no reasonable doubts to be raised (44) and fictionalized facts (53). Indeed, using the very terms of the paradox of intolerance earlier noted, Friedan pointed to the polemical force of the ideology when it was most reasonably open to doubt.

> [This is] the basic paradox of the feminine mystique: that it emerged to glorify women's role as housewife at the very moment when the barriers to her full participation in society were lowered, at the very moment when science and education and her own ingenuity made it possible for a woman to be

91. See Betty Friedan, *The Feminine Mystique* (1963; London: Penguin, 1982).

92. For the changes in the 1940s, see Chafe, *The Paradox of Change*, 166–72; for the 1950s, see ibid., 188–92.

93. On the importance of Friedan's book, see Chafe, *The Paradox of Change*, 195; Jo Freeman, *The Politics of Women's Liberation: A Case Study of an Emerging Social Movement and Its Relation to the Policy Process* (New York: Longman 1975), 27, 53; Judith Hole and Ellen Levine, *Rebirth of Feminism* (New York: Quadrangle, 1971), 17, 82; Nancy E. McGlen and Karen O'Connor, *Women's Rights: The Struggle for Equality in the Nineteenth and Twentieth Centuries* (New York: Praeger, 1983), 29; Carl N. Degler, *At Odds: Women and the Family in America from the Revolution to the Present* (New York: Oxford University Press, 1980), 443.

94. Friedan, *The Feminine Mystique*, 81–82.

both wife and mother and to take an active part in the world outside the home. The glorification of 'woman's role', then, seems to be in proportion to society's reluctance to treat women as complete human beings; for the less real function that role has, the more it is decorated with meaningless details to conceal its emptiness. (210)

The general terms of the analysis are, of course, familiar from our earlier examination of the argument for toleration. What was so striking and original in Friedan's analysis was the way she plausibly applied it both to popular American culture and the uncritical social scientists (149) who supported its cult of women's domesticity in the mid–twentieth century.[95] Friedan self-consciously saw herself quite rightly as in a similar position to leading advocates of abolitionist feminism like Theodore Parker and Elizabeth Stanton against the background of the way suffrage feminism had undercut their rights-based critique of American gender roles and thus reinforced women's moral slavery (72–90). All the terms of the abolitionist feminist analysis of moral slavery were in place in Friedan's critique. The force of the sectarian ideology of gender roles depended on the abridgment of basic human rights to critical mind and speech (59, 282–83), associated rights to critical education (155, 158, 211, 223), fair terms for rights to intimate life (148–49), and the right to creative work (289–91). The result was the cultural dehumanization of women (244, 251, 264, 265–68) in terms of an objectified sexuality (72, 228, 233) or biology (275). Women's struggle was thus one for personal identity (67–68, 289–91) on terms responsive to a morally independent basis to live a life from convictions of conscience, the voice within (29, 207, 331).

Friedan importantly made early reference to Simone de Beauvoir's path-breaking *The Second Sex* (16),[96] which had prominently explored analogies among anti-Semitism, racism, and sexism.[97] The terms of Friedan's analysis were drawn from a tradition, certainly familiar to her, that had recently applied all her terms of analysis to the criticism of American racism; she acknowledged as much when she criticized the application of separate-but-equal to women's education (which had been struck down by the Supreme Court in 1954 as applied to the education of African Americans) on the ground that such "sex-directed education segregated recent generations of able American women as surely as separate-but-equal education segregated able American Ne-

95. For social background, see Glenna Matthews, *"Just a Housewife" The Rise and Fall of Domesticity in America* (New York: Oxford University Press, 1987).
96. See Simone de Beauvoir, *The Second Sex*, trans. H. M. Parshley (1953; New York: Vintage, 1974).
97. Ibid., xvi, xx, xxi, 131, 144 (citing Sartre and Myrdal), 335.

groes from the opportunity to realize their full abilities in the mainstream of American life."[98] Friedan used the analogy to address a constitutional culture on whom "[t]he black civil rights movement had a
very profound effect."[99] Gunnar Myrdal himself, at the conclusion of
his massive 1944 cultural analysis of American racism, noted that the
status of women had been "the nearest and most natural analogy"[100]
for those justifying slavery and racism and might be subject to similar
rights-based criticism, as indeed the abolitionist feminists had urged.
Friedan's argument assumed the analogy, including the very terms
of a personal struggle for moral identity and self-consciousness that
Du Bois had brought to the black struggle for a stronger antiracist
constitutional principle of equal protection.

The Friedan also assumed and used another critical principle that had
led to the stronger antiracist principle that the Supreme Court had
accepted, namely, the Boasian cultural science that had reframed issues from the pseudo-science of race to an unjust culture of racist
subjugation. That principle was plausibly applied not only to race but,
as Myrdal suggested, to gender as well. Boas had laid the foundations,[101] but his students Margaret Mead (213–19, 226–32) and Ruth
Benedict (223–26) had elaborated the point. Indeed, such skepticism
may first have been suggested about gender differences by those skeptical of the dominant suffrage feminist ideology of basic differences
(41, 111, 176–77, 236) and then extended to race differences (108,
195, 245). The greater and earlier political success of the racial case
may be due to historical accident (an organized black movement that
powerfully used the argument, a divided woman's movement many of
whom espoused physical differences), not to the underlying issues of
principle (245). Friedan both acknowledged Mead for having made a
form of the argument, and then criticized her for not carrying it far
enough.[102] Clearly, the recent success of the argument in the racial
area made it much easier to deploy a form of the argument, as a matter
of principle, in the criticism of the unjust cultural construction of gender. If *The Feminine Mystique* was about anything, it was about that.

The dimensions of the analogy of principle became explicit in the
moral experience of the black and white women who participated in

98. See Friedan, *The Feminine Mystique*, 158,211.
99. See Freeman, *The Politics of Women's Liberation*, 27.
100. See Gunnar Myrdal, *An American Dilemma* (New York: Harper & Row, 1944), 2:
1073, appendix 5, "A Parallel to the Negro Problem."
101. See Rosalind Rosenberg, *Beyond Separate Spheres: Intellectual Roots of Modern
Feminism* (New Haven: Yale University Press, 1982), 162–69, 177.
102. See Friedan, *The Feminine Mystique*, 129–31.

the civil rights movement of the 1960s, as Sara Evans has made clear in her now classic study of this period.[103] Drawing an explicit analogy to the transformative experience of the Grimke sisters as path-breaking abolitionist feminists (24–26, 57, 101, 120), Evans noted how the struggle of black and white women to end racial discrimination led women to develop a heightened consciousness of their own oppression. In the 1950s, the civil rights movement had grown in both confidence and sense of vision. Black women played major roles in this effort, from the actions of Rosa Parks and Jo Ann Robinson in starting the Montgomery bus boycott in 1955 to Ella Baker's part in giving birth to the Student Non-Violent Coordinating Committee in 1960.[104] As the civil rights movement became a central topic in American news media, Americans became sensitized to the existence of profound constitutional injustices (including racial segregation and antimiscegenation laws) that had been rationalized on grounds that denied whole classes of persons any decent respect for their basic human rights. Like their abolitionist feminist ancestors, many women who became active in this movement only came to a realization of the comparable injustices to which they were subjected when they experienced sexism from their own male colleagues in the movement.

One group of women who realized the link between race and sex discrimination were young Southern activists who took part in the direct-action civil rights struggle of the Student Non-Violent Coordinating Committee (SNCC). Both black and white, these women found their moral voice in the protests, including sit-ins, of the civil rights movement; as one white woman later testified, "To this day I am amazed. I just did it."[105] For the white women, in particular, such activism constituted a moral revolt, similar in moral force to that of the Grimke sisters, against the idealized conception of white women central to Southern racism: "In the 1830s and again in the 1960s the first voices to link racial and sexual oppression were those of Southern white women" (25). These women, responsive to a Protestant sense of radical personal conscience and ethical responsibility, modeled themselves after black women like Ella Baker, whose life realized in practice Anna Cooper's transformative model of "[w]omen in stepping from the pedestal of statue-like inactivity in the domestic shrine, and daring to think and move and speak."[106] In so doing, these white women spiritually

103. See Sara Evans, *Personal Politics: The Roots of Women's Liberation in the Civil Rights Movement and the New Left* (New York: Vintage, 1980).

104. See Chafe, *The Paradox of Change,* 197.

105. Evans, *Personal Politics,* 38.

106. Cooper, *A Voice from the South,* 121–22.

exiled themselves from their own mothers in as radical a way as Angelina and Sarah Grimke's physical exile from the South: an experience, like the Grimkes, "exceptionally lonely, for it shattered once-supportive ties with family and friends."[107] Falling back upon personal resources they did not know they had, "they developed a sense of self that enabled them to recognize the enemy within as well—the image of the 'southern lady' " (43). In contrast to northern students who came and left the South, "southern white students were in an important sense fighting for their own identities" (45).

These white dissenting women were struggling with and against the idealized conception of white women's sphere that enforced the correlative dehumanization of black men and women as sexually animalistic. No action more outraged this ideology than the idea of consensual sexual relations between white women and black men. Antimiscegenation laws, indeed the whole structure of Southern apartheid, were rationalized as measures directed against this ultimate mythological evil. The participation of white women in interracial co-operation protesting these and other such laws represented for many of their southern white parents "a breakdown in the social order" (44); one such father, when his daughter announced "she wanted to leave school to work in a small-town black community accused her of being a whore and chased her out of the house in a drunken rage, shouting that she was disowned" (44). Within a movement of antiracist struggle led by Southern black men and women, such young white women had "to forge a new sense of themselves, to redefine the meaning of being a woman quite apart from the flawed image they had inherited" (57); their struggle was the one Du Bois had earlier defined as the antiracist struggle for a new kind of identity and self-consciousness. They self-critically recognized that the struggle for racial equality called for fundamental changes in gender roles, including what they now recognized and condemned as a conspicuously sectarian religiously-based moral "defense of white women's sexual purity in a racist society [that] held them separate from and innocent of the 'real world' of politics" (58).

The catalyst for the development of a rights-based feminism, on the model of abolitionist feminism, was the experience these women encountered of pervasive attitudes of male supremacy within SNCC. Their self-critical development and support of antiracist principles had required them to question and reject traditional gender roles, regarding "the term 'southern lady' [as] an obscene epithet" (57); they thus asserted their own human rights to conscience, speech, intimate life,

107. Evans, *Personal Politics*, 43.

and work against a sectarian racist orthodoxy that had traditionally abridged these rights. Now, within SNCC, these hard-fought personal rights were again at hazard: rights of conscience and speech were subordinated in decision making, rights of intimate life compromised by expectations that women would automatically acquiesce when men asked them to sleep with them, rights of work by limiting them to the sphere of housework (83–101). More and more of these young women began to talk with one another about their common experiences. Initially, the hope was that simply pointing out the problem in an anonymous memorandum would bring change (233–35). Stokely Carmichael's rebuttal, "The only position for women in SNCC is prone" (87), led them to conclude that they must be assertive in defense of their own rights as they had been—together with men—in the struggle for racial equality.

Increasingly, their moral experience in this rights-based struggle led them to link the two causes directly. In a summation of their thinking addressed to women in the peace and freedom movement, Casey Hayden and Mary King declared in the fall of 1965 that women, like blacks, "seem to be caught up in a common-law caste system that operates, sometime subtly, forcing them to work around or outside hierarchical structures of power which may exclude them. Women seem to be placed in the same position of assumed subordination in personal situations too. It is a caste system which, at its worst, uses and exploits women" (235). The identity-transforming struggle for a morally independent exercise of basic rights, which had led them "to think radically about the personal worth and abilities of people whose role in society had gone unchallenged before" (236), required the same analysis and criticism of "the racial caste system" and "the sexual caste system" (236). Failure to extend the criticism of racial caste to sexual caste mirrored, Hayden and King argued, the depth of the injustice of the sexual caste system and the dimensions of the problem of remedy. In particular, they pleaded for open discussion of these issues among women, creating "a community of support for each other so we can deal with ourselves and others with integrity and can therefore keep working" (237), thus identifying the centrality to rights-based feminism of the praxis of consciousness raising (203–4, 214–15). As the Black Power movement grew, it was increasingly difficult for white and black women to cooperate across racial lines; the white women veterans of the civil rights struggle took such sentiments into the student movement and the antiwar movement becoming in the process the cutting edge of second wave feminism as itself a civil rights movement (156–232).

Both the emerging feminism of these women and of Betty Friedan directed feminist discourse to the criticism, on rights-based grounds, of the normative gender roles that had theretofore been immunized from such criticism. Rather than idealizing these gender roles as the source of a higher morality (on the model of a Catharine Beecher or Frances Willard), the roles themselves and their idealization were now critically examined in the light of morally independent values of human rights. A new centrality was accorded to both the appeal to basic human rights (conscience, free speech, association, and work) and to the lack of the kind of compelling secular public justification constitutionally required before such rights might be abridged. Indeed, books like Kate Millett's 1969 *Sexual Politics*[108] and Shulamith Firestone's 1970 *Dialectic of Sex*[109] initiated the serious American study of the cultural depth and polemical power of the traditional sectarian ideology of gender, its fundamental rights-denying injustice, and the extent of imaginative (even utopian) theory and practice of change that might be required to dislodge and subvert this ideology and make space available for women to understand and claim their human rights, as persons, on fair terms.

It was such criticism of gender roles (already, as we have seen, an ingredient of the stronger antiracist principle that many black and white women now defended) that made normative space available on which black and white women could reasonably aspire to find common ground.[110] The very terms of rights-based feminism required white women to raise questions about racialized ideals of gender[111] and suggested as well that the integrity of both the stronger antiracism and antisexism appealed to common principles of nondiscrimination that should be pursued together.

Certainly, for second wave feminists, the achievements of the civil rights movement offered both a normatively powerful and relevant model of how to proceed to secure change. Virtually every legislative act, judicial decree, and executive order that applied to race could, in their view, apply to gender as well. Hence it was principled that one of the great legislative achievements of the civil rights movement (the Civil Rights Act of 1964) should, in Title VII, prohibit discrimination in

---

108. See Kate Millett, *Sexual Politics* (New York: Avon, 1969).

109. See Shulamith Firestone, *The Dialectic of Sex: The Case for Feminist Revolution* (1970; London: Woman's Press, 1988).

110. On this development, see, in general, Giddings, *When and Where I Enter*.

111. See, for example, Ruth Frankenberg, *The Social Construction of Whiteness: White Women, Race Matters* (Minneapolis: University of Minnesota Press, 1993).

employment on grounds of sex as well as race. Although a conservative opponent of the bill had proposed the additional grounds as a ludicrous attempt to cripple support for the legislation and liberal supporters opposed it for that reason,[112] the leading feminist in the House, Martha Griffiths of Michigan, held off from sponsoring the addition because she knew that the conservative's addition would bring 100 votes with him. Determined leadership by the congresswomen supporting the addition and vigorous lobbying by its supporters, including the National Woman's Party, used the logic of the connection between race and sex to persuade a majority to support the new language.[113]

The civil rights movement also supplied a model of how to proceed organizationally to implement the changes that the new legislation required. In response to the failure of implementation of the ban on sex discrimination in employment, women in the various states who had served on the various state commissions on the status of women joined with activists like Betty Friedan to form in 1966 the National Organization for Women (NOW), an organization in the civil rights mode that vowed to use lobbying, litigation, and other political means to force the Equal Employment Opportunities Commission (EEOC) to make women's issues as central to its mandate as racial issues. Friedan was elected to be NOW's first president.[114] Groups like NOW and others[115] took responsibility not only for securing compliance with progress in women's rights already achieved, but initiating new struggles to secure further victories for gender equality. Second wave feminism embraced a range of issues and concerns, from abortion rights to equal pay to ERA itself.[116]

The ERA's placement at the top of the second wave feminist agenda shows how far it had departed from its predecessors. What had once been a marginal position among feminists now became mainstream. One effect of Title VII of the Civil Rights Act was numerous court rulings invalidating state laws protective of women. Many groups, formerly opposed to ERA because of their support for these laws, had changed their minds.[117] ERA was sent to the states in 1972, where, after a spirited right-wing opposition, it failed in 1982,[118] but the level

112. See Hole and Levine, *Rebirth of Feminism,* 30–31.

113. See Freeman, *The Politics of Women's Liberation,* 53–54; McGlen and O'Connor, *Women's Rights,* 175–76.

114. See Hole Levine, *Rebirth of Feminism,* 81–95.

115. Ibid., 95–107.

116. See Chafe, *The Paradox of Change,* 201.

117. See Freeman, *The Politics of Women's Liberation,* 212.

118. See, on this political struggle, Donald G. Mathews and Jane Sherron De Hart, *Sex, Gender, and the Politics of ERA: A State and the Nation* (New York: Oxford University Press,

of support it now enjoyed both among feminists and the nation at large (the Congress and thirty-five states had ratified[119]) suggests the crucial importance in the appeal of contemporary rights-based feminist theory and practice of arguments about the unjust cultural construction of gender and the need to alter such arrangements accordingly. The appeal to differences, which had been accepted as axiomatic and the basis for a higher morality of women by Frances Willard and Jane Addams,[120] was now the basis for rights-based criticism (the differences, being unjustly culturally constructed, could be criticized and changed in light of justice).

In all of this, the civil rights movement was the impetus both for the new forms of substantive argument women now made and for women organizing themselves into a civil rights movement. It was also indispensable in preparing the constitutional mind of the nation for greater concern for related issues of constitutional justice, and indeed urging the judiciary interpretively to recognize such claims. The Supreme Court would both respond to and encourage such claims.

CONSTITUTIONAL PRINCIPLES

As recently as 1961 the Supreme Court had unanimously affirmed, as the measure of women's rights and responsibilities, their ascribed status "as the center of home and family life."[121] Even the three justices who had dissented from the enforcement of this conception in 1948 assumed that, in principle, truly benign protective legislation of women would be constitutional.[122] However, subsequent cases have interpreted relevant constitutional principles in a very different way that gave expression to and indeed forged a constitutionally enforceable conception of the rights of women in terms of rights-based principles

---

1990); Jane J. Mansbridge, *Why We Lost the ERA* (Chicago: University of Chicago Press, 1986).

    119. See Mansbridge, *Why We Lost the ERA,* 1.

    120. See Rosalind Rosenberg, *Beyond Separate Spheres,* 41.

    121. See *Hoyt v. Florida,* 368 U.S. 57, 62 (1961).

    122. In *Goesaert v. Cleary,* 335 U.S. 464 (1948), the three dissenters (Justice Rutledge, joined by Justices Douglas and Murphy) dissented because the statute drew an arbitrary distinction "between male and female owners of liquor establishments." 335 U.S. at 468. A female owner might neither work as a barmaid nor employ her daughter in that position (even if a man were there to keep order), whereas a male owner might employ his wife and daughter as barmaids though he was always absent from the bar. The dissent thus questioned not protective legislation as such, but whether this legislation (with its inadequate fit between means and ends) was properly protective.

of second wave feminism. To make clear the extent of the constitutional developments that reflect this conception, I first examine the relevant case law in various domains, and then offer in the next section a general normative perspective on how this interpretive development (including its conspicuous analogies to the race cases) should be not only understood, but critically evaluated.

The argument of toleration, applied as the abolitionist feminists did to both racism and slavery, would suggest dimensions of argument that would focus on both the basic human rights that have been unjustly denied and on the inadequate sectarian grounds that rationalized such abridgments of basic rights. The basic rights cluster in four areas: conscience, speech, intimate life, and work. The inadequate sectarian grounds would be expressed in constitutional skepticism about arguments, like racism and sexism, rooted in rights-denying injustice. In fact, we find important and relevant case law in all these areas.

Basic Human Rights

It is fundamental to the kind of criticism that the argument for toleration has brought to American racism and sexism that the political power of these ideologies reflected dehumanizing cultural stereotypes that abridged basic human rights of moral personality. Basic human rights like conscience, speech, intimate life, and work are culture-creating rights, affording appropriate space for the free exercise of our powers of moral personality in responsibly creating, forging, and sustaining the cultural and institutional forms through which we reasonably find and sustain permanent humane value in living both for ourselves and, if the values are reasonable and enduring, for later generations. Systematic abridgment of these rights is the fundamental insult and indignity that it is because of the role the free exercise of such rights plays in self-respect for our creative moral freedom to originate claims and reasonably to forge and sustain the cultural forms of life that give enduring personal sense and moral meaning to living a life as a responsible moral agent. Persons systematically deprived of such rights, in a constitutional community like the United States that otherwise respects such rights, are denationalized as both persons and citizens: useful as tools are useful, lovable and amusing as pets are, but not equal subjects of rights and responsibility and thus members of the constitutional community. Accordingly, any serious attention to such injustice requires correlative attention to guaranteeing on equal terms each of these basic rights.

CONSCIENCE. The tradition of rights-based feminism, from Woll-stonecraft to Sarah Grimke to Lucretia Mott to Elizabeth Stanton, has given weight, consistent with the significance of the inalienable right to conscience in the argument for toleration, to claims for equal rights to conscience and correlative rights to equal educational opportunity (including, as Wollstonecraft argued, integrated public education[123]). For Grimke and Mott, the argument called for the equal right of women to be scholars, theologians, and ministers and thus to bring their moral independence to bear on the criticism of misogynist Bible interpretation and the political power it had unjustly been allowed to enjoy; Stanton published *The Woman's Bible* very much in this spirit.[124] Women had in nineteenth-century American culture used constitutional guarantees of religious liberty not only in fomenting, as Grimke and Mott did, abolitionist feminist dissent within a religion like Quakerism that traditionally accorded a more central role to women in the works of conscience,[125] but in generating and fostering either highly personal forms of spirituality like that of Sojourner Truth[126] or religious organizations founded by women like Shakerism, Christian Science, and spiritualism.[127] But the censure of Stanton by the suffrage movement she had founded suggests the degree to which suffrage feminism had compromised the argument for toleration that had made it norma-

123. See Wollstonecraft, *A Vindication of the Rights of Woman,* 237–60.

124. See Mary D. Pellauer, *Toward a Tradition of Feminist Theology: The Religious Social Thought of Elizabeth Cady Stanton, Susan B. Anthony, and Anna Howard Shaw* (Brooklyn: Carlson Publishing Inc., 1991).

125. See, in general, Bacon, *Mothers of Feminism.*

126. See Jacquelyn Grant, *White Women's Christ and Black Women's Jesus: Feminist Christology and Womanist Response* (Atlanta: Scholars Press, 1989), 214, 219–20, 222.

127. See, in general, Susan Starr Sered, *Priestess, Mother, Sacred Sister: Religions Dominated by Women* (New York: Oxford University Press, 1994). On spiritualism in particular, see Braude, *Radical Spirits;* on Shakerism, see Nardi Reeder Campion, *Ann the Word: The Life of Mother Ann Lee, Founder of the Shakers* (Boston: Little, Brown, 1976); Lawrence Foster, *Women, Family, and Utopia: Communal Experiments of the Shakers, the Oneida Community, and the Mormons* (Syracuse: Syracuse University Press, 1991), 17–71; Henri Desroche, *The American Shakers: From Neo-Christianity to Presocialism,* trans. John K. Savacool (Amherst: University of Massachusetts Press, 1971); Marjorie Procter-Smith, *Women in Shaker Community and Worship: A Feminist Analysis of the Uses of Religious Symbolism* (Lewiston, N.Y.: Edwin Mellen Press, 1985); Stephen J. Stein, *The Shaker Experience in America* (New Haven: Yale University Press, 1992); Jean M. Humez, *Mother's First-Born Daughters: Early Shaker Writings on Women and Religion* (Bloomington: Indiana University Press, 1993); Louis J. Kern, *An Ordered Love: Sex Roles and Sexuality in Victorian Utopias— the Shakers, the Mormons, and the Oneida Community* (Chapel Hill: University of North Carolina Press, 1981), 71–136.

tively possible, cramping the scope of acceptable feminist conscience to the sectarian measure of a Frances Willard.[128]

An important background condition for the emergence of second wave feminism after World War II was thus not only the increasing numbers of American women who worked,[129] but the formative cultural importance of the Supreme Court's increasing insistence that, consistent with the guarantees of both religious free exercise and of antiestablishment in the First Amendment, the state not engage in or support what in contemporary circumstances was sectarian religious teaching, but extend respect to all forms of conscience, secular and religious.[130] While these doctrinal developments did not deal specifically with issues of gender or gender roles, they affirmed limits on legitimate state power to enforce sectarian purposes that were of generative importance in the constitutional legitimation of new forms of conscientious dissent, both antiracist and antisexist, on such grounds. In the areas of free speech and privacy, as we shall see, interpretations of such principles were reasonably extended specifically to protect the rights of women.

Equal respect for rights of conscience also required that constitutional attention be paid, as it had in the area of race, to forms of state-imposed segregation that were inconsistent with equal educational opportunity. It was no accident that the NAACP had directed its antiracist litigation strategy on first attacking such segregation in basic public education.[131] Consistent with the Boasian theory of the cultural construction of racism, no set of institutions could be more fundamental

---

128. See, in general, Betty A. DeBerg, *Ungodly Women: Gender and the First Wave of American Fundamentalism* (Minneapolis: Fortress Press, 1990).

129. See Chafe, *The Paradox of Change*, 166–72, 188–92.

130. Important anti-establishment cases include *McCollum v. Board of Education*, 333 U.S. 203 (1948) (release time for religious education unconstitutional); cf. *Zorach v. Clauson*, 343 U.S. 306 (1952) (not unconstitutional if release time is for religious teaching off site); *Engel v. Vitale*, 370 U.S. 421 (1962); *Abington School District v. Schempp*, 374 U.S. 203 (1963) (requirements of sectarian prayers unconstitutional); *Epperson v. Arkansas*, 393 U.S. 97 (1968) (banning teaching Darwin unconstitutional). Important free exercise cases include *United States v. Ballard*, 322 U.S. 78 (1944) (truth or falsity of religious belief not subject to state inquiry); *Torcaso v. Watkins*, 367 U.S. 488 (1960) (requirement that officials must swear belief in God held unconstitutional); *United States v. Seeger*, 380 U.S. 163 (1965) (conscientious exemption for those who object to all wars must extend to all beliefs, religious and nonreligious); *Welsh v. United States*, 398 U.S. 333 (1970) (accord); but cf. *Gillette v. United States*, 401 U.S. 437 (1970) (failure to exempt selective conscientious objectors supported by adequate secular purpose). For commentary on these developments, see, in general, Richards, *Toleration and the Constitution*, 67–162.

131. See, in general, Tushnet, *The NAACP's Legal Strategy against Segregated Education, 1925–1950*.

in framing such racism than the basic public school education that artificially divided and stigmatized minority students on grounds of race. Accordingly, the needed remedial statement of inclusion into the common culture on equal terms was eloquently made by integration of the basic institutions of universal public education. The Supreme Court has decided two cases that, consistent with Betty Friedan's early application of our growing antiracist worries about separate-but-equal to antisexism as well,[132] suggest common concerns in the area of gender.

In *Mississippi University for Women v. Hogan*,[133] the Court narrowly sustained a male's constitutional challenge to the state's policy of excluding men from the Mississippi University for Women (MUW) School of Nursing. Justice Powell in his dissent emphasized not only that coeducational public nursing schools were open to Hogan, but that the American practice of single-sex schools was supported by a long history that has only recently been largely abandoned (736–39) and that served today legitimate values of educational diversity (745). Justice O'Connor, writing for the majority, found that the State's primary justification for the single-sex admissions policy of MUW, namely, compensation for discrimination against women, was disingenuous. There was no showing that women lacked opportunities to obtain training in nursing that would call for such a policy. Instead, "MUW's policy of excluding males from admission to the School of Nursing tends to perpetuate the stereotyped view of nursing as an exclusively woman's job" (729). That was objectionable because it "lends credibility to the old view that women, not men, should become nurses, and makes the assumption that nursing is a field for women a self-fulfilling prophecy" (730). In effect, a traditional conception of gender roles, itself based on denying equal educational opportunities to women, could not, *pace* Justice Powell, be a constitutionally reasonable measure of equal opportunity today. Justice O'Connor's skepticism about the enforcement "of fixed notions concerning the roles and abilities of males and females" (725) in the educational context suggests the same Boasian themes we have already identified in the area of racial segregation, only now transposed into the key of gender. Inclusion of women into the common culture, on terms of equal respect for conscience, suggests at least a strong presumption of integrated educational opportunities.

The recent decision of the Supreme Court, 7–1, in *United States*

---

132. See Friedan, *The Feminine Mystique*, 157–59.
133. *Mississippi University for Women v. Hogan*, 458 U.S. 718 (1982) (5–4 decision).

v. Virginia[134] has, if anything, strengthened this presumption. The Virginia Military Institute (VMI) was the sole single sex institution among Virginia's current institutions of higher learning; its exclusion of women was based on its purposes (the production of citizen-soldiers for leadership in civilian and military life) and its highly demanding, adversarial mode of education based on the model of English public schools. Invoking the tests of Justice O'Connor's opinion in *Hogan*, Justice Ginsburg, writing for the Court, examined VMI's justifications for single-sex admissions and found them not to rest on compensatory purposes but on once traditional "views about women's proper place" (2277) that, themselves reflecting historical patterns of discrimination, may not be a reasonable measure of opportunity today (2280). In reaching this assessment, Justice Ginsburg noted the parallel historical uses of arguments, like those of VMI, to rationalize the exclusion of women from higher education (2277–78) as well as from the practice of law, from law and medical schools, and from policing (2280–82). In all these cases, "women's categorical exclusion, in total disregard of their individual merit" (2282), failed to do justice to women "as citizens in our American democracy equal in stature to men" (2282). The inclusion of women into VMI was called for on the same grounds that, in *Sweatt v. Painter*,[135] blacks were admitted to the University of Texas Law School: only integration into common public educational institutions can do justice to the equal rights of women as persons.[136]

FREE SPEECH.   Obscenity law was the main weapon against a wide range of dissenting late nineteenth- and early twentieth-century views on matters of sexuality and gender, including the poems of Walt Whitman, the advocacy of free love by Victoria Woodhull, Ezra Heywood, and Lois Waisbrooker, the advocacy of contraception and abortion by Margaret Sanger, and similar such advocacy, including of consensual homosexuality, by Emma Goldman. Assessed from this historical perspective, obscenity law was the main weapon to abridge the fundamental rights of free speech of dissenters to the gender orthodoxy of the Gilded Age, including rights-based feminists like Woodhull, Sanger, and Goldman and their allies. Such abridgments of rights of free speech compromised, in turn, the more basic right to conscience, on

134. See *United States v. Virginia*, 116 S. Ct. 2264 (1996).
135. *Sweatt v. Painter*, 339 U.S. 629 (1950).
136. See *United States v. Virginia*, 116 S. Ct. at 2285–86.

which the right to free speech is often grounded.[137] A number of highly
conscientious dissenting speakers and the dissenting convictions they
held were repressed on the ground that they contested the dominant
majoritarian orthodoxy of gender and sexuality. The consequences
were devastating to them and to American public discourse and debate; no one could reasonably be expected to even undertake such
debate when they saw the consequences to a Woodhull or a Goldman.
Rather, the message was either to go silent or to self-censor and accommodate one's views and public image to the mainstream in order to
make progress on one issue (e.g., Sanger's strategy on contraception).
The growing marginalization of rights-based feminism in favor of suffrage feminism was thus by no means the consequence of fair discourse
and debate, but rather of a highly cynical, blatantly unconstitutional
political manipulation of the public agenda. The normative theory of
gender roles of Catharine Beecher and Frances Willard were politically privileged; dissent was actively repressed with the full force of
criminal law. A nation, which in the antebellum period sustained a
public stage (at least outside the South) for the radical moral criticism
of a Garrison or the Grimke sisters, could not in the twentieth century
extend similar constitutional civility to the comparable rights-based
moral protests of an Emma Goldman against the shallow conventional-
ities of the Gilded Age.

The suggestion of stronger judicial protections for freedom of
speech began in the United States in 1918 in the dissent of Justice
Holmes (joined by Justice Brandeis) to *Abrams v. United States*,[138] a
federal criminal prosecution for protests of American participation in
World War I. (Emma Goldman was also successfully prosecuted for
her antiwar and antidraft advocacy under one of these statutes.[139])
Holmes and Brandeis persisted in their path-breaking dissents in several important later cases,[140] but the view began to command majorities
on clear First Amendment grounds[141] only in 1937 in cases protecting
the rights of dissent of American Communists, one of which crucially

137. For elaboration on this point, see Richards, *Toleration and the Constitution*,
166–74.

138. *Abrams v. United States*, 250 U.S. 616 (1919).

139. See Drinnon, *Rebel in Paradise*, 184–99.

140. See, in particular, *Gitlow v. New York*, 268 U.S. 652 (1925) (Holmes, J., dissenting,
joined by Brandeis, J.); *Whitney v. California*, 274 U.S. 357 (1927) (Brandeis, J., concurring,
joined by Holmes, J.).

141. See *Fiske v. Kansas*, 274 U.S. 380 (1927) (application of state criminal syndicalism
statute to the terms of the preamble to the IWW constitution found to lack any due process
factual support).

involved antiracist dissent in Georgia that was subject to the death penalty.[142] With some backtracking,[143] the federal judiciary later elaborated even stronger protections of free speech often in the context of protecting the rights of conscience and dissent of the antiracist civil rights movement.[144] On this clearly correct view, the measure of constitutional protection for conscientiously dissenting speech could not be the dominant orthodoxy that it challenged, for that would trivialize the protection of free speech to whatever massaged the prejudices of dominant majorities. Rather, as the judicial protection of the increasingly successful antiracist advocacy of the civil rights movement showed, it was the speech most critical of and offensive to the dominant racist orthodoxy in the United States that most needed to be publicly questioned and challenged if the unjust, indeed unconstitutional, basis for such racism was to be publicly understood as the rights-denying evil it was and remedially addressed with an appropriate sense of communal ethical responsibility.

No laws had been more aggressively used against the claims of rights-based feminism than anti-obscenity laws. It was against the background of growing judicial protection of antiracist dissent that the Supreme Court reconsidered as well the role that obscenity law had been allowed to play, as we have seen, against conscientious rights-based dissent from the dominant orthodoxy of gender and sexuality.

142. See *Herndon v. Lowry*, 301 U.S. 242 (1937) (5–4 decision holding unconstitutional on free speech and vagueness grounds conviction for antiracist civil rights advocacy of black member of American Communist Party under state anti-incitement-to-insurrection statute). See also *De Jonge v. Oregon*, 299 U.S. 353 (1937) (criminal prosecution under state criminal syndicalism statute of member of Communist Party for assisting in public meeting held unconstitutional under First Amendment).

143. See, most notably, *Dennis v. United States*, 341 U.S. 494 (1951) (federal Smith Act, making criminal organization and teaching of Communist Party for advocacy of overthrow of government, held facially constitutional). But see *Yates v. United States,* 354 U.S. 298 (1957) (Smith Act unconstitutional as applied); *Noto v. United States*, 367 U.S. 290 (1961) (accord); cf. *Scales v. United States*, 367 U.S. 203 (1961) (Smith Act constitutional as applied). But see also *Brandenburg v. Ohio*, 395 U.S. 444 (1969) (invalidating state criminal syndicalism statute that criminalized the advocating of government's overthrow).

144. Notable examples include *Edwards v. California*, 372 U.S. 229 (1963) (breach of peace prosecution of civil rights demonstrators on grounds of South Carolina State House held unconstitutional); *New York Times v. Sullivan*, 376 U.S. 254 (1964) (libel action for false reporting of *New York Times* of Martin Luther King's protests in Alabama held unconstitutional); *Cox v. Louisiana*, 379 U.S. 536 (1965) (criminal prosecution of civil rights demonstration for breach of peace and obstructing public passages held unconstitutional); *Brown v. Louisiana*, 383 U.S. 131 (1966) (breach of peace conviction for black sit-in of segregated public library held unconstitutional); *Shuttlesworth v. Birmingham*, 394 U.S. 147 (1969) (state ordinance, requiring permit before civil rights demonstration could take place, held unconstitutional); *Street v. New York*, 394 U.S. 576 (1969) (state prosecution for use of burning flag to protest murder of civil rights leader in Mississippi held unconstitutional).

In 1957 in *Roth v. United States*,[145] the Supreme Court, addressing the abstract question of whether obscene material was constitutionally protected, attempted to preserve the traditional immunity of obscene materials from free speech scrutiny. However, subsequent cases required it to address the more concrete question of whether certain materials were or were not obscene, and thus, within *Roth*, did not or did raise free speech questions. During this period, as issues of gender and sexuality became more publicly contested and contestable, the Supreme Court began constitutionally to reverse obscenity prosecutions on diverse constitutional theories none of which commanded a majority of the Court.[146] The view that commanded most support focused on whether the material had exclusively prurient appeal, was offensive to national community standards of sexual representation, and utterly lacked redeeming social value (excluding prurience from counting as such social value).[147] Increasingly, under this standard, only hard-core pornography could be constitutionally repressed. In 1973 in *Miller v. California*[148] and *Paris Adult Theatre I v. Slaton*,[149] the Court, 5–4, narrowly retained the structure of *Roth* but limited the scope of the constitutionally obscene effectively to hard-core pornographic depictions of sexual organs (coming to climax) that appealed exclusively to prurient interest, violated local community standards, and lacked serious value (excluding its prurient value); Justice Brennan, the original author of *Roth*, admitted that his earlier abstract view that obscene versus nonobscene material could be distinguished without compromising free speech interests had proven untenable, and dissented.

The development of obscenity law has been, first, a struggle over how appropriately to narrow the scope of what could constitutionally count as obscene and thus be immune from free speech analysis, and, second, whether, as a category immune from free speech analysis, it should be narrowed to the vanishing point. The development of Justice Brennan's thought, for example, reflects this chronology exactly. Both these interpretive developments aim to protect the basic conscientiously dissenting rights of free speech on matters of gender and sexuality that have historically been abridged by the abusively repressive use of obscenity laws. Proponents of these two interpretive perspectives disagree about precisely how those rights should be understood; both largely agree, however, that all the historical prosecutions for obscenity

145. See *Roth v. United States*, 354 U.S. 476 (1957).
146. See *Redrup v. New York*, 386 U.S. 767 (1967).
147. See *Memoirs v. Massachusetts*, 383 U.S. 413 (1966).
148. See *Miller v. California*, 413 U.S. 15 (1973).
149. See *Paris Adult Theatre I v. Slaton*, 413 U.S. 49 (1973).

so far discussed could not be reached under an appropriately narrowed conception of obscenity. That clearly reflects the important emphasis now accorded, against the background of historical repression, one of the basic rights claimed by rights-based feminism.

Catharine MacKinnon has been a notable critic of traditional obscenity law (because it targets eroticism as such) and would certainly repudiate many laws that could constitutionally be used against rights-based feminists. However, she has urged, on self-consciously feminist grounds, that obscenity law be functionally reconstructed in terms of sexual representations whose availability harms the civil rights of women, portraying them in degraded, sexually objectified ways that disable men from regarding women as persons and claimants to equal civil rights; such representations may be repressed on the ground that no basic right is thus infringed and the unjust subordination of women is combated.[150] MacKinnon was the architect, with Andrea Dworkin, of an Indianapolis civil rights ordinance that used her revised definition of pornography. This ordinance was later struck down as unconstitutional on the ground that its definition did not satisfy the *Miller* guidelines and thus unconstitutionally abridged protected-speech;[151] the Canadian Supreme Court has, however, accepted her approach not just in the form of a civil rights ordinance, but as the constitutional measure of criminalization of obscene materials.[152]

Nan Hunter, Sylvia Law, and Nadine Strossen have, again on self-consciously feminist grounds, urged that the position more consistent with the rights of women would be neither to use nor to revise the current constitutional conception of obscenity, but to get rid of it altogether. They object to MacKinnon's conception because it reintroduces the power of state censorship allegedly to protect women from moral harms that reinforces, rather than rebuts, sexist stereotypes of women in the long and now largely constitutionally repudiated tradition of protective legislation for women.[153] It would be one thing for women themselves to organize to combat any sexist material (whether

150. See, in general, Catharine A. MacKinnon, *Only Words* (Cambridge: Harvard University Press, 1993). See also id., *Feminism Unmodified: Discourses on Life and Law* (Cambridge: Harvard University Press, 1987), 127–213; id., *Toward a Feminist Theory of the State* (Cambridge: Harvard University Press, 1989), 195–214.

151. See *American Booksellers Association v. Hudnut*, 771 F.2d 323 (7th Cir. 1985), *affirmed*, 475 U.S. 1001 (1986).

152. See *Butler v. Regina*, 1 S.C.R. 452 (Can. 1992).

153. See Nan D. Hunter and Sylvia Law, "The FACT Brief," in Lisa Duggan and Nan D. Hunter, *Sex, Sexual Dissent, and Political Culture* (New York: Routledge, 1995); Nadine Strossen, *Defending Pornography: Free Speech, Sex, and the Fight for Women's Rights* (New York: Scribner, 1995).

sexually explicit or not), but quite a different matter to empower the state to make inherently controversial interpretive judgments about the degradation of women. The record in Canada, for example, has been that the state power of censorship has been used largely against gay and lesbian materials, not the mainstream hard-core pornographic materials that are MacKinnon's real concern.[154]

Obscenity law, whatever its more circumscribed or revised form, requires interpretive judgments to be made by the state about the worth or value of sexually explicit materials on the ground that they embody or elicit fantasies that are inconsistent with proper sexuality or appropriate gender roles. A theory of the obscene is a theory of the unnatural in matters of sex or gender. It should not be at all surprising that the enforcement of Canada's revised obscenity laws has given expression to a traditional conception of the unnatural, not at all to the more enlightened conception of MacKinnon or Dworkin. No such conception, no matter what its ostensibly appealing form in the abstract (including that of MacKinnon or Dworkin), has any place as a ground for censorship in a free society in contemporary circumstances, certainly not in a society with our history that now self-critically claims to respect the rights of women. No group, except perhaps gays and lesbians, has suffered more acutely than women from the imposition of traditional sexual roles, or been more often silenced and intimidated by the invocation of the unnatural in response to any legitimate form of dissent from such roles (including the cultivation of erotic imagination on their own terms). It does not advance rights-based feminism, but compromises it, to ascribe stereotypically to any communicative material in the area of sexuality or gender a depersonalized meaning or simplistic causal script (life imitates pornographic art) in the place of the varied imaginative lives of persons, the different roles sexually explicit materials play in such lives[155] and, in light of such variety, the lack of any reliable evidence of a causal significance of harm to women.[156]

MacKinnon's proposal rests on a form of antisubordination argument, but it is a quite bad one. First, it assumes that no free speech right of any weight is at stake; but, as feminists have argued against MacKinnon, such rights are at stake, namely, rights of women autonomously to define and express their own erotic imaginations free of the unjust imposition of illegitimate stereotypes of proper gender roles.

154. See Strossen, *Defending Pornography*, 229–46.
155. Ibid., 142–60.
156. Ibid., 253–56, 272–73.

244   CHAPTER FIVE

Canada's experience confirms this worry. Second, her argument demonizes the harms from such materials in ways unsupported by impartial evidence, raising worries that (like the purity movement) one's polemics, based on the search for a shallow, scapegoating populist consensus as a basis for political solidarity, are perversely enforcing subordination, not advancing antisubordination. Third, her argument assumes an undefended view of the focal importance of pornographic material in enforcing the subordination of women in contrast to other more reasonable understandings of such sources of subordination (for example, the illegitimate enforcement of sectarian religious or mythological views, or the systemically unjust economic subordination of women in family and job roles). A rights-based feminism need not indulge in yet another polemical, mythological stereotype of gender, but should contest and subvert them precisely because they do not do justice to individualized moral personality and experience, indeed have been the traditional rationale of gender inequality. The use of such stereotypes in this discourse uncritically repeats the mistake of Catharine Beecher or Frances Willard.[157] Our attention, like Willard's, is thus distracted from the intractable sectarian sources of gender inequality (which are left unexamined, and sometimes reinforced) toward an unreal issue whose pursuit, like the temperance or purity movements, retards, rather than advances human rights.[158]

INTIMATE LIFE.   We have now examined at some length the role that the abridgment of basic human rights of intimate life played in the racist dehumanization of African Americans both under slavery and in later patterns of state-supported segregation and antimiscegenation laws. It was a symptom of the depth of the comparable dehumanization of women that the very proposal of such a right in their case was greeted with the full ferocity of the Wollstonecraft repudiation of Woodhull and the free love argument she came to represent in the American public mind, including the obscenity prosecutions she and others endured. Against this background, the struggle for a rights-based feminism could reasonably be measured by the seriousness with which American constitutional culture would be willing to take the protection of so basic a human right.

In 1965 the Supreme Court in *Griswold v. Connecticut*[159] constitutionalized the argument for a basic human right to contraception that

157. On the analogy of MacKinnon's arguments to those of the temperance movement, see ibid., 269.
158. Cf. Ibid., 261–62, 266.
159. *Griswold v. Connecticut*, 381 U.S. 479 (1965).

had been persistently and eloquently defended and advocated by Margaret Sanger for well over forty years, a decision which Sanger lived to see.[160] The Court extended the right to abortion services in 1973 in *Roe v. Wade*[161] (reaffirming its central principle in 1992[162]), and denied its application in 1986 to consensual homosexual sex acts in *Bowers v. Hardwick;*[163] a related form of analysis was used, albeit inconclusively, in cases involving the right to die.[164] Three of these cases (contraception, abortion, homosexuality) can be understood on the grounds of a basic right to intimate personal life, and the remaining of them (death) involved another basic right (an aspect of the right to life or meaningful life).[165] I focus here on the first three cases.

Sanger's and Goldman's arguments for the right to contraception, as we have seen, were very much rooted in rights-based feminism. Sanger's opponents certainly made that point very clear. When her husband, Bill Sanger, was convicted of obscenity for distributing one of his wife's publications, the judge emphasized that the dispute was over woman's role: "Your crime is not only a violation of the laws of man, but of the law of God as well, in your scheme to prevent mother-hood. Too many persons have the idea that it is wrong to have children. Some women are so selfish that they do not want to be bothered with them. If some persons would go around and urge Christian women to bear children, instead of wasting their time on woman suffrage, this city and society would be better off."[166]

Sanger's and Goldman's arguments had two prongs, both of which were implicit in the Supreme Court's decisions in *Griswold* and later cases: first, a basic human right to intimate life and the role of the right to contraception as an instance of that right; second, the assessment of whether laws abridging such a fundamental right met the heavy burden of secular justification that was required.

160. See Chesler, *Woman of Valor,* 11, 230, 376, 467.

161. *Roe v. Wade,* 410 U.S. 113 (1973).

162. See *Planned Parenthood of Southeastern Pennsylvania v. Casey,* 112 S. Ct. 2791 (1992).

163. *Bowers v. Hardwick,* 478 U.S. 186 (1986).

164. See *Cruzan v. Director, Missouri Department of Health,* 496 U.S. 261 (1990). Justice Rehnquist, writing for a 5–4 majority, accepts that a right to die exists and applies to the case (refusing medical treatment) but denies that the state has imposed an unreasonable restriction on the right on the facts of the case. See also *Vacco v. Quill,* 1997 WL 348037 (U.S.) (unanimously holding that prohibition on assisted suicide is not constitutionally unreasonable).

165. For further discussion, see David A. J. Richards, *Sex, Drugs, Death, and the Law: An Essay on Human Rights and Overcriminalization* (Totowa, N.J.: Rowman and Littlefield, 1982), 215–70.

166. Chesler, *Woman of Valor,* 127.

The basis of the fundamental human right to intimate life was, as Lydia Maria Child, Stephen Andrews, and Victoria Woodhull had earlier made clear (see chapter 4), as basic an inalienable right of moral personality (respect for which is central to the argument for toleration) as the right to conscience. Like the right to conscience, it protects intimately personal moral resources (thoughts and beliefs, intellect, emotions, self-image and self-identity) and the way of life that expresses and sustains them in facing and meeting rationally and reasonably the challenge of a life worth living—one touched by enduring personal and ethical value. The right to intimate life centers on protecting these moral resources as they bear on the role of loving and being loved in the tender and caring exfoliation of moral personality, morally finding one's self, as a person, in love for and the love of another moral self.

The human right of intimate life was not only an important right in the argument for toleration central to American constitutionalism, but a right interpretively implicit in the historical traditions of American rights-based constitutionalism. In both of the two great revolutionary moments that framed the trajectory of American constitutionalism (the American Revolution and the Civil War), the right to intimate life was one of the central human rights the abridgment of which rendered political power illegitimate and gave rise to the Lockean right to revolution.[167]

At the time of the American Revolution, the background literature on human rights, known to and assumed by the American revolutionaries and founding constitutionalists, included what the influential Scottish philosopher Francis Hutcheson called "the natural right each one to enter into the matrimonial relation with any one who consents."[168] Indeed, John Witherspoon, whose lectures Madison heard at Princeton, followed Hutcheson in listing even more abstractly as a basic human and natural right a "right to associate, if he so incline, with any person or persons, whom he can persuade (not force)—under this is contained the right to marriage."[169] Accordingly, leading statesmen at the state conventions ratifying the Constitution, both those for and

167. See, on American revolutionary constitutionalism as framed by these events, Richards, *Foundations of American Constitutionalism;* id., *Conscience and the Constitution.*

168. See Francis Hutcheson, *A System of Moral Philosophy* (1755; New York: Augustus M. Kelley, 1968), 1:299.

169. See John Witherspoon, *Lectures of Moral Philosophy,* ed. Jack Scott (East Brunswick, N.J.: Associated University Presses, 1982), 123. For further development of this point, see Richards, *Toleration and the Constitution,* 232–33.

against adoption, assumed that the Constitution could not interfere in the domestic sphere. Alexander Hamilton of New York denied that the Constitution did or could "penetrate the recesses of domestic life, and control, in all respects, the private conduct of individuals,"[170] and Patrick Henry of Virginia spoke of the core of our rights to liberty as the sphere where a person "enjoys the fruits of his labor, under his own fig-tree, with his wife and children around him, in peace and security."[171] The arguments of reserved rights both of leading proponents (Hamilton) and opponents (Henry) of adoption of the Constitution thus converged on the private sphere of domestic married life.

At the time of the Civil War, the understanding of marriage as a basic human right took on a new depth and urgency because of the antebellum abolitionist rights-based attack on the peculiar nature of American slavery; such slavery failed to recognize the marriage or family rights of slaves,[172] and indeed inflicted on the black family the moral horror of breaking them up by selling family members separately.[173] One in six slave marriages thus were ended by force or sale.[174] No aspect of American slavery more dramatized its radical evil than its brutal deprivation of intimate personal life, including undermining the moral authority of parents over children. Slaves, Weld argued, had "as little control over [their children], as have domestic animals over the disposal of their young."[175] Slavery, thus understood as an attack on intimate personal life,[176] stripped persons of essential attributes of their humanity.

This historical background (as well as background rights-based political theory) makes it interpretively correct to regard the right to intimate life as one of the unenumerated rights protected both by the Ninth Amendment and the privileges and immunities clause of the

---

170. See Jonathan Elliot, *The Debates in the Several State Conventions on the Adoption of the Federal Constitution* (Washington, D.C.: Printed for the Editor, 1836), 2:269.

171. Ibid., 3:54.

172. See Kenneth M. Stampp, *The Peculiar Institution* (New York: Vintage, 1956), 198, 340–49; Eugence D. Genovese, *Roll, Jordan, Roll: The World the Slaves Made* (New York: Vintage Books, 1974), 32, 52–53, 125, 451–58.

173. See Stampp, *The Peculiar Institution,* 199–201, 204–6, 333, 348–49; Herbert G. Gutman, *The Black Family in Slavery and Freedom, 1750–1925* (New York: Vintage Books, 1976), 146, 318, 349.

174. See Gutman, *The Black Family in Slavery and Freedom,* 318.

175. See Weld, *American Slavery As It Is,* 56.

176. See Ronald G. Walters, *The Antislavery Appeal: American Abolitionism after 1830* (New York: W. W. Norton, 1978), 95–96.

Fourteenth Amendment, as Justice Harlan may be regarded as arguing in his concurrence in *Griswold*.[177] The Supreme Court quite properly interpreted the Fourteenth Amendment in particular as protecting this basic human right against unjustified state abridgment, and, as Sanger and Goldman had urged, regarding the right to use contraceptives as an instance of this right. The right to contraception was, for Sanger and Goldman, a fundamental human right for women because it would enable women, perhaps for the first time in human history, reliably to decide whether and when their sexual lives will be reproductive. Respect for this right was an aspect of the more basic right of intimate life in two ways. It would enable women to exercise control over their intimate relations to men, deciding whether and when such relations will be reproductive, and it would secure to women the right to decide whether and when they will form the intimate relationship to a child. Both choices threatened the traditional gender-defined role of women's sexuality as both exclusively and mandatorily procreational and maternally self-sacrificing, and were resisted, as by Bill Sanger's judge, for that reason.

Like other such rights, this human right may only be regulated or limited on terms of public reason not themselves hostage to an entrenched political hierarchy (for example, compulsorily arranged marriages[178]) resting on the abridgment of such rights. For example, from the perspective of the general abolitionist criticism of slavery and racism, the proslavery arguments in support of Southern slavery's treatment of family life were transparently inadequate, not remotely affording adequate public justification for the abridgment of such a fundamental right. These arguments were in their nature essentially racist: "His natural affection is not strong, and consequently he is cruel to his own offspring, and suffers little by separation from them."[179] "Another striking trait of negro character is lasciviousness. Lust is his strongest passion; and hence, rape is an offence of too frequent occurrence. Fidelity to the marriage relation they do not understand and do not expect, neither in their native country nor in a state of bond-

177. Justice Harlan, in fact, grounds his argument on the due process clause of the Fourteenth Amendment, but the argument is more plausibly understood, as a matter of text, history, and political theory, as based on the privileges and immunities clause of the Fourteenth Amendment for reasons I give in Richards, *Conscience and the Constitution,* chap. 6. For further elaboration of this interpretation of *Griswold,* see Richards, *Toleration and the Constitution,* 256–61.

178. See Werner Sollors, *Beyond Ethnicity: Consent and Descent in American Culture* (New York: Oxford University Press, 1986), 112.

179. Cobb, *An Inquiry into the Law of Negro Slavery in the United States of America,* 39.

age."[180] The blind moral callousness of Southern proslavery thought was nowhere more evident than its treatment of what were in fact agonizing, crushing, and demeaning family separations:[181] "He is also liable to be separated from wife or child . . . —but from native character and temperament, the separation is much less severely felt"[182]; "With regard to the separation of husbands and wives, parents and children, . . . Negroes are themselves both perverse and comparatively indifferent about this matter."[183]

The irrationalist racist sexualization of black slaves was evident in the frequent justification of slavery in terms of maintaining the higher standards of sexual purity of Southern white women.[184] Viewed through the polemically distorted prism of such thought, the relation of master and slave was itself justified as an intimate relationship like husband and wife that should similarly be immunized from outside interference.[185] Through the Orwellian distortion of truth by power, the defense of slavery became the defense of freedom.[186] Arguments of these sorts expressed interpretations of facts and values completely hostage to the polemical defense of entrenched political institutions whose stability required the abridgment of basic rights of blacks and of any whites who ventured reasonable criticism of such institutions.

If the antebellum experience of state abridgments of basic rights informs a reasonable interpretation of the privileges and immunities clause,[187] the protection of intimate personal life must be one among the basic human rights thus worthy of national protection. The remaining question is whether there is any adequate basis for the abridgment of so basic a right, namely, in the case of contraception, the right to decide whether or when one's sexual life will lead to offspring, or,

180. Ibid., 40.

181. See, in general, Gutman, *The Black Family in Slavery and Freedom, 1750–1925.*

182. See William Harper, "Memoir on Slavery," in *The Ideology of Slavery: Proslavery Thought in the Antebellum South, 1830–1860,* ed. Drew Gilpin Faust (Baton Rouge: Louisiana State University Press, 1981), 110.

183. See James Henry Hammond, "Letter to an English Abolitionist," in *The Ideology of Slavery,*191–92.

184. See, for example, Harper, "Memoir on Slavery," 107, 118–19; Hammond, "Letter to an English Abolitionist," 182–84.

185. See, for example, Thomas Roderick Dew, "Abolition of Negro Slavery," in *The Ideology of Slavery,* 65; William Harper, "Memoir on Slavery," 100 (citing Dew).

186. For a good general discussion of such inversions, see Kenneth S. Greenberg, *Masters and Statesman: The Political Culture of American Slavery* (Baltimore: The Johns Hopkins University Press, 1985).

187. For further defense of this position, see Richards, *Conscience and the Constitution,* chap. 6.

for that matter, the right to explore one's sexual and emotional life in personal life as an end in itself.

That right can only be justified by a compelling public reason, not on the grounds of reasons that are internal to a moral tradition not based on reasons available and accessible to all. In fact, the only argument that could sustain such laws (namely, the Augustinian[188] and Thomistic[189] view that it is immoral to engage in nonprocreative sex) is not today a view of sexuality that can reasonably be enforced on people at large. Many people regard sexual love as an end in itself and view the control of reproduction as a reasonable way to regulate when and whether they have children consistent with their own personal and larger ethical interests, that of their children, and of an overpopulated society at large. Even the question of having children at all is today a highly personal matter, certainly no longer governed by the perhaps once compelling secular need to have children for necessary work in a largely agrarian society with high rates of infant and adult mortality.[190] From the perspective of women, as Sanger and Goldman made so clear, the enforcement of an anticontraceptive morality on society at large not only harms women's interests (as well as that of an overpopulated society more generally), but impersonally demeans them to a purely reproductive function, depriving them of the rational dignity of deciding as moral agents and persons, perhaps for the first time in human history, whether, when, and on what terms they will have children consistent with their other legitimate aims and ambitions (including the free exercise of all their basic human rights). Enforcement of such a morality gives effect to a now conspicuously sectarian conception of gender hierarchy in which women's sexuality is defined by mandatory procreative role and responsibility. That conception—the basis of the unjust construction of gender hierarchy—cannot reasonably be the measure of human rights today.[191]

188. See Augustine, *The City of God*, trans. Henry Bettenson (Harmondsworth: Penguin, 1972), 577–94.

189. Thomas Aquinas elaborates Augustine's conception of the exclusive legitimacy of procreative sex in a striking way. Of the emision of semen apart from procreation in marriage, he wrote: "[A]fter the sin of homicide whereby a human nature already in existence is destroyed, this type of sin appears to take next place, for by it the generation of human nature is precluded." Thomas Aquinas, *On the Truth of the Catholic Faith: Summa Contra Gentiles*, trans. Vernon Bourke (New York: Image, 1956), pt. 2, chap. 122(9), p. 146.

190. On how personal this decision now is, see, in general, Elaine Tyler May, *Barren in the Promised Land: Childless Americans and the Pursuit of Happiness* (New York: Basic-Books, 1995).

191. For further discussion of the right to privacy and contraception, see Richards, *Toleration and the Constitution*, 256–61.

Similar considerations explain the grounds for doubt about the putative public, nonsectarian justifications for laws criminalizing abortion and homosexual sexuality. Antiabortion laws, grounded in the alleged protection of a neutral good ("life"), unreasonably equate the moral weight of a fetus in the early stages of pregnancy with that of a person; such laws fail to take seriously the weight that should be accorded a woman's basic right to reproductive autonomy in making highly personal moral choices central to her most intimate bodily and personal life against the background of the lack of reasonable public consensus that fetal life, as such, can be equated with that of a moral person.[192] There are legitimate interests that society has in giving weight at some point to fetal life as part of making a symbolic statement about the importance of taking the lives of children seriously and caring for them, analogous to the symbolic interest society may have in preventing cruelty to animals or in securing humane treatment to the irretrievably comatose, but such interests do not constitutionally justify forbidding abortion as such throughout all stages of pregnancy.[193] Rather, such interests can be accorded their legitimate weight after a reasonable period has been allowed for the proper scope of a woman's exercise of her decision whether to have an abortion.

The moral arguments for the prohibition of abortion cluster around certain traditional conceptions of the natural processes of sexuality and gender. The argument for criminalizing abortion is not a constitutionally reasonable argument for regarding abortion as homicide, but a proxy for complex background assumptions often no longer reasonably believed in the society at large, namely, a now-controversial, sectarian ideology about proper sexuality and gender roles. From this perspective, the prohibitions on abortion encumber what many now reasonably regard as a highly conscientious choice by women regarding their bodies, their sexuality and gender, and the nature and place of pregnancy, birth, and childrearing in their personal and ethical lives. The traditional condemnation of abortion fails, at a deep ethical level, to take seriously the moral independence of women as free and rational persons, lending the force of law, like comparable anticontraceptive laws, to theological ideas of biological naturalness and gender hierarchy that degrade the constructive moral powers of women themselves to establish the meaning of their sexual and reproductive life histories. The underlying conception appears to be at one with the sexist idea that

---

192. For further discussion, see Richards, *Toleration and the Constitution*, 261–69; Ronald Dworkin, *Life's Dominion: An Argument about Abortion, Euthanasia, and Individual Freedom* (New York: Knopf, 1993), 3–178.

193. See Richards, *Toleration and the Constitution*, 266–67.

women's minds and bodies are not their own, but the property of others, namely, men or their masculine God, who may conscript them and their bodies, like cattle on the farm, for the greater good.

The abortion choice is thus one of the choices essential to the just moral independence of women, centering their lives in a body image and aspirations expressive of their moral powers; it is a just application of the right to intimate life, for it protects women from the traditional degradation of their moral powers, reflected in the assumptions underlying antiabortion laws.

Antihomosexuality laws have even less of a semblance of a public justification (like fetal life) that would be acceptably enforced on society at large. They brutally abridge the sexual expression of the companionate loving relationships to which homosexuals, like heterosexuals, have an inalienable human right. That right encompasses the free moral powers through which persons forge enduring personal and ethical value in living a complete life. The decision in *Bowers v. Hardwick* was, for this reason, an interpretively unprincipled failure properly to elaborate the principle of constitutional privacy in an area of populist prejudice where the protection of that right was exigently required.[194]

In the background of the laws at issue in all these cases lies a normative view of gender roles (this is quite clear in the case of *Griswold v. Connecticut*, less obviously so in *Roe v. Wade* and *Bowers v. Hardwick*). On analysis, however, the small weight accorded women's interests and the decisive weight accorded the fetus in antiabortion laws make sense only against the background of the still powerful traditional conception of mandatory procreational, self-sacrificing, caring, and nurturant gender roles for women; its symbolic violation of that normative idea transforms abortion into murder. Similarly, the failure of the majority of the Supreme Court in *Bowers* to accord *any* weight whatsoever to the rights to privacy of homosexuals and decisive weight to incoherently anachronistic traditional moralism reflect a still powerful ideology of unnatural gender roles that renders homosexuals constitutionally invisible, voiceless, and marginal.

THE RIGHT TO WORK. Increasing numbers of women worked during and after World War II. Consistent with this development, the first achievements of second wave feminism were the Equal Pay Act of 1963, the addition of gender to race as a forbidden ground for discrimination in employment under Title VII of the Civil Rights Act of

---

194. For further discussion, see Richards, *Toleration and the Constitution*, 269–80; id., *Foundations of American Constitutionalism*, 202–47.

1964, and the mobilization of NOW and other organizations to ensure that Title VII was enforced.[195] The right to work in the public sphere (i.e., outside the traditionally private domestic sphere) was a cutting edge issue because it was the issue that put most pressure on what the rising rights-based expectations of women like Betty Friedan found so frustrating in the reigning ideology of women's essentially domestic gender roles, namely, that "more and more of the work important to the world, more and more of the work that used their human abilities and through which they were able to find self-realization, was taken from them."[196] To this extent, the right to work, contesting, as it did, the reigning romanticized ideology of gender roles, became a trope for rights-based feminist argument as such, for all its central rights (conscience, speech, intimate life, and work) contested the traditional form of the public/private distinction as, stereotypically, the male/female distinction. The privatization of women was, on this view, the basis for their oppression. Work in the public sphere became a metaphor for the legitimate entrance of women into public culture on equal terms as bearers of inalienable human rights. To this extent, the claim of the right to work was and is a way of making the larger point about the injustice of sexism as such.

Nonetheless, even as more narrowly conceived, the right to work has been central to both political and increasingly successful constitutional claims of rights-based feminism. The increasingly skeptical stance of the Supreme Court about gender-segregated public schools, reflected in the earlier discussed development from *Mississippi University for Women v. Hogan* to *United States v. Virginia,* may be interpreted not only in terms of the equal right to conscience and education, but the equal right to work: both cases suggest skepticism about a state role in enforcing gender-defined conceptions of work in the public sphere. Other cases have constitutionally opened up roles for women in administering estates,[197] serving on juries,[198] and asserting control over marital property,[199] and insisted on the equal rights and opportunities of working women in many contexts.[200] The antisex discrimination

195. See Judith Hole and Ellen Levine, *Rebirth of Feminism,* 17–54, 81–107.

196. See Friedan, *The Feminine Mystique,* 291.

197. See *Reed v. Reed,* 404 U.S. 71 (1971) (preference for males over equally situated females as administrators of wills held unconstitutional).

198. See *Taylor v. Louisiana,* 419 U.S. 522 (1975) (systematic exclusion of women from state jury duty held unconstitutional).

199. See *Kirchberg v. Feenstra,* 450 U.S. 455 (1981) (state law granting husbands unilateral control over marital property held unconstitutional).

200. See, for example, *Frontiero v. Richardson,* 411 U.S. 677 (1973) (requirement that only women army officers prove actual dependency of spouse for benefits held unconstitu-

provisions of Title VII have also been applied to eligibility to be prison guards,[201] to promotions (and failures to promote) in law firms[202] and accounting firms,[203] to deprivation of seniority benefits keyed to maternity leaves[204] or failure to provide maternity benefits on equal terms,[205] and to sexual harassment in employment,[206] and have been held not to bar affirmative action programs that opened jobs to women from which they had traditionally been excluded.[207] State antisex discrimina-

---

tional); *Califano v. Goldfarb*, 430 U.S. 199 (1977) (denying social security benefits to surviving male spouses who could not prove actual dependency on their wives held unconstitutional); cf. *Weinberg v. Wiesenfeld*, 420 U.S. 636 (1975) (denial of social security benefits to sole surviving, poor male parents of dependent children held unconstitutional); *Califano v. West-cott*, 443 U.S. 76 (1979) (providing welfare benefits to families with unemployed father, but not unemployed mother, held unconstitutional); *Wengler v. Druggists Mutual Insurance*, 446 U.S. 142 (1980) (state workmen's compensation program providing death benefits to widows, but not widowers, of workers held unconstitutional); *Corning Glass v. Brennan*, 417 U.S. 188 (1974) (policy of paying night inspectors (usually men) more than day inspectors (historically women) held violation of Equal Pay Act of 1963); cf. *Washington County v. Gunther*, 452 U.S. 161 (1981) (paying women jail guards less than the amount that it is assumed would be paid to men held violation of Title VII).

201. See *Dothard v. Rawlinson*, 433 U.S. 321 (1977) (minimum height and weight requirements for prison guards held violation of Title VII; males-only requirement for contact positions within male penitentiaries not a violation).

202. See *Hishon v. King & Spaulding*, 467 U.S. 69 (1984) (sex discrimination in promotion to law firm partner held violation of Title VII).

203. See *Price Waterhouse v. Hopkins*, 490 U.S. 228 (1989) (employers have burden of proving that their refusal to hire or promote was based on legitimate and not, as here, predominantly discriminatory reasons).

204. See *Nashville Gas v. Satty*, 434 U.S. 136 (1977) (deprivation of seniority benefits of women returning from maternity leave held violation of Title VII); cf. *Cleveland Board of Education v. LaFleur*, 414 U.S. 632 (1974) (requirement that schoolteachers leave job when five months pregnant held unconstitutional); *Turner v. Department of Employment Security*, 423 U.S. 44 (1975) (denial of unemployment compensation to women in last three months of pregnancy held unconstitutional).

205. See *Newport News Shipbuilding v. EEOC*, 462 U.S. 669 (1983) (refusal to provide maternity benefits for wives of male workers when husbands of female workers received full coverage held violation of Title VII, as amended by Pregnancy Discrimination Act of 1978).

206. See *Meritor Savings Bank v. Vinson*, 447 U.S. 57 (1986) (hostile environment sexual harassment held violation of Title VII); *Harris v. Forklift Systems, Inc.*, 114 S. Ct. 367 (1993) (victims of hostile environment sexual harassment not required to prove that they have suffered psychological injury in order to validate Title VII claim).

207. See *Johnson v. Transportation Agency, Santa Clara County, California*, 480 U.S. 616 (1987) (affirmative action hiring programs for jobs from which women have traditionally been excluded not a violation of Title VII). Cf. *Schlesinger v. Ballard*, 419 U.S. 498 (1975) (permitting women members of the armed forces more time than men to attain promotions as officers is, in light of past gender discrimination, constitutional); *Califano v. Webster*, 430 U.S. 313 (1977) (in light of past sex discrimination, providing women with a more generous technique than men for calculating social security benefits held constitutional).

tion laws have also been upheld that admitted women to the Jaycees,[208] Rotary Clubs,[209] and to private clubs.[210] While judicial opinions have by no means been uniformly affirmative of such strong antidiscrimination principles in employment,[211] the pattern suggests a serious rights-based judicial concern with enforceable guarantees of equal opportunity in the right to work.

Sexism as a Constitutional Evil

The judicial concern with recognition of basic human rights in all these four areas (conscience, speech, intimate life, and work) has been paralleled by an emerging constitutional doctrine that condemns as unconstitutional the basis on which such rights (and other less fundamental rights and opportunities) had been traditionally abridged, namely, the dehumanizing attitude we call sexism. The pertinent analogy has been the race cases and the condemnation of racism as a ground for public action.

Judicial concern along these lines was first suggested in 1971 in *Reed v. Reed*,[212] representing a sharp turn from the very different approach taken in 1948 by Justice Frankfurter for the Court in *Goesaert v. Cleary*[213] and in 1961 by Justice Harlan in *Hoyt v. Florida*.[214] In these latter cases, the Court invoked the traditional conception of gender roles as the reasonable basis for its decision upholding, in the one case, the exclusion of women from bartending and, in the other, from jury duty. In *Reed*, the Court unanimously struck down, as an unconstitu-

208. See *Roberts v. Jaycees*, 468 U.S. 609 (1984) (state law forbidding gender discrimination applicable to association open on a nonselective basis to all 35-year-old males held constitutional).

209. See *Rotary International v. Rotary Club of Duarte*, 481 U.S. 537 (1987) (state law requiring Rotary Clubs to admit women held constitutional).

210. See *New York State Club Association v. City of New York*, 487 U.S. 1 (1988) (city law prohibiting gender discrimination in certain private clubs, found to be nonprivate in nature, held constitutional).

211. See, for example, *Geduldig v. Aiello*, 419 U.S. 498 (1975) (denial of pregnancy disability benefits to employees held constitutional); *General Electric Co. v. Gilbert*, 429 U.S. 125 (1976) (denial of medical benefits for maternity-related reasons held not a violation of Title VII) (result reversed by Pregnancy Discrimination Act of 1978, amending Title VII, see *Newport News Shipbuilding v. EEOC*, 462 U.S. 669 [1983]); *Personnel Administrator v. Feeney*, 442 U.S. 256 (1979) (state law providing veterans' preference for nonclerical civil service jobs in setting where 98 percent of veterans were male held constitutional); *Rostker v. Goldberg*, 453 U.S. 57 (1981) (requiring only males to register for draft held constitutional).

212. *Reed v. Reed*, 404 U.S. 71 (1971).

213. *Goesaert v. Cleary*, 335 U.S. 464 (1948) (prohibiting women from working as bartender, except when supervised by husband or father, held constitutional).

214. *Hoyt v. Florida*, 368 U.S. 57 (1961) (exclusion of women from state jury held constitutional).

tional violation of equal protection, a state's mandatory preference for men over women in the appointment of the administrator of a decedent's estate. The state had defended the statute as a way of eliminating an area of controversy (and the need for a hearing) between relatives otherwise equally qualified. Chief Justice Burger, writing for the Court, conceded that the state's purpose was "not without some legitimacy,"[215] but struck the statute down nonetheless because it drew a distinction that was "the very kind of arbitrary legislative choice forbidden by the equal protection clause of the Fourteenth Amendment."[216] In light of *Goesaert* and *Hoyt* and previous cases, such a choice, based on traditional normative gender roles, would appear to have a rational basis, perhaps one that could be relevantly rationalized further in terms of statistically significant differences in the experience of men (in the public world of business and affairs) and women (in a largely domestic life) that the acculturation in traditional gender roles had produced. The doctrinal oddity of *Reed* was its claim that, without heightening the standard of review as it would for a suspect class like race[217] or a fundamental right like voting,[218] it could find such a statute irrational when almost all comparable cases, subjected to rational basis view, had been upheld as valid.[219] The legislative classification in *Reed* was no less overinclusive or underinclusive than many other such statutes, and was, on this basis, no less rational.[220] The result in *Reed*, however doctrinally anomalous, suggested growing judicial skepticism about the place traditional gender roles had been permitted to enjoy in the interpretation of equal protection.

The extent and basis of such judicial skepticism were clarified in

215. *Reed,* 404 U.S. at 76.
216. Id.
217. See *Loving v. Virginia,* 388 U.S. 1 (1967) (antimiscegenation laws, using a racial classification, are subject to strictest scrutiny and held unconstitutional); *Palmore v. Sidoti,* 466 U.S. 429 (1984) (use of race to determine custody held unconstitutional).
218. See *Harper v. Virginia Board of Elections,* 383 U.S. 663 (1966) (use of poll tax for voting, trenching on fundamental right, held unconstitutional); *Reynolds v. Sims,* 377 U.S. 533 (1964) (malapportionment of state legislature, burdening fundamental equal right to vote, held unconstitutional).
219. See, for example, *Railway Express Agency v. New York,* 336 U.S. 106 (1949) (New York City prohibition of advertising on vehicles, except self-advertising, subject to rational basis scrutiny, and held constitutional); *Williamson v. Lee Optical Co.,* 348 U.S. 483 (1955) (subjecting opticians, but not sellers of ready-to-wear glasses, to requirement that buyer have had eye examination subject to rational basis, and held constitutional).
220. On this mode of analysis of equal protection questions, see Joseph Tussman and Jacobus tenBroek, "The Equal Protection of the Laws," *California Law Review* 37 (1949): 341.

1973 in *Frontiero v. Richardson*[221] in which the Court struck down a federal law permitting male members of the armed forces an automatic dependency allowance for their wives but requiring servicewomen to prove that their husbands were dependent. Justice Brennan, writing for himself and Justices Douglas, White, and Marshall, interpreted *Reed v. Reed* as calling for heightened scrutiny for gender classifications, and indeed defended applying to gender at least the level of scrutiny accorded race. In support of such scrutiny, Justice Brennan acknowledged the nation's "long and unfortunate history of sex discrimination" that was "rationalized by an attitude of 'romantic paternalism' which, in practical effect, put women, not on a pedestal, but in a cage" (684). To evidence the degree to which "this paternalistic attitude became so firmly rooted in our national consciousness" (684), Brennan cited Justice Bradley's concurring opinion in *Bradwell v. State* that had made Catharine Beecher's normative theory of gender roles the measure of women's shriveled human and civil rights (684–85). In defending the analogy between race and gender, Brennan observed:

> As a result of notions such as these, our statute books gradually became laden with gross, stereotyped distinctions between the sexes and, indeed, throughout much of the 19th century the position of women in our society was, in many respects, comparable to that of blacks under the pre-Civil War slave codes. Neither slaves nor women could hold office, serve on juries, or bring suit in their own names, and married women traditionally were denied the legal capacity to hold or convey property or to serve as legal guardians of their own children. . . . And although blacks were guaranteed the right to vote in 1870, women were denied even that right—which is itself "preservative of other basic civil and political rights"—until adoption of the Nineteenth Amendment half a century later. (685)

To further support the analogy between gender and race, Justice Brennan also pointed to "the high visibility of the sex characteristic," that, "like race and national origin, is an immutable characteristic" frequently bearing "no relation to ability to perform or contribute to society" (686). In a footnote, Brennan conceded "that when viewed in the abstract, women do not constitute a small and powerless minority" but emphasized that

> in part because of past discrimination, women are vastly underrepresented in this Nation's decision-making councils. There has never been a female President, nor a female member of this Court. Not a single woman presently sits in the United States Senate, and only 14 women hold seats in the House of Representatives. And, as appellants point out, this underrepresentation

221. See *Frontiero v. Richardson*, 411 U.S. 677 (1973) (8–1 decision).

is present throughout all levels of our State and Federal Government. (686 n. 17)

Brennan concluded "that classifications based on sex, like classifica-tions based upon race, alienage, or national origin, are inherently sus-pect, and must therefore be subject to strict judicial scrutiny" (688). Subjecting the statutory classification to this standard, Brennan found that its claimed purpose, administrative convenience (more spouses of men than of women are likely to be dependent), did not justify use of the gender distinction when a more individualized assessment of dependence was available at little cost and was likely to save the government money on balance (many wives of male servicemem-bers would fail to qualify for benefits under an individualized test) (688–91).

Four other justices concurred in Brennan's judgment for the Court but on the rational basis standard of *Reed v. Reed*. Justice Powell, writ-ing for himself, Chief Justice Burger, and Justice Blackmun, argued that *Reed* "abundantly supports our decision today" without adding "sex to the narrowly limited group of classifications which are inher-ently suspect" (692).

A majority of the Supreme Court finally agreed in 1976 in *Craig v. Boren*[222] that gender classifications were subject to "heightened scru-tiny," an intermediate standard of review certainly stronger than the "rationally related" basis but not as demanding as the "strict scrutiny" accorded race. Justice Brennan, writing for the Court, characterized this heightened scrutiny as applying both to the purpose and the means-end reasoning of the statute: "classifications by gender must serve important governmental objectives and must be substantially re-lated to achievement of these objectives" (197). The statute in question in *Craig* drew a gender distinction between men and women in drink-ing age (men at 21, women at 18) allegedly on the ground that statisti-cal evidence suggested higher rates of drunk driving and traffic injuries for men. On its face, the statute, in contrast to *Frontiero* and related cases of blatantly unconstitutional sex discrimination against women,[223] advantaged women in contrast to men. Brennan's analysis framed the constitutional issue in terms of cultural stereotypes. Assessing the stat-ute in terms of appropriately heightened intermediate scrutiny, the Court accepted the legitimacy of the state's ostensible purpose for the

222. *Craig v. Boren*, 429 U.S. 190 (1976).
223. See, for example, *Stanton v. Stanton*, 421 U.S. 7 (1975) (establishing female adult-hood at 18 and male adulthood at 21 for purposes of child support payments held unconstitu-tional).

statute, traffic safety,[224] but found its means-end reasoning constitutionally defective, in particular, the role statistical evidence played
in rationalizing the use of a legislative classification in terms of
gender.

The problem was not merely doubts about the accuracy of the statistical evidence. Even taking the most reliable such evidence presented,
the statistics on driving while under the influence established that 0.18
percent of females and 2.00 percent of males were arrested for this
offense. While conceding that "such a disparity is not trivial in a statistical sense, it hardly can form the basis for employment of a gender line
as a classifying device" (201). The point was not only that a 2 percent
correlation hardly makes gender a reliable proxy for drinking and driving, for the use of gender would be constitutionally problematic even
if it were much more accurate. The basis for the gender distinctions
used in *Reed v. Reed* and *Frontiero v. Richardson* may be much more
statistically reliable measures of, in the one case, relevant business experience and, in the other, dependency, but were nonetheless problematic (202 n. 13). The constitutional evil, rather, was giving expression through public law to the unjust political force that a gender
stereotype has traditionally enjoyed, often, as a consequence, creating
reality in its own unjust image. Brennan made this point about age-
differential laws like that in *Craig* in terms of the degree to which
unjust social stereotypes may themselves distort the statistics: " 'reck-
less' young men who drink and drive are transformed into arrest statistics, where their female counterparts are chivalrously escorted home"
(202 n. 14).

The analogy to race and ethnicity was, Brennan argued, exact:

> [I]f statistics were to govern the permissibility of state alcohol regulation
> without regard to the equal protection clause as a limiting principle, it might
> follow that States could freely favor Jews and Italian Catholics at the expense
> of all other Americans, since available studies regularly demonstrate that the
> former two groups exhibit the lowest rates of problem drinking. . . . Similarly,
> if a State were allowed simply to depend upon demographic characteristics
> of adolescents in identifying problem drinkers, statistics might support the
> conclusion that only black teenagers should be permitted to drink, followed
> by Asian-Americans and Spanish-Americans. "Whites and American Indians
> have the lowest proportions of abstainers and the highest proportions of
> moderate/heavy and heavy drinkers." (208–9 n. 22)

We would not permit the use of even accurate statistics to justify racial,
ethnic, or religious classifications in such cases for the same reasons
that gender classifications should not be permitted on such a basis: the

224. *Boren*, 429 U.S. at 199.

classifications themselves reflect a long history of unjust and unconstitutional treatment that has shaped reality in its image. Laws can no more constitutionally give expression to such classifications than they can to the facts such classifications have shaped. Brennan thus took the argument he earlier made in *Frontiero* about the unjust force a rights-denying conception of gender roles had been allowed to enjoy in American public law and culture (including its stark endorsement by members of the Supreme Court) and applied it to the unjust gender stereotypes such a conception had sustained. To condemn the political imposition of such gender roles was to condemn as well the cultural stereotypes such roles enforced on reality. From this perspective, not only men but women suffered from the political enforcement of such stereotypes, inflicting a rights-denying, dehumanizing idealization (women's higher morality on the pedestal) from which women in particular have suffered.

The constitutional standard of heightened scrutiny of gender classifications has certainly moved the constitutional treatment of gender closer to race. Heightened scrutiny is not, however, strict scrutiny. While many gender classifications have, as we have seen, been struck down, others have survived, albeit sometimes by narrow majorities. In *Michael M. v. Superior Court*,[225] for example, the Court narrowly accepted the constitutionality of a state's statutory rape law that subjected men to criminal liability for intercourse with a female under 18, largely on the ground that women bore the risks of pregnancy. And in *Rostker v. Goldberg*,[226] the Court ruled, 6–3, that Congress could limit registration for the draft to men because women were categorically excluded from combat.

United States v. Virginia[227] suggests that the Supreme Court may be shifting the standard of review accorded gender to a level of scrutiny much closer to that of race. In striking down the exclusion of women from the Virginia Military Institute, the Court invoked the standard of whether the justification for exclusion was "exceedingly persuasive,"[228] was quite skeptical of the weight accorded putative gender differences as a rationale for the exclusion,[229] and expressly invoked an important racial case, *Sweatt v. Painter*, as a relevant analogy for the unconstitutionality of separate-but-equal in the realm of gender.[230] If

225. See *Michael M. v. Superior Court,* 450 U.S. 464 (1981).
226. See *Rostker v. Goldberg,* 453 U.S. 57 (1981).
227. See *United States v. Virginia,* 116 S. Ct. 2264 (1996).
228. Id. at 2274.
229. Id. at 2276, 2280.
230. Id. at 2285, 2286.

so, the result in cases like *Michael M.* and even *Rostker* may now be constitutionally problematic.

NORMATIVE AND CONSTITUTIONAL THEORY: RACE, GENDER, AND MORAL SLAVERY

When these interpretive developments are placed in a larger historical and normative perspective, we are able to understand them and to develop a normative position from which we may assess and criticize them. In particular, I want to investigate the important interpretive analogy between race and gender that has become increasingly central to American public law in light of the arguments of abolitionist feminism, and, on this basis, propose a general framework for interpreting the Thirteenth Amendment and the central substantive principles of the Fourteenth Amendment; I then further explore here and in later chapters the interpretive fertility of the proposed framework by investigating the light it sheds on one of the central principles of the Fourteenth Amendment, the heightened scrutiny under equal protection doctrine of suspect classifications.

Our interpretive interest in abolitionist feminists lies, I believe, in the self-conscious unity of principle they brought to their rights-based criticism of the evils of racism and sexism and the institutions of slavery and the subjection of women they sustained. The principle that was central to these criticisms was moral slavery: the laws, institutions, conventions, practices, and attitudes that illegitimately abridged the human rights of conscience, speech, association, and work, and rationalized a servile status on that basis. Moral slavery was, for the Grimke sisters, radical moral evil because of the unity among the rights it illegitimately abridged, enforcing a total moral subjugation, in central areas of rights-based moral sovereignty, to the will of another. The moral slave was thus stripped of the human and cultural resources through which we acknowledge persons, as persons, capable of freedom and reason in private and public life. The Grimkes' severest criticisms of moral slavery came in their indictment of a religiously and ethically bankrupt political epistemology (including practices of Bible interpretation) that, consistent with the paradox of intolerance, corrupted reason and crushed freedom in order further to entrench an illegitimate hierarchy of order and submission.

The Grimkes insisted that abolitionist political morality placed all persons "on the same platform of human rights"[231] and demanded the

---

231. See Sarah M. Grimke, *Letters on the Equality of the Sexes and the Condition of Woman*, 239.

condemnation of all forms of the radical rights-denying evil of moral slavery on that basis. The Reconstruction Amendments are properly interpreted[232] in terms of the abolitionist political morality they clearly express, affirming the equal status of all persons as bearers of human rights and condemning both slavery and rights-denying subjugation on that basis. Our best interpretation of these principles cannot be always reliably guided by how political institutions at one point or another would have construed them, for abolitionist principles are sometimes best reforged in the moral conscience of outcast rights-based dissenters to dominant political institutions. We more reasonably interpret these principles, consistent with their protection of the human rights of all persons, when we interpret them today as a continuing community of principle best elaborating such traditions of dissent in our circumstances. On this basis, we best interpret the enduring moral meaning of the Reconstruction Amendments for the American community of principle when we hermeneutically frame our interpretations in terms of condemnation of the radical rights-denying evil of moral slavery and interpret its affirmative guarantees of basic rights and equal protection against that background.

No aspect of the abolitionist feminism of the Grimkes is more interpretively suggestive today that their linkage, as a matter of principle, of antiracism and antisexism. They argued not only that these evils shared a common moral subjugation, but suggested as well that they might share a common sexual mythology. Both their analysis and its underlying moral motivations (their radical struggle to a moral independence of established orthodoxies) united their abolitionist feminism with that distinctively forged by black women like Sojourner Truth and Harriet Jacobs, and indeed prefigured the remarkable analysis of the interlinked pathologies of racism and sexism later so brilliantly offered by Ida Wells-Barnett. If uncritically racist assumptions were later to discredit suffrage feminism,[233] contemporary feminism may interpretively reforge common antiracist and antisexist principles by recovering the lost thread of abolitionist feminism. Indeed, contemporary interest in the intersection of race and gender may be interpretively explored as the recovery of a great and brilliant tradition of fundamental moral criticism originated by pioneering black and white women who recognized, articulated, and criticized the common and interlinked evils of racism and sexism, a tradition self-consciously redis-

232. See also, in general, Richards, *Conscience and the Constitution*.

233. For a cogent general treatment, see Paula Giddings, *When and Where I Enter. . . : The Impact of Black Women on Race and Sex in America* (New York: William Morrow, 1984), 124–31.

covered and reaffirmed, as we have seen, in the collaboration of black and white women in the civil rights movement in the 1960s.[234]

Such contemporary advocates may reasonably lay claim to the Grimkes' piercing analysis of the incommensurable rights-based wrong of moral slavery as the hermeneutic background to the proper interpretation today of the prohibition on slavery and involuntary servitude in the Thirteenth Amendment and the ancillary normative requirements of both the Fourteenth and Fifteenth Amendments. The Grimkes articulated a general rights-based moral theory condemning, as moral slavery, both racism and sexism and, by implication, any comparable institutions that illegitimately subjugated persons on terms that deprived them of a fair respect for their central human rights of conscience, speech, association, and work. The evil of moral slavery is subjugation of persons to the terms of a political orthodoxy tainted by such rights-denying illegitimacy. Racism and sexism exemplified, for the Grimkes, institutions condemned as moral slavery because they shared such a political orthodoxy, in particular, one that crucially *depended* on an historically entrenched public culture of exclusion, marginalization, and colonialization of, respectively, blacks and women; racism and sexism exemplified the radical evil of denying classes of persons their full status as bearers of basic rights like conscience, speech, association, and work. On this view of moral slavery, its abolition required deconstruction of the illegitimate force of such a public culture along all its rights-denying dimensions of exclusion, marginalization, and colonialization, and the full and equal guarantee to all of their basic human rights of conscience, speech, association, and work. The constitutional principles of the Fourteenth and Fifteenth Amendments would, on this view, embody various dimensions of the general prohibition on moral slavery in the Thirteenth Amendment.

To interpret the Reconstruction Amendments in this way makes powerful normative sense of their volcanic significance in American constitutional history and interpretation, both retrospectively and prospectively. Retrospectively, it makes enduring sense of the Reconstruction Amendments as the culmination of the most profound moral struggle of the American people over the meaning of their Constitution since its founding. The struggle clarified for Americans the ultimate justification of legitimate political power, namely, the protection of hu-

234. On the intersectionality of race and gender, see Kimberle Crenshaw, "Demarginalizing the Intersection of Race and Sex: A Black Feminist Critique of Antidiscrimination Doctrine, Feminist Theory and Antiracist Politics," 1989 *University of Chicago Legislative Forum* 139; Angela P. Harris, "Race and Essentialism in Feminist Legal Theory," *Stanford Law Review* 42 (1990): 581.

man rights, and the gravest threats to such rights, to wit, rights-denying institutions of moral slavery (including, as we have seen, arguments condemning in such terms both racism and sexism). Interpreting the amendments as a central condemnation of moral slavery makes powerful normative sense of this struggle in the only terms adequate to its rights-based emancipatory meaning. Americans of that generation interpretively disagreed about what counted as moral slavery; most, for example, did not accept the abolitionist feminist view that it included the subjection of women and sexism. Some abolitionist feminists, notably Elizabeth Stanton, Susan B. Anthony, and Victoria Woodhull, did publicly take that view, and indeed brought their views publicly to bear on the apparently decisive roles they played in advocacy for the ratification of the Thirteenth Amendment; they brought the same normative views to bear on interpretive arguments about how the Fourteenth Amendment should be interpreted, namely, to guarantee women the right to vote and run for public office. Our contemporary interpretive issue is to select among these interpretive traditions of what counts as moral slavery, and decide which of them makes the best interpretive sense in our circumstances.

In fact, the Supreme Court has issued contemporary interpretations of the Reconstruction Amendments that are much more antiracist and certainly more antisexist than the dominant views of the Reconstruction Congress in 1865–1870. The modern Court's views of the protection of voting rights as a fundamental right guaranteed by the equal protection clause are much closer to the views of Woodhull, Stanton, and Anthony than of the Reconstruction Congress or of the earlier Supreme Court.[235] We need to understand as well as to evaluate such interpretive developments. Abolitionist feminist theory meets both our interpretive and normative needs. It better fits much of this interpretive development than its historical competitors, indeed clarifying how and why contemporary rights-based political theory informs and guides such interpretive elaborations of our historical traditions. It may also better meet our normative needs to evaluate such interpretive developments, including criticism of them when they fail adequately to implement underlying principles.

Prospectively, this interpretation preserves and elaborates the Re-

235. Among the modern cases holding voting rights to be a fundamental right and thus entitled to more aggressive judicial protection, see *Reynolds v. Sims,* 377 U.S. 533 (1964); *Harper v. Virginia State Board of Elections,* 383 U.S. 663 (1966); *Kramer v. Union Free School District No. 15,* 395 U.S. 621 (1969). For the Supreme Court's earlier view in 1874 that voting rights were not protected by the Fourteenth Amendment, see *Minor v. Happersett,* 88 U.S. 162 (1874).

construction Amendments as a permanent normative heritage to posterity, condemning all forms of moral slavery that entrench the illegitimate subjugation of persons. Each generation has the interpretive responsibility to make the best sense of the Reconstruction Amendments in its own terms of public reason, including its best interpretation of moral slavery. Such interpretation must in its nature not only identify the basic rights (like those to conscience, speech, association, and work) that have been denied, but also both the inadequate grounds on which they have been denied and the institutional structures that have sustained such subjugation. It may reasonably elaborate, on grounds of principle, pertinent analogies among forms of moral slavery anticipated by strands of abolitionist feminist moral and political analysis that made precisely such arguments about rights, inadequate grounds, and supporting structures. On this basis, we may analogize, as a matter of rights-based principle (on the platform of human rights), between racism and sexism in ways that illuminate modern interpretive developments and offer normative perspectives that identify and criticize defects of principle in such developments, such as failures to draw analogies between racism, sexism, religious prejudice, and homophobia. In each case, a group of persons has been radically excluded from the central human rights of conscience, speech, association, and work on inadequate grounds and has been degraded by such an unjust public and private culture to a servile, marginal, and, in the case of homosexuals, unspeakable status, deprived of the resources that enable persons to come to know, understand, and claim their rights as free and equal persons.

The idea of moral slavery, thus understood, may have fertile and far-reaching consequences for the interpretation of the Reconstruction Amendments along the lines of interpretive work already in play.[236] It

236. For examples of recent interpretive work that might plausibly be regarded as exploring analogies to the theory of moral slavery and would be analytically strengthened by explicit use of this theory, see, for example, Akhil Reed Amar, "Remember the Thirteenth," *Constitutional Commentary* 10 (1993): 403; Akhil Reed Amar and Daniel Widawsky, "Child Abuse as Slavery: A Thirteenth Amendment Reponse to *DeShaney*," *Harvard University Law Review* 105 (1992): 1359; Akhil Reed Amar, "The Case of the Missing Amendments: R.A.V. v. City of St. Paul," *Harvard University Law Review* 106 (1992): 124; id., "Forty Acres and a Mule: A Republican Theory of Minimal Entitlements," *Harvard Journal of Law and Public Policy* 13 (1990): 37; Douglas L. Colbert, "Challenging the Challenge: Thirteenth Amendment as Prohibition against the Racial Use of Peremptory Challenges," *Cornell Law Review* 76 (1990): 1; Douglas L. Colbert, "Affirming the Thirteenth Amendment," 1995 *Annual Survey of American Law* 403; Neal Kumar Katyal, "Men Who Own Women: A Thirteenth Amendment Critique of Forced Prostitution," *Yale Law Journal* 103 (1993): 791; Andrew Koppelman, "Forced Labor: A Thirteenth Amendment Defense of Abortion," *Northwestern University Law Review* 84 (1990): 480; Joyce E. McConnell, "Beyond Metaphor: Battered

may, for example, usefully reconfigure the shape of current ongoing interpretive developments of and controversies over central principles of the Fourteenth Amendment.

Our analysis has already advanced interpretive understanding of one such principle, the nationalization of the protection of basic human rights. The condemnation of moral slavery by the Thirteenth Amendment crucially appealed, on the view I have taken, to the abridgment of the basic human rights of a class of persons on inadequate grounds. That analysis thus advances understanding of the structurally connected principle of the Fourteenth Amendment that nationalizes the enforceable protection of basic human rights against both state and national governments. To be specific, I have argued that the principle has properly been interpreted to include basic rights like conscience, speech, intimate life, and work, the abridgment of which on inadequate grounds was fundamental to the unjust construction of moral slavery. The analysis of the constitutional evil of moral slavery thus advances interpretive understanding of the legitimate basis for and scope of the nationalization of the protection of certain basic human rights.

Another central principle of the Fourteenth Amendment is that of equal protection. Equal protection expresses the general requirement, rooted in abolitionist political theory, that political power must be reasonably justifiable in terms of equal respect for basic human rights and the pursuit of public purposes like justice and the common good.[237] It has various dimensions, including one demanding form of analysis associated with the protection of fundamental rights and another with the protection of suspect classes (for example, racial minorities) from oppression; outside these categories, its demand for reasonable justification is much more deferential to democratic politics.[238] Fundamental rights analysis protects human rights subject to the principle nationaliz-

---

Women, Involuntary Servitude and the Thirteenth Amendment," *Yale Journal of Law and Feminism* 4 (1992): 207; Lea S. VanderVelde, "The Labor Vision of the Thirteenth Amendment," *University of Pennsylvania Law Review* 138 (1989): 437; Lea S. VanderVelde, "The Gendered Origins of the *Lumley* Doctrine: Binding Men's Consciences and Women's Fidelity," *Yale Law Journal* 101 (1992): 775; Robin West, "Toward an Abolitionist Interpretation of the Fourteenth Amendment," *West Virginia Law Review* 94 (1991): 111, 138–50. Cf. Michelle J. Anderson, Note, "A License to Abuse: The Impact of Conditional Status on Female Immigrants," *Yale Law Journal* 102 (1993): 1401, 1428–30.

237. For the classic statement of equal protection as a form of public reasonableness, see Joseph Tussman and Jacobus tenBroek, "The Equal Protection of the Laws," *California Law Review* 37 (1949): 341. For pertinent historical background, see Richards, *Conscience and the Constitution*, chap. 4.

238. On the various modes of strict and rational basis analysis, see "Developments in the Law—Equal Protection," *Harvard University Law Review* 82 (1969): 1; for further discussion and background, see Richards, *Conscience and the Constitution*, chaps. 4–5.

ing the protection of such rights, and is thus interpretively clarified by the theory of moral slavery in the same way the latter principle was. In particular, the theory of moral slavery, marking the abridgment of basic human rights on inadequate grounds, naturally clarifies related principles that call both for the national protection of such rights (the nationalization principle) and the better protection of such rights (the fundamental rights ground of equal protection) against both state and national governments. The focus of the theory on the inadequate grounds, on which such rights have been abridged, makes possible an interpretively powerful theory of suspect classification analysis. Such analysis, on this view, subjects to skeptical scrutiny, as illegitimate bases for law, the grounds condemned as inadequate by the theory of moral slavery.

A Theory of Suspect Classification Analysis: Race and Gender

Suspect classification analysis is now a well-developed form of constitutional analysis subjecting classifications on certain kinds of disfavored grounds to exacting constitutional scrutiny. A plausible general theory of the current scope of application of such analysis must unify, on grounds of principle, the claims to such analysis not only of African Americans and women, but, under recent law,[239] lesbians and gays; it must also address whether and to what extent such analysis would apply to other arguably suspect groups, including the poor,[240] the mentally retarded,[241] legal aliens,[242] the undocumented immigrant,[243] children born out of wedlock,[244] and children generally.[245]

239. See *Romer v. Evans*, 116 S. Ct. 1620 (1996) (Colorado Amendment Two, forbidding all laws that protect gays and lesbians from discrimination, held unconstitutional).

240. See, for example, Frank Michelman, "Foreword: On Protecting the Poor through the Fourteenth Amendment," *Harvard University Law Review* 83 (1969): 7–59.

241. See *Cleburne v. Cleburne Living Center, Inc.*, 473 U.S. 432 (1985) (zoning requirement of special use permit for the operation of a group home for mentally retarded held unconstitutional).

242. See *Graham v. Richardson*, 403 U.S. 365 (1971) (state welfare benefits cannot constitutionally be denied to legal aliens resident here).

243. See *Plyer v. Doe*, 457 U.S. 202 (1982) (children of undocumented aliens may not constitutionally be deprived of public school education).

244. See, for example, *Trimble v. Gordon*, 430 U.S. 762 (1977) (state statute barring intestate succession by nonmarital children from fathers held unconstitutional); but cf. *Lalli v. Lalli*, 439 U.S. 259 (1978) (state requirement of judicial finding of paternity during father's lifetime held constitutional requirement for eligibility of nonmarital children for intestate succession).

245. See, for example, David A. J. Richards, "The Individual, the Family, and the Constitution," *New York University Law Review* 55 (1980): 1.

Much scholarly argument about this matter centers on alleged analogies between the suspectness of race and gender along the lines of the immutability and salience of a trait or the political powerlessness of the group marked by the trait. Neither view is defensible even as an account of the now-settled constitutional suspectness of race and gender. The theory of moral slavery may assist us in forging a better view. I begin by exploring difficulties in current arguments about the suspectness on such grounds of race and gender, and then offer my alternative view. In later chapters, I elaborate the implications of my analysis for the suspectness of sexual preference and explore the implications of my analysis for the suspectness of other groups.

Political Powerlessness

A plausible general theory of suspect classification analysis must, under current authoritative case law, explain the claims to such analysis of African Americans and women; political powerlessness alone cannot do so. Lack of political power—measured either by some statistical norm (Ackerman[246]) or by the utilitarian principle (Ely[247])—fails to capture the plane of rights-based ethical discourse fundamental to suspect classification analysis as it has been developed in authoritative case law. It wrongly suggests, as Ackerman does, that the gains in political solidarity of groups subjected to deep racial or sexist or religious prejudice (in virtue of resistance to such prejudice) disentitle them to constitutional protection, as if the often meager political gains blacks, women, lesbians, and gays have achieved (when measured against their claims of justice) are the measure of constitutional justice.[248] It preposterously denies constitutional protection to women, as Ely does, because they are, statistically, a majority of voters.[249] The view also proves too much: any political group, though subject to no history of rights-denying prejudice, is extended protection solely because it has not been as politically successful as it might have been (say, dentists).[250]

246. See Bruce Ackerman, "Beyond *Carolene Products*," *Harvard University Law Review* 98 (1985): 713.

247. See John Hart Ely, *Democracy and Distrust: A Theory of Judicial Review* (Cambridge: Harvard University Press, 1980).

248. Racial classifications, for example, remain as suspect as they have ever been irrespective of the political advances of African Americans. See, for example, *Palmore v. Sidoti*, 466 U.S. 429 (1984) (award of custody of child on grounds of race of adoptive father held unconstitutional).

249. The Supreme Court has expressly regarded gender as a suspect classification irrespective of the status of women as a political majority. See, for example, *Frontiero v. Richardson*, 411 U.S. 677 (1973); cf. *Craig v. Boren*, 429 U.S. 190 (1976).

250. The Supreme Court has declined to regard the mere fact of the greater political success of one interest group over another as relevant to according closer scrutiny to legisla-

Procedural models of suspect classification analysis suppress the underlying substantive rights-based normative judgments in terms of which equal protection should be and certainly has been interpreted. Such models neither explanatorily fit the case law, nor afford a sound normative model in terms of which the case law should be criticized.

Suspect classification analysis focuses, I shall argue below, on the political expression of irrational prejudices of a certain sort, namely, those rooted in the background structural injustice I call moral slavery. The fundamental wrong of racism and sexism has been the intolerant exclusion of blacks and women from the rights of public culture, exiling them to cultural marginality in supposedly morally inferior realms, and unjustly stigmatizing identity on such grounds.

Immutability

Immutability and salience do not coherently explain even the historical paradigm of a suspect classification (namely, race) and therefore cannot normatively define the terms of principle reasonably applicable to other claims to suspect classification analysis. The principle of *Brown v. Board of Education*[251] itself cannot reasonably be understood in terms of the abstract ethical ideal that state benefits and burdens should never turn on an immutable and salient characteristic as such. Many cases show this is not a reasonable ideal or principle. The disabled are born with handicaps that often cannot be changed; nonetheless, people with such handicaps are certainly owed, on grounds of justice, a distinctive measure of concern aimed to accord them some fair approximation of the opportunities of nondisabled persons. It is no moral objection to such measures that they turn on immutable characteristics because the larger theory of distributive justice has identified such factors as here reasonably relevant to its concerns.

The example is not an isolated one; its principle pervades the justice of rewards and of fair distribution. For example, we reward certain athletic achievements very highly, and do not finely calibrate the components of our rewards attributable to acts of self-disciplined will from those based on natural endowments. Achievement itself suffices to elicit reward, even though some significant part of it turns on immutable physical endowments that some have and others lack. Or we allocate scarce places in institutions of higher learning on the basis of an immutable factor such as geographic distribution, an educational pol-

---

tion favorable to one group over another. See, for example, *Williamson v. Lee Optical Co.*, 348 U.S. 483 (1965); cf. *U.S. Railroad Retirement Board v. Fritz*, 449 U.S. 166 (1980).

251. *Brown v. Board of Education*, 347 U.S. 483 (1954).

icy we properly regard as sensible and not unfair. The point can be reasonably generalized to include that part of the theory of distributive justice concerned with both maintaining an economic and social minimum and with some structure of differential rewards to elicit better performance for the public good. The idea of a just minimum turns on certain facts about levels of subsistence, not on acts of will; we would not regard such a minimum as any the less justly due if some component of it turned on immutable factors. Differential rewards perform the role of incentives for the kind of performance required by modern industrial market economies such as the United States and Western Europe; immutable factors such as genetic endowment may play some significant role in such performance. Nonetheless, we do not regard it as unjust to reward such performance so long as the incentives work out with the consequences specified by our theory of distributive justice. Our conclusion, from a wide range of diverse examples, must be that immutability and salience do not identify an ethically reasonable principle of suspect classification analysis.

Race is a suspect classification, when it is, not on these grounds, but when it expresses a rights-denying culture of irrational political prejudice reflective of moral slavery. Persons are not regarded as victimized by this prejudice because they are physically unable to change or mask the trait defining the class, but because the prejudice itself assigns intrinsically unreasonable weight to and burdens on identifications central to moral personality. Race in America is culturally defined by the "one-drop rule" under which quite small proportions of black genes suffice to be regarded as black, including persons who are to all visibly salient purposes nonblack.[252] Persons, who are (by this definition) black, could pass as white; most, including some historically important African American leaders, chose not to do so (7, 56–57, 77–78, 178–79). Choosing to pass would cut them off from intimately personal relationships to family and community that nurture and sustain self-respect and personal integrity (56–57); the price of avoiding racial prejudice is an unreasonable sacrifice of basic resources of personal and ethical identity that they will not accept. In effect, one is to avoid injustice by a denial of one's moral powers to protest injustice, degrading moral integrity into silent complicity with evil. The same terms of cultural degradation apply to all victims of racism whether visibly or nonvisibly black, the demand of supine acceptance of an identity unjustly devalued.

---

252. See, in general, F. James Davis, *Who Is Black?: One Nation's Definition* (University Park: Pennsylvania State University Press, 1991).

Racial prejudice is the political evil it is because it is thus directed against central aspects of a person's cultural and moral identity on irrationalist grounds of moral slavery in virtue of that identity. The central point is not that its irrationalist object is some brute fact that cannot be changed, but that it is a central feature of moral personality—"the way people think, feel, and believe, not how they look," the identifications that make them "members of the black ethnic community" (179). Racial prejudice, thus analyzed, shares common features with certain forms of religious intolerance, for example, anti-Semitism; witness the irrationalist fear, common to both, of invisible blackness or the secret Jew, persons who can pass as white or Christian but who are allegedly tainted by some fundamental incapacity fully to identity themselves as authentically a member of the majoritarian race or religion (55–56, 145). Such incapacity is ascribed to persons on the basis of "perceived attitudes and social participation, rather than on . . . appearance or lineage" (145). In effect, any dissent from the dominant racist or anti-Semitic orthodoxy, let alone sympathetic association with the stigmatized minority, is interpreted as evidence of being a member of the defective minority, thus imposing a reign of intellectual terror on any morally independent criticism of racial or religious intolerance as such (and encouraging a stigmatized minority to accept the legitimacy of subordination, as, for example, in Jewish anti-Semitism[253]). The structural resemblance of racism to a form of religious intolerance is an important feature of its American historical background, fundamental, in my judgment, to a sound interpretation of the suspectness of race under American constitutional law.

The interpretive status of race, as the paradigm interpretive case of a suspect classification under the American constitutional law of the equal protection clause, arose against the background of the interdependent institutions of American slavery and racism and the persistence of racism, supported by its constitutional legitimation in cases like *Plessy v. Ferguson*,[254] long after the formal abolition of slavery. Racist institutions, like race-based slavery and its legacy of American apartheid,[255] importantly evolved from an unjust and constitutionally illegitimate religious intolerance against African Americans held in slavery. Racist prejudice was thus, in its origins, an instance of religious

---

253. See, for exploration of this theme, Michael Lerner, *The Socialism of Fools: Anti-Semitism on the Left* (Oakland, Cal.: Tikkun Books, 1992).

254. *Plessy v. Ferguson*, 163 U.S. 537 (1896).

255. For a recent important study of the persistence of this injustice, see Douglas S. Massey and Nancy A. Denton, *American Apartheid: Segregation and the Making of the Underclass* (Cambridge: Harvard University Press, 1993).

discrimination, that later developed, in ideological support of the institution of American slavery, into a systematically unjust cultural intolerance of African Americans as an ethnic group, reflected in the degradation of their status as bearers of human rights.[256] Race is constitutionally suspect when and to the extent public law expresses such unjust racial prejudice.[257] The evil of such prejudice is its systematic degradation of identifications central to free moral personality, including powers to protest injustice in the name and voice of one's human rights.

The suspectness of gender,[258] ethnicity,[259] alienage,[260] or illegitimacy[261] also cannot be plausibly understood in terms of some physical immutability. People not only can have operations to change their sex, but can and have successfully passed as members of the opposite gender.[262] Latinos can pass as Anglos; aliens can become citizens; the status of illegitimate children can be changed. The suspectness of the underlying prejudice in each case is its irrationalist interpretation of central aspects of human personality and the unjust degradation of the culture with which a person reasonably identifies.[263]

Neither immutability nor political powerlessness would afford sufficient reasons of constitutional suspectness in the absence of a background of a continuing pattern of the radical rights-denying evil of moral slavery in the domains of race and gender; neither immutability nor salience is even necessary when the background evil of moral slavery is in place. We must bring to bear on our interpretation of this constitutional evil a historically informed understanding of its American background.

256. I develop this argument at greater length in Richards, *Conscience and the Constitution*, 80–89, 150–70.

257. For further development of this argument, see Richards, *Conscience and the Constitution*, 170–77.

258. See, for example, *Frontiero v. Richardson*, 411 U.S. 677 (1973); *Craig v. Boren*, 429 U.S. 190 (1976).

259. *Hernandez v. Texas*, 347 U.S. 475 (1954).

260. See, for example, *Graham v. Richardson*, 403 U.S. 365 (1971).

261. See, for example, *Levy v. Louisiana*, 391 U.S. 68 (1968); *Trimble v. Gordon*, 430 U.S. 762 (1977).

262. See, for example, Lillian Faderman, *Surpassing the Lover of Men: Romantic Friendship and Love Between Women from the Renaissance to the Present* (New York: William Morrow, 1981), 292; Lillian Faderman, *Odd Girls and Twilight Lovers: A History of Lesbian Life in Twentieth-Century America* (New York: Columbia University Press, 1991), 42–43.

263. The suspectness of gender, in particular, reflects a history of unjust degradation and resulting irrationalist prejudice, which account for when and why gender is constitutionally suspect. For further development of this argument, see Richards, *Conscience and the Constitution*, 178–91.

SECOND WAVE FEMINISM AS ABOLITIONIST FEMINISM

Moral Slavery as the Ground for Suspectness

Abolitionist criticism of the evil of moral slavery centered on the distinctively American experience of slavery. In contrast to contemporary forms of slavery in Latin America, the enslaved population was a Creole population increasingly isolated from its African origins and living in much closer relationship to slaveowners, who largely lived on their land and held relatively small numbers of slaves per economic unit; the numbers of slaves, with the notable exception of South Carolina, also significantly did not outnumber the white population (slaves comprising, in 1860, one-third of the population of the South[264]). Strikingly, only some 6 percent of the Africans brought to the New World as slaves (650,000 persons out of a total current estimate of 11 million persons) were sold in the United States or its antecedent colonies, yet that number grew largely without replenishment to some 4 million persons by 1860.[265] From the Southern perspective, American slavery grew and indeed prospered because of its close symbiotic relationship to the hegemonically supervisory culture of white slaveowners, including, of course, the sometimes close living relationships of Southern blacks and whites that often shocked Northern visitors.[266] Such symbiosis, expressed also in attendant forms of sexual exploitation, gave rise to the peculiarly American proslavery rationalization of slavery in terms of moral paternalism.[267]

Proslavery paternalism appealed, in its nature, to the racist ascription to blacks of the capacities of permanent children who must be guided firmly to the ends set for them by the mature adults (the slaveowners) who served as their moral parents. Such racist moral paternalism construed the tangled symbiosis of black-white living relations under slavery on the model of intimate relations, claiming that the relation of master and slave was itself justified as an intimate relationship, like husband and wife or parent and child, that should similarly be immunized from outside interference.[268] In this Orwellian moral world, slavery was a kind of intensely close and loving intimacy of a parent with a quite young, prerational child without the capacities to define either ends or means; the parent must firmly supply both, also meeting needs of the dependent creature in the way one meets those of an otherwise helpless infant or a pet.

264. See Peter Kolchin, *American Slavery, 1619–1877* (New York: Hill & Wang, 1993), 94.
265. Ibid., 22.
266. Ibid., 117.
267. Ibid., 111–32, especially 123–25.
268. See Richards, *Conscience and the Constitution*, 227.

The special cultural power of a fundamentally hegemonic ideology like American proslavery paternalism is the self-blinding ascription to its victims of an unquestioning attachment and devotion (an assumption rudely shattered by the events of the Civil War).[269] In effect, the power of the ideology presumed the complicity of its victims. Whites and blacks had lived together closely under antebellum slavery, but, as white Southerners painfully learned, in different worlds, one hegemonically and polemically assertive, the other resignedly withdrawn into a compulsory silence mistaken for consent.

The antiracist strand of antebellum abolitionist thought had carefully analyzed not only the rights-based injustice of the evil this ideology defended, but the deeper injustice of the pathological political power of the ideology itself. Proslavery ideology drew its totalizing ideological power from its entrenchment as an unquestionable political epistemology that, consistent with the paradox of intolerance, repressed any views that might reasonably challenge its claims. American slavery itself illegitimately degraded the sole class of persons (the slaves) who would most forthrightly have challenged its claims, and Southern repression extended to all dissent, white and black—a fact that gave rise to the convincing abolitionist claim that slavery as an institution now undermined the basic rights of all Americans.[270]

This radical rights-denying feature of American slavery underlay the idea of moral slavery of abolitionist critical thought and condemned on this basis by the Thirteenth Amendment. Whites and blacks under Southern slavery lived in different worlds constructed by the rights-denying features of the institution, in particular, the creation of a status of persons denied basic rights on illegitimately circular grounds based on their deprivation of rights. The white world, thus constructed, ascribed to its victims a naturally servile status in love with its dependency; the outcast black world, brutally deprived of basic rights on specious grounds, withdrew into a silence mistaken for natural love of dependency. In fact, the silence of slaves was itself the product of moral slavery. Deprivation of such culture-creating rights enforced social death, a vacuum of the cultural resources through which persons express in public and private culture their reasonable moral powers as free and equal persons and shape public and private culture accordingly.[271]

269. Kolchin, *American Slavery*, chap. 7.

270. For further discussion of the slave power conspiracy, see Richards, *Conscience and the Constitution*, 79, 91, 119, 125–26, 129, 134, 237–39, 245, 249.

271. I adapt the idea of social death from Orlando Patterson, *Slavery and Social Death: A Comparative Study* (Cambridge: Harvard University Press, 1982).

Moral slavery, thus understood, reflects the illegitimate degradation of classes of persons to a servile status based on the unjust deprivation of culture-creating rights. Its essential evil is an unjust moral paternalism that dehumanizes one class of persons from their status as bearers of rights to servile dependents of another class of persons. Its mechanism of degradation is a totalizing political epistemology of natural dependency whose force rests on a long-standing and entrenched illegitimate failure to accord the degraded group fair respect for basic rights. American slavery was a form of moral slavery because it essentially rested on such moral degradation; its associated and supporting evil, American racism, was equally condemned by abolitionists like Maria Child as a more fundamental form of moral slavery, inflicting, as it did, unjust cultural degradation of blacks from their status as bearers of human rights.

The continuing force of this unjust culture was brilliantly described by Richard Wright in his autobiographical novel, *Black Boy*, about what it was like to grow up black in the South of apartheid.[272] Wright provided a remarkable insight into how Southerners controlled the lives and aspirations of African Americans. A series of patterns of control—physical intimidation and its pervasive fear (including lynching as a mode of terror), economic domination, the psychological power of whites both to define and circumscribe the aspirations of blacks— were devastatingly effective in limiting the life options of young blacks to two alternatives—either conformity to the white system or exile. Even modes of resistance were, Wright argued, shaped by the need to accommodate dominant white culture.[273] Wright gave a searing insight into the experience of moral slavery and the kind of moral independence, often forged (as it was by the Grimke sisters) in self-conscious exile from the South, that was often required to combat it. It is surely significant, in this connection, that two of America's best black writers and critics of American racism were expatriates, Richard Wright and James Baldwin.[274]

In forming their arguments about the evils of moral slavery in the context of race, abolitionist feminists articulated comparable arguments about the moral slavery of American women. Sarah Grimke made this point exactly when she condemned the illegitimate degrada-

272. See Richard Wright, *Black Boy*, in *Richard Wright: Later Works*, ed. Arnold Rampersad (New York: The Library of America, 1991), 5–365. For illuminating commentary, from which I have profited, see William H. Chafe, *Women and Equality: Changing Patterns in American Culture* (Oxford: Oxford University Press, 1977), 59–65, 73–74.
273. For commentary, see Chafe, *Women and Equality*, 62–65.
274. See, for useful commentary on this and related points, Leeming, *James Baldwin*.

tion of women from their status as bearers of basic rights of conscience, speech, association, and work to a servile dependence on men. The essential evil of such treatment was its unjust moral paternalism which, like the rationalization of Southern slavery as intimate life, construed women as naturally, lovingly, and intimately dependent on men, incapable of the competence necessary for morally independent assertion of their basic rights of conscience, speech, association, and work. The proslavery reading of slavery as an intimately private matter was malignly duplicated in the sexist reading of the right to privacy to legitimate women's subjection as an aspect of the sacrosanct core of private life (analogous to the thought that the right to privacy encompasses rape or other spouse abuse in marriage[275]). Men and women of both the North and South lived as closely together as blacks and whites under antebellum slavery, but they lived, on Grimke's piercing analysis, in different worlds; the one polemically assertive that its victims were in love with their dependency, the other withdrawn into a silence mistaken for a natural reticence and consensual acceptance. As in the case of race, the mechanism of such degradation was a culturally entrenched, powerful political epistemology of natural dependency (including Bible interpretation) that illegitimately failed to accord women respect for their culture-creating rights of conscience, speech, intimate life, and work, and indeed drew its hegemonic power, consistent with the paradox of intolerance, from such unjust degradation. Women, as much as blacks, had been rendered socially dead through their systematic exclusion from the public culture that, for that reason, so illegitimately dehumanized them. For Sarah Grimke, the critical analysis of such moral slavery in the domain of gender required nothing less than a new Reformation or Enlightenment in matters of gender in which women would, on fair and equal terms, invoke their basic rights of conscience, speech, intimate life, and work foundationally to reconstruct in their own authentic voice (as prophets or priests or scholars or persons of affairs) a religious and moral culture that had been illegitimately based on the denial of such basic rights. The illegitimacy of such degradation had, as in the case of race, been speciously based on stereotypical assumptions that themselves depended on such rights-denying degradation. We call the evils such assumptions inflict sexism, and Grimke condemned them as forms of moral slavery for the same reason she condemned racism.

275. For an important judicial rejection of this view, see *People v. Liberta*, 474 N.E.2d 567 (N.Y. 1984) (holding unconstitutional New York's marital exemption from its law of rape).

The claim of a rights-based analogy between racism and sexism was in the similar method of structural injustice inflicted in both cases, namely, "that others have controlled the power to define one's existence."[276] From the perspective of the constitutional condemnation of moral slavery, race and gender should be equally suspect as grounds for state action or inaction because blacks and women share a common history of rights-denying moral degradation that continued with the complicitous support of law long after their formal emancipation and enfranchisement—and powerfully and unjustly persists today. The guarantee of equal protection in the Fourteenth Amendment was ratified in 1868, but was held inapplicable to women until 1971[277] and was interpreted until 1954[278] to allow racial segregation. In both cases, the Supreme Court and the constitutional culture it shapes acted as powerful agents in the transmission and reinforcement of moral slavery in the domains of gender and race. The betrayal of basic rights expressly guaranteed is functionally often equivalent to the express deprivation of such rights, and may be even less morally excusable or justifiable when such betrayal powerfully reinforces, through the rationalizing power of the paradox of intolerance, the political force of sexism and racism as forms of moral slavery. Racial apartheid in the United States was an instrument of racial subjugation of blacks, isolating them from their basic rights of fair access on equal terms to public culture on specious racist grounds; as such, it gave powerful political legitimacy to the illegitimate force of racism in American public and private life, and thus to a continuing unjust cultural pattern of moral slavery in the domain of race that persists in various illegitimate forms today.[279] The wholesale failure even to acknowledge the evils of the subjugation of women gave powerful constitutional support to the illegitimate force of sexism in American public and private life, and thus to moral slavery in the domain of gender; gender segregation in separate spheres was, as in the case of race, an important institutional mechanism of such degradation; and a still largely unchallenged sexist political epistemology of gender roles, central to still powerful sectarian religious and moral traditions, undercuts the resources of public reason by which such mechanisms might be subjected to criticism and reform. Such

276. See Chafe, *Women and Equality*, 77; on the similar methods of repression, see ibid., 58–59, 75–76.

277. See *Reed v. Reed*, 404 U.S. 71 (1971).

278. See *Brown v. Board of Education*, 347 U.S. 483 (1954).

279. See, for example, Douglas S. Massey and Nancy A. Denton, *American Apartheid: Segregation and the Making of the Underclass* (Cambridge: Harvard University Press, 1993).

silencing of the morally independent critical voice of reason rendered unjustly entrenched patterns of gender hierarchy largely unquestioned and unquestionable.

From the perspective of the theory of moral slavery, the constitutional injury of racism and sexism was the unjust cultural burden of contempt placed on identifications central to moral personality. W. E. B. Du Bois made this point in characterizing the struggle of African Americans as two souls in one body: the one an African, the other an American identity, and the struggle to reconstruct both identities on terms of rights-based justice central to American revolutionary constitutionalism. Betty Friedan also defined women's struggle on similar grounds as "a problem of identity,"[280] the struggle to reconstruct American culture on terms of justice that would reconcile the identity of oneself as a woman and as a rights-bearing person and equal citizen. In both cases, the struggle for constitutional justice would by its nature reconstruct both personal identity and public (including constitutional) culture. In both cases, the personal and the political would become inextricably intertwined questions of both personal and moral-constitutional identity.

This perspective clarifies the justice of the remarkable interpretive development in American public law in the twentieth century that, on the basis of a radical abolitionist interpretation of the argument for toleration, subjected the cultural construction of racism and later of sexism to increasingly demanding skeptical constitutional principles. Arguments of toleration and antisubordination are, on this analysis, not contradictory and, properly understood, not even in conflict. Antisubordination is, on analysis, a structurally more profound form of cultural intolerance along the two dimensions of the argument for toleration: identification of certain basic rights of the moral person and the requirement of a compelling form of reasonably public justification for the abridgment of such basic rights. In particular, moral slavery, as I develop that idea, identifies a structural injustice marked by both its abridgment of such basic rights to a certain class of persons and the unjust enforcement at large of irrationalist stereotypical views whose illegitimate force has traditionally degraded the class of persons from their status as full bearers of human rights. European anti-Semitism is a case study that, in my approach, classically exemplifies a form of structural injustice along these two dimensions: it is certainly a species of religious intolerance but, in its European forms, a form of unjust subordination as well. Suspect classification analysis, on this view, skep-

---

280. See Friedan, *The Feminine Mystique*, 68.

tically condemns the expression through law of the structural injustices central to such unjust subordination (reflected in the cultural stereotypes of religion and race and gender that express such unjust subordination). Equal protection, as we earlier saw, requires that political power must be reasonably justifiable in terms of equal respect for human rights and the pursuit of public purposes of justice and the common good. Suspect classification analysis enforces this principle by rendering constitutionally suspect grounds for laws that not only lack such public reasons, but war against public reason by illegitimately rationalizing, on inadequate grounds, structural injustice. Laws, whose irrationalist bases thus war on public reason, lack constitutional legitimacy and are, for this reason, subjected to demanding tests of constitutional skepticism. The unconstitutionality of state-sponsored racial segregation and antimiscegenation laws show the force of this constitutional skepticism in the area of race; the comparable developments we have now reviewed at length in the sphere of gender reflect a comparable skepticism (both in protecting basic rights and in subjecting gender classifications to a constitutional scrutiny increasingly close to that accorded race). All these interpretive developments are systematically clarified and organized by the insights afforded by the theory and practice of abolitionist feminism.

The recent interpretive heightening of the standard of review for gender closer to that for race is supported by the theory of moral slavery, the terms of which were quite self-consciously invoked in Justice Brennan's important opinion in *Frontiero v. Richardson*. Justice Brennan's skepticism about the enforcement of gender stereotypes through public law in *Craig v. Boren* also is well explained by this theory. On the view taken by the theory of moral slavery, the proper interpretation of gender, as a suspect classification, must be contextually sensitive to the rights-denying cultural background of appeals to gender in the illegitimate service of the moral slavery of women as nonbearers of human rights. Such illegitimate appeals to gender are culturally centered in unjust moral paternalism; a public and private culture, unjustly based on the exclusion of women from central rights of conscience, speech, association, and work, illegitimately dehumanized its victims in terms of a nature in love with and only capable of their servile dependency, and on that basis paternalistically moralized their dependency. Accordingly, the constitutional scrutiny of both express and implied gender-based classifications must be skeptical of those gender distinctions that support the unjust cultural ascription to women of stereotypes of dependency, passivity, or lack of autonomous judgmental and other capacities linked to the traditional cultural forms that illegitimately rationalized their subjugation. In terms of Angelina and Sarah Grimke's framework of analysis, indulging such gender stereotypes through law distorts public understanding and acknowledgment of the principles of ethical responsibility incumbent on all persons, as such, and for this reason flouts constitutional principles of equal citizenship. On this normative view, it should be irrelevant to the constitutional analysis of the suspectness of gender distinctions of such sorts that they reflect gender-linked statistical probabilities. Otherwise, the fact of the long-standing enforcement of an unjust sexist orthodoxy, to which its victims have accommodated themselves as best they can, would undercut the legitimacy of constitutional scrutiny where it is, in fact, exigently needed on grounds of justice.

In addition, the antiracist and antisexist practice of abolitionist feminism was as central to these interpretive developments as was their theory. Rights-based arguments against moral slavery, whether by African Americans or women, took the form of originating claims of basic human rights in one's own voice that, skeptical as they were of traditionally dominant orthodoxies of race or gender (the mythologizing pedestal being common to both), morally transformed personal identity in the way the civil rights movement transformed both racial and gender identity; second wave feminism as a civil rights movement, if anything, reinforced this momentum. To give voice to one's human rights of moral independence, against the background of a subjugating tradition of moral slavery, is to forge a new personal and moral-constitutional identity on the platform of human rights that demands, on grounds of principle, basic rights of moral personality and rights to a private and public culture that no longer gives expression to an unjust tradition of dehumanization and marginalization. The practice of such dissent both expresses and elaborates not only new forms of identity but of consciousness and the dissident associations that sustain such consciousness. Consciousness in turn gives rise to the need for new forms of critical theory. Personally, morally, and politically transformative arguments of human rights require a complementary and mutually reinforcing theory and practice.

The theory of moral slavery affords as well a critical normative perspective on interpretive developments that fail adequately to enforce underlying arguments of rights-based principle. On this basis, both race and gender should be subject to the same strict standard of constitutional scrutiny, and the cases, which have survived such scrutiny under the *Craig v. Boren* standard of intermediate level scrutiny, would have to be argued and possibly decided differently under such strict scrutiny.[281] And, from the perspective of the theory of moral slavery, a constitutional distinction must be drawn between the uses of racial and gender classifications that perpetuate and enforce moral slavery and those that, taking this moral evil seriously, reasonably use such classifications as a way of addressing such evils (e.g., in reasonable affirmative action plans in both the areas of race and gender). If the rights-denying evil of moral slavery has been the segregation of African Americans or women into morally inferior spheres, it must be constitutionally reasonable to take steps to integrate them into the spheres to which they have unjustly been denied access. To the extent the current Supreme Court takes a different view, it cannot be justified and should be reconsidered.[282]

The ever-increasing level of constitutional skepticism about the enforcement of gender stereotypes through law may be reasonably understood and evaluated against the background of the abolitionist feminist skepticism about the ways in which unjust cultural traditions of gender roles had been and were enforced through law. The very exclusion of women from the traditional understanding of basic human rights (of conscience, speech, intimate association, and work) rested on an unjustly gendered conception of the person that provided the uncritical benchmark for questions of equality; the abolitionist feminist criticism of this exclusion crucially demanded that the background ideal of moral personality must not assume such unjust culturally constructed differences, but the demands of moral personality reasonably accessible to all. The objection of this rights-based feminism to the trajectory of suffrage feminism was along these lines, namely, the temperance and purity movements unjustly assumed gender differences that failed to subject their claims to an appropriately reasonable standpoint on the demands of moral personality (to which all persons are

281. See, in particular, *Michael M. v. Superior Court*, 450 U.S. 464 (1981) (statutory rape law, excluding women from criminal liability, held constitutional); *Rostker v. Goldberg*, 453 U.S. 57 (1981) (federal requirement that only males register for draft held constitutional). I critically examine *Rostker* further in chapter 8; my skepticism about *Michael M.*, derives from its endorsement of gender as a proxy for victimization, thus reenforcing unjust gender stereotypes; but, for some of the complexities of this issue, see Frances Olsen, "Statutory Rape: A Feminist Critique of Rights," *Texas Law Review* 63 (1984): 387–432.

282. Among the cases suggesting skepticism about race-based affirmative action plans, see *Regents v. University of California v. Bakke*, 438 U.S. 265 (1978); *Richmond v. J. A. Croson Co.*, 488 U.S. 469 (1989); *Adarand Constructors, Inc. v. Pena*, 115 S. Ct. 2097 (1995); *Shaw v. Reno*, 113 S. Ct. 2816 (1993); *Miller v. Johnson*, 115 S. Ct. 2475 (1995). For further elaboration of my criticism of this line of cases, see Richards, *Conscience and the Constitution*, 170–76.

subject), thus enforcing not only sexism but racism and ethnocentrism as well.

Even the abolitionist feminists, however, appealed to those aspects of women's moral experience that, in their view, better stated and enforced the appropriately demanding normative standpoint of universal justice on issues of race and gender (for example, the appeal to white women's experience as wives and mothers to yield moral insight into the indignities inflicted on the intimate lives of African American men and women). Such ideas of women's distinctive moral experience are often metaphors or tropes calling for interpretation and lend themselves to quite inconsistent interpretations.[283] Abolitionist feminism suggests an interpretation that enhances appropriate respect for universal human rights. Perhaps, as some contemporary feminists have argued,[284] some such arguments (exploring women's moral experience to enlarge public understanding of the critical demands of universal human rights) may be appropriate in our circumstances as well.[285]

We have now discussed at some length the abusive use of uncritical conceptions of gender roles (including, as in the case of Frances Willard, their roles as mothers) to abridge the basic rights of both women and men. We need to be both interpretively charitable and yet appropriately critical of the force of such women-centered arguments in the history of American feminism (on the importance of judging history, for contemporary interpretive constitutional purposes, in such a critical spirit, see chapter 1). Such interpretations of women's roles were not only empowering of voice but often rooted in strategic political judgments based on some real concerns (for example, interspousal violence linked to alcohol abuse). On the other hand, such an insular politics often ideologically obfuscated basic issues of human rights in service of reinforcing uncritical conceptions of gender roles that legitimated sexism as well as racism along various dimensions discussed earlier at length. In light of this historical experience and our contemporary interpretive concerns for articulating and elaborating common antiracist and antisexist constitutional principles properly contextualized

283. For example, the idea of protecting the home, which had been used by temperance women to advocate constitutional entrenchment of Prohibition, was later to be used by women to urge constitutional repeal of Prohibition. For recent illuminating discussion of this paradoxical ideological point, see Kenneth D. Rose, *American Women and the Repeal of Prohibition* (New York: New York University Press, 1996), 63–89.

284. For an argument along these lines, see Sara Ruddick, *Maternal Thinking: Towards a Politics of Peace* (Boston: Beacon Press, 1989).

285. For some sense of the range of views among contemporary feminists on the merits of equality versus difference feminism in contemporary circumstances, see Marianne Hirsch and Evelyn Fox Keller, *Conflicts in Feminism* (New York: Routledge, 1990).

in our circumstances, we must, at least as a matter of constitutional law, set a high standard of skepticism for the enforcement through law of conventional gender roles particularly when such roles are alleged uncritically to reflect the appropriate normative weight to be accorded "natural" facts like pregnancy or mothering. The tradition of moral slavery rationalized the subjugation of women in terms of the unjust interpretation accorded pregnancy. The ground for the abridgment of basic rights was the reduction of women solely to this biological possibility, to which they were consigned on terms that did even acknowledge their basic equal rights of moral personality, in terms of which they might rationally and reasonably decide (against a background of equal justice and fair opportunity in public and private life) what weight, if any, this biological possibility, among manifold other such possibilities, should and would play in their conception of a good and ethical life. Against this unjust background, any interpretation giving pregnancy as a basis for differential treatment must be skeptically scrutinized to insure that it does not unjustly impose an uncritical conception of gender roles that enforces, rather than contests the traditional moral slavery of women. In my judgment, the Supreme Court's endorsement of pregnancy as a ground for upholding a gender-based statutory rape law wrongly endorsed rather than contested the unjust cultural stereotype of women's sexual passivity.[286] For similar reasons, my argument would contest the Court's legitimation of the exclusion of pregnancy from the list of disabilities subject to a state insurance system, because it enforced a sexist interpretation of pregnancy (excluding, as it did, pregnancy from equal treatment with other forms of disability, thus enforcing the unjustly gendered conception that pregnancy disqualifies from the equal treatment and fair opportunity otherwise owed persons).[287] Much of the traditional conception of the

---

286. See *Michael M. v. Superior Court*, 450 U.S. 464 (1981). But see Frances Olsen, "Statutory Rape: A Feminist Critique of Rights Analysis," *Texas Law Review* 63 (1984): 387.

287. *Geduldig v. Aiello*, 417 U.S. 484 (1974) (exclusion of pregnancy from California's disability insurance system held constitutional) was, on this basis, wrongly decided, as was also I believe *General Electric Co. v. Gilbert*, 429 U.S. 125 (1976) (holding that Title VII of the Civil Rights Act of 1964 did not bar exclusions of pregnancies from private disability plans); but see *Nashville Gas Co. v. Satty*, 434 U.S. 136 (1977) (*Gilbert* distinguished in case where pregnant employees were not only required to take pregnancy leaves and denied sick pay while on leave, but also lost all accumulated job seniority when they returned to work). *Gilbert* was overturned by Congress when it amended Title VII in 1978; see 92 Stat. 2076. For a recent decision that gives proper weight to the relevant considerations, see *International Union v. Johnson Controls, Inc.*, 499 U.S. 187 (1991) (violation of Title VII for an employer to preclude women from holding certain jobs because of a fear that those jobs would endanger the health of a fetus).

role of gender in family roles should, for similar reasons, be subjected to much more skeptical treatment in light of its enforcement of an unjust conception of gender roles.[288]

Further, the condemnation of moral slavery in the Thirteenth Amendment should extend as broadly as the underlying rights-denying evil, which, on the view here taken, extends to both American slavery and the subjection of women. Moral slavery was as much an injury to private as it was to public life; indeed, the attempt to privatize injustice was one of its most insidious and morally corrupting evils (one's slave or one's wife as most intimately oneself). Therefore, this evil must be understood to embrace both private and public dimensions, both of which must be constitutionally addressed if the evil and its remedy are to be taken seriously. The Supreme Court, which has correctly found no state action requirement in the scope of congressional power to enforce section 1 of the amendment in the racial area,[289] should apply the same standard to gender and forms of sexism as badges of slavery on the basis of the theory of moral slavery.[290] Such a perspective may illuminate how and why ostensibly private forms of interspousal vio-

288. On such grounds, laws that reinforce gender stereotypy in maternal and paternal roles should, in my judgment, be struck down. For a decision to this effect, see *Caban v. Mohammed,* 411 U.S. 380 (1979) (state law, granting mother but not father of an illegitimate child the right to block the child's adoption by withholding consent held unconstitutional); for a decision inconsistent with this approach, see *Parham v. Hughes,* 441 U.S. 347 (1979) (state law, denying the father but not mother the right to sue for his illegitimate child's wrongful death, held constitutional). See, for an incisive general argument to similar effect, Susan Moller Okin, *Justice, Gender, and the Family* (New York: Basis Books, 1989). See also David A. J. Richards, "The Individual, the Family, and the Constitution," *New York University Law Review* 55 (1980): 1.

289. See *Jones v. Alfred H. Mayer Co.,* 392 U.S. 409 (1968) (under the Thirteenth Amendment, Congress has power to forbid racial discrimination in both public and private sales and rentals of property); *Sullivan v. Little Hunting Park, Inc.,* 396 U.S. 229 (1969) (congressional power under Thirteenth Amendment reaches racial discrimination in leasing by residents' association); *Runyon v. McCrary,* 427 U.S. 160 (1976) (Congressional power under Thirteenth Amendment extends to racial discrimination by private, nonsectarian schools).

290. For a different argument to the same effect, see Emily Calhoun, "The Thirteenth and Fourteenth Amendments: Constitutional Authority for Federal Legislation against Private Sex Discrimination," *Minnesota Law Review* 61 (1977): 355–58. For the background of such arguments, see Note, "The 'New' Thirteenth Amendment: A Preliminary Analysis," *Harvard University Law Review* 82 (1969): 1294; Note, "Jones v. Mayer: The Thirteenth Amendment and the Federal AntiDiscrimination Laws," *Columbia Law Review* 69 (1969): 1019. For a classic background historical study arguing for the pivotal role of the Thirteenth Amendment in the structure of the Reconstruction Amendments, see Jacobus tenBroek, "Thirteenth Amendment to the Constitution of the United States: Consummation to Abolition and Key to the Fourteenth Amendment," *California Law Review* 39 (1951): 171.

lence and resistance thereto raise rights-based normative issues of constitutional dimensions.[291]

Correlative with this understanding of the dimensions of the constitutional wrong of moral slavery, the principle of suspect classification review should be framed in terms of state action or omission.[292] This proposal addresses the interpretive question both of how the judicially enforceable state action requirement of the Fourteenth Amendment should be understood and the further issue of how constitutional proof of dominant racist motivation should be understood. The doctrine of equal protection imposes an ongoing ethical and constitutional responsibility on the nation to deconstruct the culture of American racism and sexism. That responsibility arises both from active support for such racism and sexism and from culpable inaction in not circumscribing its political power. In both cases, all three branches of the government failed to perform their obligations under the Reconstruction Amendments. The judiciary, deciding cases like *Plessy,* legitimated racist segregation and, in related cases, narrowly construed the state action requirement[293] and hobbled the power of Congress reasonably to circumscribe public practices of exclusion and degradation that legitimated a public culture of racism. Such complicity, based on both culpable action and omission, gives rise to a corresponding constitutional obligation to deconstruct the political force of the American culture of racism. That obligation must, in its nature, afford grounds for condemning both public actions supporting racism and omissions to take reasonable actions to circumscribe the force of racism in public life.

This argument of enforceable constitutional obligation condemns as interpretively mistaken the Supreme Court's early quite narrow construction of state action[294] and supports those more recent judicial attempts to expand what can count as state action under the equal protection clause.[295] The narrow judicial construction of state action was

---

291. For an important exploration of this issue along these lines, see Jane Maslow Cohen, "Regimes of Private Tyranny: What Do They Mean to Morality and for the Criminal Law?" *University of Pittsburgh Law Review* 57 (1996): 757.

292. For a similar view, see Jacobus tenBroek, *Equal under Law* (New York: Collier, 1969), 119, 188, 221–23.

293. See *Civil Rights Cases,* 109 U.S. 3 (1883).

294. Id.

295. See, for example, *Marsh v. Alabama,* 326 U.S. 501 (1946) (company towns); *Evans v. Newton,* 382 U.S. 296 (1966) (private park); *Shelley v. Kraemer,* 334 U.S. 1 (1948) (enforcement of racially restrictive covenant); *Burton v. Wilmington Parking Authority,* 365 U.S. 715 (1961) (lessee of space for private restaurant from state); *Reitman v. Mulkey,* 387 U.S. 369 (1967) (state constitutional amendment forbidding fair housing laws).

of a piece with the interpretively indefensible judicial evisceration of the privileges and immunities clause[296] and the legitimation of state-sponsored segregation in *Plessy*. American racism did not, as it were, grow spontaneously outside the constitutional culture; it enjoyed, at crucial points, its support, encouragement, and legitimation. A constitutional culture, now perhaps ethically capable of sustaining the vision of the Reconstruction Amendments, should fundamentally reexamine the judicially enforceable conception of state action behind which it tried to conceal its culpable abdication of ethical and constitutional responsibility for the fetid growth of a characteristically American culture of racist and sexist exclusion and degradation.

The same conception of constitutional responsibility should extend to the interpretive issue of both the nature of unconstitutional motivation and the associated burden of argument appropriate to its proof. The focus of constitutional analysis should be not only on dominant racist or sexist political motivation but on the forms of culpable political action and omission that have sustained a complex structure of social institutions constructive of racist and sexist culture, a structural racism and sexism with unjust disparate impact on the life chances of subjugated groups.[297] To the extent the judiciary has not made room for standards of proof appropriate to such structural racism and sexism,[298] its decisions are interpretively unsound and should be reexamined. And to the extent affirmative action plans are a constitutionally reasonable way to remedy such structural racial or sexual disadvantage, they should be judicially encouraged, not hobbled.[299]

These criticisms of the interpretive structure of the current constitu-

296. See *Slaughter-House Cases*, 83 U.S. (16 Wall.) 36 (1873). For criticism, see Richards, *Conscience and the Constitution*, chap. 6.

297. Cf. Owen M. Fiss, "The Fate of An Idea Whose Time Has Come: Antidiscrimination Law in the Second Decade after *Brown v. Board of Education*," *University of Chicago Law Review* 41 (1974): 742; "Groups and the Equal Protection Clause," *Philosophy and Public Affairs* 5 (1976): 107.

298. See, for example, *Washington v. Davis*, 426 U.S. 229 (1976); *Arlington Heights v. Metropolitan Housing Corp.*, 429 U.S. 252 (1977); *Personnel Administrator of Massachusetts v. Feeney*, 442 U.S. 256 (1979). The Supreme Court has, however, employed such a test in the interpretation of the Title VII, the employment discrimination provision of the Civil Rights Act of 1964. See *Griggs v. Duke Power Co.*, 401 U.S. 424 (1971) (racially disparate impact of qualifications for employment must be shown to be job-related). But see *Wards Cove Packing Co., Inc. v. Antonio*, 490 U.S. 642 (1989) (plaintiff's burden of proof must go beyond mere racial disparity in work force), statutorily modified by the Civil Rights Act of 1991, 105 Stat. 1071, reinstating *Griggs*.

299. See, for example, *Richmond v. J. A. Croson Co.*, 488 U.S. 469 (1989) (Richmond's 30 percent minority set-aside for construction contracts held unconstitutional). For an illuminating criticism of such decisions, see Michel Rosenfeld, *Affirmative Action and Justice: A Philosophical and Constitutional Inquiry* (New Haven: Yale University Press, 1991).

tional skepticism of both race and gender leave unscathed the integrity of the larger interpretive development, which has evolved, on the basis of the theory of moral slavery, strong antiracist and antisexist constitutional principles. We turn now to a body of law in which there is a much more substantial gap between the current state of constitutional interpretation and the demands of the theory of moral slavery, namely, arguments for gay rights.

6   The Case for Gay Rights

The interpretive roots of advocacy of gay rights, on the same platform of human rights as the antiracist and antisexist arguments
we have now examined at some length, lie in the poetry and prose
of Walt Whitman and the pivotal role Whitman played in the serious
development of arguments for gay rights not only in America (Emma
Goldman) but in Europe as well (Edward Carpenter, John Addington
Symonds, and Havelock Ellis, the mentor of Margaret Sanger). Against
this background, the contemporary case for gay rights, both as human
and as constitutional rights, can be cogently made not only on the normative basis of the argument for toleration but on the sound interpretive basis of the role that argument plays in American constitutional
interpretation. In particular, the application of that argument to gay
rights forges, in a principled and reasonable way, an interpretation of
the theory of moral slavery (on the basis of compelling analogies to
religious intolerance, racism, and sexism) that clarifies the dignity of
such constitutional rights in American public law. To make an argument along these lines, I begin with the historical background of Whitman's arguments in struggles over the meaning of gender in American
egalitarian democracy and the role the homosexual, as a cultural symbol, apparently played in such cultural struggles. I then turn to an interpretation of Whitman, and, on that basis, examine his impact on the
emergence of a largely European movement for gay rights and the
impact of suffrage feminism in general and the purity movement in
particular on American unreceptiveness to such arguments; I then turn

to the emergence of an American movement for gay rights in the wake of the successes of the antiracist and antisexist civil rights movements, and offer a proposal (based on the theory of moral slavery) of how we should understand and weigh its claims both in the areas of basic rights (including the right to intimate life) and the suspectness of sexual preference. In later chapters, I apply this normative perspective to various constitutional cases and controversies, including antigay/lesbian ordinances and the exclusion of publicly identified homosexuals from the military and of all homosexual couples from the right to marriage.

EQUALITY, GENDER, AND THE SCAPEGOATING OF THE HOMOSEXUAL

The struggles internal to nineteenth-century American women's thought arose from the tension between the rights-based egalitarianism of American democracy and traditions of gender inequality. Drawing on de Tocqueville, Catharine Beecher would abandon neither American equality in general nor gender inequality in particular, but rationalized the tension in her influential normative model of women's selfless subordination as in service of a higher utilitarian morality of maternal self-sacrifice for others (chapter 3). The arguments of the Grimke sisters for the human rights of both blacks and women doubly challenged this conception: first, its skeptical scrutiny of the traditional roles of both blacks and women in terms of anti-utilitarian values of universal human rights; second, women making such demands in public in their own voice and behalf, originating claims as persons not selflessly subordinating themselves to the will of another. Beecher's conception obviously had appeal not only for American men but for many women as well, laying the ideological foundation for Frances Willard's organized mother-love and the increasingly rights-denying character of suffrage feminism. It found polemical appeal in the way it religiously idealized women's inequality as indispensable to the personal value Americans increasingly placed on companionate, romantic love between spouses as tender companions. The force of this obfuscating idealization was nowhere more evident than in the way it crucially mythologized the mother-child relationship (one of radical inequality, asymmetrical devotion, and total dependence) as the higher morality that would stand judge over lesser moralities, including, of course, the morality of respect for human rights. Inequality thus became not only equal but better; radical devotion and dependence the model for all ethical relationships; private life the measure of public values. Precisely during a period when, in light of abolitionist feminist dissent, such traditional gender roles were subject to reasonable doubt, Beecher and others, consistent with the paradox of intolerance, repressed such doubts and increasingly silenced the women and men who would challenge this orthodoxy of politically enforceable normative gender roles in ways we have already examined (chapter 4).

The growing appeal of companionate marriage could be construed on a model of genuine equality or, as in Beecher's view, a model of suitably rationalized gender inequality. The unjust political enforcement at large of this latter model called for, if anything, more rigidly defined, impermeable boundaries of gender, which established the different gender roles appropriate for men and women as such. On the one hand, woman's status was ostensibly more valued on the terms of Beecher's model, but, on the other, the price for such heightened value was a rigidification in the boundaries of gender, mythologically immunized, as they were, from the skeptical rights-based doubts of abolitionist feminism. Homosexuals were the scapegoats of the repression of such doubt about the impermeability of the boundaries of gender in the same way blacks had been the scapegoats of Southern self-doubt and European Jews the victims of Christian doubt.

Homosexuality, as I will use the term, describes a dominant erotic preference for persons of one's own sex; it is a structure of sexual fantasies and vulnerabilities that has existed in all human cultures.[1] Cultures have dealt very differently with this erotic preference, including the cultural role, if any, they offer persons with such dominant erotic preferences. Ancient Greek culture not only tolerated, but idealized pederastic male homosexual relations as central elements in Greek pedagogy and artistic and political culture.[2] Christian moral teaching, sharply critical of Greek sexual morality, went well beyond the traditional Pa-

---

1. For development and defense of this position, see Edward Stein, "Conclusion: The Essentials of Constructionism and the Construction of Essentialism," in *Forms of Desire: Sexual Orientation and the Social Constructionist Controversy*, ed. Edward Stein (New York: Routledge, 1990), 325–53.

2. Important studies include William Armstrong Percy III, *Pederasty and Pedagogy in Archaic Greece* (Urbana: University of Illinois Press, 1996); Kenneth J. Dover, *Greek Popular Morality in the Time of Plato and Aristotle* (Oxford: Basil Blackwell, 1974); id., *Greek Homosexuality* (London: Duckworth, 1978); id., "Greek Homosexuality and Initiation," in K. J. Dover, *The Greeks and Their Legacy* (Oxford: Blackwell, 1988), 115–34; Peter Green, "Sex and Classical Literature," in Peter Green, *Classical Bearings: Interpreting Ancient History and Culture* (New York: Thames and Hudson, 1989), 130–50; Eva Cantarella, *Bisexuality in the Ancient World*, trans. Cormac O Cuilleanain (New Haven: Yale University Press, 1992); David M. Halperin, *One Hundred Years of Homosexuality: And Other Essays on Greek Love* (New York: Routledge, 1990); David M. Halperin, John J. Winkler, and Froma I. Zeitlin, eds., *Before Sexuality: The Construction of Erotic Experience in the Ancient Greek World* (Princeton: Princeton University Press, 1990).

gan distaste for men taking the passive (female) role in being penetrated by another man (the active role was quite a different matter)[3]
to a remarkably cruel reprobation of homosexual relations as such:

> For the first time in history, in 390 [C.E.], the Roman people witnessed the
> public burning of male prostitutes, dragged from the homosexual brothels
> of Rome. The Emperor Theodosius' edict (preserved in full, significantly by
> a writer anxious to prove the agreement of the Mosaic with the Roman laws)
> shows clearly, in the very incoherence of its moral indignation, the slow turn-
> ing of the tide. For a male to play a female role, by allowing himself to
> become the passive partner in a sexual act, had long been repugnant. . . . But
> it was now assumed to be equally shocking that a soul allotted in perpetuity to
> the "sacrosanct dwelling-place" of a recognizably male body should have
> tried to force that body into female poses.[4]

Christian moral thought on sexuality and gender had implicit within
it a valuation of asexuality (or the renunciation of sexuality) that made
a moral space possible for a theory and practice treating women as
persons and as equals.[5] Such a suspension of gender differences might
reasonably have been interpreted to justify gender equality and even
more humane treatment of homosexual love as a variation on the
theme of gender equality. Certainly, abolitionist feminist women in
the antebellum period interpreted their Christian convictions as man-
dating gender equality, and some gay Christians today not unreasonably interpret their tradition as requiring recognition of the dignity of
homosexual love.[6] The idea of gender equality in early Christianity was
increasingly interpreted in otherworldly terms without relevance to
gender roles in this world, indeed hardening the impermeability of
gender roles in this world (as the edict of Theodosius clearly does).

3. See Peter Brown, *The Body and Society: Men, Women and Sexual Renunciation in
Early Christianity* (New York: Columbia University Press, 1988), 30.
4. See Brown, *The Body and Society*, 383. For the text of Theodosius's edict, see Derrick
Sherwin Bailey, *Homosexuality and the Western Christian Tradition* (1955; Hamden, Conn.:
Archon Books, 1975), 71–72.
5. See Brown, *The Body and Society*, 118–19, 146, 170, 288, 369–71.
6. See, for an important such view, mustering historical evidence in its support, John
Boswell, *Christianity, Social Tolerance, and Homosexuality* (Chicago: University of Chicago
Press, 1980); for more recent studies, rather more critical of the Christian tradition but also
urging rethinking of these issues on grounds internal to the Christian tradition, see Bernadette
J. Brooten, *Love Between Women: Early Christian Responses to Female Homoeroticism* (Chicago: University of Chicago Press, 1996); Mark D. Jordan, *The Invention of Sodomy in Christian Theology* (Chicago: University of Chicago Press, 1997). For more popular forms of advocacy along these lines, see Andrew Sullivan, *Virtually Normal: An Argument about
Homosexuality* (New York: Knopf, 1995); Bruce Bawer, *A Place at the Table: The Gay Individual in American Society* (New York: Poseidon Press, 1993); Bruce Bawer, *Beyond Queer:
Challenging Gay Left Orthodoxy* (New York: Free Press, 1996).

And while there were periods of relative tolerance of homosexuals,[7] the dominant religious and political culture of Christian Europe was given classic legal expression for Americans at the founding of the republic by William Blackstone's hesitation to even discuss something "the very mention of which is a disgrace to human nature . . . a crime not fit to be named; *'peccatum illud horrible, inter christianos non nominandum.'*"[8] Citing with approval Constantine's sanguinary edict,[9] Blackstone grounded capital punishment for the offense not only in "the voice of nature and of reason" but "the express law of God" in the Biblical "destruction of two cities by fire from heaven," a punishment imitated by "our antient [*sic*] law . . . by commanding such miscreants to be burnt to death."[10] By Blackstone's time, however, the standard capital punishment applied to this crime as it did to other capital offenses, namely, hanging.[11]

During this long period of quite punitive reprobation, homosexual activity existed outside the law, as a kind of ultimate heresy in religion[12] or treason in law,[13] and took the form, as it did in renaissance Venice, of sometimes barbarously punished active partners (burned alive, or after decapitation) and much less severely punished passive (often younger) partners (sometimes including sodomy with women).[14] Homosexual activity was thus interpreted as an atavistic vestige of animalistic sexual barbarism at war with civilization as such. Its presence, as the tolerated cultural form of the berdache among the Amerindians of the New World,[15] was thus one of the aspects of those cultures that,

7. For the historical evidence on this point, see Boswell, *Christianity, Social Tolerance, and Homosexuality.*

8. See William Blackstone, *Commentaries on the Laws of England* (1765–69; Chicago: University of Chicago Press, 1979), 4:215–16.

9. The edict called for "exquisite punishment"; see text cited in Bailey, *Homosexuality and the Western Christian Tradition,* 70; Theodosius's later edict explicitly called for "avenging flames in the sight of the people," ibid., 72.

10. Ibid., 216.

11. Ibid.

12. See Alan Bray, *Homosexuality in Renaissance England* (London: Gay Men's Press, 1982), 19, 65.

13. Ibid., 20.

14. See Guido Ruggiero, *The Boundaries of Eros: Sex Crime and Sexuality in Renaissance Venice* (New York: Oxford University Press, 1985), 109–45; for a useful comparison, see Michael Rocke, *Forbidden Friendship: Homosexuality and Male Culture in Renaissance Florence* (New York: Oxford University Press, 1996).

15. The berdache was a man, who cross dressed and lived as a woman, who was valued for shamanic and other powers in Amerindian cultures, living sometimes as the wife of another man. For important treatments of the violent European reaction to this cultural role in Amerindian cultures, see Walter L. Williams, *The Spirit and the Flesh: Sexual Diversity in American Indian Culture* (Boston: Beacon Press, 1986); Richard C. Trexler, *Sex and Con-*

like the powerful role of women[16] or cannibalism,[17] simply outraged European colonialists; such uncritical outrage led them, sometimes through the prism of their own sectarian convictions, to interpret Amerindian cultures as barbarous and thus rationalized the normative judgment that the Amerindians were, in Aristotle's terms, natural slaves, who might justly be enslaved.[18] From this undiscriminating perspective, Amerindian sodomy was conflated, as a form of diabolic evil in the Amerindians, with cannibalism.[19] This perspective rationalized as well related judgments notably in the minds of the Spanish conquerors in particular (in light of Spain's powerfully irrationalist inquisitorial anti-Semitism and expulsion of the Jews in 1492, the year of Columbus's discovery of America for the Spanish monarchy[20]); these included the judgments of the Amerindians as women,[21] as diabolic heretics like the Jews (thus, also subject to inquisitions),[22] and, prophetically for the later history of American slavery and racism, as the descendants of comparably degraded African cultures.[23] Similarly, in British North America, the Amerindians were analogized to the Jews[24] (as well as to the Irish[25]). Such reinforcing prejudices (homophobia, sexism, anti-Semitism, racism) naturally lay the foundation, in turn, for developing forms of Spanish and British racism and the later enslavement of Africans; their African culture was interpreted also as involving comparably degraded forms of intimate life (for example, allegations of selling children[26] and sexual incontinence[27]) that rationalized their natural slavery.

---

quest: *Gendered Violence, Political Order, and the European Conquest of the Americas* (Ithaca: Cornell University Press, 1995); Rudi C. Bleys, *The Geography of Perversion: Male-to-Male Sexual Behavior Outside the West and the Ethnographic Imagination, 1750–1918* (New York: New York University Press, 1995).

16. See Anthony Pagden, *The Fall of Natural Man: The American Indian and the Origins of Comparative Ethnology* (Cambridge: Cambridge University Press, 1982), 52–53.

17. Ibid., 86.

18. See Pagden, *The Fall of Natural Man*, 86, 174–79. See also Williams, *The Spirit and the Flesh;* Trexler, *Sex and Conquest;* Bleys, *The Geography of Perversion*.

19. See Fernando Cervantes, *The Devil in the New World: The Impact of Diabolism in New Spain* (New Haven: Yale University Press, 1994), 9, 29–30.

20. For an important recent study of Spanish anti-Semitism, suggesting a much earlier racialized interpretation of the prejudice than previously supposed, see Benzion Netanyahu, *The Origins of the Inquisition in Fifteenth Century Spain* (New York: Random House, 1995).

21. See Pagden, *The Fall of Natural Man*, 43–44, 46, 116.

22. See Cervantes, *The Devil in the New World*, 39.

23. See Pagden, *The Fall of Natural Man*, 174–79.

24. See Alden T. Vaughan, *Roots of American Racism: Essays on the Colonial Experience* (New York: Oxford University Press, 1995), 49–57.

25. Ibid., 42.

26. See Pagden, *The Fall of Natural Man*, 161, 174–79.

27. See Vaughan, *Roots of American Racism*, 164–65.

Indeed, the largely successful rebuttal of the argument of natural slavery of the Amerindians by Las Casas was companioned with the quite uncritical application of such arguments to Africans.[28] Such attitudes of reprobation rested on the European rejection of any cultural legitimation of the homosexual role (largely understood in terms of men having sex with boys) as an animalistic barbarism.

However, the role of the homosexual in European cultures in the eighteenth and nineteenth centuries underwent a significant change, associated with the development of urban anonymity and a new ethics of gender relations, from a man who had sex with boys and women to men in subcultures who "are effeminate members of a third or intermediate gender, who surrender their rights to be treated as dominant males, and are exposed instead to a merited contempt as a species of male whore."[29] Homosexual activity was, if anything, even more persecuted, as it was in Britain, because it now took more publicly organized subcultural forms.[30] But persecution now had a different focus. The sodomite was labeled a "he-whore," a transvestite, and was no longer a promiscuous rake "but a species of outcast woman of the lowest standing."[31] Randolph Trumbach has eloquently explained this development in terms of rising anxieties about gender associated with "the rise of the egalitarian family":

> The degree of equality between men and women, and parents and children, that resulted from companionate marriage and closer attachment to one's children, raised profound anxiety in both men and women. The anxiety resulted in a compromise with full equality that historians have called domesticity. Men and women were equal, but they were supposed to live in separate spheres, he dominant in the economy, she in the home. Women were

28. See, in general, Pagden, *The Fall of Natural Man;* Vaughan, *Roots of American Racism.*

29. See Randolph Trumbach, "Gender and the Homosexual Role in Modern Western Culture: The 18th and 19th Centuries Compared," in Dennis Altman et al., *Homosexuality, Which Homosexuality?* (London: DMP Publishers, 1989), 153. See also Randolph Trumbach, "Sex, Gender, and Sexual Identity in Modern Culture: Male Sodomy and Female Prostitution in Enlightenment London," in *Forbidden History: The State, Society, and the Regulation of Sexuality in Modern Europe,* ed. John C. Fout (Chicago: University of Chicago Press, 1992); Randolph Trumbach, "The Birth of the Queen: Sodomy and the Emergence of Gender Equality in Modern Culture, 1660–1750," in *Hidden from History: Reclaiming the Gay and Lesbian Past,* ed. Martin Bauml Duberman et al. (New York: New American Books, 1989); Randolph Trumbach, "The Origin and Development of the Modern Lesbian Role in the Western Gender System: Northwestern Europe and the United States, 1750–1990," *Historical Reflections* 20, no. 2 (1994), 288–320; Alan Bray, *Homosexuality in Renaissance England* (London: Gay Men's Press, 1982).

30. See Bray, *Homosexuality in Renaissance England,* 81–114.

31. See Trumbach, "Gender and the Homosexual Role in Modern Western Culture," 157.

no longer supposed to have bodies which were inferior copies of men's; instead, as Thomas Laqueur has shown, their bodies were now seen to be biologically different; and of course, on these differences could be founded supposed inescapable differences in gender role, despite the morality of equality.[32]

The cultural transformation of the homosexual role was very much a form of symbolic scapegoating to rigidify the new pattern of gender roles:

> [T]he transvestite was a wall that guaranteed the permanent, lifelong separation of the majority of men and women, in societies where their relative equality must have been a perpetual danger to patriarchy. A minority of adult males were allowed to be passive, but the overwhelming majority of males can never have had the experience of being sexually submissive in their boyhood. The transvestite was the dike that held back the flood of true equality between men and women, where both genders would experience power and submission in equal degrees. All women in societies with transvestites experienced sexual domination all their lives, but only the transvestite minority of males ever did so.[33]

This cultural construction of the homosexual role guaranteed that men lived "in a sphere completely separated by biological nature from women":[34] only women desired men in the appropriately subordinated mode. An ostensible man, who violated this norm, was simply not a man, but a woman. By the late nineteenth century, women too were drawn into this normative world: a woman desiring a woman must be a man.[35]

As George Chauncey has made clear about the later development of this role in the United States, male homosexuals and prostitutes were culturally assimilated. Indeed, the word "gay," applying originally to prostitutes, was transposed to homosexuals.[36] The American cultural construction of the male homosexual as a female prostitute powerfully reinforced the embattled normative theory of radically different spheres of gender in ways our earlier discussion of the purity movement has already explored (chapter 4). As we saw there, to immunize women's traditional normative sphere from the rights-based skepti-

32. Ibid., 155. See also Thomas Laqueur, *Making Sex: Body and Gender from the Greeks to Freud* (Cambridge: Harvard University Press, 1990).
33. Trumbach, "Gender and the Homosexual Role in Modern Western Culture," 155.
34. Ibid., 156.
35. Ibid.
36. See George Chauncey, *Gay New York: Gender, Urban Culture, and the Making of the Gay Male World, 1890–1940* (New York: BasicBooks, 1994), 61, 67, 69–70, 81–85, 97, 185–86, 286. On "gay" applying to prostitutes, see Timothy J. Gilfoyle, *City of Eros: New York City, Prostitution, and the Commercialization of Sex, 1790–1920* (New York: W. W. Norton, 1992), 157.

cism of abolitionist feminism, a reactionary moral and political episte-mology of gender roles was defended and aggressively used against dissenting views, including those of advocates of free love. Women's normative sphere was, from this perspective, religiously idealized as the source of a superior maternal morality, which was to stand as judge over lesser rights-based moralities. Such a sectarian religion of rigid gender orthodoxy made its idealization of intimately domestic maternal purity the measure of what could count as a woman and degraded dissenters to this conception as fallen nonwomen, thus the scape-goating of the prostitute as outside the reasonable scope of what a woman, as such, could do or be. The male homosexual, traditionally even more culturally marginalized, was the dissident to male gender that the female prostitute was to her gender: the male homosexual's love for other men not only challenged the male gender norm of ag-gressive competition with other men, but its very object (love between men) unspeakably affirmed what the traditional model of heterosexual love anxiously did not want even to discuss, let alone debate (real equality in love). Such embattled sectarian anxieties fastened on the most symbolically marginal form of dissenting gender role (male homosexuality), and mythologically erased homosexual love in light of its sectarian image of gender hierarchy as the essence of anything that could even count as romantic love: the very idea of homosexual love was a conceptual absurdity, an unnatural act, which made such a man loving another man doubly disgraced and stigmatized (not a man, and, as a woman, a fallen woman). The measure of the even greater dehu-manization of the homosexual over the prostitute was a disgrace that could not even be spoken.

An ideology of gender roles, very much embattled against the rights-based doubts of abolitionist feminism, enforced its sectarian orthodoxy by remaking reality in its own mythological image. The measure of its mythologizing character was its frenzied reinterpretation of the tradi-tional unspeakability of the homosexual role (its role as never to have voice) in terms of the image of the most degraded of women, dehu-manized as a sexual animal owed nothing by the community of civil discourse. In a constitutional community otherwise committed to hu-man rights, it was easy enough not to extend such rights to women if an appropriate idealization could ostensibly invest them, in exchange, with a higher moral value. It was quite another matter not to extend such rights to men (and often white men at that). That could be ratio-nalized only by ascribing to such men, already traditionally voiceless as heretics and traitors to moral and religious community, a more radical dehumanization that would, as it were, legitimate their exile from the realm of the publicly speakable and thus of the thinkable or the imaginable. The homosexual thus was the placeholder for the most threatening anxieties and doubts of the embattled hierarchy of gender at the intimate heart of self-consciously egalitarian America. Such creatures must at all costs keep their degraded and silenced place in the hierarchical order of things if that order was to remain so unconscious of itself as in normative contradiction to American equal liberty.

WHITMAN ON HOMOSEXUAL LOVE AND DEMOCRACY

Whitman's towering role in American public culture is based on his remarkably direct rights-based assault on this gender hierarchy. He addressed the radical moral silencing of gay and lesbian Americans by forging a language that would give them a central place in an appealing moral vision of American democracy and what it could bring to the larger moral imagination of humankind.

Whitman described his great American poem, *Leaves of Grass*,[37] as "a language experiment—that it is an attempt to give the spirit, the body, the man, new words, new potentialities of speech—an American, a cosmopolitan . . . range of self-expression. The new world, the new times, the new peoples, the new vista, need a tongue according—yes, what is more, will have such a tongue—will not be satisfied until it is evolved."[38] The poem—successively revised in editions in 1855, 1856, 1860, and 1867[39]—spanned a period of extraordinary ferment in American public life, culminating in the sweeping changes in American public opinion worked by the Civil War and expressed in the Reconstruction Amendments. Whitman's unashamed frankness about male homoerotic feeling reflected the largely antebellum period in which the bulk of the work was written when "same-sex intimacy was then commonplace";[40] contemporary eyebrows were not raised at the homo-

---

37. See Walt Whitman, *The Complete Poems*, ed. Francis Murphy (Harmondsworth: Penguin, 1975), 37–568.

38. Cited in Betsy Erkkila, *Whitman the Political Poet* (New York: Oxford University Press, 1989), 82.

39. On the important revisions in each successive edition, see Michael Moon, *Disseminating Whitman: Revision and Corporeality in* Leaves of Grass (Cambridge: Harvard University Press, 1991).

40. See David S. Reynolds, *Walt Whitman's America: A Cultural Biography* (New York: Knopf, 1995), 403. Such homoeroticism extended evidently even to dissident religious groups like the Mormons; see D. Michael Quinn, *Same-Sex Dynamics Among Nineteenth-Century Americans: A Mormon Example* (Urbana: University of Illinois Press, 1996). On such love between women, see, in general, Lillian Faderman, *Surpassing the Love of Men: Romantic Friendship and Love Between Women from the Renaissance to the Present* (New York: William Morrow, 1981).

erotic content of the "Calamus" poems[41] but at the sexually explicit discussion and celebration of female sexuality in the "Enfans d'Adam" poems,[42] to which Emerson, for example, had sharply objected in his famous 1860 walk with Whitman on Boston Common.[43] These poems were the main subject of the 1882 obscenity prosecutions in Boston[44] and Philadelphia[45] and the 1886 and 1892 expurgated editions of the poem.[46]

Whitman's frank treatment of the power of sexuality was at the center of his distinctive interpretation of antebellum rights-based feminism and the way he brought it to bear on the expression of homoerotic feeling and conviction. Whitman had admiringly heard Frances Wright lecture,[47] and venerated leading antebellum feminists like Margaret Fuller and George Sand;[48] Elias Hicks, whose version of Quakerism was a formative influence on abolitionist feminists, remained a lifelong hero for Whitman.[49] However the linguistic innovation of *Leaves of Grass* was not its frequent homage to the equality of women,[50] which can certainly be faulted for its acquiescence in the then-common idealization of the maternal role.[51]

The core of Whitman's linguistic experiment was, consistent with the argument for toleration, forging a way of speaking publicly, in one's own personal voice, about erotic feeling, imagination, and conviction, as moral resources for democratic friendship and love, against the background of a repressive sectarian orthodoxy that blighted the scope of discourse about sexuality and gender to its cramped measure. In his 1856 preface to *Leaves of Grass*, Whitman criticized this sectarian orthodoxy for its lack of conviction about "the divinity of sex, the perfect eligibility of the female with the male,"[52] thus starving the moral

---

41. See Whitman, *Leaves of Grass*, 146–254.
42. Ibid., 125–45.
43. See Reynolds, *Walt Whitman's America*, 194–95, 198–99, 403–4.
44. Ibid., 540–1.
45. See Erkkila, *Whitman the Political Poet*, 310–11.
46. See Reynolds, *Walt Whitman's America*, 569.
47. See Justin Kaplan, *Walt Whitman: A Life* (New York: Simon and Schuster, 1980), 57.
48. Ibid., 63, 100, 164.
49. Ibid., 68–69, 190.
50. See Whitman, *Leaves of Grass*, 37, 57, 83, 136–37, 219, 241, 366, 420–21, 471, 744, 770.
51. See, on this point, Vivian R. Pollak, " 'In Loftiest Spheres': Whitman's Visionary Feminism," in Betsy Erkkila and Jay Grossman, eds., *Breaking Bounds: Whitman and American Cultural Studies* (New York: Oxford University Press, 1996), 92–111; but see Erkkila, *Whitman the Political Poet*, 100–101, 135ff., 257–59, 298, 308–17.
52. See Whitman, *Leaves of Grass*, 770.

resources that alone would enable men and women, as persons possessed of their own minds and bodies, to contest the rights-denying
rigidities of gender roles. The issue of the right to one's sexuality was,
for Whitman, central to any reasonable understanding of women's liberation.[53]

> Infidelism usurps most with foetid polite face; among the rest infidelism
> about sex. By silence or obedience the pens of savans [*sic*], poets, historians,
> biographers, and the rest, have long connived at the filthy law, and books
> enslaved to it, that what makes the manhood of a man, that sex, womanhood,
> maternity, desires, lusty animations, organs, acts, are unmentionable and to
> be ashamed of, to be driven to skulk out of literature with whatever belongs
> to them. This filthy law has to be repealed—it stands in the way of great
> reforms. Of women just as much as men, it is the interest that there should
> not be infidelism about sex, but perfect faith. Women in These States ap-
> proach the day of that organic equality with men, without which, I see, men
> cannot have organic equality among themselves. This empty dish, gallantry,
> will then be filled with something. This tepid wash, this diluted deferential
> love . . . is enough to make a man vomit; as to manly friendship, everywhere
> observed in The States, there is not the first breath of it to be observed in
> print. I say that the body of a man or women, the main matter, is so far
> quite unexpressed in poems; but that the body is to be expressed, and sex
> is. Of bards for These States, if it come to a question, it is whether they shall
> celebrate in poems the eternal decency of the amativeness of Nature, the
> motherhood of all, or whether they shall be the bards of the fashionable
> delusion of the inherent nastiness of sex, and of the feeble and querulous
> modesty of deprivation.[54]

From Whitman's perspective, a rights-based feminism could not
reasonably contest the idealization of women that deprived them of
basic rights of moral personality until the just moral freedom of all
(women and men) was understood to dignify giving public voice to
erotic feeling, imagination, and conviction as moral resources of egalitarian friendship and love in a free and democratic society. This is
the woman, guaranteed this and other basic human rights, who, in
Whitman's words, "waits for me":

> They are not one jot less than I am,
> They are tann'd in the face by shining suns and blowing winds,
> Their flesh has the old divine suppleness and strength,
> They know how to swim, row, wrestle, shoot, run, strike, retreat, advance,
>   resist, defend themselves,

---

53. For illuminating commentary, see Reynolds, *Walt Whitman's America*, 195, 210, 213,
227, 231–34.
54. See Whitman, *Leaves of Grass*, 770–71.

They are ultimate in their own rights—they are calm, clear, well-
    possess'd of themselves.[55]

Whitman was taken to such task by contemporaries, including Emerson, for extending this basic right to and on behalf of women, and for
creating a language of erotic imagination that aspired self-consciously
to take seriously their sexual needs and experiences; extending rights
so far challenged the gender hierarchy (and its double standard) believed to be essential to religiously idealized romantic love. The same
gender hierarchy that reacted so aggressively to advocacy of free love
by Victoria Woodhull reacted in the same spirit to Whitman.[56]

Consistent with these views, Whitman, like Woodhull, deplored the
treatment of prostitutes (which in the public mind included gay men).
He thus prominently attacked the persecution of prostitutes[57] and ex-
tolled the benefits of licensing brothels,[58] even suggesting legalization.[59]
His new language of respect for sexual autonomy necessarily encom-
passed prostitutes, reflected in the charity and largeness of spirit of
his "To a Common Prostitute":

Be composed—be at ease with me—I am Walt Whitman, liberal and
    lusty as Nature,
Not till the sun excludes you do I exclude you,
Not till the waters refuse to glisten for you and the leaves to rustle for
    you, do my words refuse to glisten and rustle for you.
My girl I appoint with you an appointment, and I charge you that you
    make preparation to be worthy to meet me,
And I charge you that you be patient and perfect till I come
Till then I salute you with a significant look that you do not forget me.[60]

Whitman's most innovative interpretation of rights-based feminism
was his inclusion of homoerotic experience in his discourse of erotic
experience and conviction. The "Calamus" poems, in particular, exqui-
sitely captured furtive moments of homoerotic tenderness:

Or else by stealth in some wood for trial,
Or back of a rock in the open air, . . .

55. Ibid., 136–37.
56. Whitman remarked: "Free love? Is there any other kind of love?" Kaplan, *Walt Whitman: A Life*, 43.
57. Ibid., 96.
58. Ibid., 232, 248.
59. See Reynolds, *Walt Whitman's America*, 229.
60. See Whitman, *Leaves of Grass*, 408. For illuminating commentary, see Reynolds,
Walt Whitman's America, 227–30.

But just possibly with you on a high hill, first watching lest any person
  for miles around approach unawares,
Or possibly with you sailing at sea, or on the beach of the sea or
  some quiet island,
Here to put your lips upon mine I permit you,
With the comrade's long-dwelling kiss or the new husband's kiss
For I am the new husband and I am the comrade.[61]

Or, they evoked the sufficiency of love:

When he whom I love travels with me or sits a long while holding
  me by the hand,
When the subtle air, the impalpable, the sense that words and reason
  hold not, surround us and pervade us,
Then I am charged with untold and untellable wisdom, I am silent, I
  require nothing further
I cannot answer the question of appearances or that of identity
  beyond the grave,
But I walk or sit indifferent, I am satisfied,
He ahold of my hand has completely satisfied me. (153)

The poems harnessed an empowering moral resource to forming public institutions: "[t]he institution of the dear love of comrades" (161),
where "I wish to infuse myself among you till I see it common for you
to walk hand in hand" (164). The ambition is nothing less than to put
democracy on a sound footing:

Come, I will make the continent indissoluble,
I will make the most splendid race the sun ever shone upon,
I will make the divine magnetic lands,
With the love of comrades,
With the life-long love of comrades.
I will plant companionship thick as trees along all the rivers of America,
  and along the shores of the great lakes, and all over the prairies
I will make inseparable cities with their arms about each other's necks,
By the love of comrades,
By the manly love of comrades. (150)

Whitman regarded homoerotic love as a resource fundamental to
the best religion and philosophy (in "The Base of All Metaphysics"
[154]), and as a crucial building block in the realization of the moral
values of American democracy. In his visionary essay, "Democratic Vis-

---

61. See Whitman, *Leaves of Grass*, 149.

tas,"[62] Whitman characterized these values, as had the abolitionist feminists, in terms of respect for "individuality, the pride and centripetal isolation of a human being in himself—identity—personalism" (958) "on one broad, primary, universal, common platform" (947), which required respect for the right to conscience against organized sectarian religion (964–65). In trying to come to terms with the problem of realizing these values, Whitman concluded that "[i]ntense and loving comradeship, the personal and passionate attachment of man to man" represents "the most substantial hope and safety of the future of these States" (981). Whitman explained in a footnote: "It is to the development, identification, and general prevalence of that fervid comradeship, (the adhesive love, at least rivaling the amative love hitherto possessing imaginative literature, if not going beyond it,) that I look for the counterbalance and offset of our materialistic and vulgar American democracy, and for the spiritualization thereof" (981–82). In the midst of the aggressive selfishness, materialism, and corruption of the Gilded Age, Whitman did not look to traditional marriage or the family but to "the personal and passionate attachment of man to man" (981) as the moral basis and hope for the American republic: "I say democracy infers such loving comradeship, as its most inevitable twin or counterpart, without which it will be incomplete, in vain, and incapable of perpetuating itself" (982).

The moral promise Whitman saw in homosexual love was illustrated, as Betsy Erkkila has eloquently argued, by his role as a nurse in the Civil War:

> Rather than sublimating his feelings for men, the historical role Whitman played in visiting thousands of soldiers in the Washington hospitals and the poetic role he played as the "wound-dresser" actually enabled a range of socially prohibited physical contacts and emotional exchanges among men. Soothing, touching, hugging, and kissing the sick and dying soldiers, the private poet merges with the public, female with male, "wound-dresser" with soldier, lover with democratic patriot, in Whitman's poems of the Civil War. "Many a soldier's loving arms about this neck have cross'd and rested,/Many a soldier's kiss on these bearded lips." ("The Dresser")[63]

In his 1876 preface to *Leaves of Grass*, Whitman stated that he meant the work to be "the Poem of Identity,"[64] a work that would foster in the reader an imaginative space for the forging of identity in relationship to

62. See Walt Whitman, "Democratic Vistas," in *Walt Whitman: Complete Poetry and Collected Prose*, ed. Justin Kaplan (New York: Library of America, 1982), 929–94.
63. See Erkkila, "Whitman and the Homosexual Republic," 153–171, in *Walt Whitman: The Centennial Essays*, ed. Ed Folsom (Iowa City: University of Iowa Press, 1994), 163.
64. See Whitman, *Leaves of Grass*, 783.

the author's struggle for his own identity, which Whitman confesses to be his own insatiable yearning for "this universal democratic comradeship."[65] Whitman, self-consciously claiming an identity conscientiously based on homosexual love, created a new kind of imaginative space in which these erotic feelings and convictions could be acknowledged and brought into fruitful moral relationship to fulfilling and perfecting the humane moral promise of American revolutionary constitutionalism. My own experience, as a gay person reading *Leaves of Grass*, was one of being erotically touched and imaginatively awakened by the possibility of a homoerotic love as powerful, as humane, as just, and as democratic as Whitman's. As we shall see, John Addington Symonds, Edward Carpenter, Oscar Wilde, and many others read Whitman in this spirit of awakening consciousness of one's legitimate ethical demands as a gay person, and brought those demands to bear on both private and public life.

Whitman, himself a gender dissident who obviously identified his plight with that of women,[66] brought his hard-fought moral independence to bear on their situation as well as his own "on the same platform of human rights." He thus as a poet not only forged a new poetic language of morally independent sexual voice but, as a man, resisted gender stereotypy by undertaking the role of a nurse in national service that brought his homoerotic feelings and convictions to bear on the care of men who served in the Civil War, the event more than any other that enabled Americans to rethink and reforge their democratic constitutionalism.[67] Whitman's theory and practice were very much engaged in and by that great reconstructive project.

In his life and work, Whitman contested the traditional conception of gender roles (including the norms of masculine identity) that condemned homosexual relations as a degenerate effeminacy. Whitman certainly affirmed his identity as a man and as a gay man, but, in so doing, he challenged the conventional conception of both, which supposed one to be exclusive of the other. Whitman thus affirmed the legitimate permeability of gender categories if the American dream of rights-based democracy was to be made real, and he crucially interpreted the rights-based feminist struggle for such rights as including, on grounds of principle, the rights of gay people.

It is this conception of identity as a gay man that may best explain

65. Ibid., 784.
66. On Whitman's identification with Quaker women, see Reynolds, *Walt Whitman's America*, 219; and with prostitutes, see ibid., 230. See also Erkkila, *Whitman the Political Poet*, 100–101, 135–38, 257–59, 298, 308–17.
67. See Kaplan, *Walt Whitman*, 280.

Whitman's otherwise surprising 1890 letter that responded to John Addington Symonds's repeated queries over twenty years about the nature of Whitman's advocacy of love between men.[68] Symonds made yet another query in 1890 after having sent him an essay on democratic art and Whitman, querying, "do you contemplate the possible intrusion of those semi-sexual emotions and actions which no doubt do occur between men?"[69] Whitman, obviously exasperated, responded that "L of G is only to be rightly construed by and within its own atmosphere and essential character," and Symonds's interpretation was "gratuitous and quite at the time entirely undream'd & unreck'd possibility of morbid inferences";[70] Whitman went on to mention that, though unmarried, he had had six children. Whitman's remarks about the six children were certainly at worst disingenuous fantasies[71] and at best elliptical parables about his fathering love for "some of the 'illegitimate sons' he adopted, fathered, and mothered over the course of his life"[72] (including during his nursing in the Civil War), but what about the rest? Edward Carpenter, a Briton who had visited Whitman twice in America and was much closer in temperament, lifestyle (Carpenter lived with his homosexual lover openly for thirty years), and philosophy to Whitman than was Symonds,[73] certainly gave part of the explanation when he complained at Symonds's nescience in even eliciting, let alone publishing, such a letter when the state of press censorship in the United States under the influence of the powerful purity movement was "ten times worse" than that in Britain.[74] Whitman, who would certainly have expected Symonds to make public any such correspondence (Symonds was shortly to publish in 1893 a major study of Whitman's work dealing prominently with his sexuality[75]), could hardly in such an environment have been candid. But, there may be more to it

68. For important commentaries on this correspondence, see Kaplan, *Walt Whitman,* 44–49; Reynolds, *Walt Whitman's America,* 198–99, 391, 396–97, 526–27, 577–79; Erkkila, "Whitman and the Homosexual Republic," 166–68.

69. Kaplan, *Walt Whitman,* 46.

70. Ibid., 47.

71. Ibid., 47–48.

72. See Erkkila, "Whitman and the Homosexual Republic," 167.

73. See, in general, Chushichi Tsuzuki, *Edward Carpenter, 1844–1929: Prophet of Human Fellowship* (Cambridge: Cambridge University Press, 1980).

74. See Edward Carpenter, *Some Friends of Walt Whitman: A Study in Sex-Psychology* (London: J. E. Francis, 1924), 12.

75. See John Addington Symonds, *Walt Whitman: A Study* (1893; New York: Benjamin Blom, 1967). In contrast, Symonds's sexually explicit memoirs were not published until 1984; see Phyllis Grosskurth, ed., *The Memoirs of John Addington Symonds* (London: Hutchinson, 1984).

than that, suggesting larger issues about Whitman's distinctive approach to an identity based on homosexual love that would have repudiated the way of thinking about these matters of a John Addington Symonds and the pathologizing European tradition he would have represented to Whitman.

A prolific British historian and critic, Symonds was married and had children, but was powerfully attracted to teenage boys; he had several affairs with Swiss boys that may have involved sex. Symonds read *Leaves of Grass* as a personal revelation, and wrote Whitman in 1872 that as a scholar he had "traced passionate friendship through Greece, Rome, the medieval and modern world," but only when he read Whitman a few years previously did he "learn confidently to believe that the comradeship which I conceived on a par with the sexual feeling for depth and strength and purity and capability of all good, was *real.*" He was "burning for a revelation of your more developed meaning" of "Calamus"[76] (and was to burn for twenty years). Symonds was certainly aware of the medical studies of so-called sexual inversion pioneered in the 1860s by Carl Ulrichs[77] and Karl Westfal;[78] Ulrichs had explained homosexual sexual preference as "third-sex" Uranians who were in some sense congenitally female (perhaps, reflecting features of the common stereotype of male homosexuals).[79] Summarizing this development, Foucault observed: "The sodomite had been a temporary aberration; the homosexual was now a species."[80] Consistent with this perspective, Symonds wrote back to Whitman that he was surprised at Whitman's ignorance that there were some people "whose sexual instincts are what the Germans call 'inverted'," explaining, "During the last 25 years much attention, in France, Germany, Austria, & Italy, has been directed to the psychology & pathology of these abnormal persons."[81] Both Havelock Ellis and Symonds were important forma-

---

76. Reynolds, *Walt Whitman's America,* 527.

77. See David Greenberg, *The Construction of Homosexuality* (Chicago: University of Chicago Press, 1988), 408–9, 414–15.

78. Ibid., 380.

79. Ibid., 408–9. The word "homosexual" (*homosexualitat*) was coined in 1869 by Karl Maria Benkert, but it took decades for the concept and term, homosexuality, to enter Anglo-American discourse. See Quinn, *Same-Sex Dynamics Among Nineteenth-Century Americans,* 33. It was not introduced into English until the 1890s, not used in the *New York Times* until 1926, and did not gain widespread cultural use until the 1930s. Reynolds, *Walt Whitman's America,* 578.

80. See Michel Foucault, *The History of Sexuality,* trans. Robert Hurley (New York: Pantheon, 1978), 1:43.

81. See David Reynolds, *Walt Whitman's America,* 396–97.

tive figures in the Anglo-American tradition of medicalizing the homosexual as subject to a congenital abnormality[82] and, for that reason, not properly subject to criminal liability.[83]

Whitman's rejection of Symonds's interpretation of his work as "morbid inferences . . . disavow'd by me & . . . damnable"[84] was not far from the mark if understood as a rejection not only of the pathological model of homosexuality but of the cultural stereotype of debased femininity that it apparently assumed and rationalized. Whitman's work was one of visionary rights-based ethical protest, as Lydia Maria Child's had been of racism and Sarah Grimke's of sexism, and was profoundly rooted, as were theirs, in the ethical conviction that new forms of conscience had to be forged against the background of a tradition of moral slavery that cramped respect for human rights to its own cramped sectarian measure. It was not for this reason merely poetic metaphor for Whitman, near the opening of *Leaves of Grass,* to speak of his religious ambitions[85]:

> I too, following many and follow'd by many, inaugurate a religion, I
>   descend into the arena,
> (It may be I am destin'd to utter the loudest cries there, the
>   winner's pealing shouts,
> Who knows? they may rise from me yet, and soar above every
>   thing.)
> Each is not for its own sake,
> I say the whole earth and all the stars in the sky are for religion's
>   sake.[86]

To argue, as Whitman did, for a basic human right of homosexual love against the background of the tradition of reprobation earlier discussed was to use the argument for toleration to make two central claims: first, that basic human rights are owed persons who love persons of the same gender; and second, that the tradition of reprobation had unjustly enforced at large a sectarian conception of sexuality and gender and remade reality in its own unjust image (thus, rendering un-

82. See, in general, Havelock Ellis and John Addington Symonds, *Sexual Inversion* (London: Wilson and Macmillan 1897). Only in his memoirs, not published until long after his death, did Symonds take a more skeptical stance to this pathologizing approach to homosexuality; for illuminating commentary on this point, see Joseph Bristow, *Effeminate England: Homoerotic Writing after 1885* (New York: Columbia University Press, 1995), 134–37.

83. See Havelock Ellis and John Addington Symonds, *Sexual Inversion,* 153, 155–56.

84. Kaplan, *Walt Whitman,* 47.

85. On Whitman as a religious innovator, see Reynolds, *Walt Whitman's America,* 251–59.

86. See Whitman, *Leaves of Grass,* 54.

speakable and unthinkable the legitimacy of such love). For such an argument to succeed, a new form of conscience would have to be created (and thus the personal and ethical convictions of meaning in living central to religion) and the political force that the sectarian orthodoxy had been allowed unjustly to enjoy would have to be circumscribed. Such a process would, in turn, more justly reconstruct American constitutional democracy, unleashing, in Whitman's view, moral resources central to its continuing health and vitality as a community of mutual respect for basic rights. It was Whitman's ambition that his project be understood as one of ethical, religious, and constitutional emancipation and that its critical object should be the power that the traditional orthodoxy of gender roles had been allowed to enjoy, which included the degrading stereotype of homosexual love as an unspeakably debased femininity. Whitman thus objected in principle to any pathologizing treatment of sexual preference because it failed to take seriously the central issues of rights-based conviction—ethical, political, and religious. Homosexual love was, for Whitman, no more exclusively about sexuality (let alone, a debased sexuality) than heterosexual love. To live conscientiously as a lover of another person of the same gender was, for Whitman as it was for Carpenter, something more full hearted and authentic than the ambivalent and conflicted theory and practice of a John Addington Symonds (who may have thought he heard from Whitman precisely what he wanted to hear[87]). Such a life also meant one must criticize and repudiate the political enforcement at large of any sectarian theory of gender and sexuality (including a medicalizing one) that unjustly framed the facts of homosexual love to the measure of the cultural stereotype that condemned homosexual men as debased women.[88]

The appropriate recognition of the right to love (including the right to homosexual love) would, to Whitman, make possible the reforging of personal and moral identity on terms of rights-based democratic justice, and such recognition was as important to the just reconstruction of American revolutionary constitutionalism as any of the other moral changes worked by the Reconstruction Amendments. Long before W. E. B. Du Bois wrote of reconstructing racial and American identity, or Betty Friedan called for a rethinking of gender and political

87. See Reynolds, *Walt Whitman's America*, 578; Carpenter, *Some Friends of Walt Whitman*, 11–12. Symonds's more authentic treatment of his life and thought was only to be published long after his death; see Phyllis Grosskurth, ed., *The Memoirs of John Addington Symonds*.

88. See, for a similar reading, Erkkila, "Whitman and the Homosexual Republic," 166–67.

identity, Whitman identified the same issue (the personal linked to the political) to be at the heart of the struggle for identity of gay and lesbian persons. Certainly, in a historical period of confusion about issues of gender and sexuality (a period that lacked even the word "homosexual," let alone any reasonable consensus of how sexual preference should be understood), Whitman could hardly have meant by gay and lesbian identity all the things we mean by such terms.[89] But, understood as I believe he should reasonably be (within the framework of the argument for toleration), Whitman established the structure of thinking of these issues in terms of a rights-based struggle for the personal and ethical identity of gay and lesbian persons against the background of unjustly enforced traditions of moral slavery. We must make the best sense of that structure we can in our circumstances, but the structure of a transformative rights-based identity-focused struggle for gay and lesbian persons, as part of the larger rights-based feminist struggle, was Whitman's great contribution to American ethical, religious, and constitutional thought.

Whitman's contribution was, I believe, interpretive of the American tradition of revolutionary constitutionalism in the same way the abolitionist feminists were. He creatively reforged the best rights-based moral, religious, and constitutional thought of his age to demand that basic human rights (conscience, speech, association, and work) be extended to homosexuals on the platform of human rights. Persons whose erotic and affectional life was thus homosexual should, on this view, be guaranteed respect for their basic human rights by the public culture, allowing them to bring their personal and ethical convictions of the value of such relationships to bear on both private and public life. The struggle for such rights would be transformative personally, politically, and constitutionally: the terms of one's identity, unjustly stigmatized as homosexual, would be recast on terms of constitutional justice. The struggle would as well enlarge and refine larger patterns of reasonable discourse that contest the impermeability of gender definitions and boundaries in general.

Whitman was a rights-based visionary in the fashion of Garrison, Child, and the Grimke sisters. Grounding his arguments in the rights-based feminism of a radical woman like Frances Wright and the

89. See, for example, Anthony R. D'Augelli and Charlotte J. Patterson, eds., *Lesbian, Gay, and Bisexual Identities over the Lifespan: Psychological Perspectives* (New York: Oxford University Press, 1995); Kwame Anthony Appiah and Henry Louis Gates, Jr., eds., *Identities* (Chicago: University of Chicago Press, 1995); Dan Danielsen and Karen Engle, eds., *After Identity: A Reader in Law and Culture* (New York: Routledge, 1995); Henry Harris, ed., *Identity* (Oxford: Clarendon Press, 1995).

searching moral independence of religious orthodoxies of an Elias Hicks, Whitman deepened and expanded the argument for toleration both to apply arguments of basic human rights to homosexual love and skeptically to scrutinize the political enforcement at large of traditional normative conceptions of gender roles in new ways. He did so by construing the basic right of intimate life in a more expansively abstract way (applying to both women and homosexuals) and by exploring the unjust use of traditional conceptions of gender roles against those who would challenge such conceptions. Whitman's protest against gender stereotypy makes clear its rights-denying damage to both women and men: that is, its failure to note, let alone take seriously, the bonds of love between persons of the same gender that were facts of private and public life in the culture Whitman knew and understood so well.[90] The issue of democratic justice was, for Whitman, to begin taking such facts seriously, to forge a rights-respecting culture adequate to them in contrast to the unjust political enforcement of mythologically idealized, impermeable, rigidly defined boundaries of gender that created cultural reality in its own cramped image. Whitman's insistence on the masculine character of the love between men must be understood as an example of his larger protest against the malignity of unjust gender stereotypy, which insisted on reducing the complex reality of homosexual love to the terms of a crude sexist fantasy. The struggle for gay and lesbian identity would be, like the struggle of blacks and women, a struggle for the resources that would enable people to define their own lives on terms of justice, making space for homosexualities as complex and varied and humane as heterosexualities.

When Whitman insisted in *Democratic Vistas* that giving love between men its proper cultural space was crucial to the reconstruction of American democracy on sound terms of justice, he was, I believe, making this larger point about the rights-denying damage of uncritical gender stereotypy to American democratic culture, private and public. Abolitionist feminists had made quite clear the extent of its damage to women as full participants in American democratic culture. It remained for Whitman, the moral visionary, to deepen our understanding of its damage to men locked, as they were, in rigidly impermeable gender roles that made love between men, whatever its form, unspeakable and unthinkable. Whitman protested the interlinked cultural deg-

90. See, for example, Reynolds, *Walt Whitman's America*, 391–403; Quinn, *Same-Sex Dynamics Among Nineteenth-Century Americans;* Lillian Faderman, *Surpassing the Love of Men: Romantic Friendship and Love Between Women from the Renaissance to the Present* (New York: William Morrow, 1981); Emma Donoghue, *Passions Between Women: British Lesbian Culture, 1668–1801* (New York: HarperCollins, 1993).

radation of the homosexual and the prostitute because the unjust image of their degraded, subhuman evil was, for men as for women, a way of removing from debate and discussion any doubts one might reasonably have about the impermeable boundaries of gender, making of fallen women (whether men or women) the scapegoats of one's self-doubt. Failure to entertain such doubts removed from debate and discussion the unjust gender hierarchy at the intimate center of private and public life and the corruption of democratic moral feeling that it inflicted on private and public life. The hope for American democracy that Whitman placed on the legitimation of love between men was that its might unleash, in the culturally central domains of conscience, speech, intimate life and work, resources of moral feeling, imagination, and identification that would finally render speakable and thinkable and thus subject to question the injustice of such gender hierarchy by acknowledging an image of love between equals. The legitimacy of love between homosexuals would make culturally possible not just love between persons of the same gender, but love between equals in all relationships; gender hierarchy would no longer be the uncritical sectarian measure of love as such. Whitman's vision thus challenged the heart of darkness of American masculinity, the "real" man narcissistically frozen in stereotyped moral feeling and conviction, in speech either polemically aggressive or emotionally shallow and inexpressive, armored and manipulative in intimate life, competitive and callous in work. At the heart of the matter he saw a terror of loving and being loved as an equal and tender companion that impoverished the empathic resources of the reciprocities of civic friendship that were the moral bonds of democracy as a community of equals in both public and private life. The legitimation of love between equals would deepen and invigorate the theory and practice of rights-based democratic community.

The Response to Whitman: Abroad and at Home

Whitman was a more inspirational figure to the development of self-consciously public gay and lesbian identity abroad than at home, a fact obviously connected to our earlier discussion of the trajectory of American suffrage feminism and its aftermath. We need now to investigate further both developments as a preface to our examination of the rebirth of such rights-based arguments for gay and lesbian identity in the wake of the increasingly successful antiracist and antisexist civil rights movements in the 1960s.

Whitman Abroad

Whitman was interpreted as a visionary prophet of a new view of sexuality in general and homosexuality in particular by, as we have already observed, a number of important figures in British cultural life (including John Addington Symonds, Oscar Wilde, and Edward Carpenter). I begin by discussing Symonds and Wilde, and then turn to Carpenter.

Symonds and Wilde interpreted Whitman from the perspective of the reawakening interest in Pagan high cultures, like Greece, as models for legitimate homoeroticism. Such interest was revived by the art history of Winckelmann[91] and, more recently at Oxford, by the interpretive work of Walter Pater.[92] A liberal reformer, Benjamin Jowett, sought curricular changes in Oxford University to shift the search for transcendental value from Christian theology to Plato and Greek studies. The unforeseen consequence was the development of a homosocial culture and, through the exquisite interpretive sensibility of Walter Pater, of a coded language of moral legitimacy for homosexuality; thus, Pater would note appreciatively in his essay on Winckelmann, "[t]hat his affinity with Hellenism was not merely intellectual, that the subtler threads of temperament were inwoven in it, is proved by his romantic, fervent friendships with young men."[93] Winckelmann's homosexuality was thus implicitly affirmed as enabling him better to translate the enduring values of Greek high culture in terms that made these values more available to modern Europeans. Both Symonds and Wilde found legitimation for their homosexuality in this emerging Oxford culture, that is, a way of thinking affirmatively about forming an identity in which their homosexuality would play an increasingly important part.[94]

For Symonds, this took the form of writing and publishing privately (10 copies) in 1873 his *A Problem in Greek Ethics* and in 1883 his *A Problem in Modern Ethics* (50 copies).[95] *A Problem in Greek Ethics*

91. See, for an important recent treatment, Alex Potts, *Flesh and the Ideal: Winckelmann and the Origins of Art History* (New Haven: Yale University Press, 1994).

92. See, for an important recent treatment, Linda Dowling, *Hellenism and Homosexuality in Victorian Oxford* (Ithaca: Cornell University Press, 1994). On Pater, in particular, see Denis Donoghue, *Walter Pater: Love of Strange Souls* (New York: Knopf, 1995). For his most influential work, see Walter Pater, *The Renaissance: Studies in Art the Poetry (the 1893 text),* ed. Donald L. Hill (Berkeley and Los Angeles: University of California Press, 1980).

93. See Pater, *The Renaissance,* 152.

94. See, in general, Dowling, *Hellenism and Homosexuality in Victorian Oxford.* Useful recent general studies include Joseph Bristow, *Effeminate England: Homoerotic Writing after 1885* (New York: Columbia University Press, 1995); Alan Sinfield, *The Wilde Century: Effeminacy, Oscar Wilde, and the Queer Movement* (New York: Columbia University Press, 1994).

95. See, for the original texts and useful commentary, John Addington Symonds, *Male Love: A Problem in Greek Ethics and Other Writings,* ed. John Lauritsen (New York: Pagan

312   CHAPTER SIX

was included as an appendix to the publication in 1897 (four years after Symonds's death) of Symonds's and Havelock Ellis's *Sexual Inversion*.[96] For Symonds, the example of Greece decisively rebutted the now conventional view that "a man who loves his own sex" must be "incapable of humane or generous sentiments."[97] Symonds's quite insightful interpretation of Greek homosexuality in *A Problem in Greek Ethics* focused on its idealization of homosexual love,[98] its markedly masculine character (3, 8, 18, 22, 36, 65–66), its political uses in military solidarity (9) and in combating tyranny (10–13, 20–21), and its association with sports, libraries, and education (44). Symonds contextualized the Greek institution of "paiderastia" (4) both to needs for population control (15) (citing Aristotle) and to the degraded condition of women that rendered idealizing romantic love between people of opposite genders impossible (26, 51, 62–64). Symonds's own ambivalence is apparent in the emphasis he placed on Plato's late views on the unnaturalness of homosexual sex (48–50) and the contrast of the Greek subjection of women to the modern romantic cult of women, which suggested the anachronism of Greek homosexuality for the modern world (72–73).

As we earlier noted, Symonds's passionate interest in Whitman's work was in its clear claim that love between men played a desirable role in the modern world, and indeed was decisively important in the better realization of democratic values and culture. Symonds ultimately found in Whitman what he wanted to find. His extensive discussion of Whitman's sexuality in his 1893 *Walt Whitman*[99] ascribed to Whitman, on the basis of the correspondence earlier discussed (67–85), a Platonically idealized conception of romantic homoerotic love, "a new chivalrous enthusiasm, analogous to that of primitive Hellenic society" (76–77), without sexual desire or consummation.[100] Whitman played a comparable role in the 1896 edition of Symonds's *A Problem in Modern Ethics*.

In this work Symonds deplored the lack of investigation and preju-

Press, 1983). For another edition, see John Addington Symonds, *A Problem in Modern Ethics* (London, 1896).

96. See Havelock Ellis and John Addington Symonds, *Sexual Inversion* (London: Wilson and Macmillan, 1897).

97. See Symonds, *A Problem in Modern Ethics* (1896 edition), 11.

98. See Symonds, *A Problem in Greek Ethics*, in Symonds, *Male Love*, 1–73.

99. See John Addington Symonds, *Walt Whitman: A Study* (first published, 1893) (New York: Benjamin Blom, 1967).

100. Symonds accepts, however, as legitimate expressions of love "honest delight in hand-touch, meeting lips, hours of privacy, close personal contact," ibid., 82.

dice underlying the Christian reprobation of Greek love[101] and urged the relevance of ancient Greek homosexuality in disproving the modern conception of homosexuality "as a form of hereditary neuropathy, a link between reason and madness" (34). He suggested that the alleged morbidity of homosexuality reflected the vicious circle of condemning the product of unjust cultural condemnation ("the never-ending hypocrisies and concealments he must practise in order to cloak his indwelling inclination" [74]), rather than the injustice itself. On the other hand, while Symonds denied that all homosexuals were effeminate (15), he discussed at length and credited Ulrichs's theory of male homosexuality as a congenital condition of a female soul in a male body (84–114).[102] Since it was wrong to punish any congenital state, it was wrong, Symonds suggested, to punish homosexuality.[103] Such sexual relations were not inconsistent with human dignity (in part because sodomy was not the exclusive or even common mode of intercourse) (109–11), but their criminalization and reprobation, in violation of "their natural right to toleration" (113), unjustly inflicted on homosexuals an unjust slavery (111–12).

Symonds, who elsewhere characterized Whitman "as more truly Greek than other man of modern times,"[104] introduced Whitman at this point as a way of putting his plea for tolerance in a more positive Hellenic light. Symonds used an interpretation of Whitman as a way of recharacterizing what he theretofore, on the basis of Ulrichs, had discussed as "anomalous, abnormal, vicious, or diseased forms of the emotion which males entertain for males."[105] Whitman, however, offered an alternative model for such love, namely the chivalrous idealization of homoeroticism in service of larger cultural ideals.[106] The only price was that such homoeroticism, to be culturally affirmed in this way, must be asexual. The choice was thus between grudging toleration, on the model of a sexuality rooted in congenital defect, or an affirmative homoerotic identity that was decidedly asexual.

Symonds's thinking about these matters in turn influenced Havelock Ellis's, *Sexual Inversion.*[107] Ellis praised Whitman as one of the archi-

101. See Symonds, *A Problem in Modern Ethics* (1896 edition), 5–7.

102. Symonds offered a more skeptical reading of this view in his posthumously published memoirs; for commentary on this point, see Bristow, *Effeminate England,* 134–37.

103. See Symonds, *A Problem in Modern Ethics* (1896 edition), 99–101, 105, 112.

104. See John Addington Symonds, *Studies of the Greek Poets* (originally published, 1873), reprinted in part in Symonds, *Male Love,* 119–45, 144n.

105. Symonds, *A Problem in Modern Ethics* (1896 edition), 115.

106. Ibid., 115–25.

107. See Ellis and Symonds, *Sexual Inversion,* v–xvi, 1–159.

tects of the modern mind, in particular, his "naturalism . . . the reassertion of the Greek attitude"[108] and his valuation, like Blake,[109] of sex as a human good (122–25). On the other hand, Ellis, like Symonds, interpreted Whitman's praise of love between men as founded on Greek precedents, and thus Whitman failed to take seriously "the degradation of women with which [Greek homosexuality] is always correlated"; indeed, paradoxically, the American poet lamented "the much slighter degradation of women in modern times" (104). In *Sexual Inversion*, Ellis largely followed the etiological position on homosexual preference that Symonds had taken in *A Problem of Modern Ethics*, namely, homosexuality as a congenital abnormality (40–42, 129, 131–32) in both gender and sexuality (119–20).[110] Conduct motivated by such an abnormality was not the proper subject of criminal sanction (153, 155–56), condemning on this ground the recent trial and punishment of Oscar Wilde (156–57). On the other hand, steps might be taken to prevent public homosexuality (158). While Ellis doubted whether steps to cure homosexuality could reasonably or sensibly be taken, he explicitly invoked the example of Whitman for an appropriate asexual idealization of one's homoeroticism—"the ideal of chastity, rather than normal sexuality, which the congenital invert should hold before his eyes" (147).[111] The cultural legitimation of one's homosexuality required celibacy.

Oscar Wilde made a point of visiting Whitman when he lectured in the United States in 1882, telling a batch of reporters, "There is something so Greek and sane about his poetry."[112] Whitman evidently made no effort, as he would later do with Symonds (Whitman and Symonds never met personally), to conceal his homosexuality. Wilde later said: "The kiss of Walt Whitman is still on my lips."[113] Wilde, like Symonds, married and had children, but other than their common Hellenism and homosexuality, the similarity ends there. Symonds lived mainly abroad, did not publish his works on homosexuality to a general public in his lifetime, and, even then, did so in a defensive and ambiva-

108. See Havelock Ellis, *The New Spirit* (Washington, D.C.: National Home Library Foundation Edition, 1935), 106.

109. See Ellis and Symonds, *Sexual Inversion*, 108–9.

110. Ellis questioned, however, whether the abnormality could be well explained by the precise model urged by Ulrichs; see ibid., 131–32. He also distinguished the abnormality of homosexuality from any question of its being a disease. See ibid., 135.

111. For Ellis's discussions of Whitman, see ibid., xiii, 19–21, 142–47.

112. Quoted at Richard Ellmann, *Oscar Wilde* (London: Penguin, 1988), 159–60.

113. Ibid., 163–64.

lent way that certainly was not wholly honest to his convictions.[114] Life
and art were, for Wilde, increasingly one; as he put the point in *De
Profundis,* "What the paradox was to me in the sphere of thought,
perversity became to me in the sphere of passion."[115] Wilde forged a
style of living and writing that explored homosexuality and ironic wit
subversively to question and probe the Victorian rigid boundaries of
gender and class.[116] If the reprobation of male homosexuality was the
ultimate metaphor for the impermeability of masculine gender roles,
Wilde would in his elliptical 1889 story, "The Portrait of Mr. W.H."[117]
at least play with contesting such impermeability, suggesting the humane imaginative value of homosexual passion in producing great artists and art[118] precisely because they enlarge public and private imagination by their fertile explorations of the subtle fascinations of "the
ambiguity of the sexes."[119] Wilde's life would finally imitate his art,[120]
only now with a transparency that left behind elliptical paradoxicality
for a candor worthy of Whitman; in his 1895 speech at his first trial
for consensual homosexual sex acts, Wilde declared:

> The "Love that dare not speak its name" in this century is such a great
> affection of an elder for a younger man as there was between David and
> Jonathan, such as Plato made the very basis of his philosophy, and such as
> you may find in the sonnets of Michaelangelo and Shakespeare. It is that
> deep, spiritual affection that is as pure as it is perfect. . . . It is beautiful, it
> is fine, it is the noblest form of affection. There is nothing unnatural about
> it. It is intellectual; and it repeatedly exists between an older and a younger
> man, when the elder man has intellect, and younger man has all the joy,
> hope, and glamour of life before him. That it should be so the world does
> not understand. The world mocks at it and sometimes puts one in the pillory
> for it.[121]

114. For Symonds's private hopes for and disappointments in Whitman, quite suppressed
in his published writings, see his letters of Edward Carpenter, reprinted in Symonds, *Male
Love,* 149–54; for Symonds's much more frank treatment of these matters in his memoirs
(only published in 1984), see Phyllis Grosskurth, ed., *The Memoirs of John Addington Symonds.*

115. See Oscar Wilde, *De Profundis,* in *Complete Works of Oscar Wilde,* ed. Vyvyan
Holland (New York: Harper & Row, 1989), 913.

116. See, for a magisterial study along these lines, Richard Ellman, *Oscar Wilde;* see
also Jonathan Dollimore, *Sexual Dissidence: Augustine to Wilde, Freud to Foucault* (Oxford:
Clarendon Press, 1991), 307–13; Alan Sinfield, *The Wilde Century,* 1–129; Joseph Bristow,
Effeminate England, 16–54. On Wilde's psychology, see Melissa Knox, *Oscar Wilde: A Long
and Lovely Suicide* (New Haven: Yale University Press, 1994).

117. See Wilde, *Complete Works,* 1150–201.

118. Ibid., 1174–77, 1194–96; cf. Wilde's remarks on Pater, ibid., 1177, 1190.

119. Ibid., 1180.

120. Wilde, of course, originated the phrase, "Life imitates art," in his "The Decay of
Lying," in *The Complete Works,* 970–92, 982.

121. Ellmann, *Oscar Wilde,* 435.

Wilde's model for homosexuality, both in his theory and practice, was decidedly ancient Greek, but after his second trial (the first jury was hung) his conviction and punishment (two years hard labor) were homophobically modernist.[122] He would serve the full sentence, live abroad in exile thereafter, and die, a broken man, at 46 in 1900.[123]

Wilde's trial and punishment were a defining moment in the history of the more public struggle for the rights of gay and lesbian persons. On the hand, it created a moral panic that initiated a period of heightened censorship affecting both advanced women and homosexuals. In 1898, Havelock Ellis's *Sexual Inversion* was successfully prosecuted for obscenity and was never sold in England during Ellis's lifetime. On the other hand, the Wilde trial crystallized the homosexual emancipation movement in Germany, the first such self-consciously political movement.[124] In Germany, under the leadership of Magnus Hirschfeld, the Scientific Humanitarian Committee (founded in 1897) accepted Ulrichs's third sex theory and used the argument of the congenitality of homosexuality as a ground for ending legal persecution. Those, however, in the antifeminist wing of the movement viewed male homosexuality as an expression of male superiority and viewed the Ulrichs-Hirschfeld position as insulting.[125] The Nazi Party regarded homosexuality as inconsistent with appropriately fascist male gender roles and, when it came to power, genocidally warred on it.[126]

Wilde's homosexual Hellenism also crucially influenced the life and work of André Gide. Wilde met Gide in Algiers at a crucial point in Gide's struggles with his homosexuality, helping him to recognize and realize his sexual desires and needs in Gide's first satisfying sexual relationship (with an Arab boy).[127] Wilde, the homosexual transgressive ironist, brought Gide to a sense of authentic personal self-knowledge

122. Ibid., 448–49.
123. Ibid., 450–550.
124. See, for illuminating discussion, Elaine Showalter, *Sexual Anarchy: Gender and Culture in the Fin de Siecle* (New York: Viking, 1990), 168–87; John Lauritsen and David Thorstad, *The Early Homosexual Rights Movement (1864–1935)* (New York: Times Change Press, 1974); James D. Steakley, *The Homosexual Emancipation Movement in Germany* (New York: Arno Press, 1975). For Wilde's influence on German art, see Sander L. Gilman, *Disease and Representation: Images of Illness from Madness to AIDS* (Ithaca: Cornell University Press, 1988), 156–62.
125. See Steakley, *The Homosexual Emancipation Movement in Germany,* 48–49; Greenberg, *The Construction of Homosexuality,* 410.
126. See Steakley, *The Homosexual Emancipation Movement in Germany,* 84, 106, 109–10; see also Richard Plant, *The Pink Triangle: The Nazi War against Homosexuals* (New York: Henry Holt and Co., 1986).
127. For an illuminating discussion of this meeting, see Jonathan Dollimore, *Sexual Dissidence,* 3–18.

that Gide later described as "the very moment I was beginning to discover myself—and in myself the tables of a new law."[128] When a debate over Whitman's homosexuality arose in France, Gide responded by publishing his apologia for homosexuality, *Corydon*,[129] for the general public in 1924. Gide self-consciously sought to propose a model for homosexuality tied not to Ulrichs's third-sex theory (as Proust's was[130]), but appealed, very much in the spirit of Wilde's defense at his first trial, to natural facts and the positive achievements of ancient Greek civilization and its institution of pederasty.[131]

Walt Whitman was as potent an influence on Edward Carpenter as he was on Symonds and Wilde, indeed more so, because Carpenter, who attended Cambridge (not Oxford), did not bring to his relationship to Whitman the distorting prism of the rather doctrinaire Hellenism through which both Symonds and Wilde read Whitman. When Carpenter collected an anthology of readings on homosexual love, he dutifully paid homage to the ancient Greeks' institutionalization of male comradeship,[132] but Whitman was "the inaugurator of a new era to mankind; and it is especially interesting to find that this idea of comradeship, and of its establishment as a *social institution,* plays so important a role with him."[133]

Carpenter had found reading Whitman in 1868 a revelation: "It was not till (at the age of twenty-five) I read Whitman—and then with a great leap of joy—that I met with the treatment of sex which accorded with my sentiments."[134] Finally, in 1873 Carpenter wrote a long letter to Whitman, which Whitman treasured, confessing: "I seem to get very near to his heart and he to mine."[135] The letter suggests several of the larger themes that marked Carpenter's distinctive interpretation of Whitman: a full-hearted rights-based feminism;[136] the practice, not

128. See André Gide, *If It Die . . .* , trans. Dorothy Bussy (London: Penguin, 1977), 298.

129. See André Gide, *Corydon,* trans. Richard Howard (New York: Farrar, Straus, Giroux, 1983).

130. See Gide, *Corydon,* xx. For support for Gide's reading of Proust, see Marcel Proust, *Cities of the Plain,* trans. C. K. Scott Moncrieff (New York: Vintage, 1970), 16–18.

131. See Gide, *Corydon,* 75–126. For useful commentary on Gide, see Wayne R. Dynes, *Encyclopedia of Homosexuality* (New York: Garland, 1990), 1:477–79; Michael Lucey, *Gide's Bent: Sexuality, Politics, Writing* (New York: Oxford University Press, 1995).

132. See Edward Carpenter, *Iolaus: An Anthology of Friendship* (Mitchell: New York, 1917), 188–92.

133. Ibid., 188.

134. See Edward Carpenter, *My Days and Dreams* (London: George Allen & Unwin, 1921), 30.

135. Tsuzuki, *Edward Carpenter,* 29.

136. On Wilde's somewhat contradictory position, see Showalter, *Sexual Anarchy,* 175–76.

just the theory (as in Wilde's case[137]), of socialism; a self-respecting identity as a gay man (Carpenter would live publicly in Britain with his lover for thirty years); skepticism about dominant Western religious orthodoxies including the university and intellectual elites that sustained them; and the need to construct from pluralistic sources an ethically acceptable alternative practice as well as theory of living.[138] The letter, which announced at its end Carpenter's departure from the clergy and the beginning his life with working people, read in pertinent part:

> My chief reason for writing (so I put it to myself) is that I can't help wishing you should know that there are many here in England to whom your writings have been as the waking up to a new day. . . . All that you have said, the thoughts that you have given us, are vital—they will grow—that is certain. You cannot know anything better than that you have spoken the word which is on the lips of God today. . . . There is no hope, almost none, from English respectability. Money eats into it, to the core. The Church is effete. At school the sin which cannot be forgiven is a false quantity. There men are blindly material; even—to the most intellectual—Art and the desire for something like religion are only known as an emotional sense of pain. Yet the women will save us. I wish I could tell you what is being done by them—everywhere—in private and in public. The artisans—too are shaping themselves.
>
> You hardly know, I think, in America (where the life, though as yet material, is so intense) what the relief is here to turn from the languid insanity of the well-fed to the clear hard lines of the workman's face. Yesterday there came (to mend my door) a young workman with the old divine light in his eyes—even I call it old though I am not thirty—and perhaps, more than all, he has made me write to you.
>
> Because you have, as it were, given me a ground for the love of men I thank you continually in my heart. (—And others thank you though they do not say so.) For you have made men to be not ashamed of the noblest instinct of their nature. Women are beautiful; but, to some, there is that which passes the love of women.
>
> It is enough to live wherever the divine beauty of love may flash on men; but indeed its real and enduring light seems infinitely far from us in this our day. Between the splendid dawn of Greek civilization and the high universal noon of Democracy there is a strange horror of darkness on us. We look face to face upon each other, but we do not know. At the last, it is enough to know that the longed-for realization is possible. . . . Slowly—I think—

137. See, for example, for Wilde's quite Hellenic socialism, Oscar Wilde, "The Soul of Man under Socialism," in *Complete Works*, 1079–1104.

138. See, in general, Tsuzuki, *Edward Carpenter;* Sheila Rowbotham and Jeffrey Weeks, *Socialism and the New Light: The Personal and Sexual Politics of Edward Carpenter and Havelock Ellis* (London: Pluto Press, 1977), 25–138; Tony Brown, ed., *Edward Carpenter and Late Victorian Radicalism* (London: Frank Cass, 1990).

the fetters are falling from men's feet, the cramps and crazes of the old superstitions are relaxing, the idiotic ignorance of class contempt is dissipating. If men shall learn to accept one another simply and without complaint, if they shall cease to regard themselves because the emptiness of vanity is filled up with love, and yet shall honor the free, immeasurable gift of their own personality, delight in it and bask in it without false shames and affectations—then your work will be accomplished; and men for the first time will know of what happiness they are capable . . .

As to myself, I was in orders; but I have given that up—utterly. It was no good. Nor does the University do: there is nothing vital in it. Now I am going away to lecture to working men and women in the North. They at least desire to lay hold of something with a real grasp. And I can give something of mathematics and science. It may be of no use, but I shall see . . .

I have finished this at night. All is silent again; and as at first I am yours

Edward Carpenter[139]

Carpenter made what can only be called a pilgrimage to the United States expressly to meet Whitman in 1877 (spending a week with Whitman at his home, and later meeting Emerson as well), and a second visit to meet Thoreau as well as Whitman in 1884.[140] Carpenter discussed both visits in his *Days with Walt Whitman*[141] and emphasized his retrospective sense of Whitman, both in his life and work, as a prophet "annunciative of a new order."[142] Carpenter underscored the pluralistic religious and philosophical sources on which Whitman implicitly drew[143] in order to reveal this new order, in particular, "the Vedic scriptures, and, in lineal succession from these, in the Buddhist and Platonist and Christian writings, in the Taoists of China, the Sufis of Persia, the root is to be found" (77). In one respect, Whitman was even their superior, "that is in the universality of breadth of his appeal. He seems to *liberate* the good tidings and give it a democratic scope and world-wide application unknown in the elder prophets, even in the sayings of Buddha" (78–79). Carpenter explained:

Many things conspired, with him, to this result—the girdling of the earth in his time, and the extraordinary developments of locomotion and intercom-

139. Tsuzuki, *Edward Carpenter*, 30–31.

140. Ibid., 33–34, 55–56.

141. See Edward Carpenter, *Days with Walt Whitman: With Some Notes on His Life and Work* (London: George Allen, 1906); for a related work, concentrating on the relationship of Symonds to Whitman, see Edward Carpenter, *Some Friends of Walt Whitman: A Study in Sex-Psychology* (London: J. E. Francis, Atheneum Press, 1924).

142. Carpenter, *Days with Walt Whitman*, 74.

143. Carpenter conceded: "How much exactly Walt Whitman may have known of the Vedic and other early writings is doubtful; but that he had read here and there among them, quite enough to gain an insight into the heart of them, and to know that his messages was continuous with them, is quite certain." Ibid., 76–77.

munication which were bringing together East and West, and all races and classes, creeds and customs, into close touch and acknowledgement of each other. The peoples were being compelled to see that none of them has a monopoly of excellence or defect, but that all illustrate, in their various ways, forms of necessary life. . . . The fences were breaking down; a new Era was shaping; and Whitman himself, by a nature and temperament of extraordinary balance and fulness, physical, mental, and moral ("I can resist anything better than my own diversity"), was fitted to respond to it all—to swim in this ocean of humanity as in a sea. (82–83)

The theme of "this new Era, with all its splendours and terrors" (84) was both universality and the individuality of moral personality, "an irresistible impulse . . . a strange torrential paean of identity" (86). More even than his superiors

in the matter of pure philosophical statement . . . in two respects at least his work is unique: namely, in the universality and determination of his appeal to, and brotherhood with, all creation, and in his insistence on the root-existence of every Individual from everlasting to everlasting—his protest, in fact . . . , against a mere doctrine of absorption in the Universal. (90–91)

Such prophecy must, in its nature, have an

inevitable spontaneous character, as of something arising from below the ordinary consciousness . . . —something almost inarticulate, hardly gaining the sphere of definition; irrational, and out of joint with accepted things; subversive, inconvenient, contrary. . . . The prophets are stoned; for they are obviously liars and iconoclasts. They are charged with inconsistency, and, poor things! they cannot deny the charge. They cannot help themselves. The flower unfolding out of its own roots cannot unfold other than it does. (74)

Carpenter's mission would be to translate such a mysteriously moving and prophetic moral vision into a theory and practice of social and political reconstruction on grounds of justice.

Carpenter began by publishing a long poem, *Towards Democracy;*[144] closely modeled on *Leaves of Grass*, it was a work Whitman (whose response is unknown) "might well have regarded as an imitation or even plagiarism of his own work."[145] But, he shortly went on to affirm his own distinctive interpretation of Whitman's moral vision by exploring the relevance of Eastern and other modes of inquiry to thinking about these issues[146] and bringing a rights-based feminism

144. See Edward Carpenter, *Towards Democracy* (1883; London: George Allen & Unwin, 1912).

145. See Tsuzuki, *Edward Carpenter,* 45.

146. See Edward Carpenter, *From Adam's Peak to Elephanta: Sketches in Ceylon and India* (London: George Allen & Unwin, 1892), 143, 133–35, 163–81, 170, 177–81 (superiority of Western emphasis on Love, as in Whitman, over Eastern emphasis on Will). For later developments of a similar kind of speculative inquiry, see Edward Carpenter, *The Art of*

centrally to bear on the critical examination of issues of sexuality and gender roles.[147]

In his autobiography *My Days and Dreams,* Carpenter wrote of his indignation at the wasted lives of his unmarried sisters: "More than once girls of whom I least expected it told me that their lives were miserable 'with nothing on earth to do.' Multiply this picture by thousands and hundreds of thousands all over the country, and it is easy to see how, when the causes of the misery were understood, it led to the powerful growth of the modern 'Women's Movement.' "[148] Carpenter, consistent with the American abolitionist feminists, analyzed such injustice in the condition of woman as her subjection to a moral slavery, "reducing her . . . to a mere chattel, a slave and a plaything."[149] Such unjust degradation depended both on the abridgment of basic human rights of "the self-dependence and self-ownership of women" (100) and the enforcement of a sectarian conception of gender roles that, in effect, created reality in its own image, making women "into a separate species from man—so that in the later civilizations the males and females, except when the sex-attraction has compelled them as it were to come together, have been wont to congregate in separate herds, and talk languages each unintelligible to the other" (45).[150] For the socialist Carpenter, like Emma Goldman later, the key structural feature of such injustice was depriving women of both sexual and economic independence, reflected in the demonization of the prostitute for her violation of both unjustly gender-defined imperatives (her sexual freedom and her earning money). To attack such injustice frontally, women must acknowledge the common grounds of rights-based principle applicable to all women and no longer acquiesce in the use of "free love" or "free woman" as terms of abuse:

Creation: Essays on the Self and Its Powers (London: George Allen & Unwin, 1904); id., *The Drama of Love and Death: A Study of Human Evolution and Transfiguration* (New York: Mitchell Kennerley, 1912); id., *Pagan and Christian Creeds: Their Origin and Meaning* (New York: Harcourt, Brace, 1920).

147. See Edward Carpenter, *Woman, and Her Place in a Free Society* (Manchester: Labour Press Society, 1894); id., *Marriage in Free Society* (Manchester: Labour Press Society, 1894); id., *Love's Coming of Age: A Series of Papers on the Relations of the Sexes* (1896; New York: Vanguard Press, 1926).

148. See Carpenter, *My Days and Dreams,* 32.

149. See Carpenter, *Love's Coming of Age,* 39; see also ibid., 38–39, 44, 46, 48, 60–62, 106.

150. E. M. Forster, a friend of Carpenter's, elaborates this theme in his novel *Howards End* in the rumination of Margaret Schlegel: "Are the sexes really races, each with its own code of morality, and their mutual love a mere device of Nature to keep things going?" E. M. Forster, *Howards End* (1910; New York: Vintage, 1989), 251–52.

> Let every woman whose heart bleeds for the sufferings of her sex, hasten
> to declare herself and to constitute herself, as far as she possibly can, a free
> woman. Let her accept the term with all the odium that belongs to it; let
> her insist on her right to speak, dress, think, act, and above all to use her
> sex, as she deems best; let her face the scorn and the ridicule; let her "lose
> her own life" if she likes; assured that only so can come deliverance, and
> that only when the free women is honored will the prostitute cease to exist.
> And let every man who really would respect his counterpart, entreat her also
> to act so; let him never by word or deed tempt her to grant as a bargain
> what can only be precious as a gift; let him see her with pleasure stand a
> little aloof; let him help her to gain her feet; so at last, by what slight sacrifices
> on his part such a course may involve, will it dawn upon him that he has
> gained a real companion and helpmate on life's journey. (62–63)

Carpenter's innovative next step was, consistent with our earlier interpretation of the roots of Whitman's argument in rights-based feminism, to extend this analysis to homosexuals. In effect, the injustice of the reprobation of prostitutes, as fallen women, applied, *a fortiori*, to homosexuals, also socially understood as fallen women. Carpenter made this point assuming, for purposes of argument, Ulrichs's intermediate sex model for homosexuality (114–30). While Carpenter expressed some skepticism about the terms, soul and body, on which the model depended, he credited it, as a working hypothesis, because it had at least made an attempt "to recognise the existence of what might called an Intermediate sex, and to give at any rate *some* explanation of it" (115). Lesbians or gay men represent, on this view, unconventionally larger components of masculine or feminine temperament in, respectively, a female or male body. Carpenter's larger argument of rights-based feminism had critically urged that

> the sexes do not or should not normally form two groups hopelessly isolated
> in habit and feeling from one another, but that they should represent the
> two poles of *one* group—which is the human race; so that while certainly
> the extreme specimens at either pole are vastly divergent, there are great
> numbers in the middle region who (though differing corporeally as men and
> women) are by emotional and temperament very near to each other. (112)

Lesbians and gay men were, for Carpenter, simply a variation on this theme: women or men, respectively, with larger components of male or female temperament, and therefore as much entitled as any other woman or man not to be unjustly limited to a rigidly defined sphere. Indeed, since homosexuals were in this way endowed with the temperament of the opposite gender, "these people become to a great extent the interpreters of men and women to each other" (113). Homosexuality was thus politically valorized as a way of assisting what rights-based feminism required, breaking down rights-denying boundaries of gender.

Carpenter further elaborated these themes in his more extensive considerations of "the intermediate sex."[151] Taking Whitman on love between men as his biblical text,[152] Carpenter again framed his discussion of homosexuality in terms of the rights-based feminist case for changing sex roles. Homosexuals act as translators and interpreters[153] so that men and women will no longer "absolutely cease to understand each other."[154] To make his emancipatory point, Carpenter offered interpretations of two theses central to Whitman's rights-based case for homosexual love: first, its legitimacy as a public identity; and second, its contributions to the theory and practice of democracy.

On the first point, much of Carpenter's discussion of gay men and lesbians, like his comparable discussions of heterosexual women, uncritically reflected rather than contested dominant gender stereotypes. Just as he often took gender differences as fixed points[155] and celebrated, following Whitman,[156] motherhood as women's great work,[157] his discussion of gay men and lesbians, like the work of Ulrichs that he accepted as a working hypothesis, took as uncritical fixed points dominant stereotypes of homosexual men as largely effeminate and of lesbians as masculine.[158] But within these limits, Carpenter, in contrast to Symonds and Ellis and even Wilde, was struggling to forge a new kind of discourse for gay and lesbian persons that did not depend on an anachronistic and often quite misogynist Hellenism,[159] but on central principles of rights-based feminism and the legitimate role that homosexual personal and moral identity should play in that struggle. Carpenter thus included women in the network of love; in addition, Carpenter recognized that it was absurd to restrict any form of love (including homosexual love) to a kind of philosophical, intellectual affinity, as Sy-

---

151. See Edward Carpenter, *The Intermediate Sex: A Study of Some Transitional Types of Men and Women* (New York: Mitchell Kennerley, 1912); id., *Intermediate Types among Primitive Folk* (London: George Allen & Unwin, 1919).

152. See Carpenter, *The Intermediate Sex*, 44, 70–72, 109–10.

153. Ibid., 36, 113–14.

154. Ibid., 17.

155. See Carpenter, *Love's Coming of Age*, 30–31, 42–43, 52–53, 59.

156. Ibid., 65, 71.

157. Ibid., 56, 68. For further criticism along these lines, see Showalter, *Sexual Anarchy*, 172–74; Brown, *Edward Carpenter and Late Victorian Radicalism*, 113–15, 119, 122.

158. See Carpenter, *The Intermediate Sex*, 25–30.

159. Carpenter even struggled to show that ancient Greek homosexuality was not, as Symonds had suggested, rooted in misogyny; see Carpenter, *Intermediate Types among Primitive Folk*, 105–10.

monds and Ellis had suggested; instead, he advocated the development of complex relationships involving a constellation of physical, mental, and spiritual elements.[160] Importantly, while Carpenter carefully reviewed all the uses to which many cultures had put the homosexual role (ranging from shaman to military comradeship to cultivating new plateaus of artistic and intellectual genius),[161] the case he made for the modern world was a rights-based argument that linked the case for the legitimacy of a public identity for gays and lesbians to the case for respecting the rights of free women. Carpenter thus perceptively observed the grounds of principle that sometimes linked the struggle for the rights of free women to the struggle for lesbian identity:

> It is noticeable, too, in this deepest relation to politics that the movement among women towards their own liberation and emancipation, which is taking place all over the civilised world, has been accompanied by a marked development of the homogenic passion among the female sex. It may be said that a certain strain in the relations between the opposite sexes which has come about owing to a growing consciousness among women that they have been oppressed and unfairly treated by men, and a growing unwillingness to ally themselves unequally in marriage—that this strain has caused the womenkind to draw more closely together and to cement alliances of their own. But whatever the cause may be it is pretty certain that such comrade-alliances—and of quite devoted kind—are becoming increasingly common and especially perhaps among the more cultured classes of women, who are working out the great cause of their sex's liberation; nor is it difficult to see the importance of such alliances in such a campaign. In the United States where the battle of women's independence is also being fought, the tendency mentioned is as strongly marked.[162]

Carpenter's plea for homosexual love was, like that of his teacher Whitman, at bottom a plea for quite basic human rights of conscience, speech, association, and work, the rights the free exercise of which express respect for our powers of moral personality. It was for this reason, I believe, that the only cultural stereotype about homosexuals that Carpenter *was* careful to criticize was that which reduced them to sex acts in general or one sex act in particular,[163] because he quite properly understood that their dehumanization turned, like the comparable dehumanization of women, on such obsessive sexualization. In contrast, Carpenter emphasized the dimensions of emotion (friendship

---

160. See Carpenter, *The Drama of Love and Death*, 36–37.
161. See, in general, Carpenter, *Intermediate Types among Primitive Folk*.
162. See Carpenter, *The Intermediate Sex*, 72–73.
163. Ibid., 25–30, 54, 65, 74; *Intermediate Types among Primitive Folk*, 164–65; *Love's Coming of Age*, 120. On Carpenter's distaste for sodomy, see Brown, *Edward Carpenter and Late Victorian Radicalism*, 107.

and love), intellect, imagination, and moral and political reasoning and conduct that the legitimacy of a public gay or lesbian identity would bring to public life and the range of different forms of and attitudes to sexuality that such identity involved. He was, unlike Symonds and Ellis but like Whitman, not concerned for a mere grudging toleration for sex acts, but for the equal dignity of the moral personality of gays and lesbians on terms of justice, equal rights, and opportunities for homosexualities as complex and varied and humane as heterosexualities. On this ground, Carpenter quite properly advocated the extension to homosexuals of the right to same-sex marriage[164] (see chapter 8).

Such respect for the moral personality of gays and lesbians would, in turn, make significant contributions to democracy along the lines Whitman had suggested. We have already seen the specific role homosexuals would, in Carpenter's view, play in the struggle for the rights of women. In public life, their independence of traditional family roles might also inspire desirable forms of larger political participation and action[165] across traditional barriers of class[166] in the interest of humanity as such.[167] And in private life, the weight they place on personal love, as an end in itself, might afford a desirable model of the intrinsic value of love for the larger society.[168] In addition, history would suggest that recognition of such a legitimate identity might be "a cradle of social chivalry and heroic life"[169] and foster desirable forms of creative cultural freedom from which all would profit.[170]

Carpenter also entertained more speculative views based on Lamarckian principles of psychological evolution through states of consciousness.[171] Love, for Carpenter, was the primary means of regeneration by which individuals were able to escape the bounds of self-interest and to achieve higher levels of perception.[172] The cultivation of love as a "gracious, superb, and necessary part of our lives" became a means of achieving desirable political and social change.[173] Homosexuals, because they took love so seriously as an end in itself, would, on Lamarckian evolutionary principles, play a central role in this pro-

164. Carpenter, *The Intermediate Sex*, 76–77, 119.
165. Ibid., 68–69.
166. Ibid., 72–73.
167. Ibid., 107–10.
168. Ibid., 114–15, 119–21.
169. Ibid., 67.
170. See Carpenter, *Intermediate Types among Primitive Folk*, 57–60, 171–74.
171. See Carpenter, *The Art of Creation*, chap. 4; id., *Pagan and Christian Creeds*, chap. 14.
172. See Carpenter, *The Drama of Love and Death*, 284–85.
173. Ibid., 34.

cess of desirable expansion of moral consciousness, including a role as transformative moral leaders.[174]

Carpenter was an important figure in the development of British socialism[175] and more recently a central figure in the British movement for the rights of gay and lesbian persons.[176] His work set the framework for discussion of these issues in Britain. Radclyffe Hall's important lesbian novel, *The Well of Loneliness*, interpreted its central relationship very much in terms of his intermediate sex theory.[177] E. M. Forster, who was a friend of Carpenter's (Forster's gay affirmative novel, *Maurice*, was inspired by a visit to Carpenter's home, Millthorpe),[178] would certainly have had Carpenter in mind when he introduced his defense of Democracy in terms of Swinburne's linkage: "Even love, the beloved Republic, that feeds upon freedom and lives."[179] Writing for a more skeptical age when democracy was more seriously at threat than Carpenter, a late Victorian, could have imagined, Forster denied that Democracy was a Beloved Republic "and never will be."[180] But, it de-

---

174. See, for example, Carpenter, *Intermediate Types among Primitive Folk*, 82–83. For commentary, see Rowbotham and Weeks, *Socialism and the New Life*, 111; Brown, *Edward Carpenter and Late Victorian Radicalism*, 5–6.

175. See, in general, Brown, *Edward Carpenter and Late Victorian Radicalism;* Sheila Rowbotham and Jeffrey Weeks, *Socialism and the New Life*.

176. See, for good general treatments, Jeffrey Weeks, *Sex, Politics, and Society: The Regulation of Sexuality since 1800*, 2d ed. (London: Longman, 1981); *Coming Out: Homosexual Politics in Britain from the Nineteenth Century to the Present*, rev. ed. (London: Quartet Books, 1990).

177. See Radclyffe Hall, *The Well of Loneliness* (1928; London: Virago Press, 1982), 23, 207, 301. The novel, of course, had the unhappy ending that the culture of the period apparently required, and was, in any event, banned as obscene in Britain. See Una, Lady Troubridge, *The Life and Death of Radclyffe Hall* (London: Hammond, 1961), 93–94; on Hall's friendship with Noel Coward, see Terry Castle, *Noel Coward and Radclyffe Hall: Kindred Spirits* (New York: Columbia University Press, 1996). For Henry James's earlier, more elliptical treatment of similar material (in the passion of Olive Chancellor for Verena Tarrant, ending, of course, unhappily with Tarrant's marriage to Basil Ransom), see Henry James, *The Bostonians* (1885–86; London: Penguin, 1986). Later comparable American novels by gay men have similarly unhappy endings. See Gore Vidal, *The City and the Pillar* (1948; London: Andre Deutsch 1994); James Baldwin, *Giovanni's Room* (New York: Laurel, 1956). For a more recent, rather happier autobiographical treatment, see Paul Monette, *Becoming a Man: Half a Life Story* (New York: HarperCollins, 1993).

178. See Rowbotham and Weeks, *Socialism and the New Life*, 123–25, 127–28. See also E. M. Forster, *Maurice* (Toronto: Macmillan, 1971). For useful commentary on Forster's fiction from the perspective of his homosexuality, see Bristow, *Effeminate England*, 55–99.

179. Cited in E. M. Forster, "What I Believe," in E. M. Forster, *Two Cheers for Democracy* (New York: Harcourt, Brace, & World, 1938), 69. There is no reference in this text; the poet is, in fact, Swinburne, and the poem "Hertha"; for the citation, see Swinburne, "Hertha," in *The Complete Works of Algernon Charles Swinburne*, ed. Sir Edmund Gosse and Thomas James Wise (London: William Heinemann, 1925), 2:137–45, 2:144.

180. See Forster, "What I Believe," 69.

served our support not only because "less hateful than other contemporary forms of government," but because, at bottom, it starts "from the assumption that the individual is important, and that all types are needed to make a civilisation."[181] Carpenter, interpreting Whitman, was one of the architects of that increasingly powerful, sexually pluralistic assumption in Britain and Europe, leading in Britain to the decriminalization of homosexuality in 1967.[182] America, founded in 1787 and refounded in 1865–70 on rights-based revolutionary constitutionalism, was sadly a very different story.

Whitman at Home

The role that the interpretation of Whitman played in the development of European thought on homosexuality had no correlative development in Whitman's own country. A homosexual subculture flourished in cities like New York in the period 1890–1940,[183] but as one American commentator noted with dismay in 1913: "It is rather odd that homosexuals, at least in America, do not regard Whitman as one of themselves or brag about him."[184] Europeans (Carpenter prominently among them), not Americans, in the early twentieth century publicly connected Whitman with homosexuality.[185] Whitman played a role within the thriving New York City gay subculture in arguments for a more masculine interpretation of homosexual love[186] or as evidence of a larger gay culture;[187] the Spanish gay poet, Federico García Lorca, made this latter point ("the faggots, Walt Whitman, point you out") in his harrowing "Ode to Whitman" written on the basis of the Spanish gay poet's visit to New York City during this period.[188] But Lorca's dark picture of gay life in early twentieth-century New York City made a devastating comparative point about the repressive state of American culture in this period by its ironic counterpoint to Whitman's generously optimistic antebellum vision of the promise that gay life in his

181. Ibid.

182. For discussion, see Weeks, *Coming Out*, 168–82.

183. See, in general, George Chauncey, *Gay New York: Gender, Urban Culture, and the Making of the Gay Male World, 1890–1940* (New York: BasicBooks, 1994).

184. Reynolds, *Walt Whitman's America*, 579.

185. Ibid.

186. See George Chauncey, *Gay New York*, 104–5.

187. Ibid., 284–85.

188. See Federico García Lorca, *Poet in New York*, trans. Greg Simon and Steven White (New York: Noonday Press, 1988), 157. I am grateful to Professor Jose Luis Colomer, who brought this poem and its significance to my attention during a recent visit to New York City from Madrid.

beloved New York City held for democratic life in America, concluding:

And you, lovely Walt Whitman, stay asleep on the Hudson's banks
with your beard toward the pole, openhanded.
Soft clay or snow, your tongue calls for
comrades to keep watch over your unbodied gazelle.

Sleep on, nothing remains.
Dancing walls stir the prairies
and America drowns itself in machinery and lament.[189]

The published texts using Whitman to address the larger culture in explicitly gay affirmative terms were mainly European, particularly those of Carpenter and the work of the German homosexual emancipationist Magnus Hirschfeld.[190] Ironically, whatever self-conscious political organization there was around the issues of gay rights during this period in the United States was inspired by travels in Europe. Take, for example, the short-lived homosexual-rights group, the Society for Human Rights, which was organized by the writer Henry Gerber in Chicago in 1924 and was promptly suppressed by the Chicago police.[191] In 1932 Gerber denounced American repression in contrast to European (in particular, French and German) toleration. He noted that many "homosexuals live in happy, blissful unions, especially in Europe, where homosexuals are unmolested as long as they mind their own business, and are not, as in England and in the United States, driven to the underworld of perversions and crime for satisfaction of their very real craving for love."[192]

If Whitman was not during this period self-consciously invoked in America (as he was in Europe) as the democratic prophet of homosexual love, he was notably claimed as a source of inspiration for the development of more inclusively democratic American culture by leading figures in the Harlem renaissance and associated movements of black and socialist emancipation.[193] Both the black gay critic, Alain Locke, and the poet, Langston Hughes, interpreted Whitman as making possible a distinctive form of black protest and art, one that, in Locke's

189. Ibid., 163.
190. See Chauncey, *Gay New York,* 107, 144, 231, 284, 285.
191. Ibid., 144–45.
192. Ibid., *Gay New York,* 144–45.
193. For an informative treatment of this influence, see George Hutchinson, *The Harlem Renaissance in Black and White* (Cambridge: Harvard University Press, 1995), 40–41, 107–10, 138–39, 141, 150, 251–56, 282–85, 319, 410, 414–16.

case, self-consciously included a revolt against American puritanism.[194] Even if covertly, Whitman thus was interpreted by leading gay figures in the ongoing American antiracist struggle as making possible a distinctive procedure and substance of critical voice and protest.

The repressiveness of American political culture during this period was very much framed by a development we have already explored and criticized at some length: the compromises of rights-based principle central to the alliance of suffrage feminism with the temperance and the purity movements, typified by the obscenity prosecutions of advocates of free love and contraception and the striking success of the purity movement in the repression of prostitution.[195] In the gender symbolism current in the period, advocacy of homosexuality was regarded as obscene and homosexual activity, as prostitution.[196] ("Gay," for example, etymologically derived from the self-referring slang of female prostitutes.[197]) After their success in repressing prostitution proper, the purity leagues turned their repressive focus on gay activity and were as generally uncontradicted in their sectarian political moralism there as they had been earlier.[198]

The exception that proves the rule was, of course, Emma Goldman. Goldman was a publicly articulate advocate not only of the right to contraception but of homosexuality,[199] and acknowledged the influence on her thought of the poetry of Whitman.[200] The authorities would not "tolerate her speaking publicly on homosexuality and on how to practice birth control,"[201] using obscenity prosecutions to silence her; she was eventually deported. Her advocacy of these positions was very much of a piece with her opposition to both suffrage feminism and the purity movement. Suffrage feminism's exclusive focus on voting rights, including its alliance with the temperance and purity movements, had led to its outright hostility to the deeper issues of women's human rights, including the rights to economic independence and to

194. On the appeal of Whitman for Locke along these lines, see George Hutchinson, *The Harlem Renaissance in Black and White*, 40–41, 109–10, 282–83; on the appeal of Whitman for Hughes, see ibid., 414–16.

195. On this latter development, see, in general, Gilfoyle, *City of Eros: New York City, Prostitution, and the Commercialization of Sex, 1790–1920*.

196. See Chauncey, *Gay New York*, 61, 67, 69–70, 81–85, 97, 185–86, 286.

197. Ibid., 286.

198. Ibid., 138–41, 143, 146–49.

199. Ibid., 231–32.

200. See Drinnon, *Rebel in Paradise*, 160–62; see also Richard and Anna Maria Drinnon, *Nowhere at Home*, 140–41.

201. See Alix Shulman, "The Most Dangerous Woman in the World," in Emma Goldman, *The Traffic in Women and Other Essays on Feminism* (New York: Times Change Press, 1970), 13.

love.[202] The purity leagues had unjustly demonized prostitution, enforcing on society at large a sectarian conception of gender and sexuality that rationalized, rather than contested, the abridgment of basic human rights of women.[203] If any person were capable of forging in America the kind of "comrade-alliances" between homosexuals and women that Carpenter had earlier urged in Britain, it was and would have been Goldman. But, in America, Goldman's views were interpreted as those of an antifeminist (meaning an antisuffrage feminist) and an anti-American to boot. There was no public space in America, whose once searing abolitionist feminist vision of the human rights of women had been trivialized to the measure of suffrage feminism, for Emma Goldman and the alternative rights-based feminist tradition that she might, interpreting Whitman (as Carpenter had), have eloquently embodied for Americans. Carpenter's proposed rights-based alliances between women and homosexuals could hardly be even plausible in America in light of the trajectory of suffrage feminism into increasing hostility to rights-based feminism as such. A culture of American censorship had rendered Goldman's inspiration, Whitman, as Edith Wharton sadly noted, an obscenity to be "kept under lock and key, and brought out, like tobacco, only in the absence of 'the ladies,' to whom the name of Walt Whitman was unmentionable, if not utterly unknown."[204] While Whitman was an influence on women artists like Wharton and Kate Chopin,[205] this was very much against the grain of America's repressive conception of women's proper roles.

This repressive culture of censorship effectively cut off any possibility of exploring links between arguments for feminism and gay rights. (Radclyffe Hall's explicitly lesbian novel, for example, had been declared obscene.[206]) Undoubtedly, there were strong, sometimes implicitly or explicitly lesbian connections among various women involved in the struggles of abolitionist and suffrage feminism and their aftermath, but their practice could not, in this repressive cultural environment, be theorized and publicly defended, as it would later be, as a

202. For important statements of this position, see Emma Goldman, "Woman Suffrage" and "The Tragedy of Woman's Emancipation," in *Anarchism and Other Essays,* 195–211, 213–25.

203. For important statements of this position, see Emma Goldman, "The Hypocrisy of Puritanism" and "The Traffic in Women," in *Anarchism and Other Essays,* 167–94.

204. See Edith Wharton, *The Uncollected Critical Writings,* ed. Frederick Wegener (Princeton: Princeton University Press, 1996), 282.

205. See Kenneth M. Price, *Whitman and Tradition: The Poet in His Century* (New Haven: Yale University Press, 1990), 114–21.

206. See Una, Lady Troubridge, *The Life and Death of Radclyffe Hall* (London: Hammond, 1961), 93–94.

lesbian alternative central to rights-based feminism.[207] Gertrude Stein could in France develop a hermetic style that we now understand to encode lesbian material,[208] as could Virginia Woolf in Britain.[209] And Woolf would implicitly draw upon her lesbian experience[210] to write her important feminist statement, A Room of One's Own.[211] The later development of lesbian feminism, as an interpretation of second wave feminism, thus had its roots in the lesbian practice, if not the explicit theory, of these earlier feminists.

Matters were not helped by the fact that leading advocates of more humane treatment of homosexuals (Ulrichs, Symonds, Ellis, and even Carpenter himself) had advocated a model of homosexuality as a congenital abnormality. Even respected European psychiatrists like Richard von Krafft-Ebing linked homosexuality to a Lamarckian history of past ancestors' hypersexualized degeneracy.[212] While Krafft-Ebing, like the progay advocates, called for decriminalization of homosexuality on the ground of a psychiatric abnormality for which the agent bore no responsibility,[213] the model itself reinforced the stereotypes on which the traditional moral reprobation of homosexuality uncritically rested. Krafft-Ebing had thus idealized monogamous, heterosexual marriage in terms worthy of the American antipolygamy movement;[214] Ulrichs's model of gay men (as women) and lesbians (as men) replicated the traditionally stereotypical grounds for moral reprobation (a degradation of men to women, or women to men).

Gender-stereotypical interpretations of homosexuality were thus

207. For an important general treatment, see Lillian Faderman, Surpassing the Love of Men: Romantic Friendship and Love Between Women from the Renaissance to the Present (New York: William Morrow, 1981), 145–415. See also Lilliam Faderman, Odd Girls and Twilight Lovers: A History of Lesbian Life in Twentieth-Century America (New York: Columbia University Press, 1991).

208. On Stein, see Lillian Faderman, ed., Chloe Plus Olivia: An Anthology of Lesbian Literature from the Seventeenth Century to the Present (New York: Viking, 1994), 452–59.

209. On Woolf, see ibid., 489–97. See, in general, for many other examples, Faderman, Chloe Plus Olivia, 17–544.

210. Ibid., 491–92.

211. See Virginia Woolf, A Room of One's Own (New York: Harcourt, Brace, 1929).

212. See Richard von Krafft-Ebing, Psychopathia Sexualis, trans. Franklin S. Klaf (1886; New York: Bell Publishing Co., 1965), 186–307. Krafft-Ebing revised his views in 1901 to the effect that homosexuality was not a manifestation of degeneracy or pathology, but could occur in otherwise normal subjects. But the retraction written shortly before his death did little to alter the public's impression—twelve editions of his book had by then been translated into many languages. See Wayne R. Dynes, ed., Encyclopedia of Homosexuality (New York: Garland Publishing, Inc., 1990), 1:668–69.

213. See Krafft-Ebing, 334–35, 381–88.

214. See, for illuminating discussion, Sander L. Gilman, Difference and Pathology: Stereotypes of Sexuality, Race, and Madness (Ithaca: Cornell University Press, 1985), 197–98.

hardened into medical granite and could themselves easily be uncritically used by some progay advocates as the basis for rationalizing disdain for the opposite gender: the man who identified with other men
was more valuable as a man, or more manly.[215] Such misogyny on the
part of gay affirmative advocates further widened the yawning chasm
between them and feminists of the period, who could hardly find any
reasonable common ground in what amounted to unjust mutual contempt between the two groups.

The most extraordinary development of such an interpretation into
a radical metaphysical misogyny was Otto Weininger's *Sex and Character*.[216] (Compared to Weininger, Schopenhauer's notorious misogyny
was moderate.[217]) Interpreting his own homosexuality in Ulrichs's
terms,[218] Weininger advocated decriminalization of homosexuality[219]
and argued its existence was not an illness but a human adaptation
(46–47, citing Krafft-Ebing's change of view on this issue). He also
morally idealized the contributions of gays and lesbians to human culture. His argument postulated that all people have differing components of the mutually exclusive properties, male and female, and that
maximum sexual attraction was determined by a person seeking in the
other what he or she lacks in these properties (a homosexual man,
predominantly feminine, thus sought men because they best comple-
mented his needs for masculinity) (29–31). Gay men, having less need
for women, were more ethically impartial about issues of gender (57)
(lesbians were morally superior because they were masculine [66]),
and on this basis Weininger rationalized as metaphysical truths highly
personal misogynist fantasies of women as sexually rapacious (88–89,
92, 102), lacking a soul (186–213) or any of the properties of the soul
(including memory, identity, and logic [145–52]), and therefore lacking the Kantian capacity for ethics (153–62, 177, 210, 331). Ostensible
moral reasoning in women was duplicitous (260), parroting (262–63),
and a hysterical parody (278). The "nullity and inanity of women" (294)
explained, in turn, the feminized inferiority of non-Aryan races (302)

215. See Elaine Showalter, *Sexual Anarchy*, 172–74; Bram Dijkstra, *Idols of Perversity:
Fantasies of Feminine Evil in Fin-de-Siecle Culture* (New York: Oxford University Press,
1986), 200–209.
216. Otto Weininger, *Sex and Character* (London: William Heinemann, 1907).
217. See Arthur Schopenhauer, "On Women," *Essays and Aphorisms,* trans. R. J. Hollindale (Harmondsworth: Penguin, 1970), 80–88.
218. Weininger, *Sex and Character,* 45–52. On Weininger's life and early suicide, see
David Abrahamsen, *The Mind and Death of a Genius* (New York: Columbia University Press,
1946).
219. Weininger, *Sex and Character,* 51.

and of the Jews (Weininger was also Jewish) (306).[220] The only hope for humankind, preserving the uniquely masculine competence for high culture and Kantian ethics untainted by feminine hypersexualized degradation of our higher powers, would be to give up coitus (336–37, 343, 345–47).

This farrago would be more amusing and less disturbing had it not been taken so seriously—reading Weininger, for example, pivotally influenced Ludwig Wittgenstein[221] and shaped the thought of Sigmund Freud.[222] Notably, its argument pointedly discredited the emancipation of women as, in Weininger's terms, "a prostitute emancipation."[223] Charlotte Perkins Gilman, the American feminist, was baffled at the book's paradoxical marriage of elevated metaphysical ideality with the crudest sexist stereotyping of women: "a mystical exaltation of the ideal, with an unspeakable grossness in apprehension of the real."[224] A feminist like Gilman could barely understand, let alone find common ground with, a gay affirmative advocate like Weininger, whose affirmation of homosexuality required the radical dehumanization of women, blacks, and Jews. That even Carpenter could endorse Weininger's model (as serving the goals of the homosexual rights movement) indicates the extent of the problem.[225]

The case of Weininger brings out in more dramatic form a problematic feature of all the gay affirmative views we have so far examined: their uncritical dependence on a model of homosexuality that reflects, rather than contests, the unjust gender stereotyping to which homosexuals have been subjected. The rights-based case for gay and lesbian identity is thus subverted while, for this very reason, the rights-denying evils of sexism, racism, and anti-Semitism are advanced.

Weininger's argument starkly illustrates in a different context the

220. For Weininger on Chamberlain, see ibid., 303, 312, 314, 325, 328; on Richard Wagner and German anti-Semitism, see ibid., 304–6, 319, 344; on Jewish anti-Semitism, see ibid., 304.

221. See, for example, Ray Monk, *Ludwig Wittgenstein: The Duty of Genius* (New York: Free Press, 1990), 19–25.

222. See Sander L. Gilman, *Freud, Race, and Gender* (Princeton: Princeton University Press, 1993), 77–92, 154; id., *Jewish Self-Hatred: Anti-Semitism and the Hidden Language of the Jews* (Baltimore: Johns Hopkins University Press, 1986), 250–51, 267–69, 293–94.

223. Weininger, *Sex and Character*, 332; on not giving women suffrage, see ibid., 339. See, in general, on homosexual antifeminism during this period, Dijkstra, *Idols of Perversity*, 200–209.

224. See Charlotte Perkins Gilman, "Dr. Weininger's 'Sex and Character'," in *The Critic*, 48, no. 5 (May, 1906), 416.

225. See Carpenter, *The Intermediate Sex*, 5, 155–56. For Carpenter on women's primitiveness, see Bram Dijkstra, *Idols of Perversity*, 242–43.

general rights-denying dynamic that results from the abandoning of a principled normative perspective on the platform of human rights. The failure of political abolitionists to condemn sexism on the same basis as racism rendered their antiracism shallow and culturally reinforced the degradation of women; the compromise by suffrage feminists of antiracist principles worsened American racism and rendered their antisexism increasingly vapid; their abandonment of rights-based feminism in general led to their uncritical idealization of unjust gender roles, and to their aggressive war on basic claims to human rights of women, including various aspects of the right to love, as Sanger bitterly complained.[226] Similarly, Weininger's idealization of a gender-stereotypical interpretation of homosexuality not only failed to address the central issues in the abridgment of the human rights of gays and lesbians, but enforced uncritical gender stereotypes of women as morally depraved as the basis for the dehumanization of women, racial minorities, and Jews. The study of Weininger, a classic figure in the history of European anti-Semitism (including Jewish anti-Semitism),[227] thus offers insight into the intersectionality of the unjust cultural and political construction of irrationalist prejudices based, as they often are, on rights-denying culturally and politically enforced stereotypes of difference.

Anti-Semitism, as we earlier saw, was regarded as a paradigm exemplar of such irrationalist prejudice by the American radical abolitionists because its history so clearly exemplified the intolerance condemned by a principled understanding of the argument for toleration: first, the abridgment of the basic rights of a group; second, the rationalization of such abridgment on grounds that were themselves the consequences of the history of such abridgment. The radical abolitionists generalized this analysis to condemn racism, and the abolitionist feminists among them extended the theory, as we have seen, to sexism. In all these cases, the vicious circle in question had dehumanized an entire class of persons from their status as bearers of basic human rights. The irrationalist political force of such prejudices was shown by the ways in which any doubts that might now be raised about the political order

226. See Margaret Sanger, *Woman and the New Race* (1920; Elmsford, N.Y.: Maxwell Reprint Company, 1969), 2, 94–95, 186–97, 210–11.

227. For useful general studies, see Sander L. Gilman, *Difference and Pathology: Stereotypes of Sexuality, Race, and Madness* (Ithaca: Cornell University Press, 1985); id., *Jewish Self-Hatred: Anti-Semitism and the Hidden Language of the Jews* (Baltimore: The Johns Hopkins University Press, 1986); id., *Disease and Representation: Images of Illness from Madness to AIDS* (Ithaca: Cornell University Press, 1988); id., *Freud, Race, and Gender* (Princeton: Princeton University Press, 1993).

enforcing such unjust stereotypes (in light of movements self-consciously opposing anti-Semitism, racism, and sexism) were not reasonably allowed debate and discussion, consistent with respect for human rights and the role of public reason in constitutionally legitimate politics. Rather, the paradox of intolerance aggressively repressed any such doubts through the illegitimate enforcement at large of now-embattled sectarian readings of facts and values that remade reality in their own irrationalist image. Victims were thus imaginatively transformed into aggressors, slavery into freedom, terror and even genocide into self-defense.

Weininger's pivotal use of gender stereotypy dehumanized women, non-Aryans, and Jews, and, as I earlier suggested, homosexuals. His argument thus illustrates the rights-denying intersectionality of such prejudices, the common ways in which they are enforced, and the ease with which, once the platform of human rights is abandoned, such prejudices are uncritically reinforced and allowed much more aggressive scope in their war against the theory and practice of human rights well beyond any dream of their original proponent. In periods when roles are under debate in light of reasonable rights-based pressure for change, the very foundations of personal as well as political identity are put at risk—one's sense of oneself, for example, as a man and as an American.[228] In the absence of any strong institutions or a consensus protective of human rights, identity—personal and national—knows no limits in hardening itself against change. What emerges is an often highly gendered national identity, rooted in unjust gender stereotypes, that constructs its personal and national identity in stereotypical hatred of traditionally dehumanized groups (such as fascist Germany's hatred of Jews and homosexuals).[229] The Nazi campaign against homosexuality included, for example, the criminalization of "a kiss, an embrace, even homosexual fantasies."[230] Weininger, a Jew and an advocate of homo-

228. For the important recent literature on this topic, see, in general, Mark C. Carnes and Clyde Griffen, eds., *Meanings for Manhood: Constructions of Masculinity in Victorian America* (Chicago: University of Chicago Press, 1990); David D. Gilmore, *Manhood in the Making: Cultural Concepts of Masculinity* (New Haven: Yale University Press, 1990); Harry Brod, ed., *The Making of Masculinities: The New Men's Studies* (New York: Routledge, 1987); R. W. Connell, *Masculinities* (Berkeley and Los Angeles: University of California Press, 1995); Michael Kimmel, *Manhood in America: A Cultural History* (New York: Free Press, 1996).

229. For important recent treatments, see, in general, George L. Mosse, *Nationalism and Sexuality: Middle-Class Morality and Sexual Norms in Modern Europe* (Madison: University of Wisconsin Press, 1985); *The Image of Man: The Creation of Modern Masculinity* (New York: Oxford University Press, 1996); Andrew Parker, Mary Russo, Doris Sommer, and Patricia Yaeger, eds., *Nationalisms and Sexualities* (New York: Routledge, 1992).

230. See Steakley, *The Homosexual Emancipation Movement in Germany*, 110.

sexuality, had culturally legitimated the rights-denying stereotypes on the basis of which this savagery against Jews and homosexuals worked its tyrannical will.[231]

A salient feature of such dehumanization in the modern era was, as we earlier saw in the development of both racism and sexism and see again in Weininger, its reinterpretation in terms of an abusive science of race or gender or sexuality.[232] As one astute historian of this period observed: "To combat the already diminishing influence of the orthodox religious conceptions which had formed a solid basis for anti-discriminatory activity in the fields of sex and race at midcentury, evolutionary theory had arrived in the nick of time, a resplendent white knight in the service of discrimination."[233] No argument was more abusive in this way than the translation of what had traditionally been a sectarian argument of moral condemnation (for example, of Jews as heretics) into the pseudo-scientific discourse of degeneration or madness.[234] The blatantly rights-denying character of such claims is transparent when Jewish madness was adduced as the discrediting explanation for their claims of basic rights[235] or medical claims of disease or insanity used in response to claims of women's rights.[236] The effect was, of course, exactly the same as the traditional sectarian ideological views: reducing the scope of legitimate public discussion to its own sectarian measure, excluding, in principle, any claim of Jews or women to originate claims of basic human rights in their own voice.

The same indignity was inflicted on homosexuals in the United States during much of the twentieth century. Advocacy on behalf of the rights of gays and lesbians was, as we have seen, quashed by obscenity and related police prosecutions. No fair discussion by homosexuals in their own voice was tolerable during a period when such arguments by African Americans and women were increasingly allowed fuller critical scope. The deepest damage to the normative possibility

231. See Mosse, *Nationalism and Sexuality,* 17, 145–46. For Himmler on the need for rigid gender roles, see ibid., 162–70. See, in general, for Weininger's influence on Nazi anti-Semitism, Nancy A. Harrowitz and Barbara Hyams, eds., *Jews and Gender: Responses to Otto Weininger* (Philadelphia: Temple University Press, 1996).

232. See, in general, Stephen Jay Gould, *The Mismeasure of Man* (New York: W. W. Norton, 1981).

233. See Dijkstra, *Idols of Perversity,* 164.

234. See Gilman, *Jewish Self-Hatred,* 211–12.

235. See Gilman, *Difference and Pathology,* 152–53, 162; id., *Freud, Race, and Gender,* 113.

236. See G. J. Barker-Benfield, *The Horrors of the Half-Known Life: Male Attitudes toward Women and Sexuality in Nineteenth-Century America* (New York: Harper & Row, 1976), 84–90, 122–26, 189–93, 206–14.

of such gay and lesbian conscientious voice was inflicted, however, by establishment American psychiatry. Freud and his early followers had offered a surprisingly subtle and compassionate view of homosexuality as one of a wide variety of healthy outcomes of psychosexual development, but in America, psychoanalysis changed from an open-minded and humane study to an increasingly insular and sectarian orthodoxy whose view of sexual preference as a mental disease more reflected American moral orthodoxy than it did careful empirical study. After some internal struggle, only in 1973 did the Board of Trustees of the American Psychiatric Association decide to remove homosexuality from the *Diagnostic and Statistical Manual of Psychiatric Disorders.*[237] This development was very much an outgrowth of a new American struggle to understand and elaborate the human and civil rights of African Americans and women and the impact of that struggle on forging claims of human and constitutional rights by gay and lesbian persons.

THE CIVIL RIGHTS MOVEMENT AND THE CASE FOR GAY RIGHTS

The modern American case for gay rights derives, I believe, from a practice and theory of the basic human rights of gay and lesbian persons importantly fostered by the comparable practice and theory of the increasingly successful antiracist civil rights movement and second wave rights-based feminism that followed World War II. I first discuss here this theory and practice and its background, and then in the next section turn to a constructive view of how its constitutional claims should be understood, building on the model of moral slavery.

Both the antiracist and antisexist struggles crucially required making moral independent claims on the basis of one's human rights and bringing those claims to bear on the constitutionally reasonable criticism of the illegitimate enforcement through public law of a sectarian orthodoxy of race and gender that depended on the dehumanizing abridgment of basic human rights to conscience, speech, intimate life, and work. Against the background of a tradition of rights-denying moral slavery, making such arguments was in its nature transformative of personal and political-constitutional identity: one's traditional iden-

---

237. See, for an excellent study of this development, its criticism, and its change, Kenneth Lewes, *The Psychoanalytic Theory of Male Homosexuality* (New York: Simon and Schuster, 1988). See also Ronald Bayer, *Homosexuality and American Psychiatry: The Politics of Diagnosis* (New York: Basic Books, 1981).

tity as a black or women and as an American was transformed by making claims that demanded respect for one's moral personality as a person and a citizen. African Americans and women did so by further elaborating certain radical strands of long-standing rights-based dissenting traditions that were rooted in the interpretation of American revolutionary constitutionalism, in which both groups were important participants. For gays and lesbians to take up a similar position on the platform of human rights, they too would have to build upon and further elaborate such dissenting traditions (for example, Whitman's interpretive marriage of arguments for rights-based feminism and the right to homosexual love).

World War II advanced the public mind of America toward recognizing stronger antiracist principles and unsettled gender roles (women entering the job markets) as a preliminary to second wave feminism. Many gay and lesbian Americans, in military service away from their homes and serving with wider ranges of persons of the same gender and sexual preference, experienced transformative opportunities for a new dissenting practice of gay life, including protests on grounds of justice about the treatment of homosexuals in the military.[238] In 1951 Donald Webster Cory argued in *The Homosexual in America* that there were convincing analogies between such protests of justice on behalf of homosexuals and the claims of civil rights of other minority groups (blacks and Jews).[239] While Cory noted some other differences (the involuntary character of sexual preference [5, 183, 239], lack of an associated philosophy of life [6], not being rooted in the family [10]), he pointed to the main difference which

> separates the homosexual minority from all others, and that is its lack of recognition, its lack of respectability in the eyes of the public. . . . As a minority, we homosexuals are therefore caught in a particularly vicious circle. . . . Until the world is able to accept us on an equal basis as human beings entitled to the full rights of life, we are unlikely to have any great numbers willing to become martyrs by carrying the burden of the cross. But until we are willing to speak out openly and frankly in defense of our activities, we are unlikely to find the attitudes of the world undergoing any significant change. (14)

238. See, in general, Allan Berube, *Coming Out under Fire: The History of Gay Men and Women in World War Two* (New York: Free Press, 1990). For lesbian community life during this period, see Elizabeth Lapovsky Kennedy and Madeline D. Davis, *Boots of Leather, Slippers of Gold: The History of a Lesbian Community* (New York: Routledge, 1993).
239. See Donald Webster Cory (pseud.), *The Homosexual in America: A Subjective Approach* (New York: Castle Books, 1951), 4–6, 13–14, 38–48, 152.

Cory (itself a pseudonym[240]) thus identified an unjust culture that immunized itself from criticism of its degrading stereotypes[241] (drawing an express analogy to Du Bois on race [39]). American homosexuals needed (Cory argued) cultural heroes who would break the silence (157–66), along the lines of a Carpenter (106, 152, 237) or an even more forthright Whitman (158, 163–65). They also simply needed a public culture in which they could find themselves represented as persons: one that fairly explored relevant history (for example, the Amerindians [15–16]), wrote truer fictional narratives (citing Gore Vidal [21]),[242] and offered better speculative models for the proper place of homosexuality in nature and culture (citing Gide's *Corydon*, 30, 87, 107, 165).

As the judicial protection of freedom of speech (including, eventually, the constitutional narrowing of anti-obscenity laws) expanded, some homosexual Americans were ready as early as 1951 to organize politically for gay rights. In that year the founding of the Mattachine Society in Los Angeles marked the beginning of what would grow into a nationwide effort. Henry Hay, an ex-Communist, brought his organizational skills to bear on the new organization[243] and sought to develop an appropriate theory of the movement as a dissenting cultural minority. Importantly, Hay explicitly built upon Carpenter's earlier work on the Amerindian homosexual role.[244] Other groups, including separatist lesbian groups, would shortly follow.[245] By the 1990s, there would be a wide range of such groups, some of them specifically concerned with gay issues relating to the AIDS health crisis.[246]

Neither the antiracist civil rights movement nor second wave feminism were initially hospitable to the claims made by such groups. As we have seen, women in the civil rights movement had raised troubling questions about its sexism that were among the motivating sources of second wave feminism. It is not surprising, in light of this, that James

240. On Cory's later manifestation as Edward Sagarin, see John D'Emilio, *Sexual Politics, Sexual Communities: The Making of a Homosexual Minority in the United States, 1940–1970* (Chicago: University of Chicago Press, 1983), 168.

241. Cory, *The Homosexual in America*, 34–35, 41.

242. See Vidal, *The City and the Pillar*.

243. See, in general, D'Emilio, *Sexual Politics*, 57–74.

244. See, in general, Harry Hay, *Radically Gay*, ed. Will Roscoe (Boston: Beacon Press, 1996); on the berdache, see ibid., 92–119.

245. See, in general, D'Emilio, *Sexual Politics*.

246. For an illuminating general discussion of the dynamics of these groups and their interaction with the wider society, see Urvashi Vaid, *Virtual Equality: The Mainstreaming of Gay and Lesbian Liberation* (New York: Anchor, 1995). See also David Mixner, *Stranger among Friends* (New York: Bantam Books, 1996).

Baldwin, a gay black man and influential antiracist advocate, should
have been subject to homophobic attacks from heterosexual male black
leaders.[247] And Betty Friedan notoriously stereotyped gay men in *The
Feminine Mystique;*[248] as a leader of NOW, she warned against the
"lavender menace"[249] and, when Kate Millett's lesbianism was publi-
cized, she failed to support her.[250] Views, of course, later changed but
only in response to growing challenge on grounds of rights-based principle by increasingly vocal gay and lesbian persons and their allies in
the antiracist and antisexist movements.[251]

If the case for gay rights was to be understood and acknowledged,

---

247. See Eldridge Cleaver, *Soul on Ice* (New York: Dell, 1968), 96–107; for a more muted
example, see Stanley Crouch, *Notes of a Hanging Judge: Essays and Reviews, 1979–1989*
(New York: Oxford University Press, 1990), 37–41, 231–36. For illuminating commentary,
see Dennis Altman, *Homosexual Oppression and Liberation* (New York: Avon, 1971),
190–205.

248. See Friedan, *The Feminine Mystique,* 238–42.

249. See Chafe, *The Paradox of Change,* 210; but see ibid., 211.

250. See Marcia Cohen, *The Sisterhood: The True Story of the Women Who Changed
the World* (New York: Simon and Schuster, 1988), 248–51; see also ibid., 271–72, 369, 382.

251. For the important challenge of a black lesbian to black sexism and homophobia,
see, in general, Audre Lourde, *Sister Outsider: Essays and Speeches* (Freedom, Cal.: Crossing
Press, 1983); for the comparable challenge of a black women, see bell hooks, *Ain't I a Woman:
Black Women and Feminism,* 96; id., *Feminist Theory: From Margin to Center,* 23, 150–51;
id., *Killing Rage: Ending Racism* (New York: Henry Holt, 1995), 244. For comparable challenges of white lesbians to feminist homophobia, see, in general, Estelle B. Freedman,
Barbara C. Gelpi, Susan L. Johnson, and Kathless M. Weston, eds., *The Lesbian Issue* (Chi-
cago: University of Chicago Press, 1982); Marilyn Frye, *The Politics of Reality: Essays in
Feminist Theory* (Trumansburg, N.Y.: Crossing Press, 1983); *Willful Virgin: Essays in Femi-
nism, 1976–1992* (Freedom, Cal.: Crossing Press, 1992); Claudia Card, *Lesbian Choices* (New
York: Columbia University Press, 1995); Naomi Scheman, *Engenderings: Constructions of
Knowledge, Authority, and Privilege* (London: Routledge, 1993); Celia Kitzinger, *The Social
Construction of Lesbianism* (London: SAGE, 1987); Sarah Lucia Hoagland, *Lesbian Ethics:
Toward New Value* (Palo Alto: Institute of Lesbian Studies, 1988); Boston Lesbian Psycholo-
gies Collective, *Lesbian Psychologies: Explorations and Challenges* (Urbana: University of
Illinois Press, 1987). For an example of the black response to such criticism, see Cornel West,
Race Matters (Boston: Beacon Press, 1993), 25–28, 45–46, 89; for an example of the feminist
response, see Deborah Rhode, *Justice and Gender* (Cambridge: Harvard University Press,
1989), 141–42; Patricia Ireland, *What Women Want* (New York: Dutton, 1996), 226–29,
241. (Ireland, currently NOW's president, publicly acknowledges both a husband and lesbian
companion. Ibid., 220, 239.) Though NOW changed its position to one more affirmative of
the rights of lesbians and gay men, the issue remains divisive. Ibid., 226–29, 241. See, on
these points, Sherrye Henry, *The Deep Divide: Why American Women Resist Equality* (New
York: Macmillan, 1994), 259–63, 273–75, 287, 291. For example, the implications of ERA
for gay rights were prominently used against ratification of the amendment. See Jane
J. Mansbridge, *Why We Lost the ERA,* 109, 128–29, 136–37, 144–45; Andrew Kopkind, *The
Thirty Years' War: Dispatches and Diversions of a Radical Journalist, 1965–1994,* ed. JoAnn
Wypijewski (London: Verso, 1995), 298–308.

THE CASE FOR GAY RIGHTS

it would have to be made by gay people in their own voice and on their own terms; they would have to originate their claims to their basic human rights to conscience, speech, intimate life, and work against the dominant moral orthodoxy that dehumanized, degraded, and marginalized them. By 1971, when Dennis Altman published his *Homosexual Oppression and Liberation* after the defining moment of the Stonewall resistance in 1969,[252] the main rights-based point was construed as a search for identity[253] and analogies were drawn to the comparable identity-transformative struggles of women (125) (including consciousness raising [135–36, 207]) and blacks (128–29, 143–44, 152, 186).[254] Such a rights-based search required skepticism about the unjustly self-fulfilling stereotypes so fundamental to homophobia as well as racism (61–62, 64). For historical models of dissent, we should look to Allen Ginsberg's retelling in contemporary terms of Whitman's defense of homosexual love (180). By 1982, Altman would be struck, following Susan Sontag, by analogies (first suggested by Proust[255]) between developments of gay and Jewish identity expressive of similar styles of critical moral independence[256] against comparable sectarian sexual mythologies (analogies we shall later pursue).[257] The rights-based struggle for gay identity had forged a new kind of community and culture in which that identity could find personal and ethical meaning.[258] Writers like Jean Genet (and unlike Proust and Gide) wrote conspicuously as a gay man[259] and others developed serious work in history and social theory bearing on alternative cultural constructions of the homosexual role.[260] Increasingly, such claims were interpreted, by myself among

252. See Altman, *Homosexual Oppression and Liberation,* 117–18. For a good discussion of Stonewall, see Martin Duberman, *Stonewall* (New York: Plume, 1993).

253. See Altman, *Homosexual Oppression and Liberation,* 12, 121.

254. See, for a similar argument from a lesbian perspective, Claudia Card, *The Unnatural Lottery: Character and Moral Luck* (Philadelphia: Temple University Press, 1996), 163–82.

255. See Marcel Proust, *Cities of the Plain,* 13–14; for commentary, see Leo Bersani, *Homos* (Cambridge: Harvard University Press, 1995), 129–51.

256. See Dennis Altman, *The Homosexualization of America, The Americanization of the Homosexual* (New York: St. Martin's Press, 1982), 146.

257. Ibid., 198–99.

258. Ibid., 146–68; Andrew Kopkind, *The Thirty Years' War,* 324–32, 501–10, 514.

259. For an important study of Genet along these lines, see Edmund White, *Genet: A Biography* (New York: Knopf, 1993).

260. See, for example, Gilbert Herdt, *Third Sex, Third Gender: Beyond Sexual Dimorphism in Culture and History* (New York: Zone Books, 1994); Walter L. Williams, *The Spirit and the Flesh;* David F. Greenberg, *The Construction of Homosexuality;* Martin Bauml Duberman et al., eds., *Hidden from History: Reclaiming the Gay and Lesbian Past;* Michael Warner, ed., *Fear of a Queer Planet: Queer Politics and Social Theory* (Minneapolis: University of Minnesota Press, 1993).

others, as grounding arguments of basic constitutional rights in America, Canada, and Europe.[261]

The making of the case for gay rights in terms of rights-based feminism, bringing to the interpretation of such feminism the insights forged by the just struggles for personal and ethical identity of women in general and lesbian women in particular was one important and illuminating form of that personal and constitutional-political rights-based argument. Poet and essayist, Adrienne Rich powerfully explored (citing the Grimke sisters) the importance to women's emancipation of independent moral voice[262] and the ways in which a still largely mythologically idealized conception of maternal gender roles (both mother-son and mother-daughter) unjustly subordinated that voice to the claims and needs of male supremacy (112, 191, 207, 225, 247). Rich thus brought a rights-based feminism much more critically to bear on the normative heart of the traditional conception of gender roles that, since Catharine Beecher, had warred upon rights-based feminism. Beecher's normative conception basically rationalized women's gender subordination in terms of a complementary idealization of their moral superiority as self-sacrificing mothers. On the basis of her own experience as a wife and mother, Rich carefully analyzed the profound sexuality of mothering as an interest many women legitimately have (174, 183). She also analyzed the unjust moral degradation inflicted on women by imposing on them both a sectarian orthodoxy of compulsory motherhood (including when, how, and on what terms they have children) (210) and an unjust burden of an idealized duty

261. See, for example, David A. J. Richards, "Unnatural Acts and the Constitutional Right to Privacy: a Moral Theory," *Fordham Law Review* 45 (1977): 1282; id., "Sexual Autonomy and the Constitutional Right to Privacy: A Case Study in Human Rights and the Unwritten Constitution," *Hastings Law Journal* 30 (1979): 957; id., *The Moral Criticism of Law* (Encino, Cal.: Dickenson-Wadsworth, 1977); id., *Sex, Drugs, Death, and the Law: An Essay on Human Rights and Overcriminalization* (Totowa, N.J.: Rowman & Littlefield, 1982); id., *Toleration and the Constitution;* id., *Foundations of American Constitutionalism;* id., *Conscience and the Constitution;* Richard D. Mohn, *Gays/Justice: A Study of Ethics, Society, and Law* (New York: Columbia University Press, 1988); id., *Gay Ideas: Outing and Other Controversies* (Boston: Beacon Press, 1992); id., *A More Perfect Union: Why Straight America Must Stand Up for Gay Rights* (Boston: Beacon Press, 1994); Michael Nava and Robert Davidoff, *Created Equal: Why Gay Rights Matter to America* (New York: St. Martin's Press, 1994); Lisa Duggan and Nan D. Hunter, *Sex Wars: Sexual Dissent and Political Culture* (New York: Routledge, 1995); Robert Wintemute, *Sexual Orientation and Human Rights: The United States Constitution, the European Convention, and the Canadian Charter* (Oxford: Clarendon Press, 1995).

262. See Adrienne Rich, *Of Woman Born: Motherhood as Experience and Institution* (New York: W. W. Norton, 1976), 69.

of maternal self-sacrifice (212–13).[263] Such "unchosen, indentured motherhood"[264] (including the sectarian conceptions of women's duty that support it [273–74]) stultified the complex personal and ethical aims of women's free moral personality, and unreasonably burdened mothers and children with an unbalanced mother-dominated child-rearing (211–12, 216–17) (a theme notably explored as well by other feminist social theorists and psychoanalysts[265]). Only a critical rethinking of the justice of such maternal gender roles would insure women sufficient scope for their rational and reasonable moral powers, in personal and public life, so that children need no longer "live under the burden of their mother's unlived lives."[266]

Rich has generalized her argument about the need critically to reexamine women's gender roles (so that motherhood is no longer an enforced identity for women[267]) in two ways. First, contemporary feminism must rediscover the roots of the American feminist criticism of gender roles in the antiracism struggle,[268] in ways we have already explored. Second, a rights-based feminism calls for the legitimacy of lesbianism as an option for women, precisely because it so fundamentally challenges unjust gender roles.[269] I focus here on the second point.

If the rights-based feminist struggle is one for identity on terms of

263. See, for an important recent treatment of this issue in law, Joan Williams, "Gender Wars: Selfless Women in the Republic of Choice," *New York University Law Review* 66 (1991): 1559.

264. Rich, *Of Woman Born*, 285.

265. See, for variant explorations of this theme, Dorothy Dinnerstein, *The Mermaid and The Minotaur: Sexual Arrangements and Human Malaise* (New York: Harper & Row, 1976); Nancy Chodorow, *The Reproduction of Mothering: Psychoanalysis and the Sociology of Gender* (Berkeley and Los Angeles: University of California Press, 1978); *Feminism and Psychoanalytic Theory* (London: Polity, 1989); *Femininities Masculinities Sexualities: Freud and Beyond* (London: Free Association Press, 1994); Jane Flax, *Thinking Fragments: Psychoanalysis, Feminism, and Postmodernism in the Contemporary West* (Berkeley and Los Angeles: University of California Press, 1990); Jessica Benjamin, *The Bonds of Love: Psychoanalysis, Feminism, and the Problem of Domination* (London: Virgo, 1988). But, for the constructive strengths of the maternal role for ethical theory and practice, see Sara Ruddick, *Maternal Thinking: Toward a Politics of Peace* (Boston: Beacon Press, 1989); Nel Noddings, *Caring: A Feminine Approach to Ethics and Moral Education* (Berkeley and Los Angeles: University of California Press, 1984); *Women and Evil* (Berkeley and Los Angeles: University of California Press, 1989).

266. Rich, *Of Woman Born*, 207; see also ibid., 193–95.

267. See Adrienne Rich, *On Lies, Secrets, and Silence: Selected Prose, 1966–1978* (New York: W. W. Norton, 1979), 261.

268. Ibid., 57, 232, 239–40, 282–83, 286–87, 294.

269. See ibid., 10, 17, 224–25. See also Adrienne Rich, "Compulsory Heterosexuality and Lesbian Existence," in Catharine R. Stimpson and Ethel Spector Person, *Women: Sex and Sexuality* (Chicago: University of Chicago Press, 1980), 62–91.

respect for basic human rights against an unjustly enforceable ortho-doxy of gender roles, lesbianism must be regarded as a legitimate femi-nist option for women because it is both based on such basic rights and represents so fundamental a criticism of the sectarian orthodoxy. For Rich, the rights include not only the right to intimate life, but basic rights to moral independence of the feminist struggle of all women. In particular, such rights encompass the right morally to identify one's personality with other women in what Rich calls a "lesbian contin-uum"[270] and to live a "lesbian existence"[271] centering on such moral identifications, which may or may not include sexual relations or having and raising children.[272] The important feminist issue is to foster both the wider exercise of such rights and such cultural criticism which ad-vantage all women in their rights-based struggle. Much of the unjust sectarian orthodoxy rests, Rich argues, on compulsory heterosexuality: the insistence that women, to be women, must form a sense of self based on attachments to and dependence upon the authority of men.[273] Lesbianism, as a legitimate, indeed desirable feminist experiment in living, morally empowers all women along both the dimensions (guar-antee of basic rights and skepticism about traditional gender roles) requisite to their liberation from their unjust moral slavery.

Nothing in Rich's argument requires that it be limited to lesbians as opposed to gay men, though she herself regards her perspective as a step beyond general advocacy of toleration.[274] The case for gay rights crucially depends, for both men and women, on both the ingredients of Rich's rights-based case: its insistence on the range of basic human rights at stake and skepticism about the legitimacy of enforcing a sec-tarian theory of normative gender roles at large. If lesbians may exer-cise such rights in desirable moral identifications with other women, gay men may comparably exercise such rights identifying with both gay men and lesbians, both of whom embody ways of life that are critical of compulsory heterosexuality.[275] Indeed, both lesbians and gay men may deepen our understanding of the case for rights-based feminism by

270. See Rich, "Compulsory Heterosexuality," 79 (emphasis omitted).

271. Ibid. (emphasis omitted).

272. For an asexual variant, see Esther D. Rothblum and Kathleen A. Brehony, *Boston Marriages: Romantic But Asexual Relationships among Contemporary Lesbians* (Amherst: University of Massachusetts Press, 1993).

273. On the impact on the sense of self, see, for example, Naomi Wolf, *The Beauty Myth: How Images of Beauty Are Used against Women* (New York: Anchor, 1991).

274. Rich, "Compulsary Heterosexuality," 63.

275. For a lesbian encomium to the cultural creativity of gay men, see Camille Paglia, *Sexual Personae: Art and Decadence from Nefertiti to Emily Dickinson* (New York: Vintage, 1991), 14–15, 100, 157–58, 380, 434, 653–54.

providing reasonable perspective on and challenges to possibly stale and even oppressive feminist orthodoxies (some of them uncritical remnants of suffrage feminism) that must be rethought and reevaluated.[276] Certainly, relationships of love between gay men and between lesbians directly challenge the conception, perhaps central to traditional gender hierarchy and its conception of masculine and feminine identity, that love in its intimate nature cannot be between equals and that relationships between men or between women must be fraught with competition and hostility;[277] very much to the contrary, such relationships embody a normative model for intimate life that apparently more fully develops features of egalitarian sharing in intimate life that are more often the theory than the practice of heterosexual relations.[278] Gay men, precisely because they do not sexualize women but nonetheless often have and form profound moral identifications with them, may indeed contribute something unique to rights-based feminism: moral identifications with women not based on and therefore sometimes distorted by sexual objectification.[279] It is controversial whether and how sexual desire embodies sexual objectification and whether, if so, it is necessarily a bad thing,[280] but it is certainly a good thing for rights-based feminism to legitimate relationships not only between women, but between men and between men and women, all of which, in different ways, challenge the rights-denying evils of compulsory heterosexuality as the exclusive normative model for moral relationships

276. For a provocative challenge, see Camille Paglia, *Sexual Personae; Sex, Art, and American Culture: Essays* (New York: Vintage Books, 1992); id., *Vamps and Tramps: New Essays* (New York: Vintage Books, 1994). For related challenges from dissident feminists, see Daphne Patai and Noretta Koertge, *Professing Feminism: Cautionary Tales from the Strange World of Women's Studies* (New York: BasicBooks, 1994); Rene Denfeld, *The New Victorians: A Young Woman's Challenge to the Old Feminist Order* (New York: Warner Books, 1995); Katie Roiphe, *The Morning After: Sex, Fear, and Feminism* (Boston: Little, Brown, 1993); Christina Hoff Sommers, *Who Stole Feminism: How Women Have Betrayed Women* (New York: Simon & Schuster, 1994).

277. See, for the discussion of some of these points in the context of a larger discussion of changes in masculine role and identity, Elisabeth Badinter, *On Masculine Identity,* trans. Lydia Davis (New York: Columbia University Press, 1995). See also Elisabeth Badinter, *Man/Woman: The One Is the Other,* trans. Barbara Wright (London: Collins Harvill, 1989).

278. On this point, see Susan Moller Okin, "Sexual Orientation and Gender: Dichotomizing Differences," in David M. Estlund and Martha C. Nussbaum, eds., *Sex, Preference, and Family: Essays on Law and Nature* (New York: Oxford University Press, 1997), 44–59.

279. On this point, see Kaja Silverman, *Male Subjectivity at the Margins* (New York: Routledge, 1992), 342–51, 354, 372–73. Of course, some such identifications may be subject to their own special distortions; see, for example, Wayne Koestenbaum, *The Queen's Throat: Opera, Homosexuality, and the Mystery of Desire* (New York: Poseidon Press, 1993).

280. See, on this and related points, Martha Nussbaum, "Objectification," *Philosophy and Public Affairs* 24 (1995): 249.

between men and women. Rights-based feminism might, on such grounds, redefine its aims in terms of claims for the basic human rights of all persons (whether men or women) against all forms of politically enforced gender stereotypes that have unjustly usurped moral sovereignty over framing the meaning of gender in one's personal and ethical life.

THE CASE FOR GAY RIGHTS

We need now further to explore the case for gay rights in two steps: first, to bring to bear on this question the abolitionist feminist theory of moral slavery; and second, to articulate the dimensions of constitutional rights that this theory makes possible (including both the basic human rights owed gays and lesbians as well as the reasons for regarding classifications in terms of sexual preference as constitutionally suspect). Gays and lesbians suffer, I argue, from the moral slavery condemned by the Thirteenth Amendment. Both the central substantive principles under the Fourteenth Amendment should be interpreted accordingly; the principle nationalizing the protection of basic human rights must protect their basic rights to conscience, speech, intimate life, and work; and the principle of heightened scrutiny under equal protection for abridgment of basic rights and use of suspect classifications must be construed both to acknowledge the fundamental rights owed them and to condemn, as suspect, the illegitimate grounds on which such abridgment of basic rights has been rationalized. In later chapters, I apply this theory to various current constitutional cases and controversies.

Moral Slavery as the Reprobation of Homosexuality

We may and should, on grounds of principle, extend our earlier analysis of moral slavery to the traditional reprobation of homosexuality. Homophobia reflects a cultural tradition of rights-denying moral slavery similar to and indeed overlapping with the American tradition of sexist degradation; the root of homophobia is, like sexism, a rigid conception of gender roles and spheres, only here focusing specifically on gender roles in intimate sexual and emotional life.[281] Homosexuals, because they violate these gender roles, are traditionally supposed to

---

281. See Suzanne Pharr, *Homophobia: A Weapon of Sexism* (Inverness, Cal.: Chardon Press, 1988); Sylvia A. Law, "Homosexuality and the Social Meaning of Gender," *Wisconsin Law Review* (1988): 187; Young-Bruehl, *The Anatomy of Prejudices*, 35–36, 143–51; Okin, "Sexual Orientation and Gender: Dichotomizing Differences."

be outcasts from the human race as well, and thus incapable and indeed unworthy of being accorded what all persons are, on equal terms, owed: respect for their basic human rights to conscience, speech, intimate life, and work. As we shall see in the next section, cases like *Bowers v. Hardwick*[282] are plausibly condemned as themselves expressing homophobia to the extent, on wholly unprincipled and inadequate grounds, homosexuals are uncritically excluded from the scope of a basic human right of intimate life now liberally extended to all other persons.

A way of making this point is to observe that homophobic prejudice, like racism and sexism, unjustly distorts the idea of human rights applicable to both public and private life. The political evil of racism expressed itself in a contemptuous interpretation of black family life (enforced by antimiscegenation laws that confined blacks, as a separate species, to an inferior sphere).[283] The political evil of sexism expressed itself in a morally degraded interpretation of private life to which women, as morally inferior, were confined as, in effect, a different species.[284] In similar fashion, the evil of homophobic prejudice is its degradation of homosexual love to the unspeakably private and secretive not only politically and socially, but intrapsychically in the person whose sexuality is homosexual; the intellectual reign of terror that once aimed to impose racism and anti-Semitism on the larger society and even on these stigmatized minorities themselves today aims to enforce homophobia at large and self-hating homophobia in particular on homosexuals as well.[285] Its vehicle is the denigration of gay and lesbian identity as a devalued form of conscience with which no one, under pain of ascribed membership in such a devalued species, can or should identify. Such degradation constructs not, as in the case of gender, merely a morally inferior sphere, but an unspeakably and inhumanly evil sphere, a culturally constructed and imagined diabolic hell to which gays and lesbians must be compulsively exiled on the same irrationalist mythological terms to which societies we condemn as

282. *Bowers v. Hardwick*, 478 U.S. 186 (1986).
283. See *Loving v. Virginia*, 388 U.S. 1 (1967) (antimiscegenation laws held unconstitutional expression of racial prejudice).
284. See Lillian Faderman, *Surpassing the Love of Men* (New York: William Morrow, 1981), 85–86, 157–58, 181, 236.
285. I develop this analogy in Richards, "Sexual Preference as a Suspect (Religious) Classification: An Alternative Perspective on the Unconstitutionality of Anti-Lesbian/Gay Initiatives," *Ohio State Law Journal* 55 (1994): 491. I argue that Colorado Amendment Two enforces a dehumanizing, irrationalist prejudice traditionally expressed against Jews and African Americans toward gay and lesbian persons. See also chapter 7.

348   CHAPTER SIX

primitive exiled devils and witches and werewolves;[286] homosexuals, self-consciously demonized (as devils) as they are by contemporary sectarian groups, must be kept in the sphere consistent with their inhumanity.[287] Gays and lesbians are thus culturally dehumanized as a non-human or inhuman species whose moral interests in love and friendship and nurturing care are, in their nature, radically discontinuous with anything recognizably human. The culture of such degradation is pervasive and deep, legitimating the uncritically irrationalist outrage at the very idea of gay and lesbian marriage,[288] which unjustly constructs the inhumanity of homosexual identity on the basis of exactly the same kind of vicious circle of cultural degradation unjustly imposed on African Americans through antimiscegenation laws.[289] Groups, thus marked off as ineligible for the central institutions of intimate life and cultural transmission, are deemed subculturally nonhuman or inhuman: an alien species incapable of the humane forms of culture that express and sustain our inexhaustibly varied search, as free moral persons, for enduring personal and ethical meaning and value in living.

Both racism and sexism arose in the context of close living relationships between the hegemonic and oppressed groups, drew their potent political power from such allegedly loving relationships, and were rationalized accordingly as protections of intimate personal life. As James Madison saw in his constitutionally seminal elaborations of his theory of faction, factions are most powerful when they are most local and

286. On the imaginative processes that sustain such a sphere, see Alan E. Bernstein, *The Formation of Hell: Death and Retribution in the Ancient and Early Christian Worlds* (Ithaca: Cornell University Press, 1993); Elaine Pagels, *The Origin of Satan* (New York: Random House, 1996).

287. For the view of public identified gays and lesbians as, from within the perspective of sectarian theology, devils or demonic, see Didi Herman, *The Antigay Agenda: Orthodox Vision and the Christian Right* (Chicago: University of Chicago Press, 1997), 82–91, 143; for the similar sectarian view taken of Jews and the analogy to scapegoating homosexuals today, see Elain Pagels, *The Origin of Satan*, 102–5.

288. For a powerful argument for same-sex marriages as a matter of constitutional justice, see Mark Strasser, "Family, Definitions, and the Constitution: On the Antimiscegenation Analogy," *Suffolk University Law Review* 25 (1991): 981; *Baehr v. Lewin*, 852 P.2d 44 (Haw. 1993) (denial of marriage license to same-sex couple held violative of Hawaii constitutional guarantee of equal protection strict scrutiny applicable to gender discrimination). For historical background on unions regarded as analogous to modern claims for same-sex marriage, see William N. Eskridge, Jr., "A History of Same-Sex Marriage," *Virginia Law Review* 79 (1993): 1419.

289. See, for eloquent development of this point, Andrew Koppelman, "The Miscegenation Analogy: Sodomy Law as Sex Discrimination," *Yale Law Journal* 98 (1988): 145. See also Andrew Koppelman, *Antidiscrimination Law and Social Equality* (New Haven: Yale University Press, 1996), 146–76.

parochial;[290] consistent with this view, racism and sexism are the prepo-
tent forms of faction they are because they culturally arose and were
sustained in the most local and personal of intimate relationships as
forms of moral paternalism.

Homophobia shares a comparable cultural background of moral
slavery. Heterosexuals and homosexuals lived together closely under
the moral slavery of homosexuals,[291] but, as heterosexuals have now
learned, in different worlds—one hegemonically and polemically assertive, the other resignedly withdrawn into a compulsory and silent
servitude mistaken for consent. Homosexuals were not remitted to servile status as blacks and women were under their forms of moral slavery; rather their moral slavery was more hegemonically absolute—servitude to an unjust moral paternalism that, based on crushing their
basic rights (to conscience, speech, association, and work), exiled them
from any legitimate space in public or private life into the realm of
the unspeakable. Homosexuals were thus radically denied the very resources of self-respecting personal and ethical identity as homosexuals.
Homophobia thus naturally takes, as its dominant contemporary form,
the violent attack on the relatively recent development of conscientious
moral claims to such a self-respecting identity either in public or private life.[292] The essentially hegemonic and subjugating force of this
prejudice is shown in its insistence that homosexuality remain an unspeakably privatized debasement, tolerable only on terms of a servile,
apologetic, and shrunken self-contempt, not on terms of respect for
basic human rights (including the inalienable right to conscience) owed
all persons. The oppression of homosexuals, like that of blacks and
women under moral slavery, is perversely rationalized as itself a protection of intimate life (family values) when it, in fact, wars on a legitimate
form of intimate life. This marks the roots of the prejudice, like other
forms of moral slavery, in the most intimately debasing forms of unjust
moral paternalism: the totalizing assumption that the community legiti-

290. See Jacob E. Cooke, ed., *The Federalist* (Middletown, Conn.: Wesleyan University Press, 1961), No. 10, 56–65; for background and commentary, see Richards, *Foundations of American Constitutionalism*, 32–39.

291. For a powerful study of this phenomenon in Renaissance England, see Alan Bray, *Homosexuality in Renaissance England* (London: Gay Men's Press, 1982).

292. For the history of this development in Great Britain, see Jeffrey Weeks, *Sex, Politics, and Society: The Regulation of Sexuality since 1800*, 2d ed. (London: Longman, 1989); *Coming Out: Homosexual Politics in Britain from the Nineteenth Century to the Present*, rev. ed. (London: Quartet Books, 1990). For the American development of this movement, see D'Emilio, *Sexual Politics;* John D'Emilio and Estelle B. Freedman, *Intimate Matters: A History of Sexuality in America* (New York: Harper & Row, 1988).

mately can and should know and control the very heart and mind of another's most intimate resources of moral personality. Indeed, consistent with our earlier Madisonian observations, homophobia, which enforces unjust gender roles in intimate life, may be regarded as among the most intractable and virulent of factions. It manifests an intrapsychic landscape of the gendered meaning of love in terms of sexist degradation in intimate life itself (as if, the equality traditionally understood to exist among men or among women could never be fertile soil for the garden of love).[293]

The ethical and constitutional argument about the nature of this evil was implicit in Sarah Grimke's identification of associational liberty as one among the central human rights that had been unjustly denied to women as a class. As we have seen, Grimke condemned, as heretical idolatry, women's moral dependence on men in matters of conscience, and analyzed the evil as a failure to respect women's associational liberty in deciding whether to marry and on what terms. In effect, Grimke analyzed the moral slavery of sexism (systematic deprivation of rights of conscience, speech, association, and work) in terms of the dehumanization focally inflicted on women by the ways in which (including deprivations of associated basic rights of conscience, speech, and work) they have not been accorded fair respect for the associational liberties of relating or not relating to men (and on what terms) that make possible basic control over their minds, emotions, and bodies as free persons. Failure to respect such liberties and associated rights effectively dehumanized women to a kind of sexual pet in the same way comparable failures to respect the intimate family life of African American women and men under slavery dehumanized them to the level of cattle. In the case of women and African Americans, gender or race (or some combination of both) mandated a narrow and servile way of life, often supported by sexual mythology, whose stability rested on the deprivation of the basic rights that would enable free persons reasonably to challenge such unjustly imposed servile roles. Grimke's argument stated an issue of rights-based principle on which later feminists (men and women) insisted with growing force as central to the emancipation of women from their moral slavery:[294] sovereignty in love is as central to respect for human rights as such recognized rights as con-

293. Cf. Okin, "Sexual Orientation and Gender: Dichotomizing Differences."

294. For the historical background and development of the argument, see John C. Spurlock, *Free Love: Marriage and Middle-Class Radicalism in America, 1825–1860* (New York: New York University Press, 1988). For its later development, see Linda Gordon, *Woman's Body, Woman's Right: A Social History of Birth Control in America* (New York: Penguin, 1976).

science and speech and work. This is an argument made with great force, as we have seen, by Stephen Pearl Andrews,[295] Victoria Wood-hull,[296] Ezra H. Heywood,[297] Elizabeth Cady Stanton,[298] and Margaret Sanger.[299]

As Walt Whitman surely assumed[300] and his English follower, Edward Carpenter, clearly argued,[301] the condemnation of homosexual love violates this right, as does the dominant orthodoxy that later feminists like Rich condemned as compulsory heterosexuality. In both cases, homophobic laws and practices deprived persons of the resources of the creative moral freedom of an intimate life expressive of their authentic moral powers, as persons, not as stereotypical genders. The moral power of romantic personal love lies in the imaginative, emotional, and intellectual powers that loving and being loved nurtures, sustains, and fructifies in aspects of one's moral individuality,

295. See Stephen Pearl Andrews, ed., *Love, Marriage, and Divorce* (1853; New York: Source Book Press, 1972), 33, 66, 68, 86, 89, 95, 97, 106–8.

296. See Victoria C. Woodhull, "A Speech on the Principles of Social Freedom" (New York: Woodhull, Claflin & Co., 1871), in *The Victoria Woodhull Reader,* ed. Madeleine B. Stern (Weston, Mass.: M & S Press, 1974).

297. Ezra H. Heywood, "Uncivil Liberty: An Essay to Show the Injustice and Impolicy of Ruling Woman against Her Consent" in *The Collected Works of Ezra H. Heywood,* ed. Martin Blatt (1871; Weston, Mass.: M & S Press, 1985).

298. See Elizabeth Cady Stanton, "Speech on Marriage and Divorce" and "The Solitude of Self," in Beth M. Waggenspack, *The Search for Self-Sovereignty: The Oratory of Elizabeth Cady Stanton* (1869 and 1892; Greenwood Press: New York, 1989), 121–25, 159–67.

299. See Margaret Sanger, *Woman Rebel,* ed. Alex Baskin (New York: Archives of Social History, 1976), 25; id., *The Pivot of Civilization* (Elmsford, N.Y.: Maxwell Reprint Company, 1969), 140, 211–19, 259; *Woman and the New Race* (Elmsford, N.Y.: Maxwell Reprint Company, 1969), 167, 226–34.

300. The best evidence for this is surely the poetry and essays. See, in particular, "Calamus," in *Leaves of Grass,* in *Walt Whitman: The Complete Poems,* ed. Francis Murphy (Harmondsworth: Penguin, 1975), 146–67; *Democratic Vistas,* in *Walt Whitman: Complete Poetry and Collected Prose,* ed. Justin Kaplan (New York: The Library of America, 1982), 929–94, especially 929 (praise of John Stuart Mill's *On Liberty*) and 981 (defense of "[i]ntense and loving comradeship, the personal and passionate attachment of man to men"). Whitman remarked: "Free love? Is there any other kind of love?" Justin Kaplan, *Walt Whitman: A Life* (New York: Simon and Schuster, 1980), 43. The only contrary evidence is Whitman's puzzling and surely disingenuous 1890 letter to John Addington Symonds in which he disavowed the "morbid inferences" of homosexuality Symonds apparently ascribed to Whitman. For discussion of this letter, see earlier discussion in this chapter.

301. See Edward Carpenter, *The Intermediate Sex: A Study of Some Transitional Types of Men and Women* (New York: Mitchell Kennerley, 1912), 73–75 (criticizing application of criminal sanctions to "an attachment . . . of great value in the national life"). For other works advocating reform, see John Addington Symonds, *A Problem in Modern Ethics* (London, 1896); id., *A Problem in Greek Ethics,* in John Addington Symonds, *Male Love: A Problem in Greek Ethics and Other Writings* (1901; New York: Pagan Press, 1983), 1–73; Havelock Ellis and John Addington Symonds, *Sexual Inversion* (London: Wilson and Macmillan, 1897), 153, 155–56 (homosexual conduct not properly criminal).

originality, and sensibility theretofore repressed in a mechanical conventionality and barren narcissism. Such moral power of love, unencumbered of the sexist requirements of gender, expresses a critical form of the moral independence Grimke thought essential to the emancipation of women from their moral slavery in both public and private life, as well as the competence to cultivate and realize in love one's authenticating moral powers as a person, including the identifications central to one's conscientiously defined personal identity and moral character. Grimke made this point, as we have seen, by observing the use of epithets like "unfeminine" to crush women's critical powers of moral independence; and we may note the comparable forms of unjust moral terror used historically to chill women's just moral freedom by reductive criticism of any feminist argument, made by either heterosexual or homosexual women, as, dismissively, "lesbian."[302] Adrienne Rich urged feminists to embrace the criticism as a point of honor for the integrity of their rights-based agenda. The same point applies, of course, to gay men, who suffer the same sexist degradation for a critical moral life and imaginative identifications in which men are not rigidly locked in the dominant conventionality of mutual distrust and combative competition, but mutually nurtured in love and respect for one another.[303] From this perspective, homophobic laws and practices express a residual form of sexist degradation in intimate life, unjustly enforcing gender stereotypes as the procrustean measure of the moral powers of romantic love.[304] The enforcement of such an unjust political epistemology through law impoverishes the resources of public reason of us all about issues of justice, gender, sexual preference, the family, and other central ethical issues of a well-lived life. It rests on the rights-based constitutional evil of moral slavery, which unjustly subjugates both lesbians and gay men in the same way that it has historically subjugated African Americans and women.

The background of homophobia is that a class of persons has been degraded from their status as bearers of rights on the basis of a cultural

302. See, for example, O'Neill, *Everyone Was Brave,* 290. On the consequences for feminism of disowning or espousing gay and lesbian issues as ways of responding to this criticism, see Deborah L. Rhode, *Justice and Gender* (Cambridge: Harvard University Press, 1989), 61, 310.

303. For an important study of the range of critical standards of morally independent social and political criticism implicit in the development of a gay voice in public culture, in particular, the contrasting approaches of Wilde and Gide, see Jonathan Dollimore, *Sexual Dissidence: Augustine to Wilde, Freud to Foucault* (Oxford: Clarendon Press, 1991).

304. On the struggle for gay rights as based on a principled defense of romantic love as a basic right of the person in the modern world, see Paul Berman, *A Tale of Two Utopias* (New York: W. W. Norton, 1996), 165, 180.

tradition that unjustly deprived them of the rights of conscience, speech, association, and work central to reasonable moral freedom. The moral slavery of homosexuals has, like that of African Americans and women, crucially turned on the ways in which the deprivation of basic human rights to them, through the force of the paradox of intolerance, crucially clustered on the rationalization of their dehumanization (often associated with sexual mythology) as subhuman monsters (or, in contemporary sectarian terms, devils[305]), in terms of lacking even the right to name, let alone claim, the intimate life that is the basic human right of all other persons. Homosexuals may reasonably and publicly reclaim these rights today against the unjust cultural orthodoxy and political epistemology that has traditionally silenced and degraded them[306] in the same moral voice of emancipated moral freedom that Angelina and Sarah Grimke demanded for African Americans and women in their day against a comparable degrading and silencing orthodoxy.

The Grimkes made their claims on the basis of a moral independence progressively fostered by their exile from family, region, religion, and, finally, their own gender. Public claims to basic rights by homosexuals today share a strikingly common experience of painful exile from family, ethnicity, religion, gender, and even, sometimes, sexual preference. It was because abolitionist feminists made their arguments as multiple outcasts from the dominant political consensus that they reasonably engage our interpretive interests today as among the most principled arguments that have been made in our constitutional tradition about the enduring meaning of the abolitionist political and moral theory central to the legitimate interpretation of the Reconstruction Amendments. For this reason, gay and lesbian persons today, among whom I include myself, may find in abolitionist feminism a deeper interpretive understanding of the redemptive personal, moral, and constitutional meaning of our multiple exiles and identifications. Our struggles to personal and moral integrity and authenticity, on the model of our abolitionist feminist forebears, deepen the collective interpretive understanding of all Americans about the meaning of our constitutional principles "on the platform of human rights." My interpretive argument has been that those principles are best tested, as arguments of principle, not by dominant political consensus but by the outcasts from such consensus who have raised and tested the integrity

305. For this contemporary sectarian view of the Christian Right, see Didi Herman, *The Antigay Agenda*, 82–91, 143.

306. For an exploration of some of the issues, see Eve Kosofsky Sedgwick, *Epistemology of the Closet* (Berkeley and Los Angeles: University of California Press, 1990).

of our claim, as a people, that constitutional arguments of principle reasonably extend to all persons on fair terms. Advocacy for gay and lesbian rights interpretively stands in that tradition, reinvigorating in contemporary circumstances one of our best traditions, that of abolitionist feminism as interpreted by Whitman, on the same grounds of rights-based principle.

On this view, homosexuals have been culturally subjected to the moral slavery condemned by the Thirteenth Amendment. Such condemnation interpretively clarifies the proper scope in this area of the central principles of the Fourteenth Amendment: the nationalization of the protection of basic human rights and equal protection. With respect to the former, gays and lesbians are, on terms of principle, owed the basic human rights of conscience, speech, intimate life, and work; with respect to the latter, gays and lesbians are entitled not only to equal respect for their basic rights but to suspect classification analysis. These forms of analysis are related. As the theory of moral slavery makes clear, basic human rights have been systematically denied gays and lesbians, as a class, on inadequate grounds; they have thus suffered indignities resting both on the abridgment of basic rights (nationally owed all persons) and on the wholly inadequate grounds on the basis of which they have thus been thus unjustly treated. The two indignities are, of course, mutually reinforcing: the abridgment of basic rights constructs the dehumanized status on the basis of which such abridgments are rationalized; and the inadequate grounds, in turn, rationalize the abridgments of such rights. Because these constitutional indignities have been less responsibly addressed in this case than in others we earlier discussed, both indignities still flourish, reinforcing one another. Our discussion of the issues of constitutional principle must thus reasonably embrace both issues and address the role the unjust abridgment of one such basic right (intimate life) has pivotally played today in reinforcing the moral slavery of homosexuals.

Sexual Preference as a Suspect Classification

On the basis of this analysis of moral slavery (applicable alike to race, gender, and sexual preference), we are now in a position to complete the normative analysis of suspect classification analysis proposed earlier (chapter 5), including some remarks on the scope and limits of this mode of constitutional analysis. I argued there that neither immutability or salience of a trait nor the political powerlessness of the group associated with the trait were necessary conditions for the constitutional suspectness of race and gender under current authoritative case law. African Americans, who reasonably identify themselves as such, are no less subject to unjust racial prejudice because their racial identification is not in the usual way immutable or salient; gender classifications are no less suspect for this reason or because women are a statistical majority of the American voting electorate and thus not obviously politically powerless. Rather, both racial and sexist prejudice are constitutional evils when they are unjustly directed against stigmatizing central aspects of a person's cultural and moral identity on irrationalist grounds reflective of the continuing force of the structural injustice of moral slavery. In each case its irrationalist object is not some brute fact that cannot be changed, but central features of moral personality— identifications that make one a self-respecting member of a community that one reasonably values. The suspectness of the underlying prejudice in each case is its irrationalist interpretation of central aspects of human personality and the unjust degradation of the culture (moral slavery) with which a person reasonably identifies. Such prejudice, thus analyzed, shares common features, I suggested, with forms of religious intolerance and the long-standing American tradition that condemns, as suspect, any classification on constitutionally inadequate sectarian religious grounds. We constitutionally condemn, as suspect, such prejudice because it is directed at aspects of moral personality on grounds that we condemn as inadequate (denying basic rights on historical grounds that, on examination, uncritically rest on dehumanizing failures to accord basic rights to a certain class of persons—religious, racial, or sexual).

Suspect classification analysis focuses on the political expression of irrational prejudices of moral slavery. The fundamental wrong of racism and sexism has been the dehumanizing exclusion of blacks and women from the rights of public culture, exiling them to cultural marginality in supposedly morally inferior realms and unjustly stigmatizing identity on such grounds. Such unjust cultural marginalization and stigmatization also victimize homosexuals. Its continuing populist force, against the background of the moral slavery of homosexuals, entitles sexual preference to be recognized as a suspect classification on a par with race and gender. Indeed, under contemporary circumstances, in light of the stigma popularly directed at the self-respecting conscientious assertion of one's rights as a gay or lesbian person, the grounds for the suspectness of sexual preference forthrightly draw upon the roots of suspect classification analysis in the oldest suspect classification under American public law, religion.

The fact that sexual preference is allegedly not, like race or gender, an immutable and salient personal characteristic has sometimes been taken to disqualify sexual preference from treatment as a suspect classification.[307] The argument lacks both empirical and normative basis.

Sexual preference may be a largely settled and irreversible erotic preference for most people long before the age of responsibility.[308] The possible concealment or even repression of the preference—as a reason for disqualifying it from treatment as a suspect classification— is not a reasonable condition of political respect if sexual preference is integral to the authenticity of moral personality and the prejudice against it as politically unreasonable as racism, sexism, or a religious intolerance like anti-Semitism.

In fact (as I more fully argue below), sexual preference is as central to self-authenticating claims to personal and ethical identity (as a gay or lesbian person) as race or gender or conventional religion, and the prejudice against such claims is politically unreasonable in the same way racism, sexism, and religious intolerance are unreasonable. The sacrifice of moral authenticity is not a demand any person could reasonably be asked to accept as the price for freedom from irrational prejudice, and homosexual persons can no more be reasonably asked to make such a crippling sacrifice of self than any other person.

In fact immutability and salience do not coherently explain even the historical paradigm of a suspect classification, namely, race (let alone gender, ethnicity, illegitimacy, and alienage); in all these cases, the constitutional evil remains very much in force whether a person could take steps to evade it; the very burden placed on identity to take such steps is unreasonable and indeed constitutionally illegitimate. If immutability and salience do not define the scope of the constitutional evil here, they cannot normatively define the terms of principle reasonably applicable to other claims to suspect classification analysis. From

307. See, for example, Michael J. Perry, "Modern Equal Protection: A Conceptualization and Appraisal," *Columbia Law Review* 79 (1979): 1066–67.

308. On irreversibility, see Wainwright Churchill, *Homosexual Behavior among Males* (New York: Hawthorn, 1967), 283–91; C. A. Tripp, *The Homosexual Matrix* (New York: McGraw-Hill, 1975), 251; D. J. West, *Homosexuality* (Chicago: Aldine, 1968), 266; Michael Ruse, *Homosexuality* (Oxford: Basil Blackwell, 1988), 59–62. On the early age of its formation, see John Money and A. Ehrhardt, *Man & Woman, Boy & Girl* (Baltimore: Johns Hopkins University Press, 1972), 153–201. One study hypothesizes that gender identity and sexual object choice coincide with the development of language, that is, from 18 to 24 months of age. See J. Money, J. G. Hampson, and J. L. Hampson, "An Examination of Some Basic Sexual Concepts: The Evidence of Human Hermaphroditism," *Bulletin of Johns Hopkins Hospital* 97 (1955): 301. Cf. Alan P. Bell, Martin S. Weinberg, and Sue K. Hammersmith, *Sexual Preference* (New York: Simon & Schuster, 1978). For a recent judicious review of the relevant scientific literature, see Richard Green, *Sexual Science and the Law* (Cambridge: Harvard University Press, 1992), chap. 4.

this perspective, the issue of the immutability of sexual preference should be irrelevant to its constitutional examination as a suspect classification. What is relevant is the issue of irrational political prejudice (which does not turn on salience), in particular, the irrationalist weight and burden such prejudice places on cultural identifications reasonably central to moral personality. The insistence on immutability and salience as requirements for suspect classification analysis in the case of sexual preference would be unprincipled. It is not a requirement we impose elsewhere, and there is no good argument of principle why we should impose it here.[309] Such requirements are neither necessary nor sufficient as grounds for suspectness.

It is particularly paradoxical to hold sexual preference to these requirements when the underlying irrationalist prejudice (homophobia) transparently expresses the very origins of suspect classification analysis in the first suspect classification under American public law, religion. Such religious intolerance in its nature is directed at a disfavored religious or, more broadly, conscientiously based dissenting identity, both placing burdens on its conscientious exercise and putting pressure on dissenting conscience to change identity in line with majoritarian orthodoxy. Such intolerance focuses, more transparently than racism or sexism, on the malleabilities of conscientious identity, and thus can even less plausibly be regarded as rooted in immutable physical facts (thus, the paradox of holding religiously based intolerance of conscientious gay or lesbian identity to this requirement). If political homophobia is, on examination, a constitutionally illegitimate expression of religious intolerance, public laws reflecting this prejudice should be forthrightly held suspect on the clearest of constitutional grounds, the tradition of religious toleration under the religion clauses of the First Amendment that suspect classification analysis under the equal protection clause of the Fourteenth Amendment assumes and elaborates (and certainly does not repeal or retrench).

Against this background, there are good reasons why lesbian and gay persons should resist interpreting their claims to suspect classification analysis in the biological and genetic terms that some gay scientists have recently proposed.[310] To claim a mode of argument not required

309. Cf. *Watkins v. U.S. Army*, 847 F.2d 1329, 1347 (9th Cir. 1988); Note, "The Constitutional Status of Sexual Orientation: Homosexuality as a Suspect Classification," *Harvard University Law Review* 98 (1985): 1285, 1303.

310. For further developments of this skeptical theme, see Janet E. Halley, "Sexual Orientation and the Politics of Biology: A Critique of the Argument from Immutability," *Stanford Law Review* 46 (1994): 503; Edward Stein, "The Relevance of Scientific Research about Sexual Orientation to Lesbian and Gay Rights," in *Gay Ethics: Controversies in Outing, Civil*

for other claimants to suspect classification analysis will ethically undercut the integrity of the arguments of principle that lesbians and gays may, can, and should make as arguments available on fair terms to all persons. It also falsely and malignly biologizes what is essentially a principled argument for the just ethical emancipation of the moral powers of conscience of lesbian and gay persons in terms that subvert its emancipatory potential. Biological reductionism was central to the unjust cultural subjugation of African Americans and women as a separate species,[311] and may wreak comparable havoc on lesbians and gay men today, confirming, rather than challenging, unjust cultural stereotypes of an inferiority rooted in nature (even suggesting, as both Carpenter[312] and Proust[313] did, a biologically-based racial categorization). We need not repeat the terms of our subjugation, but instead affirm an empowering critical perspective on the cultural terms of our degradation and on our corresponding political, ethical, and intellectual responsibilities to exercise our active moral powers of criticism and reconstruction of that culture on terms of justice.[314] We need responsibly to insist on and to demand our personal and moral identity as gay and lesbian persons, and to resist, unlike the first European generation of advocates of gay liberation, any complicity with those unjustly essentialist and objectifying stereotypes that have stripped us of our powers of free, self-defining moral personality.

The contemporary constitutional issue of principle is threefold: first, to highlight the devastating impact of a heretofore unchallenged, hegemonic religio-cultural orthodoxy on the basic rights of lesbian and gay people; second, to explore the ways in which it has stunted and stultified the range of human and moral intelligence and imagination (the basic resources of conscience) that lesbian and gay persons, as individuals, may reasonably bring to the diverse patterns of a well-lived and ethical life; and, third, to underscore the ways in which it today self-

---

Rights, and Sexual Science, ed. T. F. Murphy (New York: Harrington Park Press, 1994), 269–308. For a recent statement of the case for this research by a gay scientist, see Simon LeVay, *Queer Science: The Use and Abuse of Research into Homosexuality* (Cambridge: MIT Press, 1996).

311. See Stephen Jay Gould, *The Mismeasure of Man* (New York: W. W. Norton, 1981); Carol Tavris, *The Mismeasure of Woman* (New York: Simon and Schuster, 1992).

312. See Carpenter, *The Intermediate Sex,* 29 ("the Intermediate race").

313. See Proust, *Cities of the Plain,* 13 ("that race of beings").

314. For exploration of this issue from the perspective of the responsibilities of the American law school, see David A. J. Richards, "Liberal Political Culture and the Marginalized Voice: Interpretive Responsibility and the American Law School," *Stanford Law Review* 45 (1993): 1955.

consciously and aggressively wars on the ethical empowerment of gay and lesbian persons to protest its injustice.[315] We need an interpretation of suspect classification analysis adequate to our indignation at the power this unjust culture has uncritically enjoyed and plainly continues to enjoy. While the analogy to sexism plays an important part in the critical analysis of the unjust stereotypes underlying homophobia,[316] the textually explicit constitutional objection to unjust religious persecution affords another central organizing ground for our indignation.

The most illuminating constitutional analogy for the suspectness of sexual preference in contemporary American politics is neither race nor gender, but religion.[317] The constitutional protection of religion never turned on its putative immutable and salient character (people can and do convert, and can and do conceal their religious convictions), but on the traditional place of religion in the conscientious and reasonable formation of one's moral identity in public and private life and the need for protection, consistent with respect for the inalienable right of conscience, of persons against state impositions of sectarian religious views. The identifications reasonably constitutive of one's self-respect as a person of conscience are not to be subject to sectarian impositions through public law that unreasonably burden the exercise of one's conscientious convictions (the free exercise principle[318]) or encourage change of such convictions to sectarian orthodoxy (the antiestablishment principle[319]). Normative claims by gay and lesbian persons today have exactly the same ethical and constitutional force: they are in their nature claims to a self-respecting personal and moral identity in public and private life through which they may reasonably express and realize their ethical convictions of the moral powers of love and friendship in a good, fulfilled, and responsible life against the background of an un-

315. See, for important recent studies of the distorting power of this reactionary political movement in American politics, Chris Bull and John Gallagher, *Perfect Enemies: The Religious Right, the Gay Movement, and the Politics of the 1990's* (New York: Crown Publishers, 1996); Herman, *The Antigay Agenda.*

316. See Francisco Valdes, " 'Sex,' 'Gender,' and 'Sexual Orientation' in Euro-American Law and Society," *California Law Review* 83 (1995): 1; Andrew Koppelman, "Why Discrimination against Lesbians and Gay Men Is Sex Discrimination," *New York University Law Review* 69 (1994): 197; id., *Antidiscrimination Law and Social Equality,* 146–76; Cass R. Sunstein, "Homosexuality and the Constitution," *Indiana Law Journal* 19 (1993): 1; Marc A. Fajer, "Can Two Real Men Eat Quiche Together? Storytelling, Gender-Role Stereotypes, and Legal Protection for Lesbians and Gay Men," *University of Miami Law Review* 46 (1992): 511.

317. See Richards, *Foundations of American Constitutionalism,* 260, 280.

318. For fuller discussion, see Richards, *Toleration and the Constitution,* 140–46.

319. Ibid., 146–62.

just and now quite conspicuously sectarian tradition of moral subjugation.[320]

Correspondingly, the political reaction to such claims—reflected, as we shall later see, in Colorado Amendment Two and related arguments against gays in the military and gay marriage—expressed sectarian religious objection precisely to the conscientious claims of justice made by and on behalf of gay and lesbian identity as a form of conscience entitled to equal respect under fundamental American guarantees of freedom of conscience. At the bottom of the political reaction is that the very fact of gay and lesbian identity (in virtue of its conscientiously public claims to justice) is as unworthy of respect as a traditionally despised religion (like Judaism); the practice of that form of conscience may thus be abridged, and certainly persons may be encouraged to convert from its demands or, at least, be supinely and ashamedly silent. This is the very pith and substance of constitutionally illegitimate religious intolerance, which has no proper place under the letter and spirit of American constitutionalism. Sexual preference should be a suspect classification on the most traditional and conservative readings of American constitutional principles, namely, on the ground that it has been and is the object of unjust sectarian intolerance against the essential and inalienable human right of conscience and other basic rights of the person. Gay and lesbian persons have as much right to make claims on the basis of such principles as any persons and citizens in America. It is time that they reclaimed America's traditions of toleration from the bigoted religious sectarians of the right who have so degraded and abused them.

The essential points of the suspect classification analysis of sexual preference are (1) a history and culture of unjust moral slavery of homosexuals, (2) the political legitimation of such subjugation by the exclusion of homosexuals from the constitutional community of equal rights in the transparently unreasonable way that gives rise to dehumanizing subordination and the irrational political prejudice of homophobia, and (3) the aggressive sectarian religious expression of such prejudice against the conscientious claims of gay and lesbian persons to justice in public and private life.

HISTORY OF THE MORAL SLAVERY OF HOMOSEXUALS. The history and culture of the moral subjugation of homosexuals is ancient. Plato in *The Laws* gave influential expression to the moral

320. For a related argument to similar effect to the one I offer here, see Janet E. Halley, "The Politics of the Closet: Towards Equal Protection for Gay, Lesbian, and Bisexual Identity," *UCLA. Law Review* 37 (1989): 915.

condemnation in terms of two arguments: its nonprocreative character and (in its male homosexual forms) its degradation of the passive male partner to the status of a woman.[321] Homosexuality was, on this view, an immoral and unnatural abuse of the proper human function of sexuality, marking the homosexual as subhuman and therefore wholly outside the moral community of persons. The exile of homosexuals from any just claim on moral community was given expression by the striking moral idea of homosexuality as unspeakable. It was, in Blackstone's terms, "a crime not fit to be named: *peccatum illud horribile, inter christianos non nominandum*"[322]—not mentionable, let alone discussed or assessed. Such total silencing of any reasonable discussion rendered homosexuality into a kind of cultural death, naturally thus understood and indeed condemned as a kind of ultimate heresy against essential moral values.[323]

The traditional moral condemnation of homosexuality was thus, in its historical nature, a form of intolerance that should have been subject to appropriate political and constitutional assessment in light of the argument for toleration.[324] However, liberal political theory, as in the related area of gender,[325] not only failed reasonably to extend its analysis to sexual preference, it indulged irrationalist intolerance by accepting an unreasonable conception of constitutional community excluding homosexuals as subhuman and thus unworthy of the rights of conscience, free speech, intimate life, and work central to the exercise

---

321. See Plato, *Laws,* book 8, 835d–842a, in *The Collected Dialogues of Plato,* ed. Edith Hamilton and Huntington Cairns (New York: Pantheon, 1961), 1401–2. On the moral condemnation of the passive role in homosexuality in both Greek and early Christian moral thought, see Peter Brown, *The Body and Society: Men, Women, and Sexual Renunciation in Early Christianity* (New York: Columbia University Press, 1988), 30, 382–83. But, for evidence of Greco-Roman toleration of long-term homosexual relations even between adults, see John Boswell, *Same-Sex Unions in Premodern Europe* (New York: Villard Books, 1994), 53–107. I am grateful to Stephen Morris for conversations on this point. Whether these relationships were regarded as marriages may be a very different matter. For criticism of Boswell's argument along this latter line, see Brent D. Shaw, "A Groom of One's Own?" *The New Republic,* 18 July 1994, 33–41.

322. See William Blackstone, *Commentaries on the Laws of England* (Chicago: University of Chicago Press, 1979), 4:216.

323. For further discussion of this point, see Richards, *Toleration and the Constitution,* 278–79. For a useful historical overview on the social construction of homosexuality, see David F. Greenberg, *The Construction of Homosexuality* (Chicago: University of Chicago Press, 1988).

324. For further elaboration of this argument and its implications for American constitutional law, see Richards, *Toleration and the Constitution;* id., *Foundations of American Constitutionalism;* id., *Conscience and the Constitution.*

325. For fuller development of this point, see Richards, *Conscience and the Constitution,* 178–91.

of their moral powers.[326] The same defective political epistemology of gender and sexuality that unleashed the long-standing cultural intolerance against women[327] applied, *a fortiori,* to homosexuals, a group whose sexuality was, because morally unspeakable, even less well understood or fairly discussed or empirically assessed. The vacuum of fair discussion and assessment was filled by the fears and irrationalist stereotypes reflective of the long moral tradition that exiled homosexuals from moral community.

It is consistent with this argument about homophobia as a culturally constructed irrational prejudice (an insult to culture-creating rights) to observe the extraordinarily important role homosexuals have played in the construction of Western culture, including its arts.[328] An argument of essential human rights is not directed at saints, heroes, or persons of genius, who can find creative redemption in circumstances that crush the moral powers of other people. The cultural tradition of the West may honor its women and men of genius who are homosexuals, but not as homosexuals and not homosexuals as such; basic human rights of conscience, speech, intimate life, and work were not extended to them as homosexuals. The bitter, plain truth is that ordinary people of good will, whose sexual preference was homosexual, could find in their culture only their denial as unspeakable, voiceless, dead.

THE POLITICS OF HOMOPHOBIA.   The persisting political force of irrationalist homophobia, as an independent constitutional evil, is quite apparent today when persons feel free to indulge their prejudices against homosexuals (as more fully discussed in chapters 7 and 8), although neither of the two traditional moral reasons for condemning homosexuality can any longer be legitimately and indeed constitutionally imposed by society at large on any other person or group of persons.

One such moral reason (the condemnation of nonprocreational sex) can, for example, no longer constitutionally justify laws against the sale to and use of contraceptives by married and unmarried heterosexual couples.[329] The mandatory enforcement at large of the procreational model of sexuality is, in circumstances of overpopulation and declining

326. For relevant historical background, see David A. J. Richards, *The Moral Criticism of Law* (Encino, Cal.: Dickenson-Wadsworth, 1977), 78–82.

327. For fuller elaboration, see Richards, *Conscience and the Constitution,* 178–91.

328. See, in general, Wayne R. Dynes, ed., *Encyclopedia of Homosexuality,* 2 vols. (New York: Garland Publishing, Inc., 1990).

329. See *Griswold v. Connecticut,* 381 U.S. 479 (1965); *Eisenstadt v. Baird,* 405 U.S. 438 (1972).

infant and adult mortality, a sectarian ideal lacking adequate secular basis in the general goods that can alone reasonably justify state power; accordingly, contraceptive-using heterosexuals have the constitutional right to decide when and whether their sexual lives shall be pursued to procreate or as an independent expression of mutual love, affection, and companionship.[330]

And the other moral reason for condemning homosexual sex (the degradation of a man to the passive status of a woman) assumes the sexist premise of the degraded nature of women that has been properly rejected as a reasonable basis for laws or policies on grounds of suspect classification analysis.[331] If we constitutionally accept the suspectness of gender on a par with that of race, we must in principle condemn, as a basis for law, any use of stereotypes expressive of the unjust enforcement of gender roles through law. That condemnation extends, as authoritative case law makes clear, to gender stereotypy as such whether immediately harmful to women or to men.[332]

Nonetheless, although each moral ground for the condemnation of homosexuality has been independently rejected as a reasonable justification for coercive laws enforceable on society at large (applicable to both men and women), they unreasonably retain their force when brought into specific relationship to the claims of homosexual men and women for equal justice under constitutional law.[333] These claims are today in their basic nature arguments of principle made by gay men and lesbians for the same respect for their intimate love life and other basic rights, free of unreasonable procreational and sexist requirements, now rather generously accorded men and women who are het-

330. For further discussion, see Richards, *Toleration and the Constitution,* 256–61.

331. See, for example, *Frontiero v. Richardson,* 411 U.S. 677 (1973); *Craig v. Boren,* 429 U.S. 190 (1976). On homophobia as rooted in sexism, see Elisabeth Young-Bruehl, *The Anatomy of Prejudices,* 143, 148–51.

332. For cases which protect women from such harm, see *Reed v. Reed,* 404 U.S. 71 (1971) (right to administer estates); *Frontiero v. Richardson,* 411 U.S. 677 (1973) (dependency allowances to servicewomen); *Stanton v. Stanton,* 421 U.S. 7 (1975) (child support for education). For cases that protect men, see *Wengler v. Druggists Mutual Insurance Co.,* 446 U.S. 142 (1980) (widower's right to death benefits); *Craig v. Boren,* 429 U.S. 190 (1976) (age of drinking for men).

333. On the continuities among heterosexual and homosexual forms of intimacy in the modern era, see, in general, John D'Emilio and Estelle B. Freedman, *Intimate Matters: A History of Sexuality in America* (New York: Harper & Row, 1988), 239–360; Anthony Giddens, *The Transformation of Intimacy: Sexuality, Love, and Eroticism in Modern Societies* (Cambridge, U.K.: Polity, 1992). See also Barbara Ehrenreich, Elizabeth Hess, and Gloria Jacobs, *Remaking Love: The Feminization of Sex* (New York: Anchor, 1986); Anne Snitow, Christine Stansell and Sharon Thompson, eds., *Powers of Desire* (New York: Monthly Review Press, 1983); Carole S. Vance, ed., *Pleasure and Danger: Exploring Female Sexuality* (Boston: Routledge & Kegan Paul, 1984).

erosexually coupled (including, as we have seen, even the right to abortion against the alleged weight of fetal life). Empirical issues relating to sexuality and gender are now subjected to more impartial critical assessment than they were previously, and the resulting light of public reason about issues of sexuality and gender should be available to all persons on fair terms. However, both the procreational mandates and the unjust gender stereotypy, constitutionally condemned for the benefit of heterosexual men and women, are ferociously applied to homosexual men and women.[334] It bespeaks the continuing political power of the traditional moral slavery of homosexuals that such a claim of fair treatment (an argument of basic constitutional principle if any argument is) was contemptuously dismissed by a majority of the Supreme Court of the United States (5–4) in 1986 in *Bowers v. Hardwick*.[335] No skeptical scrutiny whatsoever was accorded state purposes elsewhere acknowledged as illegitimate. Certainly, no such purpose could be offered of the alleged weight of fetal life that has been rejected as a legitimate ground for criminalization of all forms of abortion; any claim of public health could be addressed, as they would be in comparable cases of heterosexual relations involving the basic constitutional right of intimate life, by constitutionally required alternatives less restrictive and more effective than criminalization (including use of prophylactics by those otherwise at threat from transmission of AIDS).[336]

Traditional moral arguments, now clearly rejected in their application to heterosexuals, were uncritically applied to a group much more exigently in need of constitutional protection on grounds of principle.[337] Reasonable advances in the public understanding of sexuality and gender, now constitutionally available to all heterosexuals, were

334. On the unjust gender stereotypy uncritically applied to homosexual men and women, see Susan Moller Okin, "Sexual Orientation and Gender: Dichotomizing Differences," in David M. Estlund and Martha C. Nussbaum, *Sex, Preference, and Family: Essays on Law and Nature* (New York: Oxford University Press, 1997), 44–59.

335. *Bowers v. Hardwick*, 478 U.S. 186 (1986).

336. The argument applies, in any event, only to those forms of sex by gay men likely to transmit the disease; it does not reasonably apply to lesbians, nor does it apply to all forms of sex (including anal sex) by gay men. So, the argument that sex acts as such can be criminalized on this basis is constitutionally overinclusive, inconsistent with the basic right thus abridged. The regulatory point is that even gay men at threat by virtue of their sexual practices can take preventive measures against this threat (by using condoms). For a recent discussion of what further such reasonable preventive measures the gay men at threat might also take, see Gabriel Rotello, *Sexual Ecology: AIDS and the Destiny of Gay Men* (New York: Dutton, 1997).

337. For further criticism, see Richards, *Foundations of American Constitutionalism*, 209–47.

suspended in favor of an appeal to the sexual mythology of the Middle Ages.[338] The transparently unprincipled character of *Bowers* confirms the unjust continuing complicity of American constitutionalism with the legitimation of the cultural construction of the moral slavery of homosexuals.[339] If the *Plessy* court illegitimately fostered the construction of American racism, the *Bowers* court has illegitimately advanced the construction of homophobia. Such legal and related political aggression against the rights of any group, on the ground of arguments regarded as illegitimate to abridge the rights of any other persons, unjustly enforces, indeed constructs the dehumanization that sustains moral slavery.

DEPRIVATION OF RIGHTS. The moral insult of homophobia, like that of racism and sexism, cannot be limited to any particular right, but to the denigration of one's status as a bearer of basic human rights (to conscience, speech, intimate life, and work) within the moral community of equal rights, in particular, unjust contempt for conscientious personal and moral identity as a lesbian or gay person. Suspect classification analysis arose from the study of the radical political evil of a political culture, ostensibly committed to toleration on the basis of universal human rights, that unjustly denied a class of persons their inalienable human rights as persons with moral powers on the basis of the structural injustice of moral slavery. Liberal political culture, consistent with respect for this basic right, must extend to all persons the cultural resources that enable them critically to explore, define, express, and revise the identifications central to free moral person-

338. Justice Blackmun put the point acidly: "Like Justice Holmes, I believe that 'it is revolting to have no better reason for a rule of law than that so it was laid down in the time of Henry IV. It is still more revolting if the grounds upon which it was laid down have vanished long since, and the rule simply persists from blind imitation of the past.'" *Bowers*, 478 U.S. at 199, quoting Oliver Wendell Holmes, "The Path of the Law," *Harvard University Law Review* 10 (1897): 457, 469.

339. I develop this argument at greater length in Richards, *Foundations of American Constitutionalism*, chap. 6; and in David A. J. Richards, "Constitutional Legitimacy and Constitutional Privacy," *New York University Law Review* 61 (1986): 800. See also Anne D. Goldstein, "History, Homosexuality, and Political Values: Searching for the Hidden Determinants of *Bowers v. Hardwick*," *Yale Law Journal* 97 (1988): 1073; Nan D. Hunter, "Life after *Hardwick*," *Harvard Civil Rights–Civil Liberties Law Review* 27 (1992): 531; Janet E. Halley, "Reasoning about Sodomy: Act and Identity in and after *Bowers v. Hardwick*," *Virginia Law Review* 79 (1993): 1721; Anne B. Goldstein, "Reasoning about Homosexuality: A Commentary on Janet Halley's 'Reasoning about Sodomy: Act and Identity in and after *Bowers v. Hardwick*,'" *Virginia Law Review* 79 (1993): 1781; Kendall Thomas, "The Eclipse of Reason: A Rhetorical Reading of *Bowers v. Hardwick*," *Virginia Law Review* 79 (1993): 1805.

ality;[340] the constitutional evil, condemned by suspect classification analysis in the case of sexual preference, is the systematic deprivation of this basic right to a group of persons, unjustly degraded from their status as persons entitled to respect for the reasonable exercise of their free moral powers in the identifications central to an ethical life based on mutual respect. To deny such a group, already the subject of a long history and culture of moral slavery, their culture-creating rights is to silence in them the very voice of their moral freedom, rendering unspoken and unspeakable the sentiments, experience, and reason that authenticate the moral personality that a political culture of human rights owes each and every person (including, as we saw earlier, their moral powers to know and claim their basic rights and to protest injustice on such grounds). Sexual preference is and should be a fully suspect classification because homosexuals are today victimized, in the same way claims to basic rights by African Americans and women are and have been, by irrational political prejudices rooted in this radical political evil, denying them the cultural resources of free moral personality.

Such political prejudice is an evil, subject to suspect classification analysis, whatever the form of erotic and emotional life in which a homosexual finds fulfillment.[341] There is as great a variety and range in homosexual as there is in heterosexual erotic intimacy and personal relations. It is an indication of the genre of dehumanizing stereotypes at work in *Bowers v. Hardwick*, stripping a class of persons (blacks, women, Jews, homosexuals) of moral personality by reducing them to a mythologized sexuality, that the Court focused so obsessively on one sex act (sodomy); as Leo Bersani perceptively observed about the public discourse (reflected in *Bowers*), it resonates in images (inherited from the nineteenth century) of homosexuals as sexually obsessed prostitutes.[342] In fact, as Whitman insisted, homosexual love is no more exclusively about sex than heterosexuality. The Court, however, unjustly constructs a difference on the basis of the tradition of moral slavery. It thus ignored not only the manifold sensual variety of erotic intimacies of homosexual (like heterosexual) bonding, but the complex, symbolically elaborated, and idealized forms of intense, deeply loving

340. For development of this theme, see Will Kymlicka, *Liberalism, Community, and Culture* (Oxford: Clarendon Press, 1989), 162–78; Yael Tamir, *Liberal Nationalism* (Princeton: Princeton University Press, 1993), 13–56.

341. See, in general, Janet E. Halley, "Reasoning about Sodomy: Act and Identity in and after *Bowers v. Hardwick*," *Virginia Law Review* 79 (1993): 1721.

342. See Leo Bersani, "Is the Rectus as a Grave?" in Douglas Crimp, *Cultural Analysis/ Cultural Activism* (Cambridge: The MIT Press, 1988), 211–12, 222.

relationships central to homosexual (like heterosexual) friendship and love, the tender humane mutualities of nurture, transparent understanding, play, concern, and commitment that arise from a common sensibility and imaginative life, conscientious way of thinking and feeling, and shared experience. What is decisively in play in American life today is the claim for self-respecting public and private identity as lesbian and gay persons, in particular, the right to a life and culture, reflecting and expressing one's moral powers, on terms free of a rights-denying political irrationalism that would aggressively silence minds and hearts competent to understand, feel, and protest rank injustice both in public and private life callously done them by sectarian bigots. The political prejudice of homophobia remains the same evil of radical cultural intolerance, whatever the sex life in question or not in question, because it denies the cultural space through which persons of homosexual preference may reasonably define and identify themselves with a life of personal and ethical self-respect on whatever terms best give expression to their free moral powers. The suspectness of sexual preference arises precisely from the target of irrationalist homophobia on the claim of gay and lesbian identity to basic human rights, and should be constitutionally condemned for this reason.[343]

Another way of making the same point, as we earlier saw, is to observe that homophobic prejudice, like racism and sexism, unjustly distorts the idea of human rights applicable to both public and private life. Like the other main forms of moral slavery (racism and sexism), such prejudice, remitting homosexuals to a degraded private sphere, injures their basic human rights to both a public and private life. The intellectual reign of terror that we earlier saw aims to impose racism and anti-Semitism on the larger society and even on these stigmatized minorities themselves aims to enforce homophobia at large and self-hating homophobia in particular on homosexuals as well. Its vehicle is the denigration of gay and lesbian identity as a devalued form of conscience with which no one, under pain of ascribed membership in such

343. For an argument alone these lines, albeit not claiming to address the status of sexual preference as a full suspect classification, see *Steffan v. Aspin*, 8 F.3d 57 (D.C. Cir. 1993) (Mikva, J.), *rehearing en banc granted and judgment vacated* (1994). *Steffan* is distinguishable from predecessor appellate court decisions in one striking respect. In *Steffan*, in contrast to previous cases, the discharged service member did not admit to, nor did the Navy claim, any improper—specifically, homosexual—conduct on his part. For earlier cases, see, for example, *Dronenberg v. Zech*, 741 F.2d 1388 (D.C. Cir. 1984); *Woodward v. United States*, 871 F.2d 1068 (Fed. Cir. 1989); *Rich v. Secretary of the Army*, 735 F.2d 1220 (10th Cir. 1984). For one opinion that ruled on homosexual status, not alleged or admitted misconduct, relying on the military reasoning rejected by Judge Mikva as constitutionally defective, see *Ben-Shalom v. Marsh*, 881 F.2d 454 (7th Cir. 1989).

a devalued species, can or should identify. It is such claims that are currently distorted by sectarian viewpoints into claims for special rights[344] and are indeed aggressively attacked on such sectarian grounds (as I more fully show in the next chapter), thus unconstitutionally expressing sectarian religious intolerance through public law.

The political evil of this prejudice, based on the compulsory secrecy of the preference, is not always ameliorated and may indeed sometimes be aggravated by the growing practice of either not enforcing or repealing or otherwise invalidating criminal laws against homosexual sex. Such developments—without comparable antidiscrimination guarantees against homophobic prejudice—legitimate the ancient idea of something unspeakably and properly private, something all the more outrageous if given any public expression whatsoever (thus, legitimating sexist violence against forms of public expression of homosexual preference).[345] But such compulsory privatization insults homosexuals in the same way it traditionally insulted African Americans and women: it deprives them as moral persons of their right to speak and feel and live as whole persons on the terms of public and private life best expressive of their free moral powers. That is the moral right of every person in a free society, and lesbian and gay persons have a right to it on equal terms.

It is for this reason that, in my judgment, appropriate constitutional remedies for homophobic prejudice include the range of remedies appropriate in the case of race and gender. I include affirmative action among these remedies, in contrast to some commentators,[346] because the underlying constitutional concern should be the reasonable decon-

---

344. The rhetoric of "special rights" has been conspicuously used in support of antigay/ lesbian intitiatives and referenda, blatantly mischaracterizing a principled claim of persons to be free of invidious discrimination that is no more a claim to special consideration than any other claim (for example, by African Americans and women) to be protected from such discrimination. The distorting characterization has been noted by several courts in refusing to allow proposed lawmaking to include such a description of antidiscrimination laws. See, for example, *Faipeas v. Municipality of Anchorage*, 860 P.2d 1214 (Alaska 1993) (referendum petition to repeal "special homosexual ordinance" does not fairly characterize ordinance which it proposes to repeal); *Citizens for Responsible Behavior v. Superior Court*, 2 Cal. Rptr. 2d 648 (Cal. Ct. App. 1991) (proposed initiative, including notice of intent to circulate petition that described antidiscrimination legislation as conferring special rights, held to be fraud on electorate). Cf. *Mabon v. Keisling*, 856 P.2d 1023 (Or. 1993) (initiative modified to strike reference to removing homosexuality as minority status subject to special classifications).

345. Cf. Kendall Thomas, "Beyond the Privacy Principle," *Columbia Law Review* 92 (1992): 1413.

346. See Michael Ruse, *Homosexuality,* 265–67. For a good general treatment of the need for antidiscrimination protections for homosexuals, see Richard D. Mohr, *Gays/Justice: A Study of Ethics, Society, and Law* (New York: Columbia University Press, 1988), 137–211.

struction of the compulsory privatization of homosexual preference. Homosexuals cannot justly be required to be secretive as the condition of fair access to public goods; to the extent they are so required, they suffer unjust discrimination on grounds of sectarian prejudice. Such prejudice can, as in the case of race and gender, be appropriately remedied by appropriate affirmative action plans that both insure that the qualifications of public homosexuals are fairly assessed and that the presence of such homosexuals in various positions challenges and undermines political prejudice in society at large.

As my earlier analysis of the basis of the Western condemnation of homosexuality suggests, homophobia may be reasonably understood today as a persisting form of residual and quite unjust gender discrimination.[347] The nonprocreative character of homosexual sexuality may be of relatively little concern, but its cultural symbolism of disordered gender roles excites anxieties in a political culture still quite unjustly sexist in its understanding of gender roles; indeed the condemnation of homosexuality acts as a reactionary reinforcement of sexism generally. As we earlier saw, the emergence of the modern conception of homosexual identity, as intrinsically effeminate (in gay men), and later mannish (in lesbians)[348] accompanied the emergence of modern Western culture after 1700 and was associated with the reinforcement of the sexist definition of gender roles in terms of which the supposedly greater equality of men and women was interpreted.[349] Male homosexuals as such were thus symbolically understood as "effeminate members of a third or intermediate gender, who surrender their rights to be treated as dominant males, and are exposed instead to a merited contempt as a species of male whore."[350] (In the more overtly sexist and homophile ancient Greek world only the passive male partner would be thus interpreted.[351]) Homosexuals as such—both lesbians

347. Cf. Sylvia A. Law, "Homosexuality and the Social Meaning of Gender," *Wisconsin Law Review* (1988): 187.

348. On the later development of lesbian identity, see Lillian Faderman, *Odd Girls and Twilight Lovers: A History of Lesbian Life in Twentieth-Century America* (New York: Columbia University Press, 1991); Carroll Smith-Rosenberg, *Disorderly Conduct: Visions of Gender in Victorian America* (New York: Knopf, 1985), 245–97.

349. See, in general, Randolph Trumbach, "Gender and the Homosexual Role in Modern Western Culture: The 18th and 19th Centuries Compared," *Homosexuality, Which Homosexuality?: International Conference on Gay and Lesbian Studies*, ed. Dennis Altman et al. (London: GMP Publishers, 1989), 149–69.

350. Ibid., 153.

351. For a probing recent study, see Eva Cantarella, *Bisexuality in the Ancient World*, trans. Cormac O Cuilleanain (New Haven: Yale University Press, 1992); but see also Boswell, *Same-Sex Unions in Premodern Europe*, 53–107.

and male homosexuals—are, on this persisting modern view, in revolt
against what many still suppose to be the "natural" order of gender
hierarchy: women or men, as the case may be, undertaking sexual roles
improper to their gender (women loving other women (independent
of men[352]), men loving other men (independent of women), or dominance in women, passivity in men). It is plainly unjust to displace such
sexist views, no longer publicly justifiable against heterosexual women
or men, against a much more culturally marginalized and despised
group—symbolic scapegoats of the feeble and cowardly sense of self
that seeks self-respect in the unjust degradation of morally innocent
people of good will.[353] It should also be constitutionally condemned as
a form of unjust gender discrimination, perpetuating unjustly rigid and
impermeable gender stereotypes (whether of women or men) that enforce their claims by indulging the dehumanization of any gender dissident (as a degraded or fallen women).[354] Homosexuals have the right,
on grounds of the antisexist prong of suspect classification analysis, to
be protected from such irrational prejudice. In addition, they have the
constitutional right, as a matter of principle, to be protected from the
expression through public law of sectarian religious prejudice targeted
specifically against claims for justice by lesbian and gay identity based
on the reasonable elaboration of constitutional principles of antidiscrimination and privacy now accepted for all other persons. The sexist
roots of modern homophobia should only confirm the irrationalism
of the prejudice and the constitutional illegitimacy of its unprincipled
expression through public law against one group and one group exclusively, namely, a small and traditionally despised minority the legitimacy of whose claims are most invisible to uncritical public opinion.

352. For commentary on the sexism of heterosexism, see Adrienne Rich, "Compulsory
Heterosexuality and Lesbian Existence," in Catharine R. Stimpson and Ethel Spector Person,
Women: Sex and Sexuality (Chicago: University of Chicago Press, 1980). It is also reprinted
in Henry Abelove, Michele Aina Barale, David M. Halperin, eds., *The Lesbian and Gay
Studies Reader* (New York: Routledge, 1993), 227–54.

353. On the antifeminism of antigay sectarian groups, see Didi Herman, *The Antigay
Agenda,* 103–10; on their opposition, in general, to the agenda of civil rights in all areas, see
ibid., 111–36, 140.

354. For important recent arguments along these lines, see Katherine M. Franke, "The
Central Mistake of Sex Discrimination Law: The Disaggregation of Sex from Gender," *University of Pennsylvania Law Review* 144 (1995): 1; Mary Ann C. Case, "Disaggregating Gender from Sex and Sexual Orientation: The Effeminate Man in the Law and Feminist Jurisprudence," *Yale Law Journal* 105 (1995): 90.

THE SCOPE OF SUSPECT CLASSIFICATION ANALYSIS

Suspect classification analysis, on the view I defend, constitutionally condemns the expression through law of the inadequate grounds that enforce the structural injustice I call moral slavery. My view of the limits on the scope of application of this analysis correspondingly turns on the availability of compelling secular reasons (justifying the abridgment of basic rights) undistorted by the background structural injustice of moral slavery. Moral slavery marks an extreme kind of dehumanizing injustice, the abridgment of the basic human rights of an entire group on inadequate grounds; it has moral and, under American public law, constitutional force within its proper domain of structural injustice rationalized to resist the demands of rights-based principle that legitimize political power under American constitutionalism. As I have argued, homosexuals have been and are subject to this justice, and, on this ground, sexual preference should be regarded as a fully suspect class on a par with race and gender. Accordingly, any distribution of state benefits and burdens that turns on sexual preference should be subject to as demanding a standard of compelling secular justification as race or gender. As I later argue, many such current laws should, on this ground, be held unconstitutional.

There are, of course, many other kinds of injustice besides moral slavery, and some of them are addressed by other constitutional principles. Many traditional areas of law do not raise the fundamental questions of structural injustice that are the concern of the theory of moral slavery, though they may raise other constitutional questions. In these cases, no group has systematically been excluded from protection of its basic human rights on constitutionally inadequate grounds, but a reasonable attempt made to protect the basic human rights of all and to abridge such rights only on compelling secular grounds reasonably acceptable to all. The analysis would clearly thus not be applicable to much (though not all) of the traditional law of homicide or to all prohibitions on sexual relations with the underaged. The law of homicide would thus pass muster (to the extent grounded in the legitimate protection of the right to life)[355] as would reasonable limitations on sexual relations with the immature. Perhaps the analysis would raise some skeptical questions about the ways in which age is defined for

---

355. To the extent substantive doctrines of the criminal law (like self-defense) are demonstrably distorted by moral slavery, they would, of course, be subject to constitutional criticism on such grounds. For an argument brilliantly suggestive of such an analysis, see Jane Maslow Cohen, "Regimes of Private Tyranny: What Do They Mean to Morality and for the Criminal Law?" *University of Pittsburgh Law Review* 57 (1996): 757.

purposes of sexual consent or even about the ferocity of punishments in some cases,[356] but some line in this area is, in my judgment, reasonably drawn.

What about applying this analysis to analogous cases, for example, of the poor, the mentally retarded, the undocumented alien, children born out of wedlock, and children generally? Poverty should not be regarded as constitutionally suspect solely on the same basis of structural injustice (systematic abridgment of basic rights on inadequate grounds) that race or gender or sexual preference are or should be suspect. Treatment of the poor certainly raises issues of justice, and some such issues may be of constitutional dimensions, but such constitutional issues may be better addressed not in terms of irrationalist prejudice but in terms of a different kind of constitutional argument (dealing with requirements of justice for an appropriate minimum of subsistence).[357]

Similarly, not all issues of constitutional injustice to children are usefully understood as expressions of a tradition of moral slavery (young age is, within limits, a reasonable basis for not fully extending the basic rights owed others), but in terms of other constitutional principles like equal opportunity, and the like.[358] On the other hand, children born out of wedlock may appropriately fit my analysis (to the extent their unjust treatment is grounded in the traditionalist enforcement of irrationalist stereotypes of gender and sexuality against a background of moral slavery), as would at least some aspects of the other cases (for example, policies resting on what in the circumstances can only be understood as irrationalist prejudices against the mentally ill or retarded in excess of any legitimate basis in their impaired or reduced competences[359]). Legal and even undocumented aliens might raise questions of constitutional suspectness, on my analysis, to the extent policies against them evinced a gratuitous hostility in excess of any rational basis for legitimate treatment of their legal or illegal status as

356. See, for a development of this theme (among other related themes), Gayle Rubin, "Thinking Sex: Notes for a Radical Theory of the Politics of Sexuality," in *Pleasure and Danger: Exploring Female Sexuality*, ed. Carole S. Vance (Boston: Routledge & Kegan Paul, 1984), 262–319, especially 272–73, 278–79, 288, 290.

357. I treat this issue along these lines in David A. J. Richards, *Conscience and the Constitution: History, Theory, and Law of the Reconstruction Amendments* (Princeton University Press, 1993), especially 244–51. Cf. Frank Michelman, "Foreword: On Protecting the Poor through the Fourteenth Amendment," *Harvard University Law Review* 83 (1969): 7–59.

358. For development of this analysis, see David A. J. Richards, "The Individual, the Family, and the Constitution," *New York University Law Review* 55 (1980): 1.

359. On this latter point, see *Cleburne v. Cleburne Living Center, Inc.*, 473 U.S. 432 (1985).

aliens, expressing, rather, long-standing cultural patterns of irrational-ist nativism and even racism, prejudices particularly invidious when directed against children.[360]

Suspect classification analysis, on the view I take of it, has its consti-tutional force and role against a certain background that I call moral slavery. Such a view has, as I have suggested, both its scope and its limits, but an account that is sensitive in the way I have urged to rights-based dissent and the capacity for moral growth such dissent fosters makes normative space for new insights into both the nature and depth of moral slavery in contemporary circumstances. That is, in my judg-ment, an interpretive and normative advantage of the account I offer. Retrospectively, it explains, as I have argued, much in the interpretive development of our public law centering on issues of race and gender. Prospectively, it challenges us to become more constitutionally self-critical of the entrenched forms of structural injustice that we often have so much difficulty in recognizing, let alone rectifying. An account of this area of our public law is a better one if it can help us more responsibly frame these latter constitutional issues at the very cutting edge of our constitutional conscience. The next two chapters investi-gate the interpretive and normative power of my account in helping us address several such issues.

360. See, on this latter point, *Plyer v. Doe*, 457 U.S. 202 (1982).

7   Unconstitutionality of Antigay/Lesbian Initiatives

T he struggle for adequate recognition of the human rights of lesbian and gay persons in the United States today faces an aggressively organized opposition that has targeted, in particular, the some
139 jurisdictions in the United States that have enacted laws that protect lesbians, gay men, and bisexuals from various forms of discrimination.[1] This organized opposition successfully secured the adoption of
Colorado Amendment Two, which not only repealed existing state laws
that protect gay people from discrimination, but also banned all future
laws that would recognize such claims by lesbians and gay men.[2] Argu-

---

1. See Note, "Constitutional Limits on Anti-Gay-Rights Initiatives," *Harvard University
Law Review* 106 (1993): 1905.

2. See Amendment Two to Colo. Const. art. 2, §2 (adopted Nov. 3, 1992). The full text
of Amendment Two is as follows:

> Neither the State of Colorado, through any of its branches or departments, nor any
> of its agencies, political subdivisions, municipalities or school districts, shall enact,
> adopt or enforce any statute, regulation, ordinance or policy whereby homosexual,
> lesbian or bisexual orientation, conduct, practices or relationships shall constitute or
> otherwise be the basis of, or entitle any person or class of persons to have or claim
> any minority status, quota preferences, protected status or claim of discrimination.
> This Section of the Constitution shall be self-executing.

The voters of Colorado approved Amendment Two by a vote of 53 percent to 47 percent
on November 3, 1992. On July 19, 1993, the Colorado Supreme Court affirmed the grant
of a preliminary injunction against the amendment. See *Evans v. Romer*, 854 P.2d 1270
(Colo.), *cert. denied*, 114 S. Ct. 419 (1993). On December 14, 1993, Judge H. Jeffrey Bayless
granted a permanent injunction against the amendment, finding that, under the strict scrutiny
standard applicable to the constitutional assessment of the amendment under *Evans*, the state

ments for constitutional limits on such antigay/lesbian initiatives have taken a number of forms, including guaranty clause objections to their antirepublican character,[3] objections on grounds of suspect classification analysis under the equal protection clause,[4] free speech and associational liberty claims under the First Amendment,[5] and abridgments of the fundamental right of political participation under the equal protection clause.[6] The last of these was endorsed by the Supreme Court of Colorado in its judgment affirming the lower court's injunction against enforcement of Colorado Amendment Two.[7]

Justice Kennedy, writing for the majority of the U.S. Supreme Court, affirmed the decision of the Colorado Supreme Court striking down Colorado Amendment Two, but on a different ground, namely, that the classification in question was "so discontinuous with the reasons offered for it that the amendment seems inexplicable by anything but animus toward the class it affects; it lacks a rational relationship to legitimate state interests."[8] In reaching this result, the Court emphasized that the protections, withheld by Colorado Amendment Two,

---

failed to justify the amendment in terms of compelling state interests. See *Evans v. Romer*, 1993 WL 518586 (Colo. Dist. Ct. 1993), reprinted in *The Bill of Rights versus the Ballot Box: Constitutional Implications of Anti-Gay Ballot Initiatives*, Continuing Legal Education Materials, presented by the Gay-Lesbian Bisexual Law Caucus of the Ohio State University, 12 March 1994 (hereinafter cited as *CLE Materials*) (on file with *Ohio State Law Journal*), 23–32.

3. See Hans A. Linde, "When Initiative Lawmaking Is Not 'Republican Government': The Campaign against Homosexuality," *Oregon Law Review* 72 (1993): 19; John F. Niblock, "Anti-Gay Initiatives: A Call for Heightened Judicial Scrutiny," *UCLA Law Review* 41 (1993): 153, 188–97.

4. See Note, "Constitutional Limits on Anti-Gay-Rights Initiatives," *Harvard University Law Review* 106 (1993): 1905, 1912–14; Niblock, "Anti-Gay Initiatives," 167–77.

5. See Note, "Constitutional Limits on Anti-Gay-Rights Initiatives," 1919–22.

6. Ibid., 1916–18; Niblock, "Anti-Gay Initiatives," 178–88.

7. See *Evans v. Romer*, 854 P.2d 1270 (Colo. 1993). Another argument, questioning the constitutionality of these initiatives, is a form of heightened rational basis scrutiny along the lines of *City of Cleburne v. Cleburne Living Center*, 473 U.S. 432 (1985) (striking down a zoning law that prohibited mentally retarded individuals from residing in certain parts of town). See Note, "Constitutional Limits on Anti-Gay-Rights Initiatives," 1914–16. Since the force of this argument depends on analogies to already existing suspect classes and fundamental rights, it will be only as strong as those analogies. Accordingly, this chapter will not independently explore this argument, but assumes that the interpretive insights afforded here can be usefully transposed to clarify its force. For example, if these initiatives, on analysis, express constitutionally suspect religious intolerance, that fact may clarify the special critical force that heightened rational basis scrutiny has been supposed to have in the case of these initiatives. For development of similar themes, see Niblock, "Anti-Gay Initiatives."

8. See *Romer v. Evans*, 116 S. Ct. 1620, 1627 (1996). On June 17, 1996, the Supreme Court vacated, on grounds of *Romer*, the judgment in a related case that had upheld the constitutionality of an antigay/lesbian ordinance of the City of Cincinnati. *Equality Foundation of Greater Cincinnati v. City of Cincinnati*, 116 S. Ct. 2519 (1996).

were "protections taken for granted by most people either because they already have them or do not need them; these are protections against exclusion from an almost limitless number of transactions and endeavors that constitute ordinary civic life in a free society."[9] Withholding such protections from a class of citizens cannot constitutionally be based on mere "animosity toward the class of persons affected";[10] Colorado Amendment Two is, however, such "a status-based enactment divorced from any factual context from which we could discern a relationship to legitimate state interests."[11] The Court concluded "that Amendment 2 classifies homosexuals not to further a proper legislative end but to make them unequal to everyone else. This Colorado cannot do. A State cannot so deem a class of persons a stranger to its laws."[12]

The application of the rational basis test in *Romer* is reminiscent of the first case in which the Supreme Court announced its skepticism about gender classifications, namely, *Reed v. Reed*.[13] The application of the rational basis standard with the consequence of invalidating such laws was in doctrinal tension with the many cases in which comparable laws with equally overinclusive and underinclusive legislative classifications had been upheld. *Reed* suggested what later cases made clear, that the Court had interpretively come to the view that some heightened level of constitutional scrutiny was owed to gender classifications. The Supreme Court in *Romer* could have obviated this problem by adopting the standard that had been proposed by several law professors in a brief, as *amici curiae,* namely, that any classifications (even a clearly nonsuspect one like renting one's home) would be per se invalid as the basis for a constitutional provision forbidding any local or state legislation that protects renters from any harm or loss.[14] The standard would have invalidated Colorado Amendment Two, but not a more narrowly drawn constitutional provision that forbade a single form of antidiscrimination statute—for example, local rent-control statutes or laws banning discrimination against homosexuals in hiring. Justice Kennedy wrote more broadly, casting doubt on amendments

---

9. *Romer,* 116 S. Ct. at 1627.

10. Id. at 1628.

11. Id. at 1629.

12. Id.

13. *Reed v. Reed,* 404 U.S. 71 (1971).

14. Professor Laurence Tribe of Harvard Law School was counsel of record, and he was joined by Professors John Hart Elly, Gerald Gunther, and Kathleen Sullivan of the Stanford Law School, and the late Philip B. Kurland of the University of Chicago Law School. For illuminating discussion, see Ronald Dworkin, "Sex, Drugs, and the Court," *The New York Review of Books* 43, no. 13, 8 August 1996, 49–50.

of both sorts as long as they used the classification in question in the forbidden way. Accordingly, the same doctrinal criticism may be made of *Romer* as was earlier made of *Reed:* why was heightened scrutiny owed to this as opposed to other classifications? If the decision is doctrinally problematic as a rational-basis decision, we need to ask how it might better be understood; in particular, what might the analogies be that made this state law, in the words of Justice Scalia's bitter dissent, "as reprehensible as racial or religious bias."[15] Scalia questions, along these lines, the elaboration of suspectness to sexual preference when the group in question is, in proportion to its numbers, quite politically powerful.[16]

In this chapter, I take up the challenge of Justice Scalia's dissent and explain how I believe *Romer* should be interpreted. I argue that the strongest constitutional argument for constitutional limits on antigay/lesbian rights initiatives has been the one least explored in the available literature[17] and the one all other arguments impliedly depend on for their force: namely, the initiatives in question express constitutionally forbidden sectarian religious intolerance through public law against fundamental rights of conscience, speech, and association of lesbian and gay persons protected by America's first and premier civil liberty, liberty of conscience.[18] My argument will thus critically examine the various current arguments regarding constitutional limits on antigay/lesbian rights initiatives; it will then constructively suggest the clarifying explanatory and normative power of the alternative perspective on this issue offered in the last chapter. This perspective points to religious intolerance as the first suspect classification under American constitutional law and the principled characterization of antigay/lesbian rights ordinances as reflecting this suspect classification. Indeed, my larger claim is that the suspectness of sexual preference instantiates the traditional suspectness of religious classifications, in this case, classifications based on gay and lesbian personal and moral conscientious

15. *Romer,* 116 S. Ct. at 1629.

16. Id. at 1637.

17. For example, the *Harvard Law Review* note dismisses, as "beyond the scope of this Note," a possible establishment clause objection to antigay-rights initiatives. Note, *Harvard University Law Review* 106 (1993): 1905, 1921. It is not explained why a note, entitled "Constitutional Limits on Anti-Gay-Rights Initiatives," fails to consider one of the more powerful constitutional arguments against such initiatives.

18. See, in general, William Lee Miller, *The First Liberty: Religion and the American Republic* (New York: Knopf, 1987); Thomas J. Curry, *The First Freedoms: Church and State in America to the Passage of the First Amendment* (New York: Oxford University Press, 1986); Leonard W. Levy, *The Establishment Clause: Religion and the First Amendment* (New York: Macmillan, 1986).

identity. If I am right, the initiatives in question run afoul of our histori-cally most robust and most textually explicit constitutional guarantees of the rights of the person. Ironically, the sectarian religious propo-nents of these initiatives egregiously degrade and abuse the American constitutional traditions of religious liberty they claim to cherish and protect.[19] It is time for Americans to reclaim and reaffirm their central constitutional guarantees of religious toleration and pluralism, basic rights owed, on terms of principle, to all Americans, including lesbian and gay Americans.

CURRENT CONSTITUTIONAL ARGUMENTS AGAINST ANTIGAY/LESBIAN INITIATIVES

All of the important current constitutional arguments against antigay/ lesbian initiatives impliedly assume and sometimes expressly identify a feature of these initiatives as relevant to their unconstitutional status, namely, their roots in sectarian religious intolerance.

Hans Linde's important development of a guaranty clause objection to these initiatives illustrates the latter point.[20] Linde makes a powerful historical and textual case against the judiciary's general failure to in-terpret the guaranty clause to raise objections to initiatives in general and suggests compelling reasons why such arguments should, in partic-ular, be developed to invalidate initiative lawmaking against the rights of homosexuals. Linde quite properly underscores Madison's objec-tions to Athenian mass assemblies and the need for a republican alter-native that would harness democratic political power (through the del-egation of such power to representative, deliberative political bodies) in ways more likely both to respect human rights and advance the public interest.[21] Consistent with the Madisonian political theory of

19. For example, a proposed antigay/lesbian initiative in Oregon rested its case on "a Right of Conscience," *CLE Materials*, 156, reprinting *DeParrie v. Keisling*, 862 P.2d 494 (Or. 1993).

20. See Hans A. Linde, "When Initiative Lawmaking Is Not 'Republican Government': The Campaign against Homosexuality," *Oregon Law Review* 72 (1993): 19.

21. Madison makes this point most clearly in *The Federalist* No. 63 in the following terms:

From these facts, to which many others might be added, it is clear that the principle of representation was neither unknown to the antients, nor wholly overlooked in their political constitutions. The true distinction between these and the American Govern-ments lies *in the total exclusion of the people in their collective capacity* from any share in the *latter*, and not in the *total exclusion of representatives of the people*, from the administration of the *former*. The distinction however thus qualified must be admitted to leave a most advantageous superiority in favor of the United States. But to ensure to this advantage its full effect, we must be careful not to separate it from the other advantage of an extensive territory. For it cannot be believed that any

American constitutionalism, Linde argues that initiatives must be condemned as antirepublican when they are functionally most equivalent to the factionalized excesses of the Athenian mass assemblies; he thus articulates five criteria of such functional equivalence.[22] Four of Linde's criteria relate to the factionalized character of such direct lawmaking, its mobilization of majoritarian factionalized group insularity against the conscientious views of unjustly stigmatized outsiders to dominant groups.[23] Madison, following Jefferson, had regarded liberty of conscience as the central inalienable right of free persons;[24] consistent with this view, Linde frames his criteria of equivalence to identify those forms of political factionalism that most put at threat the inalienable right to conscience. It is an analytically striking feature of Linde's position that, while his argument expressly assumes this Madisonian framework, he does not focus on the substantive normative considerations that motivate both Madison's and his own argument.

Other constitutional arguments against antigay/lesbian initiatives are, if anything, less explicit about the role these substantive normative considerations play in their view of the matter, yet on examination such considerations invariably clarify and strengthen the force such arguments have and should be taken to have.

For example, the claim that initiatives like Colorado Amendment Two unconstitutionally deploy a suspect classification standardly explores judicially accepted suspect classifications like race and gender in terms of features of these classifications (for example, political powerlessness, salience, and immutability) that are alleged to be analogous to sexual preference.[25] Although important analogies of principle of the constitutional suspectness accorded race and gender apply equally to sexual preference, these analogies cannot be plausibly understood in terms of political powerlessness, salience, or immutability, for none of these terms explain even the suspectness of race and gender, let alone sexual preference. Emphasis on these analogies not only fails to do justice to the suspectness of race and gender, but it renders problematic the suspectness of sexual preference for reasons that should

form of representative government, could have succeeded within the narrow limits occupied by the democracies of Greece.

The Federalist, ed. Jacob E. Cooke (Middletown, Conn.: Wesleyan University Press, 1961), 428. See also *The Federalist*, No. 10, for further development of these themes.

22. See Linde, "The Campaign against Homosexuality," 41–43.

23. Ibid., 41–42.

24. For fuller discussion, see David A. J. Richards, *Toleration and the Constitution* (New York: Oxford University Press, 1986), 111–16; id., *Foundations of American Constitutionalism* (New York: Oxford University Press, 1989), 173–82.

25. See Note, "Constitutional Limits on Anti-Gay-Rights Initiatives," 1912–14.

be and are irrelevant (for example, controversies over its salience and immutability).[26] A reasonable approach to suspect classification analysis must not be burdened by these false analogies.

The argument that antigay/lesbian initiatives abridge central free speech rights of homosexuals builds on the important role that traditional guarantees of free speech have played in the protection of speech associated with the development and expression of lesbian and gay public identity in American political and constitutional culture.[27] Thus such initiatives are condemned as violations of free speech because their constitutional repeal and prohibition of laws forbidding discrimination on grounds of sexual preference intimidates lesbian and gay persons not to assert their rights of free speech to affirm their homosexuality as a public identity. The argument has, as an argument of free speech, limited force applicable to the censorship of speech as such, an argument that some may find strained on the facts (Colorado Amendment Two, on this view, leaves the regime of free speech quite intact, robustly deployed in the weighty constitutional criticisms of the law under discussion here). Its argumentative force would be much more powerfully targeted on Colorado Amendment Two if it were not limited to censorship of speech, but to constitutionally suspect religious censorship of the life of conscience itself (in effect, degrading one form of conscientious conviction as less worthy of equal respect than others). Perhaps (as I believe) that is what advocates of this argument impliedly assume. If so, the force of their argument would be both clarified and deepened, as a matter of constitutional principle, if it were explicitly connected with the roots of the guarantee of free speech in freedom of conscience.[28] If the argument could be re-

26. For various judicial opinions that have foundered on such false analogies (denying the suspectness of sexual orientation on such grounds), see *Ben-Shalom v. Marsh*, 881 F.2d 454, 463–66 (7th Cir. 1989); *Padula v. Webster*, 822 F.2d 97, 101–4 (D.C. Cir. 1987); *High Tech Gays v. Defense Industrial Security Clearance Office*, 895 F.2d 563, 570–74 (9th Cir. 1990); *Woodward v. United States*, 871 F.2d 1068, 1075–76 (Fed. Cir. 1989). For an example of a judicial opinion that analytically rebutted these false analogies in a principled, analytically rigorous way (finding sexual preference to be a suspect classification), see *Watkins v. United States Army*, 847 F.2d 1329, 1345–49 (9th Cir. 1988).

27. See Note, "Constitutional Limits on Anti-Gay-Rights Initiatives," 1919–22. For the important role of arguments of free speech in the struggle for the rights of gay and lesbian persons, see Jose Gomez, "The Public Expression of Lesbian/Gay Personhood as Protected Speech," *Law and Inequality* 1 (1983): 121; Nan D. Hunter, "Identity, Speech, and Equality," *Virginia Law Review* 79 (1993): 1695; Nan D. Hunter, Sherryl E. Michaelson, and Thomas B. Stoddard, *The Rights of Lesbians and Gay Men*, 3d ed. (Carbondale and Edwardsville: Southern Illinois University Press, 1992), 1–14.

28. For extended argument to this effect, see Richards, *Toleration and the Constitution*, 165–87; Richards, *Foundations of American Constitutionalism*, 172–201.

conceived in this way, it would have force not only in its application to speech as conventionally understood, but to the issues of freedom of conscience that are, in fact, the central normative considerations at issue. We need a way of thinking about these questions that can clarify these connections and thus strengthen our constitutional arguments.

Finally, the argument that antigay/lesbian initiatives abridge fundamental rights of political participation[29] is an interpretive generalization from Supreme Court decisions invalidating attempts to restructure politics in ways hostile to racial minorities;[30] the principle of these cases is not, on this view, the suspectness of race, but a more general principle that constitutional rights of political participation are abridged when politics is restructured in ways hostile to any identifiable class, including not only constitutionally recognized suspect classes like racial minorities but other groups (like homosexuals) who are not, or at least not yet, a constitutionally recognized suspect class.[31] The argument's extrapolation from existing case law might have force if it were supported by convincing arguments of democratic political theory regarding the general terms of fair representation (namely, that such representation forbids all constitutional arrangements that are detrimental to any political group). There are, however, no such remotely plausible arguments as a matter of political and constitutional theory. Some political group will be hurt by any constitutional change, a fact irrelevant to the normative merits of the change (turning, rather, on whether the change, consistent with the political theory of American constitutionalism, either better protects basic rights or channels political power to pursuit of the public interest).[32] The argument based

29. See Note, "Constitutional Limits on Anti-Gay Rights Initiatives," 1916–18; *Evans v. Romer*, 854 P.2d 1270 (Colo. 1993).

30. See *Hunter v. Erickson*, 393 U.S. 385 (1969) (invalidating city charter amendment that repealed existing local antidiscrimination ordinances and that required future voter approval of any city ordinance dealing with racial, religious, or ancestral discrimination in housing); *Reitman v. Mulkey*, 387 U.S. 369 (1967) (facially neutral amendment to the California state constitution, which would have prevented the state from interfering with a person's "absolute" right to sell or rent property to whomever she wanted, constituted constitutionally forbidden discriminatory state action); *Washington v. Seattle School District No. 1*, 458 U.S. 457 (1982) (invalidating state initiative depriving local school districts of power, absent a judicial order, to eliminate racial imbalance through mandatory busing). But cf. *Crawford v. Los Angeles Board of Education*, 458 U.S. 527 (1982) (sustaining California constitutional amendment prohibiting court-ordered busing to alleviate de facto segregation).

31. Cf. Derrick A. Bell, Jr., "The Referendum: Democracy's Barrier to Racial Equality," *Washington Law Review* 54 (1978): 1.

32. On the political theory of American constitutionalism, see Richards, *Foundations of American Constitutionalism*; David A. J. Richards, *Conscience and the Constitution: History, Theory, and Law of the Reconstruction Amendments* (Princeton: Princeton University Press, 1993).

on the right of political participation has greater force when it is interpreted, as I believe it has been by both those who have advocated and
accepted it, against the background of the rights in fact placed at threat
by Colorado Amendment Two.

In general, the argument appealing to the right of political participation has force when rooted in some deprivation of basic rights, including rights against unjust discrimination. One of the leading cases, on
the basis of which the argument of a right of political participation
allegedly claims to base its case, makes this quite clear. In *Hunter v.
Erickson*,[33] an Akron charter amendment passed by voters required
that antidiscrimination measures related to race, religion, or ancestry
receive majority voter approval prior to enactment, while other ordinances remained subject to the original rule that required approval
only by the City Council. While Akron could decide to require all of
its municipal legislation to be approved by plebiscite, the Court held
that it could not selectively burden legislation directed against discrimination on the basis of race, religion, or ancestry. While acknowledging
"the section draws no distinctions among racial and religious groups,"
and that "Negroes and whites, Jews and Catholics are all subject to
the same requirements if there is housing discrimination against them
which they wish to end,"[34] the Court nevertheless found it had a discriminatory impact: "[A]lthough the law on its fact treats Negro and
white, Jew and gentiles in an identical matter, the reality is that the
law's impact falls on the minority. The majority needs no protection
against discrimination and if it did, a referendum might be bothersome
but no more than that."[35]

The interpretation of this doctrine has its real constitutional force
not in establishing a general right of all groups as such, but rights of
groups more narrowly construed on facts analogous to Colorado
Amendment Two, to wit, the roots of such constitutional lawmaking
in forms of constitutionally invidious intolerance. Indeed, under a principled interpretation of *Hunter*, the expression of religious discrimination against one particular group would be the rankest form of unconstitutional expression of religious intolerance; it would be as if the
Hunter initiative did not apply, nondiscriminatorily, to all religious discrimination, but just to religious discrimination against, say, Jews (an
analogy I explore at some length below). The constitutional outrage
of Colorado Amendment Two is of this magnitude. We need an argument to make this quite clear.

33. *Hunter v. Erickson*, 393 U.S. 385 (1969).
34. Id. at 390.
35. Id. at 391.

When we have done so, we shall need to inquire why gay and lesbian advocates have failed explicitly to make an argument that they both clearly believe and indeed must assume as the background for the plausible interpretation of the arguments they do make. We must also explore the constitutional stakes not only for justice to lesbian and gay persons, but for the role of lesbian and gay advocacy in the interpretive integrity of our constitutionalism, resting, as it does, on arguments of principle that give full and fair expression to the claim of all Americans to protection of their universal human rights.[36]

ANTIGAY/LESBIAN INITIATIVES AS CONSTITUTIONALLY INVIDIOUS RELIGIOUS INTOLERANCE

We need to bring the perspective offered in the previous chapter to bear on the analysis of the constitutionality of antigay/lesbian initiatives. These initiatives, exemplified by Colorado Amendment Two, constitutionally entrench a prohibition on laws that forbid discrimination on grounds of sexual preference in a much more bald and visibly invidious way than the comparable initiatives struck down by the Supreme Court because they entrenched constitutionally invidious racial and religious discrimination.[37]

As I have already argued, discrimination on grounds of sexual preference is, in its nature, a form of religious intolerance: it is a ground for suspectness older than the equal protection clause itself. The free exercise clause of the First Amendment thus condemns as suspect burdens placed on exercise of conscientious convictions unsupported by a compelling secular justification (especially, burdens targeted at a specific form of conscience);[38] and its companion antiestablishment clause

36. For development of this point, see Richards, *Foundations of American Constitutionalism,* 131–71.

37. Unlike *Reitman v. Mulkey,* 387 U.S. 369 (1967), Colorado Amendment Two explicitly singles out lesbians and gay men as a group, whereas the California amendment was facially neutral; the Colorado amendment also constitutionally entrenches not only a prohibition on laws against private discrimination, but against state discrimination as well. Amendment Two imposes an even more burdensome requirement than the amendment invalidated in *Hunter v. Erickson* because, rather than requiring a majority of a particular city, any successful repeal effort requires the approval of an entire state.

38. See, in general, Richards, *Toleration and the Constitution,* 141–46. Free exercise analysis was somewhat narrowly interpreted in *Employment Division of the Oregon Department of Human Resources v. Smith,* 494 U.S. 872 (1990) (religiously inspired peyote use not constitutionally exempt from neutral criminal statute criminalizing such use, and thus state permitted to deny employment benefits to persons dismissed from their jobs because of such use). The case, however, notably acknowledges the continuing authority of leading free exercise cases like *Sherbert v. Verner,* 374 U.S. 398 (1963) (state unemployment benefits, unavail-

renders suspect state support of sectarian religious views in contexts that encourage the teaching of and conversion to such views.[39] The state may not discriminate either against or in favor of sectarian conscience, but must extend equal respect to all forms of conscience. State-imposed discrimination on ground of sexual preference violates such equal respect for all forms of conscience.

Such discrimination takes objection to a conscientious form of moral thought and sensibility that makes public ethical claims to respect for a private and public identity on equal terms with the other forms of self-organized identity central to the right of conscience (i.e., the wide range of religious and irreligious views protected by both the free exercise and antiestablishment clauses of the First Amendment).[40]

---

able to Seventh Day Adventist because of failure to work on sabbath day, unconstitutionally burdens free exercise rights) and *Wisconsin v. Yoder,* 406 U.S. 205 (1972) (state compulsory education law unconstitutionally burdens free exercise rights of Amish parents to remove children from school after eighth grade). In *Church of the Lukumi Babalu Aye, Inc. v. City of Hialeah,* 508 U.S. 520 (1993), the Supreme Court clarified that *Smith* in no way limited the availability of free exercise analysis of a state law that nonneutrally targeted a specific religion (in this case, criminalizing animal sacrifice in Santeria religious rituals). The authority of *Smith* itself was cast in doubt in light of the Religious Freedom Restoration Act of 1993, S. Rep. No. 111, 103d Cong., 1st Sess. 14 (1993); for commentary, see Douglas Laycock, "Free Exercise and the Religious Freedom Restoration Act," *Fordham Law Review* 62 (1994): 883. The constitutionality of the Religious Freedom Restoration Act of 1993 itself was recently assessed by the Supreme Court in light of whether, on grounds of section 5 of the Fourteenth Amendment, it constitutionally expands or unconstitutionally contracts the constitutional right judicially defined by the Supreme Court in its free exercise jurisprudence, including *Smith.* For relevant case law on this question, see *South Carolina v. Katzenbach,* 383 U.S. 301 (1956); *Katzenbach v. Morgan,* 384 U.S. 641 (1966); *Oregon v. Mitchell,* 400 U.S. 112 (1970). The Act was held unconstitutional. See *City of Boerne v. P. F. Flores,* 1997 WL 345322 (U.S.).

39. See Richards, *Toleration and the Constitution,* 146–62.

40. Under the free exercise clause, the Supreme Court has tended, in the interest of reasonably developing the basic value of equality, to expand the constitutional concept of religion to protect conscience as such from coercion or undue burdens. See, for example, *United States v. Ballard,* 322 U.S. 78 (1944) (forbidding any inquiry into the truth or falsity of beliefs in a mail fraud action against the bizarre "I am" movement of Guy Ballard [alias "Saint Germain, Jesus, George Washington, and Godfre Ray King"]); *Torcaso v. Watkins,* 367 U.S. 488 (1960) (declaring unconstitutional a state requirement that state officials must swear belief in God); *United States v. Seeger,* 380 U.S. 163 (1965); *Welsh v. United States,* 398 U.S. 333 (1970) (congressional statutory exemption from military service—limited to religiously motivated conscientious objectors to all wars—extended to all who conscientiously object to all wars). But see *Employment Division of Oregon Department of Human Resources v. Smith,* 494 U.S. 872 (1990) (religiously inspired peyote use not exempt from general prohibition on such drug use and thus may be properly invoked by state to deny unemployment benefits to persons dismissed from their jobs because of such religiously inspired use). And under the anti-establishment clause, the Supreme Court has notably insisted that the public education curriculum may not privilege sectarian religious rituals and views over others. See,

Gay and lesbian identity—whether irreligiously, nonreligiously, or religiously grounded—is decidedly one among these views. Such identity is grounded in critically conscientious convictions both about the empowering personal and moral good of homosexual friendship and love (founded in the basic human good of love) and arguments of public reason about the injustice and ethical wrong of its condemnation and marginalization (the unprincipled failure to respect the self-authenticating right of all persons to the humane and basic good of love). The identity expresses itself in varied personal and political associations of mutual recognition, support, and respect and in demands for equal justice and for a public culture (including institutional forms) adequate to the reasonable elaboration and cultivation of its ethical vision of humane value in public and private life. Both its constructive and critical arguments are, in their nature, ethical arguments of public reason, appealing to the fundamental and broadly shared ethical imperative of treating persons as equals.[41]

Such conscientious claims to personal and moral identity appeal to the constitutionally guaranteed right to conscience. The constitutional protections for liberty of conscience, expressive of equal respect for conscience, have not been and cannot reasonably be limited to established or traditional churches; the American tradition of liberty of conscience has protected, indeed fostered the many forms of new forms of conscience that arose uniquely in America,[42] including the claims

for example, *Engel v. Vitale,* 370 U.S. 421 (1962) (use of state-composed "nondenominational" prayer in public schools held violative of anti-establishment clause), *Abington School District v. Schempp,* 374 U.S. 203 (1963) (reading of selections from Bible and Lord's Prayer in public schools held violative of anti-establishment clause), *Wallace v. Jaffree,* 472 U.S. 38 (1985) (state authorization of one-minute period of silence in public schools "for meditation or voluntary prayer" held violative of anti-establishment clause); *Lee v. Weisman,* 504 U.S. 462 (1992) (nondenominational prayer at high school graduation held violative of anti-establishment); *Epperson v. Arkansas,* 393 U.S. 97 (1968) (state statute forbidding teaching of evolution in public schools held violative of anti-establishment clause); *Edwards v. Aguillard,* 482 U.S. 578 (1987) (state statute requiring balanced treatment of creationist and evolution science held violative of anti-establishment clause).

41. On the pervasiveness of this ideal in Western religious and ethical culture, see Richards, *Toleration and the Constitution,* 69, 71, 78, 93, 123–28, 134, 272–73, 275. For an exploration of the form, content, and force of the critical and constructive aspects of these ethical arguments on behalf of lesbian and gay identity, see ibid., 269–80; David A. J. Richards, *Sex, Drugs, Death, and the Law* (Totowa, N.J.: Rowman and Littlefield, 1982), 29–83; id., "Unnatural Acts and the Constitutional Right to Privacy: a Moral Theory," *Fordham Law Review* 45 (1977): 1281; id., "Sexual Autonomy and the Constitutional Right to Privacy: A Case Study in Human Rights and the Unwritten Constitution," *Hastings Law Journal* 30 (1979): 957.

42. See, in general, Sydney E. Ahlstrom, *A Religious History of the American People* (New Haven: Yale University Press, 1972), 491–509 (Shakers, Society of the Public Universal

of conscience expressed through the abolitionist movement that were so sharply critical of established churches.⁴³ Claims to gay and lesbian identity stand foursquare in this distinguished tradition of new forms of dissenting conscience, and are, as such, fully entitled to constitutional protection on terms of principle. Correlatively, the American tradition of religious liberty cannot be and has not been limited to theistic forms of conscience as such, but embraces all forms of conscience.⁴⁴ Nor has the tradition been limited to protect only the conscientious identities in which one has been born, for its guarantees are no less for recent converts and include robust guarantees of state neutrality in circumstances that would lend the state's sectarian encouragement to conversion to one form of belief as opposed to another.⁴⁵ All forms of conscientious conviction, whether old or new, theistic or nontheistic, are thus guaranteed equal respect on terms of a constitutional principle that renders issues of conscience morally independent of factionalized political incentives.

It would trivialize such guarantees, indeed render them nugatory, not to extend them when they are most constitutionally needed, namely, to antimajoritarian claims of conscience that challenge traditional wisdom on nonsectarian grounds of public reason. Otherwise, the mere congruence of sectarian belief among traditional religions (for example, about the alleged unspeakable evil of homosexuality) would be, as it was in antebellum America on the question of slavery,⁴⁶ the measure of religious liberty in particular and of human and constitutional rights in general. The traditional orthodoxy, to which any form of dissenting conscience takes objection on grounds of public reason, would be permitted to silence as unworthy the newly emancipated voice of such progressive claims of justice. In effect, the culture of degradation that sets the terms of social death to which homosexuals have unjustly been condemned would, on this view, set the terms of argument on their behalf. It is, however, such claims of justice of dis-

---

Friend, New Harmony, Oneida Community, Hopedale, Brook Farm, the Mormons), 1019–33 (Science of Health (Christian Science), New Thought, Positive Thinking), 1059–78 (Black Pentecostalism, Father Divine, Sweet Daddy Grace, Nation of Islam, Booker T. Washington, Martin Luther King).

43. For specific elaboration and defense of this point, see David A. J. Richards, "Public Reason and Abolitionist Dissent," *Chicago-Kent Law Review* 69 (1994): 787. See also Richards, *Conscience and the Constitution*, 58–107.

44. For further development of this argument, see Richards, *Toleration and the Constitution*, 67–162.

45. Ibid., 146–62.

46. For further development of this point, see Richards, "Public Reason and Abolitionist Dissent."

senting, antimajoritarian conscience that most require, on grounds of principle, constitutional protection against nescient majorities who would aggressively and uncritically repress such a group because it dares to make claims to justice critical of the dominant religio-cultural orthodoxy.

Finally, the grounds for discrimination against gay and lesbian conscience, thus understood, are themselves increasingly sectarian religious convictions—sectarian in the sense that they rest on perceptions internal to religious convictions, not on public arguments reasonably available in contemporary terms to all persons.[47] This is confirmed by the failure to extend to gay and lesbian persons public arguments (about the acceptability of nonprocreational sex and unacceptability of sexism) otherwise available to all persons on fair terms. The expression through public law of one form of sectarian conscience against another form of conscience, without compelling justification in public arguments available to all, is constitutionally invidious (and therefore constitutionally suspect) religious intolerance. It burdens conscience, inconsistent with free exercise principles, and advances sectarian conscience, inconsistent with antiestablishment principles. Discrimination specifically directed against the claims of justice made by and on behalf of gay and lesbian conscience expresses such constitutionally forbidden intolerance.

If discrimination against persons on grounds of sexual preference expresses constitutionally forbidden religious intolerance, the constitutional entrenchment of prohibitions on such discrimination (specifically naming a group in terms of the claims of justice it makes) is unashamedly in service of such discrimination, and, as such, an unconstitutional expression of religious intolerance through public law. The character of the advocacy for such initiatives confirms the grounds for constitutional concern. Their advocacy groups standardly distort the true nature of their organizations, rely upon discredited experts and facts, and conceal the true purpose of the proposed legislation.[48] Such

47. In its position paper, Colorado for Family Values, the sponsor of Colorado Amendment Two, invoked sectarian religious arguments to justify the initiative: "Gay behavior is what the Bible calls 'sin' because sin defines any attempt to solve human problems or meet human needs without regard to God's wisdom and solutions as found in Scripture and in His saving grace and mercy." Niblock, "Anti-Gay Initiatives," 157 n. 17.

48. See Note, "Constitutional Limits on Anti-Gay-Rights Initiatives," 1909. For important recent explorations of this reactionary political movement and its power in contemporary American politics, see Chris Bull and John Gallagher, *Perfect Enemies: The Religious Right, the Gay Movement, and the Politics of the 1990's* (New York: Crown Publishers, 1996); Didi Herman, *The Antigay Agenda: Orthodox Vision and the Christian Right* (Chicago: University of Chicago Press, 1997).

irrationalist distortion of facts and values, in polemical service of a dominant orthodoxy now under reasonable examination, is at the core of the political irrationalism condemned, as a basis for law, by the argument for toleration central to American constitutionalism.[49] In fact, advocacy of such initiatives appeals not to reasonable arguments consistently pursued, but to highly sectarian forms of controversial theological discourse that regard publicly identified gays and lesbians as devils unworthy of the most minimal standards of constitutional civility and respect.[50] If public law fails these standards (on a solely sectarian basis that uses public law in service of sectarian wars of religion), it violates basic principles of American constitutional law.

While the issue has usually been discussed in terms of the cases forbidding constitutional entrenchment of laws barring racial discrimination, the more exact analogy would be constitutional entrenchment of prohibitions on claims of religious discrimination made by the groups most likely to be victimized in Christian America by such discrimination, i.e., Jews. To understand the force of this analogy between political anti-Semitism and homophobia (well-supported in both historical and contemporary expressions of such sectarian intolerance[51]), we must remind ourselves about the nature of the constitutional evil of the expression of anti-Semitism through law, in particular, why such political anti-Semitism violates the argument for toleration central to the proper interpretation of American traditions of religious liberty.[52] Such political anti-Semitism unjustly abridged basic rights of Jews (in violation of the argument for toleration) because their beliefs and ways of life raised reasonable doubts about the dominant religious orthodoxy. In order not to allow such reasonable doubts to be entertained, the dominant orthodoxy enforced itself as the measure of tolerable belief and practice, abridging the basic rights by which the Jews might reasonably raise doubts on the grounds of irrationalist stereotypes that dehumanized them. The "paradox of intolerance" is what I called the mechanism by which such an entrenched orthodoxy unjustly constructed the dehumanized status of dissidents from the dominant or-

49. See Richards, *Conscience and the Constitution,* 63–73.

50. For ample documentation, based on interviews with the Christian Right, about the roots of their claims in Biblical inerrancy and premillential theology, see, in general, Herman, *The Antigay Agenda.*

51. For historical support of the idea of Satan to condemn Jewish unbelief and the analogy of such scapegoating to homophobia, see Elaine Pagels, *The Origin of Satan* (New York: Random House, 1996), 102–5; on the analogy between anti-Semitism and homophobia in the intolerance of the Christian Right, see Herman, *The Antigay Agenda,* 85–86, 125–28.

52. On the argument for toleration, see Richards, *Conscience and the Constitution,* 63–73; see also, in general, Richards, *Toleration and the Constitution.*

thodoxy: in effect, the views that dominant orthodoxy most reasonably needs to hear are those, paradoxically, savagely repressed on whatever grounds sustain the embattled legitimacy of the dominant orthodoxy. American constitutional principles, that express the argument for toleration, forbid laws based on such sectarian intolerance.

In light of these reasons, we would immediately condemn constitutional entrenchment of political anti-Semitism (in the form of an initiative that forbade all laws protecting Jews as such against discrimination) as an unconstitutional expression of religious intolerance because such laws serve precisely the forms of majoritarian religious intolerance that constitutional guarantees of religious toleration condemn as a basis for law. A state that entrenched such initiatives would, in clear violation of free exercise principles, unconstitutionally burden specifically named conscientious convictions in a blatantly non-neutral way,[53] and, in clear contradiction of the principles of our antiestablishment jurisprudence,[54] support a sectarian religious view as the one true church of Americanism to which all dissenters are encouraged to convert. A constitutional jurisprudence that questions the neutrality of unemployment compensation schemes that effectively impose financial burdens on the convictions of Seventh Day Adventists[55] must condemn, *a fortiori,* laws that specifically target for focused disadvantage the convictions of a religion or form of conscience, and must regard as even worse the very naming of the group in question in the relevant law.[56] In effect, a state that entrenched such initiatives would itself be the unconstitutional agent of the political evil of intolerance, branding a religious group as heretics and blasphemers to American religious orthodoxy. American constitutionalism, which recognizes neither heresy nor blasphemy as legitimate expressions of state power,[57] must forbid exercises of state power, like the contemplated initiative, that

---

53. Cf. *Church of the Lukumi Babalu Aye, Inc. v. City of Hialeah,* 508 U.S. 520 (1993) (law forbidding animal sacrifice by the Santeria religion held violative of neutrality required in state burdens on religious practices by free exercise clause).

54. See, in general, Richards, *Toleration and the Constitution,* 146–62.

55. See *Sherbert v. Verner,* 374 U.S. 398 (1963), whose authority was reaffirmed in *Employment Division of Oregon Department of Human Resources v. Smith,* 494 U.S. 872 (1990).

56. The imagined case is thus even worse than *Lukumi Babalu Aye,* in which the religion of Santeria was not specifically named in the statute that was found, on analysis, to be unconstitutionally directed against that religious group.

57. "Heresy trials are foreign to our Constitution." *United States v. Ballard,* 322 U.S. 78, 86 (1944) (Douglas, J.). On the unconstitutionality of blasphemy prosecutions under current American law of free speech and religious liberty, see Leonard W. Levy, *Blasphemy: Verbal Offense against the Sacred from Moses to Salman Rushdie* (New York: Knopf, 1993), 522–33, commenting, *inter alia,* on *Burstyn v. Wilson,* 343 U.S. 495 (1952) (censorship of movie, as sacrilege, held unconstitutional).

illegitimately assert such a power, in this case, legitimating the dehumanizing evil of political anti-Semitism. The effect of such initiatives would be to enlist the state actively in the unconstitutional construction of a class of persons lacking the status of bearers of human rights—a status so subhuman that they are excluded from the minimal rights and responsibilities of the moral community of persons. Political atrocity thus becomes thinkable and practical.

The case of antigay/lesbian initiatives is exactly parallel. A dissenting form of conscience, on the grounds of its moral independence and dissenting claims for justice, is branded *for that reason* as heresy. The message is clear and clearly intended: persons should convert from this form of conscience that is wholly unworthy of respect to the only true religion of Americanism. The initiative is as much motored by sectarian religion and directed against dissenting conscience as the intolerably anti-Semitic initiative just discussed. Homosexuals are to late twentieth-century sectarians what the Jews have traditionally been to sectarians in the Christian West throughout its history: intolerable heretics to dominant religious orthodoxy.[58]

The conception that homosexuality is a form of heresy or treason is both an ancient and modern ground for its condemnation.[59] In fact, there is no good reason to believe that the legitimacy of such forms of sexual expression destabilizes social cooperation. Homosexual relations are and will foreseeably remain the preference of small minorities of the population,[60] who are as committed to principles of social coopera-

58. On the role that anti-Semitic ideology, in fact, implicitly plays in the homophobia of the Christian Right, see Herman, *The Antigay Agenda*, 85–86, 116–28. On the historical background of such intolerance in ideas of Satan as the cause of Jewish unbelief and the analogy to contemporary homophobia, see Pagels, *The Origin of Satan*, 102–5.

59. Throughout the Middle Ages, homosexuals were prosecuted as heretics and often burned at the stake. See Derrick S. Bailey, *Homosexuality and the Western Christian Tradition* (New York: Longmans, Green, 1955), 135. "Buggery," one of the names for homosexual acts, derives from a corruption of the name of one heretical group alleged to engage in homosexual practices. Ibid., 141, 148–49. For a modern use of the idea of treason in this context, see Patrick Devlin, *The Enforcement of Morals* (London: Oxford University Press, 1965), 1–25. For rebuttal, see H. L. A. Hart, *Law, Liberty, and Morality* (Stanford: Stanford University Press, 1963); id., "Social Solidarity and the Enforcement of Morals," *University of Chicago Law Review* 35 (1967): 351.

60. The original Kinsey estimate that about 4 percent of males are exclusively homosexual throughout their lives is confirmed by comparable European studies. See Paul H. Gebhard, "Incidence of Overt Homosexuality in the United States and Western Europe," *National Institute of Mental Health Task Force on Homosexuality*, ed. J. M. Livingood (Washington, D.C.: U.S. Government Printing Office, 1972), 22–29. The incidence figure remains stable though many of the European countries do not apply the criminal penalty to consensual sex acts of the kind here under discussion. See Walter Barnett, *Sexual Freedom and the Constitution* (Albuquerque: University of New Mexico Press, 1973), 293. Recent surveys indicate that

tion and contribution as any other group in society at large; the issue, as with all suspect classes, is not one of increasing or decreasing the minority, but deciding whether we should treat such a minority justly with respect as persons or unjustly with contempt as unspeakably heretical outcasts. Indeed, the very accusation of heresy or treason brings out an important feature of the traditional moral condemnation in its contemporary vestments. It no longer appeals to generally acceptable arguments of necessary protections of the rights of persons to general goods; to the contrary, both the sexism and condemnation of nonprocreational sex of the traditional view are now inconsistent with the reasonable acceptability as general goods of both gender equality and nonprocreational sex. Today, such condemnation appeals to arguments internal to highly personal, often sectarian religious decisions about acceptable ways of belief and life-style. When a moral tradition in this way abandons certain of its essential grounds in general goods, it may justly retain its legitimacy for those internal to the tradition, all the more so because it remains more exclusively constitutive of their tradition. But if those essential grounds are constitutionally necessary for the tradition coercively to enforce its mandates through the criminal law, the abandonment of those grounds must, *pari passu*, deprive the tradition of its constitutional legitimacy as a ground for enforcement though law. The tradition now no longer expresses nonsectarian ethical arguments that may fairly be imposed on all persons, but rather perspectives reasonably authoritative only for those who adhere to the tradition.

The English legal scholar, Tony Honore, put the essential point well regarding the contemporary status of the homosexual: "It is not primarily a matter of breaking rules but of dissenting attitudes. It resembles political or religious dissent, being an atheist in Catholic Ireland or a dissident in Soviet Russia."[61] In effect, the enforcement of such sectarian perspectives through law, as through Colorado Amendment Two, is the functional equivalent of a heresy prosecution: persons of gay and lesbian identity, in virtue of their conscientious claims to equal justice, are branded as subhuman heretics to true values, and told unambiguously to convert or, at a minimum, ashamedly to return to the silence and invisibility of the closet. The grounds for prohibition are highly personal ideological or political views about which free persons reason-

---

as little as 2.8 percent of the population identify themselves as gay and less than half of that number as lesbian. See Robert T. Michael, John H. Gagnon, Edward O. Laumann, and Gina Kolata, *Sex in America: A Definitive Survey* (Boston: Little, Brown, 1994), 176.

    61. See Tony Honore, *Sex Law* (London: Duckworth, 1978), 89.

ably disagree. The continuing force of the prohibitions rests not on protection of the rights of persons, but on fears and misunderstandings directed at the alien way of life of a small and traditionally condemned minority, as if, at bottom, the legitimacy of one's own way of life requires the illegitimacy of all others. Constitutional toleration, which forbids heresy and blasphemy prosecutions and sharply circumscribes treason prosecutions,[62] must likewise be extended to condemnations through law that have the political force of heresy, blasphemy, and treason prosecutions.

Indeed, constitutional arguments of toleration are, if anything, more needed in this area than more obviously conventional forms of religious discrimination because the uncritical complacencies of American majoritarian opinion conspicuously fail to recognize the constitutional dimensions of the issue involved in the case of a traditionally despised and stigmatized minority—a fact evidently shown by majoritarian acquiescence in Colorado Amendment Two. As I earlier noted, distortions of fact and value are made and accepted in polemical support of an entrenched orthodoxy now under reasonable attack.

As we have seen, such reasonable attack has included criticism of this tradition for its mandatory procreational demands and for its sexism; and both criticisms have, under American public law, significantly been expressed through constitutional principles of privacy and antidiscrimination for the benefit of the dominant heterosexual majority of both men and women. The entrenched orthodoxy is now under reasonable critical attack certainly in almost every imaginable aspect of heterosexual sexuality.[63] The orthodoxy, now in retreat in the domain of heterosexual sexuality, does not however extend such reasonable criticisms, as a matter of principle, to the examination of its traditional orthodoxy about homosexual sexuality. Rather, consistent with the paradox of intolerance as in the case of Christian reasonable doubts about transubstantiation, it displaces its doubts from the reasonable doctrinal criticism of which it is most in need to the irrationalist scapegoating of a traditionally despised and culturally subjugated minority. It thus acquiesces in a war on homosexuals on sectarian grounds it would never accept in the other areas to which sectarians extend their religious war (for example, on feminism, or on civil rights legislation in

62. See U.S. Const. art. 3, §3.
63. See, for example, *Griswold v. Connecticut*, 381 U.S. 479 (1965); *Eisenstadt v. Baird*, 405 U.S. 438 (1972); *Roe v. Wade*, 410 U.S. 113 (1973); *Planned Parenthood of Southeastern Pennsylvania v. Casey*, 112 S. Ct. 2791 (1992); *Frontiero v. Richardson*, 411 U.S. 677 (1973); *Craig v. Boren*, 429 U.S. 190 (1976).

general).[64] To achieve such a constitutionally incoherent aim, its sectarian proponents suppress opposing views relevant to reasonable public argument, distort or misstate facts, disconnect values from ethical reasoning, indeed denigrate deliberation in politics in favor of a conception of politics that allegedly, as we shall see, *requires* the constitutional repression of dissent, a symbolic glorification of violence against claims of human rights.[65]

The arguments offered in support of Colorado Amendment Two exemplify all these features of the irrationalist politics associated with the paradox of intolerance. Six such arguments were examined and rejected, at the lower court level, by Judge Bayless in *Evans v. Romer*[66]: the factionalized character of gay and lesbian identity (25), its militant aggression (26), the protection of existing suspect classes (27), the privacy and religious rights of the heterosexual majority (28), the interest in not subsidizing political objections of interest groups (29), and the protection of children (29). All of them reflect the distortions of fact and value of the paradox of intolerance.

(1) Justifying Colorado Amendment Two as deterring political factionalism inverts what is, in fact, a political attack on basic human and constitutional rights into the alleged necessity to defend proper democratic politics by the repression of dissent. Judge Bayless properly observed that "[t]he history and policy of this country has been to encourage that which defendants seek to deter," concluding that "[t]he *opposite* of defendants' first claimed compelling interest is most probably compelling" (26). The abuse of the place of the theory of faction in American constitutionalism is a particularly striking feature of the way argument on behalf of Colorado Amendment Two makes a travesty of the American constitutional tradition it claims to honor. The theory of faction was developed by Madison to identify permanent tendencies of human nature in politics, in particular, tendencies for groups to bond on the basis of sectarian abridgment of the legitimate weight owed to the human rights and interests of outsiders; Madison gave special weight to religious factions because of their tendency to

64. On the antifeminism of the Religious Right, see Herman, *The Antigay Agenda*, 103–10; on their opposition to the civil rights agenda in general, see ibid., 111–36, 140.

65. See, for further development of these irrationalist themes, Didi Herman, *The Antigay Agenda;* for example, on manufacturing false or misleading data, see ibid., 76–80.

66. 1993 WL 518586 (Colo. Dist. Ct. 1993), reprinted in *CLE Materials,* to which reference is made hereafter in discussing this opinion. Judge Bayless examined the arguments in light of the standard of strict scrutiny required by the Colorado Supreme Court in *Evans v. Romer,* 854 P.2d 1270 (Colo. 1993), found them inadequate, and thus ordered that the preliminary injunction against Colorado Amendment Two be made permanent.

deny to outsiders respect for their inalienable right to conscience.[67] It is simply Orwellian for the sectarian advocates of Colorado Amendment Two to justify its factionalized abuse of American constitutionalism on the grounds of combating faction. They exemplify the evil they claim to combat.

(2) Judge Bayless found the argument of combating "militant gay aggression" to be factually baseless.[68] As already observed, lesbians and gay men are a small minority of the American population. While relatively affluent[69] and sometimes influential,[70] their political gains have been comparatively small[71] and they remain radically underrepresented in key government positions.[72] Against this factual background,

67. For fuller discussion, see Richards, *Foundations of American Constitutionalism*, 32–39.

68. See *CLE Materials*, 26–27.

69. Marketing studies indicate gay and lesbian incomes are far in excess of the national average. See Joya L. Wesley, "With $394 Billion in Buying Power, Gays' Money Talks; and Corporate America Increasingly Is Listening," *The Atlanta Journal & Constitution*, 1 December 1991, F5. The 1990 census, measuring statistics for gay unmarried couples for the first time, showed gay male couples to have higher incomes than any other group, including heterosexual married couples. See Margaret S. Usdansky, "Gay Couples, By the Numbers-Data Suggest They're Fewer Than Believed, But Affluent," *USA Today*, 12 April 1993, 8A.

70. For a popular media account of gay power and influence, see, for example, Joni Balter, "Gay Power Brokers—Money, Stature and Savvy Give Leaders More Clout," *Seattle Times*, 1 August 1993, A1.

71. Only a handful of states and a comparatively tiny number of municipalities protect gays and lesbians from discrimination. Of the seventy-seven jurisdictions that have any sort of legislation or other government decree protecting lesbians and gay men, sixteen are merely resolutions, guidelines, or policy statements and are not fully binding. See Affidavit of Political Science Professor Kenneth Sherrill, Defendant's Motion for Summary Judgment, *Steffan v. Cheney*, 780 F. Supp. 1 (D.D.C. 1991), *reversed sub nom. Steffan v. Aspin*, 8 F.3d 57 (D.C. Cir. 1993), *rehearing en banc granted and judgment vacated* (1994), in Marc Wolinsky and Kenneth Sherrill, eds., *Gays and the Military: Joseph Steffan versus the United States* (Princeton: Princeton University Press, 1993), 114. Only four states—Wisconsin, Massachusetts, Connecticut, and Hawaii—have any statewide legislation protecting the rights of homosexuals, while seven others have executive orders issued by governors. These executive orders are limited by the range of gubernatorial power and are rescinded more easily than legislation. In half of the states, no jurisdiction whatsoever has *any* legislation or other governmental decree or policy which protects the rights of lesbians and gay men. Ibid.

The importance of this legislation should not be overstated. As a recent *Harvard Law Review* study observes, "[V]ery little legislation protects gay men and lesbians from discrimination in the private sector. No federal statute prohibits discrimination by private citizens or organizations based on sexual orientation. Nor do the states provide protection: only Wisconsin has a comprehensive statute barring such discrimination in employment." "Developments in the Law—Sexual Orientation and the Law," *Harvard University Law Review* 102 (1989): 1667.

72. In *Frontiero v. Richardson*, 411 U.S. 677 (1973), the Supreme Court found women as a class to be relatively politically powerless, despite the fact that then, as now, they constituted a majority of the electorate, because they were "vastly underrepresented in this Nation's

making an argument of "militant gay aggression" bespeaks a use of facts and values all too familiar in the history of intolerance, most grotesquely so in the late twentieth century. Thus the argument remarkably transforms the minority status of homosexuals, analogous to the similar irrationalist appeals central to political anti-Semitism, into a secret and powerful conspiracy against which politics must be protected.[73] In effect, the very attempt by homosexuals or Jews to make any basic claims of equal citizenship and any small gains thus secured (including relative affluence and occasional influence) are irrationally interpreted as a murderous attack on dominant majorities. Normative outrage at the very idea of an outcast's claim of rights remakes reality to rationalize nullification of such rights. On this hallucinatory ground, aggression against basic rights of gay and lesbian persons is, as with Hitler's exactly comparable justification for his war on the Jews,[74] ideologically inverted into a reasonable "defensive measure"[75] justified on grounds of self-defense. No argument, offered in defense of Colorado Amendment Two, more starkly communicates the hermetically Manichean sectarian world view of its proponents—its polemical power to act as a distorting prism to remake reality in its own ideological image of the wars of religion and to rationalize its conduct accordingly. The persecutor is imaginatively transformed into the victim, thus rendering persecution innocent and indeed honorable. It is in such terms that good Germans acquiesced in Hitler's war on the Jews; it is in such terms that good Americans acquiesced in Colorado's war on gay and lesbian persons.[76]

(3) Judge Bayless rejected the justification of Colorado Amendment

decisionmaking councils." Id. at 686 n. 17. The Court based its conclusions on the fact that no woman had ever been elected president; that there had not yet been a woman Supreme Court Justice; that there were then no women in the U.S. Senate (although women had served as senators in the past); and that there were then only fourteen women in the House of Representatives. Id. By this standard, lesbians and gay men are even more radically unrepresented. There has never been neither an openly gay president, Supreme Court Justice, nor openly gay federal court judge; there are no openly gay U.S. senators today, and there have never been any. Until 1984 there were no openly gay members of the U.S. House of Representatives, and while there are currently two gay House members (Congressmen Gerry Studds and Barney Frank), neither revealed his sexual orientation until after being elected. See Defendant's Motion for Summary Judgment, in *Gays and the Military*, 20.

73. See, for an illuminating study of this argument, Herman, *The Antigay Agenda*, 116–28; on the analogy to anti-Semitism, see ibid., 85–86, 125–28.

74. For a characteristic example of the inversion of victims into aggressors and the compelling need to defend against them, see Adolf Hitler, *Mein Kampf* (New York: Reynal & Hitchcock, 1940), 824–27.

75. See *CLE Materials*, 26.

76. See, for example, Stephen Bransford, *Gay Politics vs. Colorado and America: The Inside Story of Amendment 2* (Cascade, Colorado: Sardis Press, 1994).

Two as protecting existing suspect classes, both because it lacked factual support and on the normative ground that fiscal concerns were inadequate to justify abridgment of basic rights and interests.[77] The alleged justification depends on an uncritical and indefensible inversion of a claim by gay and lesbian persons to basic equal justice, appealing to antidiscrimination principles available to all, into a claim for unequal, "special" rights subversive of guarantees of equality. Several courts have rejected as intrinsically distorting and manipulatively question-begging the wording of antigay/lesbian initiatives and referenda as opposing special laws for homosexuals.[78] But, the implicit justification of such laws, as combating "special" rights, comes to the same thing. In effect, such polemics refuse to acknowledge what they are doing and mean to do: forbidding antidiscrimination laws. They do so by willfully suppressing the issues of principle common to all antidiscrimination laws, in effect, targeting an unpopular minority for making the same kind of claim that all other groups have made for such laws. Popular hostility is thus unreasonably directed at one form of antidiscrimination law by a rhetoric (confusing antidiscrimination with affirmative action) that irrationally stimulates unreflective social prejudice against a group because it makes claims to antidiscrimination protections on grounds of principle.[79]

(4) Judge Bayless acknowledged that, in contrast to other alleged compelling state interests, the justification of Colorado Amendment Two in terms of protecting rights of personal, familial, and religious privacy at least articulated compelling state interests; but he denied that the amendment in question was, in light of its abridgment of the rights of homosexuals to nondiscrimination, sufficiently narrowly

77. See *CLE Materials*, 27.
78. See, for example, *Faipeas v. Municipality of Anchorage*, 860 P.2d 1214 (Ala. 1993); *Citizens for Responsible Behavior v. Superior Court*, 1 Cal. App. 4th, 2 Cal. Rptr. 2d 648 (1992); cf. *Mabon v. Keisling*, 856 P.2d 1023 (Or. 1993).
79. In effect, such rhetoric unreasonably confuses the case for antidiscrimination laws as such with the different though related case for affirmative action. Popular animus against affirmative action is thus unreasonably brought to bear on antidiscrimination laws as such, when antidiscrimination laws and affirmative action are quite different. In fact, strong proponents of antidiscrimination laws are sometimes skeptical of affirmative action. See, for example, Justice Powell's opinion in *Regents of University of California v. Bakke*, 438 U.S. 265 (1978). There may be a good case for affirmative action in many areas, including, as I suggested in the previous chapter, sexual preference, but the case for affirmative action is quite different from that for antidiscrimination laws. Conflating these questions uniquely in the matter of sexual preference unreasonably condemns arguments for antidiscrimination laws on grounds appropriate, if at all, for affirmative action. Such rhetoric irrationally stimulates the prejudice that antidiscrimination laws should combat.

drawn to achieve these compelling interests.[80] In fact, the justification of Colorado Amendment Two in these terms reveals quite clearly why the amendment reflects constitutionally invidious religious intolerance. As Judge Bayless noted, "[i]n the present case, the religious belief urged by defendants is that homosexuals are condemned by scripture and therefore discrimination based on that religious teaching is protected within freedom of religion."[81] On this basis, discrimination against Jews, African Americans, and women could be similarly justified as protected by religious freedom since some sectarian interpretation of the Bible or its equivalent in other religious traditions could and would regard each of them as condemned. We would reject such an argument in these cases for the same reason we should reject it in the case of Colorado Amendment Two: under the basic terms of the American tradition of both free exercise and antiestablishment, let alone equal protection, the abridgment of basic rights requires a compelling, secular, nonsectarian justification.[82] The interpretation and justification of American religious liberty, enforced through Colorado Amendment Two, is, by its own admission, a sectarian interpretation of the Bible (with which many religious people in the Christian tradition disagree[83]), and, as such, an unconstitutional expression of religious intolerance through public law.[84] In the Orwellian world of Colorado Amendment Two, sectarian religion has become the measure of respect for the inalienable right of conscience.

(5) Judge Bayless rejected the justification of Colorado Amendment Two as preventing the subsidy of political objectives by focusing on the example urged in support of it, namely, a landlord forced to rent to a homosexual couple and thus forced to accept a political ideology. Bayless found this "remarkable" conclusion to be lacking in authority as well as "logic," unsupported "by any credible evidence or any cogent

80. See *CLE Materials*, 28–29.

81. Ibid., 28.

82. For fuller development of this argument, see Richards, *Toleration and the Constitution*; Richards, *Conscience and the Constitution*.

83. See, for example, John Boswell, *Christianity, Social Tolerance and Homosexuality* (Chicago: University of Chicago, 1980); John J. McNeill, *The Church and the Homosexual* (Kansas City: Sheed, Andrews & McMeel, 1976); cf. Derrick S. Bailey, *Homosexuality and the Western Christian Tradition* (New York: Longmans, Green, 1955); Bernadette J. Brooten, *Love Between Women: Early Christian Responses to Female Homoeroticism* (Chicago: University of Chicago Press, 1996); Mark D. Jordan, *The Invention of Sodomy in Christian Theology* (Chicago: University of Chicago Press, 1997).

84. On the highly sectarian Biblical and theological basis for the war of the largely Protestant Christian Right on gays and lesbians (and its links with earlier attacks on Catholics, Jews, and communists), see Herman, *The Antigay Agenda*.

argument."[85] The same argument could, of course, be made against all antidiscrimination laws, which address, of course, acts of discrimination, not thoughts alone.[86] On the view taken by this justification for Colorado Amendment Two, the lowest level of irrational prejudice (about which everyone agreed) would fix the scope of antidiscrimination laws, which would, of course, render them ineffective in the protection of any minority. The argument is unacceptable as a matter of basic principle in any area of antidiscrimination law (including race, religion, gender, and sexual preference), which shows again the unprincipled character of the justifications urged in support of Colorado Amendment Two. (The argument here is urged only against laws prohibiting discrimination on grounds of sexual preference.)

(6) Judge Bayless dismissed the defense of Colorado Amendment Two in terms of protecting children as unsupported by evidence, noting compelling evidence "that pedophiles are predominantly heterosexuals not homosexuals."[87] Colorado for Family Values, in its basic position paper on Amendment Two, had forthrightly espoused a range of such willful factual distortions by comparing homosexual orientation to "murder, theft, fraud, necrophilia, bestiality, and pedophilia."[88] In effect, elementary demands by lesbian and gay persons for equal treatment of their claims to the rights and responsibilities of adult public and private life have been transmogrified by advocates of Colorado Amendment Two, with no factual basis whatsoever, into bizarre claims to seduce and exploit the young as well as to murder and the like. We are, literally, in the same sectarian imaginative world as medieval anti-Semitism in which fantasies of cannibalism became the rationalizing measure of the massacre of the innocent and the just, or in the polemical world of modern anti-Semitism in which false conspiracies (by use of forged pamphlets like "The Protocols of the Elders of Zion") were manufactured; thus, such false conspiracies were concocted allegedly to show a comparable gay and lesbian conspiracy.[89] There are apparently no self-critical limits of accountability to fact or argument in a politics driven by the fantasies of sectarian religious intolerance as we know both from the history of anti-Semitism and from its more recent American expression, the religious war on gay and lesbian identity.[90]

85. See *CLE Materials,* 29.

86. See, for insistence on this point, *Wisconsin v. Mitchell,* 508 U.S. 476 (1993) (penalty enhancement for battery on ground of racial bias against victim held constitutional).

87. See *CLE Materials,* 29.

88. See Niblock, "Anti-Gay Initiatives," 170.

89. See Herman, *The Antigay Agenda,* 85–86, 125–28.

90. For illuminating treatments, see Bull and Gallagher, *Perfect Enemies;* Herman, *The Antigay Agenda.*

We need now, as much as ever, to remind ourselves of, to conserve, and to give effect to the American constitutional tradition of toleration that condemns, as indecent, a self-deceived and self-deceiving polemical politics that thus, through fantasy and fraud, creates a gargantuan appetite for the rights-denying evils that it monstrously feeds upon.

The perspective of the advocates of Colorado Amendment Two is that of a now much-embattled religious orthodoxy on matters of sexuality and gender, one that frames its factual and normative distortions, reflected in all six arguments examined, by the explanatory observation that homosexuals "often express deep hostility to traditional, Judeo-Christian moral beliefs and [family] values."[91] The terms of its homophobic agenda are self-consciously those of a larger, religiously sectarian "great cultural war."[92] What makes such a sectarian normative world both plausible and so politically powerful is the same dynamic that made political anti-Semitism plausible and powerful, namely, the paradox of intolerance.

The objection to homosexuals on the basis of their criticism of certain beliefs reveals this tangled political pathology. In fact, such traditional religious beliefs have been criticized, on religious and nonreligious grounds, by a wide range of persons, most of them in fact heterosexual critics of a religion's indefensible insistence on procreational sexuality and its sexism;[93] criticisms of these sorts have significantly shaped the interpretation of basic constitutional principles both of privacy and equal protection applicable to a wide range of issues relating to sexuality and gender.[94] Crucially, however, objection is not taken to such heterosexual critics who would, as a matter of principle, be as logically prone to such sectarian condemnation as homosexual critics. The paradox of intolerance by its nature defies logic, suppressing internal critical doubts it might reasonably entertain about traditional religious views of heterosexual sexuality by singling out a symbolic scapegoat of the embattled religious orthodoxy. Thus among all the persons critical of traditional religious views, only one group is singled out by name by Colorado Amendment Two, one already the traditional object of unreasoning hatred and ignorance. The willful dy-

---

91. See Niblock, "Anti-Gay Initiatives," 165 n. 70.

92. See, for example, Robert Sullivan, "An Army of the Faithful," *New York Times Magazine*, 25 April 1993, 40.

93. For a useful history of such arguments in the area of the criticism of anticontraception laws, see Linda Gordon, *Woman's Body, Woman's Right: A Social History of Birth Control in America* (New York: Penguin, 1977).

94. See, for example, *Griswold v. Connecticut*, 381 U.S. 479 (1965); *Roe v. Wade*, 410 U.S. 113 (1973); *Planned Parenthood of Southeastern Pennsylvania v. Casey*, 112 S. Ct. 2791 (1992); *Frontiero v. Richardson*, 411 U.S. 677 (1973); *Craig v. Boren*, 429 U.S. 190 (1976).

namics of the paradox of intolerance motor whatever rationalizing distortions of facts and values support its sectarian objective. The defense of the human rights of gay and lesbian persons becomes faction; arguments for such rights, unjust aggression; equality, inequality; sectarian convictions, the measure of the religious liberty; laws against discrimination, subsidy of an ideology; factual falsehoods, truths.

These insults to reason bespeak contempt for reason. They make no appeal to impartial standards of epistemic and practical reason; as we have seen in all six arguments examined, they are blatantly flouted. The nerve of their unreasonableness is their failure to extend such impartial standards to both a certain kind of claim and to the making of such a claim by gay and lesbian persons. Rather, their intrinsically irrationalist appeal turns on the manifold strategies of self-deception through which polemically entrenched convictions conceal from themselves and others their incoherence and their unreasonable willfulness when they are under reasonable criticism and debate both internally and externally in the larger society.[95] These are motivated by the grotesquely unreasonable interpretation accorded both the substance of the claims made and the making of such claims by gay and lesbian persons, in particular, substantive arguments of basic human rights claimed by gay and lesbian persons as bearers of human rights. In each of the six arguments examined, the motivational drive centers on distortions of fact or value that aim to rationalize to those already committed to the traditional orthodoxy its failure both to recognize the substance of such arguments and the right of gay and lesbian persons to make such arguments. The effort of reasonable justification is simply not recognized or acknowledged as owing to gay and lesbian persons as persons. To the contrary, both the substance and the making of such rights-based claims, as normative claims, *must* be denied any factual or normative basis whatsoever. The threat of gay and lesbian identity is, from this perspective, its expression of the powers of moral personality to originate legitimate claims of human rights. It is this perspective and only this perspective that can explain why, in the case of each of the six arguments examined, claims of gay and lesbian identity have, as such, been inflated in the irrationalist terms of an aggressive threat, and why, in service of such irrationalism, the most minimal standards of intellectual and ethical responsibility in making political arguments have not been extended to lesbians and gay men as citizens and as persons. Such unreason violates the basic norms of civility central to

95. For an illuminating philosophical study of these issues, see Denise Meyerson, *False Consciousness* (Oxford: Clarendon Press, 1991).

the reasonable justification of political power in a constitutional democracy.[96] Its unreason strips political power of legitimacy and renders
it a work of willful political violence that shames our constitutionalism.
As one court observed in striking down a comparable initiative: "All
that is lacking is a sack of stones for throwing."[97]

Like anti-Semitism such arguments draw their irrationalist polemical power from a long history of cultural exclusion and degradation (in
this case, of homosexuals from Western religio-moral community). An
embattled religious orthodoxy chooses to suppress its own reasonable
doubts about its tradition by choosing one small, traditionally despised
group of such dissenters and engages in a politics of identity, based
on the paradox of intolerance, that effectively demonizes this group
as heretics to moral value in living. The powerful political appeal of
such polemics depends on a long cultural tradition of moral slavery of
the group in question, who, traditionally silenced and silent, are barely
recognized as human and certainly not acknowledged as persons. In
effect, a public opinion, formed on injustice, is polemically aroused to
insist on its status as the measure of justice, and thus acquiesces in the
degradation of dissenters to its injustice from the very constitutional
possibility of a person of conscience worthy of making elementary
claims to justice. The constitutional evil of this initiative is transparently revealed in and by its very terms, i.e., its constitutional entrenchment of a prohibition on precisely the claims of justice made by and
on behalf of this group and only this group.

Uncritical majoritarian complacency cannot be the measure of human rights in a constitutional community committed to the theory and
practice of human rights as the measure of the demands that the community may legitimately make on its citizens.[98] Yet it is such unreflective complacency that fails to take seriously both the conscientious
character of gay and lesbian identity as one among the legitimate forms
of conscience that a rights-respecting state must treat as equals; it likewise fails to take seriously the unconstitutionally sectarian character of
the attempt to legitimate discrimination against such forms of conscience. The measure of constitutionally protected human rights of
toleration cannot itself be intolerance. Rather, it is such sectarian insularity that most requires constitutional criticism and scrutiny in the

96. See, in general, John Rawls, *Political Liberalism* (New York: Columbia University
Press, 1993).

97. See *Citizens for Responsible Behavior v. Superior Court,* 1 Cal. App. 4th, 2 Cal. Rptr.
2d 648 (1992), in *CLE Materials,* 172.

98. For further development of this point, see Richards, *Foundations of American Constitutionalism,* 78–171.

interest of protecting human rights, like those of gay and lesbian persons, that are now so visibly at threat.

On this view, initiatives like Colorado Amendment Two unconstitutionally enlist the state as the agent of the political construction of intolerance in the same way that, in my earlier parallel example, the state unconstitutionally constructed political anti-Semitism. In neither case can or should the fact of a long history of injustice, whether of Christian or anti-Christian anti-Semitism[99] or the subjection of women and homosexuals, be the just measure of constitutional argument in this domain. In all these cases, the interpretive responsibilities imposed by constitutional guarantees of basic human rights like conscience must be critically to resist and repel the force of such history, especially when such history is aggressively used against wholly just claims of constitutional rights made by and on behalf of a group of persons who has only recently reclaimed its rights of human nature against a tradition of repressive and subjugating moral slavery.[100]

Concern for such a tradition of subjugation and its vestiges is a matter of constitutional dimension in the United States because of the Thirteenth Amendment's pivotal role in the structure of the Reconstruction Amendments, in particular, its constitutionally enforceable judgment of the wrongness of slavery and involuntary servitude on grounds of its abridgment of fundamental human rights.[101] That judgment condemns what I have called moral slavery, the unjust degradation of whole classes of persons from their status as bearers of human rights into a servile status. That judgment has been reasonably interpreted to condemn not only African American slavery but the traditional subjection of women as well.[102] It would also condemn, as a matter of principle, the long history of Christian Europe's restrictions on Jews (including access to influential occupations, intercourse with Christians, living quarters, and the like) justified, as it was, by Augustine, among others, in the quite explicit terms of moral slavery:

99. On anti-Christian anti-Semitism, see Richards, *Conscience and the Constitution,* 156–57.

100. On the relatively recent emergence of a self-identified homosexual minority in the United States, see John D'Emilio, *Sexual Politics, Sexual Communities: The Making of a Homosexual Minority in the United States, 1940–1970* (Chicago: University of Chicago Press, 1983).

101. See Richards, *Conscience and the Constitution,* 114, 116, 121, 129.

102. See, for example, Justice Brennan's opinion in *Frontiero v. Richardson,* 411 U.S. 677 (1973). For historical background in the abolitionist movement (most notably, the Grimke sisters) of the interpretive judgment that the subjection of women was moral slavery, see Richards, "Public Reason and Abolitionist Dissent." See also chapter 3 above.

"The Jew is the slave of the Christian."[103] In all these cases, unjust deprivation of basic human rights to a class of persons (African Americans, women, Jews) rendered them into a social and legal status rationalized as capable only of limited, socially conceived servile roles.[104]

Constitutional condemnation of moral slavery applies, as a matter of principle, to homosexuals. Homosexuals have been degraded from their status as bearers of basic human rights, and that status has crucially been in service of a social and legal role rationalized in terms of servile cultural marginality to dominant sexist stereotypes of the sex roles of men and women. The analogy to the rationalization of European anti-Semitism is, again, strikingly exact. Just as the Jews were condemned to servile status as the slaves of Christians because of their refusal to convert, lesbians and gay men were and are condemned to servile marginality because of their dissidence from conventional gender roles as defined and enforced by the dominant and now embattled religio-cultural orthodoxy.

The moral slavery of homosexuals may indeed today in America cut deeper and thus more unjustly into moral personality than that of African Americans, women, and Jews. For one thing, the moral slavery of these latter groups was usually rationalized in terms of some legitimate, albeit servile social space that the group might occupy; the social space occupied by homosexuals was and is that of the culturally unspeakable, which is the ultimate in cultural death and invisibility. For another, African Americans and women appeal to and elaborate a heritage of American antiracist and antisexist dissent at least as old as the abolitionist movement.[105] Jewish Americans appeal both to a long historical tradition of learned dissent from Christian orthodoxy and the constitutional principles of respect for dissenting conscience of the American tradition of both free exercise and antiestablishment.[106] The critical resources of the struggle for justice of lesbians and gay men are altogether more recent and fragile,[107] certainly not of a strength remotely

---

103. Cited in Gavin I. Langmuir, *History, Religion, and Antisemitism* (Berkeley and Los Angeles: University of California Press, 1990), 294.

104. For elaboration of this point in the case of European Jews, see ibid., 294–97, 345–46; id., *Toward a Definition of Anti-Semitism* (Berkeley and Los Angeles: University of California Press, 1990), 156–57, 165–66.

105. See, in general, Richards, *Conscience and the Constitution;* id., "Public Reason and Abolitionist Dissent."

106. See, in general, Richards, *Toleration and the Constitution;* id., *Conscience and the Constitution.*

107. For an important recent study of some of these resources, see Jonathan Dollimore, *Sexual Dissidence: Augustine to Wilde, Freud to Foucault* (Oxford: Clarendon Press, 1991).

commensurate to the strength of their arguments of justice. Indeed, the very making of such claims was, in contrast to such claims by African Americans and women, the object of repressive censorship in the United States until well after World War II. It is against this repressive background that the making of such claims is regarded today by many Americans as, at best, laughable, and, at worst, the object of vilifying unreason, reflecting a constitutionally decadent public opinion in which a lowest common denominator of unreflective majoritarian preferences is taken to be the measure of human and constitutional rights. A nation in which majorities are thus demogogically persuaded realizes the darkest nightmare of the tyrannical majority that worried America's Founders.[108]

It could not be a reasonable constitutional argument of principle that we should only extend basic protections of civil liberties to groups who already have a significant tradition of dissent already recognized and, to some extent, vindicated. Indeed, to the contrary, the relative recentness and frailty of claims of constitutional justice to lesbian and gay identity surely render the constitutional protection of such claims of conscience, as claims of conscience, all the more exigent as a matter of constitutional principle. Both the recentness and fragility of the critical resources of gay and lesbian identity reflect not the merits of their case, but the extraordinary history of moral subjugation of homosexuals and the reality-shaping power that dehumanizing history evidently possesses. In effect, one of the gravest forms of constitutionally condemned traditions of moral slavery still flourishing in the late twentieth century is, in virtue of the power of the tradition of subjugation, the one most invisible to the complacent American public mind. Such a public mind is for this reason so uncritically and so easily polemically aroused to inflict with such guiltless self-righteousness the tyrannies that moral slavery wreaks on moral personality.

The devastating cultural force of this tradition of subjugation has traditionally been its claim of unspeakability, which deprived persons of homosexual sexual orientation of the resources of speech and thought and thus of critical conscience central to an independent moral life. It is this tradition of compulsory unspeakability that has responded so aggressively to ethical, political, and constitutional claims of lesbian and gay identity that rest on the deeper claim to voice and speech, in effect, claiming the most basic right of every person, the inalienable

108. For Madison's worries about the tyrannical propensities of majority rule and the role of constitutionalism in limiting these propensities, see Richards, *Foundations of American Constitutionalism*, 107–9, 135, 180.

right of conscience. The aggressive target of Colorado Amendment Two is this claim and this right. The considerable political power of the unjust tradition of silencing the humanity of homosexuals remains easily deployed, as in passage of Colorado Amendment Two, to quash the vulnerable voice of recently emancipated conscientious dissent precisely because and on the ground of its arguments for justice. That is a voice central to the integrity of American constitutionalism and one most worthy of constitutional protection when thus most at threat. The claims for justice of lesbians and gay men in the late twentieth century are based on the most insistent demand of American constitutionalism itself, the right to conscience.

Claims of gay and lesbian identity have this status and force, and the attack on these claims, reflected in the complacent majoritarian nescience underlying the adoption of Colorado Amendment Two, unconstitutionally enlists the state as the agent not just to deny basic rights but to construct the political evil of the intolerant subjugation of persons from their status as bearers of human rights. As with anti-Semitism, this is the stuff of basic dehumanization that renders atrocity thinkable and practical. It should have no place in a constitutional order committed to conserve guarantees of basic human rights owed all persons on terms of principle.

Constitutional Arguments against Antigay/Lesbian Initiatives Reviewed

A striking feature of the constitutional arguments against antigay/lesbian initiatives is their failure to bring into play the alternative perspective on these matters I have proposed. Yet, in each case, this perspective either clarifies or strengthens these arguments.

Hans Linde's development of a guaranty clause objection to these initiatives frames its interpretive position with clear reference to what we may now acknowledge to be the constitutionally protected right to conscience. Linde urges the force of a guaranty clause objection in those cases most likely to implicate the constitutional evil of politically powerful religious intolerance.[109] Guaranty clause objections to initiatives surely have their greatest constitutional force in such contexts and should be aggressively pressed for this reason.

The argument for the constitutional suspectness of sexual preference is, if anything, clarified and strengthened by reconceiving the argument in terms of religious intolerance. In effect, the argument for

109. See Linde, "The Campaign against Homosexuality," 41–42.

the suspectness of sexual preference draws upon the historically oldest and textually clearest guarantees of human rights in the American constitutional tradition, the religion clauses of the First Amendment. Sexual preference is and should be constitutionally suspect because state action on this ground reflects sectarian intolerance of claims to ethical, political, and constitutional identity central to the right to conscience; in effect, the point of initiatives like Colorado Amendment Two is unconstitutionally both to burden such claims of conscience and to encourage conversion to sectarian moral orthodoxy. It is the unjust sectarian degradation of the identity of gay and lesbian persons that compels the suspectness of sexual preference, thus linking the suspectness of sexual preference to the comparable reasons (the unjust degradation of African American and gender identity) for the suspectness of race and gender. In all these cases, the constitutional evil of the underlying prejudice is its systematic degradation of identifications central to free moral personality, including powers to protest injustice in the name and voice of one's human rights. The suspectness of sexual preference should not, for this reason, be supposed marginal or peripheral to a responsible interpretation of the American constitutional tradition, but a central conservative case of the enduring meaning in contemporary circumstances of American constitutional values of human rights and toleration.

The objection to antigay/lesbian initiatives, on grounds of their violation of free speech, is deepened when reinterpreted as an aspect of the constitutionally guaranteed right of conscience. Censorship of speech is certainly one aspect of the constitutional issue, but the deeper constitutional insult of such initiatives is their expression through public law of sectarian discrimination against legitimate forms of conscience that, on grounds of principle, have as much a claim to equal protection as any other form of conscience. The emphasis of the free speech argument on gay and lesbian identity may, in light of the alternative perspective here proposed, reasonably be interpreted to mean to make this point exactly.

The political participation objection to these initiatives, however dubious as a general argument of either constitutional or political theory, may reasonably be understood to make a narrower point about their unconstitutional entrenchment of rights-denying forms of prejudice. *Hunter v. Erickson,* on my interpretation, makes this point exactly: issues of discrimination on grounds of race, religion, and ancestry may not be selectively removed from the political process. Colorado Amendment Two violates this principle *a fortiori:* it selectively removes not all grounds for discrimination on grounds of conscience from the ordinary political process, but discrimination on the basis of one named form of conscience, namely, discrimination on grounds of gay and lesbian identity. The state may no more be complicitous with the construction of the rights-denying dehumanization of gays and lesbians than it may be with that of Jews or African Americans or women.

Finally, the argument of the Supreme Court in *Romer v. Evans* is best interpreted not in terms of rational basis analysis, as the Court states, but in terms of the heightened scrutiny properly accorded laws grounded in sectarian prejudice against conscientious identity. The Court's analysis, at crucial points, rests on this approach. Its skeptical treatment of the alleged state purposes of Colorado Amendment Two requires a constitutional principle, which the argument offered here cogently supplies. Its concluding suggestion that the amendment seeks "not to further a proper legislative end but to make them [homosexuals] unequal"[110] makes my argument's point exactly about state complicity with dehumanization. The argument also answers directly Justice Scalia's challenge: the suspectness is that of a religious classification—a classification forbidden as a matter of principle irrespective of calculations of comparative political power.[111]

One might be struck by the paradox that these arguments, invariably clarified or strengthened by the alternative perspective here proposed, make no reference to it when, on examination, their legitimacy expressly or impliedly assumes this perspective. The paradox is all the more puzzling because these arguments much more closely capture and express the reality of the situation, the emancipation of self-respecting gay and lesbian conscience to voice its claims to basic justice and the aggressively reactionary religious war on these claims to respect for such a form of conscience, let alone for its claims to justice. Lesbians and gay men should, on this reactionary view, supinely return to the closet of their cultural invisibility and silence, surrendering their minds and hearts to the measure of the dehumanized stereotype that has historically shrunk and degraded them.

But, proponents of basically sound constitutional arguments are understandably as much under the sway of dominant, uncritical majoritarian assumptions as their opponents. Advocates of the rights of gay and lesbian persons may uncritically assume that their understanding of these rights is so opposed by dominant religious understandings that these rights cannot, in their nature, be protected by guarantees that

110. See *Romer v. Evans*, 116 S. Ct. 1620, 1629 (1996).

111. Indeed, Scalia's rather overwrought dissent echoes, both in style and substance, the anti-Semitic overtones of the comparable argument by the Religious Right; see Herman, *The Antigay Agenda*, 120.

include protections of religious conscience. Such assumptions commit a startling *non sequitur:* if the arguments of one's opponents depend on religion or conscience, one's own arguments cannot depend on anything remotely of that sort (as if sectarian conscience must be the measure of all arguments of conscience). Erroneous assumptions of these sorts not only underestimate the capacity of traditionally religious people to rethink and recast their own traditions on grounds of justice, but fail also to take seriously what is, I believe, fundamental to all serious advocacy for the basic rights of lesbian and gay persons, namely, that the grounds for claims to gay and lesbian identity are the most basic rights owed all persons under American constitutionalism. We can no more permit sectarians to define for us the meaning of constitutional values like conscience and toleration than we can permit them to define the meaning of our lives and struggles as free people.

The emphasis placed here on the right to conscience may have been resisted for another, more weighty reason. Most serious discussion of the suspectness of sexual preference has assumed that, to qualify as a suspect classification, it must be pressed into the procrustean model of immutability, salience, and powerlessness. The emphasis on these three factors is an interpretive mistake both as a matter of the constitutional principle of suspect classification analysis in general and the suspectness of sexual preference in particular. All compelling arguments for suspect classification status turn on the irrationalist burdens placed on reasonable identifications expressive of moral personality; sexual preference is suspect forthrightly because irrationalist burdens are today placed on the identifications increasingly central to the moral personality of gay and lesbian persons as free and equal people and citizens. We need a new approach, one closer to our experience and closer to the reality of our struggle.

The appeal of such an approach is its truth: its truth as a matter of constitutional interpretation but, equally importantly, its self-respecting truth to ourselves. The shape we give to constitutional arguments is not merely or only or perhaps even primarily whether they will be fully accepted by a court or president or Congress now. The shape we give to constitutional arguments constructs the shape of our moral identity as gay and lesbian persons, and we must responsibly define ourselves in the way most adequate to the common grievances of our diverse lives and experiences.[112] The appeal to the right to conscience

112. On the need for gay and lesbian scholars to frame their arguments in ways that reflect a reasonable consensus among them, see Janet E. Halley, "Sexual Orientation and the Politics of Biology: A Critique of the Argument from Immutability," *Stanford Law Review* 46 (1994): 503.

UNCONSTITUTIONALITY OF INITIATIVES

is, in my judgment, compelling because it most responsibly articulates our common grievances and thus our demands for self-respect that will not again acquiesce in the silence of the grave that has been the destiny assigned us by the dominant religio-cultural orthodoxy that we must challenge.

Lesbian and gay persons demand personal and moral identity on grounds of justice appealing to the inalienable right of conscience that is the right of very American, and they have the right to demand on that ground that their difference from the heterosexual majority is no longer a ground for the expression through public law of the constitutionally condemned irrationalism of sectarian identity politics. Identity and difference must be reconstructed on grounds of justice; that has been the struggle for constitutional decency and integrity of African Americans and women under constitutional law, and it is the same struggle, on grounds of principle, of gays and lesbians.[113]

Gay and lesbian persons must reclaim their constitutional tradition from the sectarian bigots who make their narrow minds and cramped souls the measure of human and constitutional rights and responsibilities. By remaking American constitutionalism in their own image, gays and lesbians will, like the comparable demands of the radical abolitionists and their successors (including Martin Luther King), confirm the moral power of outcasts to lead the nation into a deeper understanding of the meaning of a community not of race or gender or sexual preference, but a moral community of human rights.[114] That is a morally constructive task which touches with ethically prophetic fire the lives and struggles not only of gay and lesbian persons, but the meaning of life for all Americans. Life is thus lived not in the vacancies of consumerist distractions or the insipidities of mobility without aim, but in distinguished service of the better interpretation of one of the world's most humane constitutional traditions in light of its normative promise and demand of respect for universal human rights under law. One thus dignifies one's life as a gay or lesbian person and as an American. Few lives could be better lived than in such service.

Claims of lesbian and gay identity rest on the most fundamental principles of human rights in our tradition, in particular, the right to conscience, a right central to any sound understanding and conservation of the enduring values of American constitutionalism. Their claims

---

113. For exploration of similar themes, see William E. Connolly, *Identity/Difference: Democratic Negotiations of Political Paradox* (Ithaca: Cornell University Press, 1991), 64–94, 158–97.

114. See, for some further discussion, Richards, *Conscience and the Constitution*, 257–58.

are, in their nature, claims of conscience, of ethical emancipation and empowerment resting on conscientious convictions about how a life is well and responsibly lived. Their opponents aggressively condemn them essentially in terms of heresy and blasphemy from what, in their view, can alone be the measure of religious truth; a constitutional tradition that knows neither heresy nor blasphemy as constitutionally acceptable forms of law must condemn as well attempts, like Colorado Amendment Two, to use law to condemn gay and lesbian identity as heresy and blasphemy against true value in living.

The struggle for lesbian and gay identity, on terms of justice, is our contemporary retelling of the oldest narrative of civil liberty, the struggle for the inalienable right of conscience against the manifold forms of subjugation of the moral power to understand, let alone to claim, the rights of one's human nature as a free and responsible person and ethical agent. To be adequate to our responsibilities in this struggle, we must understand the stakes, namely, the central role of the struggle of gay and lesbian identity in a both reasonable and conservative public understanding in contemporary circumstances of the struggle against intolerance and the demand that constitutional institutions refuse complicity, on grounds of principle, with its dehumanizing evils.

Colorado Amendment Two and its imitations are unconstitutional for this reason: they enlist the state in active complicity with the evil of denying persons the most basic right of their moral personalities, the right conscientiously to forge a mind and heart that demands justice. To crush the human spirit in this way prepares a nation, as twentieth-century experience shows so clearly, to accept injustice and to rationalize atrocity. Americans have the responsibilities that go with the good fortune of living under a constitutional order that, properly interpreted, refuses complicity with such a denial of the most basic human rights. We must make clear that what is at stake is nothing less than the interpretive integrity and conservation of our most basic constitutional principles, which are not suspended when a minority is irrationally despised and degraded. Indeed, the test of our constitutional principles is to stand by them when they are needed, not when they are not. We must stand on these principles, and dignify ourselves and our nation by the integrity of our demands for no more but certainly no less than respect for the basic human rights due all Americans.

8   The Case for Gay Rights: The Military and Marriage

The issue of gay rights has recently come to national attention in two contexts: President Clinton's initiation of a review of the current policy of exclusion of homosexuals from the military (leading to Congressional adoption of Clinton's proposed change in policy, "Don't Ask, Don't Tell"), and congressional consideration of the Defense of Marriage Act (supported also by Clinton) that tries to limit the effect, under the full faith and credit clause,[1] of the possible legalization of same-sex marriage in Hawaii. Such federal legislation raises troubling constitutional questions in light of the evident judicial concern over sexist exclusion from state-supported military academies[2] and comparable concern with discrimination on grounds of sexual preference and identity.[3] I want to explore these troubling constitutional questions in light of the normative approach to gay rights defended in the previous two chapters. In both cases, the legislation in question uses the classification of sexual preference (in particular, conscientious claims of gay and lesbian identity) in a constitutionally suspect way, and neither can survive the level of scrutiny in terms of compelling state secular purposes such laws must survive in order to be constitutional. Neither the congressional and presidential consensus on the military exclusion nor on same-sex marriage can be regarded as constitutionally legitimate.

1. See U.S. Const. art. 4, §1.
2. See *United States v. Virginia*, 116 S. Ct. 2264 (1996).
3. See *Romer v. Evans*, 116 S. Ct. 1620 (1996).

Drawing on the analysis of constitutional principles developed earlier particularly those derived from the tradition of the abolitionist feminists, I hope to show why this is so.

There are, of course, arguments of institutional competence and even prudence that might caution the judiciary from embracing the full extent of the arguments of principle owed gay and lesbian persons in these or other contexts. As Sunstein has recently urged, these principles may be used to invalidate antigay/lesbian ordinances yet not to protect a right to same-sex marriages or even to sexual relations as such.[4] But before we can know what weight such arguments should have, we must be clear about what the best interpretive arguments of constitutional principle are. Only in light of such a normative standard can we reasonably assess the gap between current practice and the appropriate standard and ask ourselves what role the judiciary can and should play in narrowing that gap, acknowledging the complementary constitutional role played by other institutions.[5] I begin with the military exclusion question, then turn to same-sex marriage, and finally assess the case for a limited judicial role in one or another of these areas.

EXCLUSION FROM THE MILITARY

The pertinent law currently in constitutional dispute is popularly known as the "Don't Ask, Don't Tell" policy.[6] In question as well are the accompanying directives issued by the Department of Defense ("DoD") and the Secretary of Transportation. The background of this legislation lay in a debate, initiated by President Clinton, over the continued exclusion of homosexuals from service in the military.[7] Under the policy, in force at that time and promulgated by the DoD in 1982,[8] a service member was to be separated from the armed services if one or more of the following findings was made:

---

4. See Cass R. Sunstein, "Homosexuality and the Constitution," *Indiana Law Journal* 70 (1994): 1.

5. See, in general, Lawrence G. Sager, "The Legal Status of Underenforced Constitutional Norms," *Harvard University Law Review* 91 (1978): 1212.

6. 10 U.S.C. §654 (1996).

7. For a good review of the historical background, see Lawrence J. Korb, "The President, the Congress, and the Pentagon: Obstacles to Implementing the 'Don't Ask, Don't Tell' Policy," in Gregory M. Herek, Jared. B. Jobe, and Ralph M. Carney, *Out in Force: Sexual Orientation and the Military* (Chicago: University of Chicago Press, 1996), 290–301.

8. See 47 Fed. Reg. 10,162 (1982).

(1) The member has engaged in, attempted to engage in, or solicited another to engage in a homosexual act or acts unless there are approved further findings that:

(a) Such conduct is a departure from the member's usual and customary behavior;

(b) Such conduct under all the circumstances is unlikely to recur;

(c) Such conduct was not accomplished by use of force, coercion, or intimidation by the member during a period of military service;

(d) Under the particular circumstances of the case, the member's continued presence in the Service is consistent with the interest of the Service in proper discipline, good order, and morale; and

(e) The member does not desire to engage in or intend to engage in homosexual acts.

(2) The member has stated that he or she is a homosexual or bisexual unless there is a further finding that the member is not a homosexual or bisexual.

(3) The member has married or attempted to marry a person known to be of the same biological sex (as evidenced by the external anatomy of the persons involved) unless there are further findings that the member is not a homosexual or bisexual and that the purpose of the marriage or attempt was the avoidance or termination of military service.[9]

In January 1993, Clinton directed the Secretary of Defense to review this policy, which led to such review and extensive hearings in both houses of Congress on the question of military service by homosexuals.[10] Several months later, the President announced a new policy that was the basis for §654. In the legislation, Congress grounded its basis for enactment in considerations of unit cohesion in combat and long-standing traditions of military restrictions on personal behavior that would not be acceptable in civilian society. "[T]he presence in the armed forces of persons who demonstrate a propensity or intent to engage in homosexual acts would create an unacceptable risk to the high standards of morale, good order, and discipline, and unit cohesion that are the essence of military capability."[11] Based on such findings, Congress provided that a service member would be separated from the armed services, pursuant to regulations to be promulgated by the Secretary of Defense, in terms that generally tracked the previous policy with the exception of the second ground for separation which now read:

(2) That the member has stated that he or she is a homosexual or bisexual, or words to that effect, unless there is a further finding, made and approved in accordance with procedures set forth in the regulations, that the member has demonstrated that he or she is not a person who engages in, or attempts

9. See 32 C.F.R. pt. 41, app. A, pt. 1, at H.c (1992).
10. See, for example, S. Rep. No. 112, 103d Cong., 1st Sess. 269–70 (1993).
11. 10 U.S.C. §654(a).

to engage in, has a propensity to engage in, or intends to engage in homosexual acts.[12]

The regulations implementing the new policy state that its purpose is not aimed at the separation of homosexuals on status grounds alone,[13] and the new policy sharply restricts the circumstances under which the military authorities may initiate an investigation of a service member: such an investigation may not be initiated without cause and a criminal investigation based on consensual gay sex acts must be based on credible evidence; credible evidence of homosexual acts does not include "associational activity such as going to a gay bar, possessing or reading homosexual publications, associating with known homosexuals, or marching in a gay rights rally in civilian clothes. Such activity, in and of itself, does not provide evidence of homosexual conduct."[14] And applicants "shall not be asked or required to reveal whether they are heterosexual, homosexual, or bisexual."[15]

A number of constitutional difficulties may be raised about each of the grounds for exclusion under both the old and new policies: the ground of all homosexual sex acts in contrast to sexual relations or untoward sexual exploitation or harassment as such, heterosexual or homosexual, that prejudice legitimate military interests; self-identifying speech as a homosexual; same-sex marriage.

The exclusion on the basis of gay consensual sex may have been regarded as unproblematic when *Bowers v. Hardwick* (allowing the criminalization of gay sex in the privacy of the home) was good law, but *Bowers* assumed decisively the Court's acceptance of mere majoritarian moral opinion as the measure of constitutional toleration. If that were still acceptable, *Romer v. Evans* could not have been decided as it was by six justices of the Supreme Court. The state's arguments in support of Colorado Amendment Two reflected the strength of majoritarian moral opinion about homosexuality. When the Court found the amendment to lack a rational basis, it repudiated the force of such moral opinions as the measure of constitutional rights. If that is true in a case dealing with a state constitutional amendment forbidding antidiscrimination laws, it must apply, *a fortiori*, to the much deeper intrusion into moral sovereignty at stake in *Bowers*. *Bowers*, for this

---

12. 10 U.S.C. §654(b).

13. See DoD Directive No. 1332.14, encl. 3, pt. 1, at H.1b(2).

14. See Guidelines for Fact-Finding into Homosexual Conduct, Enclosure 4 to DoDD 1332.14, Enlisted Administrative Separations and Enclosure 8 to DoDD 1332.30, Separations of Regular Commissioned Officers, News Release No. 605-93, Office of Assistant Secretary of Defense (Public Affairs), Washington, D.C., 22 December 1993, 4-4.

15. See DoD Directive No. 1304.26, encl. 1, at B.8.a.

reason, must be regarded as no longer authoritative. If so, *Bowers* can no longer be regarded as good authority for the blunderbuss prohibition of gay sex as such in the exclusion policy.

If exclusion on the ground of gay sex simpliciter was problematic, the case for the unconstitutionality of the speech-based ground would be quite straightforward. Indeed, the new policy makes even clearer than the old policy that the speech-based ground is justified as good rebuttable evidence of gay sex acts. If such sex acts could not be crudely forbidden in the way both the new and old policies contemplate, both policies would be in doubt, the new policy quite clearly so. Even the ground of same-sex marriage might be problematic if the illegitimacy of *Bowers* was interpreted in terms of a sufficiently robust basic right of the person to moral independence in making decisions central to one's intimate life. I postpone further discussion of this last point until the discussion of the constitutional basis for same-sex marriage, and turn here to constitutional discussion of the other grounds, in particular, self-identifying speech.[16]

The provision might be constitutionally problematic even if *Bowers v. Hardwick* were good law, or at least good law in the military context. The measure of free speech protection, under well-accepted American principles of free speech, is not limited to speech endorsing acts that are legal. The very core of the modern law of free speech is the protection of subversive advocacy—speech offering reasons for why current institutions are so fundamentally unjust that they should be rejected.[17] It is the speech that confronts American institutions with the most fundamental criticism (going to their basic worth) that most deserves judicial protection on grounds of free speech, not the speech that limits its criticisms to the measure of what is currently legal and acceptable. If so, constitutional protection of speech involving illegal acts would be called for though no one challenged the legitimacy of making such acts illegal.

In fact, of course, the moral and political reality of the exclusion policy is that there is enormous public controversy over the legitimacy of the traditional premise of the policy, condemning gay sex as im-

---

16. For similar discussions, see Nan D. Hunter, "Life after *Hardwick*," in *Sex Wars*, 85–100; id., "Identity, Speech, and Equality," 123–43. See also David Cole and William N. Eskridge, Jr., "From Hand-Holding to Sodomy: First Amendment Protection of Homosexual (Expressive) Conduct," *Harvard Civil Rights–Civil Liberties Law Review* 29 (1994): 319.

17. See *Brandenburg v. Ohio*, 395 U.S. 444 (1969) (speech advocating violent overthrow of government held protected and subject to demanding test of high probability of very grave harms not rebuttable in the normal course). For discussion and defense of this development in American public law, see Richards, *Toleration and the Constitution*, 178–87.

moral. Any discussion of the self-identifying speech ground, as an independent basis, must therefore in its nature be highly artificial, treating as a free speech issue what is as much an issue of legitimate criminalization; indeed, as several commentators have critically observed, the new policy disingenuously confuses speech with conduct and conduct with speech in an unstable semiotics that may indulge (if not encourage) prejudiced enforcement by military authorities.[18] The issues are especially closely linked in the context of the military exclusion if the interlinked grounds for both exclusions are the normative conception of religious, racial, or gender roles that are, on grounds of constitutional principle, increasingly rejected as the measure of public rights and responsibilities. These constitutionally illegitimate purposes find fertile grounds in the military context because, of all forms of state action, it has been the one most traditionally associated with a defining, indeed constitutive sense of American nationality and citizenship that has historically unjustly excluded classes of persons, on constitutionally illegitimate grounds, from such a national identity as fully citizens. A constitutionally defective conception of national citizenship has been constructed on the basis of such exclusions.

Many of the great struggles for inclusion of such groups in American citizenship have thus been over access on equal terms to military service. Perhaps the best evidence of how constitutive such participation in the military has been of American nationality and citizenship is the African American experience in the Civil War.[19] Until surprisingly late in the Civil War, Lincoln was considering various measures that would colonize the freed slaves abroad, where they could establish their own national forms.[20] Lincoln, though morally opposed to slavery, could not contemplate a national community that included African Americans on equal terms.[21] Under the pressures of abolitionist advocacy and military exigency, Lincoln authorized raising African American troops to serve in the war effort,[22] and they played an important role in the Union

18. See Janet E. Halley, "The Status/Conduct Distinction in the 1993 Revisions to Military Anti-Gay Policy," *GLQ: A Journal of Lesbian and Gay Studies,* 3:159–252 (1996); Theodore R. Sarbin, "The Deconstruction of Stereotypes: Homosexuals and Military Policy," in *Out in Force: Sexual Orientation and the Military,* ed. Gregory M. Herek, Jared B. Jobe, and Ralph M. Carney (Chicago: University of Chicago Press, 1996), 189; Gail L. Zellman, "Implementing Policy Changes in Large Organizations: The Case of Gays and Lesbians in the Military," in *Out in Force,* 283.

19. See McPherson, *The Struggle for Equality,* 192–220.

20. See Donald, *Lincoln,* 166–67, 343–44, 346–48, 396–97.

21. For an important recent study of Jefferson and his racist legacy to America, see Paul Finkelman, *Slavery and the Founders: Race and Liberty in the Age of Jefferson* (Armonk, N.Y.: M. E. Sharpe, 1996), 105–67.

22. See McPherson, *The Struggle for Equality,* 193–97.

victory.[23] Under the moral pressure of such participation (albeit in segregated regiments), Lincoln gradually came to the view that African
Americans were now morally owed what he had once, like most Americans, assumed to be unthinkable: the radical abolitionist dream of full
inclusion into the American political and moral community with equal
rights and responsibilities.[24] Military service was the moralizing practice of equal responsibilities that gave birth to America's moral growth
into at least the serious beginning of an American constitutional theory
and practice of equal rights.

The later struggle of African Americans to serve in a racially integrated military culminated in President Truman's 1948 executive order
calling for desegregation of the armed services, which was finally embraced by the military after the outbreak of the Korean War in June
1950.[25] That struggle was as important to the antiracist aims of the civil
rights movement as integration in public education was. If integration
in public education would make feasible a new public culture of inclusive educational and cultural opportunity, integration in the military
would take the equally important step of forging a practice of the equal
responsibilities of all citizens that would institutionalize as well a more
profound sense of the equal rights of all Americans.

It was fundamental to the cultural construction of American racism,
against the background of its tension with American rights-based revolutionary constitutionalism, that African Americans be dehumanized
in a way that would rationalize their denationalization as a part of the
American people. The crucial exclusionary point was to sustain the
image of such inferiority so that no rights-bearing constitutional guarantee could, in their favor, acknowledge or confer the basic rights of
American citizenship. In *Dred Scott v. Sanford*, Chief Justice Roger
Taney vividly described this tradition and its force:

> They [African Americans] had for more than a century before been regarded
> as beings of an inferior order, and altogether unfit to associate with the white
> race, either in social or political relations; and so far inferior, that they had
> no rights which the white man was bound to respect; and that the negro
> might justly and lawfully be reduced to slavery for his benefit. . . . It was
> regarded as an axiom in morals as well as in politics, which no one thought
> of disputing, or supposed to be open to dispute; and men in every grade
> and position in society daily and habitually acted upon it in their private

23. Ibid., 197–220.
24. See Donald, *Lincoln*, 430, 456–57, 526–27, 556.
25. See Donald G. Nieman, *Promises to Keep: African-Americans and the Constitutional
Order, 1776 to the Present* (New York: Oxford University Press, 1991), 139–42; Michael R.
Kauth and Dan Landis, "Applying Lessons Learned from Minority Integration in the Military," in *Out in Force*, 86–105.

pursuits, as well as in matters of public concern, without doubting for a moment the correctness of this opinion.[26]

The alleged grounds of Taney's pronouncement were as important as its substance: most notably, the claim of racism as "an axiom in morals as well as in politics," whose truth no one could or would doubt. The paradox of intolerance thus wreaked its rights-denying havoc on the American public mind. The reasonable debate most needed was repressed. To assert in 1857 that racism could not be doubted, after over thirty years of radical abolitionist dissent, was to ignore reasonable doubts about the racist composition of American national identity. Such doubts were wholly suppressed by, first, the invention of an originalist history and, second, making such history interpretively decisive. Justice Curtis's dissent decisively showed Taney's history to be false,[27] and Justice McLean's dissent made clear the large number of legitimate sources of interpretive authority (including relevant history, interpretive practices, applicable principles of human rights) that were cavalierly ignored by Taney.[28] Taney's opinion, so lacking in good interpretive reasons, achieved whatever appeal it had by his skillfully question-begging manipulation of the rhetoric of American national identity.

An interpretive performance as disastrous as *Dred Scott*[29] had this basically conclusory rhetorical appeal, which massaged uncritical assumptions that rationalized the continued existence and even the extension of slavery, as an institution, in otherwise republican America. A concept like national identity lends itself to such interpretive abuse as we can see in the parallel case of the use of the concept in Nazi Germany to rationalize political anti-Semitism. The comparison to America is instructive, and well worth exploring.

If American politics in the nineteenth century was preoccupied by the issue of the terms and scope of political community (including the status of blacks), the comparable political issue in Europe was posed by the emancipation of the Jews against the background of the principles of Enlightenment thought embodied in the French Revolution[30] and the ancient anti-Judaism and anti-Semitism we earlier discussed

26. *Dred Scott v. Sanford*, 60 U.S. (19 How.) 393, 407 (1857).

27. *Dred Scott*, 60 U.S. at 572–86.

28. Id. at 529–64.

29. For critical exploration in depth of the opinion and its consequences, see Don E. Fehrenbacher, *The Dred Scott Case: Its Significance in American Law and Politics* (New York: Oxford University Press, 1978).

30. See Arthur Hertzberg, *The French Enlightenment and the Jews* (New York: Columbia University Press, 1990).

(chapter 2). In the medieval period, both the expulsions of the Jews and their segregation were justified on the ground that they were legitimately the serfs or slaves of Christian princes because of their culpable failure to adopt Christian belief.[31] The segregation of Jewish communities from the life and occupations and responsibilities of Christian communities—intended, as it was, to stigmatize their culpability—created a Christian image of Jewish culture as inferior, the kind of cultural degradation that was, as we have seen in the case of American blacks, the context of American racism. It was also part of the historical background of the modern European form of racism we call anti-Semitism.

Modern European anti-Semitism, sometimes marked by its students as anti-Christian anti-Semitism,[32] arose in the context of the tense relationship between emerging European principles of universal human rights, sponsored by the French Revolution, and nineteenth-century struggles for a sense of national identity and self-determination. When the French Revolution took the form of Napoleonic world revolution, these forces became fatally contradictory. The emancipation of the Jews fatally occurred in this tense environment, and became over time its most terrible victim. The Jews, whose emancipation was sponsored by the appeal to universal human rights, were identified with a culture hostile to the emergence of national self-determination. Their very attempts at assimilation into that culture were, on this view, marks of their degraded inability for true national culture.

The struggles for national identity in nineteenth-century Europe—against the background of balkanized Germany principalities, Italian kingdoms, and imperialistic domination by non-Germans and non-Italians—were not obviously religious struggles. Indeed, many of them were self-consciously secular in nature and some of them deeply anti-religious (thus, German anti-Christian anti-Semitism). Religion was not usually the rallying call of national identity, but culture was—culture often understood in terms of linguistic unity as the basis of a larger cultural and ultimate national unity (thus, Pan-Germanism). For example, national unity in Germany was increasingly identified with the forging of a cultural orthodoxy of the purity of the German language, its ancient "Aryan" myths,[33] and its high culture. This search for cul-

31. See Gavin I. Langmuir, *Toward a Definition of Antisemitism* (Berkeley and Los Angeles: University of California Press, 1990), 156–57.

32. See, in general, Uriel Tal, *Christians and Jews in Germany,* trans. Noah Jonathan Jacobs (Ithaca: Cornell University Press, 1975).

33. For a superb treatment, see Leon Poliakov, *The Aryan Myth: A History of Racist and Nationalist Ideas in Europe,* trans. Edmund Howard (London: Sussex University Press, 1971).

tural unity arose in part in reaction to the French imperialistic and assimilationist interpretation of universal human rights. That history invited the search for an alternative linguistically and culturally centered concept of national unity.

But cultural unity—when hostile to universal human rights—is, as under Southern slavery, an unstable, highly unprincipled, and sometimes ethically regressive basis for national unity. It may unreasonably enforce highly sectarian values by deadly polemical reaction to its imagined spiritual enemies and it is all too historically comfortable to identify those enemies with a group already historically degraded as culturally inferior. Blacks were this group in America; in Europe, this role was performed by Jews, a highly vulnerable, historically stigmatized cultural minority—the paradigm case of cultural heresy, as it were. In the German case, where there was little solid humane historical background of moral pluralism on which to build, romantic aesthetic values overcame ethical ones; Italy's Mussolini, in contrast, had the history of Roman pluralistic toleration of Jews to appeal to in rebuking Hitler's very German anti-Semitism.[34] Richard Wagner, a major influence on the development of German anti-Semitism, thus preposterously regarded his artistic genius as sufficient to entitle him to articulate, as a prophetic moral leader like Lincoln, an ethical vision for the German people in the Aryan myth embodied in *Parsifal.* Such a confusion of the categories of aesthetic and ethical leadership reflected the underlying crisis in ethical and political culture.[35]

These deadly confusions were brilliantly displayed in Houston Chamberlain's immensely influential *The Foundations of the Nineteenth Century,*[36] a work much admired and indeed used by Hitler.[37] Chamberlain, Wagner's son-in-law, offered a cultural history of the world in which Aryan culture was the repository and vehicle of all value and Jews, as rationalists lacking creative imagination, the embodiment

34. See Poliakov, *The Aryan Myth,* 70.

35. Ibid., 380–457. On Wagner's actual confused state of belief, see Jacob Katz, *The Darker Side of Genius* (Hanover: University Press of New England, 1986). For good general studies of Wagner and Wagnerism (including their political uses by Hitler), see L. J. Rather, *Reading Wagner: A Study in the History of Ideas* (Baton Rouge: Louisiana State University Press, 1990); David C. Large and William Weber, eds., *Wagnerism in European Culture and Politics* (Ithaca: Cornell University Press, 1984).

36. Houston Stewart Chamberlain, *The Foundations of the Nineteenth Century,* trans. John Lees, 2 vols. (London: John Lane, 1911).

37. See Hitler, *Mein Kampf,* 116, 307, 325, 359, 369, 395, 413, 605. On Chamberlain's admiration and support for Hitler, see Large and Weber, *Wagnerism in European Culture and Politics,* 124–25.

of negative value. In effect, Chamberlain called for a politically enforceable cultural orthodoxy centering on Aryan culture against corrupting non-Aryan (Jewish) culture.

Chamberlain's argument clearly exemplified the paradox of intolerance; he admitted that there were reasonable scientific doubts about
the equation of language and race (which underlay his thesis), but resolved these doubts by appeal to a certitude expressive of the political
irrationalism of the will: "Though it were proved that there never was
an Aryan race in the past, yet we desire that in the future there may
be one. That is the decisive standpoint for men for action."[38] Jesus of
Nazareth, whom Chamberlain claimed to much admire, must, of
course, be a non-Jew, an Aryan in fact; we are in the never-neverland
where wishes magically become facts.

As in the evolution of American racism, religious intolerance became racist subjugation under the impact of decadent standards of
public reason. Chamberlain thus gave an essentially cultural argument
a racial interpretation (transmogrifying religious or cultural intolerance
into racism) at a time when such scientific racism, as he (like Hitler[39])
clearly recognized, was under examination and attack among students
of language and culture.[40]

The malignant consequences of the dynamic of such irrationalism,
when it is actually seriously harnessed to political power aggressively
hostile to human rights, was played out in the history of modern politi-

---

38. Chamberlain, *The Foundations of the Nineteenth Century*, 1:266.

39. For Hitler's clear recognition "that in the scientific sense there is no such thing as
race," see Rather, *Reading Wagner*, 286 (quoting conversation with Hitler reported by
Rauschning).

40. Franz Boas, a German Jew and anthropologist who emigrated to the United States
where he became a central architect of the modern human sciences of culture, had begun
seriously to debunk the racial assumptions of European and American anthropology as early
as the 1890s. In a way that had not been the case when the American ethnologists wrote,
racial theory was now under sharp attack as scientifically unsound. Yet it was in this context
that the increasingly well-understood irrationalism of racial thinking was accorded its fullest
and most dangerous political expression in the legitimation of a new conception of the basis
of political unity and identity. See Franz Boas, "Human Faculty as Determined by Race,"
in *A Franz Boas Reader*, ed. George W. Stocking, Jr. (1894; Chicago: University of Chicago
Press, 1974), 221–42. For Boas's fullest statement of his views, see Franz Boas, *The Mind
of Primitive Man* (1911; Westport, Conn.: Greenwood Press, 1963). On Boas's critical influence on modern social theory, see George W. Stocking, *Race, Culture, and Evolution* (New
York: The Free Press, 1968); Carl J. Degler, *In Search of Human Nature* (New York: Oxford
University Press, 1991). For a useful comparison of American and British antiracist thought
and argument, see Elazar Barkan, *The Retreat of Scientific Racism: Changing Concepts of
Race in Britain and the United States Between the World Wars* (Cambridge: Cambridge
University Press, 1992).

cal anti-Semitism and the racial genocide of some five million European Jews to which it ruthlessly led.[41] Political leaders obtained or retained populist political support for governments that violated human rights (and whose legitimacy was therefore in doubt) by appealing to racist fears as the basis of national unity. This strategy included the blatant falsification and distortion of facts that, consistent with Chamberlain and Hitler, inspired the national will with an unreasonable certitude (for example, the Dreyfus Affair in France, and "The Protocols of the Elders of Zion" in Imperial Russia[42]).

Political anti-Semitism became, under Hitler's leadership, the very core of the success of Nazi politics in a nation humiliated by the triumphant democracies in World War I.[43] Reasonable standards of discussion and debate on issues of race and human rights were brutally suppressed by a government-sponsored pseudo-science of race enforced by totalitarian terror.[44] Nazism was self-consciously at war with the idea and practice of human rights, including the institutions of constitutional government motivated by the construction of a politics of public reason that respects human rights.[45] Its politics of an artificially constructed group solidarity of myth, ritual, and pseudo-science, having no basis whatsoever in public reason, was motivated by the internal dynamic of the paradox of intolerance to manufacture a basis of unity in an irrationalist will to believe in the fantasized degraded evils of the Jews. The social construction of racism was carried in Nazi politics to its most irrationalist and immoral extremes because the basis of unity of Nazi politics was essentially a social solidarity of political unreason.

Against this comparative background, the decisive role that the concept of national identity played in an interpretive opinion on American constitutionalism like *Dred Scott* is even more inexcusable because the American constitutional tradition is a cultural tradition in which substantive moral values of respect for human rights play such a central role. *Dred Scott* was an interpretively incompetent performance because it drained the interpretation of the Constitution of any reference whatsoever to critical standards of universal human rights as tests of

41. See Raul Hilberg, *The Destruction of the European Jews* (New York: Holmes & Meier, 1985), 3:1201–20. On anti-Semitism, see, in general, Poliakov, *The History of Anti-Semitism.*

42. Poliakov, *The History of Anti-Semitism,* vol. 4.

43. See Peter Pulzer, *The Rise of Political Anti-Semitism in Germany and Austria,* rev. ed. (Cambridge: Harvard University Press, 1988); Jacob Katz, *From Prejudice to Destruction* (Cambridge: Harvard University Press, 1980).

44. See, in general, Hannah Arendt, *The Origins of Totalitarianism* (New York: Harcourt Brace Jovanovich, 1973).

45. Ibid.

legitimate political power. Public opinion, which had grown complacent about the moral evils of slavery, was not subjected to any measure
of critical assessment in light of the text, history, interpretive practice,
and rights-based political theory of the Constitution; rather, such public opinion was presented with its own narcissistic image of itself as
the measure of American constitutional demands, "blowing out," as
Lincoln put this point, "the moral lights around us."[46] Appeals to national identity are the way this point is made because they so easily lend
themselves to highly unstable, often insular and parochial aesthetic
judgments of the groups with which dominant majorities uncritically
identify, rather than more ethically demanding standards of constitutional justice.

The struggle of African Americans to claim their basic rights as
Americans was in its nature a hard-fought argument against the conception of national identity that had historically denationalized them
as part of the American people in terms of the dehumanizing abridgment of culture-creating rights (the basic equal rights of conscience,
speech, intimate life, and work). After slavery, institutions of segregation and antimiscegenation laws maintained that dehumanized image
and status by enforcing exclusion from the institutions central to American cultural life and the exercise of culture-creating rights. Integration
into these institutions was so important to the civil rights movement
because such access, on terms of respect for culture-creating rights,
affirmed that alternative normative conception of American constitutionalism central to their rights-based claims as persons and as citizens.

Integration into the military had the focal significance that it did
because such participation affirmed the status of African Americans
as equal bearers of rights and responsibilities in the role of citizen-
soldier historically central to the theory and practice of republican government.[47] In particular, American revolutionary constitutionalism,
both in the wake of the American Revolution and of the Civil War,
made possible a constitutional theory and practice of respect for inalienable human rights, tested the legitimacy of political power in
terms of such rights, and affirmed the right of persons and citizens to
question and resist illegitimate laws on constitutional grounds.[48] A theory and practice thus based on respect for inalienable human rights
morally empowered persons freely to exercise their basic rights, in-

46. See Johannsen, *The Lincoln-Douglas Debates,* 233.
47. For illuminating discussion of this point from a skeptical feminist perspective, see
Jean Bethke Elshtain, *Women and War* (New York: Basic Books, 1987), 47–91.
48. See, in general, Richards, *Foundations of American Constitutionalism;* id., *Conscience
and the Constitution.*

cluding taking steps, when necessary, to assert and defend their rights. One of the most insidious consequences of slavery under American revolutionary constitutionalism was that its racist rationalization required that African Americans be so dehumanized that they lacked such rights and thus the right to resist and, if necessary, revolt. Otherwise, the very foundations of American constitutionalism would legitimate the slave revolts that were the terror of the American South.[49] Participation of African Americans in the Union armies was so transformative for American racist public opinion because it directly challenged the dehumanized image of African Americans as natural slaves. On the basis of such participation, American blacks laid claim to their human right and responsibility to resist the total abridgment of their rights that American slavery involved. Integration of African Americans into the American military powerfully made this deeper point in the deconstruction of American racism. It was central to this struggle that the sense of indignation at segregation in the military would become most intense after American participation in wars justified in terms of American rights-respecting republican values and principles, to wit, World War I and World War II.[50] The latter war, conceived in terms of the defeat of an aggressively racist power, particularly called for full integration of African Americans in the struggle against such a racist power.[51] It is striking, along these lines, that such integration should have taken place by order of President Truman in 1948[52] and be followed in 1954 by *Brown v. Board of Education.*

Military service has a special character and role under American revolutionary constitutionalism as a public institution concerned to protect and defend rights-based constitutional institutions (of which the military itself is one). Accordingly, as the African American struggle makes abundantly clear, military service in the United States cannot be cordoned off from the larger struggles of rights-based justice under

49. The black abolitionist, David Walker, had thus asked in his 1829 *Appeal:* "Now, Americans! I ask you candidly, was your sufferings under Great Britain, one hundredth part as cruel and tyrannical as you have rendered ours under you?" See David Walker, *Walker's Appeal, in Four Articles, Together with a Preamble, to the Coloured Citizens of the World* (1829), in *A Documentary History of the Negro People in the United States,* ed. Herbert Aptheker (New York: Citadel Press Books, 1990), 1:97. For good general studies of the slave revolts, see Eugene D. Genovese, *From Rebellion to Revolution: Afro-American Slave Revolts in the Making of the Modern World* (Baton Rouge: Louisiana State University Press, 1979); Herbert Aptheker, *American Negro Slave Revolts* (New York: International Publishers, 1952).
50. See Nieman, *Promises to Keep,* 114–15, 139–40.
51. See Mary L. Dudziak, "Desegregation as a Cold War Imperative," *Stanford Law Review* 41 (1988): 61.
52. See Nieman, *Promises to Keep,* 141.

American constitutionalism. It is not and never has been a bystander to these struggles, but itself has been, by its nature, crucially involved in some of the nation's most disgraceful rights-denying exclusions and its most significant steps taken to remedy such constitutional evils. The claim that, by its nature, it must be immunized from civilian principles of constitutional analysis cannot reasonably be extended to rights-denying exclusions which, by their nature, compromise the very legitimacy of the role of the military under American rights-based constitutionalism. We must, rather, in each case inquire whether a ground for exclusion uncritically enforces a conception of national identity inconsistent with the demands of American constitutionalism.[53]

Issues of this sort are important in ongoing public discussions in the United States about the place and terms of the service of women, if any, in the military. Two issues should be distinguished: whether women may serve in the military at all and whether they should be excluded from combat. The two issues are related in the following way: if women can reasonably be excluded from combat, the case for exclusion from the military as such may be stronger. For example, in *Rostker v. Goldberg*,[54] the Supreme Court considered the constitutionality of the exclusion of women from the requirement to register for the draft, and decided, 6–3, that the exclusion was constitutional. All justices assumed that the combat exclusion was legitimate. On that basis, it was easier for the majority to find the exclusion to be reasonable because considerably lesser numbers of women than men would be needed to serve in combat roles.

Women now serve in the American military; indeed, there are more women in the military in the United States than any other country.[55] The main dispute has been over the legitimacy of the combat exclusion.[56] A 1991 presidential commission's report on this matter unanimously recommended exclusion of women from ground combat,[57] and

---

53. On the relevance of this experience to the integration of gays and lesbians into the military, see Kauth and Landis, "Applying Lessons Learned from Minority Integration in the Military."

54. See *Rostker v. Goldberg*, 453 U.S. 57 (1981).

55. See Jean Bethke Elshtain, *Women and War* (New York: Basic Books, 1987), 241.

56. See, in general, Presidential Commission on the Assignment of Women in the Armed Forces, *Women in Combat: Report to the President* (Washington, D.C.: Brassey's (U.S.), 1991) (hereinafter *Women in Combat*); Nancy Loring Goldman, *Female Soldiers—Combatants or Noncombatants* (Westport, Conn.: Greenwood Press, 1982). But for general skepticism about service of women in the military at all, see Brian Mitchell, *Weak Link: The Feminization of the American Military* (Washington, D.C.: Regnery Gateway, 1989).

57. Presidential Commission on the Assignment of Women in the Armed Forces, *Women in Combat* [hereinafter *Women in Combat*], 24–27.

narrowly (8–7) recommended exclusion of women from service on air-craft in combat missions (28–30) and that women be allowed to serve on combatant vessels except submarine and amphibious vessels (31–33). The grounds offered for the combat exclusion clustered in three categories: physical differences (bearing on "muscular strength and aerobic capacity" relevant to "tasks central to ground combat" [24]); unit-cohesion factors (in particular, forced intimacy on the battlefield, paternalistic attitudes to women that undermine "such key ingredients [of unit cohesion] as mutual confidence, commonality of experience, and equitable treatment," and "dysfunctional relationships (e.g., sexual misconduct)"; and mistreatment of women after capture (which "could have negative impact on male captives" [25]). None of these factors would reasonably justify exclusion in all cases. For example, the seven dissenters to the exclusion of women from combat aircraft have the stronger case for integration on the basis of the indisputable fact of "women's physical capability to perform in combat aviation." Unit co-hesion "is a function of leadership, shared purposes, and common risks and rewards," and should not be a bar when there is no demonstrated difference that would "be a contributing factor to the deterioration of unit performance" (81); and, as to worries about capture, it is not reasonable that "women who are willing to accept those risks should be restricted from competing for combat aviation assignments because of the protective tendencies of others" (83).

The force of arguments of rights-based feminism in this domain has recently been underscored by the Supreme Court's 7–1 decision in *United States v. Virginia*.[58] In ruling that gender-based exclusion from a Virginia public military college was unconstitutional, Justice Gins-burg, writing for the Court, critically examined the college's arguments of alleged gender differences in light of a constitutionally-based skepti-cism about crude gender stereotypes that themselves reflect a history of unjust gender-based discrimination in basic rights and opportunities (2280–84). Ginsburg conceded, "for purposes of this decision, that most women would not choose VMI's adversarial method" (2280), but in the same spirit of Justice Brennan's skepticism about giving effect to statistically significant factual differences between men and women rooted in unjust gender stereotypes in *Craig v. Boren*, the Court de-nied that such differences can "constitutionally deny to women who have the will and capacity, the training and attendant opportunities that VMI uniquely affords" (2280). In this connection, the Court em-phasized that women's integration into both federal military academies

58. See *United States v. Virginia*, 116 S. Ct. 2264 (1996).

and the armed forces abundantly confirmed the equal competence of women as citizen-soldiers once they were afforded an equal opportunity (2281). Accordingly, any exclusion of women from a public military academy, on the grounds of cultural stereotypes of incapacity to be citizen-soldiers, must be held to a high standard of constitutional scrutiny in terms of an exceedingly persuasive justification; only such a level of heightened scrutiny can make sure that the operative generalization was supported by compelling grounds independent of the rights-denying cultural stereotype. Such a justification was lacking here, and the exclusion was accordingly unconstitutional (2281–87).

Justice Ginsburg brings powerful arguments of rights-based feminism to bear on the military domain, suggesting that gender integration in the military may be as important to the equality of women as racial integration was to African Americans (2285–86).[59] Our earlier examination of the African American struggle for integration suggests why this should be so. Sexist, like racist, exclusion from the military affirms a dehumanized stereotype of servile dependence, certainly not the status of persons with moral powers that originate and demand claims of basic human rights, test the legitimacy of political power in those terms, and stand ready, if necessary to uphold their basic rights, whether by self-defense, by resistance, or, if necessary, by revolution. Such defensive rights (to protect one's rights) dignify moral personality as a bearer of rights; for this reason, recognition of such rights (for groups previously subjugated) humanizes its members as bearers of human rights (contesting the stereotype of subhumanity that subjugated them).[60] As Mary Wollstonecraft put this point in her pathbreaking essay on rights-based feminism, "if defensive war, the only justifiable war, in the present advanced state of society, where virtue can shew its face and ripen amidst the rigours which purify the air on the mountain's top, were alone to be adopted as just and glorious, the true heroism of antiquity might again animate female bosoms."[61] If Justice Ginsburg is correct about the importance to a rights-based con-

59. The Court indeed cites *Sweatt v. Painter,* 339 U.S. 629 (1950) (admitting African Americans to University of Texas Law School) as a relevant analogy.

60. For an important exploration of this theme in terms of a normative argument for rights of resistance, by battered women, to violence from their spouses, see Jane Maslow Cohen, "Regimes of Private Tyranny: What Do They Mean to Morality and for the Criminal Law?" *University of Pittsburgh Law Review* 57 (1996): 757.

61. See Wollstonecraft, *Vindication of the Rights of Woman,* 216. Wollstonecraft does not, however, ultimately endorse the proposition that women "turn their distaff into a musket," having "recreated an imagination" of a properly rights-based reform of the conception of gender roles that includes, in the military domain, separate gender roles for men and women (men serving in the military, women in family and related life). Ibid.

stitutional feminism of gender integration in the military domain, the admission of women to the American volunteer military may now be regarded as constitutionally compelled. If that is so, then Jean Bethke Elshtain may be correct that "[t]here seems little point in maintaining the pretense of combat exclusion for 'their protection.' Nobody can be protected any longer in the old sense of being 'immune from possible destruction.' "[62] In fact, perhaps reflecting the force of such arguments, incremental change in both congressional legislation and Department of Defense rules has substantially eroded the combat exclusion for women.[63] Both the integration of African Americans and of women into the military support the analogous case, on grounds of principle, for inclusion of gays and lesbians.[64] The experience of such inclusion both in foreign militaries[65] and in domestic police and fire departments[66] suggests that appropriately articulated and enforced policies of integration are as reasonable and feasible as they have been in the cases of the integration of African Americans and women.[67]

It is certainly striking in this connection that the institutional crucible for the development of the modern American movement for gay rights was the experience of gay men and lesbians in the military during World War II, including their resistance on grounds of justice to discrimination in the military.[68] Long before it had any publicly articulated theory, the practice of gay rights in America was thus formed around a sense of common identity in resisting injustice in the military service they rendered to the United States, as citizens, in perhaps the greatest struggle for human rights in history. If participation in this struggle

62. See Elshtain, *Women and War,* 244.
63. For a useful overview of these changes, see Madeline Morris, "By Force of Arms: Rape, War and Military Culture," *Duke Law Journal* 45 (1996): 732–38. For a recent expression of doubt by an anthropologist, see Anna Simons, "In War, Let Men Be Men," *New York Times,* 23 April 1997, A23.
64. On the parallel to African-American integration, see Kauth and Landis, "Applying Lessons Learned from Minority Integration in the Military"; on the parallel to the integration of women, see Patricia J. Thomas and Marie D. Thomas, "Integration of Women in the Military: Parallels to the Progress of Homosexuals?" in *Out in Force,* 65–85.
65. See Paul A. Gade, David R. Segal, and Edgar M. Johnson, "The Experience of Foreign Militaries," in *Out in Force,* 106–30.
66. See Paul Koegel, "Lessons Learned from the Experience of Domestic Police and Fire Departments," in *Out in Force,* 131–56.
67. For discussion of how such policy changes should be understood and implemented, see Gail L. Zellman, "Implementing Policy Changes in Large Organizations: The Case of Gays and Lesbians in the Military," in *Out in Force,* 266–89; on the relevance of unit cohesion, properly analyzed, see Robert J. MacCoun, "Sexual Orientation and Military Cohesion: A Critical Review of the Evidence," in *Out in Force,* 157–76.
68. See, in general, Allan Berube, *Coming Out under Fire: The History of Gay Men and Women in World War Two* (New York: Free Press, 1990).

energized previously existing claims of justice on behalf of African Americans, it literally forged the practice of making such claims of justice by American gay men and lesbians, who self-defined their previously unspeakable common identity in terms of making such claims.[69]

The distance gay men and lesbians traveled in this period was the distance from moral slavery to freedom, from submissive unspeakability to morally independent voice on grounds of the rights-based principles of American constitutionalism. It would take time for such practices to become self-consciously political and to develop a sense of their place in the larger fabric of an emerging rights-based civil rights movement. The first test of their moral voice occurred in the military context because both its homosocial context, away from traditional ties and communities, and larger rights-based purposes made such a personal and political growth in moral consciousness factually and normatively possible.[70] For this reason, quite unsurprisingly, there may be a higher rate of same-gender sexual behavior in the military than in the general population.[71] Ironically, the institution that gave rise to and indeed sustained the practice of gay rights is now the state institution that most vigorously represses its claims.

Some aspects of the "Don't Ask, Don't Tell" policy are an advance over the previous policy. It clearly repudiates, for example, the use of sexual preference as a ground for separation, an aspect of the earlier policy that several federal courts have correctly found unconstitutional.[72] It carefully limits the kinds of evidence that may credibly be used to show homosexual acts, excluding, for example, going to gay bars or attending a gay rights parade (thus, protecting, to some degree,

69. Ibid.; Randy Shilts, *Conduct Unbecoming: Gays and Lesbians in the U.S. Military* (New York: St. Martin's Press, 1993).

70. See, in general, Berube, *Coming Out under Fire.*

71. See, for relevant studies, Janet Lever and David E. Kanouse, "Sexual Orientation and Proscribed Sexual Behaviors," in *Out in Force,* 22 (gay men); Thomas and Thomas, "Integration of Women in the Military: Parallels to the Progress of Homosexuals?" in *Out in Force,* 72 (lesbians).

72. See, for example, *Watkins v. United States Army,* 837 F.2d 1428 (9th Cir. 1988) (regulation barring gays violates equal protection by discriminating on basis of homosexual orientation); cf. *Watkins v. United States Army,* 875 F.2d 699 (9th Cir. 1989) (en banc) (Army estopped from barring soldier's enlistment solely because of his acknowledged homosexuality); *Cammermeyer v. Aspin,* 850 F. Supp. 910 (W.D. Wash. 1994) (national guard officer's discharge for sexual orientation violated equal protection); *Pruitt v. Cheney,* 963 F.2d 1160 (9th Cir. 1992) (discharged Reverend's First Amendment rights not violated, but did state an equal protection claim (discrimination on grounds of sexual orientation), on which relief could be granted); *Dahl v. Secretary of U.S. Navy,* 830 F. Supp. 1319 (E.D. Cal. 1993) (homosexual exclusion policy violated equal protection in that it could not be based on anything but illegitimate prejudice).

associational rights). It draws the line, however, at self-identifying one-self as gay or lesbian and, *a fortiori*, same-sex marriage, literally making such self-identifying exercises of speech a *per se* ground for separation. Once having made such a self-identifying statement, it is practically impossible to rebut the inference, which the policy requires one to rebut, namely, that one has a "propensity" to gay sex. As Judge Nicker-son made clear in an opinion (later reversed), striking down the policy as unconstitutional, "propensity" here comes to mean the same thing as having a gay sexual orientation.[73] The ground for exclusion from the military under the new policy is thus the public assertion of one's iden-tity as a gay and lesbian person. This represents an unconstitutional abridgment by the state of human rights of personal and ethical con-science and of speech, that is, the capacity of a person to entertain and to express ethical convictions and identifications at the center of what gives enduring meaning to personal and ethical life. The Ameri-can military is a central institution of legitimate government; its uncon-stitutional war on a form of conscientious personal and ethical identity amounts to the unconstitutional enlisting of the state on one highly sectarian side of our contemporary wars of religion—a war in which the state must, as a matter of basic constitutional principle, be impar-tial.

A review of the new policy makes quite clear that the war is rather disingenuously on gay and lesbian *identity* much more than on gay sex *acts*. Even under a policy of full inclusion of gays and lesbians in the military, the evidence suggests that there would be few acknowledged homosexuals in the military.[74] Against this background, the policy's fo-cus on public statements of gay and lesbian identity appears all the more constitutionally problematic, focusing, as it does, on unfounded worries about rampant self-identifying speech acts (as gay or lesbian), rather than on the sex acts that are the supposed evil against which the policy is directed. Circumspection about one's sex life should, un-der the policy, render one immune from separation from the military; associational acts, highly probative of gay sex like attending gay bars or gay rights demonstrations, are not to be regarded as credible evi-dence of such acts. The only things that are given such decisive proba-tive weight are self-identifying speech acts as a gay and lesbian person, including undertaking same-sex marriage.

To rationalize the constitutionality of such a policy, federal circuit

73. See *Able v. United States*, 880 F. Supp. 968, 974–75 (E.D.N.Y. 1995), *reversed*, 1996 WL 391210 (2d Cir. 1996).

74. See MacCoun, "Sexual Orientation and Military Cohesion," 165, 172; Zellman, "Im-plementing Policy Changes in Large Organizations," 281.

courts have implausibly either denied that it significantly restricts speech, or claimed that the restriction is in any event a reasonable way of pursuing the clearly justifiable purpose of limiting gay sex.[75] Analogies to support the speech claim, used by two of the circuit courts, have included cases involving the regulation of obscene materials[76] or sexually harassing or provocative fighting words.[77] Neither opinion explains or attempts to explain how a self-identifying statement of one's homosexuality can reasonably be regarded as obscene or sexually harassing or fighting words. The statement, "I am gay," is not a hard-core pornographic representation of turgid genitals offensive to community values and lacking serious value under current judicial tests for the constitutionally obscene.[78] Nor is the statement in its nature sexually harassing, or a provocative epithet like "damned Fascist."[79]

Judge Nickerson, in a lower court opinion reversed and remanded by the appellate court in one of these cases, observed a tendency in the statute and regulations dealing with this policy to indulge uses of language that are "nothing less than Orwellian."[80] The same Orwellian distortions are seen in the judicial opinions of these circuit courts. Self-identifying statements like "I am gay" are expressions of gay and lesbian moral identity that specifically protest the unjustly enforced tradition of moral slavery by asserting conscientiously a self-respecting moral identity that protests on grounds of justice the political and legal force that tradition has uncritically enjoyed. To choose such an expres-

75. See *Able v. United States*, 1996 WL 391210 (2d Cir. 1996) (speech restriction of the policy not unconstitutional, but remanded for consideration of constitutionality of act restriction of policy and reconsideration of speech restriction in light of that analysis); *Thomasson v. Perry*, 80 F.3d 915 (4th Cir. 1996) ("Don't Ask, Don't Tell" policy subject to rational basis; there is no fundamental right to engage in homosexual acts, and there is legitimate interest in preventing them); *Philips v. Perry*, 1997 U.S. App. LEXIS 2646 (9th Cir. 1997) (policy, including restrictions on speech, has adequate basis in prohibiting sex acts).

76. See *Able v. United States*, 1996 WL 391210, at °13 (2d Cir. 1996), citing *City of Renton v. Playtime Theatres, Inc.*, 475 U.S. 41 (1986) (scattering zoning of adult theatre held constitutional).

77. See *Thomasson*, 80 F.3d at 930, citing *Price Waterhouse v. Hopkins*, 490 U.S. 228 (1989) (discriminatory words may be basis for Title VII action) and *R.A.V. v. City of St. Paul*, 505 U.S. 377 (1992) (sexually derogatory fighting words may produce violation of Title IV).

78. See *Miller v. California*, 413 U.S. 15 (1973).

79. See *Chaplinsky v. New Hampshire*, 315 U.S. 568 (1942).

80. See *Able v. United States*, 880 F. Supp. 968, 974 (E.D.N.Y. 1995) (section of "Don't Ask, Don't Tell," which permitted removal of service members for self-identification as homosexuals, held violation of free speech), *reversed and remanded*, 1996 WL 391210 (2d Cir. 1996). In a recent decision on the remand from the Second Circuit, Judge Nickerson found the restriction of the policy on acts (applying to a homosexual, but not a heterosexual, who "kisses or holds hands off base or in private or before entering the service") unconstitutional. *Able v. United States*, 1997 WL 369504, at °8 (E.D.N.Y. July 2, 1997).

sion for detrimental state treatment, in the terms of current constitutional principles of free speech, not only censors a kind of speech (a content-based expression of speech), but censors a point of view within one of the kinds of speech (conscientious dissent about issues of justice) that is one of the most clearly protected forms of speech.[81] This is the most blatantly unconstitutional censorship of certain kinds of conscientious protests, namely, those that protest on grounds of justice the tradition of the unspeakability of homosexuality by speaking of it not as a pathology or an evil but as a self-affirming conscientious identity that gives meaning to personal and ethical life. The circuit courts, however, engage in Orwellian transformations of ethical claims into pornography, of dissent into sexual harassment, and of a challenge to dominant orthodoxy into fighting words. The measure of judicially protected speech has become, in this area, the entrenched sexual orthodoxy that such dissenters self-consciously challenge and mean to challenge. That cannot be an acceptable measure for the judicial protection of freedom of speech in a period when reasonable doubts about traditional conceptions of both gender and sexuality are very much in play, and indeed fundamental to the growing judicial skepticism about both gender and sexual preference as suspect classifications.

The second judicial rationalization for the policy of exclusion on the ground of making self-identifying statements as a homosexual (namely, its rational basis in forbidding gay sex) is no more constitutionally reasonable. To begin with, such exclusion is a viewpoint-based discrimination about clearly protected speech. It is for this reason wholly inappropriate to apply to its constitutional analysis, as one circuit court has, the more deferential standards of review appropriate to time, place, and manner regulations or symbolic speech;[82] it is equally wrong doctrinally to analyze such a viewpoint-based restriction on distinctive forms of public speech, as another circuit court has, on the model of bias crimes or sexual harassment.[83]

81. On the centrality of both viewpoint-based and content-based restrictions as constitutional violations of free speech, see Stone, "Content Regulation and the First Amendment," 25 *William and Mary Law Review* 25 (1983): 189. On conscientious dissent as the core of protected speech, see Richards, *Toleration and the Constitution*, 165–227.

82. See *Able v. United States*, 1996 WL 391210, at °12–13 (2d Cir. 1996), citing, for example, *Madsen v. Women's Health Center, Inc.*, 114 S. Ct. 2516 (1996) (reviewing regulations of abortion protests under time, place, and manner standards), and related cases, and *United States v. O'Brien*, 391 U.S. 367 (1968) (upholding criminalizing draft-card burning as based on dominant conduct element).

83. See *Thomasson*, 80 F.3d at 918, citing *Wisconsin v. Mitchell*, 508 U.S. 476 (1993) (speech elements may be used in aggravation of bias crime); *Price Waterhouse v. Hopkins*,

Crude doctrinal manipulations of the standard of review appropriate to viewpoint-based restrictions are constitutionally unprincipled in exactly the context that such evasions of principle work the most damage on traditionally stigmatized minorities subject to an unjust history of moral slavery, that is, they express and reinforce rights-denying cultural stereotypes of moral slavery. The core of the argument for the constitutionality of the new policy is along lines that the policy's concern for gay self-identifying speech focuses not on the speech, but on the gay sex acts of which such speech is highly probative,[84] but the attention of the new policy is decidedly on identity, not acts, which is doubly constitutionally unreasonable.

First, public assertion of gay or lesbian identity is not, in its nature, a statement about sex acts any more than a comparable statement of dissenting religious or racial or gender identity is when made against the tradition of moral slavery. There has in fact been a long history of rights-denying dehumanization of persons, often in terms of politically enforced sectarian sexual mythologies of black or female sexuality or Jewish or gay femininity (Weininger). Indeed, the culturally dominant Euro-American stereotype of homosexuals has been as a sexualized fallen woman (whether the feminization of gay men or the masculinization of lesbians). Against this background, to ascribe to a statement "I am gay" a statement or even a prediction of sex acts is not fairly to hear what is being said but to degrade the speaker to the terms of a dehumanized and dehumanizing stereotype. Such a self-ascribing claim of gay or lesbian identity makes, as we have seen, a claim of justice protesting an unjust cultural tradition of moral slavery and the political force its rights-denying cultural stereotypes have uncritically been allowed to enjoy. It claims what that tradition denied: speakability and moral voice, indeed, the basic human rights of conscience, speech, intimate life, and work. It claims the moral powers rationally and reasonably to live a life founded in, among other things, convictions of the moral value of homosexual love, care, and passion and the intimate identifications and personal and moral growth to which they give expression. These convictions center in ethical arguments of justice, some of which interpret rights-based feminism as grounding a right to homosexual love as part of a just moral protest about compulsory heterosexuality. The lives that give expression to these convictions are as various as the people who claim such basic rights. There is no funda-

---

490 U.S. 228 (1989) (discriminatory words in proper context may be used to prove discriminatory acts under Title VII).

84. See *Thomasson*, 80 F.3d at 931–32; *Able*, 1996 WL 391210, at °14–15.

mentalist orthodoxy of sex acts integral to their moral claims, nor should there be. Rather, the resistance to any such orthodoxy is surely what may be most humane about its larger moral promise of emancipated moral imagination about love, as a basic human good, for the culture at large. Resistance to such stereotypes (including their sexualization as homosexuals) may indeed distinguish such claimants of gay and lesbian identity from other homosexuals who have accommodated themselves to what they cannot or will not challenge.[85] Part of their challenge may be to insist, on grounds of justice like Whitman's, that homosexuality should no more be only about sex than heterosexuality, challenging, on grounds of justice, the common assumption to the contrary.[86] From this perspective, the judicial mantra that claims of homosexual identity equate to sex acts is not made more reasonable by repetition,[87] but bespeaks the uncritical force of the cultural stereotype, as a still uncontested and unchallenged stereotype, controlling even the judicial mind ready to manipulate constitutional principles to indulge irrationalist forms of homophobic and sexist prejudice.

As Judge Betty Fletcher observed in her dissent to her circuit court's disposition of this issue, the military's treatment of public statements of gay or lesbian identity ascribes to such statements, in the name of unit cohesion, an interpretation in terms of "biases that cannot be tolerated under the laws."[88] Effectively, the discomfort of heterosexual men with homosexuality, as a kind of irrationalist sense of tribal pollution,[89] is made the measure of unit cohesion. Unit cohesion, as a measure of the performance of groups, is most reasonably understood as a measure of task cohesion, not of generalized social cohesion[90]—a critical

85. See, on this conflict, Larry Gross, *Contested Closets: The Politics and Ethics of Outing* (Minneapolis: University of Minnesota Press, 1993); Michelangelo Signorile, *Queer in America: Sex, the Media, and the Closets of Power* (New York: Random House, 1993). The lowest rates of homosexuality are reported when people are asked whether they identify themselves as homosexuals, in contrast to attraction to the same sex or having had sex with members of the same sex; see Michael et al., *Sex in America: A Definitive Survey,* 174–76. Even within the group who identify themselves as homosexual in such a study, there will be differences between those who more publicly disclose their identity in contrast to those who do not.

86. For support that this is the common assumption, see Gregory M. Herek, "Why Tell If You're Not Asked? Self-Disclosure, Intergroup Contact, and Heterosexuals' Attitudes toward Lesbians and Gay Men," in *Out in Force*, 203, 207–8.

87. See, for citation to other cases making the same mistake, *Able,* 1996 WL 391210, at °17; *Thomasson,* 80 F.3d at 930–31.

88. See *Philips v. Perry,* 1997 U.S. App. LEXIS 2646, at °52 (9th Cir. 1997).

89. For support for this interpretation, see Theodore R. Sarbin, "The Deconstruction of Stereotypes: Homosexuals and Military Policy," in *Out in Force,* 181.

90. See, for an illuminating treatment of this issue, MacCoun, "Sexual Orientation and Military Cohesion."

understanding that facilitated the integration of both African Americans and women into the military. Social discomfort based on bias cannot be a reasonable measure of task cohesion under properly stated and enforced policies of nondiscriminatory treatment in the military.[91] Sexist worries about sexuality, which were inadequate to bar the integration of African Americans or women into the military, cannot, in principle, bar the integration of gays and lesbians on similar terms of justice (including appropriate protections from sexual harassment, heterosexual or homosexual). The experience of foreign militaries and of domestic police and fire departments with the integration of homosexuals support the common grounds, methods, and success of such policies.[92] In all these cases, clearly stated and appropriately mandated policies enforced a professionally appropriate etiquette of disregard of sexual issues so that all persons could attend to their tasks ably and well.[93] Judge Fletcher properly regards heterosexual fear that gays or lesbians could not (contrary to all evidence) appropriately observe such an etiquette in their professional lives (as they have done and continue to do in all professions) as homophobic; such bias, for bias it is, cannot be the constitutionally reasonable measure of service in the American military.

Second, if the policy had been concerned with gay sex acts, it would not reasonably have gone about its business in the way it in fact did. Many of the courses of conduct that were expressly ruled out as probative of such sex acts (attending a gay bar or a gay rights rally or having homosexual friends) surely are probative of such acts, and some of them are much more probative than making a claim of gay identity. The structure of the new policy is hospitable to gay sex acts, as long as they are clandestine, secretive, and, of course, discreet. The homage the new policy pays to the prohibition of gay sex acts is a matter of constitutional form, not substance: it is concerned with prohibiting gay sex only insofar as such concern is the necessary gesture to constitutional virtue that must be paid to rationalize its constitutional vice. Its real concern is to eliminate assertions of gay identity, a viewpoint-based discrimination against conscience and speech that should have been subjected to much more demanding judicial scrutiny than it was.

91. See Thomas and Thomas, "Integration of Women in the Military;" Kauth and Landis, "Applying Lessons Learned from Minority Integration in the Military."

92. See Gade, Segal, and Johnson, "The Experience of Foreign Militaries;" Koegel, "Lessons Learned from the Experience of Domestic Police and Fire Departments."

93. See, for an illuminating treatment of this issue, Lois Shawver, "Sexual Modesty, the Etiquette of Disregard, and the Question of Gays and Lesbians in the Military," in *Out in Force*, 226–46.

As it is, the dilution of such standards of review in this case indulges the hypocritical subterfuge that the new policy, in fact concerned with identity, is focused on acts. Such abuse of language is Orwellian indeed, pandering to the exigencies of politicians not measuring political power by arguments of integrity that reflect deliberation of and about constitutional principles.

All the circuit courts put decisive weight on one last consideration: the deference the judiciary owes the expertise of the legislative and executive branches in running an orderly and effective military service.[94] *Rostker v. Goldberg*[95] is directly in point: the Supreme Court applied the applicable standard of heightened scrutiny[96] deferentially in view of the judgment of the Congress that only men should be required to register for the draft. *Rostker,* decided in 1981, crucially assumed the acceptance by all justices of the legitimacy of the gender-based combat exclusion and may have been superseded both by the erosion of the combat exclusion and by the even higher level of scrutiny that may now be applicable to such gender classifications in light of *United States v. Virginia.*[97] As I earlier suggested, there may now be a compelling constitutional argument why women could not be excluded from the current all-volunteer military.

Whatever may be the appropriate level of judicial scrutiny for constitutional issues involving military service in other contexts, there are, I believe, compelling arguments of principle why a higher level of scrutiny should be accorded exclusions which express and reinforce dehumanizing stereotypes that deprive whole classes of citizens of their equal rights of citizenship. The issue at stake here is nothing less than the constitutional conception of national citizenship, including the equal rights and responsibilities central to rights-based, republican citizenship. That is not a conception on which the judgments of military leaders can be regarded as decisive in the way they might reasonably be regarded in other areas relating to issues of military discipline, organization, and readiness. Such judgments of national citizenship may uncritically reflect not impartial judgments of competence and merit in military service but the traditional military's sense of themselves as

94. See *Thomasson,* 80 F.3d at 921–26; *Able,* 1996 WL 391210, at °11–12; *Philips,* 1997 U.S. App. LEXIS 2646, at °13–20 (Rymer, J.), °30–39 (Noonan, J., concurring).

95. See *Rostker v. Goldberg,* 453 U.S. 57 (1981) (women may constitutionally be excluded from requirement to register for draft).

96. See *Craig v. Boren,* 429 U.S. 190 (1976) (intermediate level standard of review applicable to gender-based classification, in age at which beer may be sold to men and women, and classification found unconstitutional).

97. See *United States v. Virginia,* 116 S. Ct. 2264 (1996).

men—a sense that is unjustly constructed, as racism and sexism surely are, on the unjust dehumanization of African Americans and women through long-standing traditions of racial or gender segregation. All of the struggles central to our moral growth as a people under American revolutionary constitutionalism have been over the insistence that the conditions of American citizenship must be rights-based, subjecting our religious, racial, ethnic and (most recently) gendered sense of our identities as Americans to critical scrutiny in terms of more demanding ethical principles. We cannot reasonably put such a strong conception of rights-based moral community at hazard by allowing uncritical conceptions of true manhood, which may have no more basis than Aryan brotherhood, to be the defining measure of American national identity. The analogy to Aryan brotherhood is, I believe, exact if the exclusion of conscientiously identified homosexuals from the military is in principle the same as excluding from such service a religious identity (Judaism) on that sectarian basis. We would reject such a constitutional outrage on grounds of constitutional principle that apply, in contemporary circumstances, to gays and lesbians as well.[98]

I therefore propose that the appropriate standard of judicial review for such exclusions should scrutinize closely the grounds alleged in their support. In particular, conclusory statements about the conditions of group solidarity should be, as Judge Fletcher urged, closely examined to determine whether such statements express prejudices derived from a constitutionally condemned history of rights-denying dehumanization. Policies of exclusion that express such prejudices should be constitutionally rejected. In fact, as our earlier discussion of the "Don't Ask, Don't Tell" policy makes clear, the grounds urged in its support, including those mentioned in the legislation itself, are essentially constitutionally suspect grounds about conditions of group solidarity. Such exclusions should not be constitutionally tolerated.[99]

The American military, which gave birth to the modern American struggle for gay rights, has been among its most intransigent antago-

---

98. A different, perhaps closer case would be posed by a neutral military regulation requiring uniform dress regulations barring the wearing of headgear indoors (forbidding the wearing of a yarmulke by an Orthodox Jew). See *Goldman v. Weinberger*, 475 U.S. 503 (1986) (regulation held constitutional against free exercise challenge). Even *Goldman* may be a doubtful constitutional result as Congress apparently believed in reversing it. See 10 U.S.C. §774 (1988) (granting relief from the regulation).

99. For a similar analysis, see Kenneth I. Karst, "The Pursuit of Manhood and the Segregation of the Armed Forces," *UCLA Law Review* 38 (1991): 499. See also Seth Harris, "Permitting Prejudice to Govern: Equal Protection, Military Deference, and the Exclusion of Lesbians and Gay Men from the Military," *New York University Review of Law and Social Change* 17 (1989–90): 171.

nists. Military life fostered this struggle because many gay men and lesbians found their lives to be validated by its demands and purposes (including a war against a power hostile, in principle, to the theory and practice of human rights). The rather homophobic attempts of the military to construct a difference between gay men and lesbians and all other persons in the military, including the rather rank record of persecution recorded by Randy Shilts in his important study of the post-World War II period,[100] try to deny what seems all too obvious: the demands and purposes of military life are, in fact, quite congenial to and supportive of gay and lesbian identity.[101] The analogy between homophobia and anti-Semitism is again informative. Freud observed of anti-Semitism that its irrationalism was its heightening of small, morally irrelevant differences into Manichean stereotypical truths.[102] The homophobia of the military builds upon small, morally irrelevant differences to paint a dehumanized portrait of self-identified homosexuals as incapable of the responsible exercise of the duties of military service. The military could reasonably acknowledge what it clearly knows to be true (that homosexuals are as good soldiers as heterosexuals in republican military service judged on the basis of merit and contribution). Instead, it self-destructively wars on its republican children, who have learned better than their parents the inward moral meaning of rights-based military service. We should not rest until they are fully satisfied in their wholly just quest for full republican citizenship on terms of equal respect.

SAME-SEX MARRIAGE

Another ground for the military exclusion is same-sex marriage which, itself a heightened expression of gay or lesbian identity, raises the same constitutional issues as the focus of the new policy on self-identified gay or lesbian identity as such. Certainly, claims for same-sex marriage, after they have been rejected on the constitutional merits, have then also been the basis for firing people on the ground of "flaunting" gay

100. See Shilts, *Conduct Unbecoming.*

101. One severe critic of women in the military noted that, of the women in the military, lesbians were much the best soldiers. See Mitchell, *Weak Link,* 178–82. On the higher incidence of homosexuals in the military than in civilian life, see Lever and Kanouse, "Sexual Orientation and Proscribed Sexual Behaviors," 22 (gay men); Thomas and Thomas, "Integration of Women in the Military," 72 (lesbians).

102. On "the narcissism of small differences," see Sigmund Freud, *Civilization and Its Discontents,* in *Standard Edition of the Complete Psychological Works of Sigmund Freud,* ed. and trans. James Strachey (London: Hogarth Press, 1961), 21:114; see also *Moses and Monotheism* (1964), 23:91.

or lesbian identity—firings that have usually been upheld.[103] If all such forms of state action discriminating against gay and lesbian identity are, as I have argued, presumptively unconstitutional, then these certainly should be as well, as one circuit court recently has held.[104] If, however, there are compelling constitutional arguments why same-sex marriage itself may not be denied, that would afford an additional ground for the unconstitutionality of the military exclusion on that ground. We need to address the latter question of the constitutionality of banning same-sex marriage.

The question came to the forefront of national attention in light of the Hawaii Supreme Court's decision in *Baehr v. Lewin*,[105] followed by legislation approved by Congress and signed by the President to limit the force of that decision. I begin with the discussion of *Baehr* on its merits and then turn to the legislation.

Baehr held, under the Hawaii state constitution, that the denial of marriage in Hawaii to same-sex couples must be subjected to strict scrutiny under Hawaii's Equal Rights Amendment (ERA). In reaching this result, the Hawaii Supreme Court declined to find that there was a fundamental right to gay marriage, a finding of which would also have subjected the case to demanding judicial scrutiny. The case was remanded for trial of the issue whether the denial of same-sex marriage could satisfy this demanding standard; unsurprisingly, the trial court recently found that the denial could not survive such scrutiny.[106] It now appears not unlikely that an amendment to the Hawaii state constitution will be approved next year that would ban same-sex marriages but give gay and lesbian couples some rights and benefits available to married couples.[107] *Baehr* will, however, continue to challenge the

---

103. See *Singer v. Hara*, 522 P.2d 1187 (Wash. Ct. App. 1974) (statutory prohibition of same-sex marriage not violative of Washington Equal Rights Amendment) followed by *Singer v. United States Civil Service Commission*, 530 F.2d 247 (9th Cir. 1976) (U.S. Government's firing of man who "flaunted" his homosexuality by *inter alia* commencing same-sex marriage suit did not violate First Amendment rights). See also *Baker v. Nelson*, 191 N.W.2d 185 (Minn. 1971) (same-sex couple not permitted to marry and denial not violative of constitutional provisions), followed by *McConnell v. Anderson*, 451 F.2d 193 (8th Cir. 1971) (university library permitted to withdraw offer to gay man because he had publicly applied for marriage license with another man).

104. See *Shahar v. Bowers*, 70 F.3d 1218 (11th Cir. 1995) (Georgia Attorney General's withdrawal of job offer to attorney after learning of her plans for same-sex marriage held subject to heightened scrutiny based upon First Amendment claims).

105. See *Baehr v. Lewin*, 852 P.2d 44 (Haw. 1993).

106. See *Baehr v. Miike*, 1996 WL 694235 (Haw. Cir. Ct. 1996).

107. See "Hawaii Seeks Law to Block Gay Marriage," *New York Times*, 18 April 1997, A15; David Orgon Coolidge, "At Last, Hawaiians Have Their Say on Gay Marriage," *Wall Street Journal*, 23 April 1997, A19.

American constitutional conscience to the extent it raises valid issues of constitutional principle that must be responsibly addressed. The populist failure to address them may, if the arguments of basic principle are valid, measure the depth of the constitutional evil of moral slavery now so visibly at work in our constitutionally decadent politics.

Baehr v. Lewin is a path-breaking departure from the usual interpretation of applicable constitutional principles in the area of same-sex marriage. Almost all American courts have held, both under state and federal constitutional law, that failure to recognize same-sex marriage is not unconstitutional[108] and have correlatively failed to accord same-same couples benefits like employee insurance coverage[109] or spousal rights under the law of wills[110] or the immigration laws[111] or the law of veteran benefits.[112] *Baehr* suggests it may be timely to rethink this question fundamentally.

Studies by William Eskridge[113] and Mark Strasser[114] have to my mind argued cogently that the denial of same-sex marriage is presumptively unconstitutional not only on the suspectness ground urged in *Baehr* but on the independent ground of abridging the basic human

---

108. See, for example, *Dean v. District of Columbia,* 653 A.2d 307 (D.C. 1995) (District of Columbia marriage law prohibits clerk from issuing marriage license to same-sex couple and does not unlawfully discriminate against couples under D.C. Human Rights Act or U.S. Constitution); *DeSanto v. Barnsley,* 476 A.2d 952 (Pa. Super. Ct. 1984) (man could not seek divorce from other man because same-sex common law marriages are not permitted in Pennsylvania); *Singer v. Hara,* 522 P.2d 1187 (Wash. Ct. App. 1974) (statutory prohibition of same-sex marriage not violative of Washington Equal Rights Amendment); *Jones v. Hallahan,* 501 S.W.2d 588 (Ky. Ct. App. 1973) (same-sex couple incapable of obtaining marriage license because same-sex marriage would not be a marriage); *Baker v. Nelson,* 191 N.W.2d 185 (Minn. 1971) (same-sex couple not permitted to marry and denial not violative of constitutional protections); *Anonymous v. Anonymous,* 325 N.Y.S.2d 499 (Sup. Ct. 1971) (marriage between males a nullity despite fact husband thought wife was a female at time of marriage and she subsequently underwent reassignment surgery). But see *M.T. v. J.T.,* 355 A.2d 204 (N.J. Super. Ct. 1976) (absent fraud, man not allowed to void marriage to post-operative transsexual female); *In re Matter of Marley,* 1996 WL 280890 (Del. Super. Ct. 1996).

109. See *Lilly v. City of Minneapolis,* 1994 WL 315620 (Minn. Dist. Ct. 1994) (registered domestic partners are not spousal dependants for purposes of extending employee insurance coverage).

110. See *In re Matter of Cooper,* 592 N.Y.S.2d 797 (App. Div. 1993) (surviving partner of same-sex relationship not entitled to spousal right of election against decedent's will).

111. See *Adams v. Howerton,* 673 F.2d 1036 (9th Cir. 1982) (an Australian and an American male citizen who had been married by minister in Colorado not married for purposes of Immigration and Nationality Act).

112. See *McConnell v. Nooner,* 547 F.2d 54 (8th Cir. 1976) (spousal veteran benefits denied to same-sex partner of veteran who had gone through same-sex marriage ceremony).

113. See William N. Eskridge, Jr., *The Case for Same-Sex Marriage: From Sexual Liberty to Civilized Commitment* (New York: Free Press, 1996).

114. See Mark Strasser, *Legally Wed: Same-Sex Marriage and the Constitution* (Ithaca: Cornell University Press, 1997).

right to intimate life, of which the right to marriage is an important institutional expression. If such statutes are subject to heightened scrutiny whether on the ground of their suspectness or their abridgment of a fundamental right, both scholars make clear that no compelling justification could constitutionally legitimate such invidious treatment.[115] I hope to complement their arguments by placing them in the context of the larger argument for gay rights that I have offered and defended in this book.

On the view I have taken, the moral slavery of homosexuals is constitutionally condemned by the Thirteenth Amendment just like that of African Americans and women, and the correlative guarantees of the Fourteenth Amendment must be interpreted accordingly to give effect to this rights-based normative judgment in all its relevant dimensions. These dimensions include the abridgment of the basic human rights (conscience, speech, intimate life, and work) and the inadequate sectarian grounds on which such abridgments have been, inconsistent with the argument for toleration, rationalized. These dimensions are systematically interconnected; the rectification of such rights-denying evils has resulted in striking interpretive developments both recognizing such basic rights and in constitutional doctrines increasingly suspicious of the expression through public law of the dehumanizing prejudices that have traditionally abridged such rights. Even discrimination on grounds of sexual preference has now been acknowledged by the Supreme Court as a ground to some degree thus suspect.[116]

The right to intimate life has played a central role in each of these interpretive developments both because of the moral fundamentality of the right itself and because its abridgment has been so historically salient in the cultural formation and support of rights-denying dehumanizing prejudices and the political expression they have uncritically been permitted to enjoy through public law and policies. Antimiscegenation laws perpetuated, long after the Civil War, the dehumanizing attitudes to African Americans that had, under slavery, deprived them of the basic rights to intimate life (including marriage and control of family relations) and thus dehumanized their treatment to the level

---

115. For example, as Eskridge argues, having children is not a constitutionally reasonable requirement for heterosexual marriage and, therefore, not having children could not be a compelling reason for excluding homosexuals from the institution. See, for a compelling rebuttal of a range of such arguments, William N. Eskridge, Jr., *The Case for Same-Sex Marriage*, 127–52. See, for judicial support of the premise of Eskridge's argument, *Turner v. Safley*, 482 U.S. 78 (1987) (state bar to marriage by prison inmates, on ground could not procreate, held unconstitutional).

116. See *Romer v. Evans*, 116 S. Ct. 1620 (1996).

of cattle, reduced to their utility (including reproductive fertility in producing further slaves) to the master class. As Lydia Maria Child first pointed out and Harriet Jacobs explored from the perspective of a former slave woman, antimiscegenation laws abridged the basic human right of intimate life in a way that sustained the sectarian sexual mythology of the subhuman image of African Americans. As James Baldwin observed of his own sexual exploitation at the hands of a white man, such a mythology could certainly easily sexualize and exploit African Americans by whites, meeting their "enormous need to debase other men."[117] What they could not do was to dignify the lives of African Americans as persons capable of the free exercise of the moral powers of intimate life, including the right to marriage on whatever terms rationally and reasonably give expression to these powers for them in conferring enduring meaning on personal and ethical life. Abridgment of the right to intimate life played so significant a role in this unjust dehumanization because the free exercise of this right centrally frames enduring moral interests in loving and being loved, caring and being care for, intimately giving value to the lives of others and having value given to one's own life; to be denied respect for such powers is, literally, to be deemed subhuman, incapable of the moral interests that give enduring value to living and sustain that value in others often over the generations.

In the case of women the abridgment of all their basic rights was focally rationalized in terms of a sectarian mythology of mandatory gender roles central to their moral slavery. To the extent such a mythology was uncritically sustained by suffrage feminism, it wreaked havoc centrally on women's rights to intimate life in what we called and explored as the Wollstonecraft repudiation. Indeed, suffrage feminists and their allies censored reasonable public argument not only about the right to free love, properly so called, but more concrete interpretations of that right, including the right to contraception, abortion, and consensual homosexuality. These rights have been so important in the emergence and constitutionalization of rights-based feminism since World War II because of their intrinsic fundamentality to moral sovereignty and because their recognition reflects constitutional skepticism about the political force that the traditional grounds for their abridgment had been uncritically allowed to enjoy. No robust constitutional understanding of women's human right to intimate life was possible as long as the political orthodoxy of mandatory gender roles was the measure of such rights. Nothing is, in my judgment, more central to

117. See Baldwin, *No Name in the Street,* 63.

the emancipatory meaning and promise of rights-based feminism (building on and elaborating abolitionist feminism) than its skepticism about the political enforcement at large of such mandatory gender roles, its insistence that women and men be accorded respect for their freedom and rationality in taking responsibility for how and on what terms gender may or should play a role in framing their private and public lives. Such growing constitutional skepticism about the legitimate enforcement through public law of such sectarian conceptions of mandatory gender roles has cleared normative space to acknowledge and respect not only women's rights to intimate life, but all their basic human rights (both public and private).

Rights-based feminism grounds respect for the basic human rights of homosexuals (to conscience, speech, intimate life, and work) as well as skepticism about the traditional grounds for the abridgment of such rights (including compulsory heterosexuality). Against the background of the distinctive moral slavery of homosexuals (their degraded unspeakability), the claim of any human rights at all must be regarded as an outrageous heresy against traditional values, as it was by the majority of Coloradans who approved Colorado Amendment Two. The outrage is most polemically overwrought in contemplation of the recognition of the human right of homosexuals, on equal terms with heterosexuals, to intimate life and its reasonable corollary, the right to marriage. Such a right has the force it has, both for its proponents and opponents, because its acknowledgment so critically addresses the grounds of dehumanization that had excluded the stigmatized group from the moral community of equal rights. In the case of homosexuals, such dehumanization stigmatized them as fallen women, or as sexualized prostitutes incapable of exercising the powers of moral personality protected by basic human rights. The consequence of the unjust enforcement of this political epistemology is the common uncritical populist assumption that homosexuality, unlike heterosexuality, is exclusively about sex.[118] This assumption is, I believe, the basis for the wounded sense of outrage surrounding even the suggestion of the legitimacy of extending the humane values of the institutions central to protecting the dignity of heterosexual intimate life to homosexuals. Homosexuals, on this view, no more can marry than animals.

There are two dimensions to any reasonable discussion of this matter: the nature of the constitutional right, and the appropriate constitutional burden of justification for any abridgment or regulation of such a right. On the first point, the basic right to intimate life—the right

---

118. See, on this point, Herek, "Why Tell If You're Not Asked?" 203, 207–8.

to bring to bear on intimate matters of love and care one's ethical convictions and to live a life centered in such convictions and the relationships of love and care to which they give rise—applies to all persons heterosexuals and homosexuals alike.

On the second point, such a basic human right (like other such rights) can only be abridged, consistent with the argument for toleration, on compelling grounds of public reason not themselves hostage to a sectarian view that, whatever may once have been the case, can no longer be regarded as justifiable to the public reason of all persons in the community. On this ground, the Supreme Court, as we have seen, correctly struck down both anticontraception and antiabortion laws. Anticontraception laws rested on a view that was, in contemporary circumstances, an unjustly sectarian view of mandatory procreational sexuality that many reasonable people no longer accept as the measure of sexual love, and antiabortion laws rest on a conception of fetal life in early pregnancy that cannot be legitimately enforced to abridge the reproductive autonomy of the many women who do not regard that conception of fetal life as a reasonable conception of moral personality. For the same reason, no compelling argument of public reason exists in contemporary circumstances that could justify the abridgment of the right to love of homosexuals. Neither of the two arguments traditionally regarded as justifying such abridgment (the evil of nonprocreational sex, and the conception of homosexual love as lowering one party to the status of a woman, a degraded status to be), can be regarded as publicly reasonable today. The first argument was justly repudiated by the contraception cases; the second by the many cases repudiating the force of sexist stereotypes in public law. As I earlier argued (chapter 6), *Bowers v. Hardwick*[119] was wrongly decided and should be overruled; a reasonable interpretation of *Romer v. Evans*[120] suggests implicitly that it has been.

A Catholic moral conservative like John Finnis has argued that, even if *Bowers* were properly overruled (as he suggests it should be), it would still be appropriate to make the exclusively procreational model of sexuality the measure of the right to marriage.[121] On this view, as another moral conservative put the point, the right to marriage is determined not solely by commitments arising from love as such but by "the

---

119. See *Bowers v. Hardwick*, 478 U.S. 186 (1986).

120. See *Romer v. Evans*, 116 S. Ct. 1620 (1996).

121. See John Finnis, "Law, Morality, and 'Sexual Orientation,'" *Notre Dame Journal of Law, Ethics, and Public Policy* 9 (1995): 11.

natural teleology of the body."[122] There is, however, no difference of principle between the sectarian character of such arguments in the one context (*Bowers*) as opposed to the other (the right to marriage). Heterosexual couples who are childless, whether by design or by force of circumstances, are not for that reason disqualified from the right to marry, nor could they reasonably be.[123] If the natural teleology of the body made any sense as a basis for public law, such childlessness as much violates the natural teleology of the body as that of a homosexual couple. The natural teleology of the body, whatever its legitimate force within sectarian moral and religious traditions, is not a publicly reasonable basis for law. Arguments of such sorts are based on appeals to nature of the sort David Hume considered as an illegitimate basis for prohibiting suicide:

> 'Tis impious, says the *French* superstition, to inoculate for the small-pox, or usurp the business of providence, by voluntarily producing distempers and maladies. 'Tis impious, says the modern *European* superstition, to put a period to our own life, and thereby rebel against our creator. And why not impious, say I, to build houses, cultivate the ground, and sail upon the ocean? In all these actions, we employ our powers of mind and body to produce some innovation in the course of nature; and in none of them do we any more. They are all of them, therefore, equally innocent or equally criminal.[124]

The natural teleology of the body (like the teleology of nature more generally) cannot reasonably be a basis for public law in a morally and religiously pluralistic society that lacks any reasonable common ground to ascribe to such natural facts a politically enforceable normative purpose. We can no more reasonably impose such a normative conception on homosexual than on heterosexual intimate relations. In both cases, as free and rational persons, we may "employ our powers of mind and body to produce some innovation in the course of nature," including taking pleasure in one another's bodies in whatever forms one gives or receives mutual pleasure in expressing and sustaining companionate sexual love as an end in itself.

122. See Hadley Arkes, "Testimony on the Defense of Marriage Act, 1996," Judiciary Committee, House of Representatives, 1996 WL 246693 (F.D.C.H.), °11; see also Hadley Arkes, "Questions of Principle, Not Predictions," *Georgetown Law Journal* 84 (1995): 321; and, to similar effect, Robert P. George and Gerard V. Bradley, "Marriage and the Liberal Imagination," *Georgetown Law Journal* 84 (1995): 301. For cogent criticism, see Stephen Macedo, "Homosexuality and the Conservative Mind," *Georgetown Law Journal* 84 (1995): 261; and, "Reply to Critics," *Georgetown Law Journal* 84 (1995): 329.

123. Cf. *Turner v. Safley*, 482 U.S. 78 (1987) (denial of marriage right to prison inmates, on ground could not procreate, held unconstitutional). For discussion, see Eskridge, *The Case for Same-Sex Marriage*, 128–30.

124. See David Hume, "Of Suicide," in *Essays Moral Political and Literary*, ed. Eugene F. Miller (1777; Indianapolis: LibertyClassics, 1985), 585.

The imposition, on either heterosexual or homosexual love, of the model of mandatory procreational sex is surely, in contemporary circumstances, constitutionally unjust because it politically remakes reality in its own anachronistic sectarian image. In particular, it conspicuously fails to acknowledge what any reasonable understanding of modern life, not hostage to such a sectarian conception, must acknowledge: the force in human life of sexual love as an end in itself that sustains intimate relations of loving and being loved central to giving meaning to personal and ethical life.[125] From this perspective, the political demand that human love, to be maritally legitimate, must conform to the natural teleology of the body usurps the moral sovereignty of the person over the transformative moral powers of love in intimate relations and the identifications central to sustaining personal and ethical value in living, in effect, dehumanizing human sexuality to its purely biological, reproductive aspect. As a Catholic critic of his church's condemnation of homosexuality recently put this point (against, among others, Finnis), "it is extraordinary that so many branches of Christianity should have now degenerated into fertility cults."[126] Such a view, dubious even today on internal religious grounds, can hardly reasonably be the measure of rights and responsibilities in a secular society.[127] The role of human sexuality in the imaginative life and transformative moral passions and identifications of free personality would, by force of law, be unreasonably degraded to the procrustean sectarian measure of a purely animal sexuality.[128]

125. See, in general, Giddens, *The Transformation of Intimacy;* D'Emilio and Freedman, *Intimate Matters,* 239–360; Ehrenreich, Hess, and Jacobs, *Remaking Love: The Feminization of Sex;* Anitow, Stansell, and Thompson, *Powers of Desire: The Politics of Sexuality;* Vance, *Pleasure and Danger: Exploring Female Sexuality.*

126. See Jordan, *The Invention of Sodomy in Christian Theology,* 174.

127. As Mark Jordan observes: "The Christian criterion of fertility, of parenting, of filiation, is not bodily. That much was worked out with painstaking care in the early Trinitarian debates." Ibid., 174.

128. For important studies of the differences between human and animal sexuality, see Clellan S. Ford and Frank A. Beach, *Patterns of Sexual Behavior* (New York: Harper & Row, 1951); Irenaus Eibl-Eibesfeldt, *Love and Hate: The Natural History of Behavior Patterns,* trans. Geoffrey Strachan (New York: Holt, Rinehart, and Winston, 1971). The insight is also central to Freud's exploration of the imaginative role of sexuality in human personality; see Sigmund Freud, " 'Civilized' Sexual Morality and Modern Nervous Illness," in *Standard Edition,* 9:181.

> The sexual instinct . . . is probably more strong developed in man than in most of the higher animals; it is certainly more constant, since it has almost entirely overcome the periodicity to which it is tied in animals. It places extraordinarily large amounts of force at the disposal of civilized activity, and it does this in virtue of its especially marked characteristic of being able to displace its aim without materially diminishing

At bottom, the insistence on opposite sexes as the legitimate measure of the right to marriage indulges, as the *Baehr* court saw, constitutionally illegitimate gender stereotypes. Andrew Koppelman has persuasively explored, in this connection, the analogy of the antimiscegenation laws.[129] The prohibition of racial intermarriage was to the cultural construction of racism what the prohibition of same-sex marriage is to sexism and homophobia: "just as miscegenation was threatening because it called into question the distinctive and superior status of being white, homosexuality is threatening because it calls into question the distinctive and superior status of being male."[130] The condemnation of same-sex marriage is a crucial aspect of the cultural construction of the dehumanization of the homosexual as a sexualized fallen woman.

Such dehumanization retains popular appeal when brought into relation to claims for same-sex marriage because, consistent with Freud's observation of the narcissism of small differences, it enables a culture with a long history of uncritical moral slavery of women and homosexuals to disregard the growing convergences of heterosexual and homosexual human love in the modern world. These include: shared economic contributions to the household and convergent styles of nonprocreational sex and elaboration of erotic play as an end in itself; the interest in sex as an expressive bond central to companionate relationships of friendship and love as ends in themselves; several partners over a lifetime; when there is interest in children, only in few of them; and the insistence on the romantic love of tender and equal companions as the democratized center of sharing intimate daily life.[131] Indeed,

---

its intensity. This capacity to exchange its originally sexual aim for another one, which is no longer sexual but which is physically related to the first aim, is called the capacity for sublimation. (9:187)

129. See Andrew Koppelman, "The Miscegenation Analogy: Sodomy Laws as Sex Discrimination," *Yale Law Journal* 98 (1988): 145.

130. Ibid., 159–60.

131. See, on the continuities among heterosexual and homosexual forms of intimacy in the modern world, in general, Giddens, *The Transformation of Intimacy;* D'Emilio and Freedman, *Intimate Matters: A History of Sexuality in America*, 239–360; Philip Blumstein and Pepper Schwartz, *American Couples* (New York: William Morrow, 1983), 332–545. On declining fertility rates, see Claudia Goldin, *Understanding the Gender Gap: An Economic History of American Women* (New York: Oxford University Press, 1990), 139–42; on childlessness, see, in general, May, *Barren in the Promised Land;* on rising divorce rates, see Degler, *At Odds,* 165–68, 175–76. See also Barbara Ehrenreich, Elizabeth Hess, and Gloria Jacobs, *Remaking Love: The Feminization of Sex* (New York: Anchor, 1986); Ann Anitow, Christine Stansell and Sharon Thompson, eds., *Powers of Desire* (New York: Monthly Review Press, 1983); Carol S. Vance, ed., *Pleasure and Danger: Exploring Female Sexuality* (Boston: Routledge & Kegan Paul, 1984).

some studies suggest that, if anything, homosexual relationships more fully develop features of egalitarian sharing that are more often the theory than the practice of heterosexual relations.[132]

The uncritical ferocity of contemporary political homophobia draws its populist power from the compulsive need to construct Manichean differences where none reasonably exist, thus reinforcing institutions of gender hierarchy perceived now to be at threat. In particular, as Whitman argued, democratic equality in homosexual intimate life threatens the core of traditional gender roles and the hierarchy central to such roles. Consistent with the paradox of intolerance, the embattled sectarian orthodoxy does not explore such reasonable doubts, but polemically represses them by remaking reality in its own sectarian image of marriage, powerfully deploying the uncritical traditional stereotype of the homosexual as the scapegoat of one's suppressed doubts (excluding the homosexual from the moral community of human rights, including the basic human right to intimate life). Homosexuals are the natural scapegoat for this uncritical feminist backlash[133] because they, unlike women, remain a largely marginalized and despised minority. Traditional sectarian orthodoxy objects as strongly to many of the achievements of the feminist movement (some to the decriminalization of contraception, others to that of abortion, still others to now mainstream feminist issues like ERA[134]), but they have lost many of these battles and the sectarian hard core of the orthodoxy, in fact hostile to feminism and civil rights measures in general,[135] takes its stand strategically where it still can against members of a traditionally stigmatized and silenced minority who are, like the Jews in Europe, easily demonized.[136]

132. On this point, see Susan Moller Okin, "Sexual Orientation and Gender: Dichotomizing Differences," in David M. Estlund and Martha C. Nussbaum, eds., *Sex, Preference, and Family: Essays on Law and Nature* (New York: Oxford University Press, 1997), 44–59.

133. See, in general, Susan Faludi, *Backlash: The Undeclared War against American Women* (New York: Doubleday, 1991); Marilyn French, *The War against Women* (London: Penguin, 1992).

134. For some sense of the range of such views and their supporting reasons, see Sherrye Henry, *The Deep Divide: Why American Women Resist Equality;* Elizabeth Fox-Genovese, *"Feminism Is Not the Story of My Life": How Today's Feminist Elite Has Lost Touch with the Real Concerns of Women* (New York: Doubleday, 1996); *Feminism without Illusions: A Critique of Individualism* (Chapel Hill: University of North Carolina Press, 1991).

135. For its antifeminism, see Herman, *The Antigay Agenda,* 103–10; for its opposition to the civil rights agenda in general, see ibid., 111–36, 140.

136. On the analogy of such contemporary homophobia to anti-Semitism, see Didi Herman, *The Antigay Agenda,* 82–91, 125–28; cf. Elaine Pagels, *The Origin of Satan,* 102–5.

A revealing historical analogy has been drawn upon in the resistance to contemporary same-sex marriage, namely, arguments taken from the earlier discussed antipolygamy movement of the nineteenth century. Conservative commentators like George Will[137] and William Bennett[138] have thus questioned the allegedly conservative advocacy of same-sex marriage, by Andrew Sullivan among others,[139] as affording no limiting principle that would not extend the right to polygamy as well. Arguments against polygamy had two crucial features: a defense of monogamy as central to the values of Western civilization, and a critique of polygamy as reinforcing the unjust subjection of women. But the contemporary gay defense of same-sex marriage does not question monogamy, it insists on it;[140] it does so on the basis of a forceful repudiation of sexist gender-roles in the name of the principles of rights-based feminism.[141] Polygamy, as traditionally understood, reinforced such unjust gender roles and thus cannot be regarded as a constitutionally reasonable form of intimate life consistent with these principles. As Nancy Rosenblum recently observed:

> Despite rare exceptions, patriarchy has been the dominant form of polygamy. It has never had its basis in reciprocity or friendship, not even ideally. Its justification has never been the expansiveness of affection or cooperation. It has rested on ideological or spiritual accounts of male authority and female subjection, on status associated with numbers of wives, and of course on beliefs about male sexual power (or the need to temper women's sexual

See also, for a useful study of the reactionary populist politics of this group, Chris Bull and John Gallagher, *Perfect Enemies*.

137. See George Will, "And Now Pronounce Them Spouse and Spouse," *Washington Post*, 19 May 1996, C9.

138. See William Bennett, "Leave Marriage Alone (legalizing same-sex marriage would tamper with centuries of tradition and demean the institution of marriage)," *Newsweek* 127, n. 23, 3 June 1996, 27.

139. See, for example, Andrew Sullivan, "Here Comes the Groom: A (Conservative) Case for Gay Marriage," in Bawer, *Beyond Queer*, 252–58. See also Jonathan Rauch, "For Better or Worse?" *The New Republic*, 6 May 1996, 18–23.

140. See William N. Eskridge, Jr., *The Case for Same-Sex Marriage*. For a similar argument by a gay man defending the humane need within gay and lesbian culture for institutional incentives for fidelity, see Gabriel Rotello, *Sexual Ecology: AIDS and the Destiny of Gay Men* (New York: Dutton, 1997), 233–61.

141. But, for an argument that some forms of polygamy would be consistent with rights-based feminism if based on modern values giving "perfect freedom and independence to women in their relation to men," see Carpenter, *Love's Coming of Age,* 134. It would, on this view, be a factual question whether any such form of polygamy could reasonably be proposed in contemporary circumstances. Many advocates of gay marriage might reasonably deny, consistent with Nancy Rosenblum's view cited in the text, that it could be. See Eskridge, *The Case for Same-Sex Marriage,* 148–49.

450   CHAPTER EIGHT

power) and male entitlements. It is doubtful that the known doctrinal supports for polygamy could be rehabilitated and made congruent with democratic sex.[142]

The antipolygamy appeal is not then reasonably on point: the arguments for same-sex marriage do not support such an extension any more than they would justify spouse abuse or adultery or, for that matter, no-fault divorce.[143] Compelling secular arguments of gender equality support the limitation of the right to marriage to monogamous couples.[144]

The spirit of the antipolygamy movement is, I believe, very much in play in such arguments. They attempt, like the demonizing of Mormon polygamy, to insist on an uncritical conception of gender hierarchy in marriage, thus further immunizing the conventional theory of gender

142. See Nancy L. Rosenblum, "Democratic Sex: *Reynolds v. U.S.*, Sexual Relations, and Community," in *Sex, Preference, and Family: Essays on Law and Nature*, ed. David M. Estlund and Martha C. Nussbaum (New York: Oxford University Press, 1997), 80.

143. For the debate in social science and law surrounding what this development factually comes to and what normative sense we should make of it, see Lenore J. Weitzman, *The Divorce Revolution: The Unexpected Social and Economic Consequences for Woman and Children in America* (New York: Free Press, 1985); Martha Albertson Fineman, *The Illusion of Equality: The Rhetoric and Reality of Divorce Reform* (Chicago: University of Chicago Press, 1991); Ira Mark Ellman, Paul M. Kurtz, Katharine T. Bartlett, eds., *Family Law: Cases, Text, Problems*, 2d ed. (Charlottesville, Va.: The Michie Company, 1991), 292–301; Howard S. Erlanger, ed., "Review Symposium on Weitzman's *Divorce Revolution*," *American Bar Foundation Research Journal* 4 (1986): 759–97; James B. McLindon, "Separate But Unequal: The Economic Disaster of Divorce of Women and Children," 21 *Family Law Quarterly* 21 (1987): 351–409; Greg J. Duncan and Saul D. Hoffman, "A Reconsideration of the Economic Consequences of Marital Dissolution," *Demography* 22 (1985): 485; Judith A. Seltzer and Irwin Garfinkel, "Inequality in Divorce Settlements: An Investigation of Property Settlements and Child Support Awards," *Social Science Research* 19 (1990): 82; Susan Moller Okin, "Economic Equality After Divorce," *Dissent* (summer 1991): 383; Martha L. Fineman, "Implementing Equality: Ideology, Contradiction and Social Change, A Study of Rhetoric and Results in the Regulation of the Consequences of Divorce," *Wisconsin Law Review* (1983): 789; Jane Rutherford, "Duty in Divorce: Shares Income as a Path of Equality," *Fordham Law Review* 58 (1990): 539; Joan Williams, "Is Coverture Dead? Beyond a New Theory of Alimony," *Georgetown Law Journal* 82 (1994): 2227; Isabel Marcus, "Locked In and Locked Out: Reflections on the History of Divorce Law Reform in New York State," *Buffalo Law Review* 37 (1989): 375; Marsha Garrison, "Good Intentions Gone Awry: The Impact of New York's Equitable Distribution Law on Divorce Outcomes," *Brooklyn Law Review* 57 (1991): 621.

144. It is a different question whether such principles would justify, in contemporary circumstances, the use of criminal law against polygamous unions as such (in particular, such unions undertaken in accord with religious conscience). Legitimate state purposes that might be sufficiently powerful to disallow the extension of marriage to such unions may be insufficient to justify the use of criminal sanctions in this area for the same reasons that one might reasonably believe adultery should no longer be condemned by the criminal law. (Such laws inflict a preponderance of harm over good in areas better regulated or addressed in other ways.)

roles from much-needed rights-based feminist critique. (It was on this ground that John Stuart Mill, an advocate of feminist equality,[145] condemned the hypocrisy of the American persecution of the Mormons.[146]) The antipolygamy movement, like suffrage feminism and the temperance and purity movements, thus importantly censored from public debate and discussion important arguments of rights-based feminism, rationalizing the shrunken and decrepit thing suffrage feminism became. The ferocity of the populist attack on gay marriage has a similarly reactionary character and basis polemically to insist on a symbolism of marriage as an immovable rock (impermeable to reasonable doubt about gender roles) that is factually unreal and normatively unfair, using homosexuals as the normative scapegoat politically to reify gender hierarchy in marriage.

Same-sex marriage is not a threat to marriage, but a recognition of marriage's deeper moral values and the principled elaboration of those values to all persons; the case for the legitimacy of gay marriage crucially rests on the value (real and symbolic) reasonably placed in our culture on marriage and family life, and argues, as a matter of principle, for fair extension of that value to all persons on fair terms. Homosexuality is no more exclusively about sex than heterosexuality. The culturally marked difference between them is the product of a culture of moral slavery, constructed, in part, by the unthinkability of extending the right to marriage (as an aspect of the basic human right to intimate life) to homosexuals (because they are assumed to be subhuman, if not animalistic, in their intimate lives). Homosexuals thus justly resist the traditional terms of their dehumanization by insisting on their constitutional right to marriage as an aspect of the basic human right to respect for the dignity of intimate life, the transformative moral passion of mutual love and care in personal and ethical life. Their argument gives, if you will, a distinctly liberal interpretation to the moral appeal of the argument for family values. The idea that gay marriage is a threat to marriage as such can barely be credited, as an argument, when an ethical wrong like adultery goes quite unmentioned in such ostensibly promarriage discourse. The difference, of course, is that adultery is a reasonably popular heterosexual vice;[147] there is no interest in tackling in a responsible way such serious ethical issues which require a chal-

---

145. See John Stuart Mill, *The Subjection of Women.*

146. See John Stuart Mill, *On Liberty,* ed. Alburey Castell (1859; New York: Appleton-Century-Crofts, 1947), 92–94.

147. See, in general, Edward O. Laumann, John H. Gagnon, Robert T. Michael, and Stuart Michaels, *The Organization of Sexuality: Sexual Practices in the United States* (Chicago: University of Chicago Press, 1994), 172–224.

lenge to be made to uncritical public opinion. Rather, same-sex marriage is demonized as a threat to marriage from within an embattled sectarian perspective on gender orthodoxy that still has a hold on uncritical public opinion. Arguments for same-sex marriage, which in fact depend on respect for the dignity of marriage, are thus irresponsibly but conveniently inverted into an attack on marriage—yet another instance of the paradox of forging irrationalist intolerance precisely when public opinion most needs reasonable discussion and debate of real, not unreal ethical issues.

Such populist uncritical scapegoating is, I believe, quite clearly in play in the passage of the Defense of Marriage Act of 1996.[148] The act's purpose is to exercise federal power to limit the force of the possible legality of same-sex marriage in Hawaii. It does so in two ways. First, it expressly excludes same-sex marriage from any of the benefits that accrue to married couples under federal law (thus, discouraging even gay and lesbian couples in Hawaii from exercising their rights to marry). Second, it ordains that no other state shall be required to give effect to such same-sex marriage.[149] The purpose of the second provision is to limit any extraterritorial effect of the Hawaii legitimation of same-sex marriage under the full faith and credit clause of the Constitution.[150] Even assuming same-sex marriage were not a constitutional right, this provision would be constitutionally problematic since it claims for Congress a power over the substantive law of marriage that, under the federal system, it does not have; the recognition of Hawaii same-sex marriages by other states is decisively a matter for state, not federal, law.[151] Since same-sex marriage is, however, a constitutional right, the first provision is unconstitutional as well, illegitimately exercising viewpoint discrimination with respect to a fundamental right.

Once same-sex marriage were recognized as a constitutional right, questions relating to the custody and adoption of children must be reasonably discussed in terms of general principles that equitably ac-

148. See 1 U.S.C.A. §7, 28 U.S.C.A. §1738C, as amended by Congress on September 21, 1996, Pub. L. No. 104-199, 110 Stat. 2419.

149. See H.R. 3396, 104th Cong., 2d Sess. (Discussion Draft, May 2, 1996).

150. The provision reads as follows: "Full faith and credit shall be given in each State to the public acts, records, and judicial proceedings of every other State. And the Congress may by general laws prescribe the manner in which such acts, records, and proceedings shall be proved, and the effect thereof." U.S. Const. art. 4, §1.

151. See Laurence H. Tribe, "Toward a Less Perfect Union," New York Times, 26 May 1966, E–11; Laurence Tribe to Sen. Edward M. Kennedy, 142 Cong. Rec. S5931-01, at S5932–33 (daily ed. June 6, 1966) (statement of Sen. Kennedy). See also Mark Strasser, "Loving the Romer Out for Baehr: On Acts in Defense of Marriage and the Constitution," University of Pittsburgh Law Review 58 (1997): 279.

knowledge both the rights of all married couples and the rights of children to the care and nurturance of good parents. There is no reason, in principle, why homosexual couples should not constitutionally be guaranteed, under this analysis, many of the rights, as good and loving parents, they are increasingly claiming in practice.[152]

CONSTITUTIONAL PRUDENCE AND INSTITUTIONAL COMPETENCE

The arguments of constitutional principle I have offered against the military exclusion and in favor of a right to same-sex marriage run very much against the grain of the contemporary political consensus in the United States. If such arguments are indeed valid, it may be suggested[153] that, in such a reactionary political environment, more harm than good may be done by the judiciary's acknowledgment of the weight of these arguments as arguments of principle.

This argument may be made in two ways. First, as an argument of simple prudence, no judicial defense even of an argument of principle should be taken if its predictable consequences will be more to retard than to advance the practice of human rights in the United States. The suggestion here is that either judicial invalidation of the military exclusion or the bar on same-sex marriage would lead to an overall reaction in the nation that was, on balance, more hostile to than supportive of good arguments of human rights; Sunstein cites *Roe v. Wade* as such a decision, because it "prematurely committed the nation to a principle toward which it was in any case steadily moving, and that ... premature judicial decision had a range of harmful consequences," including "the creation of the Moral Majority, the death of the Equal Rights Amendment, the galvanizing of general opposition to the women's movement, the identification of the movement with the single issue of abortion, the dampening of desirable political activity by women, and the general transformation of the political landscape in a way deeply damaging to women's interests."[154] Second, constitutional law is not only for the courts, but for all public officials. It may thus be

152. For a judicious treatment of these developments and a compelling constitutional analysis of their implications, see Strasser, *Legally Wed*, chap. 4; see also Nancy D. Polikoff, "Needs of Children in Lesbian-Mother and Other Nontraditional Families," *Georgetown Law Journal* 78 (1990): 459. For an argument that such rights may reasonably inhere in motherhood simpliciter, see Martha Albertson Fineman, *The Neutered Mother, the Sexual Family, and Other Twentieth Century Tragedies* (Routledge: New York, 1995).

153. See Cass R. Sunstein, "Homosexuality and the Constitution," *Indiana Law Journal* 70 (1993): 1.

154. Ibid., 25.

appropriate for the judiciary to underenforce a constitutional principle when another branch of government may be much better positioned institutionally to make and enforce the correct constitutional argument of principle.[155]

The first argument is, in its own terms, misconceived. Sunstein's objection to *Roe* is an objection to the constitutional analysis of the case in terms of a principle of constitutional privacy; he prefers an analysis in terms of equal protection.[156] Sunstein's argument, both as a criticism of privacy analysis and a defense of an alternative equal protection approach, is fundamentally flawed. He certainly offers no good interpretive argument why the same abstract interpretive approach that he advocates in the area of equal protection should not reasonably also be taken in the arena of constitutional privacy. He also claims that equal protection analysis somehow can avoid the hard question of the status of fetal life that privacy analysis at least faces and resolves on the basis of justifiability in terms of nonsectarian public reasons available to and accessible, in principle, to all persons;[157] but, it simply cannot beg this question, without compromising the whole integrity of its analysis. If abortion is equivalent to the murder of a full moral person, nothing in the equality of women can justify such a moral price. To the extent Sunstein takes a similar view of the right to gay sex, as he clearly does,[158] his argument of principle is no more plausible. Nor does his account of the wrongness of discrimination on grounds of sexual preference take sufficiently seriously the cultural background of homophobia in moral slavery, which is as much an indignity to self-respecting identity as in other cases of suspectness.[159]

Even if Sunstein's equal protection analysis were more plausible than it is as an argument of principle protecting either abortion or gay sex, it would be unacceptable for the judiciary to compromise the interpretive integrity of an argument of principle in the way Sunstein suggests. Many of the most important and defensible interpretive decisions of the modern period, advancing the judicial protection of basic

155. See Lawrence G. Sager, "The Legal Status of Underenforced Constitutional Norms," *Harvard University Law Review* 91 (1978): 1212.

156. See Cass R. Sunstein, *The Partial Constitution* (Cambridge: Harvard University Press, 1993), 272–85.

157. Ibid., 274–76.

158. See Cass R. Sunstein, "Sexual Orientation and the Constitution: A Note on the Relationship Between Due Process and Equal Protection," *University of Chicago Law Review* 55 (1988): 1161.

159. For Sunstein's denial that homosexuality (because not a salient characteristic) should get the benefit of the anticaste principle, see Cass R. Sunstein, "The Anticaste Principle," *Michigan Law Review* 92 (1994): 2431, 2443.

human rights, would not have been decided if the judiciary regarded itself as having the kind of political discretion that Sunstein ascribes to it. It is, in my judgment, an important discipline on the interpretive integrity of the American judiciary that it not have such discretion when it comes to the interpretation of the central rights-bearing normative guarantees of the Constitution.[160] Only such interpretive discipline can assure the kind of access of despised minorities to fair adjudication of central constitutional arguments of principle by an independent judiciary, an adjudication which is a basic right American citizens enjoy. *Roe v. Wade* was, in my judgment, an appropriate exercise of this disciplined interpretive power on grounds of rights-based principle. It gave a basic human right of women the kind of judicial protection it deserved and afforded a much-needed forum of principle for public discussion and debate among Americans on the meaning of human rights in contemporary circumstances.[161]

The second underenforcement argument is more substantial, and might plausibly be accorded more weight than I have given it in, for example, the military exclusion issue. On this view, both the executive and legislative branches have ample constitutional power and responsibility to bring the military more in line with basic constitutional principles. Whatever the problems in the "Don't Ask, Don't Tell" policy, it represents an advance over the older policy initiated by the executive and negotiated with the military and Congress in a direction more respectful of the rights to nondiscrimination of homosexuals. The policy is, of course, flawed, but the judiciary should not intervene when the direction of reform is one that is more respectful of constitutional principles than the policy it supplants.[162] I have acknowledged the weight of this argument by proposing a principle of judicial review limited to certain kinds of dehumanizing exclusions that bear on the conception of national citizenship. For reasons I have suggested, such deference

160. See, for an argument to similar effect, Gerald Gunther, "The Subtle Vices of the 'Passive Virtues'—a Comment on Principle and Expediency in Judicial Review," *Columbia Law Review* 64 (1964): 1.

161. In reaching his critical judgment on *Roe*, Sunstein places much weight on the court-skeptical argument of Gerald Rosenberg, questioning whether the judiciary itself has been responsible for much rights-based social change in contrast to other agencies of government and social movements. See Gerald N. Rosenberg, *The Hollow Hope: Can Courts Bring about Social Change?* (Chicago: University of Chicago Press, 1991). Nothing in Rosenberg's argument bears on issues of interpretive principle, and it is these issues that Sunstein fails adequately to address.

162. For a powerful statement of this argument, see *Thomasson v. Perry*, 80 F.3d 915, 919–26 (4th Cir. 1996) (Wilkinson, C.J.).

cannot reasonably justify wholesale judicial abdication of interpretive responsibility when central principles of human rights, in particular freedom of conscience and speech, are thus put at hazard.

Whatever weight this argument may have in the context of the military exclusion, it has none in the area either of overruling *Bowers v. Hardwick* or acknowledging a constitutional right to marry. *Bowers* is, in my judgment, ripe for overruling in light of *Romer v. Evans*. It was wrong when decided (as Justice Powell, the swing vote, later acknowledged[163]), has done incalculable damage to public understanding of the human rights of gays and lesbians, and now, in light of the reaffirmance of a women's right to abortion in *Planned Parenthood v. Casey*,[164] is a conspicuously unprincipled application of the right to privacy. The constitutional right to marriage is similarly a matter that, when the judiciary is appropriately convinced of its merits, it must and should face in a principled way. In light of the gap in time between the Court's path-breaking public school desegregation decision in *Brown v. Board of Education*[165] in 1954 and its decision in *Loving v. Virginia*[166] in 1967 against antimiscegenation laws, it would not be surprising if any favorable decision in the area of same-sex marriage would take place some considerable time after the overruling of *Bowers*. That, however, may be as much a matter of convincing the judiciary and the nation at large of the underlying merits of the constitutional argument of principle as it is a matter of either prudence or underenforcement. Much hard interpretive work and public argument, on the platform of human rights, obviously remain to be done.

Both the theory and practice of abolitionist feminism afford a conspicuous model of the kind of intelligence, integrity, and courage that gay and lesbian people must bring to this challenge. If we carry this project forward on its terms of principle, we must conscientiously identify and protest, in a voice empowered by our sense of universal human rights, the terms of our unjust subjugation, what I have called our moral slavery. Consistent with our historic mission (retelling, as we do,

163. Justice Powell on October 25, 1990 acknowledged that his vote in *Bowers* was a mistake. See *New York Times*, 26 October 1990, A11, col. 4.

164. See *Planned Parenthood of Southeastern Pennsylvania v. Casey*, 112 S. Ct. 2791 (1992) (reaffirming central holding of *Roe*, that women's access to abortion services may not be criminalized until the point of fetal viability).

165. See *Brown v. Board of Education*, 347 U.S. 483 (1954).

166. See *Loving v. Virginia*, 388 U.S. 1 (1967). See also *McLaughlin v. Florida*, 379 U.S. 184 (1964) (invalidating state criminal statute prohibiting cohabitation by interracial married couples). In 1955 and 1956, the Supreme Court conspicuously refused to address the question of the constitutionality of the antimiscegenation laws in the wake of *Brown*. See *Naim v. Naim* litigation, 350 U.S. 891 (1955) and 350 U.S. 985 (1956).

the oldest and most contemporary narrative of American civil liberties), we must measure ourselves, as the abolitionist feminists did, by the integrity of our reasonable demands for nothing less and nothing more than the arguments of principle that are each American's birthright of equal liberty under law.

9   Conclusion: Identity and Justice

T his book has explored the interpretive fertility of antebellum abolitionist feminism in both the understanding and criticism of contemporary interpretive developments in the areas of gender and sexual
preference. The power of abolitionist feminism was, I have argued, its
normative stance on the platform of human rights and the way it
brought that stance to bear on an interlinked analysis of the ethical
and constitutional wrongs of both slavery and racism and the subjection
of women and sexism. The later history of suffrage feminism, its victory
and collapse, and the rebirth of second wave feminism can, I have
argued, be both understood and critically evaluated in terms of the
rights-based feminism that abolitionist feminism had so brilliantly
stated. Such an analysis illuminates as well the increasing importance
of rights-based arguments of such sorts in American constitutional interpretation, building on analogies between racism and sexism first articulated by the abolitionist feminists.

On this basis, I proposed a new constructive approach to the interpretation of the Reconstruction Amendments. This approach ascribes
to the Thirteenth Amendment a constitutional condemnation of what
I have called moral slavery, a structural injustice based on the abridgment of basic human rights to a whole class of persons on illegitimate
grounds. The normative guarantees of the Fourteenth Amendment
should, in turn, be interpreted along the various dimensions made relevant by the condemnation of moral slavery in the Thirteenth Amend-

ment. This includes both robust national protections of rights of conscience, free speech, intimate life, and work, and a demanding constitutional suspicion (in the terms of suspect classification analysis under the equal protection clause) of the enforcement through public law of cultural stereotypes that rest on a history of moral slavery. Congressional powers would accordingly also be interpreted more broadly in light of the condemnation of moral slavery in the Thirteenth Amendment in both the public and private spheres.

Finally, I argued that the traditional reprobation of homosexuals should, on the same platform of human rights, be regarded (in light of abolitionist feminist arguments first suggested by Walt Whitman) as rights-denying moral slavery, condemned by the abstract normative judgment central to the Thirteenth Amendment. In light of that analysis, guarantees of the Fourteenth Amendment should, in my view, be interpreted both to protect basic human rights of gays and lesbians, and to protect such persons from the dehumanizing expression through public law of the cultural stereotypes that reflect this unjust cultural history of moral slavery; classifications on the basis of sexual preference should, on grounds of principle, be regarded as a fully suspect class. This analysis was then extended to develop interpretive arguments for the unconstitutionality of antigay/lesbian initiatives as well as of the exclusion of homosexuals from the military and from the right to marriage.

These main points of my interpretive argument were developed by way of building a practice and theory of human rights from the interpretive struggles of dissenting movements who contested traditional readings of American constitutional principles and institutions and sought to imagine and realize an alternative American constitutionalism. The study of their struggles, in light of the argument for toleration central to them, makes available to contemporary constitutional interpretation an interpretive strand of our constitutionalism that powerfully reminds us of what the tradition of American constitutionalism is, on whose shoulders we stand, and of our interpretive responsibility to make the best sense in our circumstances of that tradition, including its cumulative insights into the interlinked rights-denying evils of moral slavery.

The practice and theory of human rights that we have now studied in various domains featured not only rights-based arguments but the remarkable people who, on the basis of making such arguments, transformed their own identities and contested that of the larger constitutional culture to make a space of justice for their revised identities both as persons and as citizens. Our study has thus included the close examination of Lydia Maria Child, the Grimke sisters, Lucretia Mott, Elizabeth Stanton, Susan B. Anthony, Victoria Woodhull, Harriet Jacobs, Sojourner Truth, Ida Wells-Barnett, Emma Goldman, Margaret Sanger, Betty Friedan, Frederick Douglass, Franz Boas, W. E. B. Du Bois, James Baldwin, Walt Whitman, Edward Carpenter, Adrienne Rich, and many others. In the terms Du Bois seminally put the point, each protested, on grounds of justice, the stigmatized role the dominant culture had accorded both their personal and constitutional identities: whether their culturally degraded role as an African American, a Jew, a woman, or a homosexual (or some combination thereof). Each stood on the platform of human rights of American revolutionary constitutionalism, and, on that ground, demanded a new kind of identity for themselves personally and at the same time, a new place and role for themselves in the larger constitutional culture.

I have suggested that their struggles can, consistent with their common platform of human rights, be clarified in terms both of the grounds of their self-originating claims as persons (namely, the basic human rights of conscience, speech, intimate life, and work) and the kinds of skeptical criticisms they offered of traditionally enforced politically epistemologies of race, religion, gender, or sexual preference. There were, of course, different dynamics in each case. The traditional family was often a source of strength and resistance for many of the rights-based claims of African Americans and Jews, whereas women and homosexuals have often found their common identities on grounds of justice independent of and sometimes quite critical of the traditional family.[1] Indeed, in the case of women and homosexuals, their demands often called for redefinitions of the family and of marriage more consistent with both respect for human rights and an appropriate constitutionally based skepticism about politically enforceable irrationalist prejudices based on an unjust gender hierarchy centered in the traditional family.

But, as I conclude the argument of the book, let me point to the following common features in these struggles, thus indicating further the interpretive and critical fertility of the approach here developed.

First, our analysis of the intractable character of the politically enforceable prejudices in each area has emphasized their common roots

---

1. On the special problems of intergenerational support that this raises for gays and lesbians, see Anthony R. D'Augelli and Charlotte J. Patterson, *Lesbian, Gay, and Bisexual Identities over the Lifespan* (New York: Oxford University Press, 1995), 41, 304–6.

in variant forms of moral slavery. The institutional feature of such slavery, common to all its different expressions, is the intimacy of the servile dependence not so much on the part of the oppressed (who often silently resist) but of the oppressor. Proslavery thought rationalized American slavery on the basis of the slave being an intimate part of their family, indeed of themselves, often self-consciously using the same model on the basis of which the subjection of women was rationalized. Both anti-Semitism and homophobia prominently have similarly featured the subjection of women as the model: the Jew or homosexual as a woman or fallen woman. Such rationalization of irrationalist prejudice on the basis of private life suggests that its criticism must always contest the ways in which the public/private distinction has illegitimately been drawn, immunizing such a rights-denying evil from scrutiny on the basis that it is at the center of private life or even part of one's self. Such moral inversions are familiar features of prejudices rationalized in the terms described in this book as the paradox of intolerance. Any reasonable criticism of such inversions must press its inquiry into both traditionally private and public life, reconstructing such distinctions on a sound basis in respect for human rights. The theory of moral slavery, that I argue should be central to the just interpretation of the Reconstruction Amendments, insists on this point.

Second, we have observed various interlinkages among the prejudices we have studied, including several already noted. To elaborate, the rationalizing pedestal of women's traditional role was, as we have seen, central not only to racism but to sexism as well. African Americans were dehumanized, both as men and women, in terms of a politically enforceable sexual mythology that depended on the abridgment of, among other basic rights, the right of intimate life. Black women, in particular, were not women at all in the terms defined by the idealizing pedestal (as Sojourner Truth made clear), but fallen women available for sexual abuse and exploitation; and black men, as James Baldwin testified, were mythologized as sexual animals, so any intercourse with idealized white women must be rape (Ida Wells-Barnett). The persistence of the pedestal, in the forms rationalized by suffrage feminism and its allies, was at the root of the intractable power of American sexism over the lives of American women; any serious deviation thus stigmatized them as fallen women, not really women but prostitutes unworthy of any respect or concern. In similar ways, both anti-Semitism and homophobia were rationalized on the basis of models of fallen women (Weininger).

Third, the criticism of such prejudices crucially included, in each case, a cultural analysis of the ways in which the results of an unjust culture of moral slavery had been rationalized on the basis of nature, supported by pseudo-science manufactured to support the sectarian political epistemology of race, or religion, or gender, or sexual preference. Such rationalization included, as we have seen, a good deal of gender role idealization: women as unequal and subordinated but also as morally superior along lines that obfuscated the rights-denying ravages of mandatory self-sacrifice based on unjustly enforced gender roles, the pedestal that was a cage.

Fourth, the struggle in each case was founded on originating claims in one's one voice and responsive to one's own morally independent conscience in terms of basic human rights to conscience, speech, intimate life, and work. Such moral independence had often severe costs in dislocation from family and home and religion, as we saw in the Grimke sisters who found, in one another as sisters (and as Stanton and Susan B. Anthony later found as friends), the moral strength to undertake the difficult role of moral exile in the search for an identity, as a woman and an American, based on rights-based constitutional justice. The very marginality of figures like the Grimke sisters or Whitman to the dominant culture was the key to what was so valuable to our constitutional culture in the rigor and impartiality and inclusive largeness of humane imagination of their morally independent readings of American revolutionary constitutionalism, as making space, on equal terms, for women and for gays and lesbians. The platform of human rights, the enduring legacy of abolitionist feminism to American revolutionary constitutionalism, requires on grounds of principle a generative respect for conscience and speech through which persons come to understand and to claim all their basic human rights against an unjustly enforceable sectarian orthodoxy.

Fifth, such a rights-based struggle called for a demanding criticism of traditional sectarian views of race, religion, gender, and sexual preference. Such moral exiles must, in the nature of their rights-based struggle, be morally independent critics of dominant orthodoxies that have, inconsistent with the argument for toleration, enjoyed hegemonic force as the measure of public and private rights and responsibilities. Often, as in the case of antebellum radical abolitionists (including abolitionist feminists), this has required religious heterodoxy and heresy and the willingness to construct new forms of public conscience, of modes and epistemologies of inquiry, of culture that would be more hospitable to claims of rights-based justice. The struggle for human rights in the United States has always been energized and often inspired by the independent moral criticism made possible by insisting on strong guarantees of separation of church and state.[2]

Sixth, in each case, the upshot of such rights-based struggle was the contesting of traditional roles based on religion, race, gender, and sexual preference: in effect, the debunking of the unjust force the political imposition of these roles had uncritically enjoyed for much too long. No such natural hierarchy of roles can, consistent with the argument of this book, be justly enforced to the extent such enforcement fails the tests of respect for human rights and of reasonable justification in terms of public reasons.

Contesting such ideas of natural hierarchy is what inspires the moral freedom central to the theory and practice so many of the persons studied in this book have brought to our better understanding of the demands of American revolutionary constitutionalism. Their contribution does not arise from their interest or participation in ordinary politics as we know it today, for some of the most important contributors among them (the Garrisonian moral abolitionists, including many leading abolitionist feminists) despised ordinary politics and condemned both voting and serving in public office. Their contribution of critical thought and ethical practice, rather, was to our moral growth as a constitutional people. The nature of their claims, on the platform of human rights, was always profoundly antimajoritarian, reminding complacent American democratic majorities of the deeper rights-based arguments of principle requisite to the legitimacy of any politics under American revolutionary constitutionalism. That is a requirement that, when Americans forget it, leads to the tragic corruption of our constitutionalism in the antebellum period and gives the Civil War and the Reconstruction Amendments the significance they have for us as a rebirth of American revolutionary constitutionalism.[3] The legacy of the abolitionist feminists and their progeny is a theory and practice of rights-based dissent that, when most needed, will be most antimajoritarian, most demanding in its respect for basic human rights of conscience and speech, most insistent in its morally independent criticism of the most popular uncritical stereotypes of religion or race or gender or sexual preference.

Such advocates are unlikely to win elections, let alone popularity contests. Their struggle, expressing the demands of moral personality,

2. For further exploration of some of these points, see David A. J. Richards, "Public Reason and Abolitionist Dissent," *Chicago-Kent Law Review* 69 (1994): 787; id., *Toleration and the Constitution;* id., *Conscience and the Constitution.*

3. See Richards, *Conscience and the Constitution.*

transforms their own identities as much as that of the larger constitutional culture (in this sense, for all such advocates the personal is the political). A struggle of this sort does not renegotiate all the terms of personal identity; one's identity, as a person, is never infinitely malleable. Certain cultural assumptions must always be taken as given if any rights-based criticism and reform are to go forward sensibly. The struggle for identity, as we have studied it, must be understood in terms of the distinctive arguments of rights-based justice central to each person's sense of integrity, the sense in which, for example, gay and lesbian identity is literally defined and renegotiated by the self-respecting claims of basic rights and the reasonable criticisms thus made against the traditional force of one's unspeakable moral slavery.[4]

We have now studied such struggles for the renegotiation of identity in various domains of race, religion, gender, and sexual preference, investigating them in terms of both abstract normative principles of universal human rights and their detailed, often interlinked historical contextualizations. Our methodology suggests that both a normative philosophy of universal human rights and of close interpretive study of the historical contextualizations of such arguments are mutually complementary and illuminate the interpretive purposes of American public law; our study gives a distinctively American moral interpretation and indeed foundation to the anti-essentialist idea of such reinventions of identity. My account has linked this question to a structural injustice centering on indignities to legitimate moral freedom undermined by the uncritical enforcement of traditions of moral slavery in the domains of religion, race, gender, and sexual preference. Such traditions unjustly ascribe a devalued or degraded status that dehumanizes a class of persons in terms of essentialist stereotypes and, on this basis, abridges their inalienable rights. If persons have any such human rights, they must have the right rationally and reasonably to reinvent

4. See, on such identity-altering forms of dissent in various domains, Iris Marion Young, *Justice and the Politics of Difference* (Princeton: Princeton University Press, 1990); D'Augelli and Patterson, *Lesbian, Gay, and Bisexual Identities over the Lifespan;* Michael Warner, *Fear of a Queer Planet: Queer Politics and Social Theory* (Minneapolis: University of Minnesota Press, 1993); Judith Butler, *Gender Trouble: Feminism and the Subversion of Identity* (New York: Routledge, 1990); *Bodies That Matter: On the Discursive Limits of "Sex"* (New York: Routledge, 1993); Marjorie Garber, *Vested Interests: Cross-Dressing and Cultural Anxiety* (New York: Routledge, 1992); *Vice Versa: Bisexuality and the Eroticism of Everyday Life* (New York: Simon and Schuster, 1995); Dan Danielsen and Karen Engle, *After Identity: A Reader in Law and Culture* (New York: Routledge, 1995); Kwame Anthony Appiah and Henry Louis Gates, Jr., eds., *Identities* (Chicago: University of Chicago Press, 1995). For discussion of a range of philosophical issues, see Henry Harris, ed., *Identity* (Oxford: Clarendon Press, 1995).

their identities on terms free of such fundamental injustice. The story I have now told in such detail is the narrative, in each domain we have studied, of coming to understand, recognize, and demand one's basic human right of self-invention of one's personal and ethical life (including the role of religion, race, gender, and sexual preference in one's life) as an expression of the moral powers of free personality on the dignifying basis of one's claims to human rights against traditions constructed on the basis of unjust stereotypes that abridge such rights. What are contested and questioned, in such terms, are those often deep aspects of identity that rest on and are sustained by such traditional patterns of moral slavery. That is not to protest everything that should be protested, but it is more than enough to justify one's ethical admiration for the persons whose lives have such integrity that they can undertake, for shorter or longer periods in their lives, such profound questioning of both themselves and of their cultures. Their theory and practice constitute the rights-based public conscience of their community, and they are, under American constitutionalism, often its constitutional conscience as well.

Sometimes one kind of rights-based advance may compromise another (as antiracism was to compromise antisexism, and conversely). The enduring legacy of the abolitionist feminists is the insistence on the platform of human rights and the price paid for such compromise in the dilution of rights-based principles in all areas (for example in both the antiracist and antisexist struggles). They set us a standard, particularly in the interpretation of the Reconstruction Amendments, against which we test the integrity of our own arguments of constitutional principle and insist that our theory and practice should be always more reasonably principled and inclusive.

If gays and lesbians have much to gain from demanding of others such inclusive terms of American basic arguments of principle, they must demand no less of themselves. Gays and lesbians, the newest advocates retelling the oldest and most contemporary narrative of American civil liberties, must resist the temptation to compromise such arguments of principle, as earlier advocates of gay rights sometimes did, by scapegoating women and even Jews (Weininger). If we can learn anything from the historical struggle for human rights, in which we are central contemporary participants, it must be our proper place on the platform of human rights; we must demand, on this basis, the full application of basic constitutional principles of antidiscrimination applicable in both public and private life for African Americans, women, religious minorities, and gays and lesbians, including inclusive policies of affirmative action. Contemporary arguments to the contrary, even by so perceptive an advocate of gay rights as Andrew Sullivan, bespeak the compromise of basic constitutional principles we must and should resist.[5] We have much to learn from the rich historical tradition of theory and practice of abolitionist feminism, not least that we, like our forebears, stand most secure when we stand on the common principles that condemn, the interlinked evils of moral slavery (including religious intolerance, racism, sexism, and homophobia).

I have tried to suggest what the reasonable interpretation of the legacy of abolitionist feminism should mean in our circumstances. Their theory of moral slavery enables us both to understand how far we have come and how far we have yet to go. We can reasonably interpret much of our contemporary public law as an elaboration in our circumstances of the interpretive strand of our revolutionary constitutionalism on which they insisted on the platform of human rights. We can also see other parts of our public law (for example, in the area of sexual preference) as falling critically short of meeting in our circumstances such demands. In light of this normative gap, this area more than any other tests ourselves in terms of appropriately demanding standards of constitutional conscience, requiring a theory and practice that stands its rights-based ground against the most majoritarian and popular of laws and policies. I have already argued that the contemporary American populist homophobia, so easily aroused to pass Colorado Amendment Two, was normatively the same as the populist anti-Semitism of European politics, and made a similar case against the exclusion of gays and lesbians from the military and the right to marriage, both of which enjoy and continue to enjoy populist support. We may have the same difficulty in seeing this today as Americans in the antebellum period had in seeing their racism and sexism; we thus jocularly dismiss gay marriage, dehumanizing the intimate life of gay and lesbian persons, with the same nescient popular complacency that led antebellum Americans, on the basis of institutions of racial and sexual subordination they assumed to be in the nature of things, to reduce African Americans and women to a servile stereotype, as vacant and empty of moral personality as a cruelly unjust political mythology of race and gender required them to be. Such simplistic insults to moral intelligence and complexity, precisely because they are so powerfully majoritarian and thus so apparently irresistible to our populist politicians, make it all the more important today, consistent with our legacy

5. For Sullivan's opposition to antidiscrimination laws that extend beyond prohibition of state-imposed exclusions of minorities, see Andrew Sullivan, *Virtually Normal: An Argument about Homosexuality* (New York: Knopf, 1995), 133–68.

of abolitionist feminism, to take our stand, as a matter of elementary constitutional justice, on the platform of human rights as we best understand it against such popular consensus and the constitutionally decadent politics that feeds on it. It is such rights-denying bromides and complacencies, the common sense structured by uncritical traditions of moral slavery, that most need our critical attention as persons and as citizens under American revolutionary constitutionalism.

If America stands for something of enduring value in human politics, it is, in my judgment, the proven moral competence of traditionally marginalized Americans—African Americans, Jews, women, homosexuals—to insist that universal human rights be the measure of legitimate politics under American constitutionalism. The outcast or exile, empowered with such cleansing moral fire, becomes the insistent conscience and demanding prophet of American rights-based moral community. Their theory and practice have been the study of this book. If I am right, no Americans speak more authentically and critically to the values that make us, when our hearts are imaginatively responsive and our minds are open to their strenuous ethical demands, a moral people because capable of moral growth on fundamental terms of constitutional principle. Through such struggle, we stand in union not on grounds of our ethnicity or race or gender or sexual preference, but on the demanding terms of our collective constitutional conscience to which Lincoln appealed, against antebellum majoritarian acquiescence in the evils of moral slavery, as the enduring basis of American union, "the light of reason and the love of liberty in this American people."[6]

6. See Robert W. Johannsen, ed., *The Lincoln-Douglas Debates* (New York: Oxford University Press, 1965), 67.

BIBLIOGRAPHY

Abelove, Henry, Michele Aina Barale, and David M. Halperin, eds. *The Lesbian and Gay Studies Reader.* New York: Routledge, 1993.

Abrahamsen, David. *The Mind and Death of a Genius.* New York: Columbia University Press, 1946.

Abzug, Robert H. *Cosmos Crumbling: American Reform and the Religious Imagination.* New York: Oxford University Press, 1994.

Ackerman, Bruce. "Beyond *Carolene Products.*" *Harvard Law Review* 98 (1985): 713.

Addams, Jane. *A New Conscience and an Ancient Evil.* New York: Macmillan, 1913.

Ahlstrom, Sydney E. *A Religious History of the American People.* New Haven: Yale University Press, 1972.

Altman, Dennis. *Homosexual Oppression and Liberation.* New York: Avon, 1971.

——. *The Homosexualization of America, The Americanization of the Homosexual.* New York: St. Martin's Press, 1982.

Altman, Dennis, et al. *Homosexuality, Which Homosexuality?* London: DMP Publishers, 1989.

Amar, Akhil Reed. "Forty Acres and a Mule: A Republican Theory of Minimal Entitlements." *Harvard Journal of Law and Public Policy* 13 (1990): 37.

——. "Remember the Thirteenth." *Constitutional Commentary* 10 (1993): 403.

——. "The Bill of Rights and the Fourteenth Amendment." *Yale Law Journal* 101 (1992): 1193.

——. "The Case of the Missing Amendments: *R. A. V. v. City of St. Paul.*" *Harvard Law Review* 106 (1992): 124.

Amar, Akhil Reed and Daniel Widawsky. "Child Abuse as Slavery: A Thirteenth Amendment Response to *DeShaney.*" *Harvard Law Review* 105 (1992): 1359.

Amsterdam, Anthony G. "Thurgood Marshall's Image of the Blue-Eyed Child in *Brown.*" *New York University Law Review* 68 (1993): 226.

Andersen, Kristi. *After Suffrage: Woman in Partisan and Electoral Politics before the New Deal.* Chicago: University of Chicago Press, 1996.

Anderson, Michelle J. "A License to Abuse: The Impact of Conditional Status on Female Immigrants." *Yale Law Journal* 102 (1993): 1401.

Andrews, Stephen Pearl, ed. *Love, Marriage, and Divorce.* 1853. Reprint, New York: Source Book Press, 1972.

Appiah, Kwame Anthony, and Henry Louis Gates, Jr., eds. *Identities.* Chicago: University of Chicago Press, 1995.

Aptheker, Herbert. *American Negro Slave Revolts.* New York: International Publishers, 1952.

———, ed. *A Documentary History of the Negro People in the United States.* 4 vols. New York: Citadel Press Books, 1990.

Aquinas, Thomas. *On the Truth of the Catholic Faith: Summa Contra Gentiles.* Translated by Vernon Bourke. New York: Image, 1956.

Arendt, Hannah. *The Origins of Totalitarianism.* New York: Harcourt Brace Jovanovich, 1973.

Arkes, Hadley. "Questions of Principle, Not Predictions." *Georgetown Law Journal* 84 (1995): 321.

———. "Testimony on the Defense of Marriage Act, 1996," Judiciary Committee, House of Representatives, 1996 WL 246693 (F.D.C.H.).

Augustine. *The City of God.* Translated by Henry Bettenson. Harmondsworth: Penguin, 1972.

Bacon, Margaret Hope. *Mothers of Feminism: The Story of Quaker Women in America.* San Francisco: Harper & Row, 1989.

Badinter, Elisabeth. *Man/Woman: The One Is the Other.* Translated by Barbara Wright. London: Collins Harvill, 1989.

———. *On Masculine Identity.* Translated by Lydia Davis. New York: Columbia University Press, 1995.

Bailey, Derrick Sherwin. *Homosexuality and the Western Christian Tradition.* Originally published, 1955. Hamden, Conn.: Archon Books, 1975.

Bailyn, Bernard, ed. *Pamphlets of the American Revolution, 1750–1776.* Vol. 1. Cambridge: Harvard University Press, Belknap Press, 1965.

Baker, Paula. "The Domestication of Politics: Woman and American Political Society, 1780–1920." *American Historical Review* (June 1984): 89.

Baldwin, James. *Giovanni's Room.* New York: Laurel, 1956.

———. *No Name in the Street.* New York: Dell, 1972.

———. *The Price of the Ticket: Collected Nonfiction, 1948–1985.* New York: St. Martin's, 1985.

Balint, Michael. *Primary Love and Psycho-Analytic Technique.* New York: Liveright, 1965.

Balter, Joni. "Gay Power Brokers—Money, Stature and Savvy Give Leaders More Clout." *Seattle Times,* 1 August 1993, A1.

Barkan, Elazar. *The Retreat of Scientific Racism: Changing Concepts of Race in Britain and the United States between the World Wars.* Cambridge: Cambridge University Press, 1992.

Barker-Benfield, G. J. *The Horrors of the Half-Known Life: Male Attitudes toward Women and Sexuality in Nineteenth-Century America.* New York: Harper & Row, 1976.

Barnes, Gilbert H., and Dwight L. Dumond. *Letters of Theodore Dwight Weld, Angelina Grimke Weld, and Sarah Grimke, 1822–1844.* 2 vols. Gloucester, Mass.: Peter Smith, 1965.

Barnes, Gilbert Hobbs. *The Antislavery Impulse, 1830–1844.* New York: D. Appleton-Century Co., 1933.

Barnett, Walter. *Sexual Freedom and the Constitution.* Albuquerque: University of New Mexico Press, 1973.

Baskin, Alex, ed. *Woman Rebel.* New York: Archives of Social History, 1976.

Bawer, Bruce. *A Place at the Table: The Gay Individual in American Society.* New York: Poseidon Press, 1993.

———. *Beyond Queer: Challenging Gay Left Orthodoxy.* New York: Free Press, 1996.

Bayer, Ronald. *Homosexuality and American Psychiatry: The Politics of Diagnosis.* New York: Basic Books, 1981.

Bayle, Pierre, *Philosophical Commentary.* Translated by Amie Godman Tannenbaum. New York: Peter Lang, 1987.

Beattie, James. *An Essay on the Nature and Immutability of Truth.* 1770. Reprint edited by Lewis White Beck. New York: Garland Publishing, 1983.

———. *Elements of Moral Science.* Delmar, N.Y.: Scholars' Facsimiles & Reprints, 1976.

Beauvoir, Simone de. *The Second Sex.* Translated by H. M. Parshley. New York: Vintage Books, 1974.

Bederman, Gail. *Manliness and Civilization: A Cultural History of Gender and Race in the United States, 1880–1917.* Chicago: University of Chicago Press, 1995.

Beecher, Catharine E. *A Treatise on Domestic Economy.* 1841. Reprint edited by Kathryn Kish Sklar. New York: Schocken Books, 1977.

Beecher, Catharine E. *An Appeal to the People in Behalf of Their Rights as Authorized Interpreters of the Bible.* New York: Harper & Bros., 1860.

———. *Common Sense Applied to Religion; or, The Bible and the People.* New York: Harper & Bros., 1857.

———. "Essay on Slavery and Abolitionism, with Reference to the Duty of American Females." Philadelphia: H. Perkins; Boston: Perkins & Marvin, 1837.

———. "The Duty of American Women to Their Country." New York: Harper & Bros., 1845.

———. "The Evils Suffered by American Women and American Children: The Cause and the Remedy." New York: Harper & Bros., 1846.

———. "The True Remedy for the Wrongs of Women." Boston: Phillips, Sampson, 1851.

———. "Woman Suffrage and Woman's Profession." Hartford: Brown and Gross, 1871.

Beecher, Jonathan. *Charles Fourier: The Visionary and His World.* Berkeley and Los Angeles: University of California Press, 1986.

Beecher, Jonathan, and Richard Bienvenu. *The Utopian Vision of Charles Fourier.* Boston: Beacon Press, 1971.

Bell, Alan P., Martin S. Weinberg, and Sue K. Hammersmith. *Sexual Preference.* New York: Simon & Schuster, 1978.

Bell, Jr., Derrick A. "The Referendum: Democracy's Barrier to Racial Equality." *Washington Law Review* 54 (1978): 1.

Bem, Sandra Lipsitz. *The Lenses of Gender: Transforming the Debate on Sexual Equality.* New Haven: Yale University Press, 1993.

Benedict, Michael Les. *A Compromise of Principle: Congressional Republicans and Reconstruction, 1863–1869.* New York: W. W. Norton, 1974.

Benedict, Ruth. *Race: Science and Politics.* New York: The Viking Press, 1945.

Benjamin, Jessica. *The Bonds of Love: Psychoanalysis, Feminism, and the Problem of Domination.* London: Virgo, 1988.

Bennett, William. "Leave Marriage Alone." *Newsweek,* 3 June 1996, 27.

Berg, Barbara J. *The Remembered Gate: Origins of American Feminism—The Woman and the City, 1800–1860.* New York: Oxford University Press, 1978.

Berger, Raoul. *Government by Judiciary: The Transformation of the Fourteenth Amendment.* Cambridge: Harvard University Press, 1977.

Berghe, Pierre L. van den. *Race and Racism.* New York: John Wiley & Sons, 1967.

Berlin, Ira. *Slaves Without Masters: The Free Negro in the Antebellum South.* New York: Pantheon Books, 1974.

Berman, Paul. *A Tale of Two Utopias.* New York: W. W. Norton, 1996.

Bernstein, Alan E. *The Formation of Hell: Death and Retribution in the Ancient and Early Christian Worlds.* Ithaca: Cornell University Press, 1993.

Bersani, Leo. *Homos.* Cambridge: Harvard University Press, 1995.

Berube, Allan. *Coming Out under Fire: The History of Gay Men and Women in World War Two.* New York: Free Press, 1990.

Birney, James G. *Letter on Colonization Addressed to the Rev. Thornton J. Mills, Corresponding Secretary of the Kentucky Colonization Society.* New York, 1834.

Blackstone, William. *Commentaries on the Laws of England.* 1765–1769. Vol. 4. Facsimile of first edition edited by Thomas A. Green. Chicago: University of Chicago Press, 1979.

Blassingame, John W. *The Slave Community: Plantation Life in the Antebellum South.* 2d ed. New York: Oxford University Press, 1979.

Blatt, Martin, ed. *The Collected Works of Ezra H. Heywood.* Weston, Mass.: M & S Press, 1985.

Bleys, Rudi C. *The Geography of Perversion: Male-to-Male Sexual Behavior Outside the West and the Ethnographic Imagination, 1750–1918.* New York: New York University Press, 1995.

Bloom, Harold, ed. *Walt Whitman.* New York: Chelsea House Publishers, 1985.

Boas, Franz. "Race." In *Encyclopaedia of the Social Sciences,* edited by Edwin R. A. Seligman, 7:25–36. New York: Macmillan, 1937.

———. *The Mind of Primitive Man.* 1911. Rev. ed. Westport, Conn.: Greenwood Press, 1983.

Bordin, Ruth, *Frances Willard: A Biography.* Chapel Hill: University of North Carolina Press, 1986.

———. *Woman and Temperance: The Quest for Power and Liberty, 1873–1900.* New Brunswick, N.J.: Rutgers University Press, 1990.

Bork, Robert. *The Tempting of America: The Political Seduction of the Law.* New York: The Free Press, 1990.

Boston Lesbian Psychologies Collective. *Lesbian Psychologies: Explorations and Challenges*. Urbana: University of Illinois Press, 1987.

Boswell, John. *Christianity, Social Tolerance, and Homosexuality*. Chicago: University of Chicago Press, 1980.

———. *Same-Sex Unions in Premodern Europe*. New York: Villard Books, 1994.

Boydston, Jeanne, Mary Kelley, and Anne Margolis. *The Limits of Sisterhood: The Beecher Sisters on Women's Rights and Woman's Sphere*. Chapel Hill: University of North Carolina Press, 1988.

Branch, Taylor. *Parting the Waters: Martin Luther King and the Civil Rights Movement, 1954–63*. London: Papermac, 1990.

Bransford, Stephen. *Gay Politics vs. Colorado and America: The Inside Story of Amendment 2*. Cascade, Colorado: Sardis Press, 1994.

Braude, Ann. *Radical Spirits: Spiritualism and Women's Rights in Nineteenth-Century America*. Boston: Beacon Press, 1989.

Bray, Alan. *Homosexuality in Renaissance England*. London: Gay Men's Press, 1982.

Bristow, Joseph. *Effeminate England: Homoerotic Writing after 1885*. New York: Columbia University Press, 1995.

Brod, Harry, ed. *The Making of Masculinities: The New Men's Studies*. New York: Routledge, 1987.

Brodie, Janet Farrell. *Contraception and Abortion in 19th-Century America*. Ithaca: Cornell University Press, 1994.

Brooten, Bernadette J. *Love Between Women: Early Christian Responses to Female Homoeroticism*. Chicago: University of Chicago Press, 1996.

Brown, Peter. *The Body and Society: Men, Women and Sexual Renunciation in Early Christianity*. New York: Columbia University Press, 1988.

Brown, Tony, ed. *Edward Carpenter and Late Victorian Radicalism*. London: Frank Cass, 1990.

Buhle, Mari Jo. *Woman and American Socialism, 1870–1920*. Urbana: University of Illinois Press, 1981.

Bull, Chris, and John Gallagher. *Perfect Enemies: The Religious Right, the Gay Movement, and the Politics of the 1990's*. New York: Crown Publishers, 1996.

Bushnell, Horace. *Christian Nurture*. 1861. Edited by Luther A. Weigle. New Haven: Yale University Press, 1916.

———. *Views of Christian Nurture and of Subjects Adjacent Thereto*. 1847. Edited by Philip B. Eppard. New York: Delmar, 1975.

———. *Women's Suffrage: The Reform against Nature*. New York: Charles Scribner and Co., 1869.

Butler, Judith. *Bodies That Matter: On the Discursive Limits of "Sex."* New York: Routledge, 1993.

———. *Gender Trouble: Feminism and the Subversion of Identity*. New York: Routledge, 1990.

Bynum, Caroline Walker. *Jesus as Mother: Studies in the Spirituality of the High Middle Ages*. Berkeley and Los Angeles: University of California Press, 1982.

Cahn, Edmond. "Jurisprudence." *New York University Law Review* 30 (1955): 150.

Caine, Barbara. *Victorian Feminists*. Oxford: Oxford University Press, 1992.

Calhoun, Emily. "The Thirteenth and Fourteenth Amendments: Constitutional Authority for Federal Legislation against Private Sex Discrimination." *Minnesota Law Review* 61 (1977): 355–58.

Campion, Nardi Reeder. *Ann the Word: The Life of Mother Ann Lee, Founder of the Shakers*. Boston: Little, Brown, 1976.

Cantarella, Eva. *Bisexuality in the Ancient World*. Translated by Cormac O Cuilleanain. New Haven: Yale University Press, 1992.

Carby, Hazel V. *Reconstructing Womanhood: The Emergence of the Afro-American Woman Novelist*. New York: Oxford University Press, 1987.

Card, Claudia. *Lesbian Choices*. New York: Columbia University Press, 1995.

———. *The Unnatural Lottery: Character and Moral Luck*. Philadelphia: Temple University Press, 1996.

Carnes, Mark C., and Clyde Griffen, eds. *Meanings for Manhood: Constructions of Masculinity in Victorian America*. Chicago: University of Chicago Press, 1990.

Carpenter, Edward. *Days with Walt Whitman: With some Notes on his Life and Work*. London: George Allend, 1906.

———. *From Adam's Peak to Elephanta: Sketches in Ceylon and India*. London: Geroge, Allen & Unwin, 1892.

———. *Intermediate Types among Primitive Folk*. London: George Allen & Unwin, 1919.

———. *Iolaus: An Anthology of Friendship*. Mitchell: New York, 1917.

———. *Love's Coming of Age: A Series of Papers on the Relations of the Sexes*. 1896. New York: Vanguard Press, 1926.

———. *Marriage in Free Society*. Manchester: Labour Press Society, 1894.

———. *My Days and Dreams: Being Autobiographical Notes*. London: George Allen, 1921.

———. *Pagan and Christian Creeds: Their Origin and Meaning*. New York: Harcourt, Brace, 1920.

———. *Some Friends of Walt Whitman: A Study in Sex-Psychology*. London: J. E. Francis, 1924.

———. *The Art of Creation: Essays on the Self and Its Powers*. London: George Allen & Unwin, 1904.

———. *The Drama of Love and Death: A Study of Human Evolution and Transfiguration*. New York: Mitchell Kennerley, 1912.

———. *The Intermediate Sex: A Study of Some Transitional Types of Men and Women*. New York: Mitchell Kennerley, 1912.

———. *Towards Democracy*. 1883. London: George Allen & Unwin, 1912.

———. *Woman, and Her Place in a Free Society*. Manchester: Labour Press Society, 1894.

Case, Mary Ann C. "Disaggregating Gender from Sex and Sexual Orientation: The Effeminate Man in the Law and Feminist Jurisprudence." *Yale Law Journal* 105 (1995): 90.

Cash, W. J. *The Mind of the South*. New York: Vintage Books, 1941.

Castle, Terry. *Noel Coward and Radclyffe Hall: Kindred Spirits*. New York: Columbia University Press, 1996.

Ceplair, Larry, ed. *The Public Years of Sarah and Angelina Grimke: Selected Writings, 1835–1839*. New York: Columbia University Press, 1989.

Cervantes, Fernando. *The Devil in the New World: The Impact of Diabolism in New Spain*. New Haven: Yale University Press, 1994.

Chafe, William Henry. *The American Woman: Her Changing Social, Economic, and Political Roles, 1920–1970*. New York: Oxford University Press, 1972.

————. *The Paradox of Change: American Women in the 20th Century.* New York: Oxford University Press, 1991.

————. *Women and Equality: Changing Patterns in American Culture.* Oxford: Oxford University Press, 1977.

Chamberlain, Houston Stewart. *The Foundations of the Nineteenth Century.* Translated by John Lees. 2 vols. London: John Lane, 1911.

Chandler, Elizabeth Margaret. *Essays, Philanthropic and Moral, Principally Relating to the Abolition of Slavery in America.* Philadelphia: T. E. Chapman, 1845.

Channing, William E. *The Works of William E. Channing.* New York: Burt Franklin 1970.

Chauncey, George. *Gay New York: Gender, Urban Culture, and the Making of the Gay Male World, 1890–1940.* New York: BasicBooks, 1994.

Chesler, Ellen. *Woman of Valor: Margaret Sanger and the Birth Control Movement in America.* New York: Anchor, 1992.

Child, L. Maria. *An Appeal in Favor of Americans Called Africans.* 1833. New York: Arno Press and New York Times, 1968.

————. *Letters from New York.* London: Richard Bentley, 1843.

————. *The History of the Condition of Women, in Various Ages and Nations.* 2 vols. Boston: Otis, Broaders & Co., 1838.

————. *The Progress of Religious Ideas through Successive Ages.* 3 vols. New York: C. S. Francis, 1855.

Chodorow, Nancy. *Femininities Masculinities Sexualities: Freud and Beyond.* London: Free Association Press, 1994.

————. *Feminism and Psychoanalytic Theory.* London: Polity, 1989.

————. *The Reproduction of Mothering: Psychoanalysis and the Sociology of Gender.* Berkeley and Los Angeles: University of California Press, 1978.

Churchill, Wainwright. *Homosexual Behavior among Males.* New York: Hawthorn, 1967.

Claflin, Tennie C. *Constitutional Equality a Right of Woman.* New York: Woodhull, Claflin & Co., 1871.

Clark, Elizabeth B. "Self-Ownership and the Political Theory of Elizabeth Cady Stanton." *Connecticut Law Review* 21 (1989): 905.

————. "The Politics of God and the Woman's Vote: Religion in the American Suffrage Movement, 1848–1895." Ph.D. diss., Princeton University, 1989.

Cleaver, Eldridge. *Soul On Ice.* New York: Dell, 1968.

Cleveland, Henry. *Alexander H. Stephens, in Public and Private.* Philadelphia: National Publishing Co., 1866.

Clifford, Deborah Pickman. *Crusader for Freedom: A Life of Lydia Maria Child.* Boston: Beacon Press, 1992.

Cobb, Thomas R. R. *An Inquiry into the Law of Negro Slavery in the United States of America.* New York: Negro Universities Press, 1968. originally published, 1858.

Code, Lorraine. *What Can She Know?: Feminist Theory and the Construction of Knowledge.* Ithaca: Cornell University Press, 1991.

Cohen, Bernard I., ed. *Puritanism and the Rise of Modern Science: The Merton Thesis.* New Brunswick, N.J.: Rutgers University Press, 1990.

Cohen, Jane Maslow. "Regimes of Private Tyranny: What Do They Mean to Morality and for the Criminal Law?" *University of Pittsburgh Law Review* 57 (1996): 757.

Cohen, Marcia. *The Sisterhood: The True Story of the Women Who Changed the World.* New York: Simon and Schuster, 1988.

Colbert, Douglas L. "Affirming the Thirteenth Amendment." 1995 *Annual Survey of American Law* (1995): 403.

———. "Challenging the Challenge: Thirteenth Amendment as Prohibition against the Racial Use of Peremptory Challenges." *Cornell Law Review* 76 (1990): 1.

Cole, David, and William N. Eskridge, Jr. "From Hand-Holding to Sodomy: First Amendment Protection of Homosexual Expressive Conduct." *Harvard Civil Rights–Civil Liberties Law Review* 29 (1994): 319.

Commager, Henry Steele. *Theodore Parker.* Boston: Little, Brown, 1936.

Connell, R. W. *Masculinities.* Berkeley and Los Angeles: University of California Press, 1995.

Connelly, Mark Thomas. *The Response to Prostitution in the Progressive Era.* Chapel Hill: University of North Carolina Press, 1980.

Connolly, William E. *Identity/Difference: Democratic Negotiations of Political Paradox.* Ithaca: Cornell University Press, 1991.

Continuing Legal Education Materials. *The Bill of Rights versus the Ballot Box: Constitutional Implications of Anti-Gay Ballot Initiatives,* presented by the Gay-Lesbian Bisexual Law Caucus of The Ohio State University, March, 12, 1994 (on file with Ohio State Law Journal).

Cooke, Jacob E., ed. *The Federalist.* Middletown, Conn.: Wesleyan University Press, 1961.

Coolidge, David Orgon. "At Last, Hawaiians Have Their Say on Gay Marriage." *Wall Street Journal,* 23 April 1997, A19.

Cooper, Anna Julia. *A Voice from the South.* 1892. Reprint edited by Mary Helen Washington. New York: Oxford University Press, 1988.

Cory, Donald Webster [pseud.]. *The Homosexual in America: A Subjective Approach.* New York: Castle Books, 1951.

Cott, Nancy F. "Passionlessness: An Interpretation of Victorian Sexual Ideology, 1790–1850." *Signs* 4, no. 2 (winter, 1978): 219–36.

———. *The Grounding of Modern Feminism.* New Haven: Yale University Press, 1987.

Crenshaw, Kimberle. "Demarginalizing the Intersection of Race and Sex: A Black Feminist Critique of Antidiscrimination Doctrine, Feminist Theory and Antiracist Politics." *University of Chicago Legislative Forum* (1989): 139.

Crimp, Douglas. *Cultural Analysis/Cultural Activism.* Cambridge: The MIT Press, 1988.

Cross, Barbara M. *Horace Bushnell: Minister to a Changing America.* Chicago: University of Chicago Press, 1958.

Crouch, Stanley. *Notes of a Hanging Judge: Essays and Reviews, 1979–1989.* New York: Oxford University Press, 1990.

Curry, Thomas J. *The First Freedoms: Church and State in America to the Passage of the First Amendment.* New York: Oxford University Press, 1986.

Dall, Caroline H. *The College, the Market, and the Court.* Boston: Lee and Shepard, 1867.

Daly, Mary. *Beyond God the Father: Towards a Philosophy of Women's Liberation*. London: Women's Press, 1986.

Danielsen, Dan, and Karen Engle, eds. *After Identity: A Reader in Law and Culture*. New York: Routledge, 1995.

Dannenbaum, Jed. *Drink and Disorder: Temperance Reform in Cincinnati from the Washingtonian Revival to the WCTU*. Urbana: University of Illinois Press, 1984.

D'Augelli, Anthony, and Charlotte J. Patterson, eds. *Lesbian, Gay, and Bisexual Identities over the Lifespan: Psychological Perspectives*. New York: Oxford University Press, 1995.

Davis, David Brion. *The Problem of Slavery in Western Culture*. Ithaca: Cornell University Press, 1967.

―――. *The Slave Power Conspiracy and the Paranoid Style*. Baton Rouge: Louisiana State University Press, 1969.

Davis, F. James. *Who Is Black?: One Nation's Definition*. University Park, Pennsylvania: Pennsylvania State University Press, 1991.

Davis, Peggy Cooper. "Neglected Stories and the Lawfulness of *Roe v. Wade*." *Harvard Civil Rights–Civil Liberties Law Review* 28 (1993): 299.

DeBerg, Betty A. *Ungodly Women: Gender and the First Wave of American Fundamentalism*. Minneapolis: Fortress Press, 1990.

Degler, Carl N. *At Odds: Women and the Family in America from the Revolution to the Present*. New York: Oxford University Press, 1980.

―――. *In Search of Human Nature: The Decline and Revival of Darwinism in American Social Thought*. New York: Oxford University Press, 1991.

―――. *Neither Black Nor White*. Madison: University of Wisconsin Press, 1986.

―――. *Out of Our Past: The Forces That Shaped Modern America*. 3d ed. New York: Harper and Row, 1984.

Delbanco, Andrew. *William Ellery Channing: An Essay on the Liberal Spirit in America*. Cambridge: Harvard University Press, 1981.

D'Emilio, John. *Sexual Politics, Sexual Communities: The Making of a Homosexual Minority in the United States, 1940–1970*. Chicago: University of Chicago Press, 1983.

D'Emilio, John, and Estelle B. Freedman. *Intimate Matters: A History of Sexuality in America*. New York: Harper & Row, 1988.

Denfeld, Rene. *The New Victorians: A Young Woman's Challenge to the Old Feminist Order*. New York: Warner Books, 1995.

d'Entremont, John. *Southern Emancipator: Moncure Conway, The American Years, 1832–1865*. New York: Oxford University Press, 1987.

Desroche, Henri. *The American Shakers: From Neo-Christianity to Presocialism*. Translated by John K. Savacool. Amherst: University of Massachusetts Press, 1971.

"Developments in the Law—Equal Protection." *Harvard Law Review* 82 (1969): 86.

"Developments in the Law—Sexual Orientation." *Harvard Law Review* 102 (1939): 1508.

Devlin, Patrick. *The Enforcement of Morals*. London: Oxford University Press, 1965.

Dijkstra, Bram. *Idols of Perversity: Fantasies of Feminine Evil in Fin-de-Siecle Culture.* New York: Oxford University Press,1986.

Dillon, Merton L. *The Abolitionists: The Growth of a Dissenting Minority.* New York: W. W. Norton, 1974.

Dinnerstein, Dorothy. *The Mermaid and The Minotaur: Sexual Arrangements and Human Malaise.* New York: Harper & Row, 1976.

Dirks, John Edward. *The Critical Theology of Theodore Parker.* New York: Columbia University Press, 1948.

Dollimore, Jonathan. *Sexual Dissidence: Augustine to Wilde, Freud to Foucault.* Oxford: Clarendon Press, 1991.

Donald, David Herbert. *Charles Sumner and the Coming of the Civil War.* New York: Alfred A. Knopf, 1960.

———. *Charles Sumner and the Rights of Man.* New York: Alfred A. Knopf, 1970.

———. *Lincoln.* New York: Simon & Schuster, 1995.

Donoghue, Denis. *Walter Pater: Love of Strange Souls.* New York: Knopf, 1995.

Donoghue, Emma. *Passions Between Women: British Lesbian Culture, 1668–1801.* New York: HarperCollins, 1993.

Douglas, Ann. *The Feminization of American Culture.* New York: Knopf, 1977.

Douglass, Frederick. *Narrative of the Life of Frederick Douglass: An American Slave Written by Himself.* 1845. Harmondsworth: Signey, 1968.

Dover, Kenneth J. *Greek Homosexuality.* London: Duckworth, 1978.

———. *Greek Popular Morality in the Time of Plato and Aristotle.* Oxford: Basil Blackwell, 1974.

———. *The Greeks and Their Legacy.* Oxford: Blackwell, 1988.

Dowling, Linda. *Hellenism and Homosexuality in Victorian Oxford.* Ithaca: Cornell University Press, 1994.

Drinnon, Richard. *Rebel in Paradise: A Biography of Emma Goldman.* Chicago: University of Chicago Press, 1961.

Drinnon, Richard and Anna Maria. *Nowhere At Home: Letters from Exile of Emma Goldman and Alexander Berkman.* New York: Schocken, 1975.

Duberman, Martin. *Stonewall.* New York: Plume, 1993.

———, ed. *The Antislavery Vanguard: New Essays on the Abolitionists.* Princeton: Princeton University Press, 1965.

Duberman, Martin Bauml, Martha Vicinus, and George Chauncey, Jr. *Hidden from History: Reclaiming the Gay and Lesbian Past.* New York: New American Library, 1989.

DuBois, Ellen Carol. *Feminism and Suffrage: The Emergence of an Independent Women's Movement in the America, 1848–1869.* Ithaca: Cornell University Press, 1978.

———. "On Labor and Free Love: Two Unpublished Speeches of Elizabeth Cady Stanton." *Signs* 1, no. 1 (1975): 265–68.

———, ed. *The Elizabeth Cady Stanton-Susan B. Anthony Reader: Correspondence, Writings, Speeches.* Rev. ed. Boston: Northeastern University Press, 1992.

Du Bois, W. E. B. *Black Reconstruction in America, 1860–1880.* 1935. New York: Atheneum, 1969.

Duby, Georges, and Michelle Perrot, eds. *A History of Women in the West.* 5

vols. Translated by Arthur Goldhammer. Cambridge: Harvard University Press, 1992–1994.

Dudziak, Mary L. "Desegregation as a Cold War Imperative." *Stanford Law Review* 41 (1988): 61.

Duggan, Lisa, and Nan D. Hunter. *Sex Wars: Sexual Dissent and Political Culture.* New York: Routledge, 1995.

Dumond, Dwight Lowell. *Antislavery: The Crusade for Freedom in America.* Ann Arbor: University of Michigan Press, 1961.

Duncan, Greg J., and Saul D. Hoffman. "A Reconsideration of the Economic Consequences of Marital Dissolution." *Demography* 22 (1985): 485.

Duster, Alfreda M., ed. *Crusade for Justice: The Autobiography of Ida B. Wells.* Chicago: University of Chicago Press, 1970.

Dworkin, Ronald. *Life's Dominion: An Argument about Abortion, Euthanasia, and Individual Freedom.* New York: Knopf, 1993.

———. "Sex, Drugs, and the Court." *The New York Review of Books* 43, no. 13, 8 August 1996, 44–50.

———. "What Is Equality? Part I: Equality of Welfare." *Philosophy and Public Affairs* 10 (1981): 185.

———. "What Is Equality? Part II: Equality of Resources." *Philosophy and Public Affairs* 10 (1981): 283.

———. "What Is Equality? Part III: The Place of Liberty." *Iowa Law Review* 73 (1987): 1.

———. "What Is Equality? Part IV: Political Equality." *University of San Francisco Law Review* 22 (1987): 1.

Dynes, Wayne R. *Encyclopedia of Homosexuality* 2 vols. New York: Garland, 1990.

Eaton, Clement. *The Freedom-of-Thought Struggle in the Old South.* New York: Harper and Row, 1940.

Ehrenreich, Barbara, Elizabeth Hess, and Gloria Jacobs. *Remaking Love: The Feminization of Sex.* New York: Anchor, 1986.

Eibl-Eibesfeldt, Irenaus. *Love and Hate: The Natural History of Behavior Patterns.* Translated by Geoffrey Strachan. New York: Holt, Rinehart, and Winston, 1971.

Elkins, Stanley M. *Slavery: A Problem in American Institutional and Intellectual Life.* 3d ed. Chicago: University of Chicago Press, 1976.

Elliot, Jonathan. *The Debates in the Several State Conventions on the Adoption of the Federal Constitution.* Vol. 2. Washington, D.C.: Printed for the Editor, 1836.

Ellis, Havelock. *The New Spirit.* Washington, D.C.: National Home Library Foundation, 1935.

Ellis, Havelock, and John Addington Symonds. *Sexual Inversion.* London: Wilson and Macmillan, 1897.

Ellman, Ira Mark, Paul M. Kurtz, Katharine T. Bartlett, eds. *Family Law: Cases, Text, Problems.* 2d ed. Charlottesville, Va.: The Michie Co., 1991.

Ellmann, Richard. *Oscar Wilde.* London: Penguin, 1988.

Elshtain, Jean Bethke. *Women and War.* New York: Basic Books, 1987.

Ely, John Hart. *Democracy and Distrust: A Theory of Judicial Review.* Cambridge: Harvard University Press, 1980.

Epstein, Barbara Leslie. *The Politics of Domesticity: Women, Evangelism and Temperance in Nineteenth-Century America.* Middletown, Conn.: Wesleyan University Press, 1981.

Epstein, Cynthia Fuchs. *Deceptive Distinctions: Sex, Gender, and the Social Order.* New Haven: Yale University Press, 1988.

Erkkila, Betsy. *Whitman: The Political Poet.* New York: Oxford University Press, 1989.

Erkkila, Betsy, and Jay Grossman, eds. *Breaking Bounds: Whitman and American Cultural Studies.* New York: Oxford University Press, 1996.

Erlanger, Howard S., ed. "Review Symposium on Weitzman's *Divorce Revolution.*" *American Bar Foundation Research Journal* 4 (1986): 759–97.

Eskridge, Jr., William N. "A History of Same-Sex Marriage." *Virginia Law Review* 79 (1993): 1419.

———. *The Case for Same-Sex Marriage: From Sexual Liberty to Civilized Commitment.* New York: Free Press, 1996.

Estlund, David M., and Martha C. Nussbaum, eds. *Sex, Preference, and Family: Essays on Law and Nature.* New York: Oxford University Press, 1997.

Evans, Sara. *Personal Politics: The Roots of Women's Liberation in the Civil Rights Movement and the New Left.* New York: Vintage Books, 1979.

Faderman, Lillian, ed. *Chloe Plus Olivia: An Anthology of Lesbian Literature from the Seventeenth Century to the Present.* New York: Viking, 1994.

———. *Odd Girls and Twilight Lovers: A History of Lesbian Life in Twentieth-Century America.* New York: Columbia University Press, 1991.

———. *Surpassing the Love of Men: Romantic Friendship and Love Between Women from the Renaissance to the Present.* New York: William Morrow, 1981.

Fajer, Marc A. "Can Two Real Men Eat Quiche Together? Storytelling, Gender-Role Stereotypes, and Legal Protection for Lesbians and Gay Men." *University of Miami Law Review* 46 (1992): 511.

Faludi, Susan. *Backlash: The Undeclared War against American Women.* New York: Doubleday, 1991.

Farrand, Max, ed. *The Records of the Federal Convention of 1787.* Vol. 1. New Haven: Yale University Press, 1966.

Faust, Drew Gilpin. *Mothers of Invention: Women of the Slaveholding South in the American Civil War.* Chapel Hill: University of North Carolina Press, 1996.

———. *The Ideology of Slavery.* Baton Rouge: Louisiana State University Press, 1981.

Fausto-Sterling, Anne. *Myths of Gender: Biological Theories about Women and Men.* New York: Basic Books, 1985.

Fehrenbacher, Don E., ed. *Abraham Lincoln: Speeches and Writings, 1832–1858.* New York: The Library of America, 1989.

———. *Abraham Lincoln: Speeches and Writings, 1859–1865.* New York: The Library of America, 1989.

———. *The Dred Scott Case: Its Significance in American Law and Politics.* New York: Oxford University Press, 1978.

Filler, Louis. *The Crusade against Slavery, 1830–1860.* New York: Harper & Row, 1960.

Filmer, Robert. *Patriarcha*. 1680. In *Patriarcha and Other Writings*. Edited by Johann P. Sommerville. Cambridge: Cambridge University Press, 1991.

Fineman, Martha Albertson. "Implementing Equality: Ideology, Contradiction and Social Change, A Study of Rhetoric and Results in the Regulation of the Consequences of Divorce." *Wisconsin Law Review* (1983): 789.

———. *The Illusion of Equality: The Rhetoric and Reality of Divorce Reform*. Chicago: University of Chicago Press, 1991.

———. *The Neutered Mother, the Sexual Family, and Other Twentieth Century Tragedies*. Routledge: New York, 1995.

Finkelman, Paul. "Prelude to the Fourteenth Amendment: Black Legal Rights in the Antebellum North." *Rutgers Law Journal* 17 (1986): 415.

———. *Slavery and the Founders: Race and Liberty in the Age of Jefferson*. Armonk, N.Y.: M. E. Sharpe, 1996.

———. "The Constitution and the Intentions of the Framers: The Limits of Historical Analysis." *University of Pittsburgh Law Review* 50 (1989): 392–93.

Finnis, John. "Law, Morality, and 'Sexual Orientation.'" *Notre Dame Journal of Law, Ethics, and Public Policy* 9 (1995): 11.

Firestone, Shulamith. *The Dialectic of Sex: The Case for Feminist Revolution*. 1970. London: Woman's Press, 1988.

Fiss, Owen M. "Groups and the Equal Protection Clause." *Philosophy and Public Affairs* 5 (1976): 107.

———. "The Fate of an Idea Whose Time Has Come: Antidiscrimination Law in the Second Decade after *Brown v. Board of Education*." *University of Chicago Law Review* 41 (1974): 742.

Fitzhugh, George. *Cannibals All! or, Slaves without Masters*. Edited by C. Vann Woodward. Cambridge: Harvard University Press, Belknap Press, 1960.

Flax, Jane. *Thinking Fragments: Psychoanalysis, Feminism, and Postmodernism in the Contemporary West*. Berkeley and Los Angeles: University of California Press, 1990.

Flexner, Eleanor. *Century of Struggle: The Woman's Rights Movement in the United States*. Rev. ed. Cambridge: Harvard University Press, Belknap Press, 1975.

Folsom, Ed, ed. *Walt Whitman*. Iowa City: University of Iowa Press, 1994.

Foner, Eric. *Reconstruction: America's Unfinished Revolution, 1863–1877*. New York: Harper & Row, 1988.

———. *Free Soil, Free Labor, Free Men: The Ideology of the Republican Party before the Civil War*. New York: Oxford University Press, 1970.

Foner, Philip S., ed. *Frederick Douglass on Women's Rights*. New York: Da Capo Press, 1992.

———. *The Life and Writings of Frederick Douglass*. 5 vols. New York: International Publishers, 1950–70.

Ford, Clellan S., and Frank A. Beach. *Patterns of Sexual Behavior*. New York: Harper & Row, 1951.

Forster, E. M. *Howards End*. New York: Vintage, 1989.

———. *Maurice*. Toronto: Macmillan, 1971.

———. *Two Cheers for Democracy*. New York: Harcourt, Brace, & World, 1938.

Foster, Lawrence. *Women, Family, and Utopia: Communal Experiments of the*

Shakers, the Oneida Community, and the Mormons. Syracuse: Syracuse University Press, 1991.

Foucault, Michel. *The History of Sexuality.* Translated by Robert Hurley. Vol. 1. New York: Pantheon, 1978.

Fout, John C., ed. *Forbidden History: The State, Society, and the Regulation of Sexuality in Modern Europe.* Chicago: University of Chicago Press, 1992.

Fox-Genovese, Elizabeth. *"Feminism Is Not the Story of My Life": How Today's Feminist Elite Has Lost Touch with the Real Concerns of Women.* New York: Doubleday, 1996.

———. *Feminism without Illusions: A Critique of Individualism.* Chapel Hill: University of North Carolina Press, 1991.

———. *Within the Plantation Household: Black and White Women in the Old South.* Chapel Hill: University of North Carolina Press, 1988.

Franke, Katherine M. "The Central Mistake of Sex Discrimination Law: The Dissaggregation of Sex from Gender." *University of Pennsylvania Law Review* 144 (1995): 1.

Frankenberg, Ruth. *The Social Construction of Whiteness: White Women, Race Matters.* Minneapolis: University of Minnesota Press, 1993.

Franklin, John Hope. *The Militant South, 1800–1861.* Cambridge: Harvard University Press, Belknap Press, 1956.

Franklin, John Hope, and Alfred A. Moss, Jr. *From Slavery to Freedom: A History of Negro Americans.* 6th ed. New York: Knopf, 1988.

Fredrickson, George M. *The Black Image in the White Mind: The Debate on Afro-American Character and Destiny, 1817–1914.* Middletown, Conn.: Wesleyan University Press, 1971.

———. *White Supremacy: A Comparative Study in American and South African History.* Oxford: Oxford University Press, 1981.

Freedman, Estelle B., Barbara C. Gelpi, Susan L. Johnson, and Kathleen M. Weston, eds. *The Lesbian Issue.* Chicago: University of Chicago Press, 1982.

Freeman, Jo. *The Politics of Women's Liberation: A Case Study of an Emerging Social Movement and Its Relation to the Policy Process.* New York: Longman 1975.

Freidel, Frank, ed. *Union Pamphlets of the Civil War, 1861–1865.* Cambridge: Harvard University Press, Belknap Press, 1967.

French, Marilyn. *The War against Women.* London: Penguin, 1992.

Friedan, Betty. *The Feminine Mystique.* 1963. London: Penguin, 1982.

Friedman, Jean E. *The Enclosed Garden: Women and Community in the Evangelical South, 1830–1900.* Chapel Hill: University of North Carolina Press, 1985.

Friedman, Lawrence J. *Gregarious Saints: Self and Community in American Abolitionism, 1830–1870.* Cambridge: Cambridge University Press, 1982.

Frye, Marilyn. *The Politics of Reality: Essays in Feminist Theory.* Trumansburg, N.Y.: Crossing Press, 1983.

———. *Willful Virgin: Essays in Feminism, 1976–1992.* Freedom, Cal.: Crossing Press, 1992.

Fuchs, Victor R., *Women's Quest for Economic Equality.* Cambridge: Harvard University Press, 1988.

Fuller, S. Margaret. *Woman in the Nineteenth Century.* 1845 ed. edited by Madeleine B. Stern. Columbia: University of South Carolina, 1980.

Gager, John A. *The Origins of Anti-Semitism: Attitudes toward Judaism in Pagan and Christian Antiquity.* New York: Oxford University Press, 1983.

Garber, Marjorie. *Vested Interests: Cross-Dressing and Cultural Anxiety.* New York: Routledge, 1992.

———. *Vice Versa: Bisexuality and the Eroticism of Everyday Life.* New York: Simon and Schuster, 1995.

García Lorca, Federico. *Poet in New York.* Translated by Greg Simon and Steven White. New York: Noonday Press, 1988.

Garfield, Deborah M., and Rafia Zafar, eds. *Harriet Jacobs and Incidents in the Life of a Slave Girl.* Cambridge: Cambridge University Press, 1996.

Garrison, Marsha."Good Intentions Gone Awry: The Impact of New York's Equitable Distribution Law on Divorce Outcomes." *Brooklyn Law Review* 57 (1991): 621.

Garrison, Wendell Phillips, and Francis Jackson Garrison. *William Lloyd Garrison, 1805–1879.* 4 vols. New York: Century Co., 1889.

Garrison, William Lloyd. *Selections from the Writings and Speeches of William Lloyd Garrison.* Boston: R. F. Wallcut, 1852.

———. *Thoughts on African Colonization.* 1832. New York: Arno Press and The New York Times, 1968.

Gates, Jr., Henry Louis, ed. *Frederick Douglass: Autobiographies.* New York: The Library of America, 1994.

Geinapp, William E. *The Origins of the Republican Party, 1852–1956.* New York: Oxford University Press, 1987.

Genovese, Eugene D. *From Rebellion to Revolution: Afro-American Slave Revolts in the Making of the Modern World.* Baton Rouge: Louisiana State University Press, 1979.

———. *Roll, Jordan, Roll: The World the Slaves Made.* New York: Vintage Books, 1974.

———. *The World the Slaveholders Made.* Middletown, Conn.: Wesleyan University Press, 1979.

George, Robert P. and Gerard V. Bradley. "Marriage and the Liberal Imagination." *Georgetown Law Journal* 84 (1995): 301.

Giddens, Anthony. *The Transformation of Intimacy: Sexuality, Love, and Eroticism in Modern Societies.* Cambridge, U.K.: Polity, 1992.

Giddings, Paula. *When and Where I Enter: The Impact of Black Woman on Race and Sex in America.* New York: William Morrow, 1984.

Gide, André. *Corydon.* Translated by Richard Howard. New York: Farrar, Straus, Giroux, 1983.

———. *If I Die. . .* Translated by Dorothy Bussy. London: Penguin, 1977.

Gilfoyle, Timothy J. *City of Eros: New York City, Prostitution, and the Commercialization of Sex, 1790–1920.* New York: W. W. Norton, 1992.

Gilman, Charlotte Perkins. "Dr. Weininger's 'Sex and Character.'" *The Critic* 48, no. 5. (May 1906): 387–417.

———. *Women and Economics: A Study of the Economic Relation Between Men and Women as a Factor in Social Evolution.* 1898. Edited by Carl N. Degler. New York: Harper & Row, 1966.

Gilman, Sander L. *Difference and Pathology: Stereotypes of Sexuality, Race, and Madness.* Ithaca: Cornell University Press, 1985.

―――. *Disease and Representation: Images of Illness from Madness to AIDS.* Ithaca: Cornell University Press, 1988.

―――. *Freud, Race, and Gender.* Princeton: Princeton University Press, 1993.

―――. *Jewish Self-Hatred: Anti-Semitism and the Hidden Language of the Jews.* Baltimore: Johns Hopkins University Press, 1986.

Gilmore, David D. *Manhood in the Making: Cultural Concepts of Masculinity.* New Haven: Yale University Press, 1990.

Godwin, William. *Memoirs of the Author of a Vindication of the Rights of Woman.* London: J. Johnson, 1798.

Goldin, Claudia, *Understanding the Gender Gap: An Economic History of American Women.* New York: Oxford University Press, 1990.

Goldman, Emma. *Anarchism and Other Essays.* Edited by Richard Drinnon. New York: Dover, 1969.

―――. *The Traffic in Women and Other Essays on Feminism.* Edited by Alisx Shulman. New York: Times Change Press, 1970.

Goldman, Nancy Loring. *Female Soldiers—Combatants or Noncombatants?* Westport, Conn.: Greenwood Press, 1982.

Goldstein, Anne B. "History, Homosexuality, and Political Values: Searching for the Hidden Determinants of *Bowers v. Hardwick.*" *Yale Law Journal* 97 (1988): 1073.

―――. "Reasoning about Homosexuality: A Commentary on Janet Halley's 'Reasoning about Sodomy: Act and Identity in and after *Bowers v. Hardwick.*'" *Virginia Law Review* 79 (1993): 1781.

Gomez, Jose. "The Public Expression of Lesbian/Gay Personhood as Protected Speech." *Law and Inequality* 1 (1983): 121.

Gordon, Linda. *Woman's Body, Woman's Right: A Social History of Birth Control in America.* New York: Penguin, 1976.

Gordon, Sarah B. "'The Twin Relic of Barbarism': A Legal History of Anti-Polygamy in Nineteenth-Century America." Ph.D. diss., Princeton University, History Department, June 1995.

Gosse, Sir Edmund, and Thomas James Wise, eds. *The Complete Works of Algernon Charles Swinburne.* Vol. 2. London: William Heinemann, 1925.

Gossett, Thomas F. *Race: The History of an Idea in America.* New York: Schocken Books, 1965.

Gougeon, Len. *Virtue's Hero: Emerson, Antislavery, and Reform.* Athens: University of Georgia Press, 1990.

Gould, Stephen Jay. *The Mismeasure of Man.* New York: W. W. Norton, 1981.

Graham, Sara Hunter. *Woman Suffrage and the New Democracy.* New Haven: Yale University Press, 1996.

Grant, Jacquelyn. *White Women's Christ and Black Women's Jesus: Feminist Christology and Womanist Response.* Atlanta: Scholars Press, 1989.

Grant, Madison. *The Passing of the Great Race or The Racial Basis of European History.* New York: Charles Scribner's Sons, 1919.

Grant, Ruth W. *John Locke's Liberalism.* Chicago: University of Chicago Press, 1987.

Green, Peter. *Classical Bearings: Interpreting Ancient History and Culture.* New York: Thames and Hudson, 1989.

Green, Richard. *Sexual Science and the Law*. Cambridge: Harvard University Press, 1992.

Greenberg, David. *The Construction of Homosexuality*. Chicago: University of Chicago Press, 1988.

Greenberg, Jack. *Crusaders in the Courts: How a Dedicated Band of Lawyers Fought for the Civil Rights Revolution*. New York: BasicBooks, 1994.

Greenberg, Kenneth S. *Masters and Statesman: The Political Culture of American Slavery*. Baltimore: The Johns Hopkins University Press, 1985.

Greene, Dana, ed. *Lucretia Mott: Her Complete Speeches and Sermons*. New York: Edwin Mellen Press, 1980.

Griffith, Elisabeth. *In Her Own Right: The Life of Elizabeth Cady Stanton*. New York: Oxford University Press, 1984.

Grimke, Angelina. *Appeal to the Women of the Nominally Free States*. New York: William S. Dorr, 1837.

Grimke, Archibald H. *William Lloyd Garrison: The Abolitionist*. New York: Funk & Wagnal, 1891.

———. *William Lloyd Garrison: The Abolitionist*. New York: Negro Universities Press, 1969.

Gross, Larry. *Contested Closets: The Politics and Ethics of Outing*. Minneapolis: University of Minnesota Press, 1993.

Grosskurth, Phyllis, ed., *The Memoirs of John Addington Symonds*. London: Hutchinson, 1984.

Gunther, Gerald. "Newer Equal Protection." *Harvard Law Review* 86 (1972): 1.

———. "The Subtle Vices of the 'Passive Virtues'—a Comment on Principle and Expediency in Judicial Review." *Columbia Law Review* 64 (1964): 1.

Gutman, Herbert G. *The Black Family in Slavery and Freedom, 1750–1925*. New York: Vintage Books, 1976.

Haaland, Bonnie. *Emma Goldman: Sexuality and the Impurity of the State*. Montreal: Black Rose Books, 1993.

Hacker, Andrew. *Two Nations: Black and White, Separate, Hostile, Unequal*. New York: Charles Scribner's Sons, 1992.

Hall, Radclyffe. *The Well of Loneliness*. 1928. London: Virago Press, 1982.

Haller, Jr., John S. *Outcasts from Evolution: Scientific Attitudes of Racial Inferiority, 1859–1900*. New York: McGraw-Hill, 1971.

Halley, Janet E. "Reasoning about Sodomy: Act and Identity in and after *Bowers v. Hardwick*." *Virginia Law Review* 79 (1993): 1721.

———. "Sexual Orientation and the Politics of Biology: A Critique of the Argument from Immutability." *Stanford Law Review* 46 (1994): 503.

———. "The Politics of the Closet: Towards Equal Protection for Gay, Lesbian, and Bisexual Identity." *UCLA Law Review* 37 (1989): 915.

———. "The Status/Conduct Distinction in the 1993 Revisions to Military Anti-Gay Policy." *GLQ: A Journal of Lesbian and Gay Studies* 3 (1996): 159–252.

Hallowell, Anna. *James and Lucretia Mott Life and Letters*. Boston: Houghton, Mifflin, 1884.

Halperin, David M. *One Hundred Years of Homosexuality and Other Essays on Greek Love*. New York: Routledge, 1990.

Halperin, David M., John J. Winkler, and Froma I. Zeitlin, eds. *Before Sexuality:*

The Construction of Erotic Experience in the Ancient Greek World. Princeton: Princeton University Press, 1990.

Hamilton, Edith, and Huntington Cairns, eds. *The Collected Dialogues of Plato.* New York: Pantheon, 1961.

Harding, Sandra. *The Science Question in Feminism.* Ithaca: Cornell University Press, 1986.

———. *Whose Science? Whose Lives?: Thinking from Women's Lives.* Ithaca: Cornell University Press, 1991.

Harding, Sandra, and Merill B. Hintikka, eds. *Discovering Reality: Feminist Perspectives on Epistemology, Metaphysics, Methodology, and Philosophy of Science.* Dordrecht: D. Reidel, 1983.

Harris, Angela P. "Race and Essentialism in Feminist Legal Theory." *Stanford Law Review* 542 (1990): 81.

Harris, Henry, ed. *Identity.* Oxford: Clarendon Press, 1995.

Harris, Seth. "Permitting Prejudice to Govern: Equal Protection, Military Deference, and the Exclusion of Lesbians and Gay Men from the Military." *New York University Review of Law and Social Change* 17 (1989–90): 171.

Harris, Trudier, ed. *Selected Works of Ida B. Wells-Barnett.* New York: Oxford University Press, 1991.

Harrowitz, Nancy A., and Barbara Hyams, eds. *Jews and Gender: Responses to Otto Weininger.* Philadelphia: Temple University Press, 1996.

Hart, H. L. A. *Law, Liberty, and Morality.* Stanford: Stanford University Press, 1963.

———. "Social Solidarity and the Enforcement of Morals." *University of Chicago Law Review* 35 (1967): 1.

"Hawaii Seeks Law to Block Gay Marriage." *New York Times,* 18 April 1997, A15.

Hay, Harry. *Radically Gay.* Edited by Will Roscoe. Boston: Beacon Press, 1996.

Hedrick, Joan D. *Harriet Beecher Stowe: A Life.* New York: Oxford University Press, 1994.

Henry, Sherrye. *The Deep Divide: Why American Women Resist Equality.* New York: Macmillan, 1994.

Herdt, Gilbert. *Third Sex, Third Gender: Beyond Sexual Dimorphism in Culture and History.* New York: Zone Books, 1994.

Herek, Gregory M., Jared. B. Jobe, Ralph M. Carney. *Out in Force: Sexual Orientation and the Military.* Chicago: University of Chicago Press, 1996.

Herman, Didi. *The Antigay Agenda: Orthodox Vision and the Christian Right.* Chicago: University of Chicago Press, 1997.

Herndon, William H., and Jesse W. Weik. *Life of Lincoln.* New York: Da Capo, 1983.

Hersh, Blanche Glassman. *The Slavery of Sex: Feminist-Abolitionists in America.* Urbana: University of Illinois Press, 1978.

Hertzberg, Arthur. *The French Enlightenment and the Jews.* New York: Columbia University Press, 1990.

Higginbotham, Evelyn Brooks, *Righteous Discontent: The Women's Movement in the Black Baptist Church, 1880–1920.* Cambridge: Harvard University Press, 1993.

Higham, John. *Strangers in the Land: Patterns of American Nativism, 1860–1925.* New Brunswick, N.J.: Rutgers University Press, 1988.

Hilberg, Raul. *The Destruction of the European Jews.* 3 vols. New York: Holmes & Meier, 1985.

Hirsch, Marianne, and Evelyn Fox Keller. *Conflicts in Feminism.* New York: Routledge, 1990.

Hitler, Adolf. *Mein Kampf.* New York: Reynal & Hitchcock, 1940.

Hoagland, Sarah Lucia. *Lesbian Ethics: Toward New Value.* Palo Alto: Institute of Lesbian Ethics, 1988.

Hobson, Barbara Meil. *Uneasy Virtue: The Politics of Prostitution and the American Reform Tradition.* Chicago: University of Chicago Press, 1990.

Hoemann, George H. *What Hath God Wrought: The Embodiment of Freedom in the Thirteenth Amendment.* New York: Garland Publishing, Inc., 1987.

Hoffman, Ross J. S., and Paul Levack, eds. *Burke's Politics.* New York: Knopf, 1959.

Hole, Judith, and Ellen Levine. *Rebirth of Feminism.* New York: Quadrangle, 1971.

Holmes, Oliver Wendell. "The Path of the Law." *Harvard Law Review* 10 (1897): 45.

Honore, Tony. *Sex Law.* London: Duckworth, 1978.

hooks, bell. *Ain't I a Woman: Black Women and Feminism.* Boston: South End Press, 1981.

———. *Feminist Theory: From Margin to Center.* Boston: South End Press, 1984.

———. *Killing Rage: Ending Racism.* New York: Henry Holt, 1995.

Hopkins, Samuel. *Timely Articles on Slavery.* 1776. Miami: Mnemosyne Publishing Inc., 1969.

Horsman, Reginald. *Race and Manifest Destiny: The Origins of American Racial Anglo-Saxonism.* Cambridge: Harvard University Press, 1981.

Hosmer, William. *The Higher Law in its Relations to Civil Government.* Auburn: Derby & Miller, 1852.

Howe, Daniel Walker. "Henry David Thoreau on the Duty of Civil Disobedience." An Inaugural Lecture delivered before the University of Oxford on 21 May 1990. Oxford: Clarendon Press, 1990.

———. *The Unitarian Conscience: Harvard Moral Philosophy, 1805–1861.* Middletown, Conn.: Wesleyan University Press, 1988.

Huggins, Nathan, ed. *W. E. B. DuBois: Writings.* New York: The Library of America, 1986.

Hume, David. *Essays Moral Political Literary.* Edited by Eugene F. Miller. Indianapolis: LibertyClassics, 1987.

Humez, Jean M. *Mother's First-Born Daughters: Early Shaker Writings on Women and Religion.* Bloomington: Indiana University Press, 1993.

Hunter, Nan D. "Identity, Speech, and Equality." *Virginia Law Review* 79 (1993): 1695.

———. "Life after *Hardwick.*" *Harvard Civil Rights–Civil Liberties Law Review* 27 (1992): 531.

Hunter, Nan D., Sherryl E. Michaelson, and Thomas B. Stoddard. *The Rights of Lesbians and Gay Men.* 3d ed. Carbondale and Edwardsville: Southern Illinois University Press, 1992.

Hurlbut, E. P. *Essays on Human Rights and Their Political Guaranties.* New York: Greeley & McElrath, 1845.

Hutcheson, Francis, *A Short Introduction to Moral Philosophy*. 1747. Hildesheim: Georg Olms Verlagsbuchhandlung, 1969.

———. *A System of Moral Philosophy*. 1755. New York: Augustus M. Kelley, 1968.

———. *A System of Moral Philosophy*. 1755. Hildesheim: Georg Olms Verlagsbuchhandlung, 1969.

Hutchinson, George. *The Harlem Renaissance in Black and White*. Cambridge: Harvard University Press, 1995.

Hyman, Harold M. *A More Perfect Union: The Impact of the Civil War and Reconstruction on the Constitution*. New York: Knopf, 1973.

Hyman, Harold M., and William M. Wiecek. *Equal Justice under Law: Constitutional Development, 1835–1975*. New York: Harper & Row, 1982.

Ingle, H. Larry. *First Among Friends: George Fox and the Creation of Quakerism*. New York: Oxford University Press, 1994.

Inikori, Joseph E., and Stanley L. Engerman, eds. *The Atlantic Slave Trade: Effects on Economies, Societies, and Peoples in Africa, the Americas, and Europe*. Durham: Duke University Press, 1992.

Ireland, Patricia. *What Women Want*. New York: Dutton, 1996.

Jacobs, Harriet A. *Incidents in the Life of a Slave Girl Written by Herself*. Edited by Jean Fagan Yellin. Cambridge: Harvard University Press, 1987.

James, Henry. *The Bostonians*. 1885–86. London: Penguin, 1986.

James, Henry, Horace Greeley, and Stephen Pearl Andrews. *Love, Marriage, and Divorce*. 1853. New York: Source Book Press, 1972.

Jay, William. *Inquiry into the Character and Tendency of the American Colonization, and American Anti-Slavery Societies*. 1835. In William Jay, ed., *Miscellaneous Writings on Slavery*. New York: Negro Universities Press, 1968.

Jefferson, Thomas. *Notes on the State of Virginia*. Edited by William Peden. New York: W. W. Norton, 1982.

Jeffreys, Sheila, ed. *The Sexuality Debates*. New York: Routledge & Kegan Paul 1987.

Johannsen, Robert W. *The Lincoln-Douglas Debates of 1858*. New York: Oxford University Press, 1965.

Johnson, Michael P. "Twisted Truth." *The New Republic*, 4 November 1996, 37–41.

Johnson, Paul E., and Sean Wilentz. *The Kingdom of Matthias*. New York: Oxford University Press, 1994.

Johnston, Johanna. *Mrs. Satan: The Incredible Saga of Victoria C. Woodhull*. New York: G. P. Putnam's Sons, 1967.

Jordan, Mark D. *The Invention of Sodomy in Christian Theology*. Chicago: University of Chicago Press, 1997.

Jordan, Winthrop D. *White over Black: American Attitudes toward the Negro, 1550–1812*. New York: W. W. Norton, 1977.

Kalven, Jr., Harry. *The Negro and the First Amendment*. Chicago: University of Chicago Press, 1965.

Kant, Immanuel. *Observations on the Feeling of the Beautiful and Sublime*. Edited by John T. Goldthwait. Berkeley and Los Angeles: University of California Press, 1965.

Kaplan, Justin. *Walt Whitman: A Life*. New York: Simon and Schuster, 1980.

————, ed. *Walt Whitman: Complete Poetry and Collected Prose.* New York: Library of America, 1982.

Karcher, Carolyn L. *The First Woman in the Republic: A Cultural Biography of Lydia Maria Child.* Durham: Duke University Press, 1994.

Karst, Kenneth I. "The Pursuit of Manhood and the Segregation of the Armed Forces." *UCLA Law Review* 38 (1991): 499.

Kateb, George. *The Inner Ocean: Individualism and Democratic Culture.* Ithaca: Cornell University Press, 1992.

Katyal, Neal Kumar. "Men Who Own Women: A Thirteenth Amendment Critique of Forced Prostitution." *Yale Law Journal* 103 (1993): 791.

Katz, Jacob. *From Prejudice to Destruction.* Cambridge: Harvard University Press, 1980.

————. *The Darker Side of Genius.* Hanover: University Press of New England, 1986.

Katz, Jonathan Ned. *Gay American History: Lesbians and Gay Men in the U.S.A.* New York: Meridian, 1992.

Kelly, Joan. *Women, History, and Theory.* Chicago: University of Chicago Press, 1984.

Kennedy, Elizabeth Lapovsky, and Madeline D. Davis. *Boots of Leather, Slippers of Gold: The History of a Lesbian Community.* New York: Routledge, 1993.

Kerber, Linda K. *Women of the Republic: Intellect and Ideology in Revolutionary America.* New York: W. W. Norton, 1980.

Kern, Louis J. *An Ordered Love: Sex Roles and Sexuality in Victorian Utopias— The Shakers, the Mormons, and the Oneida Community.* Chapel Hill: University of North Carolina Press, 1981.

Kerr, Andrea Moore. *Lucy Stone: Speaking Out for Equality.* New Brunswick: N.J.: Rutgers University Press, 1992.

Key, Ellen. *The Renaissance of Motherhood.* 1914. New York: Source Book Press, 1970.

Kimmel, Michael. *Manhood in America: A Cultural History.* New York: Free Press, 1996.

Kitzinger, Celia. *The Social Construction of Lesbianism.* London: Sage, 1987.

Klein, Herbert S. *Slavery in the Americas: A Comparative Study of Virginia and Cuba.* Chicago: Elephant Paperbacks, 1989.

Klineberg, Otto. *Race Differences.* New York: Harper & Brothers, 1935.

Knox, Melissa. *Oscar Wilde: A Long and Lovely Suicide.* New Haven: Yale University Press, 1994.

Koestenbaum, Wayne. *The Queen's Throat: Opera, Homosexuality, and the Mystery of Desire.* New York: Poseidon Press, 1993.

Kolchin, Peter. *American Slavery, 1619–1877.* New York: Hill and Wang, 1987.

————. *Unfree Labor: American Slavery and Russian Serfdom.* Cambridge: Harvard University Press, 1987.

Kopkind, Andrew. *The Thirty Years' War: Dispatches and Diversions of a Radical Journalist, 1965–1994.* Edited by JoAnn Wypijewski. London: Verson, 1995.

Koppelman, Andrew. *Antidiscrimination Law and Social Equality.* New Haven: Yale University Press, 1996.

————. "Forced Labor: A Thirteenth Amendment Defense of Abortion." *Northwestern University Law Review* 84 (1990): 480.

————. "The Miscegenation Analogy: Sodomy Law as Sex Discrimination." *Yale Law Journal* 98 (1988): 145.

————. "Why Discrimination against Lesbians and Gay Men Is Sex Discrimination." *New York University Law Review* 69 (1994): 197.

Kraditor, Aileen S. *Means and Ends in American Abolitionism: Garrison and His Critics on Strategy and Tactics, 1834–1850.* New York: Pantheon, 1969.

————. *The Ideas of the Woman Suffrage Movement, 1890–1920.* New York: Columbia University Pres, 1965.

Krafft-Ebing, Richard von. *Psychopathia Sexualis.* 1886. Translated by Franklin S. Klaf. New York: Bell Publishing Co., 1965.

Kymlicka, Will. *Liberalism, Community, and Culture.* Oxford: Clarendon Press, 1989.

Lane, Ann J., ed. *The Debate over Slavery: Stanley Elkins and His Critics.* Urbana: University of Illinois Press, 1971.

Langmuir, Gavin I. *History, Religion, and Antisemitism.* Berkeley and Los Angeles: University of California Press, 1990.

————. *Toward a Definition of Antisemitism.* Berkeley and Los Angeles: University of California Press, 1990.

Laqueur, Thomas. *Making Sex: Body and Gender from the Greeks to Freud.* Cambridge: Harvard University Press, 1990.

Large, David C., and William Weber, eds. *Wagnerism in European Culture and Politics.* Ithaca: Cornell University Press, 1984.

Lauritsen, John, and David Thorstad. *The Early Homosexual Rights Movement. 1864–1935.* New York: Times Change Press, 1974.

Law, Sylvia A. "Homosexuality and the Social Meaning of Gender." *Wisconsin Law Review* (1988): 187.

————. "Women, Work, Welfare, and the Preservation of Patriarchy." *University of Pennsylvania Law Review* 131 (1983): 1249.

Laycock, Douglas. "Free Exercise and the Religious Freedom Restoration Act." *Fordham Law Review* 62 (1994): 883.

Lebsock, Suzanne. "Across the Great Divide: Women and Politics, 1890–1920." In *Women, Politics, and Change in Twentieth-Century America,* edited by Louise Tilly and Patricia Gurin. New York: Russell Sage Foundation, 1990.

Leeming, David. *James Baldwin.* New York: Knopf, 1994.

Lerner, Gerda. *The Creation of Feminist Consciousness: From the Middle Ages to 1870.* New York: Oxford University Press, 1993.

————. *The Creation of Patriarchy.* New York: Oxford University Press, 1986.

————. *The Grimke Sisters from South Carolina: Pioneers for Woman's Rights and Abolition.* New York: Schocken Books, 1971.

Lerner, Michael. *The Socialism of Fools: Anti-Semitism on the Left.* Oakland, Cal.: Tikkun Books, 1992.

LeVay, Simon. *Queer Science: The Use and Abuse of Research into Homosexuality.* Cambridge: MIT Press, 1996.

Levy, Leonard W. *Blasphemy: Verbal Offense against the Sacred from Moses to Salman Rushdie.* New York: Knopf, 1993.

Levy, Leonard W. *The Establishment Clause: Religion and the First Amendment.* New York: Macmillan, 1986.

Lewes, Kenneth. *The Psychoanalytic Theory of Male Homosexuality.* New York: Simon and Schuster, 1988.

Lewis, David Levering. *W. E. B. Du Bois: Biography of a Race, 1868–1919.* New York: Henry Holt, 1993.

Lieber, Francis. *Manual of Political Ethics.* 2 vols. Boston: Little, Brown, 1838–39.

Linde, Hans A. "When Initiative Lawmaking Is Not 'Republican Government': The Campaign against Homosexuality." *Oregon Law Review* 72 (1993): 19.

Litwack, Leon F. *Been in the Storm So Long: The Aftermath of Slavery.* New York: Vintage Books, 1979.

———. *North of Slavery: The Negro in the Free States, 1790–1860.* Chicago: University of Chicago Press, 1961.

Livingood, J. M., ed. *National Institute of Mental Health Task Force on Homosexuality.* Washington, D.C.: U.S. Government Printing Office, 1972.

Locke, John. *The First Treatise of Government.* In John Locke, *Two Treatises of Government.* Edited by Peter Laslett. Cambridge: Cambridge University Press, 1960.

———. *The Works of John Locke.* 10 vols. London: Tomas Tegg et al., 1823.

Loewenberg, Bert James, and Ruth Bogin, eds. *Black Women in Nineteenth-Century American Life.* University Park and London: The Pennsylvania State University Press, 1976.

Lofgren, Charles A. *The Plessy Case.* New York: Oxford University Press, 1987.

Lourde, Audre. *Sister Outsider: Essays and Speeches.* Freedom, Cal.: Crossing Press, 1983.

Lovejoy, Arthur O. *The Great Chain of Being.* Cambridge: Harvard University Press, 1964.

Lowell, James Russell, *The Anti-Slavery Papers of James Russell Lowell.* Vol. 1. Boston: Houghton Mifflin, 1902.

Lucey, Michael. *Gide's Bent: Sexuality, Politics, Writing.* New York: Oxford University Press, 1995.

Lumpkin, Katharine Du Pre. *The Emancipation of Angelina Grimke.* Chapel Hill: University of North Carolina Press, 1974.

Lundy, Benjamin. *The Poetical Works of Elizabeth Margaret Chandler.* Philadelphia: Lemuel Howell, 1836.

Lystra, Karen. *Searching the Heart: Women, Men, and Romantic Love in Nineteenth-Century America.* New York: Oxford University Press, 1989.

Macedo, Stephen. "Homosexuality and the Conservative Mind." *Georgetown Law Journal* 283 (1995): 61.

———. "Reply to Critics." *Georgetown Law Journal* 83 (1995): 329.

MacKinnon, Catharine A. *Feminism Unmodified: Discourses on Life and Law.* Cambridge: Harvard University Press, 1987.

———. *Only Words.* Cambridge: Harvard University Press, 1993.

———. *Toward a Feminist Theory of the State.* Cambridge: Harvard University Press, 1989.

Mansbridge, Jane J. *Why We Lost the ERA*. Chicago: University of Chicago Press, 1986.

Marcus, Isabel. "Locked In and Locked Out: Reflections on the History of Divorce Law Reform in New York State." *Buffalo Law Review* 37 (1989): 375.

Marilley, Suzanne M. *Woman Suffrage and the Origins of Liberal Feminism in the United States, 1820–1920*. Cambridge: Harvard University Press, 1996.

Mason, Michael. *The Making of Victorian Sexual Attitudes*. Oxford: Oxford University Press, 1994.

Mason, Michael. *The Making of Victorian Sexuality*. Oxford: Oxford University Press, 1994.

Massey, Douglas S., and Nancy A. Denton. *American Apartheid: Segregation and the Making of the Underclass*. Cambridge: Harvard University Press, 1993.

Mathews, Donald G., and Jane Sherron De Hart. *Sex, Gender, and the Politics of ERA: A State and the Nation*. New York: Oxford University Press, 1990.

Matthews, Glenna. *"Just a Housewife" The Rise and Fall of Domesticity in America*. New York: Oxford University Press, 1987.

May, Elaine Tyler. *Barren in the Promised Land: Childless Americans and the Pursuit of Happiness*. New York: Basic Books, 1995.

McConnell, Joyce E. "Beyond Metaphor: Battered Women, Involuntary Servitude and the Thirteenth Amendment." *Yale Journal of Law and Feminism* 4 (1992): 207.

McCord, Louisa. "Diversity of the Races: Its Bearing upon Negro Slavery." *Southern Quarterly Review* 19 (April 1851): 392–419.

———. "Enfranchisement of Woman." *Southern Quarterly Review* 21 (April 1852): 233–341.

[McCord, Louisa]. "Uncle Tom's Cabin." *Southern Quarterly Review* 7, n.s., no. 13 (January 1853): 81–120.

McFeely, William S., *Frederick Douglass*. New York: W. W. Norton, 1991.

McGlen, Nancy E., and Karen O'Connor. *Women's Rights: The Struggle for Equality in the Nineteenth and Twentieth Centuries*. New York: Praeger, 1983.

McKitrick, Eric L. *Andrew Johnson and Reconstruction*. New York: Oxford University Press, 1960.

———, ed. *Slavery Defended*. Englewood Cliffs, N.J.: Prentice-Hall, 1963.

McLindon, James B. "Separate But Unequal: The Economic Disaster of Divorce of Women and Children." *Family Law Quarterly* 21 (1987): 351–409.

McNeil, Genna Rae. *Groundwork: Charles Hamilton Houston and the Struggle for Civil Rights*. Philadelphia: University of Pennsylvania Press, 1983.

McNeill, John J. *The Church and the Homosexual*. Kansas City: Sheed, Andrews & McMeel, 1976.

McPherson, James M. *The Abolitionist Legacy: From Reconstruction to the NAACP*. Princeton: Princeton University Press, 1975.

———. *The Struggle for Equality: Abolitionists and the Negro in the Civil War and Reconstruction*. Princeton: Princeton University Press, 1964.

Melder, Keith E. *Beginnings of Sisterhood: The American Woman's Rights Movement, 1800–1850*. New York: Schocken, 1977.

Meltzer, Milton, and Patricia G. Holland, eds. *Lydia Maria Child: Selected Letters, 1817–1880*. Amherst: University of Massachusetts Press, 1982.

Meyer, D. H. *The Instructed Conscience: The Shaping of the American National Ethic.* Philadelphia: University of Pennsylvania Press, 1972.

Meyerson, Denise. *False Consciousness.* Oxford: Clarendon Press, 1991.

Michael, Robert T. et al. *Sex in America: A Definitive Survey.* Boston: Little, Brown, 1994.

Michelman, Frank. "Foreword: On Protecting the Poor through the Fourteenth Amendment." *Harvard Law Review* 83 (1969): 7–59.

Mill, John Stuart. *On Liberty.* 1859. Edited by Alburey Castell. New York: Appleton-Century-Crofts, 1947.

Mill, John Stuart, and Harriet Taylor Mill. *Essays on Sex Equality.* Edited by Alice S. Rossi. Chicago: University of Chicago Press, 1970.

Miller, Perry. *The New England Mind: the Seventeenth Century.* Cambridge: Harvard University Press, 1939.

Miller, William Lee. *Arguing About Slavery: The Great Battle in the United States Congress.* New York: Knopf, 1996.

———. *The First Liberty: Religion and the American Republic.* New York: Knopf, 1987.

Millett, Kate. *Sexual Politics.* New York: Avon, 1969.

Mink, Gwendolyn. *The Wages of Motherhood: Inequality in the Welfare State, 1917–1942.* Ithaca: Cornell University Press, 1995.

Mitchell, Brian. *Weak Link: The Feminization of the American Military.* Washington, D.C.: Regnery Gateway, 1989.

Mixner, David. *Stranger among Friends.* New York: Bantam Books, 1996.

Mohr, Richard D. *A More Perfect Union: Why Straight America Must Stand Up for Gay Rights.* Boston: Beacon Press, 1994.

———. *Gay Ideas: Outing and Other Controversies.* Boston: Beacon Press, 1992.

———. *Gays/Justice: A Study of Ethics, Society, and Law.* New York: Columbia University Press, 1988.

Monette, Paul. *Becoming a Man: Half a Life Story.* New York: HarperCollins, 1993.

Money, John, and A. Ehrhardt. *Man & Woman, Boy & Girl.* Baltimore: Johns Hopkins University Press, 1972.

Money, J.; J. G. Hampson; and J. L. Hampson. "An Examination of Some Basic Sexual Concepts: The Evidence of Human Hermaphroditism." *Bulletin of Johns Hopkins Hospital* 97 (1955): 301.

Monk, Ray. *Ludwig Wittgenstein: The Duty of Genius.* New York: Free Press, 1990.

Montesquieu, Baron de. *The Spirit of the Laws.* Translated by Thomas Nugent. New York: Hafner Publishing Co., 1949.

Moon, Michael. *Disseminating Whitman: Revision and Corporeality in Leaves of Grass.* Cambridge: Harvard University Press, 1991.

Moore, R. I. *The Formation of a Persecuting Society: Power and Deviance in Western Europe, 950–1250.* Oxford: Basil Blackwell, 1987.

Morgan, Edmund S. *American Slavery American Freedom.* New York: W. W. Norton, 1975.

Morris, Aldon D. *The Origins of the Civil Rights Movement: Black Communities Organizing for Change.* New York: Free Press, 1984.

Morris, Madeline. "By Force of Arms: Rape, War and Military Culture." *Duke Law Journal* 45 (1996): 651.

Mosse, George L. *Nationalism and Sexuality: Middle-Class Morality and Sexual Norms in Modern Europe.* Madison: University of Wisconsin Press, 1985.

———. *The Image of Man: The Creation of Modern Masculinity.* New York: Oxford University Press, 1996.

Munger, Theodore T. *Horace Bushnell: Preacher and Theologian.* Boston: Houghton, Mifflin, 1899.

Murphy, Francis, ed. *Walt Whitman: The Complete Poems.* Harmondsworth: Penguin, 1975.

Murphy, T. F., ed. *Gay Ethics: Controversies in Outing, Civil Rights, and Sexual Science.* New York: Harrington Park Press, 1994.

Myrdal, Gunnar. *An American Dilemma: The Negro Problem and Modern Democracy.* 1944. 2 vols. New York: Pantheon Books, 1972.

Nava, Michael, and Robert Dawidoff. *Created Equal: Why Gay Rights Matter to America.* New York: St. Martin's Press, 1994.

Nelson, William E. *The Fourteenth Amendment: From Political Principle to Judicial Doctrine.* Cambridge: Harvard University Press, 1988.

Netanyahu, Benzion. *The Origins of the Inquisition in Fifteenth Century Spain.* New York: Random House, 1995.

Niblock, John F. "Anti-Gay Initiatives: A Call for Heightened Judicial Scrutiny." *UCLA Law Review* 141 (1993): 53.

Nicholson, Linda J. *Gender and History: The Limits of Social Theory in the Age of the Family.* New York: Columbia University Press, 1986.

Nieman, Donald G. *Promises to Keep: African-Americans and the Constitutional Order, 1776 to the Present.* New York: Oxford University Press, 1991.

Noddings, Nel. *Caring: A Feminine Approach to Ethics and Moral Education.* Berkeley and Los Angeles: University of California Press, 1984.

———. *Women and Evil.* Berkeley and Los Angeles: University of California Press, 1989.

Norton, Charles Eliot, ed. *Orations and Addresses of George William Curtis.* New York: Harper & Brothers, 1894.

Norton, Mary Beth. *Founding Mothers and Fathers: Gendered Power and the Forming of American Society.* New York: Knopf, 1996.

Note, "Constitutional Limits on Anti-Gay-Rights Initiatives." *Harvard Law Review* 106 (1993): 1905.

Note, "Jones v. Mayer: The Thirteenth Amendment and the Federal Anti-Discrimination Laws." *Columbia Law Review* 69 (1969): 1019.

Note, "The Constitutional Status of Sexual Orientation: Homosexuality as a Suspect Classification." *Harvard Law Review* 98 (1985): 1285, 1303.

Note, "The 'New' Thirteenth Amendment: A Preliminary Analysis." *Harvard Law Review* 82 (1969): 1294.

Nussbaum, Martha. "Objectification." *Philosophy and Public Affairs* 24 (1995): 249.

Nye, Russel B. *Fettered Freedom: Civil Liberties and the Slavery Controversy, 1830–1860.* East Lansing: Michigan State College Park, 1949.

O'Neill, Onora. *Constructions of Reason.* Cambridge: Cambridge University Press, 1989.

O'Neill, William L. *Everyone Was Brave: The Rise and Fall of Feminism in America.* Chicago: Quadrangle Books, 1969.

————, ed. *The Woman Movement: Feminism in the United States and England.* Chicago: Quadrangle, 1969.

Okin, Susan Moller. "Economic Equality after Divorce." *Dissent* (summer 1991), 383.

————. *Justice, Gender, and the Family.* New York: Basic Books, 1989.

Olsen, Frances. "Statutory Rape: A Feminist Critique of Rights." *Texas Law Review* 63 (1984): 387–432.

Ostriker, Alicia Suskin, *Feminist Revision and the Bible.* Oxford: Blackwell, 1993.

Pagden, Anthony. *The Fall of Natural Man: The American Indians and the Origins of Comparative Ethnology.* Cambridge: Cambridge University Press, 1982.

Pagels, Elaine. *Adam, Eve, and the Serpent.* New York: Random House, 1988.

————. *The Origin of Satan.* New York: Random House, 1996.

Paglia, Camille. *Sex, Art, and American Culture: Essays.* New York: Vintage Books, 1992.

————. *Sexual Personae: Art and Decadence from Nefertiti to Emily Dickinson.* New York: Vintage, 1991.

————. *Vamps and Tramps: New Essays.* New York: Vintage Books, 1994.

Painter, Nell Irvin. *Sojourner Truth: A Life, A Symbol.* New York: W. W. Norton, 1996.

Parker, Andrew, Mary Russo, Doris Sommer, and Patricia Yaeger, eds. *Nationalisms and Sexualities.* New York: Routledge, 1992.

Parker, Theodore. *The Public Function of Woman.* London: John Chapman, 1855.

————. *The Rights of Man in America.* Edited by F. B. Sanborn. Boston: American Unitarian Association, 1911.

————. *The Slave Power.* Edited by James K. Hosmer. Boston: American Unitarian Association, n.d.

————. *The Transient and Permanent in Christianity.* Edited by George Willis Cooke. Boston: American Unitarian Association, 1908.

————. *The World of Matter and the Spirit of Man.* Boston: American Unitarian Association, 1907.

Patai, Daphne, and Noretta Koertge. *Professing Feminism: Cautionary Tales from the Strange World of Women's Studies.* New York: BasicBooks, 1994.

Pater, Walter. *The Renaissance: Studies in Art the Poetry (the 1893 text).* Edited by Donald L. Hill. Berkeley and Los Angeles: University of California Press, 1980.

Patterson, Orlando. *Slavery and Social Death: A Comparative Study.* Cambridge: Harvard University Press, 1982.

Paulson, Ross Evans. *Women's Suffrage and Prohibition: A Comparative Study of Equality and Social Control.* Glenview, Ill.: Scott, Foresman, 1973.

Pease, William H., & Jane H. Pease. *The Antislavery Argument.* Indianapolis: Bobbs-Merrill, 1965.

Pellauer, Mary D. *Toward a Tradition of Feminist Theology: The Religious Social Thought of Elizabeth Cady Stanton, Susan B. Anthony, and Anna Howard Shaw.* Brooklyn: Carlson Publishing Inc., 1991.

Percy III, William Armstrong. *Pederasty and Pedagogy in Archaic Greece.* Urbana: University of Illinois Press, 1996.

Perry, Lewis. *Radical Abolitionism: Anarchy and the Government of God in Antislavery Thought.* Ithaca: Cornell University Press, 1973.

Perry, Michael J. "Modern Equal Protection: A Conceptualization and Appraisal." *Columbia Law Review* 79 (1979): 1023.

Pharr, Suzanne. *Homophobia: A Weapon of Sexism.* Inverness, Cal.: Chardon Press, 1988.

Phillips, Wendell. *Can Abolitionists Vote or Take Office under the United States Constitution?* New York: American Anti-Slavery Society, 1845.

———. *Speeches on Rights of Women.* Philadelphia: A. J. Ferris, 1898.

———. *Speeches, Lectures, and Letters.* Boston: Lothrop, Lee, & Shepard, 1891.

Pivar, David J. *Purity Crusade: Sexual Morality and Social Control, 1868–1900.* Westport, Conn.: Greenwood Press, 1973.

Plant, Richard, *The Pink Triangle: The Nazi War against Homosexuals.* New York: Henry Holt and Co., 1986.

Poliakov, Leon. *The Aryan Myth: A History of Racist and Nationalist Ideas in Europe.* Translated by Edmund Howard. London: Sussex University Press, 1971.

———. *The History of Anti-Semitism.* Vol. 1 translated by Richard Howard. New York: Vanguard Press, 1965. Vol. 2 translated by Natalie Gerardi. New York: Vanguard Press, 1973. Vol. 3 translated by Miriam Kochan. New York: Vanguard Press, 1975. Vol. 4 translated by George Klin Oxford: Oxford University Press, 1985.

Polikoff, Nancy D. "Needs of Children in Lesbian-Mother and Other Nontraditional Families." *Georgetown Law Journal* 78 (1990): 459.

Potts, Alex. *Flesh and the Ideal: Winckelmann and the Origins of Art History.* New Haven: Yale University Press, 1994.

Presidential Commission on the Assignment of Women in the Armed Forces. *Women in Combat: Report to the President.* Washington, D.C.: Brassey's. U.S., 1991.

Price, Kenneth M. *Whitman and Tradition: The Poet in His Century.* New Haven: Yale University Press, 1990.

Price, Richard. *Richard Price: Political Writings* Edited by D. O. Thomas. Cambridge: Cambridge University Press, 1991.

Procter-Smith, Marjorie. *Women in Shaker Community and Worship: A Feminist Analysis of the Uses of Religious Symbolism.* Lewiston, N.Y.: Edwin Mellen Press, 1985.

Proust, Marcel. *Cities of the Plain.* Translated by C. K. Scott Moncrieff. New York: Vintage, 1970.

Pulzer, Peter. *The Rise of Political Anti-Semitism in Germany and Austria.* Rev. ed. Cambridge: Harvard University Press, 1988.

Quarles, Benjamin. *Black Abolitionists.* London: Oxford University Press, 1969.

Quinn, D. Michael. *Same-Sex Dynamics Among Nineteenth-Century Americans: A Mormon Example.* Urbana: University of Illinois Press, 1996.

Rampersad, Arnold, ed. *Richard Wright: Later Works.* New York: The Library of America, 1991.

Rather, L. J. *Reading Wagner: A Study in the History of Ideas.* Baton Rouge: Louisiana State University Press, 1990.

Rauch, Jonathan. "For Better or Worse?" *The New Republic,* 6 May 1996, 18–23.

Rawls, John. *A Theory of Justice.* Cambridge: Harvard University Press, 1971.

———. *Political Liberalism.* New York: Columbia University Press, 1993.

Reiss, Hans, ed. *Kant's Political Writings.* Cambridge: Cambridge University Press, 1970.

Reynolds, David S. *Walt Whitman's America.* New York: Knopf, 1995.

Rhode, Deborah. *Justice and Gender.* Cambridge: Harvard University Press, 1989.

Rich, Adrienne. *Of Woman Born: Motherhood as Experience and Institution.* 1976. 10th anniversary ed. New York: W. W. Norton, 1986.

————. *On Lies, Secrets, and Silence: Selected Prose, 1966–1978.* New York: W. W. Norton, 1979.

Richards, David A. J. *A Theory of Reasons for Action.* Oxford: Clarendon Press, 1971.

————. "Commercial Sex and the Rights of the Person: A Moral Argument for the Decriminalization of Prostitution." *University of Pennsylvania Law Review* 127 (1979): 1195.

————. *Conscience and the Constitution: History, Theory, and Law of the Reconstruction Amendments.* Princeton: Princeton University Press, 1993.

————. "Constitutional Legitimacy and Constitutional Privacy." *New York University Law Review* 61 (1986): 800.

————. "Drug Use and the Rights of the Person: A Moral Argument for the Decriminalization of Certain Forms of Drug Use." *Rutgers Law Review* 22 (1981): 607.

————. *Foundations of American Constitutionalism.* New York: Oxford University Press, 1989.

————. "Liberal Political Culture and the Marginalized Voice: Interpretive Responsibility and the American Law School." *Stanford Law Review* 45 (1993): 1955.

————. "Public Reason and Abolitionist Dissent." *Chicago-Kent Law Review* 69 (1994): 787.

————. *Sex, Drugs, Death and the Law: An Essay on Human Rights and Overcriminalization.* Totowa, N.J.: Rowman and Littlefield, 1982.

————. "Sexual Autonomy and the Constitutional Right to Privacy: A Case Study in Human Rights and the Unwritten Constitution." *Hastings Law Journal* 30 (1979): 957.

————. "Sexual Preference as a Suspect Religious Classification: An Alternative Perspective on the Unconstitutionality of Anti-Lesbian/Gay Initiatives." *Ohio Law Journal* 55 (1994): 491.

————. "The Individual, the Family, and the Constitution." *New York University Law Review* 55 (1980): 1.

————. *The Moral Criticism of Law.* Encino, Cal.: Dickenson-Wadsworth, 1977.

————. *Toleration and the Constitution.* New York: Oxford University Press, 1986.

————. "Unnatural Acts and the Constitutional Right to Privacy: a Moral Theory." 45 *Fordham Law Review* 1282 (1977).

Richards, Leonard L. *"Gentlemen of Property and Standing": Anti-Abolition Mobs in Jacksonian America.* New York: Oxford University Press, 1970.

Rocke, Michael. *Forbidden Friendship: Homosexuality and Male Culture in Renaissance Florence.* New York: Oxford University Press, 1996.

Roiphe, Katie. *The Morning After: Sex, Fear, and Feminism.* Boston: Little, Brown, 1993.

Rose, Kenneth D. *American Women and the Repeal of Prohibition.* New York: New York University Press, 1996.

Rosen, Ruth. *The Lost Sisterhood: Prostitution in America, 1900–1918.* Baltimore: Johns Hopkins University Press, 1982.

Rosenberg, Gerald N. *The Hollow Hope: Can Courts Bring about Social Change?* Chicago: University of Chicago Press, 1991.

Rosenberg, Rosalind. *Beyond Separate Spheres: Intellectual Roots of Modern Feminism.* New Haven: Yale University Press, 1982.

Rosenfeld, Michel. *Affirmative Action and Justice: A Philosophical and Constitutional Inquiry.* New Haven: Yale University Press, 1991.

Rotello, Gabriel. *Sexual Ecology: AIDS and the Destiny of Gay Men.* New York: Dutton, 1997.

Rothblum, Esther D., and Kathleen A. Brehony. *Boston Marriages: Romantic but Asexual Relationships among Contemporary Lesbians.* Amherst: University of Massachusetts Press, 1993.

Rowbotham, Sheila, and Jeffrey Weeks. *Socialism and the New Light: The Personal and Sexual Politics of Edward Carpenter and Havelock Ellis.* London: Pluto Press, 1977.

Ruddick, Sara. *Maternal Thinking: Towards a Politics of Peace.* Boston: Beacon Press, 1989.

Ruether, Rosemary Radford. *Womanguides: Readings toward a Feminist Theology.* Boston: Beacon Press, 1985.

Ruggiero, Guido. *The Boundaries of Eros: Sex Crime and Sexuality in Renaissance Venice.* New York: Oxford University Press, 1985.

Ruse, Michael. *Homosexuality.* Oxford: Basil Blackwell, 1988.

Rutherford, Jane. "Duty in Divorce: Shares Income as a Path of Equality." *Fordham Law Review* 58 (1990): 539.

Sager, Lawrence G. "The Legal Status of Underenforced Constitutional Norms." *Harvard Law Review* 91 (1978): 1212.

Sanger, Margaret, *The Pivot of Civilization.* Elmsford, N.Y.: Maxwell Reprint Company, 1969.

———. *Woman and the New Race.* 1920. Elmsford, N.Y.: Maxwell Reprint Co., 1969.

Sapiro, Virginia. *A Vindication of Political Virtue: The Political Theory of Mary Wollstonecraft.* Chicago: University of Chicago Press, 1992.

Scanlon, T. M. "Preference and Urgency." *Journal of Philosophy* 72 (1975): 655.

Scheman, Naomi. *Engenderings: Constructions of Knowledge, Authority, and Privilege.* London: Routledge, 1993.

Schopenhauer, Arthur. *Essays and Aphorisms.* Translated by R. J. Hollindale. Harmondsworth: Penguin, 1970.

Schreiner, Olive. *Woman and Labour.* London: T. Fisher Unwin, 1911.

Scott, Anne Firor. *The Southern Lady: From Pedestal to Politics, 1830–1930.* Chicago: University of Chicago Press, 1970.

Scott, Joan Wallach. *Gender and the Politics of History.* New York: Columbia University Press, 1988.

Sedgwick, Eve Kosofsky. *Epistemology of the Closet.* Berkeley and Los Angeles: University of California Press, 1990.

Seltzer, Judith A., and Irwin Garfinkel. "Inequality in Divorce Settlements: An Investigation of Property Settlements and Child Support Awards." *Social Science Research* 19 (1990): 82.

Sen, Amartya. *The Standard of Living.* Cambridge: Cambridge University Press, 1987.

Sered, Susan Starr. *Priestess, Mother, Sacred Sister: Religions Dominated by Women.* New York: Oxford University Press, 1994.

Sewell, Richard H. *Ballots for Freedom: Antislavery Politics in the United States, 1837–1860.* New York: Oxford University Press, 1976.

Shakespeare, William. *Shakespeare: Complete Works.* Edited by W. J. Craig. London: Oxford University Press, 1966.

Shaw, Brent D. "A Groom of One's Own?" *The New Republic,* 18–25 July 1994, 33–41.

Shilts, Randy. *Conduct Unbecoming: Gays and Lesbians in the U. S. Military.* New York: St. Martin's Press, 1993.

Showalter, Elaine, *Sexual Anarchy: Gender and Culture in the Fin De Siecle.* New York: Viking, 1990.

Signorile, Michelangelo. *Queer in America: Sex, the Media, and the Closets of Power.* New York: Random House, 1993.

Silverman, Kaja. *Male Subjectivity at the Margins.* New York: Routledge, 1992.

Simons, Anna. "In War, Let Men Be Men." *New York Times,* 23 April 1997, A23.

Sinfield, Alan. *The Wilde Century: Effeminacy, Oscar Wilde, and the Queer Movement.* New York: Columbia University Press, 1994.

Sklar, Kathryn Kish. *Catharine Beecher: A Study in American Domesticity.* New Haven: Yale University Press, 1973.

———. *Florence Kelley and the Nation's Work: The Rise of Women's Political Culture, 1830–1900.* New Haven: Yale University Press, 1995.

Smith, H. Shelton, ed. *Horace Bushnell.* New York: Oxford University Press, 1965.

Smith-Rosenberg, Carroll. *Disorderly Conduct: Visions of Gender in Victorian America.* New York: Knopf, 1985.

Snitow, Anne, Christine Stansell and Sharon Thompson, eds. *Powers of Desire.* New York: Monthly Review Press, 1983.

Sollors, Werner. *Beyond Ethnicity: Consent and Descent in American Culture.* New York: Oxford University Press, 1986.

Solow, Barbara L., ed., *Slavery and the Rise of the Atlantic System.* Cambridge: Cambridge University Press, 1991.

Sommers, Christina Hoff. *Who Stole Feminism: How Women Have Betrayed Women.* New York: Simon & Schuster, 1994.

Southern, David W., *Gunnar Myrdal and Black-White Relations: The Use and Abuse of An American Dilemma, 1944–1969.* Baton Rouge: Louisiana State University Press, 1987.

Spooner, Lysander. *The Unconstitutionality of Slavery.* New York: Burt Franklin, 1860.

———. *Vices Are Not Crimes: A Vindication of Moral Liberty.* 1875. Cupertino, Cal.: Tanstaafl, 1977.

Spurlock, John C. *Free Love: Marriage and Middle-Class Radicalism in America, 1825–1860.* New York: New York University Press, 1988.

Stampp, Kenneth M. *The Peculiar Institution: Slavery in the Ante-Bellum South.* New York: Vintage, 1956.

Stanley, Amy Dru. "Conjugal Bonds and Wage Labor: Rights of Contract in the Age of Emancipation." *Journal of American History* 75 (1985): 471.

Stansell, Christine. *City of Women: Sex and Class in New York, 1789–1860.* New York: Knopf, 1986.

Stanton, Elizabeth Cady. *Eighty Years and More (1815–1897).* London: T. Fisher Unwin, 1898.

———. *The Woman's Bible.* New York: European Publishing Co., 1895–98.

Stanton, Elizabeth Cady, Susan B. Anthony, and Matilda Joslyn Gage, eds. *History of Woman Suffrage.* 1881. Vol. 1. Salem, N.H.: Ayer Company, 1985.

———, eds. *History of Woman Suffrage.* 1861–76. Vol. 2. New York: Fowler & Wells, 1882.

Stanton, William. *The Leopard's Spots: Scientific Attitudes toward Race in America, 1815–59.* Chicago: University of Chicago Press, 1960.

Steakley, James D. *The Homosexual Emancipation Movement in Germany.* New York: Arno Press,1975.

Stein, Edward, ed. *Forms of Desire: Sexual Orientation and the Social Constructionist Controversy.* New York: Routledge, 1990.

Stein, Stephen J. *The Shaker Experience in America.* New Haven: Yale University Press, 1992.

Sterling, Dorothy. *Ahead of Her Time: Abby Kelley and the Politics of Antislavery.* New York: W. W. Norton, 1991.

Stern, Madeleine B. *The Pantarch: A Biography of Stephen Pearl Andrews.* Austin: University of Texas Press, 1968.

———, ed. *The Victoria Woodhull Reader.* Weston, Mass.: M & S Press, 1974.

Stevenson, Brenda E. *Life in Black and White: Family and Community in the Slave South.* New York: Oxford University Press, 1996.

Stewart, James Brewer. *Holy Warriors: The Abolitionists and American Slavery.* New York: Hill and Wang, 1976.

Stewart, Jeffrey C., ed. *Narrative of Sojourner Truth.* New York: Oxford University Press, 1991.

Stimpson, Catharine R., and Ethel Spector Person. *Women: Sex and Sexuality.* Chicago: University of Chicago Press, 1980.

Stocking, Jr., George W. *A Franz Boas Reader: The Shaping of American Anthropology, 1883–1911.* Chicago: University of Chicago Press, 1974.

———. *Race, Culture, and Evolution: Essays in the History of Anthropology.* New York: The Free Press, 1968.

Stone, Geoffrey. "Content Regulation and the First Amendment." *William & Mary Law Review* 25 (1983): 189.

Stowe, Harriet Beecher. *The Key to Uncle Tom's Cabin.* 1854. Salem, N.H.: Ayer Company, 1987.

———. *Uncle Tom's Cabin or, Life among the Lowly.* 1852. Translated and edited by Ann Douglas. New York: Penguin, 1981.

Strachey, James, ed. *Standard Edition of the Complete Psychological Works of Sigmund Freud.* Vol. 9. London: Hogarth Press, 1959. Vol. 21: 1961. Vol. 23: 1964.

Strasser, Mark. "Family, Definitions, and the Constitution: On the Antimiscegenation Analogy." *Suffolk University Law Review* 25 (1991): 981.

———. "*Loving* the *Romer* Out for *Baehr*: On Acts in Defense of Marriage and the Constitution." *University of Pittsburgh Law Review* 58 (1997): 279.

———. *Legally Wed: Same-Sex Marriage and the Constitution.* Ithaca: Cornell University Press, 1997.

Strossen, Nadine. *Defending Pornography: Free Speech, Sex, and the Fight for Women's Rights.* New York: Scribner, 1995.

Sullivan, Andrew. *Virtually Normal: An Argument about Homosexuality.* New York: Knopf, 1995.

Sullivan, Robert. "An Army of the Faithful." *New York Times,* 25 April 1993, sec. 6, Magazine, at 40.

Sumner, Charles. *Charles Sumner: His Complete Works,* 20 vols. New York: Negro Universities Press, 1969.

Sundquist, Eric J. *Frederick Douglass: New Liberary and Historical Essays.* Cambridge: Cambridge University Press, 1990.

———. *To Wake the Nations: Race in the Making of American Literature.* Cambridge: Harvard University Press, Belknap Press, 1993.

Sunstein, Cass R. "Homosexuality and the Constitution." *Indiana Law Journal* 19 (1993): 1.

———. "Naked Preferences and the Constitution." *Columbia Law Review* 84 (1984): 1689.

———. "Sexual Orientation and the Constitution: A Note on the Relationship between Due Process and Equal Protection." *University of Chicago Law Review* 55 (1988): 1161.

———. "The Anticaste Principle." *Michigan Law Review* 92 (1994): 2410.

———. *The Partial Constitution.* Cambridge: Harvard University Press, 1993.

Symonds, John Addington. *A Problem in Modern Ethics.* London, 1896.

———. *Male Love: A Problem in Greek Ethics and Other Writings.* 1901. Edited by John Lauritse. New York: Pagan Press, 1983.

———. *Walt Whitman: A Study.* 1893. New York: Benjamin Blom, 1967.

Takaki, Ronald. *Iron Cages: Race and Culture in 19th-Century America.* New York: Oxford University Press, 1990.

Tal, Uriel. *Christians and Jews in Germany.* Translated by Noah Jonathan Jacobs. Ithaca: Cornell University Press, 1975.

Tamir, Yael. *Liberal Nationalism.* Princeton: Princeton University Press, 1993.

Tavris, Carol. *The Mismeasure of Woman.* New York: Simon and Schuster, 1992.

tenBroek, Jacobus. *Equal under Law.* New York: Collier, 1965.

———. "Thirteenth Amendment to the Constitution of the United States: Consummation to Abolition and Key to the Fourteenth Amendment." *California Law Review* 39 (1951): 171.

Thomas, Kendall. "The Eclipse of Reason: A Rhetorical Reading of *Bowers v. Hardwick.*" *Virginia Law Review* 79 (1993): 1805.

Tiffany, Joel. *A Treatise on the Unconstitutionality of American Slavery.* 1849. Miami: Mnemosyme, 1969.

Tocqueville, Alexis de. *Democracy in America.* 2 vols. Edited by Phillips Bradley. New York: Vintage, 1945.

Tolles, Frederick B. *Slavery and "The Woman Question": Lucretia Mott's Diary of Her Visit to Great Britain to Attend the World's Anti-Slavery Convention of 1840.* Haverford, Pa.: Friends' Historical Association, 1952.

Trexler, Richard C. *Sex and Conquest: Gendered Violence, Political Order, and the European Conquest of the Americas.* Ithaca: Cornell University Press, 1995.

Tribe, Laurence H. "Toward a Less Perfect Union." *New York Times,* 26 May 1966, E-11.

Tripp, C. A. *The Homosexual Matrix.* New York: McGraw-Hill, 1975.

Trumbach, Randolph. "The Origin and Development of the Modern Lesbian Role in the Western Gender System: Northwestern Europe and the United States, 1750–1990." *Historical Reflections* 20, no. 2 (1994): 288–320.

Tsuzuki, Chushichi, *Edward Carpenter, 1844–1929: Prophet of Human Fellowship.* Cambridge: Cambridge University Press, 1980.

Tucker, St. George. *A Dissertation on Slavery with a Proposal for the Gradual Abolition of It, in the State of Virginia.* 1796. Westport, Conn.: Negro Universities Press, 1970.

———. Reprinted in *Blackstone's Commentaries with Notes of Reference to the Constitution and Laws of the Federal Government of the United States and of the Commonwealth of Virginia.* 5 vols. Philadelphia: Birch & Small, 1803, 2: 31–89 note H.

Tushnet, Mark V. *Making Civil Rights Law: Thurgood Marshall and the Supreme Court, 1956–1961.* New York: Oxford University Press, 1994.

———. *The NAACP's Legal Strategy against Segregated Education, 1925–1950.* Chapel Hill: University of North Carolina Press, 1987.

Tussman, Joseph, and Jacobus tenBroek. "The Equal Protection of the Laws." *California Law Review* 37 (1949): 341.

Tyrrell, Ian R. *Sobering Up: From Temperance to Prohibition in Antebellum America, 1800–1860.* Westport, Conn: Greenwood Press, 1979.

———. *Woman's World, Woman's Empire: The Women's Christian Temperance Union in International Perspective, 1800–1930.* Chapel Hill: University of North Carolina Press, 1991.

Una, Lady Troubridge. *The Life and Death of Radclyffe Hall.* London: Hammond, 1961.

Underhill, Lois Beachy. *The Woman Who Ran for President: The Many Lives of Victoria Woodhull.* Bridgehampton, N.Y.: Bridge Works Publishing Co., 1995.

Usdansky, Margaret S. "Gay Couples, By the Numbers—Data Suggest They're Fewer Than Believed, But Affluent." *USA Today,* 12 April 1993, at 8A.

Vaid, Urvashi. *Virtual Equality: The Mainstreaming of Gay and Lesbian Liberation.* New York: Anchor, 1995.

Valdes, Francisco. "'Sex,' 'Gender,' and 'Sexual Orientation' in Euro-American Law and Society." *California Law Review* 83 (1995): 1.

Vance, Carole S., ed. *Pleasure and Danger: Exploring Female Sexuality.* Boston: Routledge & Kegan Paul, 1984.

VanderVelde, Lea S. "The Gendered Origins of the *Lumley* Doctrine: Binding Men's Consciences and Women's Fidelity." *Yale Law Journal* 101 (1992): 775.

———. "The Labor Vision of the Thirteenth Amendment." *University of Pennsylvania Law Review* 138 (1989): 437.

Vaughan, Alden T. *Roots of American Racism: Essays on the Colonial Experience.* New York: Oxford University Press, 1995.

Vidal, Gore. *The City and the Pillar.* 1948. London: Andre Deutsch 1994.

Voegeli, V. Jacque. *Free but Not Equal: The Midwest and the Negro During the Civil War.* Chicago: University of Chicago Press, 1967.

Waggenspack, Beth M. *The Search for Self-Sovereignty: The Oratory of Elizabeth Cady Stanton.* Greenwood Press: New York, 1989.

Walker, Peter F. *Moral Choices: Memory, Desire, and Imagination in Nineteenth-Century American Abolition.* Baton Rouge: Louisiana State University Press, 1978.

Walkowitz, Judith R. *Prostitution and Victorian Society: Woman, Class, and the State.* Cambridge: Cambridge University Press, 1980.

Waller, Altina L. *Reverend Beecher and Mrs. Tilton: Sex and Class in Victorian America.* Amherst: University of Massachusetts Press, 1982.

Walters, Ronald G. *The Antislavery Appeal: American Abolitionism after 1830.* New York: W. W. Norton, 1978.

Warner, Michael, ed. *Fear of a Queer Planet: Queer Politics and Social Theory.* Minneapolis: University of Minnesota Press, 1993.

Washington, James M., ed. *A Testament of Hope: The Essential Writings of Martin Luther King, Jr.* San Francisco: Harper & Row, 1986.

Waterman, William Randall. *Frances Wright.* New York: Columbia University Press, 1924.

Wayland, Francis. *The Elements of Moral Science.* Cambridge: Harvard University Press, Belknap Press, 1963.

Weeks, Jeffrey. *Coming Out: Homosexual Politics in Britain from the Nineteenth Century to the Present.* Rev. ed. London: Quartet Books, 1990.

———. *Sex, Politics, and Society: The Regulation of Sexuality since 1800* 2d ed. London: Longman, 1981.

Weininger, Otto. *Sex and Character.* London: William Heinemann, 1907.

Weitzman, Lenore J. *The Divorce Revolution: The Unexpected Social and Economic Consequences for Woman and Children in America.* New York: Free Press, 1985.

Weld, Theodore Dwight. *American Slavery As It Is.* 1839. New York: Arno Press and The New York Times, 1968.

———. "Persons held to Service, Fugitive Slave, &c." 1843. Reprinted in *The Influence of the Slave Power with other Anti-Slavery Pamphlets.* Westport, Conn.: Negro Universities Press, 1970.

———. "The Power of Congress over Slavery in the District of Columbia." 1838. Reprinted in Jacobus tenBroek, *Equal under Law,* appendix A, 243–80. New York: Collier, 1965.

[Weld, Theodore]. *The Bible against Slavery.* 1838. Pittsburgh: United Presbyterian Board of Publication, 1864.

Wesley, Joya L. "With $394 Billion in Buying Power, Gays' Money Talks; and Corporate America Increasingly Is Listening." *Atlanta Journal and Constitution,* 1 December 1991, F5.

West, Cornel. *Race Matters.* Boston: Beacon Press, 1993.

West, D. J. *Homosexuality.* Chicago: Aldine, 1968.

West, Robin. "Toward an Abolitionist Interpretation of the Fourteenth Amendment." *West Virginia Law Review* 94 (1991): 111.

Wharton, Edith. *The Uncollected Critical Writings* Frederick Wegener, ed. Princeton: Princeton University Press, 1996.

White, Deborah Gray. *Ar'n't I a Woman? Female Slaves in the Plantation South.* New York: W. W. Norton, 1985.

White, Edmund. *Genet: A Biography.* New York: Knopf, 1993.

Wilde, Oscar. *Complete Works of Oscar Wilde.* Edited by Vyvyan Holland. New York: Harper & Row, 1989.

Will, George. "And Now Pronounce Them Spouse and Spouse." *Washington Post,* 19 May 1996, C9.

Willard, Frances E. *Glimpses of Fifth Years: The Autobiography of An American Woman.* Chicago: H. J. Smith, 1889.

———. *Woman and Temperance.* 1883. New York: Arno Press, 1972.

Williams, Joan. "Gender Wars: Selfless Women in the Republic of Choice." *New York University Law Review* 66 (1991): 1559.

———. "Is Coverture Dead? Beyond a New Theory of Alimony." *Georgetown Law Journal* 82 (1994): 2227.

Williams, Walter L. *The Spirit and the Flesh: Sexual Diversity in American Indian Culture.* Boston: Beacon Press, 1986.

Wintemute, Robert. *Sexual Orientation and Human Rights: The United States Constitution, the European Convention, and the Canadian Charter.* Oxford: Clarendon Press, 1995.

Witherspoon, John. *Lectures of Moral Philosophy.* Edited by Jack Scott. East Brunswick: N.J.: Associated University Presses, 1982.

Wolf, Naomi. *The Beauty Myth: How Images of Beauty Are Used against Women.* New York: Anchor, 1991.

Wolinsky, Marc, and Kenneth Sherrill, eds. *Gays and the Military: Joseph Steffan versus the United States.* Princeton: Princeton University Press, 1993.

Wollstonecraft, Mary. *The Works of Mary Wollstonecraft.* Edited by Janet Todd and Marilyn Butler. 7 vols. New York: New York University Press, 1989.

Woodward, C. Vann. *Origins of the New South, 1877–1913.* Baton Rouge: Louisiana State University Press, 1971.

———. *Reunion and Reaction: The Compromise of 1877 and the End of Reconstruction.* New York: Oxford University Press, 1966.

———. *The Future of the Past.* New York: Oxford University Press, 1989.

———. *The Strange Career of Jim Crow.* 3d rev. ed. New York: Oxford University Press, 1974.

Woodward, C. Vann, and Elisabeth Muhlenfeld. *The Private Mary Chesnut: The Unpublished Civil War Diaries.* New York: Oxford University Press, 1984.

Woolf, Virginia. *A Room of One's Own.* New York: Harcourt, Brace, 1929.

Wright D'Arusmont, Frances. *Life, Letters and Lectures, 1834/1844.* New York: Arno Press, 1972.

Wyatt-Brown, Bertram. *Honor and Violence in the Old South.* New York: Oxford University Press, 1986.

Yee, Shirley J. *Black Women Abolitionists: A Study in Activism, 1828–1860.* Knoxville: University of Tennessee Press, 1992.

Yellin, Jean Fagan. *Women and Sisters: The Antislavery Feminists in American Culture.* New Haven: Yale University Press, 1989.

Young, Iris Marion. *Justice and the Politics of Difference.* Princeton: Princeton University Press, 1990.

Young-Bruehl, Elisabeth. *The Anatomy of Prejudices.* Cambridge: Harvard University Press, 1996.

INDEX

abolitionist antiracism, 202–4, 215
  denationalization of African Americans,
    201, 234, 417
  impact on civil rights movement, 212–13
  structural analysis of evil of racism,
    200–204, 217–18, 273
    abridgment of core human rights,
      200–201, 234
    inadequate, circular grounds for
      abridgment, 201–2, 234, 274
  use of analysis in criticism of *Plessy
    v. Ferguson*, 217–18
  See also abolitionist feminism; abolition-
    ist movement; radical antislav-
    ery; racism
abolitionist feminism, 12, 14, 34–35, 73–
  74, 79–82, 83, 115
  as anti-Garrisonian political abolition-
    ism (Stanton), 107–14, 125
  effect of Civil War on, 130–32, 167
  common plight of women and prosti-
    tutes, 165, 170
  criticism of double standard of woman-
    belle ideal, 165, 166–67, 281–82
  criticism of subjection of women and
    sexism, 22–23, 234
  Friedan's use of, 226
  as Garrisonian moral abolitionism, 106–
    7, 125, 129, 130, 167, 173, 463

Grimke sisters as central architects of
  position of moral slavery of, 81–
  102, 321
as guide to constitutional interpretation,
  22–25, 28–30, 132–33, 199,
  261–63, 278–79, 458, 462, 465,
  466–67
  practice as important a guide as
    theory, 22–25, 280, 456–57
on political epistemology, 23, 141–44
support for Thirteenth Amendment,
  132–33, 140
See also moral slavery
abolitionist movement, 9–10, 55, 59, 386–
  87, 403
  criticism of slavery and racism, 20, 50–
    62, 273
  defense of conscience and free speech,
    19, 34–35
  as guide to constitutional interpretation,
    19–22
  impact on Reconstruction Amend-
    ments, 15, 17
  as moral movement (Garrison), 106–7,
    386, 463
    advocacy of not voting, 106
    Constitution "a covenant with death
      and agreement with hell,"
      106

exclusion of gays and lesbians from, 412–38

exclusion of women from, 260–61, 425
  as arguable requisite for right to vote, 139–40, 183
  from combat roles, 425–28, 436
  integration in, 427–28, 434–35
  gays and lesbians serving in World War II, 338, 428–29
  See also citizenship and military service; "Don't Ask, Don't Tell" policy on gays in the military

Miller v. California, 241

Millett, Kate, 231, 340
  Sexual Politics, 231

Mill, John Stuart Mill, 142, 151, 451
  The Subjection of Women, 142

Mississippi University for Women v. Hogan, 237, 238, 253

moderate antislavery, 136

Modern Women: The Lost Sex (Ferdinand Lundberg and Marynia Farnham), 197

Montesquieu, 49, 55, 213

Montgomery bus boycott (1955), 228

Moore, R. I., 43

moral slavery, 4, 66–67, 90–94, 105–6, 113–14, 130–31, 142, 160, 178, 180, 182, 261–63, 275, 321, 467
  anti-Semitism as, 402–3, 466
  civil rights movement and second wave feminism as protest of, 260, 337–38
  defined, 3, 155, 261, 354, 371, 458
  homophobia as evil best explained by theory of, 346–54, 364, 371, 403–5, 443, 447, 456–57, 466
  injury to both private and public life, 284
  inversion by purity advocates of theory of, 170, 176–77, 178
  rejected by Reconstruction Congress, 14, 138
  role of segregation in construction of, 281, 402
  Sarah Grimke on structural analysis of, 97–100, 106, 142, 261–63
  silencing or social death as product of, 274, 362, 366, 402–4
  as theory of analogy between racism

and sexism, 122–24, 174, 257, 277–79, 321, 402, 442–43, 447, 466
  as theory of constitutional interpretation, 5–6, 199, 200, 262, 337–38, 354, 461
  fundamental rights, 266–67, 354
  of Reconstruction Amendments, 262, 461
  suspect classifications, 267, 273–87, 354
  of Thirteenth Amendment, 199, 274, 354, 402, 461; condemning homophobia, 346, 354, 403, 441; Stanton on, 137–38, 264
  unjust moral paternalism as central to, 273–75

motherhood
  Angelina Grimke's abolitionist appeal to, 84–85, 282
  Chandler's abolitionist appeal to, 82, 282
  as idealized model for moral relationships, 73–78, 146, 147–48, 149–50, 282, 289, 298
  as moral ideal for women's roles, 78, 90, 145, 149
  pregnancy, constitutional weight to be accorded, 283–84
  progressive role in enhancing respect for universal human rights of appeals to, 282
  regressive role in advancing sexism and racism of appeals to, 282–84, 289–90, 295–96
  in advancing homophobia, 295–96
  Rich on unjust interpretation and enforcement of roles of, 148, 342–43
  Stowe's appeal to, 83, 282
  See also gender; pedestal, women on; sexism

Mott, Lucretia, 63, 70, 103–5, 139, 460
  as abolitionist feminist, 83, 102, 168
  on Bible interpretation, 104, 235
  "Discourse on Women," 105
  as Hicksite Quaker, 103–4
  as moral abolitionist, 106–7, 125
  on rights to work, 105, 168
  role at Seneca Falls, 109–12, 154
  using argument from toleration, 104, 105, 235

exemplified by sexism, 104–5, 225–26, 261, 335, 353, 461
force in compromising constitutional principles, entrenching sexism and racism, 277, 289–90
illustrated by arguments in support of Colorado Amendment Two, 393–99
See also dehumanization; stereotypes; toleration, argument for
Paris Adult Theatre I v. Slaton, 241
Parker, Theodore, 50–54, 63, 78, 108–9, 203, 226
Parks, Rosa, 228
Parsifal (Richard Wagner), 420
passing to avoid prejudice, 270, 271
Pater, Walter, 311
Paul, Alice, 104, 193–94
Paul, Saint, epistles of, 39, 95–96, 104. See also Bible interpretation
pedestal, women on, 462
abolitionist feminist critique of ethical double standard of, 84, 119, 142–43, 165, 280
as a cage, 257, 462
Cooper on stepping down from, 210, 228
as justification for racism and sexism, 116–17, 123–24, 143, 189–90, 280, 461, 462
as justification for slavery, 73–74, 148, 249, 461, 462
women working in civil rights movement challenge, 228–31
See also motherhood; proslavery argument; sexism
personal as political, 92, 111, 278, 307–8. See also public/private distinction, unjust drawing of
Phillips, Wendell, 129, 130, 139
phrenology, 29
platform of human rights, 2, 181, 280, 335, 353, 458, 459, 460
Angelina Grimke on, 92, 261, 302
as normative position against unprincipled compromise, 177–78, 458, 463, 465, 466–67
Sarah Grimke on, 98, 100, 261, 302
Whitman on, 288, 302
Planned Parenthood v. Casey, 456
Plato on the unnaturalness of homosexual sex, 312, 360–61
The Laws, 360–61

Plessy v. Ferguson, 183, 208–10, 212, 213–21, 271, 285, 286, 365
political abolitionism on free speech, free labor, and antislavery, 53–54. See also abolitionist movement, as political movement; Republican Party
"Political Atheism" (Lyman Beecher), 72
political epistemology, 23, 460
as background of argument for toleration, 40–42, 96, 135
as concern of abolitionist feminists, 23, 87, 91, 94–100, 104–5, 142, 261, 276
as concern of abolitionists, 50–51, 83, 87
as concern of contemporary feminists, 23–24
enforcing sectarian conception of gender roles, 67–69, 147–48, 149–52, 163–64, 361–62
homophobia as based on, 299–300, 302–3, 309, 352, 361–62
proslavery ideology as enforcing unjust, 248–49, 274
role in unjust enforcement of racialized conception of gender, 117, 119, 123–24, 187, 189–90, 217–18, 275
See also dehumanization; paradox of toleration; stereotypes
Political Ethics (Francis Lieber), 171
political participation, constitutional rights of
antigay/lesbian initiatives as inconsistent with, 375, 381–82, 406–7
political powerlessness, 257–58, 268–69, 379
polygamy, 171, 172, 449–51. See also antipolygamy movement
polygenetic theories of human origins, 214
popular sovereignty, 17, 18–19
pornography, 241–44
statement of gay or lesbian identity as, 431, 432
See also obscenity
"The Portrait of Mr. W.H." (Oscar Wilde), 315
Powell, Justice Lewis F., 237, 258, 456
pregnancy, constitutional weight to be accorded, 283–84. See also motherhood

sexual love relationships; love,
 moral powers of
Romer v. Evans, 9, 375–76, 377, 407, 414,
 441, 444, 456
A Room of One's Own (Virginia Woolf),
 331
Roosevelt, Eleanor, 192
Roosevelt, Theodore, 175
Rosenblum, Nancy, 449–50
Rostker v. Goldberg, 260, 261, 425, 436
Roth v. United States, 241
Rousseau, Jean-Jacques, 64, 69

same-sex marriage, right to, 411
 antipolygamy arguments used in opposition to, 449–51
 Baehr v. Lewin on, 439–40
 Carpenter on, 325
 custody and adoption of children by
  gay and lesbians, 452–53
 as ground for exclusion from military,
  413–14, 438–39
 homophobic responses to, 347–48, 443,
  451–52
 judicial treatment of constitutionality,
  until *Baehr*, of, 440
 as required by constitutional right of intimate association, 441–44
  burden of justification for abridgment not satisfied, 444–46, 459,
   466; illegitimate gender stereotyping, 447–51; analogy of antimiscegenation laws, 447
 See also companionate marriage; homosexual love relationships; intimate association, inalienable human right of; love, moral powers
  of
Sand, George, 298
Sanger, Margaret, 33, 179–81, 245, 288,
 334, 460
 Family Limitation, 178
 on moral slavery, 178, 180, 250
 obscenity prosecutions of, 156, 178,
  179, 181, 238, 334
 on principle of right to love, 26, 172,
  179–81, 245, 351
  right to contraceptives, 173, 178–
   81, 239, 245, 248, 250
 The Woman Rebel, 178, 179
Scalia, Justice Antonin E., 377, 407

scapegoats
 African Americans as, 59, 271, 290,
  335, 420
 homosexuals as, 290, 295–96, 310, 335,
  370, 392, 401, 448, 451
 Jews as, 43–44, 59, 271, 290, 335, 401,
  420, 448, 465
 prostitutes as, 164, 166–67, 169–71,
  178, 295–96, 310, 321–22, 335,
  465
Schopenhauer, Arthur, 332
Scientific Humanitarian Committee, 316
The Second Sex (Simone de Beauvoir),
 226
segregation by gender, state-sponsored
 constitutional wrongness of, 237–38,
  260–61, 277–78, 279, 281, 426–
  28, 437
  impact of judicial validation until recently, 277–78
 Friedan on, 226–27
segregation by race, state-sponsored, 207
 constitutional wrongness of, 207, 221,
  236–37, 277–78, 279, 281, 437
 Friedan's appeal to, 226–27
 role in constructing racism, 277–78,
  423, 437
Seneca Falls Convention of 1848, 103, 109,
 125, 126, 137, 144, 193, 225
separation of church and state, 133–34,
  463. *See also* establishment of religion; free exercise of religion
Sex and Character (Otto Weininger), 332–
 33
sexism, 70–71, 94–100, 226, 275–76
 as analogy to homophobia, 292–94,
  361–62
 homophobia as form of, 346–47, 352,
  369–70
 judicial recognition of evil of, 255–61
 prohibition on same-sex marriage as enforcing, 447–51
 unjust conception of public and private
  life, as resting on, 347–48, 367–
  68
 as unjust insult to identity, 355, 406
 as unjust moral paternalism, 275–76,
  348–49
 See also racism, analogy to sexism
sexism, scientific, 358. *See also* ethnology;
  nature and culture, confusion of;